200
CIVIL PROCEDURE
SUPPLEMENT

By
John J. Cound
Professor of Law
University of Minnesota

Jack H. Friedenthal
Freda H. Alverson Professor of Law
The George Washington University Law School

Arthur R. Miller
Bruce Bromley Professor of Law
Harvard University

John E. Sexton
Dean and Professor of Law
New York University

AMERICAN CASEBOOK SERIES®

WEST GROUP

ST. PAUL, MINN., 2000

West Group has created this publication to provide you with accurate and authoritative information concerning the subject matter covered. However, this publication was not necessarily prepared by persons licensed to practice law in a particular jurisdiction. West Group is not engaged in rendering legal or other professional advice, and this publication is not a substitute for the advice of an attorney. If you require legal or other expert advice, you should seek the services of a competent attorney or other professional.

 TEXT IS PRINTED ON 10% POST CONSUMER RECYCLED PAPER

Table of Contents

Page

PART I:
Federal Rules of Civil Procedure for the United States District Courts and Comparative Federal and State Provisions -------------- 1

PART II:
Selected Provisions of The Constitution of the United States and of Titles 28 and 42, United States Code plus Comparative Federal and State Provisions --- 225

PART III:
Selected State Jurisdictional Statutes and Selected State Statutes Governing the Powers of Appellate Courts ---------------------------- 284

PART IV:
Selected Portions of the Federal Rules of Appellate Procedure -------- 291

PART V:
Selected Sample Court Orders and Notices for Controlling Discovery, Pretrial Conferences, and Settlement of Class Action ---------- 332

PART VI:
Illustrative Litigation Problem with Sample Documents --------------- 357

PART VII:
Local (Civil) Rules for the United States District Courts for the Eastern and Southern Districts of New York ---------------------------- 387

PART VIII:
Recent U.S. Supreme Court Cases--- 432

PART IX:
Proposed Federal Statutes and Rules Regulating Civil Procedure ---- 495

PART X:
Index to Comparative Provisions-- 519

*

Table of Contents

2000
CIVIL PROCEDURE
SUPPLEMENT

1.
EVENT OR TRANSACTION LEADING TO LAWSUIT

2.
DECISION TO SUE
Including choice of forum and parties

3.
STARTING THE SUIT
Filing Complaint
Service of Process
Rules 3, 4, 5, 7 & 9, 10 & 11

A.
Motion for Temp. Restraining Order and/or Preliminary Injunction   R. 65

B.
Preliminary Injunction Granted

C.
Preliminary Injunction Denied

D.
Interlocutory Appeal

E.
Motion to Dismiss and Other R. 12(b), (e) & (f) motions

F.
Motion to Dismiss Granted

G.
Appeal

H.
Refile if Possible

I.
Case Over

J.
M. to D. denied: Rulings on other M's—no appeal before Judgment

4.
ANSWER
Including Affirmative Defenses, if Any
R. 7–12

K.
Default Judgment
R. 55

Go to Box 8

L.
Crossclaims & Counterclaims Filed with Ans.
R. 7–11, 13

M.
Reply to Counter- claim; Ans. to Crossclaim
R. 7–12

N.
Motion to dismiss & other R. 12 motions—similar to Boxes E–J

O.
Motion for Judgment on the Pleadings
R. 12(c)

P.
Motion denied— No appeal before Judgment

Q.
Motion granted, Judgment entered

Go to Box 8

R.
Motions re: multiparty litigation, e.g. certification of class action R. 23; Joinder, R. 19, 20; Intervention, R. 24; Interpleader, R. 22. Motions usually made before or during discovery. Usually no appeal before Judgment

S.
Motions to compel & for Protective Orders; Usually no appeal before Judgment
R. 26, 37

5.
DISCOVERY
Rules 26–37

vi

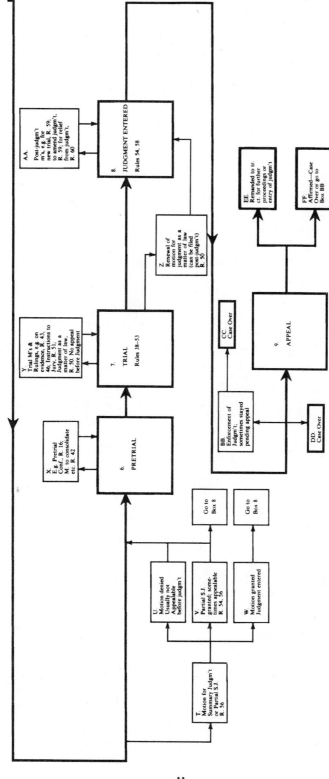

This chart was prepared by Professor Michael J. Goldberg of Widener University School of Law.

Part I

Federal Rules of Civil Procedure for the United States District Courts

and

Comparative Federal and State Provisions

TABLE OF CONTENTS

Federal Rules of Civil Procedure

I. Scope of Rules—One Form of Action

Rule		Page
1.	Scope of Rules	11
2.	One Form of Action	11

II. Commencement of Action; Service of Process, Pleadings, Motions and Orders

		Page
3.	Commencement of Action	11
4.	Summons	11

    (a) Form.
    (b) Issuance.
    (c) Service With Complaint; by Whom Made.
    (d) Waiver of Service; Duty to Save Costs of Service; Request to Waive.
    (e) Service Upon Individuals Within a Judicial District of the United States.
    (f) Service Upon Individuals in a Foreign Country.
    (g) Service Upon Infants and Incompetent Persons.
    (h) Service Upon Corporations and Associations.
    (i) Service Upon the United States, and Its Agencies, Corporations, or Officers.
    (j) Service Upon Foreign, State or Local Governments.
    (k) Territorial Limits of Effective Service.
    (*l*) Proof of Service.
    (m) Time Limit for Service.
    (n) Seizure of Property; Service of Summons Not Feasible.

4.1	Service of Other Process	22

    (a) Generally.
    (b) Enforcement of Orders; Commitment for Civil Contempt.

5.	Service and Filing of Pleadings and Other Papers	23

    (a) Service: When Required.
    (b) Same: How Made.

1

Rule   **Page**

(c) Same: Numerous Defendants.
(d) Filing; Certificate of Service.
(e) Filing With the Court Defined.

6. Time.. 24
(a) Computation.
(b) Enlargement.
(c) Rescinded.
(d) For Motions—Affidavits.
(e) Additional Time After Service by Mail.

III. Pleadings and Motions

7. Pleadings Allowed; Form of Motions........................... 26
(a) Pleadings.
(b) Motions and Other Papers.
(c) Demurrers, Pleas, etc., Abolished.
8. General Rules of Pleading..................................... 27
(a) Claims for Relief.
(b) Defenses; Form of Denials.
(c) Affirmative Defenses.
(d) Effect of Failure to Deny.
(e) Pleading to Be Concise and Direct; Consistency.
(f) Construction of Pleadings.
9. Pleading Special Matters..................................... 31
(a) Capacity.
(b) Fraud, Mistake, Condition of the Mind.
(c) Conditions Precedent.
(d) Official Document or Act.
(e) Judgment.
(f) Time and Place.
(g) Special Damage.
(h) Admiralty and Maritime Claims.
10. Form of Pleadings... 34
(a) Caption; Names of Parties.
(b) Paragraphs; Separate Statements.
(c) Adoption by Reference; Exhibits.
11. Signing of Pleadings, Motions, and Other Papers; Representations to   36
Court; Sanctions
(a) Signature.
(b) Representations to Court.
(c) Sanctions.
(d) Inapplicability to Discovery.
12. Defenses and Objections—When and How Presented—By Pleading or   39
Motion—Motion for Judgment on the Pleadings
(a) When Presented.
(b) How Presented.
(c) Motion for Judgment on the Pleadings.
(d) Preliminary Hearings.
(e) Motion for More Definite Statement.
(f) Motion to Strike.
(g) Consolidation of Defenses in Motion.
(h) Waiver or Preservation of Certain Defenses.
13. Counterclaim and Cross-Claim 47
(a) Compulsory Counterclaims.
(b) Permissive Counterclaims.
(c) Counterclaim Exceeding Opposing Claim.

2

Rule   **Page**

    (d) Counterclaim Against the United States.
    (e) Counterclaim Maturing or Acquired After Pleading.
    (f) Omitted Counterclaim.
    (g) Cross-Claim Against Co-party.
    (h) Joinder of Additional Parties.
    (i) Separate Trials; Separate Judgments.
14. Third Party Practice 49
    (a) When Defendant May Bring in Third Party.
    (b) When Plaintiff May Bring in Third Party.
    (c) Admiralty and Maritime Claims.
15. Amended and Supplemental Pleadings 50
    (a) Amendments.
    (b) Amendments to Conform to the Evidence.
    (c) Relation Back of Amendments.
    (d) Supplemental Pleadings.
16. Pretrial Conferences; Scheduling; Management 54
    (a) Pretrial Conferences; Objectives.
    (b) Scheduling and Planning.
    (c) Subjects for Consideration at Pretrial Conferences.
    (d) Final Pretrial Conference.
    (e) Pretrial Orders.
    (f) Sanctions.

IV. Parties

17. Parties Plaintiff and Defendant; Capacity 58
    (a) Real Party in Interest.
    (b) Capacity to Sue or Be Sued.
    (c) Infants or Incompetent Persons.
18. Joinder of Claims and Remedies 59
    (a) Joinder of Claims.
    (b) Joinder of Remedies; Fraudulent Conveyances.
19. Joinder of Persons Needed for Just Adjudication 60
    (a) Persons to Be Joined if Feasible.
    (b) Determination by Court Whenever Joinder Not Feasible.
    (c) Pleading Reasons for Nonjoinder.
    (d) Exception of Class Actions.
20. Permissive Joinder of Parties 64
    (a) Permissive Joinder.
    (b) Separate Trials.
21. Misjoinder and Non-joinder of Parties 65
22. Interpleader 65
23. Class Actions 68
    (a) Prerequisites to a Class Action.
    (b) Class Actions Maintainable.
    (c) Determination by Order Whether Class Action to Be Maintained;
        Notice; Judgment; Actions Conducted Partially as Class Actions.
    (d) Orders in Conduct of Actions.
    (e) Dismissal or Compromise.
    (f) Appeals.
23.1 Derivative Actions by Shareholders 74
23.2 Actions Relating to Unincorporated Associations 75
24. Intervention 75
    (a) Intervention of Right.
    (b) Permissive Intervention.
    (c) Procedure.

Rule		Page
25.	Substitution of Parties...	77

    (a) Death.
    (b) Incompetency.
    (c) Transfer of Interest.
    (d) Public Officers; Death or Separation From Office.

V. Depositions and Discovery

26. General Provisions Governing Discovery; Duty of Disclosure 78
    (a) Required Disclosures; Methods to Discover Additional Matter.
        (1) *Initial Disclosures.*
        (2) *Disclosure of Expert Testimony.*
        (3) *Pretrial Disclosures.*
        (4) *Form of Disclosures; Filing.*
        (5) *Methods to Discover Additional Matter.*
    (b) Discovery Scope and Limits.
        (1) *In General.*
        (2) *Limitations.*
        (3) *Trial Preparation: Materials.*
        (4) *Trial Preparation: Experts.*
        (5) *Claims of Privilege or Protection of Trial Preparation Materials.*
    (c) Protective Orders.
    (d) Timing and Sequence of Discovery.
    (e) Supplementation of Disclosures and Responses.
    (f) Meeting of Parties; Planning for Discovery.
    (g) Signing of Disclosures, Discovery Requests, Responses, and Objections.

27. Depositions Before Action or Pending Appeal 93
    (a) Before Action.
        (1) *Petition.*
        (2) *Notice and Service.*
        (3) *Order and Examination.*
        (4) *Use of Deposition.*
    (b) Pending Appeal.
    (c) Perpetuation by Action.

28. Persons Before Whom Depositions May Be Taken 95
    (a) Within the United States.
    (b) In Foreign Countries.
    (c) Disqualification for Interest.

29. Stipulations Regarding Discovery Procedure 97
30. Depositions Upon Oral Examination 97
    (a) When Depositions May Be Taken; When Leave Required.
    (b) Notice of Examination: General Requirements; Method of Recording; Production of Documents and Things; Deposition of Organization; Deposition by Telephone.
    (c) Examination and Cross-Examination; Record of Examination; Oath; Objections.
    (d) Schedule and Duration; Motion to Terminate or Limit Examination.
    (e) Review by Witness; Changes; Signing.
    (f) Certification and Filing by Officer; Exhibits; Copies; Notice of Filing.
    (g) Failure to Attend or to Serve Subpoena; Expenses.

31. Depositions Upon Written Questions 103
    (a) Serving Questions; Notice.

Rule   **Page**

    (b) Officer to Take Responses and Prepare Record.

    (c) Notice of Filing.

32. Use of Depositions in Court Proceedings 104

    (a) Use of Depositions.

    (b) Objections to Admissibility.

    (c) Form of Presentation.

    (d) Effect of Errors and Irregularities in Depositions.

        (1) *As to Notice.*

        (2) *As to Disqualification of Officer.*

        (3) *As to Taking of Deposition.*

        (4) *As to Completion and Return of Deposition.*

33. Interrogatories to Parties 106

    (a) Availability.

    (b) Answers and Objections.

    (c) Scope; Use at Trial.

    (d) Option to Produce Business Records.

34. Production of Documents and Things and Entry Upon Land for   109
Inspection and Other Purposes

    (a) Scope.

    (b) Procedure.

    (c) Persons Not Parties.

35. Physical and Mental Examination of Persons 112

    (a) Order for Examination.

    (b) Report of Examiner.

36. Requests for Admission 113

    (a) Request for Admission.

    (b) Effect of Admission.

37. Failure to Make or Cooperate in Discovery: Sanctions 116

    (a) Motion for Order Compelling Disclosure or Discovery.

        (1) *Appropriate Court.*

        (2) *Motion.*

        (3) *Evasive or Incomplete Disclosure, Answer, or Response.*

        (4) *Expenses and Sanctions.*

    (b) Failure to Comply With Order.

        (1) *Sanctions by Court in District Where Deposition Is Taken.*

        (2) *Sanctions by Court in Which Action Is Pending.*

    (c) Failure to Disclose; False or Misleading Disclosure; Refusal to
Admit.

    (d) Failure of Party to Attend at Own Deposition or Serve Answers
to Interrogatories or Respond to Request for Inspection.

    (e) [Abrogated.]

    (f) [Repealed.]

    (g) Failure to Participate in the Framing of a Discovery Plan.

VI. Trials

38. Jury Trial of Right 121

    (a) Right Preserved.

    (b) Demand.

    (c) Same: Specification of Issues.

    (d) Waiver.

    (e) Admiralty and Maritime Claims.

39. Trial by Jury or by the Court 123

    (a) By Jury.

    (b) By the Court.

    (c) Advisory Jury and Trial by Consent.

Rule		Page
40.	Assignment of Cases for Trial	123
41.	Dismissal of Actions	123
	(a) Voluntary Dismissal: Effect Thereof.	
	(1) *By Plaintiff; by Stipulation.*	
	(2) *By Order of Court.*	
	(b) Involuntary Dismissal: Effect Thereof.	
	(c) Dismissal of Counterclaim, Cross-Claim, or Third-Party Claim.	
	(d) Costs of Previously-Dismissed Action.	
42.	Consolidation; Separate Trials	127
	(a) Consolidation.	
	(b) Separate Trials.	
43.	Taking of Testimony	128
	(a) Form.	
	(b), (c) [Abrogated.]	
	(d) Affirmation in Lieu of Oath.	
	(e) Evidence on Motions.	
	(f) Interpreters.	
44.	Proof of Official Record	128
	(a) Authentication.	
	(1) *Domestic.*	
	(2) *Foreign.*	
	(b) Lack of Record.	
	(c) Other Proof.	
44.1	Determination of Foreign Law	129
45.	Subpoena	130
	(a) Form; Issuance.	
	(b) Service.	
	(c) Protection of Persons Subject to Subpoenas.	
	(d) Duties in Responding to Subpoena.	
	(e) Contempt.	
46.	Exceptions Unnecessary	134
47.	Jurors	134
	(a) Examination of Jurors.	
	(b) Peremptory Challenges.	
	(c) Excuse.	
48.	Number of Jurors—Participation in Verdict	135
49.	Special Verdicts and Interrogatories	136
	(a) Special Verdicts.	
	(b) General Verdict Accompanied by Answer to Interrogatories.	
50.	Judgment as a Matter of Law in Actions Tried by Jury; Alternative Motion for New Trial; Conditional Rulings	137
	(a) Judgment as a Matter of Law.	
	(b) Renewal of Motion for Judgment After Trial; Alternative Motion for New Trial.	
	(c) Same: Conditional Rulings on Grant of Motion.	
	(d) Same: Denial of Motion for Judgment as a Matter of Law.	
51.	Instructions to Jury: Objection	139
52.	Findings by the Court; Judgment on Partial Findings	141
	(a) Effect.	
	(b) Amendment.	
	(c) Judgment on Partial Findings.	
53.	Masters	142
	(a) Appointment and Compensation.	
	(b) Reference.	
	(c) Powers.	
	(d) Proceedings.	

Rule   **Page**

      (1) *Meetings.*
      (2) *Witnesses.*
      (3) *Statement of Accounts.*
    (e) Report.
      (1) *Contents and Filing.*
      (2) *In Non-jury Actions.*
      (3) *In Jury Actions.*
      (4) *Stipulation as to Findings.*
      (5) *Draft Report.*
    (f) Application to Magistrate Judge.

VII. Judgment

54. Judgments; Costs 146
    (a) Definition; Form.
    (b) Judgment Upon Multiple Claims or Involving Multiple Parties.
    (c) Demand for Judgment.
    (d) Costs; Attorneys' Fees.
      (1) *Costs Other Than Attorneys' Fees.*
      (2) *Attorneys' Fees.*
55. Default 148
    (a) Entry.
    (b) Judgment.
      (1) *By the Clerk.*
      (2) *By the Court.*
    (c) Setting Aside Default.
    (d) Plaintiffs, Counterclaimants, Cross-Claimants.
    (e) Judgment Against the United States.
56. Summary Judgment 150
    (a) For Claimant.
    (b) For Defending Party.
    (c) Motion and Proceedings Thereon.
    (d) Case Not Fully Adjudicated on Motion.
    (e) Form of Affidavits; Further Testimony; Defense Required.
    (f) When Affidavits Are Unavailable.
    (g) Affidavits Made in Bad Faith.
57. Declaratory Judgments 155
58. Entry of Judgment 155
59. New Trials; Amendment of Judgments 156
    (a) Grounds.
    (b) Time for Motion.
    (c) Time for Serving Affidavits.
    (d) On Initiative of Court.
    (e) Motion to Alter or Amend a Judgment.
60. Relief From Judgment or Order 158
    (a) Clerical Mistakes.
    (b) Mistakes; Inadvertence; Excusable Neglect; Newly Discovered
       Evidence; Fraud, etc.
61. Harmless Error 159
62. Stay of Proceedings to Enforce a Judgment 159
    (a) Automatic Stay; Exceptions—Injunctions, Receiverships, and
       Patent Accountings.
    (b) Stay on Motion for New Trial or for Judgment.
    (c) Injunction Pending Appeal.
    (d) Stay Upon Appeal.
    (e) Stay in Favor of the United States or Agency Thereof.

Rule		Page
	(f) Stay According to State Law.	
	(g) Power of Appellate Court Not Limited.	
	(h) Stay of Judgment as to Multiple Claims or Multiple Parties.	
63.	Inability of a Judge to Proceed	161

VIII. Provisional and Final Remedies

64.	Seizure of Person or Property	161
65.	Injunctions	162
	(a) Preliminary Injunction.	
	(1) *Notice*.	
	(2) *Consolidation of Hearing With Trial on Merits*.	
	(b) Temporary Restraining Order; Notice; Hearing; Duration.	
	(c) Security.	
	(d) Form and Scope of Injunction or Restraining Order.	
	(e) Employer and Employee; Interpleader; Constitutional Cases.	
65.1	Security: Proceedings Against Sureties..........................	165
66.	Receivers Appointed by Federal Courts	165
67.	Deposit in Court	166
68.	Offer of Judgment..	166
69.	Execution	168
	(a) In General.	
	(b) Against Certain Public Officers.	
70.	Judgment for Specific Acts; Vesting Title	171
71.	Process in Behalf of and Against Persons Not Parties	171

IX.   Special Proceedings

71A.	Condemnation of Property	171
	(a) Applicability of Other Rules.	
	(b) Joinder of Properties.	
	(c) Complaint.	
	(1) *Caption*.	
	(2) *Contents*.	
	(3) *Filing*.	
	(d) Process.	
	(1) *Notice; Delivery*.	
	(2) *Same; Form*.	
	(3) *Service of Notice*.	
	(4) *Return; Amendment*.	
	(e) Appearance or Answer.	
	(f) Amendment of Pleadings.	
	(g) Substitution of Parties.	
	(h) Trial.	
	(i) Dismissal of Action.	
	(1) *As of Right*.	
	(2) *By Stipulation*.	
	(3) *By Order of the Court*.	
	(4) *Effect*.	
	(j) Deposit and Its Distribution.	
	(k) Condemnation Under a State's Power of Eminent Domain.	
	(*l*) Costs.	
72.	Magistrates; Pretrial Matters	176
	(a) Nondispositive Matters.	
	(b) Dispositive Motions and Prisoner Petitions.	
73.	Magistrate Judges; Trial by Consent and Appeal Options	177

Rule   **Page**

    (a) Powers; Procedure.
    (b) Consent.
    (c) Appeal.
74–76. [Abrogated].

X. District Courts and Clerks

77. District Courts and Clerks 178
    (a) District Courts Always Open.
    (b) Trials and Hearings; Orders in Chambers.
    (c) Clerk's Office and Orders by Clerk.
    (d) Notice of Orders or Judgments.
78. Motion Day.. 179
79. Books and Records Kept by the Clerk and Entries Therein 179
    (a) Civil Docket.
    (b) Civil Judgments and Orders.
    (c) Indices; Calendars.
    (d) Other Books and Records of the Clerk.
80. Stenographer; Stenographic Report or Transcript as Evidence 180
    (a), (b) [Abrogated.]
    (c) Stenographic Report or Transcript as Evidence.

XI. General Provisions

81. Applicability in General... 180
    (a) To What Proceedings Applicable.
    (b) Scire Facias and Mandamus.
    (c) Removed Actions.
    (d) [Abrogated.]
    (e) Law Applicable.
    (f) References to Officer of the United States.
82. Jurisdiction and Venue Unaffected............................... 182
83. Rules by District Courts 182
    (a) Local Rules.
    (b) Procedures When there is No Controlling Law.
84. Forms.. 183
85. Title.. 183
86. Effective Date... 184
    (a) [Effective Date of Original Rules].
    (b) Effective Date of Amendments.
    (c) Effective Date of Amendments.
    (d) Effective Date of Amendments.
    (e) Effective Date of Amendments.

Form
1.   Summons _____ 185
1A. Notice of Lawsuit and Request for Waiver of Service of Summons ____ 186
1B. Waiver of Service of Summons_____ 187
2.   Allegation of Jurisdiction_____ 188
3.   Complaint on a Promissory Note _____ 189
4.   Complaint on an Account_____ 190
5.   Complaint for Goods Sold and Delivered _____ 190
6.   Complaint for Money Lent_____ 190
7.   Complaint for Money Paid by Mistake _____ 190
8.   Complaint for Money Had and Received_____ 190
9.   Complaint for Negligence _____ 191
10. Complaint for Negligence Where Plaintiff Is Unable to Determine
      Definitely Whether the Person Responsible Is C.D. or E.F. or

Form

Whether Both Are Responsible and Where His Evidence May Justify a Finding of Wilfulness or of Recklessness or of Negligence ... 192

11. Complaint for Conversion ... 192
12. Complaint for Specific Performance of Contract to Convey Land ... 193
13. Complaint on Claim for Debt and to Set Aside Fraudulent Conveyance Under Rule 18(b) ... 193
14. Complaint for Negligence Under Federal Employer's Liability Act ... 194
15. Complaint for Damages Under Merchant Marine Act ... 194
16. Complaint for Infringement of Patent ... 195
17. Complaint for Infringement of Copyright and Unfair Competition ... 196
18. Complaint for Interpleader and Declaratory Relief ... 197
18–A. [Abrogated] ... 198
19. Motion to Dismiss, Presenting Defenses of Failure to State a Claim, of Lack of Service of Process, of Improper Venue, and of Lack of Jurisdiction Under Rule 12(b) ... 198
20. Answer Presenting Defenses Under Rule 12(b) ... 199
21. Answer to Complaint Set Forth in Form 8, With Counterclaim for Interpleader ... 200
22. Motion to Bring in Third-Party Defendant [Eliminated] ... 200
22–A. Summons and Complaint Against Third-Party Defendant ... 201
22–B. Motion to Bring in Third-Party Defendant ... 202
23. Motion to Intervene as a Defendant Under Rule 24 ... 203
24. Request for Production of Documents, etc., Under Rule 34 ... 204
25. Request for Admission Under Rule 36 ... 205
26. Allegation of Reason for Omitting Party ... 205
27. Notice of Appeal to Court of Appeals Under Rule 73(b) [Abrogated.] ... 206
28. Notice: Condemnation ... 206
29. Complaint: Condemnation ... 207
30. Suggestion of Death Upon the Record Under Rule 25(a)(1) ... 209
31. Judgment on Jury Verdict ... 209
32. Judgment on Decision by the Court ... 210
33. Notice of Availability of a Magistrate Judge to Exercise Jurisdiction and Appeal Option ... 210
34. Consent to Exercise of Jurisdiction by a United States Magistrate Judge, Election of Appeal to District Judge ... 211
34A. Order of Reference ... 211
35. Report of Parties' Planning Meeting ... 212

Supplemental Rules for Certain Admiralty and Maritime Claims

Rule   **Page**

A. Scope of Rules ... 214
B. Attachment and Garnishment: Special Provisions ... 214
C. Actions in Rem: Special Provisions ... 215
D. Possessory, Petitory, and Partition Actions ... 218
E. Actions in Rem and Quasi in Rem: General Provisions ... 218
F. Limitation of Liability ... 222

Comparative Federal and State Provisions

(See Index to Comparative State Provisions, Part X, infra.)

———

FEDERAL RULES OF CIVIL PROCEDURE FOR THE UNITED STATES DISTRICT COURTS PLUS COMPARATIVE STATE AND FEDERAL PROVISIONS

I. SCOPE OF RULES—ONE FORM OF ACTION

Rule 1. Scope of Rules

These rules govern the procedure in the United States district courts in all suits of a civil nature whether cognizable as cases at law or in equity or in admiralty, with the exceptions stated in Rule 81. They shall be construed and administered to secure the just, speedy, and inexpensive determination of every action.

Rule 2. One Form of Action

There shall be one form of action to be known as "civil action".

II. COMMENCEMENT OF ACTION; SERVICE OF PROCESS, PLEADINGS, MOTIONS AND ORDERS

Rule 3. Commencement of Action

A civil action is commenced by filing a complaint with the court.

Comparative State Provision

Kansas Statutes Annotated § 60–203(a)

A civil action is commenced at the time of: (1) filing a petition with the clerk of the court, if service of process is obtained or the first publication is made for service by publication within 90 days after the petition is filed, except that the court may extend that time an additional 30 days upon a showing of good cause by the plaintiff; or (2) service of process or first publication, if service of process or first publication is not made within the time specified by provision (1).

Rule 4. Summons

[See proposed changes to Rule 4(i), in Part IX, infra.]

(a) Form. The summons shall be signed by the clerk, bear the seal of the court, identify the court and the parties, be directed to the defendant, and state the name and address of the plaintiff's attorney or, if unrepresented, of the plaintiff. It shall also state the time within which the defendant must appear and defend, and notify the defendant that failure to do so will result in judgment by default against the defendant for the relief demanded in the complaint. The court may allow a summons to be amended.

(b) Issuance. Upon or after filing the complaint, the plaintiff may present a summons to the clerk for signature and seal. If the summons is in proper form, the clerk shall sign, seal, and issue it to the plaintiff for service on the defendant. A summons, or a copy of the summons if addressed to multiple defendants, shall be issued for each defendant to be served.

(c) Service With Complaint; by Whom Made.

(1) A summons shall be served together with a copy of the complaint. The plaintiff is responsible for service of a summons and complaint within the time allowed under subdivision (m) and shall furnish the person effecting service with the necessary copies of the summons and complaint.

(2) Service may be effected by any person who is not a party and who is at least 18 years of age. At the request of the plaintiff, however, the court may direct that service be effected by a United States marshal, deputy United States marshal, or other person or officer specially appointed by the court for that purpose. Such an appointment must be made when plaintiff is authorized to proceed in forma pauperis pursuant to 28 U.S.C. § 1915 or is authorized to proceed as a seaman under 28 U.S.C. § 1916.

(d) Waiver of Service; Duty to Save Costs of Service; Request to Waive.

(1) A defendant who waives service of a summons does not thereby waive any objection to the venue or to the jurisdiction of the court over the person of the defendant.

(2) An individual, corporation, or association that is subject to service under subdivision (e), (f), or (h) and that receives notice of an action in the manner provided in this paragraph has a duty to avoid unnecessary costs of serving the summons. To avoid costs, the plaintiff may notify such a defendant of the commencement of the action and request that the defendant waive service of a summons. The notice and request

(A) shall be in writing and shall be addressed directly to the defendant, if an individual, or else to an officer or managing or general agent (or other agent authorized by appointment or law to receive service of process) or of a defendant subject to service under subdivision (h);

(B) shall be dispatched through first-class mail or other reliable means;

(C) shall be accompanied by a copy of the complaint and shall identify the court in which it has been filed;

(D) shall inform the defendant, by means of a text prescribed in an official form promulgated pursuant to Rule 84, of the consequences of compliance and of a failure to comply with the request;

(E) shall set forth the date on which the request is sent;

(F) shall allow the defendant a reasonable time to return the waiver, which shall be at least 30 days from the date on which the request is sent, or 60 days from that date if the defendant is addressed outside any judicial district of the United States; and

(G) shall provide the defendant with an extra copy of the notice and request, as well as a prepaid means of compliance in writing.

If a defendant located within the United States fails to comply with a request for waiver made by a plaintiff located within the United States, the court shall impose the costs subsequently incurred in effecting service on the defendant unless good cause for the failure be shown.

(3) A defendant that, before being served with process, timely returns a waiver so requested is not required to serve an answer to the complaint until 60 days after the date on which the request for waiver of service was sent, or 90 days after that date if the defendant was addressed outside any judicial district of the United States.

(4) When the plaintiff files a waiver of service with the court, the action shall proceed, except as provided in paragraph (3), as if a summons and complaint had been served at the time of filing the waiver, and no proof of service shall be required.

(5) The costs to be imposed on a defendant under paragraph (2) for failure to comply with a request to waive service of a summons shall include the costs subsequently incurred in effecting service under subdivision (e), (f), or (h), together with the costs, including a reasonable attorney's fee, of any motion required to collect the costs of service.

(e) Service Upon Individuals Within a Judicial District of the United States. Unless otherwise provided by federal law, service upon an individual from whom a waiver has not been obtained and filed, other than an infant or an incompetent person, may be effected in any judicial district of the United States:

(1) pursuant to the law of the state in which the district court is located, or in which service is effected, for the service of a summons upon the defendant in an action brought in the courts of general jurisdiction of the State; or

(2) by delivering a copy of the summons and of the complaint to the individual personally or by leaving copies thereof at the individual's dwelling house or usual place of abode with some person of suitable age and discretion then residing therein or by delivering a copy of the summons and of the complaint to an agent authorized by appointment or by law to receive service of process.

(f) Service Upon Individuals in a Foreign Country. Unless otherwise provided by federal law, service upon an individual from whom a waiver has not been obtained and filed, other than an infant or an incompetent person, may be effected in a place not within any judicial district of the United States:

(1) by any internationally agreed means reasonably calculated to give notice, such as those means authorized by the Hague Convention on the Service Abroad of Judicial and Extrajudicial Documents; or

(2) if there is no internationally agreed means of service or the applicable international agreement allows other means of service, provided that service is reasonably calculated to give notice:

(A) in the manner prescribed by the law of the foreign country for service in that country in an action in any of its courts of general jurisdiction; or

(B) as directed by the foreign authority in response to a letter rogatory or letter of request; or

(C) unless prohibited by law of the foreign country, by

(i) delivery to the individual personally of a copy of the summons and the complaint; or

(ii) any form of mail requiring a signed receipt, to be addressed and dispatched by the clerk of the court to the party to be served; or

(3) by other means not prohibited by international agreement as may be directed by the court.

(g) Service Upon Infants and Incompetent Persons. Service upon an infant or an incompetent person in a judicial district of the United States shall be effected in the manner prescribed by the law of the state in which the service is made for the service of summons or other like process upon any such defendant in an action brought in the courts of general jurisdiction of that state. Service upon an infant or an incompetent person in a place not within any judicial district of the United States shall be effected in the manner prescribed by paragraph (2)(A) or (2)(B) of subdivision (f) or by such means as the court may direct.

(h) Service Upon Corporations and Associations. Unless otherwise provided by federal law, service upon a domestic or foreign corporation or upon a partnership or other unincorporated association that is subject to suit under a common name, and from which a waiver of service has not been obtained and filed, shall be effected:

(1) in judicial district of the United States in the manner prescribed for individuals by subdivision (e)(1), or by delivering a copy of the summons and of the complaint to an officer, a managing or general agent, or to any other agent authorized by appointment or by law to receive service of process and, if the agent is one authorized by statute to receive service and the statute so requires, by also mailing a copy to the defendant, or

(2) in a place not within any judicial district of the United States in any manner prescribed for individuals by subdivision (f) except personal delivery as provided in paragraph (2)(C)(i) thereof.

(i) Service Upon the United States, and Its Agencies, Corporations, or Officers

(1) Service upon the United States shall be effected

(A) by delivering a copy of the summons and of the complaint to the United States attorney for the district in which the action is brought or to an assistant United States attorney or clerical employee designated by the United States attorney in a writing filed with the clerk of the court or by sending a copy of the summons and of the complaint by registered or certified mail addressed to the civil process clerk at the office of the United States attorney and

(B) by also sending a copy of the summons and of the complaint by registered or certified mail to the Attorney General of the United States at Washington, District of Columbia, and

(C) in any action attacking the validity of an order of an officer or agency of the United States not made a party, by also sending a copy of the summons and of the complaint by registered or certified mail to the officer or agency.

(2) Service upon an officer, agency, or corporation of the United States shall be effected by serving the United States in the manner prescribed by paragraph (1) of this subdivision and by also sending a copy of the summons and of the complaint by registered or certified mail to the officer, agency, or corporation.

(3) The court shall allow a reasonable time for service of process under this subdivision for the purpose of curing the failure to serve multiple officers, agencies, or corporations of the United States if the plaintiff has effected service on either the United States attorney or the Attorney General of the United States.

(j) Service Upon Foreign, State, or Local Governments.

(1) Service upon a foreign state or a political subdivision, agency, or instrumentality thereof shall be effected pursuant to 28 U.S.C. § 1608.

(2) Service upon a state, municipal corporation, or other governmental organization subject to suit shall be effected by delivering a copy of the summons and of the complaint to its chief executive officer or by serving the summons and complaint in the manner prescribed by the law of that state for the service of summons or other like process upon any such defendant.

(k) Territorial Limits of Effective Service.

(1) Service of a summons or filing a waiver of service is effective to establish jurisdiction over the person of a defendant

15

(A) who could be subjected to the jurisdiction of a court of general jurisdiction in the state in which the district court is located, or

The Bulge Rule

(B) who is a party joined under Rule 14 or Rule 19 and is served at a place within a judicial district of the United States and not more than 100 miles from the place from which the summons issues, or

state wouldn't have j/d

Statute

(C) who is subject to the federal interpleader jurisdiction under 28 U.S.C. § 1335, or, *ex- Ins. Co. bringing in all claimants*

(D) when authorized by a statute of the United States. *ex- Anti-Trust Law, Security Law*

(2) If the exercise of jurisdiction is consistent with the Constitution and laws of the United States, serving a summons or filing a waiver of service is also effective, with respect to claims arising under federal law, to establish personal jurisdiction over the person of any defendant who is not subject to the jurisdiction of the courts of general jurisdiction of any state.

if you can serve him + no j/d elsewhere

p. 175 only apply to Aliens but impt. (narrow)

(*l*) Proof of Service. If service is not waived, the person effecting service shall make proof thereof to the court. If service is made by a person other than a United States marshal or deputy United States marshal, the person shall make affidavit thereof. Proof of service in a place not within any judicial district of the United States shall, if effected under paragraph (1) of subdivision (f), be made pursuant to the applicable treaty or convention, and shall, if effected under paragraph (2) or (3) thereof, include a receipt signed by the addressee or other evidence of delivery to the addressee satisfactory to the court. Failure to make proof of service does not affect the validity of the service. The court may allow proof of service to be amended.

(m) Time Limit for Service. If service of the summons and complaint is not made upon a defendant within 120 days after the filing of the complaint, the court, upon motion or on its own initiative after notice to the plaintiff, shall dismiss the action without prejudice as to that defendant or direct that service be effected within a specified time; provided that if the plaintiff shows good cause for the failure, the court shall extend the time for service for an appropriate period. This subdivision does not apply to service in a foreign country pursuant to subdivision (f) or (j)(1).

(n) Seizure of Property; Service of Summons Not Feasible.

(1) If a statute of the United States so provides, the court may assert jurisdiction over property. Notice to claimants of the property shall then be sent in the manner provided by the statute or by service of a summons under this rule.

(2) Upon a showing that personal jurisdiction over a defendant cannot, in the district where the action is brought, be obtained with reasonable efforts by service of summons in any manner authorized by this rule, the court may assert jurisdiction over any of the defendant's

assets found within the district by seizing the assets under the circumstances and in the manner provided by the law of the state in which the district court is located.

Notes on Amendments to Federal Rule 4 and Comparative State Provisions

(a) *Amendments in 1993*

Rule 4 has been altered in order to facilitate service of the summons and complaint. While some provisions of the old rule have merely been reorganized by the Amendments, other provisions have been added or deleted to improve the service of summons. The provisions of Rule 4 that previously dealt with the service of process other than a summons have been removed to the new Rule 4.1, and, as a result, the caption of Rule 4 has been changed from "Process" to "Summons". Several substantive changes have been made to the rule.

The 1993 Amendment facilitates the issuance and service of a summons in several ways. Subdivision (a) (formerly subdivision (b)) no longer requires that summons follow local rule or statute in special cases, allowing instead a uniform summons form and procedure to be used by all federal courts. Subdivision (b) (formerly subdivision (a)) now makes it clear that it is the plaintiff, and not the clerk, who has the obligation to fill out the summons form. Requirements for service have been broadened to allow service to be made not only pursuant to the laws of the forum state, but, unless the defendant is a minor or incompetent, to be made according to the laws of the state in which service is effected as well.

The Amendment also clarifies the procedure for waiving service. The old Rule 4(c)(2)(C)(ii), stated that a summons and complaint may be served "by mailing a copy of the summons and of the complaint (by first-class mail, postage prepaid) to the person to be served, together with two copies of a notice and acknowledgement. * * * " Further, 4(c)(2)(D) provided for the recovery of costs of service from a defendant who did not return the acknowledgement. While this provision was commonly known as "service by mail", it did not, in fact, effect service on the defendant. Rather, the acknowledgement constituted a waiver of personal service. As amended, Rule 4(d) now clearly sets out the procedure for securing a waiver of service from a defendant and, further, explicitly states that the defendant "has a duty to avoid unnecessary costs of serving the summons." The amended rule sets forth the procedures to be followed when service is waived, and, at subsection (d)(5), lists what costs are to be recovered from a defendant who fails to waive service.

The reach of the federal courts is broadened by the Amendment. New Rule 4(e) and 4(k) permit service to be effected anywhere in the United States, and further provide that a federal court shall obtain personal jurisdiction over a defendant not subject to the jurisdiction of any single state to the fullest extent permitted under statute and the Constitution.

Rule 4 sets forth several officers who must be served when the United States is a defendant. Under the old rule, the plaintiff had to deal with the danger of failing to serve a required officer, thereby not effecting service on the United States. The revision eliminates this danger by allowing the plaintiff a reasonable time to cure the defect once it is discovered.

Finally, as amended, Rule 4(f) recommends the use of international agreements regarding service of process by permitting service to be effected on individuals in a foreign country by "any internationally agreed means * * * such as those means authorized by the Hague Convention on the Service Abroad of Judicial and Extrajudicial Documents. * * * "

(b) *Comparative State Provisions—The Illinois Scheme for Issuing and Serving Process*

1. *Issuance of process*

Illinois Compiled Statutes ch. 735, 5/2–201(a)

Every action, unless otherwise expressly provided by statute, shall be commenced by the filing of a complaint. The clerk shall issue summons upon request of the plaintiff. The form and substance of the summons, and of all other process, and the issuance of alias process and the service of copies of pleadings shall be according to rules.

2. *By whom served*

Illinois Compiled Statutes ch. 735, 5/2-202

(a) Process shall be served by a sheriff, or if the sheriff is disqualified, by a coroner of some county of the State. A sheriff of a county with a population of less than 1,000,000 may employ civilian personnel to serve process * * *. The court may, in its discretion upon motion, order service to be made by a private person over 18 years of age and not a party to the action. It is not necessary that service be made by a sheriff or coroner of the county in which service is made. If served or sought to be served by a sheriff or coroner, he or she shall endorse his or her return thereon, and if by a private person the return shall be by affidavit.

(b) Summons may be served upon the defendants wherever they may be found in the State, by any person authorized to serve process. An officer may serve summons in his or her official capacity outside his or her county, but fees for mileage outside the county of the officer cannot be taxed as costs. The person serving the process in a foreign county may make return by mail.

(c) If any sheriff, coroner, or other person to whom any process is delivered, neglects or refuses to make return of the same, the plaintiff may petition the court to enter a rule requiring the sheriff, coroner, or other person, to make return of the process on a day to be fixed by the court, or to show cause on that day why that person should not be attached for contempt of the court. The plaintiff shall then cause a written notice of the rule to be served on the sheriff, coroner, or other person. If good and sufficient cause be not shown to excuse the officer or other person, the court shall adjudge him or her guilty of a contempt, and shall impose punishment as in other cases of contempt.

* * *

3. *Personal service within the state*

Illinois Compiled Statutes ch. 735, 5/2-203(a)

Except as otherwise expressly provided, service of summons upon an individual defendant shall be made (1) by leaving a copy thereof with the defendant personally, (2) by leaving a copy at the defendant's usual place of abode, with some person of the family, or a person residing there, of the age of 13 years or upwards, and informing that person of the contents of the summons, provided the officer or other person making service shall also send a copy of the summons in a sealed envelope with postage fully prepaid, addressed to the defendant at his or her usual place of abode, or (3) as provided in section 1-2-9.2 of the Illinois Municipal Code with respect to a violation of an ordinance governing parking or standing of vehicles in cities with a population over 500,000. The certificate of the officer or affidavit of the person that he or she has sent the copy in pursuance of this Section is evidence that he or she has done so.

Illinois Compiled Statutes ch. 735, 5/2-204

A private corporation may be served (1) by leaving a copy of the process with its registered agent or any officer or agent of the corporation found anywhere in the State; or (2) in any other manner now or hereafter permitted by law. A private corporation may also be notified by publication and mail in like manner and with like effect as individuals.

Illinois Compiled Statutes ch. 735, 5/2-205

(a) A partnership sued in its firm name may be served by leaving a copy of the process with any partner personally or with any agent of the partnership found anywhere in the State. A partnership sued in its firm name may also be notified by publication and mail in like manner and with like effect as individuals.

(b) When a personal judgment is sought against a known partner for a partnership liability the partner may be served (1) in any manner provided for service on individuals or (2) by leaving a copy of the summons for him or her with any other partner and mailing a copy of the summons in a sealed envelope with postage prepaid, addressed to the partner against whom the judgment is sought at his or her usual place of abode as shown by an affidavit filed in the cause. The certificate of the officer or the affidavit of the other person making service that he or she has mailed the copy in pursuance of this section is evidence that he or she has done so. Service on a nonresident partner against whom a personal judgment is sought may be made by leaving a copy with any other partner, and mailing, as provided herein, only if the cause of action sued on is a partnership liability arising out of the transaction of business within the State.

(c) When a personal judgment is sought against an unknown owner in an action authorized under Section 6 of "An Act in relation to the use of an assumed name in the conduct or transaction of business in this State", approved July 17, 1941, as amended, service may be made by leaving a copy of the summons with any agent of the business and publishing notice in the manner provided by Section 2–206 of this Act. (Footnote omitted.)

Illinois Compiled Statutes ch. 735, 5/2–205.1

A voluntary unincorporated association sued in its own name may be served by leaving a copy of the process with any officer of the association personally or by leaving a copy of the process at the office of the association with an agent of the association. A voluntary unincorporated association sued in its own name may also be notified by publication and mail in like manner and with like effect as individuals.

Illinois Compiled Statutes ch. 735, 5/2–211

In actions against public, municipal, governmental or quasi-municipal corporations, summons may be served by leaving a copy with the chairperson of the county board or county clerk in the case of a county, with the mayor or city clerk in the case of a city, with the president of the board of trustees or village clerk in the case of a village, with the supervisor or town clerk in the case of a town, and with the president or clerk or other officer corresponding thereto in the case of any other public, municipal, governmental or quasi-municipal corporation or body.

Illinois Compiled Statutes ch. 735, 5/2–212

Any trustee of a corporation or its property or any receiver may be served with summons (1) in any manner provided for service on individuals or corporations, as is appropriate, or (2) by leaving a copy thereof with any agent in the employ of the trustee or receiver anywhere in the State. The trustee or receiver may also be notified by publication and mail in like manner and with like effect as individuals.

4. *Personal service on party not inhabitant of or found within state*

Illinois Compiled Statutes ch. 735, 5/2–208

(a) Personal service of summons may be made upon any party outside the State. If upon a citizen or resident of this State or upon a person who has submitted to the jurisdiction of the courts of this State, it shall have the force and effect of personal service of summons within this State; otherwise it shall have the force and effect of service by publication.

(b) The service of summons shall be made in like manner as service within this State, by any person over 18 years of age not a party to the action. No order of court is required. An affidavit of the server shall be filed stating the time, manner and place of service. The court may consider the affidavit, or any other competent proofs, in determining whether service has been properly made.

(c) No default shall be entered until the expiration of at least 30 days after service. A default judgment entered on such service may be set aside only on a showing which would be timely and sufficient to set aside a default judgment entered on personal service within this State.

5. *Service by publication*

Illinois Compiled Statutes ch. 735, 5/2–206(a)

Whenever, in any action affecting property or status within the jurisdiction of the court, including an action to obtain the specific performance, reformation, or rescission of a contract for the conveyance of land, plaintiff or his or her attorney shall file, at the office of the clerk of the court in which the action is pending, an affidavit showing that the defendant resides or has gone out of this State, or on due inquiry cannot be found, or is concealed within this State, so that process cannot be served upon him or her and stating the place of residence of the defendant, if known, or that upon diligent inquiry his or her place of residence cannot be ascertained, the clerk shall cause publication to be made in some newspaper published in the county in which the action is pending. If there is no newspaper published in that county, then the publication shall be in a newspaper published in an adjoining county in this State, having a circulation in the county in which action is pending. The publication shall contain notice of the pendency of the action, the title of the court, the title of the case, showing the names of the first named plaintiff and the first named defendant, the number of the case, the names of the parties to be served by publication, and the date on or after which default may be entered against such party. The clerk shall also, within 10 days of the first publication of the notice, send a copy thereof by mail, addressed to each defendant whose place of residence is stated in such affidavit. The certificate of the clerk that he or she has sent the copy in pursuance of this Section is evidence that he or she has done so.

Illinois Compiled Statutes ch. 735, 5/2–207

The notice required in the preceding section may be given at any time after the commencement of the action, and shall be published at least once in each week for 3 successive weeks. No default or proceeding shall be taken against any defendant not served with summons, or a copy of the complaint, and not appearing, unless the first publication be at least 30 days prior to the time when the default or other proceeding is sought to be taken.

6. *Service when action based on attachment*

Illinois Compiled Statutes ch. 735, 5/4–101

In any court having competent jurisdiction, a creditor having a money claim, whether liquidated or unliquidated, and whether sounding in contract or tort or based upon a statutory cause of action created by law in favor of the People of the State of Illinois, or any agency of the State, may have an attachment against the property of his or her debtor, or that of any one or more of several debtors, either at the time of commencement of the action or thereafter, when the claim exceeds $20, in any one of the following cases:

1. Where the debtor is not a resident of this State.

2. When the debtor conceals himself or herself or stands in defiance of an officer, so that process cannot be served upon him or her.

3. Where the debtor has departed from this State with the intention of having his or her effects removed from this State.

4. Where the debtor is about to depart from this State with the intention of having his or her effects removed from this State.

5. Where the debtor is about to remove his or her property from this State to the injury of such creditor.

6. Where the debtor has within 2 years preceding the filing of the affidavit required, fraudulently conveyed or assigned his or her effects, or a part thereof, so as to hinder or delay his or her creditors.

7. Where the debtor has, within 2 years prior to the filing of such affidavit, fraudulently concealed or disposed of his or her property so as to hinder or delay his or her creditors.

8. Where the debtor is about fraudulently to conceal, assign, or otherwise dispose of his or her property or effects, so as to hinder or delay his or her creditors.

9. Where the debt sued for was fraudulently contracted on the part of the debtor. The statements of the debtor, his or her agent or attorney, which constitute the fraud, shall have been reduced to writing, and his or her signature attached thereto, by himself or herself, agent or attorney.

10. When the debtor is a person convicted of first degree murder or * * * [other serious] felony, or found not guilty by reason of insanity or guilty but mentally ill of first degree murder or * * * [such other felony.]

11. When the debtor is a defendant in a suit brought by the Attorney General under Section 3–7–6 of the Unified Code of Corrections to recover the expenses incurred as a result of that debtor's cost of incarceration.

Illinois Compiled Statutes ch. 735, 5/4–126

The sheriff or any other person authorized to serve summons shall, in like manner as summons are served in ordinary civil cases, summon, wherever they may be found in the State, the persons mentioned in such order of attachment as garnishees and all other persons whom the creditor shall designate as having any property, effects, choses in action or credits in their possession or power, belonging to the defendant, or who are in any way indebted to such defendant, the same as if their names had been inserted in such order for attachment. The persons so summoned shall be considered as garnishees. The return shall state the names of all persons so summoned, and the date of such service on each.

Persons summoned as garnishees shall thereafter hold any property, effects, choses in action or credits in their possession or power belonging to the defendant which are not exempt, subject to the court's order in such proceeding, and shall not pay to the defendant any indebtedness owed to him or her subject to such order, and such property, effects, choses in action, credits and debts shall be considered to have been attached and the plaintiff's claim to have become a lien thereon pending such action.

(c) *Comparative State Provisions—California Provision for*
Service of Summons by Mail

California Civil Procedure Code § 415.30

(a) A summons may be served by mail as provided in this section. A copy of the summons and of the complaint shall be mailed (by first-class mail or airmail, postage prepaid) to the person to be served, together with two copies of the notice and acknowledgment provided for in subdivision (b) and a return envelope, postage prepaid, addressed to the sender.

(b) The notice specified in subdivision (a) shall be in substantially the following form:

(Title of court and cause, with action number, to be
inserted by the sender prior to mailing)

Notice

To: (Here state the name of the person to be served.)

This summons is served pursuant to Section 415.30 of the California Code of Civil Procedure. Failure to complete this form and return it to the sender within 20 days may subject you (or the party on whose behalf you are being served) to liability for the payment of any expenses incurred in serving a summons upon you in any other manner permitted by law. If you are served on behalf of a corporation, unincorporated association (including a partnership), or other entity,

21

this form must be signed in the name of such entity by you or by a person authorized to receive service of process on behalf of such entity. In all other cases, this form must be signed by you personally or by a person authorized by you to acknowledge receipt of summons. Section 415.30 provides that this summons is deemed served on the date of execution of an acknowledgment of receipt of summons.

....
Signature of sender

ACKNOWLEDGMENT OF RECEIPT OF SUMMONS

This acknowledges receipt on (insert date) of a copy of the summons and of the complaint at (insert address).

Date: ....
(Date this acknowledgment is executed)

....
Signature of person acknowledging receipt, with title if acknowledgment is made on behalf of another person

(c) Service of a summons pursuant to this section is deemed complete on the date a written acknowledgment of receipt of summons is executed, if such acknowledgment thereafter is returned to the sender.

(d) If the person to whom a copy of the summons and of the complaint are mailed pursuant to this section fails to complete and return the acknowledgment form set forth in subdivision (b) within 20 days from the date of such mailing, the party to whom the summons was mailed shall be liable for reasonable expenses thereafter incurred in serving or attempting to serve the party by another method permitted by this chapter, and, except for good cause shown, the court in which the action is pending, upon motion, with or without notice, shall award the party such expenses whether or not he is otherwise entitled to recover his costs in the action.

(e) A notice or acknowledgment of receipt in form approved by the Judicial Council is deemed to comply with this section.

Rule 4.1   Service of Other Process

(a) Generally. Process other than a summons as provided in Rule 4 or subpoena as provided in Rule 45 shall be served by a United States marshal, a deputy United States marshal, or a person specially appointed for that purpose, who shall make proof of service as provided in Rule 4(1). The process may be served anywhere within the territorial limits of the state in which the district court is located, and, when authorized by a statute of the United States, beyond the territorial limits of that state.

(b) Enforcement of Orders: Commitment for Civil Contempt. An order of civil commitment of a person held to be in contempt of a decree or injunction issued to enforce the laws of the United States may be served and enforced in any district. Other orders in civil contempt proceedings shall be served in the state in which the court issuing the order to be enforced is located or elsewhere within the United States if not more than 100 miles from the place at which the order to be enforced was issued.

Rule 4.1 was adopted in 1993 following the reorganization of Rule 4. Prior to 1993, Rule 4 was entitled "Process" and addressed service of all process. Rule 4 has since been retitled as "Summons" and Rule 4.1 created to govern service of process, other than a summons (governed by Rule 4) and a subpoena (governed by Rule 45).

Rule 4.1(b) provides for nationwide service of orders of civil commitment enforcing decrees of injunctions when issued to compel compliance with federal law. This change replaces the final clause of the second sentence of the former Rule 4. Nationwide service is not mandated by Rule 4.1 in cases where federally-created rights are not at issue.

As noted by the Advisory Committee on Rules, "present law [28 U.S.C. § 3041] permits criminal contempt enforcement against a contemnor wherever that person may be found." Rule 4.1 broadens the scope of the civil contempt service rule to provide greater choice in selecting the most appropriate contempt remedy, be it civil or criminal.

Rule 5. Service and Filing of Pleadings and Other Papers

[See proposed changes to Rule 5(b) and (d), in Part IX, infra.]

(a) Service: When Required. Except as otherwise provided in these rules, every order required by its terms to be served, every pleading subsequent to the original complaint unless the court otherwise orders because of numerous defendants, every paper relating to discovery required to be served upon a party unless the court otherwise orders, every written motion other than one which may be heard ex parte, and every written notice, appearance, demand, offer of judgment, designation of record on appeal, and similar paper shall be served upon each of the parties. No service need be made on parties in default for failure to appear except that pleadings asserting new or additional claims for relief against them shall be served upon them in the manner provided for service of summons in Rule 4.

In an action begun by seizure of property, in which no person need be or is named as defendant, any service required to be made prior to the filing of an answer, claim, or appearance shall be made upon the person having custody or possession of the property at the time of its seizure.

(b) Same: How Made. Whenever under these rules service is required or permitted to be made upon a party represented by an attorney the service shall be made upon the attorney unless service upon the party is ordered by the court. Service upon the attorney or upon a party shall be made by delivering a copy to the attorney or party or by mailing it to the attorney or party at the attorney's or party's last known address or, if no address is known, by leaving it with the clerk of the court. Delivery of a copy within this rule means: handing it to the attorney or to the party; or leaving it at the attorney's or party's office with a clerk or other person in charge thereof; or, if there is no one in charge, leaving it in a conspicuous place therein; or, if the office is closed or the person to be served has no office, leaving it at the person's dwelling house or usual place of abode with some person of suitable age and discretion then residing therein. Service by mail is complete upon mailing.

(c) Same: Numerous Defendants. In any action in which there are unusually large numbers of defendants, the court, upon motion or of its own initiative, may order that service of the pleadings of the defendants and replies thereto need not be made as between the defendants and that any cross-claim, counterclaim, or matter constituting an avoidance or affirmative defense contained therein shall be deemed to be denied or avoided by all other parties and that the filing of any such pleading and service thereof upon the plaintiff constitutes due notice of it to the parties. A copy of every such order shall be served upon the parties in such manner and form as the court directs.

(d) Filing; Certificate of Service. All papers after the complaint required to be served upon a party, together with a certificate of service, shall be filed with the court within a reasonable time after service but the court may on motion of a party or on its own initiative order that depositions upon oral examination and interrogatories, requests for documents, requests for admission, and answers and responses thereto not be filed unless on order of the court or for use in the proceeding.

(e) Filing With the Court Defined. The filing of papers with the court as required by these rules shall be made by filing them with the clerk of the court, except that the judge may permit the papers to be filed with the judge, in which event the judge shall note thereon the filing date and forthwith transmit them to the office of the clerk. A court may by local rule permit papers to be filed, signed, or verified by electronic means that are consistent with technical standards, if any, that the Judicial Conference of the United States establishes. A paper filed by electronic means in compliance with a local rule constitutes a written paper for the purpose of applying these rules. The clerk shall not refuse to accept for filing any paper presented for that purpose solely because it is not presented in proper form as required by these rules or any local rules or practices.

Rule 6. Time

[See proposed changes to Rule 6(e), in Part IX, infra.]

(a) Computation. In computing any period of time prescribed or allowed by these rules, by the local rules of any district court, by order of court, or by any applicable statute, the day of the act, event, or default from which the designated period of time begins to run shall not be included. The last day of the period so computed shall be included, unless it is a Saturday, a Sunday, or a legal holiday or, when the act to be done is the filing of a paper in court, a day on which weather or other conditions have made the office of the clerk of the district court inaccessible, in which event the period runs until the end of the next day which is not one of the aforementioned days. When the period of time prescribed or allowed is less than 11 days, intermediate Saturdays, Sundays, and legal holidays shall be excluded in the computation. As used in this rule and in Rule 77(c), "legal holiday" includes New Year's Day, Birthday of Martin Luther King, Jr., Washington's Birthday, Memorial Day, Independence Day, Labor Day, Columbus Day, Veterans Day, Thanksgiving Day, Christmas Day, and any other day appointed as a holiday by the President or the Congress of the United States, or by the state in which the district court is held.

(b) Enlargement. [A proposed technical amendment to Rule 6(b) to take effect in December 1999 would omit reference to Rule 74(a). Rule 74 has previously been abrogated.] When by these rules or by a notice given thereunder or by order of court an act is required or allowed to be done at or within a specified time, the court for cause shown may at any time in its discretion (1) with or without motion or notice order the period enlarged if request therefor is made before the expiration of the period originally prescribed or as extended by a previous order, or (2) upon motion made after the expiration of the specified period permit the act to be done where the failure to act was the result of excusable neglect; but it may not extend the time for taking any action under Rules 50(b) and (c)(2), 52(b), 59(b), (d) and (e), 60(b), and 74(a), except to the extent and under the conditions stated in them.

(c) [Rescinded. Feb. 28, 1966, eff. July 1, 1966.]

(d) For Motions—Affidavits. A written motion, other than one which may be heard ex parte, and notice of the hearing thereof shall be served not later than 5 days before the time specified for the hearing, unless a different period is fixed by these rules or by order of the court. Such an order may for cause shown be made on ex parte application. When a motion is supported by affidavit, the affidavit shall be served with the motion; and, except as otherwise provided in Rule 59(c), opposing affidavits may be served not later than 1 day before the hearing, unless the court permits them to be served at some other time.

(e) Additional Time After Service by Mail. Whenever a party has the right or is required to do some act or take some proceedings within a prescribed period after the service of a notice or other paper upon the party and the notice or paper is served upon the party by mail, 3 days shall be added to the prescribed period.

Note on 1985 Amendments to Federal Rule 6

The amended rule extends the exclusion of intermediate Saturdays, Sundays, and legal holidays to the computation of time periods less than 11 days. Under the prior version of Rule 6, parties bringing motions under rules with 10-day periods could have as few as 5 working days to prepare their motions. This hardship was especially acute in the case of Rules 50(b) and (c)(2), 52(b), 59(b), (d), and (e), and 60(b), which may not be enlarged at the discretion of the court. See Rule 6(b).

III. PLEADINGS AND MOTIONS

Rule 7. Pleadings Allowed; Form of Motions

(a) Pleadings. There shall be a complaint and an answer; a reply to a counterclaim denominated as such; an answer to a cross-claim, if the answer contains a cross-claim; a third-party complaint, if a person who was not an original party is summoned under the provisions of Rule 14; and a third-party answer, if a third-party complaint is served. No other pleading shall be allowed, except that the court may order a reply to an answer or a third-party answer.

(b) Motions and Other Papers.

(1) An application to the court for an order shall be by motion which, unless made during a hearing or trial, shall be made in writing, shall state with particularity the grounds therefor, and shall set forth the relief or order sought. The requirement of writing is fulfilled if the motion is stated in a written notice of the hearing of the motion.

(2) The rules applicable to captions and other matters of form of pleadings apply to all motions and other papers provided for by these rules.

(3) All motions shall be signed in accordance with Rule 11.

(c) Demurrers, Pleas, etc., Abolished. Demurrers, pleas, and exceptions for insufficiency of a pleading shall not be used.

Amendment to Federal Rule 7 and Comparative State Provisions

(a) Addition in 1983 of Rule 7(b)(3)

Rule 7(b)(3) makes clear that an "appropriate sanction" can be obtained against an attorney or party who files a motion in bad faith. One of the reasons sanctions against improper motion practice had been employed infrequently was the lack of clarity of Rule 7. It had stated only generally that the pleading requirements relating to captions, signing, and other matters of form also apply to motions and other papers. The addition of Rule 7(b)(3) explicitly expresses the applicability of the signing requirement and the sanctions of Rule 11, which have been amplified. See Amendments to Federal Rule 11, following Rule 11 infra.

(b) Comparative State Provisions

Nebraska Revised Statutes § 25–803

The only pleadings allowed are (1) the petition by the plaintiff; (2) the answer or demurrer by the defendant; (3) the demurrer or reply by the plaintiff; and (4) the demurrer to the reply by the defendant.

Nebraska Revised Statutes § 25–820

The plaintiff may demur to one or more of the defenses set up in the answer, stating in his demurrer the grounds thereof; and where the answer contains new matter the plaintiff may reply to such new matter, denying generally or specifically each allegation controverted by him; and he may allege, in ordinary and concise language, and without repetition, any new matter not inconsistent with the petition, constituting a defense to such new matter in the answer.

Rule 8. General Rules of Pleading

(a) Claims for Relief. A pleading which sets forth a claim for relief, whether an original claim, counterclaim, cross-claim, or third-party claim, shall contain (1) a short and plain statement of the grounds upon which the court's jurisdiction depends, unless the court already has jurisdiction and the claim needs no new grounds of jurisdiction to support it, (2) a short and plain statement of the claim showing that the pleader is entitled to relief, and (3) a demand for judgment for the relief the pleader seeks. Relief in the alternative or of several different types may be demanded.

(b) Defenses; Form of Denials. A party shall state in short and plain terms the party's defenses to each claim asserted and shall admit or deny the averments upon which the adverse party relies. If a party is without knowledge or information sufficient to form a belief as to the truth of an averment, the party shall so state and this has the effect of a denial. Denials shall fairly meet the substance of the averments denied. When a pleader intends in good faith to deny only a part or a qualification of an averment, the pleader shall specify so much of it as is true and material and shall deny only the remainder. Unless the pleader intends in good faith to controvert all the averments of the preceding pleading, the pleader may make denials as specific denials of designated averments or paragraphs, or may generally deny all the averments except such designated averments or paragraphs as the pleader expressly admits; but, when the pleader does so intend to controvert all its averments, including averments of the grounds upon which the court's jurisdiction depends, the pleader may do so by general denial subject to the obligations set forth in Rule 11.

(c) Affirmative Defenses. In pleading to a preceding pleading, a party shall set forth affirmatively accord and satisfaction, arbitration and award, assumption of risk, contributory negligence, discharge in bankruptcy, duress, estoppel, failure of consideration, fraud, illegality, injury by fellow servant, laches, license, payment, release, res judicata, statute of frauds, statute of limitations, waiver, and any other matter constituting an avoidance or affirmative defense. When a party has mistakenly designated a defense as a counterclaim or a counterclaim as a defense, the court on terms, if justice so requires, shall treat the pleading as if there had been a proper designation.

(d) Effect of Failure to Deny. Averments in a pleading to which a responsive pleading is required, other than those as to the amount of damage, are admitted when not denied in the responsive pleading. Averments in a pleading to which no responsive pleading is required or permitted shall be taken as denied or avoided.

(e) Pleading to Be Concise and Direct; Consistency.

(1) Each averment of a pleading shall be simple, concise, and direct. No technical forms of pleading or motions are required.

(2) A party may set forth two or more statements of a claim or defense alternately or hypothetically, either in one count or defense or in separate counts or defenses. When two or more statements are made in the alternative and one of them if made independently would be sufficient, the pleading is not made insufficient by the insufficiency of one or more of the alternative statements. A party may also state as many separate claims or defenses as the party has regardless of consistency and whether based on legal, equitable, or maritime grounds. All statements shall be made subject to the obligations set forth in Rule 11.

(f) Construction of Pleadings. All pleadings shall be so construed as to do substantial justice.

Comparative State Provisions

(a) *Rule 8(a)*

California Civil Procedure Code § 425.10(b)

[A complaint or cross-complaint shall contain:]

A demand for judgment for the relief to which the pleader claims to be entitled. If the recovery of money or damages be demanded, the amount thereof shall be stated, unless the action is brought in the superior court to recover actual or punitive damages for personal injury or wrongful death, in which case the amount thereof shall not be stated * * *.

Georgia Code Annotated § 9–11–8(a)(2)

An original complaint shall contain facts upon which the court's venue depends; and any pleading which sets forth a claim for relief, whether an original claim, counterclaim, a cross-claim, or a third-party claim, shall contain:

(A) A short and plain statement of the claims showing that the pleader is entitled to relief; and

(B) A demand for judgment for the relief to which the pleader deems himself entitled; provided, however, that in actions for medical malpractice, as defined in this Code section, in which a claim for unliquidated damages is made for $10,000.00 or less, the pleadings shall contain a demand for judgment in a sum certain; and, in actions for medical malpractice in which a claim for unliquidated damages is made for a sum exceeding $10,000.00, the demand for judgment shall state that the pleader "demands judgment in excess of $10,000.00," and no further monetary amount shall be stated.

Relief in the alternative or of several different types may be demanded.

Illinois Compiled Statutes ch. 735, 5/2–604

Every complaint and counterclaim shall contain specific prayers for the relief to which the pleader deems himself or herself entitled except that in actions for injury to the person, no ad damnum may be pleaded except to the minimum extent necessary to comply with the circuit rules of assignment where the claim is filed. Relief, whether based on one or more counts, may be requested in the alternative. Prayers for relief which the allegations of the pleadings do not sustain may be objected to on motion or in the answering pleading. In actions for injury to the person, any complaint filed which contains an ad damnum, except to the minimum extent necessary to comply with the circuit rules of assignment where the claim is filed, shall, on motion of a defendant or on the court's own motion, be dismissed without prejudice. Except in case of default, the prayer for relief does not limit the relief obtainable, but where other relief is sought the court shall, by proper orders, and upon terms that may be just, protect the adverse party against prejudice by reason of surprise. In case of default, if relief is sought, whether by amendment, counterclaim, or otherwise, beyond that prayed in the pleading to which the party is in default, notice shall be given the defaulted party as provided by rule.

Nothing in this Section shall be construed as prohibiting the defendant from requesting of the plaintiff by interrogatory the amount of damages which will be sought.

Nebraska Revised Statutes § 25–804

The petition must contain (1) the name of the court and county in which the action is brought, and the names of the parties, plaintiff and defendant; (2) a statement of the facts constituting the cause of action, in ordinary and concise language, and without repetition; and (3) a demand for the relief to which the party supposes himself entitled. If the recovery of money be demanded, the amount of special damages shall be stated but the amount of general damages shall not be stated; and if interest thereon be claimed, the time from which interest is to be computed shall also be stated.

New York Civil Practice Law and Rules 3013

Statements in a pleading shall be sufficiently particular to give the court and parties notice of the transactions, occurrences, or series of transactions or occurrences, intended to be proved and the material elements of each cause of action or defense.

New York Civil Practice Law and Rules 3017(c)

In an action for medical or dental malpractice or in an action against a municipal corporation, as defined in section two of the general municipal law, the complaint, counterclaim, cross-claim, interpleader complaint, and third-party complaint shall contain a prayer for general relief but shall not state the amount of damages to which the pleader deems himself entitled. If the action is brought in the supreme court, the pleading shall also state whether or not the amount of damages sought exceeds the jurisdictional limits of all lower courts which would otherwise have jurisdiction. Provided, however, that a party against whom an action for medical or dental malpractice is brought or the municipal corporation, may at any time request a supplemental demand setting forth the total damages to which the pleader deems himself entitled. A supplemental demand shall be provided by the party bringing the action within fifteen days of the request. In the event the supplemental demand is not served within fifteen days, the court, on motion, may order that it be served. A supplemental demand served pursuant to this subdivision shall be treated in all respects as a demand made pursuant to subdivision (a) of this section.

New York Civil Practice Law and Rules 3041

Any party may require any other party to give a bill of particulars of such party's claim, or a copy of the items of the account alleged in a pleading. * * *

New York Civil Practice Law and Rules 3043

(a) **Specified particulars.** In actions to recover for personal injuries the following particulars may be required:

(1) The date and approximate time of day of the occurrence;

(2) Its approximate location;

(3) General statement of the acts or omissions constituting the negligence claimed;

(4) Where notice of a condition is a prerequisite, whether actual or constructive notice is claimed;

(5) If actual notice is claimed, a statement of when and to whom it was given;

(6) Statement of the injuries and description of those claimed to be permanent, and in an action designated in * * * [§ 5104(a)] of the insurance law, for personal injuries arising out of negligence in the use or operation of a motor vehicle in this state, in what respect plaintiff has sustained a serious injury, as defined in * * * [§ 5102(d)] of the insurance law, or economic loss greater than basic economic loss, as defined in * * * [§ 5102(a)] of the insurance law;

(7) Length of time confined to bed and to house;

(8) Length of time incapacitated from employment; and

(9) Total amounts claimed as special damages for physicians' services and medical supplies; loss of earnings, with name and address of the employer; hospital expenses; nurses' services.

(b) Supplemental bill of particulars without leave. A party may serve a supplemental bill of particulars with respect to claims of continuing special damages and disabilities without leave of court at any time, but not less than thirty days prior to trial. Provided however that no new cause of action may be alleged or new injury claimed * * *.

(c) Discretion of court. Nothing contained in the foregoing shall be deemed to limit the court in denying in a proper case, any one or more of the foregoing particulars, or in a proper case, in granting other, further or different particulars.

See also North Carolina Rules of Civil Procedure—[Form] (3) Complaint for Negligence as set out following Form 9 of the Appendix of Forms, Federal Rules of Civil Procedure, infra.

(b) *Rule 8(b)*

1. *In general*

Illinois Compiled Statutes ch. 735, 5/2–610

(a) Every answer and subsequent pleading shall contain an explicit admission or denial of each allegation of the pleading to which it relates.

(b) Every allegation, except allegations of damages, not explicitly denied is admitted, unless the party states in his or her pleading that he or she has no knowledge thereof sufficient to form a belief, and attaches an affidavit of the truth of the statement of want of knowledge, or unless the party has had no opportunity to deny.

(c) Denials must not be evasive, but must fairly answer the substance of the allegation denied.

(d) If a party wishes to raise an issue as to the amount of damages only, he or she may do so by stating in his or her pleading that he or she desires to contest only the amount of the damages.

2. *Importance of verification*

California Civil Procedure Code § 431.30(d)

If the complaint is * * * not verified, a general denial is sufficient but only puts in issue the material allegations of the complaint. If the complaint is verified, * * * [then, with exceptions for certain actions] the denial of the allegations shall be made positively or according to the information and belief of the defendant. * * *

California Civil Procedure Code § 446(a)

Every pleading shall be subscribed by the party or his or her attorney. * * * When the complaint is verified, the answer shall be verified. * * *.

(c) *Rule 8(c)*

New York Civil Practice Law and Rules 3018(b)

A party shall plead all matters which if not pleaded would be likely to take the adverse party by surprise or would raise issues of fact not appearing on the face of a prior pleading such as arbitration and award, collateral estoppel, culpable conduct claimed in diminution of damages * * *, discharge in bankruptcy, facts showing illegality either by statute or common law, fraud, infancy or other disability of the party defending, payment, release, res judicata, statute of frauds, or statute of limitation. The application of this subdivision shall not be confined to the instances enumerated.

(d) *Rule 8(d)*

Nebraska Revised Statutes § 25–842

Every material allegation of the petition not controverted by the answer, and every material allegation of new matter in the answer not controverted by the reply, shall, for the purposes of the action, be taken as true; but the allegation of new matter in the reply shall be deemed controverted by the adverse party as upon direct denial or avoidance. Allegations of value or amount of damage shall not be considered as true by failure to controvert them.

New York Civil Practice Law and Rules 3018(a)

A party shall deny those statements known or believed by him to be untrue. He shall specify those statements as to the truth of which he lacks knowledge or information sufficient to form a belief and this shall have the effect of a denial. All other statements of a pleading are deemed admitted, except that where no responsive pleading is permitted they are deemed denied or avoided.

(e) *Rule 8(e)(1)*

Colorado Rule of Civil Procedure 8(e)(1)

Each averment of a pleading shall be simple, concise, and direct. When a pleader is without direct knowledge, allegations may be made upon information and belief. No technical forms of pleading or motions are required. Pleadings otherwise meeting the requirements of these rules shall not be considered objectionable for failure to state ultimate facts as distinguished from conclusions of law.

(f) *Rule 8(e)(2)*

Georgia Code Annotated § 9–11–8(e)(2)

A party may set forth two or more statements of a claim or defense alternatively or hypothetically, either in one count or defense or in separate counts or defenses. When two or more statements are made in the alternative and one of them, if made independently, would be sufficient, the pleading is not made insufficient by the insufficiency of one or more of the alternative statements. A party may also state as many separate claims or defenses as he has, regardless of consistency and whether based on legal or on equitable grounds or on both. All statements shall be made subject to the obligations set forth in Code Section 9–11–11.

Rule 9. Pleading Special Matters

(a) **Capacity.** It is not necessary to aver the capacity of a party to sue or be sued or the authority of a party to sue or be sued in a representative capacity or the legal existence of an organized association of persons that is made a party, except to the extent required to show the jurisdiction of the court. When a party desires to raise an issue as to the legal existence of any party or the capacity of any party to sue or be sued or the authority of a party to sue or be sued in a representative capacity, the party desiring to raise the issue shall do so by specific negative averment, which shall include such supporting particulars as are peculiarly within the pleader's knowledge.

(b) Fraud, Mistake, Condition of the Mind. In all averments of fraud or mistake, the circumstances constituting fraud or mistake shall be stated with particularity. Malice, intent, knowledge, and other condition of mind of a person may be averred generally.

(c) Conditions Precedent. In pleading the performance or occurrence of conditions precedent, it is sufficient to aver generally that all conditions precedent have been performed or have occurred. A denial of performance or occurrence shall be made specifically and with particularity.

(d) Official Document or Act. In pleading an official document or official act it is sufficient to aver that the document was issued or the act done in compliance with law.

(e) Judgment. In pleading a judgment or decision of a domestic or foreign court, judicial or quasijudicial tribunal, or of a board or officer, it is sufficient to aver the judgment or decision without setting forth matter showing jurisdiction to render it.

(f) Time and Place. For the purpose of testing the sufficiency of a pleading, averments of time and place are material and shall be considered like all other averments of material matter.

(g) Special Damage. When items of special damage are claimed, they shall be specifically stated.

(h) Admiralty and Maritime Claims. A pleading or count setting forth a claim for relief within the admiralty and maritime jurisdiction that is also within the jurisdiction of the district court on some other ground may contain a statement identifying the claim as an admiralty or maritime claim for the purposes of Rules 14(c), 38(e), 82, and the Supplemental Rules for Certain Admiralty and Maritime Claims. If the claim is cognizable only in admiralty, it is an admiralty or maritime claim for those purposes whether so identified or not. The amendment of a pleading to add or withdraw an identifying statement is governed by the principles of Rule 15. A case that includes an admiralty or maritime claim within this subdivision is an admiralty case within 28 U.S.C. § 1292(a)(3).

Comparative State Provisions and Notes on Amendment to Federal Rule 9

(a) *Comparative State Provisions*

1. *In General*

New York Civil Practice Law and Rules 3015

(a) Conditions precedent. The performance or occurrence of a condition precedent in a contract need not be pleaded. A denial of performance or occurrence shall be made specifically and with particularity. In case of such denial, the party relying upon the performance or occurrence shall be required to prove on the trial only such performance or occurrence as shall have been so specified.

(b) Corporate status. Where any party is a corporation, the complaint shall so state and, where known, it shall specify the state, country or government by or under whose laws the party was created.

(c) Judgment, decision or determination. A judgment, decision or other determination of a court, judicial or quasi-judicial tribunal, or of a board or officer, may be pleaded without stating matter showing jurisdiction to render it.

(d) Signatures. Unless specifically denied in the pleadings each signature on a negotiable instrument is admitted.

* * *

New York Civil Practice Law and Rules 3016

(a) Libel or slander. In an action for libel or slander, the particular words complained of shall be set forth in the complaint, but their application to the plaintiff may be stated generally.

(b) Fraud or mistake. Where a cause of action or defense is based upon misrepresentation, fraud, mistake, wilful default, breach of trust or undue influence, the circumstances constituting the wrong shall be stated in detail.

(c) Separation or divorce. In an action for separation or divorce, the nature and circumstances of a party's alleged misconduct, if any, and the time and place of each act complained of, if any, shall be specified in the complaint or counterclaim as the case may be.

(d) Judgment. In an action on a judgment, the complaint shall state the extent to which any judgment recovered by the plaintiff against the defendant, or against a person jointly liable with the defendant, on the same cause of action has been satisfied.

(e) Law of foreign country. Where a cause of action or defense is based upon the law of a foreign country or its political subdivision, the substance of the foreign law relied upon shall be stated.

(f) Sale and delivery of goods or performing of labor or services. In an action involving the sale and delivery of goods, or the performing of labor or services, or the furnishing of materials, the plaintiff may set forth and number in his verified complaint the items of his claim and the reasonable value or agreed price of each. Thereupon the defendant by his verified answer shall indicate specifically those items he disputes and whether in respect of delivery or performance, reasonable value or agreed price.

* * *

2. *Rule 9(c)*

New Jersey Civil Practice Rule 4:5–8(b)

In pleading the performance or occurrence of conditions precedent, it is sufficient to allege generally that all such conditions have been performed or have occurred. A denial of performance or occurrence shall be made specifically and with particularity, but when so made the party pleading the performance or occurrence has the burden of establishing it.

See also New York Civil Practice Law and Rules 3015(a) set out in 1 above.

(b) *Amendment in 1966 Adding Rule 9(h)*

Rule 9(h) was added by amendment in 1966. The Advisory Committee's Note to the Rule reads as follows:

Certain distinctive features of the admiralty practice must be preserved for what are now suits in admiralty. This raises the question: After unification, when a single form of action is established, how will the counterpart of the present suit in admiralty be identifiable? In part the question is easily answered. Some claims for relief can only be suits in admiralty, either because the admiralty jurisdiction is exclusive or because no nonmaritime ground of federal jurisdiction exists. Many claims, however, are cognizable by the district courts whether asserted in admiralty or in a civil action, assuming the existence of a nonmaritime ground of jurisdiction. Thus at present the pleader has power to determine procedural consequences by the way in which he exercises the classic privilege given by the saving-to-suitors clause (28 U.S.C. § 1333) or by equivalent statutory provisions. For example, a longshoreman's claim for personal injuries suffered by reason of the unseaworthiness of a vessel may be asserted in a suit in admiralty or, if diversity of citizenship exists, in a civil action. One of the important procedural consequences is that in the civil action either party may demand a jury trial, while in the suit in admiralty there is no right to jury trial except as provided by statute.

It is no part of the purpose of unification to inject a right to jury trial into those admiralty cases in which that right is not provided by statute. Similarly, as will be more specifically noted below, there is no disposition to change the present law as to interlocutory appeals in admiralty, or as to the venue of suits in admiralty; and, of course, there is no disposition to inject into the civil practice as it now is the distinctively maritime remedies (maritime attachment and garnishment, actions in rem, possessory, petitory, and partition actions and limitation of liability). The unified rules must therefore provide some device for preserving the present power of the pleader to determine whether these historically maritime procedures shall be applicable to his claim or not; the pleader must be afforded some means of designating his claim as the counterpart of the present suit in admiralty, where its character as such is not clear.

The problem is different from the similar one concerning the identification of claims that were formerly suits in equity. While that problem is not free from complexities, it is broadly true that the modern counterpart of the suit in equity is distinguishable from the former action at law by the character of the relief sought. This mode of identification is possible in only a limited category of admiralty cases. In large numbers of cases the relief sought in admiralty is simple money damages, indistinguishable from the remedy afforded by the common law. This is true, for example, in the case of the longshoreman's action for personal injuries stated above. After unification has abolished the distinction between civil actions and suits in admiralty, the complaint in such an action would be almost completely ambiguous as to the pleader's intentions regarding the procedure invoked. The allegation of diversity of citizenship might be regarded as a clue indicating an intention to proceed as at present under the saving-to-suitors clause; but this, too, would be ambiguous if there were also reference to the admiralty jurisdiction, and the pleader ought not be required to forego mention of all available jurisdictional grounds.

Other methods of solving the problem were carefully explored, but the Advisory Committee concluded that the preferable solution is to allow the pleader who now has power to determine procedural consequences by filing a suit in admiralty to exercise that power under unification, for the limited instances in which procedural differences will remain, by a simple statement in his pleading to the effect that the claim is an admiralty or maritime claim.

The choice made by the pleader in identifying or in failing to identify his claim as an admiralty or maritime claim is not an irrevocable election. The rule provides that the amendment of a pleading to add or withdraw an identifying statement is subject to the principles of Rule 15.

Rule 10. Form of Pleadings

(a) Caption; Names of Parties. Every pleading shall contain a caption setting forth the name of the court, the title of the action, the file number, and a designation as in Rule 7(a). In the complaint the title of the action shall include the names of all the parties, but in other pleadings it is sufficient to state the name of the first party on each side with an appropriate indication of other parties.

(b) Paragraphs; Separate Statements. All averments of claim or defense shall be made in numbered paragraphs, the contents of each of which shall be limited as far as practicable to a statement of a single set of circumstances; and a paragraph may be referred to by number in all succeeding pleadings. Each claim founded upon a separate transaction or occurrence and each defense other than denials shall be stated in a separate count or defense whenever a separation facilitates the clear presentation of the matters set forth.

(c) Adoption by Reference; Exhibits. Statements in a pleading may be adopted by reference in a different part of the same pleading or in another pleading or in any motion. A copy of any written instrument which is an exhibit to a pleading is a part thereof for all purposes.

Comparative State Provisions

(a) *Rule 10(b)*

Illinois Compiled Statutes ch. 735, 5/2–613(a)

Parties may plead as many causes of action, counterclaims, defenses, and matters in reply as they may have, and each shall be separately designated and numbered.

Illinois Compiled Statutes ch. 735, 5/2–603(b)

Each separate cause of action upon which a separate recovery might be had shall be stated in a separate count or counterclaim, as the case may be and each count, counterclaim, defense or reply, shall be separately pleaded, designated and numbered, and each shall be divided into paragraphs numbered consecutively, each paragraph containing, as nearly as may be, a separate allegation.

(b) *Rule 10(c)*

Michigan Court Rule 2.113(F)

Exhibits; Written Instruments.

(1) If a claim or defense is based on a written instrument, a copy of the instrument or its pertinent parts must be attached to the pleading as an exhibit unless the instrument is

> (a) a matter of public record in the county in which the action is commenced and its location in the record is stated in the pleading;

> (b) in the possession of the adverse party and the pleading so states;

> (c) inaccessible to the pleader and the pleading so states, giving the reason; or

> (d) of a nature that attaching the instrument would be unnecessary or impractical and the pleading so states, giving the reason.

(2) An exhibit attached or referred to under subrule (F)(1)(a) or (b) is a part of the pleading for all purposes.

Michigan Court Rule 2.113(G)

Adoption by Reference. Statements in a pleading may be adopted by reference only in another part of the same pleading.

Rule 11.   Signing of Pleadings, Motions, and Other Papers; Representations to Court; Sanctions

[See proposed congressional changes to Rule 11(c), in Part IX, infra.]

(a) Signature. Every pleading, written motion, and other paper shall be signed by at least one attorney of record in the attorney's individual name, or, if the party is not represented by an attorney, shall be signed by the party. Each paper shall state the signer's address and telephone number, if any. Except when otherwise specifically provided by rule or statute, pleadings need not be verified or accompanied by affidavit. An unsigned paper shall be stricken unless omission of the signature is corrected promptly after being called to the attention of the attorney or party.

(b) Representations to Court. By presenting to the court (whether by signing, filing, submitting, or later advocating) a pleading, written motion, or other paper, an attorney or unrepresented party is certifying that to the best of the person's knowledge, information, and belief formed after an inquiry reasonable under the circumstances,—

(1) it is not being presented or maintained for any improper purpose, such as to harass or to cause unnecessary delay or needless increase in the cost of litigation;

(2) the claims, defenses, and other legal contentions therein are warranted by existing law or by a nonfrivolous argument for the extension, modification, or reversal of existing law or the establishment of new law;

(3) the allegations and other factual contentions have evidentiary support or, if specifically so identified, are likely to have evidentiary support after a reasonable opportunity for further investigation or discovery; and

(4) the denials of factual contentions are warranted on the evidence or, if specifically so identified, are reasonably based on a lack of information and belief.

(c) Sanctions. If, after notice and a reasonable opportunity to respond, the court determines that subdivision (b) has been violated, the court may, subject to the conditions stated below, impose an appropriate sanction upon the attorneys, law firms, or parties that have violated subdivision (b) or are responsible for the violation.

(1) *How Initiated.*

(A) *By Motion.* A motion for sanctions under this rule shall be made separately from other motions or requests, and shall describe the specific conduct alleged to violate subdivision (b). It shall be served as provided in Rule 5, but shall not be filed with, or presented to, the court unless, within 21 days after service of the motion (or such other period as the court may prescribe), the challenged paper, claim, defense, contention, allegation or denial is not withdrawn or appropriately corrected. If warranted, the court may award to the party prevailing on the motion the reasonable expenses and attorney's fees incurred in presenting or opposing the motion. Absent exceptional circumstances, a law firm shall be held jointly responsible for violations committed by its partners, associates, and employees.

(B) *On Court's Initiative.* On its own initiative, the court may enter an order describing the specific conduct that appears to violate subdivision (b) and directing an attorney, law firm, or party to show cause why it has not violated subdivision (b) with respect thereto.

(2) *Nature of Sanction; Limitations.* A sanction imposed for violation of this rule shall be limited to what is sufficient to deter repetition of such conduct or comparable conduct by others similarly situated. Subject to the limitations in subparagraphs (A) and (B), the sanction may consist of, or include, directives of a nonmonetary nature, an order to pay a penalty into court, or, if imposed on motion and warranted for effective deterrence, an order directing payment to the movant of some or all of the reasonable attorney's fees and other expenses incurred as a direct result of the violation.

(A) Monetary sanctions may not be awarded against a represented party for a violation of subdivision (b)(2).

(B) Monetary sanctions may not be awarded on the court's initiative unless the court issues its order to show cause before a voluntary dismissal or settlement of the claims made by or against the party which is, or whose attorneys are, to be sanctioned.

(3) *Order.* When imposing sanctions, the court shall describe the conduct determined to constitute a violation of this rule and explain the basis for the sanction imposed.

(d) Inapplicability to Discovery. Subdivisions (a) through (c) of this rule do not apply to disclosures and discovery requests, responses, objections, and motions that are subject to the provisions of Rules 26 through 37.

Note on Amendment to Federal Rule 11 and Comparative State Provisions

(a) *Amendment in 1993 to Federal Rule 11*

Several revisions to Rule 11 were adopted in 1993 to address problems that have arisen from application of the 1983 amendments to the Rule. While the purpose of the Rule, to provide sanctions for litigants and attorneys who attempt to thwart the goals of the Federal Rules of Civil Procedure set forth in Rule 1, remains the same, the Rule has been altered to attempt to reduce the large number of motions for sanctions presented under the old Rule.

The amended Rule broadens the duty of an attorney or pro se litigant to warrant that representations to the court, by any means and at any time, are proper, as defined in subdivision (b)(1)–(4). The inclusion of the phrase "later advocating" in subdivision (b) makes clear that the duty to make truthful representations to the court is an ongoing one. Therefore, factual contentions in initial pleadings which fail to be sustained by information obtained through discovery may not, under the new Rule, continue to be advocated. The pleading party making such a contention, however, need only cease advocating the unsustainable contention and is under no duty to formally amend the initial pleading.

Two provisions included in the amended Rule 11 are expected to limit the high volume of requests for sanctions prevailing under the old Rule. First, the new Rule provides, in subdivision (c)(1)(A), that motions for sanctions under the rule should be served according to Rule 5, but not filed with the court unless the attorney served fails to withdraw or appropriately correct the challenged document or contention. This "safe harbor" provision allows an attorney possibly in violation of Rule 11 to voluntarily act to avoid potential sanctions.

A second major change to Rule 11 is that sanctions, whether prompted by motion or issued at the court's own initiative, are no longer mandatory. Subdivision (c) states that "[i]f * * * the court determines that subdivision (b) has been violated, **the court may** * * * impose and appropriate sanction." The former rule required that a court "shall impose" appropriate sanctions if a violation of the rule occurred. Additionally, the new rule makes clear that not only the attorney in violation of the rule, but also that attorney's firm, may be sanctioned, in effect overturning the Supreme Court's decision in Pavelic & Leflore v. Marvel Entertainment Group, 493 U.S. 120, 110 S.Ct. 456, 107 L.Ed.2d 438 (1989).

Finally, the language contained in subdivision (d) of the revised Rule has been added to make clear that the provisions of Rule 11 are inapplicable to discovery. Certification standards for discovery are contained in Rules 26(g) and 37.

(b) *Comparative State Provisions*

Georgia Code Annotated § 9–11–11(b)

Except when otherwise specifically provided by rule or statute, pleadings need not be verified or accompanied by affidavit.

Georgia Code Annotated § 9–10–111

In all cases where the plaintiff files a pleading with an affidavit attached to the effect that the facts stated in the pleading are true to the best of his knowledge and belief, the defendant shall in like manner verify any answer. If the defendant is a corporation, the affidavit may be made by the president, vice-president, superintendent, or any officer or agent who knows, or whose official duty it is to know, about the matters set out in the answer.

Georgia Code Annotated § 19–5–5(a)

The action for divorce shall be brought by written petition and process, the petition being verified by the petitioner.

Pennsylvania Rule of Civil Procedure 1024

(a) Every pleading containing an averment of fact not appearing of record in the action or containing a denial of fact shall state that the averment or denial is true upon the signer's personal knowledge or information and belief and shall be verified. The signer need not aver the source of the information or expectation of ability to prove the averment or denial at the trial. A pleading may be verified upon personal knowledge as to a part and upon information and belief as to the remainder.

(b) If a pleading contains averments which are inconsistent in fact, the verification shall state that the signer has been unable after reasonable investigation to ascertain which of the inconsistent averments, specifying them, are true but that the signer has knowledge or information sufficient to form a belief that one of them is true.

(c) The verification shall be made by one or more of the parties filing the pleading unless all the parties (1) lack sufficient knowledge or information, or (2) are outside the jurisdiction of the court and the verification of none of them can be obtained within the time allowed for filing the pleading. In such cases, the verification may be made by any person having sufficient knowledge or information and belief and shall set forth the source of the person's information as to matters not stated upon his or her own knowledge and the reason why the verification is not made by a party.

Rule 12. Defenses and Objections—When and How Presented—By Pleading or Motion—Motion for Judgment on the Pleadings

[See proposed changes to Rule 12(a)(3), in Part IX, infra.]

(a) When Presented.

(1) Unless a different time is prescribed in a statute of the United States, a defendant shall serve an answer

(A) within 20 days after being served with the summons and complaint, or

(B) if service of the summons has been timely waived on request under Rule 4(d), within 60 days after the date when the request for waiver was sent, or within 90 days after that date if the defendant was addressed outside any judicial district of the United States.

(2) A party served with a pleading stating a cross-claim against that party shall serve an answer thereto within 20 days after being served. The plaintiff shall serve a reply to a counterclaim in the answer within 20 days after service of the answer, or, if a reply is ordered by the court, within 20 days after service of the order, unless the order otherwise directs.

(3) The United States or an agency thereof shall serve an answer to the complaint or to a cross-claim, or a reply to a counterclaim, within 60 days after the service upon the United States attorney of the pleading in which the claim is asserted.

(4) Unless a different time is fixed by court order, the service of a motion permitted under this rule alters these periods of time as follows,

(A) if the court denies the motion or postpones its disposition until the trial on the merits, the responsive pleading shall be served within 10 days after notice of the court's action; or

(B) if the court grants a motion for a more definite statement, the responsive pleading shall be served within 10 days after the service of the more definite statement.

(b) How Presented. Every defense, in law or fact, to a claim for relief in any pleading, whether a claim, counterclaim, cross-claim, or

Direct attack - go in + contest j/d or bring a lawsuit

can join other defenses

third-party claim, shall be asserted in the responsive pleading thereto if one is required, except that the following defenses may at the option of the pleader be made by motion: (1) lack of jurisdiction over the subject matter, (2) lack of jurisdiction over the person, (3) improper venue, (4) insufficiency of process, (5) insufficiency of service of process, (6) failure to state a claim upon which relief can be granted, (7) failure to join a party under Rule 19. A motion making any of these defenses shall be made before pleading if a further pleading is permitted. No defense or objection is waived by being joined with one or more other defenses or objections in a responsive pleading or motion. If a pleading sets forth a claim for relief to which the adverse party is not required to serve a responsive pleading, the adverse party may assert at the trial any defense in law or fact to that claim for relief. If, on a motion asserting the defense numbered (6) to dismiss for failure of the pleading to state a

6 - failure to state a claim

claim upon which relief can be granted, matters outside the pleading are presented to and not excluded by the court, the motion shall be treated as one for summary judgment and disposed of as provided in Rule 56, and all parties shall be given reasonable opportunity to present all material made pertinent to such a motion by Rule 56.

(c) Motion for Judgment on the Pleadings. After the pleadings are closed but within such time as not to delay the trial, any party may move for judgment on the pleadings. If, on a motion for judgment on the pleadings, matters outside the pleadings are presented to and not excluded by the court, the motion shall be treated as one for summary judgment and disposed of as provided in Rule 56, and all parties shall be given reasonable opportunity to present all material made pertinent to such a motion by Rule 56.

(d) Preliminary Hearings. The defenses specifically enumerated (1)–(7) in subdivision (b) of this rule, whether made in a pleading or by motion, and the motion for judgment mentioned in subdivision (c) of this rule shall be heard and determined before trial on application of any party, unless the court orders that the hearing and determination thereof be deferred until the trial.

(e) Motion for More Definite Statement. If a pleading to which a responsive pleading is permitted is so vague or ambiguous that a party cannot reasonably be required to frame a responsive pleading, the

you need more info to plead back

party may move for a more definite statement before interposing a responsive pleading. The motion shall point out the defects complained of and the details desired. If the motion is granted and the order of the court is not obeyed within 10 days after notice of the order or within such other time as the court may fix, the court may strike the pleading to which the motion was directed or make such order as it deems just.

(f) Motion to Strike. Upon motion made by a party before responding to a pleading or, if no responsive pleading is permitted by these rules, upon motion made by a party within 20 days after the service of the pleading upon the party or upon the court's own initiative at any time, the court may order stricken from any pleading any insufficient defense or any redundant, immaterial, impertinent, or scandalous matter.

(g) Consolidation of Defenses in Motion. A party who makes a motion under this rule may join with it any other motions herein provided for and then available to the party. If a party makes a motion under this rule but omits therefrom any defense or objection then available to the party which this rule permits to be raised by motion, the party shall not thereafter make a motion based on the defense or objection so omitted, except a motion as provided in subdivision (h)(2) hereof on any of the grounds there stated.

in person j/d

Must raise the issue in 1st paper or waive the defense

(h) Waiver or Preservation of Certain Defenses.

(1) A defense of lack of jurisdiction over the person, improper venue, insufficiency of process, or insufficiency of service of process is waived (A) if omitted from a motion in the circumstances described in subdivision (g), or (B) if it is neither made by motion under this rule nor included in a responsive pleading or an amendment thereof permitted by Rule 15(a) to be made as a matter of course.

If not raised then gone

(2) A defense of failure to state a claim upon which relief can be granted, a defense of failure to join a party indispensable under Rule 19, and an objection of failure to state a legal defense to a claim may be made in any pleading permitted or ordered under Rule 7(a), or by motion for judgment on the pleadings, or at the trial on the merits.

(3) Whenever it appears by suggestion of the parties or otherwise that the court lacks jurisdiction of the subject matter, the court shall dismiss the action.

Comparative State Provisions and Notes on Amendments to Federal Rule 12

(a) *Rule 12(a)*

Maryland Rule 2–321

(a) General Rule. A party shall file an answer to an original complaint, counterclaim, cross-claim, or third-party claim within 30 days after being served, except as provided by sections (b) and (c) of this Rule.

(b) Exceptions.

(1) A defendant who is served with an original pleading outside of the State but within the United States shall file an answer within 60 days after being served.

(2) A defendant who is served with an original pleading by publication or posting, pursuant to Rule 2–122, shall file an answer within the time specified in the notice.

(3) A person [whose required agent is] * * * served with an original pleading by service upon the State Department of Assessments and Taxation, the Insurance Commissioner, or some other agency of the State authorized by statute to receive process shall file an answer within 60 days after being served.

(4) The United States or an officer or agency of the United States served with an original pleading pursuant to Rule 2–124(f) shall file an answer within 60 days after being served.

(5) A defendant who is served with an original pleading outside of the United States shall file an answer within 90 days after being served.

(6) If rules for special proceedings, or statutes of this State or of the United States, provide for a different time to answer, the answer shall be filed as provided by those rules or statutes.

(c) Automatic Extension. When a motion is filed pursuant to Rule 2–322, the time for filing an answer is extended without special order to 15 days after entry of the court's order on the motion or, if the court grants a motion for a more definite statement, to 15 days after the service of the more definite statement.

Missouri Rule of Civil Procedure 55.25(a)

A defendant shall file an answer within thirty days after the service of the summons and petition upon him, except where service by mail is had, in which event a defendant shall file an answer within thirty days after the acknowledgment of receipt of summons and petition or return registered or certified mail receipt is filed in the case, or within forty-five days after the first publication of notice if neither personal service nor service by mail is had.

(b) *Rule 12(b)*

1. *In general*

Nebraska Revised Statutes § 25–806

The defendant may demur to the petition only when it appears on its face (1) that the court has no jurisdiction of the person of the defendant or the subject of the action; (2) that the plaintiff has not legal capacity to sue; (3) that there is another action pending between the same parties for the same cause; (4) that there is a defect of parties, plaintiff or defendant; (5) that several causes of action are improperly joined; or (6) that the petition does not state facts sufficient to constitute a cause of action.

Nebraska Revised Statutes § 25–807

The demurrer shall specify distinctly the grounds of objection to the petition. Unless it do so, it shall be regarded as objecting only that the petition does not state facts sufficient to constitute a cause of action.

Nebraska Revised Statutes § 25–808

When any of the defects enumerated in section 25–806 do not appear upon the face of the petition, the objection may be taken by answer, and if no objection be taken either by demurrer or answer, the defendant shall be deemed to have waived the same, except only the objection to the jurisdiction of the court, and that the petition does not state facts sufficient to constitute a cause of action.

Nebraska Revised Statutes § 25–810

The defendant may demur to one or more of the several causes of action stated in the petition and answer as to the residue.

Indiana Rules of Trial Procedure, Trial Rule 8(E)(3)

All motions and pleadings of any kind addressed to two [2] or more paragraphs of any pleading, or filed by two [2] or more parties, shall be taken and construed as joint, separate, and several motions or pleadings to each of such paragraphs and by and against each of such parties. All motions or pleadings containing two [2] or more subject-matters shall be taken and construed as separate and several as to each subject-matter. All objections to rulings made by two [2] or more parties shall be taken and construed as the joint, separate, and several objections of each of such parties.

A complaint filed by or against two [2] or more plaintiffs shall be taken and construed as joint, separate, and several as to each of said plaintiffs.

2. *Challenging jurisdiction over the subject matter*

California Civil Procedure Code § 396

If an action or proceeding is commenced in a court that lacks jurisdiction of the subject matter thereof, as determined by the complaint or petition, if there is a court of this state that has subject matter jurisdiction, the action or proceeding shall not be dismissed (except as provided in Section 399, and subdivision 1 of Section 581) but shall, on the application of either party, or on the court's own motion, be transferred to a court having jurisdiction of the subject matter that may be agreed upon by the parties, or, if they do not agree, to a court having subject matter jurisdiction that is designated by law as a proper court for the trial or determination thereof, and it shall thereupon be entered and prosecuted in the court to which it is transferred as if it had been commenced therein, all prior proceedings being saved. In any such case, if summons is served prior to the filing of the action or proceeding in the court to which it is transferred, as to any defendant, so served, who has not appeared in the action or proceeding, the time to answer or otherwise plead shall date from service upon that defendant of written notice of filing of the action or proceeding in the court to which it is transferred.

If an action or proceeding is commenced in or transferred to a court that has jurisdiction of the subject matter thereof as determined by the complaint or petition, and it thereafter appears from the verified pleadings, or at the trial, or hearing, that the determination of the action or proceeding, or of a cross-complaint, will necessarily involve the determination of questions not within the jurisdiction of the court, in which the action or proceeding is pending, the court, whenever that lack of jurisdiction appears, must suspend all further proceedings therein and transfer the action or proceeding and certify the pleadings (or if the pleadings be oral, a transcript of the same), and all papers and proceedings therein to a court having jurisdiction thereof that may be agreed upon by the parties, or, it they do not agree, to a court having subject matter jurisdiction that is designated by law as a proper court for the trial or determination thereof.

An action or proceeding that is transferred under the provisions of this section shall be deemed to have been commenced at the time the complaint or petition was filed in the court from which it was originally transferred.

Nothing herein shall be construed to preclude or affect the right to amend the pleadings as provided in this code.

Nothing herein shall be construed to require the superior court to transfer any action or proceeding because the judgment to be rendered, as determined at the trial or hearing, is one that might have been rendered by a municipal court in the same county or city and county.

In any case where the lack of jurisdiction is due solely to an excess in the amount of the demand, the excess may be remitted and the action may continue in the court where it is pending.

Upon the making of an order for transfer, proceedings shall be had as provided in Section 399 of this code, the costs and fees thereof, and of filing the case in the court to which transferred, to be paid by the party filing the pleading in which the question outside the jurisdiction of the court appears unless the court ordering the transfer shall otherwise direct.

3. *Challenging venue*

Illinois Compiled Statutes ch. 735, 5/2–104(b)

All objections of improper venue are waived by a defendant unless a motion to transfer to a proper venue is made by the defendant on or before the date upon which he or she is required to appear or within any further time that may be granted him or her to answer or move with respect to the complaint, except that if a defendant upon whose residence venue depends is dismissed upon motion of plaintiff, a remaining defendant may promptly move for transfer as though the dismissed defendant had not been a party.

4. *Challenging personal jurisdiction, process, and service of process*

Illinois Compiled Statutes ch. 735, 5/2–301

(a) Prior to the filing of any other pleading or motion, other than a motion for an extension of time to answer or otherwise appear, a party may object to the court's jurisdiction over the party's person, either on the ground that the party is not amenable to process of a court of this State or on the ground of insufficiency of process or insufficiency of service of process, by filing a motion to dismiss the entire proceeding or any cause of action involved in the proceeding or by filing a motion to quash service of process. Such a motion may be made singly or included with others in a combined motion, but the parts of a combined motion must be identified in the manner described in Section 2–619.1. Unless the facts that constitute the basis for the objection are apparent from papers already on file in the case, the motion must be supported by an affidavit setting forth those facts.

(b) In disposing of a motion objecting to the court's jurisdiction over the person of the objecting party, the court shall consider all matters apparent from the papers on file in the case, affidavits submitted by any party, and any evidence adduced upon contested issues of fact. The court shall enter an appropriate order sustaining or overruling the objection. No determination of any issue of fact in connection with the objection is a determination of the merits of the case or any aspect thereof. A decision adverse to the objector does not preclude the objector from making any motion or defense which he or she might otherwise have made.

(c) Error in ruling against the objecting party on the objection is waived by the party's taking part in further proceedings unless the objection is on the ground that the party is not amenable to process issued by a court of this State.

New York Civil Practice Law and Rules 320(c)

Can make a limited appearance based on quasi-in-rem

When the court's jurisdiction is not based upon personal service on the defendant, an appearance is not equivalent to personal service upon the defendant:

1. [In quasi-in-rem attachment actions] * * * if jurisdiction is based solely upon a levy on defendant's property within the state pursuant to an order of attachment; or

2. [In in rem actions] * * * if an objection to jurisdiction * * * is asserted by motion or in the answer as provided in rule 3211, unless the defendant proceeds with the defense after asserting the objection to jurisdiction and the objection is not ultimately sustained.

Minnesota Rule of Civil Procedure 4.04(a)(2)(B)

* * *

Doesn't allow limited appearance

When quasi in rem jurisdiction has been obtained, a party defending the action thereby submits personally to the jurisdiction of the court. An appearance solely to contest the validity of quasi in rem jurisdiction is not such a submission.

(c) *Rule 12(d)*

California Civil Procedure Code § 597

When the answer pleads that the action is barred by the statute of limitations, or by a prior judgment, or that another action is pending upon the same cause of action, or sets up any other defense not involving the merits of the plaintiff's cause of action but constituting a bar or ground of abatement to the prosecution thereof, the court may, either upon its own motion or upon the motion of any party, proceed to the trial of the special defense or defenses before the trial of any other issue in the case * * *.

California Civil Procedure Code § 597.5

[In a malpractice action against a doctor, dentist, nurse, or other medical professional] * * * if the answer pleads that the action is barred by the statute of limitations, and if any party so moves or the court upon its own motion requires, the issues raised thereby must be tried separately and before any other issues in the case are tried. * * *

(d) Rule 12(e)

1. *Amendments in 1946 to Rule 12(e)*

Prior to 1946 Rule 12(e) read:

Before responding to a pleading or, if no responsive pleading is permitted by these rules, within 20 days after the service of the pleading upon him, a party may move for a more definite statement or for a bill of particulars of any matter which is not averred with sufficient definiteness or particularity to enable him properly to prepare his responsive pleading or to prepare for trial. The motion shall point out the defects complained of and the details desired. If the motion is granted and the order of the court is not obeyed within 10 days after notice of the order or within such other time as the court may fix, the court may strike the pleading to which the motion was directed or make such order as it deems just. A bill of particulars becomes a part of the pleading which it supplements.

The Advisory Committee commented on the alterations as follows:

Subdivision (e). References in this subdivision to a bill of particulars have been deleted, and the motion provided for is confined to one for a more definite statement, to be obtained only in cases where the movant cannot reasonably be required to frame an answer or other responsive pleading to the pleading in question. With respect to preparations for trial, the party is properly relegated to the various methods of examination and discovery provided in the rules for that purpose. * * *

Rule 12(e) as originally drawn has been the subject of more judicial rulings than any other part of the rules, and has been much criticized by commentators, judges and members of the bar. See general discussion and cases cited in 1 Moore's Federal Practice, 1938, Cum.Supplement, § 12.07, under "Page 657"; also, Holtzoff, New Federal Procedure and the Courts, 1940, 35–41. * * * The tendency of some courts freely to grant extended bills of particulars has served to neutralize any helpful benefits derived from Rule 8, and has overlooked the intended use of the rules on depositions and discovery. The words "or to prepare for trial"—eliminated by the proposed amendment—have sometimes been seized upon as grounds for compulsory statement in the opposing pleading of all the details which the movant would have to meet at the trial. On the other hand, many courts have in effect read these words out of the rule. See Walling v. Alabama Pipe Co., W.D.Mo.1942, 3 F.R.D. 159, 6 Fed.Rules Serv. 12e.244, Case 7 * * *. And it has been urged from the bench that the phrase be stricken. Poole v. White, N.D.W.Va.1941, 5 Fed.Rules Serv. 12e.231, Case 4, 2 F.R.D. 40. See also Bowles v. Gabel, W.D.Mo.1946, 9 Fed.Rules Serv. 12e.244, Case 10 ("The courts have never favored that portion of the rules which undertook to justify a motion of this kind for the purpose of aiding counsel in preparing his case for trial.").

2. *Comparative state provisions*

California Civil Procedure Code § 430.10

The party against whom a complaint or cross-complaint has been filed may object, by demurrer or answer as provided in Section 430.30, to the pleading on any one or more of the following grounds:

    * * *

45

(f) The pleading is uncertain. As used in this subdivision, "uncertain" includes ambiguous and unintelligible.

(g) In an action founded upon a contract, it cannot be ascertained from the pleading whether the contract is written, is oral, or is implied by conduct.

* * *

Nebraska Revised Statutes § 25–833

* * * [W]hen the allegations of a pleading are so indefinite and uncertain that the precise nature of the charge or defense is not apparent, the court may require the pleading to be made definite and certain by amendment.

(e) *Rule 12(f)*

1. *Challenging an insufficient defense*

New York Civil Practice Law and Rules 3211

* * *

(b) A party may move for judgment dismissing one or more defenses, on the ground that a defense is not stated or has no merit.

(c) Upon the hearing of a motion made under subdivision (a) or (b), either party may submit any evidence that could properly be considered on a motion for summary judgment. Whether or not issue has been joined, the court, after adequate notice to the parties, may treat the motion as a motion for summary judgment. The court may, when appropriate for the expeditious disposition of the controversy, order immediate trial of the issues raised on the motion.

* * *

2. *Striking irrelevant, impertinent matter*

New York Civil Practice Law and Rules 3024(b)

A party may move to strike any scandalous or prejudicial matter unnecessarily inserted in a pleading.

(f) *Rule 12(h)*

1. *Amendments in 1966 to Rule 12(h)*

Prior to 1966 Rule 12(h) read:

A party waives all defenses and objections which he does not present either by motion as hereinbefore provided or, if he has made no motion, in his answer or reply, except * * * [that defenses under 12(b)(1), 12(b)(6) and 12(b)(7) may be raised at any time before or at trial by pleading or motion.]

The Advisory Committee commented on the 1966 changes as follows:

The question has arisen whether an omitted defense which cannot be made the basis of a second motion may nevertheless be pleaded in the answer. Subdivision (h) called for waiver of "* * * defenses and objections which he [defendant] does not present * * * by motion * * * or, if he has made no motion, in his answer * * *." If the clause "if he has made no motion," was read literally, it seemed that the omitted defense was waived and could not be pleaded in the answer. On the other hand, the clause might be read as adding nothing of substance to the preceding words; in that event it appeared that a defense was not waived by reason of being omitted from the motion and might be set up in the answer. The decisions were divided. * * *

Amended subdivision (h)(1)(A) eliminates the ambiguity and states that certain specified defenses which were available to a party when he made a preanswer motion, but which he omitted from the motion, are waived. The specified defenses are lack of jurisdiction over the person, improper venue, insufficiency of process, and insufficiency of service of process (see Rule 12(b)(2)–

(5)). A party who by motion invites the court to pass upon a threshold defense should bring forward all the specified defenses he then has and thus allow the court to do a reasonably complete job. The waiver reinforces the policy of subdivision (g) forbidding successive motions.

By amended subdivision (h)(1)(B), the specified defenses, even if not waived by the operation of (A), are waived by the failure to raise them by a motion under Rule 12 or in the responsive pleading or any amendment thereof to which the party is entitled as a matter of course. The specified defenses are of such a character that they should not be delayed and brought up for the first time by means of an application to the court to amend the responsive pleading.

Since the language of the subdivisions is made clear, the party is put on fair notice of the effect of his actions and omissions and can guard himself against unintended waiver. It is to be noted that while the defenses specified in subdivision (h)(1) are subject to waiver as there provided, the more substantial defenses of failure to state a claim upon which relief can be granted, failure to join a party indispensable under Rule 19, and failure to state a legal defense to a claim (see Rule 12(b)(6), (7), (f)), as well as the defense of lack of jurisdiction over the subject matter (see Rule 12(b)(1)), are expressly preserved against waiver by amended subdivision (h)(2) and (3).

2. *Comparative state provisions*

See Nebraska Revised Statutes § 25–808, as set out in (b)1, above, in connection with Federal Rule 12(b).

Rule 13.   Counterclaim and Cross-Claim

(a) Compulsory Counterclaims. A pleading shall state as a counterclaim any claim which at the time of serving the pleading, the pleader has against any opposing party, if it arises out of the transaction or occurrence that is the subject matter of the opposing party's claim and does not require for its adjudication the presence of third parties of whom the court cannot acquire jurisdiction. But the pleader need not state the claim if (1) at the time the action was commenced the claim was the subject of another pending action, or (2) the opposing party brought suit upon the claim by attachment or other process by which the court did not acquire jurisdiction to render a personal judgment on that claim, and the pleader is not stating any counterclaim under this Rule 13.

(b) Permissive Counterclaims. A pleading may state as a counterclaim any claim against an opposing party not arising out of the transaction or occurrence that is the subject matter of the opposing party's claim.

(c) Counterclaim Exceeding Opposing Claim. A counterclaim may or may not diminish or defeat the recovery sought by the opposing party. It may claim relief exceeding in amount or different in kind from that sought in the pleading of the opposing party.

(d) Counterclaim Against the United States. These rules shall not be construed to enlarge beyond the limits now fixed by law the right to assert counterclaims or to claim credits against the United States or an officer or agency thereof.

(e) Counterclaim Maturing or Acquired After Pleading. A claim which either matured or was acquired by the pleader after serving a pleading may, with the permission of the court, be presented as a counterclaim by supplemental pleading.

(f) Omitted Counterclaim. When a pleader fails to set up a counterclaim through oversight, inadvertence, or excusable neglect, or when justice requires, the pleader may by leave of court set up the counterclaim by amendment.

(g) Cross-Claim Against Co-party. A pleading may state as a cross-claim any claim by one party against a co-party arising out of the transaction or occurrence that is the subject matter either of the original action or of a counterclaim therein or relating to any property that is the subject matter of the original action. Such cross-claim may include a claim that the party against whom it is asserted is or may be liable to the cross-claimant for all or part of a claim asserted in the action against the cross-claimant.

(h) Joinder of Additional Parties. Persons other than those made parties to the original action may be made parties to a counter-claim or cross-claim in accordance with the provisions of Rules 19 and 20.

(i) Separate Trials; Separate Judgments. If the court orders separate trials as provided in Rule 42(b), judgment on a counterclaim or cross-claim may be rendered in accordance with the terms of Rule 54(b) when the court has jurisdiction so to do, even if the claims of the opposing party have been dismissed or otherwise disposed of.

Notes on Amendments to Federal Rule 13 and Comparative State Provisions

(a) *Amendments in 1963 to Federal Rule 13(a)*

Rule 13(a)(2) was added by amendment in 1963. The Advisory Committee's Note on the change reads as follows:

When a defendant, if he desires to defend his interest in property, is obliged to come in and litigate in a court to whose jurisdiction he could not ordinarily be subjected, fairness suggests that he should not be required to assert counterclaims, but should rather be permitted to do so at his election. If, however, he does elect to assert a counterclaim, it seems fair to require him to assert any other which is compulsory within the meaning of Rule 13(a). Clause (2), added by amendment to Rule 13(a), carries out this idea. It will apply to various cases described in Rule 4(e), as amended, where service is effected through attachment or other process by which the court does not acquire jurisdiction to render a personal judgment against the defendant. Clause (2) will also apply to actions commenced in State courts jurisdictionally grounded on attachment or the like, and removed to the Federal courts.

(b) *Comparative State Provisions*

1. *Rules 13(a) and 13(b)*

Michigan Court Rule 2.203(B)

A pleader may join as either independent or alternate claims as many claims, legal or equitable, as the pleader has against an opposing party. If a claim is one previously cognizable only after another claim has been prosecuted to a conclusion, the two claims may be joined in a single action; but the court may grant relief only in accordance with the substantive rights of the parties.

Nebraska Revised Statutes § 25–811

The answer shall contain (1) a general or specific denial of each material allegation of the petition controverted by the defendant; and (2) a statement of any new matter constituting a defense, counterclaim or setoff, in ordinary and concise language and without repetition.

2. *Rule 13(g)*

New York Civil Practice Law and Rules 3019(b)

A cross-claim may be any cause of action in favor of one or more defendants or a person whom a defendant represents against one or more defendants, a person whom a defendant represents or a defendant and other persons alleged to be liable. A cross-claim may include a claim that the party against whom it is asserted is or may be liable to the cross-claimant for all or part of a claim asserted in the action against the cross-claimant.

Rule 14. Third Party Practice

[See discussion of proposed amendments to Rule 14(a) and (c), in Part IX, infra.]

(a) When Defendant May Bring in Third Party. At any time after commencement of the action a defending party, as a third-party plaintiff, may cause a summons and complaint to be served upon a person not a party to the action who is or may be liable to the third-party plaintiff for all or part of the plaintiff's claim against the third-party plaintiff. The third-party plaintiff need not obtain leave to make the service if the third-party plaintiff files the third-party complaint not later than 10 days after serving the original answer. Otherwise the third-party plaintiff must obtain leave on motion upon notice to all parties to the action. The person served with the summons and third-party complaint, hereinafter called the third-party defendant, shall make any defenses to the third-party plaintiff's claim as provided in Rule 12 and any counterclaims against the third-party plaintiff and cross-claims against other third-party defendants as provided in Rule 13. The third-party defendant may assert against the plaintiff any defenses which the third-party plaintiff has to the plaintiff's claim. The third-party defendant may also assert any claim against the plaintiff arising out of the transaction or occurrence that is the subject matter of the plaintiff's claim against the third-party plaintiff. The plaintiff may assert any claim against the third-party defendant arising out of the transaction or occurrence that is the subject matter of the plaintiff's claim against the third-party plaintiff, and the third-party defendant thereupon shall assert any defenses as provided in Rule 12 and any counterclaims and cross-claims as provided in Rule 13. Any party may move to strike the third-party claim, or for its severance or separate trial. A third-party defendant may proceed under this rule against any person not a party to the action who is or may be liable to the third-party defendant for all or part of the claim made in the action against the third-party defendant. The third-party complaint, if within the admiralty and maritime jurisdiction, may be in rem against a vessel, cargo, or other property subject to admiralty or maritime process in rem, in which case references in this rule to the summons include the warrant of arrest, and references to the third-party plaintiff or defendant include, where appropriate, the claimant of the property arrested.

(b) When Plaintiff May Bring in Third Party. When a counterclaim is asserted against a plaintiff, the plaintiff may cause a third party to be brought in under circumstances which under this rule would entitle a defendant to do so.

(c) Admiralty and Maritime Claims. When a plaintiff asserts an admiralty or maritime claim within the meaning of Rule 9(h), the defendant or claimant, as a third-party plaintiff, may bring in a third-party defendant who may be wholly or partly liable, either to the plaintiff or to the third-party plaintiff, by way of remedy over, contribution, or otherwise on account of the same transaction, occurrence, or series of transactions or occurrences. In such a case the third-party plaintiff may also demand judgment against the third-party defendant in favor of the plaintiff, in which event the third-party defendant shall make any defenses to the claim of the plaintiff as well as to that of the third-party plaintiff in the manner provided in Rule 12, and the action shall proceed as if the plaintiff had commenced it against the third-party defendant as well as the third-party plaintiff.

Rule 15.   Amended and Supplemental Pleadings

(a) Amendments. A party may amend the party's pleading once as a matter of course at any time before a responsive pleading is served or, if the pleading is one to which no responsive pleading is permitted and the action has not been placed upon the trial calendar, the party may so amend it at any time within 20 days after it is served. Otherwise a party may amend the party's pleading only by leave of court or by written consent of the adverse party; and leave shall be freely given when justice so requires. A party shall plead in response to an amended pleading within the time remaining for response to the original pleading or within 10 days after service of the amended pleading, whichever period may be the longer, unless the court otherwise orders.

(b) Amendments to Conform to the Evidence. When issues not raised by the pleadings are tried by express or implied consent of the parties, they shall be treated in all respects as if they had been raised in the pleadings. Such amendment of the pleadings as may be necessary to cause them to conform to the evidence and to raise these issues may be made upon motion of any party at any time, even after judgment; but failure so to amend does not affect the result of the trial of these issues. If evidence is objected to at the trial on the ground that it is not within the issues made by the pleadings, the court may allow the pleadings to be amended and shall do so freely when the presentation of the merits of the action will be subserved thereby and the objecting party fails to satisfy the court that the admission of such evidence would prejudice the party in maintaining the party's action or defense upon the merits. The court may grant a continuance to enable the objecting party to meet such evidence.

only after § o6 limit. has run

(c) Relation Back of Amendments. An amendment of a pleading relates back to the date of the original pleading when

must meet reqs. of 15c

(1) relation back is permitted by the law that provides the statute of limitations applicable to the action, or

(2) the claim or defense asserted in the amended pleading arose out of the conduct, transaction, or occurrence set forth or attempted to be set forth in the original pleading, or

(3) the amendment changes the party or the naming of the party against whom a claim is asserted if the foregoing provision (2) is satisfied and, within the period provided by Rule 4(m) for service of the summons and complaint, the party to be brought in by amendment (A) has received such notice of the institution of the action that the party will not be prejudiced in maintaining a defense on the merits, and (B) knew or should have known that, but for a mistake concerning the identity of the proper party, the action would have been brought against the party.

The delivery or mailing of process to the United States Attorney, or his designee, or the Attorney General of the United States, or an agency or officer who would have been a proper defendant if named, satisfies the requirement of subparagraphs (A) and (B) of this paragraph (3) with respect to the United States or any agency or officer thereof to be brought into the action as a defendant.

(d) Supplemental Pleadings. Upon motion of a party the court may, upon reasonable notice and upon such terms as are just, permit the party to serve a supplemental pleading setting forth transactions or occurrences or events which have happened since the date of the pleading sought to be supplemented. Permission may be granted even though the original pleading is defective in its statement of a claim for relief or defense. If the court deems it advisable that the adverse party plead to the supplemental pleading, it shall so order, specifying the time therefor.

Comparative State Provisions and Notes on Amendments to Federal Rule 15

(a) *Rule 15(a)*

New York Civil Practice Law and Rules 3025(a) & (b)

(a) A party may amend his pleading once without leave of court within twenty days after its service, or at any time before the period for responding to it expires, or within twenty days after service of a pleading responding to it.

(b) A party may amend his pleading, or supplement it by setting forth additional or subsequent transactions or occurrences, at any time by leave of court or by stipulation of all parties. Leave shall be freely given upon such terms as may be just including the granting of costs and continuances.

(b) *Rule 15(b)*

California Civil Procedure Code § 469

No variance between the allegation in a pleading and the proof is to be deemed material, unless it has actually misled the adverse party to his prejudice in maintaining his action or defense upon the merits. Whenever it appears that a party has been so misled, the Court may order the pleading to be amended upon such terms as may be just.

California Civil Procedure Code § 470

Where the variance is not material, as provided in Section 469 the Court may direct the fact to be found according to the evidence, or may order an immediate amendment, without costs.

California Civil Procedure Code § 471

Where, however, the allegation of the claim or defense to which the proof is directed, is unproved, not in some particular or particulars only, but in its general scope and meaning, it is not to be deemed a case of variance, within the meaning of Sections 469 and 470, but a failure of proof.

(c) *Rule 15(c)*

1. *Relation back of amendments to the claim*

New Jersey Civil Practice Rule 4:9–3

Whenever the claim or defense asserted in the amended pleading arose out of the conduct, transaction or occurrence set forth or attempted to be set forth in the original pleading, the amendment relates back to the date of the original pleading; but the court, in addition to its power to allow amendments may, upon terms, permit the statement of a new or different claim or defense in the pleading. * * *

2. *Relation back of amendments adding parties*

(i) *Amendments in 1991 to Federal Rule 15(c)*

The amendment has two major parts. First, it provides that an amendment relates back to the time the original pleading was filed whenever "relation back is permitted by the law that provides the statute of limitations applicable to the action." Second, it overturns the Supreme Court decision in Schiavone v. Fortune, 477 U.S. 21, 106 S.Ct. 2379, 91 L.Ed.2d 18 (1986), by modifying what is now the second sentence of Rule 15(c) to provide that an amendment *changing the name of a party* relates back to the time of the original pleading under the same circumstances as an amendment *changing a party.*

(ii) *Amendments in 1966 to Federal Rule 15(c)*

Prior to the 1966 amendments, Rule 15(c) contained only what is now its first sentence. The Advisory Committee commented upon the additions as follows:

Rule 15(c) is amplified to state more clearly when an amendment of a pleading changing the party against whom a claim is asserted (including an amendment to correct a misnomer or misdescription of a defendant) shall "relate back" to the date of the original pleading.

The problem has arisen most acutely in certain actions by private parties against officers or agencies of the United States. Thus an individual denied social security benefits by the Secretary of Health, Education, and Welfare may secure review of the decision by bringing a civil action against that officer within sixty days. 42 U.S.C. § 405(g) (Supp. III, 1962). In several recent cases the claimants instituted timely action but mistakenly named as defendant the United States, the Department of HEW, the "Federal Security Administration" (a nonexistent agency), and a Secretary who had retired from the office nineteen days before. Discovering their mistakes, the claimants moved to amend their complaints to name the proper defendant; by this time the statutory sixty-day period had expired. The motions were denied on the ground that the amendment "would amount to the commencement of a new proceeding and would not relate back in time so as to avoid the statutory provision * * * that suit be brought within sixty days. * * *" *Cohn v. Federal Security Adm.*, 199 F.Supp. 884, 885 (W.D.N.Y. 1961) * * *.

Relation back is intimately connected with the policy of the statute of limitations. The policy of the statute limiting the time for suit against the Secretary of HEW would not have been offended by allowing relation back in the situations described above. For the government was put on notice of the claim within the stated period—in the particular instances, by means of the initial delivery of process to a responsible government official (see Rule 4(d)(4) and (5)). In these circumstances, characterization of the amendment as a new proceeding is not responsive to the reality, but is merely question-begging; and to deny relation back is to defeat unjustly the claimant's opportunity to prove his case.

* * * In actions between private parties, the problem of relation back of amendments changing defendants has generally been better handled by the courts, but incorrect criteria have sometimes been applied, leading sporadically to doubtful results. * * * Rule 15(c) has been amplified to provide a general solution. * * *

The relation back of amendments changing plaintiffs is not expressly treated in revised Rule 15(c) since the problem is generally easier. Again the chief consideration of policy is that of the statute of limitations, and the attitude taken in revised Rule 15(c) toward change of defendants extends by analogy to amendments changing plaintiffs. Also relevant is the amendment of Rule 17(a) (real party in interest). To avoid forfeitures of just claims, revised Rule 17(a) would provide that no action shall be dismissed on the ground that it is not prosecuted in the name of the real party in interest until a reasonable time has been allowed for correction of the defect in the manner there stated.

(iii) *Comparative State Provision*

Illinois Compiled Statutes ch. 735, 5/2–616(d)

A cause of action against a person not originally named a defendant is not barred by lapse of time under any statute or contract prescribing or limiting the time within which an action may be brought or right asserted, if all the following terms and conditions are met: (1) the time prescribed or limited had not expired when the original action was commenced; (2) failure to join the person as a defendant was inadvertent; (3) service of summons was in fact had upon the person, his or her agent or partner, as the nature of the defendant made appropriate, even though he or she was served in the wrong capacity or as agent of another, or upon a trustee who has title to but no power of management or control over real property constituting a trust of which the person is a beneficiary; (4) the person, within the time that the action might have been brought or the right asserted against him or her, knew that the original action was pending and that it grew out a transaction or occurrence involving or concerning him or her; and (5) it appears from the original and amended pleadings that the cause of action asserted in the amended pleading grew out of the same transaction or occurrence set up in the original pleading, even though the original pleading was defective in that it failed to allege the performance of some act or the existence of some fact or some other matter which is a necessary condition precedent to the right of recovery when the condition precedent has in fact been performed, and even though the person was not named originally as a defendant. For the purpose of preserving the cause of action under those conditions, an amendment adding the person as a defendant relates back to the date of the filing of the original pleading so amended.

(d) *Rule 15(d)*

See New York Civil Practice Law and Rules 3025(b) as set out in connection with Federal Rule 15(a), supra.

Rule 16. Pretrial Conferences; Scheduling; Management

(a) Pretrial Conferences; Objectives. In any action, the court may in its discretion direct the attorneys for the parties and any unrepresented parties to appear before it for a conference or conferences before trial for such purposes as

(1) expediting the disposition of the action;

(2) establishing early and continuing control so that the case will not be protracted because of lack of management;

(3) discouraging wasteful pretrial activities;

(4) improving the quality of the trial through more thorough preparation, and;

(5) facilitating the settlement of the case.

(b) Scheduling and Planning. Except in categories of actions exempted by district court rule as inappropriate, the district judge, or a magistrate judge when authorized by district court rule, shall, after receiving the report from the parties under Rule 26(f) or after consulting with the attorneys for the parties and any unrepresented parties by a scheduling conference, telephone, mail, or other suitable means, enter a scheduling order that limits the time

(1) to join other parties and to amend the pleadings;

(2) to file motions; and

(3) to complete discovery.

The scheduling order may also include

(4) modifications of the times for disclosures under Rules 26(a) and 26(e)(1) and of the extent of discovery to be permitted;

(5) the date or dates for conferences before trial, a final pretrial conference, and trial; and

(6) any other matters appropriate in the circumstances of the case.

The order shall issue as soon as practicable but in any event within 90 days after the appearance of a defendant and within 120 days after the complaint has been served on a defendant. A schedule shall not be modified except upon a showing of good cause and by leave of the district judge or, when authorized by local rule, by a magistrate judge.

(c) Subjects for Consideration at Pretrial Conferences. At any conference under this rule consideration may be given, and the court may take appropriate action, with respect to

(1) the formulation and simplification of the issues, including the elimination of frivolous claims or defenses;

(2) the necessity or desirability of amendments to the pleadings;

(3) the possibility of obtaining admissions of fact and of documents which will avoid unnecessary proof, stipulations regarding the authenticity of documents, and advance rulings from the court on the admissibility of evidence;

(4) the avoidance of unnecessary proof and of cumulative evidence, and limitations or restrictions on the use of testimony under Rule 702 of the Federal Rules of Evidence;

(5) the appropriateness and timing of summary adjudication under Rule 56;

(6) the control and scheduling of discovery, including orders affecting disclosures and discovery pursuant to Rule 26 and Rules 29 through 37;

(7) the identification of witness[es] and documents, the need and schedule for filing and exchanging pretrial briefs, and the date or dates for further conferences and for trial;

(8) the advisability of referring matters to a magistrate judge or master;

(9) settlement and the use of special procedures to assist in resolving the dispute when authorized by statute or local rule;

(10) the form and substance of the pretrial order;

(11) the disposition of pending motions;

(12) the need for adopting special procedures for managing potentially difficult or protracted actions that may involve complex issues, multiple parties, difficult legal questions, or unusual proof problems;

(13) an order for a separate trial pursuant to Rule 42(b) with respect to a claim, counterclaim, cross-claim, or third-party claim, or with respect to any particular issue in the case;

(14) an order directing a party or parties to present evidence early in the trial with respect to a manageable issue that could, on the evidence, be the basis for a judgment as matter of law under Rule 50(a) or a judgment on partial findings under Rule 52(c);

(15) an order establishing a reasonable limit on time allowed for presenting evidence; and

(16) such other matters as may facilitate the just, speedy, and inexpensive disposition of the action.

At least one of the attorneys for each party participating in any conference before trial shall have authority to enter into stipulations and to make admissions regarding all matters that the participants may reasonably anticipate may be discussed. If appropriate, the court may require that a party or its representative be present or reasonably available by telephone in order to consider possible settlement of the dispute.

(d) Final Pretrial Conference. Any final pretrial conference shall be held as close to the time of trial as reasonable under the circumstances. The participants at any such conference shall formulate a plan for trial, including a program for facilitating the admission of evidence. The conference shall be attended by at least one of the attorneys who will conduct the trial for each of the parties and by any unrepresented parties.

(e) Pretrial Orders. After any conference held pursuant to this rule, an order shall be entered reciting the action taken. This order shall control the subsequent course of the action unless modified by a subsequent order. The order following a final pretrial conference shall be modified only to prevent manifest injustice.

(f) Sanctions. If a party or party's attorney fails to obey a scheduling or pretrial order, or if no appearance is made on behalf of a party at a scheduling or pretrial conference, or if a party or party's attorney is substantially unprepared to participate in the conference, or if a party or party's attorney fails to participate in good faith, the judge, upon motion or the judge's own initiative, may make such orders with regard thereto as are just, and among others any of the orders provided in Rule 37(b)(2)(B), (C), (D). In lieu of or in addition to any other sanction, the judge shall require the party or the attorney representing the party or both to pay the reasonable expenses incurred because of any noncompliance with this rule, including attorney's fees, unless the judge finds that the noncompliance was substantially justified or that other circumstances make an award of expenses unjust.

Amendments to Federal Rule 16 and Comparative State Provisions

(a) *Amendment in 1983 and 1993 to Federal Rule 16*

The purpose of the 1983 changes was to alter the focus of pretrial conferences to encompass all aspects of case management and not merely the conduct of the trial. The most dramatic addition was the mandatory scheduling order that must be prepared even in the absence of a formal pretrial conference (unless the case is exempted by local rule).

In 1993, Rule 16(c) was modified to broaden the scope of what may be considered at pretrial conferences. Paragraph (c)(4) now explicitly authorizes the court to consider the limits on the proposed use of expert testimony. While the old Rule referred only to "the avoidance of unnecessary proof and of cumulative evidence," the new Rule specifically allows restrictions on expert testimony where, according to the Notes of the Advisory Committee such testimony "would be unduly expensive given the needs of the case and the other evidence available at trial."

Paragraph (c)(5) was added to allow parties to discuss at pretrial conferences the possibility of summary judgment under Rule 56. Paragraph (c)(6) emphasizes that control of the discovery process is an appropriate goal of the pretrial process.

Paragraph (c)(9) was revised to refer to alternative dispute resolution techniques, especially those authorized by local rule or statute which may be mandatory.

(b) *Comparative State Provisions*

New Jersey Civil Practice Rule 4:25–1

(a) Actions to Be Pretried. Pretrial conferences shall be held in all contested actions in the Chancery Division, General Equity, and in all actions brought in lieu of Prerogative Writs. Pretrial conferences in other causes may be held in the discretion of the court either on its own motion or upon a party's written request. The request of a party for a pretrial conference shall include a statement of the facts and reasons supporting the request. * * *

(b) Pretrial Order. The court shall make a pretrial order to be dictated in open court upon the conclusion of the conference and signed forthwith by the judge and attorneys, which shall recite specifically:

(1) A concise descriptive statement of the nature of the action.

(2) The admissions or stipulations of the parties with respect to the cause of action pleaded by plaintiff or defendant-counterclaimant.

(3) The factual and legal contentions of the plaintiff as to the liability of the defendant.

(4) The factual and legal contentions of the defendant as to nonliability and affirmative defenses.

(5) All claims as to damages and the extent of injury, and admissions or stipulations with respect thereto, and this shall limit the claims thereto at the trial. * * *

(6) Any amendments to the pleadings made at the conference * * *.

(7) A specification of the issues to be determined at the trial including all special evidence problems to be determined at trial * * *.

(8) A specification of the legal issues raised by the pleadings which are abandoned or otherwise disposed of. * * *

(9) A list of the exhibits marked in evidence by consent.

(10) Any limitation on the number of expert witnesses.

(11) Any direction with respect to the filing of briefs. * * *

(12) In special circumstances the order of opening and closing to the jury at the trial.

(13) Any other matters which have been agreed upon in order to expedite the disposition of the case.

(14) In the event that a particular member or associate of a firm is to try a case, or if outside trial counsel is to try the case, the name must be specifically set forth. No change in such designated trial counsel shall be made without leave of court if such change will interfere with the trial schedule. * * *

(15) The estimated length of the trial.

(16) When the case shall be placed on the weekly call.

When entered, the pretrial order becomes part of the record, supersedes the pleadings where inconsistent therewith, and controls the subsequent course of action unless modified at or before the trial or pursuant to R. 4:9–2 to prevent manifest injustice. The matter of settlement may be discussed at the sidebar, but it shall not be mentioned in the order.

* * *

IV. PARTIES

Rule 17. Parties Plaintiff and Defendant; Capacity

(a) Real Party in Interest. Every action shall be prosecuted in the name of the real party in interest. An executor, administrator, guardian, bailee, trustee of an express trust, a party with whom or in whose name a contract has been made for the benefit of another, or a party authorized by statute may sue in that person's own name without joining the party for whose benefit the action is brought; and when a statute of the United States so provides, an action for the use or benefit of another shall be brought in the name of the United States. No action shall be dismissed on the ground that it is not prosecuted in the name of the real party in interest until a reasonable time has been allowed after objection for ratification of commencement of the action by, or joinder or substitution of, the real party in interest; and such ratification, joinder, or substitution shall have the same effect as if the action had been commenced in the name of the real party in interest.

(b) Capacity to Sue or Be Sued. The capacity of an individual, other than one acting in a representative capacity, to sue or be sued shall be determined by the law of the individual's domicile. The capacity of a corporation to sue or be sued shall be determined by the law under which it was organized. In all other cases capacity to sue or be sued shall be determined by the law of the state in which the district court is held, except (1) that a partnership or other unincorporated association, which has no such capacity by the law of such state, may sue or be sued in its common name for the purpose of enforcing for or against it a substantive right existing under the Constitution or laws of the United States, and (2) that the capacity of a receiver appointed by a court of the United States to sue or be sued in a court of the United States is governed by Title 28, U.S.C. §§ 754 and 959(a).

(c) Infants or Incompetent Persons. Whenever an infant or incompetent person has a representative, such as a general guardian, committee, conservator, or other like fiduciary, the representative may sue or defend on behalf of the infant or incompetent person. An infant or incompetent person who does not have a duly appointed representative may sue by a next friend or by a guardian ad litem. The court shall appoint a guardian ad litem for an infant or incompetent person not otherwise represented in an action or shall make such other order as it deems proper for the protection of the infant or incompetent person.

Notes on Amendments in 1966 to Federal Rule 17(a)

In 1966 Federal Rule 17(a) was amended to add the provision prohibiting dismissal until a reasonable time has been allowed for ratification, joinder, or substitution of the real party in interest.

The Advisory Committee commented on this provision as follows:

This provision keeps pace with the law as it is actually developing. Modern decisions are inclined to be lenient when an honest mistake has been made in choosing the party in whose name the action is to be filed * * *. The provision should not be misunderstood or distorted. It is intended to prevent forfeiture when determination of the proper party to sue is difficult or when an understandable mistake has been made. It does not mean, for example, that, following an airplane crash in which all aboard were killed, an action may be filed in the name of John Doe (a fictitious person), as personal representative of Richard Roe (another fictitious person), in the hope that at a later time the attorney filing the action may substitute the real name of the real personal representative of a real victim, and have the benefit of suspension of the limitation period. * * *

Rule 18.   Joinder of Claims and Remedies

(a) Joinder of Claims.   A party asserting a claim to relief as an original claim, counterclaim, cross-claim, or third-party claim, may join, either as independent or as alternate claims, as many claims, legal, equitable, or maritime, as the party has against an opposing party.

(b) Joinder of Remedies; Fraudulent Conveyances.   Whenever a claim is one heretofore cognizable only after another claim has been prosecuted to a conclusion, the two claims may be joined in a single action; but the court shall grant relief in that action only in accordance with the relative substantive rights of the parties.   In particular, a plaintiff may state a claim for money and a claim to have set aside a conveyance fraudulent as to that plaintiff, without first having obtained a judgment establishing the claim for money.

Notes on Amendments to Federal Rule 18 and Comparative State Provisions

(a) *Amendments in 1966 to Rule 18(a)*

Prior to 1966, Rule 18(a) read as follows:

(a) Joinder of Claims.   The plaintiff in his complaint or in a reply setting forth a counterclaim and the defendant in an answer setting forth a counterclaim may join either as independent or as alternate claims as many claims either legal or equitable or both as he may have against an opposing party.   There may be a like joinder of claims when there are multiple parties if the requirements of Rules 19, 20, and 22 are satisfied.   There may be a like joinder of cross-claims or third-party claims if the requirements of Rules 13 and 14 respectively are satisfied.

The Advisory Committee commented on the amendments as follows:

* * *

The liberal policy regarding joinder of claims in the pleadings extends to cases with multiple parties.   However, the language used in the second sentence of Rule 18(a)—"if the requirements of Rules 19 [necessary joinder of parties], 20 [permissive joinder of parties], and 22 [interpleader] are satisfied"—has led some courts to infer that the rules regulating joinder of parties are intended to carry back to Rule 18(a) and to impose some special limits on joinder of claims in multiparty cases.   In particular, Rule 20(a) has been read as restricting the operation of Rule 18(a) in certain situations in which a number of parties have been permissively joined in an action.   In *Federal Housing Admr. v. Christianson*, 26 F.Supp. 419 (D.Conn.1939), the indorsee of two notes sued the three comakers of one note, and sought to join in the action a count on a second note which had been made by two of the three defendants.   There was no doubt about the propriety of the joinder of the three parties defendant, for a right to relief was being asserted against all three defendants which arose out of a single "transaction" (the first note) and a question of fact or law "common" to all three defendants would arise in the action. See the text of Rule 20(a). The court, however, refused to allow the joinder of the count on the second note, on the ground that this right to relief, assumed to arise from a distinct transaction, did not involve a question common to all the defendants but only two of them. * * *

If the court's view is followed, it becomes necessary to enter at the pleading stage into speculations about the exact relation between the claim sought to be joined against fewer than all the defendants properly joined in the action, and the claims asserted against all the defendants. * * * Thus if it could be found in the *Christianson* situation that the claim on the second note arose out of the same transaction as the claim on the first or out of a transaction forming part of a "series," and that any question of fact or law with respect to the second note also arose with regard to the first, it would be held that the claim on the second note could be joined in the complaint. * * * Such pleading niceties provide a basis for delaying and wasteful maneuver. It is more compatible with the design of the rules to allow the claim to be joined in the pleading, leaving the question of possible separate trial of that claim to be later decided. * * * It is instructive to note that the court in the *Christianson* case, while holding that the claim on the second note could not be joined as a matter of pleading, held open the possibility that both claims would later be consolidated for trial under Rule 42(a). See 26 F.Supp. 419.

Rule 18(a) is now amended not only to overcome the *Christianson* decision and similar authority, but also to state clearly, as a comprehensive proposition, that a party asserting a claim (an original claim, counterclaim, cross-claim, or third-party claim) may join as many claims as he has against an opposing party. * * *

It is emphasized that amended Rule 18(a) deals only with pleading. As already indicated, a claim properly joined as a matter of pleading need not be proceeded with together with the other claims if fairness or convenience justifies separate treatment.

* * *

Free joinder of claims and remedies is one of the basic purposes of unification of the admiralty and civil procedure. The amendment accordingly provides for the inclusion in the rule of maritime claims as well as those which are legal and equitable in character.

(b) *Comparative State Provisions*

Michigan Court Rule 2.203

(A) Compulsory Joinder. In a pleading that states a claim against an opposing party, the pleader must join every claim that the pleader has against that opposing party at the time of serving the pleading, if it arises out of the transaction or occurrence that is the subject matter of the action and does not require for its adjudication the presence of third parties over whom the court cannot acquire jurisdiction.

(B) Permissive Joinder. A pleader may join as either independent or alternate claims as many claims, legal or equitable, as the pleader has against an opposing party. If a claim is one previously cognizable only after another claim has been prosecuted to a conclusion, the two claims may be joined in a single action; but the court may grant relief only in accordance with the substantive rights of the parties.

* * *

Rule 19. Joinder of Persons Needed for Just Adjudication

(a) Persons to Be Joined if Feasible. A person who is subject to service of process and whose joinder will not deprive the court of jurisdiction over the subject matter of the action shall be joined as a party in the action if (1) in the person's absence complete relief cannot be accorded among those already parties, or (2) the person claims an interest relating to the subject of the action and is so situated that the disposition of the action in the person's absence may (i) as a practical matter impair or impede the person's ability to protect that interest or (ii) leave any of the persons already parties subject to a substantial risk of incurring double, multiple, or otherwise inconsistent obligations by reason of the claimed interest. If the person has not been so joined, the court shall order that the person be made a party. If the person should join as a plaintiff but refuses to do so, the person may be made a defendant, or, in a proper case, an involuntary plaintiff. If the joined party objects to venue and joinder of that party would render the venue of the action improper, that party shall be dismissed from the action.

(b) Determination by Court Whenever Joinder Not Feasible. If a person as described in subdivision (a)(1)–(2) hereof cannot be made a party, the court shall determine whether in equity and good conscience the action should proceed among the parties before it, or should be dismissed, the absent person being thus regarded as indispensable. The factors to be considered by the court include: first, to what extent a judgment rendered in the person's absence might be prejudicial to the person or those already parties; second, the extent to which, by protective provisions in the judgment, by the shaping of relief, or other measures, the prejudice can be lessened or avoided; third, whether a judgment rendered in the person's absence will be adequate; fourth, whether the plaintiff will have an adequate remedy if the action is dismissed for nonjoinder.

(c) Pleading Reasons for Nonjoinder. A pleading asserting a claim for relief shall state the names, if known to the pleader, of any persons as described in subdivision (a)(1)–(2) hereof who are not joined, and the reasons why they are not joined.

(d) Exception of Class Actions. This rule is subject to the provisions of Rule 23.

Notes on Amendments to Federal Rule 19

Prior to 1966, Rule 19 read as follows:

(a) Necessary Joinder. Subject to the provisions of Rule 23 and of subdivision (b) of this rule, persons having a joint interest shall be made parties and be joined on the same side as plaintiffs or defendants. When a person who should join as a plaintiff refuses to do so, he may be made a defendant or, in proper cases, an involuntary plaintiff.

(b) Effect of Failure to Join. When persons who are not indispensable, but who ought to be parties if complete relief is to be accorded between those already parties, have not been made parties and are subject to the jurisdiction of the court as to both service of process and venue and can be made parties without depriving the court of jurisdiction of the parties before it, the court shall order them summoned to appear in the action. The court in its discretion may proceed in the action without making such persons parties, if its jurisdiction over them as to either service of process or venue can be acquired only by their consent or voluntary appearance or if, though they are subject to its jurisdiction, their joinder would deprive the court of jurisdiction of the parties before it; but the judgment rendered therein does not affect the rights or liabilities of absent persons.

(c) Same: Names of Omitted Persons and Reasons for Non-Joinder to be Pleaded. In any pleading in which relief is asked, the pleader shall set forth the names, if known to him, of persons who ought to be parties if complete relief is to be accorded between those already parties, but who are not joined, and shall state why they are omitted.

The Advisory Committee noted the alterations as follows:

Whenever feasible, the persons materially interested in the subject of an action—see the more detailed description of these persons in the discussion of new subdivision (a) below—should be joined as parties so that they may be heard and a complete disposition made. When this comprehensive joinder cannot be accomplished—a situation which may be encountered in Federal courts because of limitations on service of process, subject matter jurisdiction, and venue—the case should be examined pragmatically and a choice made between the alternatives of proceeding with the action in the absence of particular interested persons, and dismissing the action.

Even if the court is mistaken in its decision to proceed in the absence of an interested person, it does not by that token deprive itself of the power to adjudicate as between the parties already before it through proper service of process. But the court can make a legally binding adjudication only between the parties actually joined in the action. It is true that an adjudication between the parties before the court may on occasion adversely affect the absent person as a practical matter, or leave a party exposed to a later inconsistent recovery by the absent person. These are factors which should be considered in deciding whether the action should proceed, or should rather be dismissed; but they do not themselves negate the court's power to adjudicate as between the parties who have been joined.

Defects in the Original Rule

The foregoing propositions were well understood in the older equity practice, see Hazard, *Indispensable Party: The Historical Origin of a Procedural Phantom*, 61 Colum.L.Rev. 1254 (1961), and Rule 19 could be and often was applied in consonance with them. But experience showed that the rule was defective in its phrasing and did not point clearly to the proper basis of decision.

Textual defects. * * *

(2) The word "indispensable," appearing in original subdivision (b), was apparently intended as an inclusive reference to the interested persons in whose absence it would be advisable, all factors having been considered, to dismiss the action. Yet the sentence implied that there might be interested persons, not "indispensable," in whose absence the action ought also to be dismissed. Further, it seemed at least superficially plausible to equate the word "indispensable" with the expression "having a joint interest," appearing in subdivision (a). * * * But persons holding an interest technically "joint" are not always so related to an action that it would be unwise to proceed without joining all of them, whereas persons holding an interest not technically "joint" may have this relation to an action. See Reed, *Compulsory Joinder of Parties in Civil Actions*, 55 Mich.L.Rev. 327, 356 ff., 483 (1957).

(3) The use of "indispensable" and "joint interest" in the context of original Rule 19 directed attention to the technical or abstract character of the rights or obligations of the persons whose joinder was in question, and correspondingly distracted attention from the pragmatic considerations which should be controlling.

(4) The original rule, in dealing with the feasibility of joining a person as a party to the action, besides referring to whether the person was "subject to the jurisdiction of the court as to both service of process and venue," spoke of whether the person could be made a party "without depriving the court of jurisdiction of the parties before it." The second quoted expression used "jurisdiction" in the

sense of the competence of the court over the subject matter of the action, and in this sense the expression was apt. However, by a familiar confusion, the expression seems to have suggested to some that the absence from the lawsuit of a person who was "indispensable" or "who ought to be [a] part[y]" itself deprived the court of the power to adjudicate as between the parties already joined. * * *

Failure to point to correct basis of decision. The original rule did not state affirmatively what factors were relevant in deciding whether the action should proceed or be dismissed when joinder of interested persons was infeasible. In some instances courts did not undertake the relevant inquiry or were misled by the "jurisdiction" fallacy. In other instances there was undue preoccupation with abstract classifications of rights or obligations, as against consideration of the particular consequences of proceeding with the action and the ways by which these consequences might be ameliorated by the shaping of final relief or other precautions.

Although these difficulties cannot be said to have been general, analysis of the cases showed that there was good reason for attempting to strengthen the rule. * * *

The Amended Rule

Subdivision (a) now defines the persons whose joinder in the action is desirable. Clause (1) stresses the desirability of joining those persons in whose absence the court would be obliged to grant partial or "hollow" rather than complete relief to the parties before the court. The interests that are being furthered here are not only those of the parties, but also that of the public in avoiding repeated lawsuits on the same essential subject matter. Clause (2)(i) recognizes the importance of protecting the person whose joinder is in question against the practical prejudice to him which may arise through a disposition of the action in his absence. Clause (2)(ii) recognizes the need for considering whether a party may be left, after the adjudication, in a position where a person not joined can subject him to a double or otherwise inconsistent liability. See Reed, *supra*, 55 Mich.L.Rev. at 330, 338 * * *.

The subdivision (a) definition of persons to be joined is not couched in terms of the abstract nature of their interests—"joint," "united," "separable," or the like. * * * It should be noted particularly, however, that the description is not at variance with the settled authorities holding that a tortfeasor with the usual "joint-and several" liability is merely a permissive party to an action against another with like liability. * * * Joinder of this tortfeasors continues to be regulated by Rule 20 * * *. [See Temple v. Synthes Corp., 498 U.S. 5, 111 S.Ct. 315, 112 L.Ed.2d 263 (1990).]

If a person as described in subdivision (a)(1)–(2) is amenable to service of process and his joinder would not deprive the court of jurisdiction in the sense of competence over the action, he should be joined as a party; and if he has not been joined, the court should order him to be brought into the action. If a party joined has a valid objection to the venue and chooses to assert it, he will be dismissed from the action.

Subdivision (b). When a person as described in subdivision (a)(1)–(2) cannot be made a party, the court is to determine whether in equity and good conscience the action should proceed among the parties already before it, or should be dismissed. That this decision is to be made in the light of pragmatic considerations has often been acknowledged by the courts. See *Roos v. Texas Co.*, 23 F.2d 171 (2d Cir. 1927), *cert. denied*, 277 U.S. 587 (1928); *Niles-Bement-Pond Co. v. Iron Moulders' Union*, 254 U.S. 77, 80 (1920). The subdivision sets out four relevant considerations drawn from the experience revealed in the decided cases. The factors are to a certain extent overlapping, and they are not intended to exclude other considerations which may be applicable in particular situations.

The *first factor* brings in a consideration of what a judgment in the action would mean to the absentee. Would the absentee be adversely affected in a practical sense, and if so, would the prejudice be immediate and serious, or remote and minor? The possible collateral consequences of the judgment upon the parties already joined are also to be appraised. Would any party be exposed to a fresh action by the absentee, and if so, how serious is the threat?   * * *

The *second factor* calls attention to the measures by which prejudice may be averted or lessened. The "shaping of relief" is a familiar expedient to this end. See, *e.g.,* the award of money damages in lieu of specific relief where the latter might affect an absentee adversely. *Ward v. Deavers,* 203 F.2d 72 (D.C.Cir.1953) * * *.

The *third factor*—whether an "adequate" judgment can be rendered in the absence of a given person—calls attention to the extent of the relief that can be accorded among the parties joined. It meshes with the other factors, especially the "shaping of relief" mentioned under the second factor.   * * *

The *fourth factor,* looking to the practical effects of a dismissal, indicates that the court should consider whether there is any assurance that the plaintiff, if dismissed, could sue effectively in another forum where better joinder would be possible.   * * *

The subdivision uses the word "indispensable" only in a conclusory sense, that is, a person is "regarded as indispensable" when he cannot be made a party and, upon consideration of the factors above-mentioned, it is determined that in his absence it would be preferable to dismiss the action, rather than to retain it. * * *

Subdivision (c) parallels the predecessor subdivision (c) of Rule 19. In some situations it may be desirable to advise a person who has not been joined of the fact that the action is pending, and in particular cases the court in its discretion may itself convey this information by directing a letter or other informal notice to the absentee.

Rule 20.   Permissive Joinder of Parties

(a) Permissive Joinder. All persons may join in one action as plaintiffs if they assert any right to relief jointly, severally, or in the alternative in respect of or arising out of the same transaction, occurrence, or series of transactions or occurrences and if any question of law or fact common to all these persons will arise in the action. All persons (and any vessel, cargo or other property subject to admiralty process in rem) may be joined in one action as defendants if there is asserted against them jointly, severally, or in the alternative, any right to relief in respect of or arising out of the same transaction, occurrence, or series of transactions or occurrences and if any question of law or fact common to all defendants will arise in the action. A plaintiff or defendant need not be interested in obtaining or defending against all the relief demanded. Judgment may be given for one or more of the plaintiffs according to their respective rights to relief, and against one or more defendants according to their respective liabilities.

(b) Separate Trials. The court may make such orders as will prevent a party from being embarrassed, delayed, or put to expense by the inclusion of a party against whom the party asserts no claim and who asserts no claim against the party, and may order separate trials or make other orders to prevent delay or prejudice.

Comparative State Provisions

Michigan Court Rule 2.206(A)

(1) All persons may join in one action as plaintiffs

(a) if they assert a right to relief jointly, severally, or in the alternative, in respect of or arising out of the same transaction, occurrence, or series of transactions or occurrences and if a question of law or fact common to all of the plaintiffs will arise in the action; or

(b) if their presence in the action will promote the convenient administration of justice.

(2) All persons may be joined in one action as defendants

(a) if there is asserted against them jointly, severally, or in the alternative, a right to relief in respect of or arising out of the same transaction, occurrence, or series of transactions or occurrences and if a question of law or fact common to all of the defendants will arise in the action; or

(b) if their presence in the action will promote the convenient administration of justice.

(3) A plaintiff or defendant need not be interested in obtaining or defending against all the relief demanded. Judgment may be rendered for one or more of the parties against one or more of the parties as the rights and liabilities of the parties are determined.

New York Civil Practice Law and Rules 1002(a) & (b)

(a) Persons who assert any right to relief jointly, severally, or in the alternative arising out of the same transaction, occurrence, or series of transactions or occurrences, may join in one action as plaintiffs if any common question of law or fact would arise.

(b) Persons against whom there is asserted any right to relief jointly, severally, or in the alternative, arising out of the same transaction, occurrence, or series of transactions or occurrences, may be joined in one action as defendants if any common question of law or fact would arise.

* * *

Rule 21. Misjoinder and Non-joinder of Parties

Misjoinder of parties is not ground for dismissal of an action. Parties may be dropped or added by order of the court on motion of any party or of its own initiative at any stage of the action and on such terms as are just. Any claim against a party may be severed and proceeded with separately.

Rule 22. Interpleader

(1) Persons having claims against the plaintiff may be joined as defendants and required to interplead when their claims are such that the plaintiff is or may be exposed to double or multiple liability. It is not ground for objection to the joinder that the claims of the several claimants or the titles on which their claims depend do not have a common origin or are not identical but are adverse to and independent of one another, or that the plaintiff avers that the plaintiff is not liable in whole or in part to any or all of the claimants. A defendant exposed to similar liability may obtain such interpleader by way of cross-claim or counterclaim. The provisions of this rule supplement and do not in any way limit the joinder of parties permitted in Rule 20.

(2) The remedy herein provided is in addition to and in no way supersedes or limits the remedy provided by Title 28, U.S.C. §§ 1335,

1397, and 2361. Actions under those provisions shall be conducted in accordance with these rules.

Comparative State Provisions

California Civil Procedure Code § 386

(a) A defendant, against whom an action is pending upon a contract, or for specific personal property, may, at any time before answer, upon affidavit that a person not a party to the action makes against him, and without any collusion with him, a demand upon such contract, or for such property, upon notice to such person and the adverse party, apply to the court for an order to substitute such person in his place, and discharge him from liability to either party, on his depositing in court the amount claimed on the contract, or delivering the property or its value to such person as the court may direct; and the court may, in its discretion, make the order; or such defendant may file a verified cross-complaint in interpleader, admitting that he has no interest in such amount or such property claimed, or in a portion of such amount or such property and alleging that all or such portion of the amount or property is demanded by parties to such action or cross-action and apply to the court upon notice to such parties for an order to deliver such property or portion thereof or its value to such person as the court shall direct. And whenever conflicting claims are or may be made upon a person for or relating to personal property, or the performance of an obligation, or any portion thereof, such person may bring an action against the conflicting claimants to compel them to interplead and litigate their several claims. The order of substitution may be made and the action of interpleader may be maintained, and the applicant or interpleading party be discharged from liability to all or any of the conflicting claimants, although their titles or claims have not a common origin, or are not identical but are adverse to and independent of one another.

(b) Any person, firm, corporation, association or other entity against whom double or multiple claims are made, or may be made, by two or more persons which are such that they may give rise to double or multiple liability, may bring an action against the claimants to compel them to interplead and litigate their several claims.

When the person, firm, corporation, association or other entity against whom such claims are made, or may be made, is a defendant in an action brought upon one or more of such claims, it may either file a verified cross-complaint in interpleader, admitting that it has no interest in the money or property claimed, or in only a portion thereof, and alleging that all or such portion is demanded by parties to such action, and apply to the court upon notice to such parties for an order to deliver such money or property or such portion thereof to such person as the court shall direct; or may bring a separate action against the claimants to compel them to interplead and litigate their several claims. The action of interpleader may be maintained although the claims have not a common origin, are not identical but are adverse to and independent of one another, or the claims are unliquidated and no liability on the part of the party bringing the action or filing the cross-complaint has arisen. The applicant or interpleading party may deny liability in whole or in part to any or all of the claimants. The applicant or interpleading party may join as a defendant in such action any other party against whom claims are made by one or more of the claimants or such other party may interplead by cross-complaint; provided, however, that such claims arise out of the same transaction or occurrence.

        * * *

New York Civil Practice Law and Rules 216

(a) **Action to recover money.** 1. No action for the recovery of any sum of money due and payable under or on account of a contract, or for any part thereof, shall be commenced by any person who has made claim to the sum, after the expiration of one year from the giving of notice, as hereinafter provided, to the claimant that an action commenced by another person is pending to recover the sum, or any part thereof, exceeding fifty dollars in amount. This limitation shall not be construed to enlarge the time within which the cause of action of the claimant would otherwise be barred.

2. If any person shall make claim for the recovery of any sum of money due and payable under or on account of a contract, and an action has theretofore been, or shall thereafter be, commenced by another person to recover the sum, or any part thereof, exceeding fifty dollars in amount, the defendant in such action may, within twenty days from the date of service upon him of the complaint or from the date of receipt by him of the claim, whichever occurs later, make a motion before the court in which the action is pending for an order permitting the defendant to give notice to the claimant that the action is pending. The court in which the action is pending shall grant the order where it appears that a person not a party to the action has made claim against the defendant for the sum of money, or any part thereof, exceeding fifty dollars in amount; that the action was brought without collusion between the defendant and the plaintiff; and that the claimant cannot, with due diligence, be served with process in such a manner as to obtain jurisdiction over his person. The order shall provide, among such other terms and conditions as justice may require, that notice shall be given to the claimant by sending by registered mail a copy of the summons and complaint in the action and the order and a notice addressed to the claimant at his last known address. In the event that registration of mail directed to any country or part thereof shall be discontinued or suspended, notice to a claimant whose last known address is within such country or part thereof shall be given by ordinary mail, under such terms and conditions as the court may direct. Proof that the notice has been mailed shall be filed within ten days from the date of the order; otherwise the order becomes inoperative. Upon such filing, notice shall be deemed to have been given on the tenth day after the date of such order.

3. Upon proof by affidavit or otherwise, to the satisfaction of the court, that the conditions of this subdivision have been satisfied and that there is no collusion between the claimant and the defendant, the court shall make an order staying further prosecution of the action for a period not to exceed one year from the date when the notice shall have been given to the claimant. At the time of the granting of such order or at any time thereafter, the court, upon the motion of any party, shall, as a condition of the granting of the order or its continuation, impose upon the defendant such terms as justice may require as to the furnishing of an undertaking in an amount to be fixed by the court. The stay shall be vacated and the undertaking, if any has been given, may be discharged or modified, as justice may require, upon proof to the court by any party to the action that the claimant has intervened or has instituted another action in any court of this state to recover the said sum of money, or any part thereof, exceeding fifty dollars.

4. A motion for any relief as prescribed in this subdivision shall be made on notice to all other parties to the action.

5. Whenever claims are made by two or more persons, each claiming to be, to the exclusion of the other, the duly authorized deputy, officer or agent to demand, receive, collect, sue for or recover the same sum of money due and payable under or on account of a contract, or any part thereof, exceeding fifty dollars in amount, for and on behalf of the same person, each person making such a claim shall be deemed an adverse claimant. Notwithstanding that an action has been commenced in the name of or on behalf of the person for whom he claims to be the duly authorized deputy, officer or agent, any such adverse claimant may be notified of the pendency of an action as provided in this subdivision and may intervene in the action and be designated as claiming to be or as the alleged deputy, officer or agent.

6. Whenever an action has been commenced for the recovery of any sum of money exceeding fifty dollars due and payable under or on account of a contract and the records of the defendant show that a person other than the plaintiff has the right, exclusive of other deputies, officers or agents of the plaintiff, to demand, sue for and recover the same sum of money, or any part thereof, exceeding fifty dollars in amount, either in his own name, on his own behalf, or as the authorized deputy, officer or agent for the plaintiff, and the defendant has received no notice

of transfer, revocation, or other change in right or authority acceptable to it, the person so appearing on the records shall be deemed to have made an adverse claim to the sum of money and may be treated as an adverse claimant.

(b) Action to recover property. When an action has been commenced to recover specific personal property, including certificates of stocks, bonds, notes or other securities or obligations, exceeding fifty dollars in value, held by the defendant within the state, or to enforce a vested or contingent interest or lien upon such property, and a person not a party to the action asserts a claim to the whole or any part of the same property or to a right, interest or lien upon it which is adverse to the plaintiff's claim, and the court in which the action is pending has no jurisdiction over the adverse claimant to direct the issuance of process or if the same be issued it would be without effect notwithstanding that the action seeks to have declared, enforced, regulated, defined or limited, rights, interests or liens upon specific personal property within the state, the defendant in the action may within twenty days from the date of service upon him of the complaint or within twenty days of the date of the receipt by him of the adverse claim, whichever shall occur later, make a motion before the court for leave to give notice to the adverse claimant of the pending action in the same manner as provided in subdivision (a). Upon the granting of such an order, the provisions of subdivision (a) shall apply insofar as they are compatible with the subject matter of the action.

Rule 23. Class Actions

[See proposed congressional enactments to amend 28 U.S.C. § 1332 and to add new §§ 1453, 1712, 1713, and 1714, in Part IX, infra.]

(a) Prerequisites to a Class Action. One or more members of a class may sue or be sued as representative parties on behalf of all only if (1) the class is so numerous that joinder of all members is impracticable, (2) there are questions of law or fact common to the class, (3) the claims or defenses of the representative parties are typical of the claims or defenses of the class, and (4) the representative parties will fairly and adequately protect the interests of the class.

(b) Class Actions Maintainable. An action may be maintained as a class action if the prerequisites of subdivision (a) are satisfied, and in addition:

(1) the prosecution of separate actions by or against individual members of the class would create a risk of

(A) inconsistent or varying adjudications with respect to individual members of the class which would establish incompatible standards of conduct for the party opposing the class, or

(B) adjudications with respect to individual members of the class which would as a practical matter be dispositive of the interests of the other members not parties to the adjudications or substantially impair or impede their ability to protect their interests; or

(2) the party opposing the class has acted or refused to act on grounds generally applicable to the class, thereby making appropriate final injunctive relief or corresponding declaratory relief with respect to the class as a whole; or

(3) the court finds that the questions of law or fact common to the members of the class predominate over any questions affecting only

individual members, and that a class action is superior to other available methods for the fair and efficient adjudication of the controversy. The matters pertinent to the findings include: (A) the interest of members of the class in individually controlling the prosecution or defense of separate actions; (B) the extent and nature of any litigation concerning the controversy already commenced by or against members of the class; (C) the desirability or undesirability of concentrating the litigation of the claims in the particular forum; (D) the difficulties likely to be encountered in the management of a class action.

(c) Determination by Order Whether Class Action to Be Maintained; Notice; Judgment; Actions Conducted Partially as Class Actions.

(1) As soon as practicable after the commencement of an action brought as a class action, the court shall determine by order whether it is to be so maintained. An order under this subdivision may be conditional, and may be altered or amended before the decision on the merits.

(2) In any class action maintained under subdivision (b)(3), the court shall direct to the members of the class the best notice practicable under the circumstances, including individual notice to all members who can be identified through reasonable effort. The notice shall advise each member that (A) the court will exclude the member from the class if the member so requests by a specified date; (B) the judgment, whether favorable or not, will include all members who do not request exclusion; and (C) any member who does not request exclusion may, if the member desires, enter an appearance through counsel.

(3) The judgment in an action maintained as a class action under subdivision (b)(1) or (b)(2), whether or not favorable to the class, shall include and describe those whom the court finds to be members of the class. The judgment in an action maintained as a class action under subdivision (b)(3), whether or not favorable to the class, shall include and specify or describe those to whom the notice provided in subdivision (c)(2) was directed, and who have not requested exclusion, and whom the court finds to be members of the class.

(4) When appropriate (A) an action may be brought or maintained as a class action with respect to particular issues, or (B) a class may be divided into subclasses and each subclass treated as a class, and the provisions of this rule shall then be construed and applied accordingly.

(d) Orders in Conduct of Actions. In the conduct of actions to which this rule applies, the court may make appropriate orders: (1) determining the course of proceedings or prescribing measures to prevent undue repetition or complication in the presentation of evidence or argument; (2) requiring, for the protection of the members of the class or otherwise for the fair conduct of the action, that notice be given in such manner as the court may direct to some or all of the members of any step in the action, or of the proposed extent of the judgment, or of the opportunity of members to signify whether they consider the representation fair and adequate, to intervene and present claims or defenses, or otherwise to come into the action; (3) imposing conditions on the representative parties or on intervenors; (4) requiring that the pleadings be amended to eliminate therefrom allegations as to representation of absent persons, and that the action proceed accordingly; (5) dealing with similar procedural matters. The orders may be combined with an order under Rule 16, and may be altered or amended as may be desirable from time to time.

(e) Dismissal or Compromise. A class action shall not be dismissed or compromised without the approval of the court, and notice of the proposed dismissal or compromise shall be given to all members of the class in such manner as the court directs.

(f) Appeals. A court of appeals may in its discretion permit an appeal from an order of a district court granting or denying class action certification under this rule if application is made to it within ten days after entry of the order. An appeal does not stay proceedings in the district court unless the district judge or the court of appeals so orders.

Notes on Amendments to Federal Rule 23 and Comparative State Provision

(a) *Amendments in 1966 to Rule 23*

Prior to 1966 the basic subject matter of current Rule 23 was covered in Rules 23(a) and (c), which read as follows:

(a) Representation. If persons constituting a class are so numerous as to make it impracticable to bring them all before the court, such of them, one or more, as will fairly insure the adequate representation of all may, on behalf of all, sue or be sued, when the character of the right sought to be enforced for or against the class is

(1) joint, or common, or secondary in the sense that the owner of a primary right refuses to enforce that right and a member of the class thereby becomes entitled to enforce it;

(2) several, and the object of the action is the adjudication of claims which do or may affect specific property involved in the action; or

(3) several, and there is a common question of law or fact affecting the several rights and a common relief is sought.

(c) Dismissal or Compromise. A class action shall not be dismissed or compromised without the approval of the court. If the right sought to be enforced is one defined in paragraph (1) of subdivision (a) of this rule notice of the proposed dismissal or compromise shall be given to all members of the class in such manner as the court directs. If the right is one defined in paragraphs (2) or (3) of subdivision (a) notice shall be given only if the court requires it.

The Advisory Committee noted the changes as follows:

Difficulties with the original rule. The categories of class actions in the original rule were defined in terms of the abstract nature of the rights involved: the so-called "true" category was defined as involving "joint, common, or secondary rights"; the "hybrid" category, as involving "several" rights related to "specific property"; the "spurious" category, as involving "several" rights affected by a common question and related to common relief. It was thought that the definitions accurately described the situations amenable to the class-suit device, and also would indicate the proper extent of the judgment in each category, which would in turn help to determine the *res judicata* effect of the judgment if questioned in a later action. Thus the judgments in "true" and "hybrid" class actions would extend to the class (although in somewhat different ways); the judgment in a "spurious" class action would extend only to the parties including intervenors. See Moore, *Federal Rules of Civil Procedure: Some Problems Raised by the Preliminary Draft*, 25 Geo.L.J. 551, 570–76 (1937).

In practice the terms "joint," "common," etc., which were used as the basis of the Rule 23 classification proved obscure and uncertain. * * *

Nor did the rule provide an adequate guide to the proper extent of the judgments in class actions. First, we find instances of the courts classifying actions as "true" or intimating that the judgments would be decisive for the class where these results seemed appropriate but were reached by dint of depriving the word "several" of coherent meaning. * * * Second, we find cases classified by the courts as "spurious" in which, on a realistic view, it would seem fitting for the judgments to extend to the class. * * *

The "spurious" action envisaged by original Rule 23 was in any event an anomaly because, although denominated a "class" action and pleaded as such, it was supposed not to adjudicate the rights or liabilities of any person not a party. It was believed to be an advantage of the "spurious" category that it would invite decisions that a member of the "class" could, like a member of the class in a "true" or "hybrid" action, intervene on an ancillary basis without being required to show an independent basis of Federal jurisdiction, and have the benefit of the date of the commencement of the action for purposes of the statute of limitations. See 3 *Moore's Federal Practice* ¶¶ 23.10[1], 23.12 (2d ed. 1963). These results were attained in some instances but not in others. * * * The results, however, can hardly depend upon the mere appearance of a "spurious" category in the rule; they should turn on more basic considerations. See discussion of subdivision (c)(1) below.

Finally, the original rule did not squarely address itself to the question of the measures that might be taken during the course of the action to assure procedural fairness, particularly giving notice to members of the class, which may in turn be related in some instances to the extension of the judgment to the class. * * *

The amended rule describes in more practical terms the occasions for maintaining class actions; provides that all class actions maintained to the end as such will result in judgments including those whom the court finds to be members of the class, whether or not the judgment is favorable to the class; and refers to the measures which can be taken to assure the fair conduct of these actions.

Subdivision (a) states the prerequisites for maintaining any class action in terms of the numerousness of the class making joinder of the members impracticable, the existence of questions common to the class, and the desired qualifications of the representative parties. * * * These are necessary but not sufficient conditions for a class action. * * * Subdivision (b) describes the additional elements which in varying situations justify the use of a class action.

Subdivision (b)(1). The difficulties which would be likely to arise if resort were had to separate actions by or against the individual members of the class here furnish the reasons for, and the principal key to, the propriety and value of utilizing the class-action device. The considerations stated under clauses (A) and (B) are comparable to certain of the elements which define the persons whose joinder in an action is desirable as stated in Rule 19(a), as amended. * * *

Clause (A): One person may have rights against, or be under duties toward, numerous persons constituting a class, and be so positioned that conflicting or varying adjudications in lawsuits with individual members of the class might establish incompatible standards to govern his conduct. The class action device can be used effectively to obviate the actual or virtual dilemma which would thus confront the party opposing the class. * * * To illustrate: Separate actions by individuals against a municipality to declare a bond issue invalid or condition or limit it, to prevent or limit the making of a particular appropriation or to compel or invalidate an assessment, might create a risk of inconsistent or varying determinations. In the same way, individual litigations of the rights and duties of riparian owners, or of landowners' rights and duties respecting a claimed nuisance, could create a possibility of incompatible adjudications. Actions by or against a class provide a ready and fair means of achieving unitary adjudication. * * *

Clause (B): This clause takes in situations where the judgment in a nonclass action by or against an individual member of the class, while not technically concluding the other members, might do so as a practical matter. The vice of an individual action would lie in the fact that the other members of the class, thus practically concluded, would have had no representation in the lawsuit. In an action by policy holders against a fraternal benefit association attacking a financial reorganization of the society, it would hardly have been practical, if indeed it would have been possible, to confine the effects of a validation of the reorganization to the individual plaintiffs. Consequently a class action was called for with adequate representation of all members of the class. * * * The same reasoning applies to an action which charges a breach of trust by an indenture trustee or other fiduciary similarly affecting the members of a large class of security holders or other beneficiaries, and which requires an accounting or like measures to restore the subject of the trust. * * *

In various situations an adjudication as to one or more members of the class will necessarily or probably have an adverse practical effect on the interests of other members who should therefore be represented in the lawsuit. This is plainly the case when claims are made by numerous persons against a fund insufficient to satisfy all claims. A class action by or against representative members to settle the validity of the claims as a whole, or in groups, followed by separate proof of the amount of each valid claim and proportionate distribution of the fund, meets the problem. * * * Similar problems, however, can arise in the absence of a fund either present or potential. A negative or mandatory injunction secured by one of a numerous class may disable the opposing party from performing claimed duties toward the other members of the class or materially affect his ability to do so. An adjudication as to movie "clearances and runs" nominally affecting only one exhibitor would often have practical effects on all the exhibitors in the same territorial area. * * * Assuming a sufficiently numerous class of exhibitors, a class action would be advisable. (Here representation of subclasses of exhibitors could become necessary; see subdivision (c)(3)(B).)

Subdivision (b)(2). This subdivision is intended to reach situations where a party has taken action or refused to take action with respect to a class, and final relief of an injunctive nature or of a corresponding declaratory nature, settling the legality of the behavior with respect to the class as a whole, is appropriate. Declaratory relief "corresponds" to injunctive relief when as a practical matter it affords injunctive relief or serves as a basis for later injunctive relief. The subdivision does not extend to cases in which the appropriate final relief relates exclusively or predominantly to money damages. Action or inaction is directed to a class within the meaning of this subdivision even if it has taken effect or is threatened only as to one or a few members of the class, provided it is based on grounds which have general application to the class.

Illustrative are various actions in the civil-rights field where a party is charged with discriminating unlawfully against a class, usually one whose members are incapable of specific enumeration. * * *

Subdivision (b)(3). In the situations to which this subdivision relates, class-action treatment is not as clearly called for as in those described above, but it may nevertheless be convenient and desirable depending upon the particular facts. Subdivision (b)(3) encompasses those cases in which a class action would achieve economies of time, effort, and expense, and promote uniformity of decision as to persons similarly situated, without sacrificing procedural fairness or bringing about other undesirable results. * * *

The court is required to find, as a condition of holding that a class action may be maintained under this subdivision, that the questions common to the class predominate over the questions affecting individual members. It is only where this predominance exists that economies can be achieved by means of the class-action device. In this view a fraud perpetrated on numerous persons by the use of similar misrepresentations may be an appealing situation for a class action, and it may remain so despite the need, if liability is found, for separate determination of the damages suffered by individuals within the class. On the other hand, although having some common core, a fraud case may be unsuited for treatment as a class action if there was material variation in the representations made or in the kinds or degrees of reliance by the persons to whom they were addressed. * * *

That common questions predominate is not itself sufficient to justify a class action under subdivision (b)(3), for another method of handling the litigious situation may be available which has greater practical advantages. Thus one or more actions agreed to by the parties as test or model actions may be preferable to a class action; or it may prove feasible and preferable to consolidate actions. * * * To reinforce the point that the court with the aid of the parties ought to assess the relative advantages of alternative procedures for handling the total controversy, subdivision (b)(3) requires, as a further condition of maintaining the class action, that the court shall find that that procedure is "superior" to the others in the particular circumstances.

* * *

Subdivision (c)(2) makes special provision for class actions maintained under subdivision (b)(3). As noted in the discussion of the latter subdivision, the interests of the individuals in pursuing their own litigations may be so strong here as to warrant denial of a class action altogether. Even when a class action is maintained under subdivision (b)(3), this individual interest is respected. Thus the court is required to direct notice to the members of the class of the right of each member to be excluded from the class upon his request. A member who does not request exclusion may, if he wishes, enter an appearance in the action through his counsel; whether or not he does so, the judgment in the action will embrace him.

* * *

Subdivision (c)(3). * * *

Hitherto, in a few actions conducted as "spurious" class actions and thus nominally designed to extend only to parties and others intervening *before* the determination of liability, courts have held or intimated that class members might be permitted to intervene *after* a decision on the merits favorable to their interests, in order to secure the benefits of the decision for themselves, although they would presumably be unaffected by an unfavorable decision. * * * Under proposed subdivision (c)(3), one-way intervention is excluded; the action will have been early determined to be a class or nonclass action, and in the former case the judgment, whether or not favorable, will include the class, as above stated.

Although thus declaring that the judgment in a class action includes the class, as defined, subdivision (c)(3) does not disturb the recognized principle that the court conducting the action cannot predetermine the *res judicata* effect of the judgment; this can be tested only in a subsequent action. * * * The court, however, in framing the judgment in any suit brought as a class action, must decide what its extent or coverage shall be, and if the matter is carefully considered, questions of *res judicata* are less likely to be raised at a later time and if raised will be more satisfactorily answered. * * *

(b) *Comparative State Provision*

California Civil Procedure Code § 382

* * * [W]hen the question is one of a common or general interest, of many persons, or when the parties are numerous, and it is impracticable to bring them all before the court, one or more may sue or defend for the benefit of all.

Rule 23.1   Derivative Actions by Shareholders

In a derivative action brought by one or more shareholders or members to enforce a right of a corporation or of an unincorporated association, the corporation or association having failed to enforce a right which may properly be asserted by it, the complaint shall be verified and shall allege (1) that the plaintiff was a shareholder or member at the time of the transaction of which the plaintiff complains or that the plaintiff's share or membership thereafter devolved on the plaintiff by operation of law, and (2) that the action is not a collusive one to confer jurisdiction on a court of the United States which it would not otherwise have.   The complaint shall also allege with particularity the efforts, if any, made by the plaintiff to obtain the action the plaintiff desires from the directors or comparable authority and, if necessary, from the shareholders or members, and the reasons for the plaintiff's failure to obtain the action or for not making the effort.   The derivative action may not be maintained if it appears that the plaintiff does not fairly and adequately represent the interests of the shareholders or members similarly situated in enforcing the right of the corporation or association.   The action shall not be dismissed or compromised without the approval of the court, and notice of the proposed dismissal or compromise shall be given to shareholders or members in such manner as the court directs.

Notes on the Adoption in 1966 of Federal Rule 23.1

Prior to 1966 the substance of Rule 23.1 was contained in Rules 23 (b) and (c). Rule 23(b) stated:

Secondary Action by Shareholders.   In an action brought to enforce a secondary right on the part of one or more shareholders in an association, incorporated or unincorporated, because the association refuses to enforce rights which may properly be asserted by it, the complaint shall be verified by oath and shall aver (1) that the plaintiff was a shareholder at the time of the transaction of which he complains or that his share thereafter devolved on him by operation of law and (2) that the action is not a collusive one to confer on a court of the United States jurisdiction of any action of which it would not otherwise have jurisdiction. The complaint shall also set forth with particularity the efforts of the plaintiff to secure from the managing directors or trustees and, if necessary, from the shareholders such action as he desires, and the reasons for his failure to obtain such action or the reasons for not making such effort.

For former Rule 23(c) see the note following Rule 23.

The Advisory Committee commented as follows on the changes:

A derivative action by a shareholder of a corporation or by a member of an unincorporated association has distinctive aspects which require the special provisions set forth in the new rule.   The next-to-the-last sentence recognizes that the question of adequacy of representation may arise when the plaintiff is one of a group of shareholders or members.   *Cf.* 3 *Moore's Federal Practice* ¶ 23.08 (2d ed. 1963).

The court has inherent power to provide for the conduct of the proceedings in a derivative action, including the power to determine the course of the proceedings and require that any appropriate notice be given to shareholders or members.

Rule 23.2 Actions Relating to Unincorporated Associations

An action brought by or against the members of an unincorporated association as a class by naming certain members as representative parties may be maintained only if it appears that the representative parties will fairly and adequately protect the interests of the association and its members. In the conduct of the action the court may make appropriate orders corresponding with those described in Rule 23(d), and the procedure for dismissal or compromise of the action shall correspond with that provided in Rule 23(e).

Notes on the Adoption in 1966 of Federal Rule 23.2

The substance of Rule 23.2 was not directly treated prior to its addition in 1966. The Advisory Committee's Notes to the Rule read as follows:

Although an action by or against representatives of the membership of an unincorporated association has often been viewed as a class action, the real or main purpose of this characterization has been to give "entity treatment" to the association when for formal reasons it cannot sue or be sued as a jural person under Rule 17(b). See Louisell & Hazard, *Pleading and Procedure: State and Federal* 718 (1962); 3 *Moore's Federal Practice* ¶ 23.08 (2d ed. 1963) * * *. Rule 23.2 deals separately with these actions, referring where appropriate to Rule 23.

Rule 24. Intervention

(a) Intervention of Right. Upon timely application anyone shall be permitted to intervene in an action: (1) when a statute of the United States confers an unconditional right to intervene; or (2) when the applicant claims an interest relating to the property or transaction which is the subject of the action and the applicant is so situated that the disposition of the action may as a practical matter impair or impede the applicant's ability to protect that interest, unless the applicant's interest is adequately represented by existing parties.

(b) Permissive Intervention. Upon timely application anyone may be permitted to intervene in an action: (1) when a statute of the United States confers a conditional right to intervene; or (2) when an applicant's claim or defense and the main action have a question of law or fact in common. When a party to an action relies for ground of claim or defense upon any statute or executive order administered by a federal or state governmental officer or agency or upon any regulation, order, requirement or agreement issued or made pursuant to the statute or executive order, the officer or agency upon timely application may be permitted to intervene in the action. In exercising its discretion the court shall consider whether the intervention will unduly delay or prejudice the adjudication of the rights of the original parties.

(c) Procedure. A person desiring to intervene shall serve a motion to intervene upon the parties as provided in Rule 5. The motion shall state the grounds therefor and shall be accompanied by a pleading setting forth the claim or defense for which intervention is sought. The same procedure shall be followed when a statute of the United States gives a right to intervene. When the constitutionality of an act of Congress affecting the public interest is drawn in question in any action to which the United States or an officer, agency, or employee thereof is not a party, the court shall notify the Attorney General of the United States as provided in Title 28, U.S.C. § 2403. When the constitutionality of any statute of a State affecting the public interest is drawn in question in any action in which that State or any agency, offices, or employee thereof is not a party, the court shall notify the attorney general of the State as provided in Title 28, U.S.C. § 2403. A party challenging the constitutionality of legislation should call the attention of the court to its consequential duty, but failure to do so is not a waiver of any constitutional right otherwise timely asserted.

Notes on Amendments to Federal Rule 24 and Comparative State Provisions

(a) *Amendments in 1966 to Rule 24(a)*

Prior to 1966, Rules 24(a)(2) and (3) provided a right to intervene as follows:

(2) when the representation of the applicant's interest by existing parties is or may be inadequate and the applicant is or may be bound by a judgment in the action; or (3) when the applicant is so situated as to be adversely affected by a distribution or other disposition of property which is in the custody or subject to the control or disposition of the court or an officer thereof.

The amendment eliminated this language and substituted the present Rule 24(a)(2). The Advisory Committee's Notes on the Amendment read as follows:

In attempting to overcome certain difficulties which have arisen in the application of present Rule 24(a)(2) and (3), this amendment draws upon the revision of the related Rules 19 (joinder of persons needed for just adjudication) and 23 (class actions), and the reasoning underlying that revision.

Rule 24(a)(3) as amended in 1948 provided for intervention of right where the applicant established that he would be adversely affected by the distribution or disposition of property involved in an action to which he had not been made a party. Significantly, some decided cases virtually disregarded the language of this provision. Thus Professor Moore states: "The concept of a fund has been applied so loosely that it is possible for a court to find a fund in almost any in personam action." 4 Moore's Federal Practice, par. 24.09[3], at 55 (2d ed. 1962), and see, e.g., Formulabs, Inc. v. Hartley Pen Co., 275 F.2d 52 (9th Cir. 1960). This development was quite natural, for Rule 24(a)(3) was unduly restricted. If an absentee would be substantially affected in a practical sense by the determination made in an action, he should, as a general rule, be entitled to intervene, and his right to do so should not depend on whether there is a fund to be distributed or otherwise disposed of. Intervention of right is here seen to be a kind of counterpart to Rule 19(a)(2)(i) on joinder of persons needed for a just adjudication: where, upon motion of a party in an action, an absentee should be joined so that he may protect his interest which as a practical matter may be substantially impaired by the disposition of the action, he ought to have a right to intervene in the action on his own motion. See Louisell & Hazard, Pleading and Procedure: State and Federal 749–50 (1962).

The general purpose of original Rule 24(a)(2) was to entitle an absentee, purportedly represented by a party, to intervene in the action if he could establish with fair probability that the representation was inadequate. Thus, where an action is being prosecuted or defended by a trustee, a beneficiary of the trust should have a right to intervene if he can show that the trustee's representation of his interest probably is inadequate; similarly a member of a class should have the right to intervene in a class action if he can show the inadequacy of the representation of his interest by the representative parties before the court.

Original Rule 24(a)(2), however, made it a condition of intervention that "the applicant is or may be bound by a judgment in the action," and this created difficulties with intervention in class actions. If the "bound" language was read literally in the sense of res judicata, it could defeat intervention in some meritorious cases. A member of a class to whom a judgment in a class action extended by its terms (see Rule 23(c)(3), as amended) might be entitled to show in a later action, when the judgment in the class action was claimed to operate as res judicata against him, that the "representative" in the class action had not in fact adequately represented him. If he could make this showing, the class-action judgment might be held not to bind him. See Hansberry v. Lee, 311 U.S. 32 (1940). If a class member sought to intervene in the class action proper, while it was still pending, on grounds of inadequacy of representation, he could be met with the argument: if the representation was in fact inadequate, he would not be "bound" by the judgment when it was subsequently asserted against him as res judicata, hence he was not entitled to intervene; if the representation was in fact adequate, there was no occasion or ground for intervention. * * * This reasoning might be linguistically justified by original Rule 24(a)(2); but it could lead to poor results. * * * A class member who claims that his "representative" does not adequately represent him, and is able to establish that proposition with sufficient probability, should not be put to the risk of having a judgment entered in the action which by its terms extends to him, and be obliged to test the validity of the judgment as applied to his interest by a later collateral attack. Rather he should, as a general rule, be entitled to intervene in the action.

The amendment provides that an applicant is entitled to intervene in an action when his position is comparable to that of a person under Rule 19(a)(2)(i), as amended, unless his interest is already adequately represented in the action by existing parties. The Rule 19(a)(2)(i) criterion imports practical considerations, and the deletion of the "bound" language similarly frees the rule from undue preoccupation with strict considerations of res judicata.

The representation whose adequacy comes into question under the amended rule is not confined to formal representation like that provided by a trustee for his beneficiary or a representative party in a class action for a member of the class. A party to an action may provide practical representation to the absentee seeking intervention although no such formal relationship exists between them, and the adequacy of this practical representation will then have to be weighed. * * *

An intervention of right under the amended rule may be subject to appropriate conditions or restrictions responsive among other things to the requirements of efficient conduct of the proceedings.

(b) *Comparative State Provision*

Ohio Revised Code Annotated § 2307.27

In an action for the recovery of real or personal property, a person claiming an interest in the property, on his application, may be made a party.

Rule 25. Substitution of Parties

(a) Death.

(1) If a party dies and the claim is not thereby extinguished, the court may order substitution of the proper parties. The motion for substitution may be made by any party or by the successors or representatives of the deceased party and, together with the notice of hearing, shall be served on the parties as provided in Rule 5 and upon persons not parties in the manner provided in Rule 4 for the service of a summons, and may be served in any judicial district. Unless the motion for substitution is made not later than 90 days after the death is suggested upon the record by service of a statement of the fact of the death as

provided herein for the service of the motion, the action shall be dismissed as to the deceased party.

(2) In the event of the death of one or more of the plaintiffs or of one or more of the defendants in an action in which the right sought to be enforced survives only to the surviving plaintiffs or only against the surviving defendants, the action does not abate. The death shall be suggested upon the record and the action shall proceed in favor of or against the surviving parties.

(b) Incompetency. If a party becomes incompetent, the court upon motion served as provided in subdivision (a) of this rule may allow the action to be continued by or against the party's representative.

(c) Transfer of Interest. In case of any transfer of interest, the action may be continued by or against the original party, unless the court upon motion directs the person to whom the interest is transferred to be substituted in the action or joined with the original party. Service of the motion shall be made as provided in subdivision (a) of this rule.

(d) Public Officers; Death or Separation From Office.

(1) When a public officer is a party to an action in an official capacity and during its pendency dies, resigns, or otherwise ceases to hold office, the action does not abate and the officer's successor is automatically substituted as a party. Proceedings following the substitution shall be in the name of the substituted party, but any misnomer not affecting the substantial rights of the parties shall be disregarded. An order of substitution may be entered at any time, but the omission to enter such an order shall not affect the substitution.

(2) A public officer who sues or is sued in an official capacity may be described as a party by the officer's official title rather than by name; but the court may require the officer's name to be added.

V. DEPOSITIONS AND DISCOVERY

Rule 26. General Provisions Governing Discovery; Duty of Disclosure

497-500

[See proposed changes to Rule 26(a), (b), (d), and (f), in Part IX, infra.]

(a) Required Disclosures; Methods to Discover Additional Matter.

p. 782

(1) *Initial Disclosures.* Except to the extent otherwise stipulated or directed by order or local rule, a party shall, without awaiting a discovery request, provide to other parties;

(A) the name and, if known, the address and telephone number of each individual likely to have discoverable information relevant to disputed facts alleged with particularity in the pleadings, identifying the subjects of the information;

78

(B) a copy of, or a description by category and location of, all documents, data compilations, and tangible things in the possession, custody, or control of the party that are relevant to the disputed facts alleged with particularity in the pleadings;

(C) a computation of any category of damages claimed by the disclosing party, making available for inspection and copying as under Rule 34 the documents or other evidentiary material, not privileged or protected from disclosure, on which such computation is based, including materials bearing on the nature and extent of injuries suffered; and

(D) for inspection copying as under Rule 34 any insurance agreement under which any person carrying on an insurance business may be liable to satisfy part or all of a judgment which may be entered in the action or to indemnify or reimburse for payments made to satisfy the judgment.

Unless otherwise stipulated or directed by the court, these disclosures shall be made at or within 10 days after the meeting of the parties under subdivision (f). A party shall make its initial disclosures based on the information then reasonably available to it and is not excused from making its disclosure because it has not fully completed its investigation of the case or because it challenges the sufficiency of another party's disclosures or because another party has not made its disclosures.

(2) *Disclosure of Expert Testimony.*

(A) In addition to the disclosures required by paragraph (1), a party shall disclose to other parties the identity of any person who may be used at trial to present evidence under Rules 702, 703, or 705 of the Federal Rules of Evidence.

(B) Except as otherwise stipulated or directed by the court, this disclosure shall, with respect to a witness who is retained or specially employed to provide expert testimony in the case or whose duties as an employee of the party regularly involve giving expert testimony, be accompanied by a written report prepared and signed by the witness. The report shall contain a complete statement of all opinions to be expressed and the basis and reasons therefor; the data or other information considered by the witness in forming the opinions; any exhibits to be used as a summary of or support for the opinions; the qualifications of the witness, including a list of all publications authored by the witness within the preceding ten years; the compensation to be paid for the study and testimony; and a listing of any other cases in which the witness has testified as an expert at trial or by deposition within the preceding four years.

(C) These disclosures shall be made at the times and in the sequence directed by the court. In the absence of other directions from the court or stipulation by the parties, the disclosures shall be made at least 90 days before the trial date or the date the case is to be ready for trial or, if the evidence is intended solely to contradict or rebut evidence on the same subject matter identified by another party under paragraph (2)(B), within 30 days after the disclosure made by such other party. The parties shall supplement these disclosures when required under subdivision (e)(1).

(3) *Pretrial Disclosures.* In addition to the disclosures required in the preceding paragraphs, a party shall provide to other parties the following information regarding the evidence that it may present at trial other than solely for impeachment purposes:

(A) the name and, if not previously provided, the address and telephone number of each witness, separately identifying those whom the party expects to present and those whom the party may call if the need arises;

(B) the designation of those witnesses whose testimony is expected to be presented by means of a deposition and, if not taken by stenographic means, a transcript of the pertinent portions of the deposition testimony; and

(C) an appropriate identification of each document or other exhibit, including summaries of other evidence, separately identifying those which the party expects to offer and those which the party may offer if the need arises.

Unless otherwise directed by the court, these disclosures shall be made at least 30 days before trial. Within 14 days thereafter, unless a different time is specified by the court, a party may serve and file a list disclosing (i) any objections to the use under Rule 32(a) of a deposition designated by another party under subparagraph (B) and (ii) any objection, together with the grounds therefor, that may be made to the admissibility of materials identified under subparagraph (C). Objections not so disclosed, other than objections under Rules 402 and 403 of the Federal Rules of Evidence, shall be deemed waived unless excused by the court for good cause shown.

(4) *Form of Disclosures; Filing.* Unless otherwise directed by order or local rule, all disclosures under paragraphs (1) through (3) shall be made in writing, signed, served, and promptly filed with the court.

(5) *Methods to Discover Additional Matter.* Parties may obtain discovery by one or more of the following methods: depositions upon oral examination or written questions; written interrogatories; production of documents or things or permission to enter upon land or other property under Rule 34 or 45(a)(1)(C), for inspection and other purposes; physical and mental examinations; and requests for admission.

(b) Discovery Scope and Limits. Unless otherwise limited by order of the court in accordance with these rules, the scope of discovery is as follows:

(1) *In General.* Parties may obtain discovery regarding any matter, not privileged, which is relevant to the subject matter involved in the pending action, whether it relates to the claim or defense of the party seeking discovery or to the claim or defense of any other party, including the existence, description, nature, custody, condition and location of any books, documents, or other tangible things and the identity and location of persons having knowledge of any discoverable matter. The information sought need not be admissible at the trial if the information sought appears reasonably calculated to lead to the discovery of admissible evidence.

(2) *Limitations.* By order or by local rule, the court may alter the limits in these rules on the number of depositions and interrogatories and may also limit the length of depositions under Rule 30 and the number of requests under Rule 36. The frequency or extent of use of the discovery methods otherwise permitted under these rules and any local rule shall be limited by the court if it determines that: (i) the discovery sought is unreasonably cumulative or duplicative, or is obtainable from some other source that is more convenient, less burdensome, or less expensive; (ii) the party seeking discovery has had ample opportunity by discovery in the action to obtain the information sought; or (iii) the burden or expense of the proposed discovery outweighs its likely benefit, taking into account the needs of the case, the amount in controversy, the parties' resources, the importance of the issues at stake in the litigation, and the importance of the proposed discovery in resolving the issues. The court may act upon its own initiative after reasonable notice or pursuant to a motion under subdivision (c).

(3) *Trial Preparation: Materials.* Subject to the provisions of subdivision (b)(4) of this rule, a party may obtain discovery of documents and tangible things otherwise discoverable under subdivision (b)(1) of this rule and prepared in anticipation of litigation or for trial by or for another party or by or for that other party's representative (including the other party's attorney, consultant, surety, indemnitor, insurer, or agent) only upon a showing that the party seeking discovery has substantial need of the materials in the preparation of the party's case and that the party is unable without undue hardship to obtain the substantial equivalent of the materials by other means. In ordering discovery of such materials when the required showing has been made, the court shall protect against disclosure of the mental impressions, conclusions, opinions, or legal theories of an attorney or other representative of a party concerning the litigation.

A party may obtain without the required showing a statement concerning the action or its subject matter previously made by that party. Upon request, a person not a party may obtain without the required showing a statement concerning the action or its subject matter previously made by that person. If the request is refused, the person may move for a court order. The provisions of Rule 37(a)(4) apply to the award of expenses incurred in relation to the motion. For purposes of this paragraph, a statement previously made is (A) a written statement signed or otherwise adopted or approved by the person making it, or (B) a stenographic, mechanical, electrical, or other recording, or a transcription thereof, which is a substantially verbatim recital of an oral statement by the person making it and contemporaneously recorded.

(4) *Trial Preparation: Experts.*

(A) A party may depose any person who has been identified as an expert whose opinions may be presented at trial. If a report from the expert is required under subdivision (a)(2)(B), the deposition shall not be conducted until after the report is provided.

(B) A party may, through interrogatories or by deposition, discover facts known or opinions held by an expert who has been retained or specially employed by another party in anticipation of litigation or preparation for trial and who is not expected to be called as a witness at trial only as provided in Rule 35(b) or upon a showing of exceptional circumstances under which it is impracticable for the party seeking discovery to obtain facts or opinions on the same subject by other means.

(C) Unless manifest injustice would result, (i) the court shall require that the party seeking discovery pay the expert a reasonable fee for time spent in responding to discovery under this subdivision; and (ii) with respect to discovery obtained under subdivision (b)(4)(B) of this rule the court shall require the party seeking discovery to pay the other party a fair portion of the fees and expenses reasonably incurred by the latter party in obtaining facts and opinions from the expert.

(5) *Claims of Privilege or Protection of Trial Preparation Materials.* When a party withholds information otherwise discoverable under these rules by claiming that it is privileged or subject to protection as trial preparation material, the party shall make the claim expressly and shall describe the nature of the documents, communications, or things not produced or disclosed in a manner that, without revealing information itself privileged or protected, will enable other parties to assess the applicability of the privilege or protection.

(c) Protective Orders. Upon motion by a party or by the person from whom discovery is sought, accompanied by a certificate that the movant in good faith has conferred or attempted to confer with other affected parties in an effort to resolve the dispute without court action, and for good cause shown, the court in which the action is pending or alternatively, on matters relating to a deposition, the court in the district where the deposition is to be taken may make any order which justice requires to protect a party or person from annoyance, embarrassment, oppression, or undue burden or expense, including one or more of the following: (1) that the disclosure or discovery not be had; (2) that the disclosure or discovery may be had only on specified terms and conditions, including a designation of the time or place; (3) that the discovery may be had only by a method of discovery other than that selected by the party seeking discovery; (4) that certain matters not be inquired into, or that the scope of the disclosure or discovery be limited to certain matters; (5) that the discovery be conducted with no one present except persons designated by the court; (6) that a deposition after being sealed be opened only by order of the court; (7) that a trade secret or other confidential research, development, or commercial information not be revealed or be revealed only in a designated way; (8) that the parties simultaneously file specified documents or information enclosed in sealed envelopes to be opened as directed by the court.

If the motion for a protective order is denied in whole or in part, the court may, on such terms and conditions as are just, order that any party or other person provide or permit discovery. The provisions of Rule 37(a)(4) apply to the award of expenses incurred in relation to the motion.

(d) Timing and Sequence of Discovery. Except when authorized under these rules or by local rule, order, or agreement of the parties, a party may not seek discovery from any source before the parties have met and conferred as required by subdivision (f). Unless the court upon motion, for the convenience of parties and witnesses and in the interests of justice, orders otherwise, methods of discovery may be used in any sequence, and the fact that a party is conducting discovery, whether by deposition or otherwise, shall not operate to delay another party's discovery.

(e) Supplementation of Disclosures and Responses. A party who has made a disclosure under subdivision (a) or responded to a request for discovery with a disclosure or response is under a duty to supplement or correct the disclosure or response to include information thereafter acquired if ordered by the court or in the following circumstances:

(1) A party is under a duty to supplement at appropriate intervals its disclosures under subdivision (a) if the party learns that in some material respect the information disclosed is incomplete or incorrect and if the additional or corrective information has not otherwise been made known to the other parties during the discovery process or in writing. With respect to testimony of an expert from whom a report is required under subdivision (a)(2)(B) the duty extends both to information contained in the report and to information provided through a deposition of the expert, and any additions or other changes to this information shall be disclosed by the time the party's disclosures under Rule 26(a)(3) are due.

(2) A party is under a duty seasonably to amend a prior response to an interrogatory, request for production, or request for admission if the

party learns that the response is in some material respect incomplete or incorrect and if the additional or corrective information has not otherwise been made known to the other parties during the discovery process or in writing.

(f) Meeting of Parties; Planning for Discovery. Except in actions exempted by local rule or when otherwise ordered, the parties shall, as soon as practicable and in any event at least 14 days before a scheduling conference is held or a scheduling order is due under Rule 16(b), meet to discuss the nature and basis of their claims and defenses and the possibilities for a prompt settlement or resolution of the case, to make or arrange for the disclosures required by subdivision (a)(1), and to develop a proposed discovery plan. The plan shall indicate the parties' views and proposals concerning:

(1) what changes should be made in the timing, form, or requirement for disclosures under subdivision (a) or local rule, including a statement as to when disclosures under subdivision (a)(1) were made or will be made;

(2) the subjects on which discovery may be needed, when discovery should be completed, and whether discovery should be conducted in phases or be limited to or focused upon particular issues;

(3) what changes should be made in the limitations on discovery imposed under these rules or by local rule, and what other limitations should be imposed; and

(4) any other orders that should be entered by the court under subdivision (c) or under Rule 16(b) and (c).

The attorneys of record and all unrepresented parties that have appeared in the case are jointly responsible for arranging and being present or represented at the meeting, for attempting in good faith to agree on the proposed discovery plan, and for submitting to the court within 10 days after the meeting a written report outlining the plan.

(g) Signing of Disclosures, Discovery Requests, Responses, and Objections.

(1) Every disclosure made pursuant to subdivision (a)(1) or subdivision (a)(3) shall be signed by at least one attorney of record in the attorney's individual name, whose address shall be stated. An unrepresented party shall sign the disclosure and state the party's address. The signature of the attorney or party constitutes a certification that to the best of the signer's knowledge, information, and belief formed after a reasonable inquiry, the disclosure is complete and correct as of the time it is made.

(2) Every discovery request, response, or objection made by a party represented by an attorney shall be signed by at least one attorney of record in the attorney's individual name, whose address shall be stated. An unrepresented party shall sign the request, response, or objection and

state the party's address. The signature of the attorney or party constitutes a certification that to the best of the signer's knowledge, information, and belief, formed after a reasonable inquiry, the request, response, or objection is: (A) consistent with these rules and warranted by existing law or a good faith argument for the extension, modification, or reversal of existing law; (B) not interposed for any improper purpose, such as to harass or to cause unnecessary delay or needless increase in the cost of litigation; and (C) not unreasonable or unduly burdensome or expensive, given the needs of the case, the discovery already had in the case, the amount in controversy, and the importance of the issues at stake in the litigation.

If a request, response, or objection, is not signed, it shall be stricken unless it is signed promptly after the omission is called to the attention of the party making the request, response, or objection, and a party shall not be obligated to take any action with respect to it until it is signed.

(3) If without substantial justification a certification is made in violation of the rule, the court, upon motion or upon its own initiative, shall impose upon the person who made the certification, the party on whose behalf the disclosure, request, response, or objection is made, or both, an appropriate sanction, which may include an order to pay the amount of the reasonable expenses incurred because of the violation, including a reasonable attorney's fee.

Notes on Amendments to Federal Rule 26 and Comparative State Provisions

(a) *Advisory Committee Comments on Substantive Alterations in Rule 26 Made in 1993*

Major revisions to Rule 26 were adopted in 1993 to facilitate the exchange of pertinent information between parties early in the case. The Advisory Committee on Rules, in the Notes to the amended Rule 26, state that the revisions were based, in part, on the experience of district courts which had previously adopted similar automatic disclosure provisions. It is important to note that some of the significant new changes, such as those in 26(a) and 26(f), state that they can be superseded by local court rules. Although trial courts have been able to control discovery on a case-by-case basis, they have not been formally permitted to sidestep a Federal Rule provision entirely. This new approach raises important questions regarding the value of procedural uniformity among the federal courts.

Subdivision (a) of Rule 26 was amended to include subparagraphs (1)–(4), which impose a duty to disclose basic information necessary for parties to prepare for trial. Subparagraph (1) states that parties must now automatically exchange information such as the names of witnesses, copies of pertinent documents, computations of damages and insurance data.

Subparagraph (2) imposes a duty to disclose information regarding expert testimony, usually within 90 days before the trial date. The revision clarifies the more vague requirement in old Rule 26 that the "substance" of expert testimony be revealed by requiring that experts retained to provide testimony submit detailed and complete written reports. This requirement, along with Rule 37(c)(1), which provides that ordinarily a party will be unable to use expert testimony not so disclosed, is intended to provide parties with basic information about the testimony of the expert. Revised Rule 26(b)(4)(A) now authorizes depositions of experts, but only after the expert's report has been served.

Subparagraph (3) requires that parties automatically exchange information regarding the use of witnesses, trial deposition testimony and exhibits at least 30 days before trial.

Subparagraph (5) is amended to reflect changes to Rule 45 regarding inspection by non-parties of documents and premises without deposition.

Subdivision (b) is substantially revised, in part for organizational clarity and in part to implement provisions which limit the discovery process. Of the substantive revisions, subparagraph (4)(A) is revised to show that experts may be deposed, but as noted in subdivision (a)(2)(B), only after the expert has submitted the required detailed report. Subparagraph (4)(C), regarding compensation of experts, is revised to reflect changes in (4)(A).

Subparagraph (5) has been added to place upon a party an affirmative duty to disclose to other parties if it is withholding materials based on a claim of privilege or work product protection. The party claiming privilege must provide enough information to support its claim to enable other parties to evaluate the applicability of the claim. Sanctions may be imposed under Rule 37(b)(2) for violating this provision.

Subdivision (c) is revised to require parties to confer and attempt to resolve discovery disputes in good faith prior to seeking a protective order from the court.

Subdivision (d) is revised to prohibit the commencement of formal discovery until the parties have met pursuant to revised rule 26(f). Exceptions to this Rule are allowed under Rule 30(a)(2)(C) (deposition of a person about to leave the country) and by local rule, order or stipulation.

Subdivision (e) provides that parties are subject to a continuing duty to supplement disclosures made pursuant to Rule 26(a)(1)–(3). In addition, the revised rule clarifies that the duty to supplement formal discovery requests applies to interrogatories, requests for production, and requests for admissions, but not ordinarily to deposition testimony. Only when opinions expressed by an expert in deposition change is there a duty to supplement deposition responses.

Subdivision (f) is revised to remove provisions relating to a conference with the court regarding discovery. As noted by the Advisory Committee on Rules, "[t]his change does not signal any lessening of the importance of judicial supervision," but rather results from the relocation of such provisions to amended Rule 16 which addresses the court's role in directing the discovery process.

Subdivision (g), newly added, requires all disclosures be signed. In keeping with the revisions to Rule 11, which state that Rule is no longer applicable to discovery matters, the signature requirement is now included directly in Rule 26.

(b) *Advisory Committee Comments on Substantive Alterations
in Rule 26 Made in 1970*

The Advisory Committee commented on changes in Rule 26 as follows:

Subdivision (b)(2)—Insurance Policies. [This provision was altered in 1993 and is now covered in Rule 26(a)(1)(D).] Both the cases and commentators are sharply in conflict on the question whether defendant's liability insurance coverage is subject to discovery in the usual situation when the insurance coverage is not itself admissible and does not bear on another issue in the case. * * *

The amendment resolves this issue in favor of disclosure. Most of the decisions denying discovery, some explicitly, reason from the text of Rule 26(b) that it permits discovery only of matters which will be admissible in evidence or appear reasonably calculated to lead to such evidence; they avoid considerations of policy, regarding them as foreclosed. * * *. Some note also that facts about a defendant's financial status are not discoverable as such, prior to judgment with execution unsatisfied, and fear that, if courts hold insurance coverage discoverable, they must extend the principle to other aspects of the defendant's financial status. The cases favoring disclosure rely heavily on the practical significance of insurance in the decisions lawyers make about settlement and trial preparation.

In *Clauss v. Danker,* 264 F.Supp. 246 (S.D.N.Y.1967), the court held that the rules forbid disclosure but called for an amendment to permit it.

Disclosure of insurance coverage will enable counsel for both sides to make the same realistic appraisal of the case, so that settlement and litigation strategy are based on knowledge and not speculation. It will conduce to settlement and avoid protracted litigation in some cases, though in others it may have an opposite effect. The amendment is limited to insurance coverage, which should be distinguished from any other facts concerning defendant's financial status (1) because insurance is an asset created specifically to satisfy the claim; (2) because the insurance company ordinarily controls the litigation; (3) because information about coverage is available only from defendant or his insurer; and (4) because disclosure does not involve a significant invasion of privacy. * * *

In no instance does disclosure make the facts concerning insurance coverage admissible in evidence.

Subdivision (b)(3)—Trial Preparation: Materials. Some of the most controversial and vexing problems to emerge from the discovery rules have arisen out of requests for the production of documents or things prepared in anticipation of litigation or for trial. The existing rules make no explicit provision for such materials. Yet, two verbally distinct doctrines have developed, each conferring a qualified immunity on these materials—the "good cause" requirement in Rule 34 (now generally held applicable to discovery of documents via deposition under Rule 45 and interrogatories under Rule 33) and the work-product doctrine of *Hickman v. Taylor,* 329 U.S. 495 (1947). Both demand a showing of justification before production can be had, the one of "good cause" and the other variously described in the *Hickman* case: "necessity or justification," "denial * * * would unduly prejudice the preparation of petitioner's case," or "cause hardship or injustice" 329 U.S. at 509–510. * * *

The major difficulties visible in the existing case law are (1) confusion and disagreement as to whether "good cause" is made out by a showing of relevance and lack of privilege, or requires an additional showing of necessity, (2) confusion and disagreement as to the scope of the *Hickman* work-product doctrine, particularly whether it extends beyond work actually performed by lawyers, and (3) the resulting difficulty of relating the "good cause" required by Rule 34 and the "necessity or justification" of the work-product doctrine, so that their respective roles and the distinctions between them are understood. * * *

The rules are amended by eliminating the general requirement of "good cause" from Rule 34 but retaining a requirement of a special showing for trial preparation materials in this subdivision. The required showing is expressed, not in terms of "good cause" whose generality has tended to encourage confusion and controversy, but in terms of the elements of the special showing to be made: substantial need of the materials in the preparation of the case and inability without undue hardship to obtain the substantial equivalent of the materials by other means.

These changes conform to the holdings of the cases, when viewed in light of their facts. Apart from trial preparation, the fact that the materials sought are documentary does not in and of itself require a special showing beyond relevance and absence of privilege. * * *

Elimination of a "good cause" requirement from Rule 34 and the establishment of a requirement of a special showing in this subdivision will eliminate the confusion caused by having two verbally distinct requirements of justification that the courts have been unable to distinguish clearly. Moreover, the language of the subdivision suggests the factors which the courts should consider in determining whether the requisite showing has been made. The importance of the materials sought to the party seeking them in preparation of his case and the difficulty he will have obtaining them by other means are factors noted in the *Hickman* case. The courts should also consider the likelihood that the party, even if he obtains the information by independent means, will not have the substantial equivalent of the documents the production of which he seeks.

* * *

Materials assembled in the ordinary course of business, or pursuant to public requirements unrelated to litigation, or for other nonlitigation purposes are not under the qualified immunity provided by this subdivision. *Goosman v. A. Duie Pyle, Inc.*, 320 F.2d 45 (4th Cir.1963); *cf. United States v. New York Foreign Trade Zone Operators, Inc.*, 304 F.2d 792 (2d Cir.1962). No change is made in the existing doctrine, noted in the *Hickman* case, that one party may discover relevant facts known or available to the other party, even though such facts are contained in a document which is not itself discoverable.

Treatment of Lawyers; Special Protection of Mental Impressions, Conclusions, Opinions, and Legal Theories Concerning the Litigation.—The courts are divided as to whether the work-product doctrine extends to the preparatory work only of lawyers. The *Hickman* case left this issue open since the statements in that case were taken by a lawyer. * * *

Subdivision (b)(3) reflects the trend of the cases by requiring a special showing, not merely as to materials prepared by an attorney, but also as to materials prepared in anticipation of litigation or preparation for trial by or for a party or any representative acting on his behalf. The subdivision then goes on to protect against disclosure [of] the mental impressions, conclusions, opinions, or legal theories concerning the litigation of an attorney or other representative of a party. The *Hickman* opinion drew special attention to the need for protecting an attorney against discovery of memoranda prepared from recollection of oral interviews. The courts have steadfastly safeguarded against disclosure of lawyers' mental impressions and legal theories, as well as mental impressions and subjective evaluations of investigators and claim-agents. In enforcing this provision of the subdivision, the courts will sometimes find it necessary to order disclosure of a document but with portions deleted. * * *

Party's Right to Own Statement.—An exception to the requirement of this subdivision enables a party to secure production of his own statement without any special showing. The cases are divided. * * *

Courts which treat a party's statement as though it were that of any witness overlook the fact that the party's statement is, without more, admissible in evidence. Ordinarily, a party gives a statement without insisting on a copy because he does not yet have a lawyer and does not understand the legal consequences of his actions. Thus, the statement is given at a time when he functions at a disadvantage. Discrepancies between his trial testimony and earlier statement may result from lapse of memory or ordinary inaccuracy; a written statement produced for the first time at trial may give such discrepancies a prominence which they do not deserve. In appropriate cases the court may order a party to be deposed before his statement is produced. * * *

Witness' Right to Own Statement.—A second exception to the requirement of this subdivision permits a non-party witness to obtain a copy of his own statement without any special showing. Many, though not all, of the considerations supporting a party's right to obtain his statement apply also to the non-party witness. Insurance companies are increasingly recognizing that a witness is entitled to a copy of his statement and are modifying their regular practice accordingly.

Subdivision (b)(4)—Trial Preparation: Experts. * * *

Subsection (b)(4)(A) deals with discovery of information obtained by or through experts who will be called as witnesses at trial. The provision is responsive to problems suggested by a relatively recent line of authorities. Many of these cases present intricate and difficult issues as to which expert testimony is likely to be determinative. Prominent among them are food and drug, patent, and condemnation cases. * * *

In cases of this character, a prohibition against discovery of information held by expert witnesses produces in acute form the very evils that discovery has been created to prevent. Effective cross-examination of an expert witness requires advance preparation. The lawyer even with the help of his own experts frequently cannot anticipate the particular approach his adversary's expert will take or the data on which he will base his judgment on the stand. McGlothlin, *Some Practical Problems in Proof of Economic, Scientific, and Technical Facts*, 23 F.R.D. 467, 478 (1958). A California study of discovery and pretrial in condemnation cases notes that the only substitute for discovery of experts' valuation materials is "lengthy—and often fruitless—cross-examination during trial," and recommends pretrial exchange of such material. Calif.Law Rev.Comm'n, *Discovery in Eminent Domain Proceedings*, 707–710 (Jan.1963). Similarly, effective rebuttal requires advance knowledge of the line of testimony of the other side. If the latter is foreclosed by a rule against discovery, then the narrowing of issues and elimination of surprise which discovery normally produces are frustrated. * * *

Past judicial restrictions on discovery of an adversary's expert, particularly as to his opinions, reflect the fear that one side will benefit unduly from the other's better preparation. The procedure established in subsection (b)(4)(A) holds the risk to a minimum. Discovery is limited to trial witnesses, and may be obtained only at a time when the parties know who their expert witnesses will be. A party must as a practical matter prepare his own case in advance of that time, for he can hardly hope to build his case out of his opponent's experts. * * *

Subdivision (b)(4)(B) deals with an expert who has been retained or specially employed by the party in anticipation of litigation or preparation for trial (thus excluding an expert who is simply a general employee of the party not specially employed on the case), but who is not expected to be called as a witness. Under its provisions, a party may discover facts known or opinions held by such an expert only on a showing of exceptional circumstances under which it is impracticable for the party seeking discovery to obtain facts or opinions on the same subject by other means. * * *

Subdivision (d)—Sequence and Priority. This new provision is concerned with the sequence in which parties may proceed with discovery and with related problems of timing. The principal effects of the new provision are first, to eliminate any fixed priority in the sequence of discovery, and second, to make clear and explicit the court's power to establish priority by an order issued in a particular case.

A priority rule developed by some courts, which confers priority on the party who first serves notice of taking a deposition, is unsatisfactory in several important respects:

First, this priority rule permits a party to establish a priority running to all depositions as to which he has given earlier notice. Since he can on a given day serve notice of taking many depositions he is in a position to delay his adversary's taking of depositions for an inordinate time. * * *

Second, since notice is the key to priority, if both parties wish to take depositions first a race results. See *Caldwell–Clements, Inc. v. McGraw–Hill Pub. Co.*, 11 F.R.D. 156 (S.D.N.Y.1951) (description of tactics used by parties). But the existing rules on notice of deposition create a race with runners starting from different positions. The plaintiff may not give notice without leave of court until 20 days after commencement of the action, whereas the defendant may serve notice at any time after commencement. Thus, a careful and prompt defendant can almost always secure priority. This advantage of defendants is fortuitous, because the purpose of requiring plaintiff to wait 20 days is to afford defendant an opportunity to obtain counsel, not to confer priority.

Third, although courts have ordered a change in the normal sequence of discovery on a number of occasions, *e.g., Kaeppler v. James H. Matthews & Co.*, 200 F.Supp. 229 (E.D.Pa.1961); *Park & Tilford Distillers Corp. v. Distillers Co.*, 19 F.R.D. 169 (S.D.N.Y.1956), and have at all times avowed discretion to vary the usual priority, most commentators are agreed that courts in fact grant relief only for "the most obviously compelling reasons." * * *

It is contended by some that there is no need to alter the existing priority practice. In support, it is urged that there is no evidence that injustices in fact result from present practice and that, in any event, the courts can and do promulgate local rules, as in New York, to deal with local situations and issue orders to avoid possible injustice in particular cases.

Subdivision (d) is based on the contrary view that the rule of priority based on notice is unsatisfactory and unfair in its operation. Subdivision (d) follows an approach adapted from Civil Rule 4 of the District Court for the Southern District of New York. That rule provides that starting 40 days after commencement of the action, unless otherwise ordered by the court, the fact that one party is taking a deposition shall not prevent another party from doing so "concurrently." In practice, the depositions are not usually taken simultaneously; rather, the parties work out arrangements for alternation in the taking of depositions. One party may take a complete deposition and then the other, or, if the depositions are extensive, one party deposes for a set time, and then the other. See, *Caldwell–Clements, Inc. v. McGraw–Hill Pub. Co.*, 11 F.R.D. 156 (S.D.N.Y.1951).

In principle, one party's initiation of discovery should not wait upon the other's completion, unless delay is dictated by special considerations. Clearly the principle is feasible with respect to all methods of discovery other than depositions. And the experience of the Southern District of New York shows that the principle can be applied to depositions as well. The courts have not had an increase in motion business on this matter. * * *

Subdivision (e)—Supplementation of Responses. The rules do not now state whether interrogatories (and questions at deposition as well as requests for inspection and admissions) impose a "continuing burden" on the responding party to supplement his answers if he obtains new information. The issue is acute when new information renders substantially incomplete or inaccurate an answer which was complete and accurate when made. It is essential that the rules provide an answer to this question. The parties can adjust to a rule either way, once they know what it is. See 4 *Moore's Federal Practice* ¶ 33.25[4] (2d ed. 1966).

Arguments can be made both ways. Imposition of a continuing burden reduces the proliferation of additional sets of interrogatories. Some courts have adopted local rules establishing such a burden. * * * On the other hand, there are serious objections to the burden, especially in protracted cases. Although the party signs the answers, it is his lawyer who understands their significance and bears the responsibility to bring answers up to date. In a complex case all sorts of information reaches the party, who little understands its bearing on answers previously given to interrogatories. In practice, therefore, the lawyer under a continuing burden must periodically recheck all interrogatories and canvass all new information. * * *

The duty will normally be enforced, in those limited instances where it is imposed, through sanctions imposed by the trial court, including exclusion of evidence, continuance, or other action, as the court may deem appropriate.

(c) *Note on the Addition of Rule 26(g) in 1983*

Rule 26(g) was added to require every discovery request, or response or objection thereto, to be signed by an attorney of record or by the party if he or she is not represented by an attorney. In harmony with changes in Rules 7 and 11, Rule 26(g) provides for an "appropriate sanction" to be imposed on an attorney, or party, or both, if a certificate is made in violation of the rule.

(d) *Comparative State Provisions*

1. *Rule 26(a)—Required Disclosure*

Arizona Rule of Civil Procedure 26.1(a)

(a) Duty to Disclose, Scope. Within the times set forth in subdivision (b), each party shall disclose in writing to every other party:

(1) The factual basis of the claim or defense. In the event of multiple claims or defenses, the factual basis for each claim or defense.

(2) The legal theory upon which each claim or defense is based including, where necessary for a reasonable understanding of the claim or defense, citations of pertinent legal or case authorities.

(3) The names, addresses, and telephone numbers of any witnesses whom the disclosing party expects to call at trial with a fair description of the substance of each witness' expected testimony.

(4) The names and addresses of all persons whom the party believes may have knowledge or information relevant to the events, transactions, or occurrences that gave rise to the action, and the nature of the knowledge or information each such individual is believed to possess.

(5) The names and addresses of all persons who have given statements, whether written or recorded, signed or unsigned, and the custodian of the copies of those statements.

(6) The name and address of each person whom the disclosing party expects to call as an expert witness at trial, the subject matter on which the expert is expected to testify, the substance of the facts and opinions to which the expert is expected to testify, a summary of the grounds for each opinion, the qualifications of the witness and the name and address of the custodian of copies of any reports prepared by the expert.

(7) A computation and the measure of damage alleged by the disclosing party and the documents or testimony on which such computation and measure are based and the names, addresses, and telephone numbers of all damage witnesses.

(8) The existence, location, custodian, and general description of any tangible evidence or relevant documents that the disclosing party plans to use at trial and relevant insurance agreements.

(9) A list of the documents or, in the case of voluminous documentary information, a list of the categories of documents, known by a party to exist whether or not in the party's possession, custody or control and which that party believes may be relevant to the subject matter of the action, and those which appear reasonably calculated to lead to the discovery of admissible evidence, and the date(s) upon which those documents will be made, or have been made, available for inspection and copying. Unless good cause is stated for not doing so, a copy of each document listed shall be served with the disclosure. If production is not made, the name and address of the custodian of the document shall be indicated. A party who produces documents for inspection shall produce them as they are kept in the usual course of business.

2. *Rule 26(b)—Scope of Discovery*

Minnesota Rule of Civil Procedure 26.02(c)

[The Minnesota rule is identical to Federal Rule 26(b)(3) except that the second sentence of the second paragraph reads, "Upon request, a *party or other person* may obtain without the required showing a statement concerning the action or its subject matter previously made by that person *who is not a party*." (Emphasis added.)]

New York Civil Practice Law and Rules 3101

(a) Generally. There shall be full disclosure of all matter material and necessary in the prosecution or defense of an action, regardless of the burden of proof, by:

(1) a party, or the officer, director, member, agent or employee of a party;

(2) a person who possessed a cause of action or defense asserted in the action;

(3) a person about to depart from the state, or without the state, or residing at a greater distance from the place of trial than one hundred miles, or so sick or infirm as to afford reasonable grounds of belief that he will not

be able to attend the trial, or a person authorized to practice medicine, dentistry or podiatry who has provided medical, dental or podiatric care or diagnosis to the party demanding disclosure, or who has been retained by him as an expert witness; and

(4) any other person, upon notice stating the circumstances or reasons such disclosure is sought or required.

(b) Privileged matter. Upon objection by a person entitled to assert the privilege, privileged matter shall not be obtainable.

(c) Attorney's work product. The work product of an attorney shall not be obtainable.

(d) Trial preparation. 1. Experts. (i) Upon request, each party shall identify each person whom the party expects to call as an expert witness at trial and shall disclose in reasonable detail the subject matter on which each expert is expected to testify, the substance of the facts and opinions on which each expert is expected to testify, the qualifications of each expert witness and a summary of the grounds for each expert's opinion. However, where a party for good cause shown retains an expert an insufficient period of time before the commencement of trial to give appropriate notice thereof, the party shall not thereupon be precluded from introducing the expert's testimony at the trial solely on grounds of noncompliance with this paragraph. In that instance, upon motion of any party, made before or at trial, or on its own initiative, the court may make whatever order may be just. In an action for medical, dental or podiatric malpractice, a party, in responding to a request, may omit the names of medical, dental or podiatric experts but shall be required to disclose all other information concerning such experts otherwise required by this paragraph.

(ii) In an action for medical, dental or podiatric malpractice, any party may, by written offer made to and served upon all other parties and filed with the court, offer to disclose the name of, and to make available for examination upon oral deposition, any person the party making the offer expects to call as an expert witness at trial. Within twenty days of service of the offer, a party shall accept or reject the offer by serving a written reply upon all parties and filing a copy thereof with the court. Failure to serve a reply within twenty days of service of the offer shall be deemed a rejection of the offer. If all parties accept the offer, each party shall be required to produce his or her expert witness for examination upon oral deposition upon receipt of a notice to take oral deposition in accordance with rule thirty-one hundred seven of this chapter. If any party, having made or accepted the offer, fails to make that party's expert available for oral deposition, that party shall be precluded from offering expert testimony at the trial of the action.

(iii) Further disclosure concerning the expected testimony of any expert may be obtained only by court order upon a showing of special circumstances and subject to restrictions as to scope and provisions concerning fees and expenses as the court may deem appropriate. However, a party, without court order, may take the testimony of a person authorized to practice medicine or dentistry or podiatry who is the party's treating or retained expert, as described in paragraph three of subdivision (a) of this section, in which event any other party shall be entitled to the full disclosure authorized by this article with respect to that expert without court order.

* * *

2. Materials. ... [Identical in substance to the first paragraph of Federal Rule 26(b)(3).]

(e) Party's statement. A party may obtain a copy of his own statement.

(f) Contents of insurance agreement. * * *

(g) Accident reports. Except as otherwise provided by law, in addition to any other matter which may be subject to disclosure, there shall be full disclosure of any written report of an accident prepared in the regular course of business operations or practices of any person, firm, corporation, association or other public or private entity * * *.

(h) * * *

(i) In addition to any other matter which may be subject to disclosure, there shall be full disclosure of any films, photographs, video tapes or audio tapes, including transcripts or memoranda thereof, involving a person referred to in paragraph one of subdivision (a) of this section. There shall be disclosure of all portions of such material, including out-takes, rather than only those portions a party intends to use. * * *

2. *Rule 26(d)—Sequence and Timing of Discovery*

New York Civil Practice Law and Rules 3106

(a) Normal priority. After an action is commenced, any party may take the testimony of any person by deposition upon oral or written questions. Leave of the court, granted on motion, shall be obtained if notice of the taking of the deposition of a party is served by the plaintiff before that party's time for serving a responsive pleading has expired.

(b) Witnesses. Where the person to be examined is not a party or a person who at the time of taking the deposition is an officer, director, member or employee of a party, he shall be served with a subpoena. Unless the court orders otherwise, on motion with or without notice, such subpoena shall be served at least twenty days before the examination. Where a motion for a protective order against such an examination is made, the witness shall be notified by the moving party that the examination is stayed.

(c) Prisoners. The deposition of a person confined under legal process may be taken only by leave of the court.

(d) Designation of deponent. A party desiring to take the deposition of a particular officer, director, member or employee of a person shall include in the notice or subpoena served upon such person the identity, description or title of such individual. Such person shall produce the individual so designated unless they shall have, no later than ten days prior to the scheduled deposition, notified the requesting party that another individual would instead be produced and the identity, description or title of such individual is specified. If timely notification has been so given, such other individual shall instead be produced.

3. *Rule 26(e)—Supplementation of Responses*

New Jersey Civil Practice Rule 4:17–7

* * * [I]f a party who has furnished answers to interrogatories thereafter obtains information that renders such answers incomplete or inaccurate, amended answers shall be served not later than 20 days prior to the first date fixed for trial. Thereafter amendments may be allowed only for extraordinary or compelling reasons and to prevent manifest injustice, and upon such terms as the court directs. In no case shall amendments be allowed at trial where it appears that the evidence sought to be introduced was known to the party seeking such leave, more than 10 days prior to trial.

Rule 27. Depositions Before Action or Pending Appeal

(a) Before Action.

(1) *Petition.* A person who desires to perpetuate testimony regarding any matter that may be cognizable in any court of the United States may file a verified petition in the United States district court in the district of the residence of any expected adverse party. The petition shall be entitled in the name of the petitioner and shall show: 1, that the petitioner expects to be a party to an action cognizable in a court of the United States but is presently unable to bring it or cause it to be brought, 2, the subject matter of the expected action and the petitioner's

interest therein, 3, the facts which the petitioner desires to establish by the proposed testimony and the reasons for desiring to perpetuate it, 4, the names or a description of the persons the petitioner expects will be adverse parties and their addresses so far as known, and 5, the names and addresses of the persons to be examined and the substance of the testimony which the petitioner expects to elicit from each, and shall ask for an order authorizing the petitioner to take the depositions of the persons to be examined named in the petition, for the purpose of perpetuating their testimony.

(2) *Notice and Service.* The petitioner shall thereafter serve a notice upon each person named in the petition as an expected adverse party, together with a copy of the petition, stating that the petitioner will apply to the court, at a time and place named therein, for the order described in the petition. At least 20 days before the date of hearing the notice shall be served either within or without the district or state in the manner provided in Rule 4(d) for service of summons; but if such service cannot with due diligence be made upon any expected adverse party named in the petition, the court may make such order as is just for service by publication or otherwise, and shall appoint, for persons not served in the manner provided in Rule 4(d), an attorney who shall represent them, and, in case they are not otherwise represented, shall cross-examine the deponent. If any expected adverse party is a minor or incompetent the provisions of Rule 17(c) apply.

(3) *Order and Examination.* If the court is satisfied that the perpetuation of the testimony may prevent a failure or delay of justice, it shall make an order designating or describing the persons whose depositions may be taken and specifying the subject matter of the examination and whether the depositions shall be taken upon oral examination or written interrogatories. The depositions may then be taken in accordance with these rules; and the court may make orders of the character provided for by Rules 34 and 35. For the purpose of applying these rules to depositions for perpetuating testimony, each reference therein to the court in which the action is pending shall be deemed to refer to the court in which the petition for such deposition was filed.

(4) *Use of Deposition.* If a deposition to perpetuate testimony is taken under these rules or if, although not so taken, it would be admissible in evidence in the courts of the state in which it is taken, it may be used in any action involving the same subject matter subsequently brought in a United States district court, in accordance with the provisions of Rule 32(a).

(b) Pending Appeal. If an appeal has been taken from a judgment of a district court or before the taking of an appeal if the time therefor has not expired, the district court in which the judgment was rendered may allow the taking of the depositions of witnesses to perpetuate their testimony for use in the event of further proceedings in the district court. In such case the party who desires to perpetuate the testimony may make a motion in the district court for leave to take the depositions, upon the same notice and service thereof as if the action was pending in the district court. The motion shall show (1) the names and addresses of persons to be examined and the substance of the testimony which the party expects to elicit from each; (2) the reasons for perpetuating their testimony. If the court finds that the perpetuation of the testimony is proper to avoid a failure or delay of justice, it may make an order allowing the depositions to be taken and may make orders of the character provided for by Rules 34 and 35, and thereupon the depositions may be taken and used in the same manner and under the same conditions as are prescribed in these rules for depositions taken in actions pending in the district court.

(c) Perpetuation by Action. This rule does not limit the power of a court to entertain an action to perpetuate testimony.

Comparative State Provision

Rule 27(a)(1)

New York Civil Practice Law and Rules 3102(c)

Before an action is commenced, disclosure to aid in bringing an action, to preserve information or to aid in arbitration, may be obtained, but only by court order. The court may appoint a referee to take testimony.

Rule 28. Persons Before Whom Depositions May Be Taken

(a) Within the United States. Within the United States or within a territory or insular possession subject to the jurisdiction of the United States, depositions shall be taken before an officer authorized to administer oaths by the laws of the United States or of the place where the examination is held, or before a person appointed by the court in which the action is pending. A person so appointed has power to administer oaths and take testimony. The term officer as used in Rules 30, 31 and 32 includes a person appointed by the court or designated by the parties under Rule 29.

(b) In Foreign Countries. Depositions may be taken in a foreign country (1) pursuant to any applicable treaty or convention, or (2) pursuant to a letter of request (whether or not captioned a letter rogatory), or (3) on notice before a person authorized to administer oaths in the place where the examination is held, either by the law thereof or by the law of the United States, or (4) before a person commissioned by the court, and a person so commissioned shall have the power by virtue of the commission to administer any necessary oath and take testimony. A commission or letter of request shall be issued on application and notice and on terms that are just and appropriate. It is not requisite to the issuance of a commission or a letter of request that the taking of the deposition in any other manner is impracticable or inconvenient; and both a commission and a letter of request may be issued in proper cases.

A notice or commission may designate the person before whom the deposition is to be taken either by name or descriptive title. A letter of request may be addressed "To the Appropriate Authority in [here name the country]." When a letter of request or any other device is used pursuant to any applicable treaty or convention, it shall be captioned in the form prescribed by that treaty or convention. Evidence obtained in response to a letter of request need not be excluded merely because it is not a verbatim transcript, because the testimony was not taken under oath, or because of any similar departure from the requirements for depositions taken within the United States under these rules.

(c) Disqualification for Interest. No deposition shall be taken before a person who is a relative or employee or attorney or counsel of any of the parties, or is a relative or employee of such attorney or counsel, or is financially interested in the action.

Notes on Amendments to Federal Rule 28 and Related Federal and State Acts Providing Judicial Assistance to Foreign Tribunals

(a) *Amendments in 1993 and 1963 to Federal Rule 28(b)*

The 1993 changes were primarily linguistic, substituting the term "letter of request" for "letter rogatory" to conform to the Hague Convention.

It was in 1963 that Rule 28(b) was altered to facilitate the taking of depositions abroad. The Advisory Committee discussed the 1963 changes as follows:

The amendment of clause (1) is designed to facilitate depositions in foreign countries by enlarging the class of persons before whom the depositions may be taken on notice. The class is no longer confined, as at present, to a secretary of embassy or legation, consul general, consul, vice consul, or consular agent of the United States. In a country that regards the taking of testimony by a foreign official in aid of litigation pending in a court of another country as an infringement upon its sovereignty, it will be expedient to notice depositions before officers of the country in which the examination is taken. * * *

Clause (2) of amended subdivision (b), like the corresponding provision of subdivision (a) dealing with depositions taken in the United States, makes it clear that the appointment of a person by commission in itself confers power upon him to administer any necessary oath.

It has been held that a letter rogatory will not be issued unless the use of a notice or commission is shown to be impossible or impracticable. * * * The intent of the fourth sentence of the amended subdivision is to overcome this judicial antipathy and to permit a sound choice between depositions under a letter rogatory and on notice or by commission in the light of all the circumstances. In a case in which the foreign country will compel a witness to attend or testify in aid of a letter rogatory but not in aid of a commission, a letter rogatory may be preferred on the ground that it is less expensive to execute, even if there is plainly no need for compulsive process. A letter rogatory may also be preferred when it cannot be demonstrated that a witness will be recalcitrant or when the witness states that he is willing to testify voluntarily, but the contingency exists that he will change his mind at the last moment. In the latter case, it may be advisable to issue both a commission and a letter rogatory, the latter to be executed if the former fails. The choice between a letter rogatory and a commission may be conditioned by other factors, including the nature and extent of the assistance that the foreign country will give to the execution of either.

In executing a letter rogatory the courts of other countries may be expected to follow their customary procedure for taking testimony. See *United States* v.

Paraffin Wax, 2255 Bags, 23 F.R.D. 289 (E.D.N.Y.1959). In many non-common-law countries the judge questions the witness, sometimes without first administering an oath, the attorneys put any supplemental questions either to the witness or through the judge, and the judge dictates a summary of the testimony, which the witness acknowledges as correct. * * * The last sentence of the amended subdivision provides, contrary to the implications of some authority, that evidence recorded in such a fashion need not be excluded on that account. * * * Whether or to what degree the value or weight of the evidence may be affected by the method of taking or recording the testimony is left for determination according to the circumstances of the particular case * * *; the testimony may indeed be so devoid of substance or probative value as to warrant its exclusion altogether.

Some foreign countries are hostile to allowing a deposition to be taken in their country, especially by notice or commission, or to lending assistance in the taking of a deposition. Thus compliance with the terms of amended subdivision (b) may not in all cases ensure completion of a deposition abroad. Examination of the law and policy of the particular foreign country in advance of attempting a deposition is therefore advisable. See 4 *Moore's Federal Practice* ¶¶ 28.05–28.08 (2d ed. 1950).

(b) *Judicial Assistance to Foreign Tribunals*

See 28 U.S.C. § 1782(a) and the comparative state provision set forth in Part II, infra.

Rule 29. Stipulations Regarding Discovery Procedure

Unless otherwise directed by the court, the parties may by written stipulation (1) provide that depositions may be taken before any person, at any time or place, upon any notice, and in any manner and when so taken may be used like other depositions, and (2) modify other procedures governing or limitations placed upon discovery, except that stipulations extending the time provided in Rules 33, 34, and 36 for responses to discovery may, if they would interfere with any time set for completion of discovery, for hearing of a motion, or for trial, be made only with the approval of the court.

Rule 30. Depositions Upon Oral Examination

[See proposed changes to Rule 30(d), in Part IX, infra.]

(a) When Depositions May Be Taken; When Leave Required.

(1) A party may take the testimony of any person, including a party, by deposition upon oral examination without leave of court except as provided in paragraph (2). The attendance of witnesses may be compelled by subpoena as provided in Rule 45.

(2) A party must obtain leave of court, which shall be granted to the extent consistent with the principles stated in Rule 26(b)(2), if the person to be examined is confined in prison or if, without the written stipulation of the parties,

(A) a proposed deposition would result in more than ten depositions being taken under this rule or Rule 31 by the plaintiffs, or by the defendants, or by third-party defendants;

(B) the person to be examined already has been deposed in the case; or

(C) a party seeks to take a deposition before the time specified in Rule 26(d) unless the notice contains a certification, with supporting facts, that the person to be examined is expected to leave the United States and be unavailable for examination in this country unless deposed before that time.

(b) Notice of Examination: General Requirements; Method of Recording; Production of Documents and Things; Deposition of Organization; Deposition by Telephone.

(1) A party desiring to take the deposition of any person upon oral examination shall give reasonable notice in writing to every other party to the action. The notice shall state the time and place for taking the deposition and the name and address of each person to be examined, if known, and, if the name is not known, a general description sufficient to identify the person or the particular class or group to which the person belongs. If a subpoena duces tecum is to be served on the person to be examined, the designation of the materials to be produced as set forth in the subpoena shall be attached to or included in the notice.

(2) The party taking the deposition shall state in the notice the method by which the testimony shall be recorded. Unless the court orders otherwise, it may be recorded by sound, sound-and-visual, or stenographic means, and the party taking the deposition shall bear the cost of the recording. Any party may arrange for a transcription to be made from the recording of a deposition taken by nonstenographic means.

(3) With prior notice to the deponent and other parties, any party may designate another method to record the deponent's testimony in addition to that specified by the person taking the deposition. The additional record or transcript shall be made at that party's expense unless the court otherwise orders.

(4) Unless otherwise agreed by the parties, a deposition shall be conducted before an officer appointed or designated under Rule 28 and shall begin with a statement on the record by the officer that includes (A) the officer's name and business address; (B) the date, time, and place of the deposition; (C) the name of the deponent; (D) the administration of the oath or affirmation to the deponent; and (E) an identification of all persons present. If the deposition is recorded other than stenographically, the officer shall repeat items (A) through (C) at the beginning of each unit of recorded tape or other recording medium. The appearance or demeanor of deponents or attorneys shall not be distorted through camera or sound-recording techniques. At the end of the deposition, the officer shall state on the record that the deposition is complete and shall set forth any stipulations made by counsel concerning

the custody of the transcript or recording and the exhibits, or concerning other pertinent matters.

(5) The notice to a party deponent may be accompanied by a request made in compliance with Rule 34 for the production of documents and tangible things at the taking of the deposition. The procedure of Rule 34 shall apply to the request.

(6) A party may in the party's notice and in a subpoena name as the deponent a public or private corporation or a partnership or association or governmental agency and describe with reasonable particularity the matters on which examination is requested. In that event, the organization so named shall designate one or more officers, directors, or managing agents, or other persons who consent to testify on its behalf, and may set forth, for each person designated, the matters on which the person will testify. A subpoena shall advise a non-party organization of its duty to make such a designation. The persons so designated shall testify as to matters known or reasonably available to the organization. This subdivision (b)(6) does not preclude taking a deposition by any other procedure authorized in these rules.

(7) The parties may stipulate in writing or the court may upon motion order that a deposition be taken by telephone or other remote electronic means. For the purposes of the rule and Rules 28(a), 37(a)(1), and 37(b)(1), a deposition taken by such means is taken in the district and at the place where the deponent is to answer questions.

(c) Examination and Cross–Examination; Record of Examination; Oath; Objections. Examination and cross-examination of witnesses may proceed as permitted at the trial under the provisions of the Federal Rules of Evidence except Rules 103 and 615. The officer before whom the deposition is to be taken shall put the witness on oath or affirmation and shall personally, or by someone acting under the officer's direction and in the officer's presence, record the testimony of the witness. The testimony shall be taken stenographically or recorded by any other method authorized by subdivision (b)(2) of this rule. All objections made at the time of the examination to the qualifications of the officer taking the deposition, to the manner of taking it, to the evidence presented, to the conduct of any party, or to any other aspect of the proceedings shall be noted by the officer upon the record of the deposition; but the examination shall proceed, with the testimony being taken subject to the objections. In lieu of participating in the oral examination, parties may serve written questions in a sealed envelope on the party taking the deposition and the party taking the deposition shall transmit them to the officer, who shall propound them to the witness and record the answers verbatim.

(d) Schedule and Duration; Motion to Terminate or Limit Examination.

(1) Any objection to evidence during a deposition shall be stated concisely and in a non-argumentative and non-suggestive manner. A

party may instruct a deponent not to answer only when necessary to preserve a privilege, to enforce a limitation on evidence directed by the court, or to present a motion under paragraph (3).

(2) By order or local rule, the court may limit the time permitted for the conduct of a deposition, but shall allow additional time consistent with Rule 26(b)(2) if needed for a fair examination of the deponent or if the deponent or another party impedes or delays the examination. If the court finds such an impediment, delay, or other conduct that has frustrated the fair examination of the deponent, it may impose upon the person responsible an appropriate sanction, including the reasonable costs and attorney's fees incurred by any parties as a result thereof.

(3) At any time during a deposition, on motion of a party or of the deponent and upon a showing that the examination is being conducted in bad faith or in such a manner as unreasonable to annoy, embarrass, or oppress the deponent or party, the court in which the action is pending or the court in the district where the deposition is being taken may order the officer conducting the examination to cease forthwith from taking the deposition, or may limit the scope and manner of the taking of the deposition as provided in Rule 26(c). If the order made terminates the examination, it shall be presumed thereafter only upon the order of the court in which the action is pending. Upon demand of the objecting party or deponent, the taking of the deposition shall be suspended for the time necessary to make a motion for an order. The provisions of Rule 37(a)(4) apply to the award of expenses incurred in relation to the motion.

(e) Review by Witness; Changes; Signing. If requested by the deponent or a party before completion of the deposition, the deponent shall have 30 days after being notified by the officer that the transcript or recording is available in which to review the transcript or recording and, if there are changes in form or substance, to sign a statement reciting such changes and the reasons given by the deponent for making them. The officer shall indicate in the certificate prescribed by subdivision (f)(1) whether any review was requested and, if so, shall append any changes made by the deponent during the period allowed.

(f) Certification and Filing by Officer; Exhibits; Copies; Notice of Filing.

(1) The officer shall certify that the witness was duly sworn by the officer and that the deposition is a true record of the testimony given by the witness. This certificate shall be in writing and accompany the record of the deposition. Unless otherwise ordered by the court, the officer shall securely seal the deposition in an envelope or package indorsed with the title of the action and marked "Deposition of [here insert name of witness]" and shall promptly file it with the court in which the action is pending or send it to the attorney who arranged for the transcript or recording, who shall store it under conditions that will

protect it against loss, destruction, tampering, or deterioration. Documents and things produced for inspection during the examination of the witness, shall, upon the request of a party, be marked for identification and annexed to the deposition and may be inspected and copied by any party, except that if the person producing the materials desires to retain them the person may (A) offer copies to be marked for identification and annexed to the deposition and to serve thereafter as originals if the person affords to all parties fair opportunity to verify the copies by comparison to the originals, or (B) offer the originals to be marked for identification, after giving to each party an opportunity to inspect and copy them, in which event the materials may then be used in the same manner as if annexed to the deposition. Any party may move for an order that the original be annexed to and returned with the deposition to the court, pending final disposition of the case.

(2) Unless otherwise ordered by the court or agreed by the parties, the officer shall retain stenographic notes of any deposition taken stenographically or a copy of the recording of any deposition taken by another method. Upon payment of reasonable charges therefor, the officer shall furnish a copy of the transcript or other recording of the deposition to any party or to the deponent.

(3) The party taking the deposition shall give prompt notice of its filing to all other parties.

(g) Failure to Attend or to Serve Subpoena; Expenses.

(1) If the party giving the notice of the taking of a deposition fails to attend and proceed therewith and another party attends in person or by attorney pursuant to the notice, the court may order the party giving the notice to pay to such other party the reasonable expenses incurred by that party and that party's attorney in attending, including reasonable attorney's fees.

(2) If the party giving the notice of the taking of a deposition of a witness fails to serve a subpoena upon the witness and the witness because of such failure does not attend, and if another party attends in person or by attorney because that party expects the deposition of that witness to be taken, the court may order the party giving the notice to pay to such other party the reasonable expenses incurred by that party and that party's attorney in attending, including reasonable attorney's fees.

Notes on Amendments to Federal Rule 30

(a) *Amendments in 1993 to Rule 30*

Rule 30, in an effort to limit costs of discovery, has been modified to limit the number of depositions. Paragraph (a)2(A), containing this new limit, provides that absent leave of court or stipulation among the parties, a party is limited to ten (10) depositions. Paragraph (a)2(B) limits the number of times a witness may be deposed by requiring leave of court if a party wishes to depose a witness more than once.

Subdivision (b) has been revised to allow parties to record deposition testimony by nonstenographic means without first obtaining permission of other counsel. Parties choosing to record only by video- or audiotape should be cognizant that a transcript of such recordings will be required if the testimony is later offered as evidence at trial or on a dispositive motion under Rule 56, pursuant to Rules 26(a)(3)(B) and 32(c).

Subparagraph (b)(3) now allows parties, at their own expense, to record a deposition by any means, in addition to the method designated, and subparagraph (7) is revised to include technological improvements in the taking of depositions. In addition to the use of telephones, authorized by the 1980 Amendment to Rule 30, other remote electronic means such as satellite television are now allowed by stipulation or court order.

Subparagraph (c) is revised to clarify when other witnesses may attend a depositions. The revised Rule provides that other witnesses (potential deponents) are not automatically excluded by request, but that exclusion can be ordered pursuant to Rule 26(c)(5) when appropriate.

Subdivision (d)(2) has been added to clarify the court's authority to limit the length of depositions and to sanction attorneys, parties and non-party witnesses for the use of dilatory and obstructive tactics, and subparagraph (3) clarifies the court's authority to impose sanctions for conduct in violation of the provisions of Rule 30(d)(1).

Subdivision (e) has been modified to require pre-filing review by the deponent only if requested before the deposition is completed. Recognizing the difficulty reporters often have in obtaining signatures for pre-filing review, such signatures are now waived unless review is requested and changes are made.

(b) *Amendments in 1970 to Rule 30*

The 1970 amendments to Rule 30 included a number of important alterations in the deposition practice.

The Advisory Committee commented on these alterations as follows:

Subdivision (b)(5). A provision is added to enable a party, through service of notice, to require another party to produce documents or things at the taking of his deposition. This may now be done as to a nonparty deponent through use of a subpoena duces tecum as authorized by Rule 45, but some courts have held that documents may be secured from a party only under Rule 34. See 2A Barron & Holtzoff, *Federal Practice and Procedure* § 644.1 n. 83.2, § 792 n. 16 (Wright ed. 1961). With the elimination of "good cause" from Rule 34, the reason for this restrictive doctrine has disappeared. * * * If the discovering party insists on examining many and complex documents at the taking of the deposition, thereby causing undue burdens on others, the latter may, under Rules 26(c) or 30(d), apply for a court order that the examining party proceed via Rule 34 alone.

Subdivision (b)(6). A new provision is added, whereby a party may name a corporation, partnership, association, or governmental agency as the deponent and designate the matters on which he requests examination, and the organization shall then name one or more of its officers, directors, or managing agents, or other persons consenting to appear and testify on its behalf with respect to matters known or reasonably available to the organization. *Cf.* Alberta Sup.Ct.R. 255. The organization may designate persons other than officers, directors, and managing agents, but only with their consent. Thus, an employee or agent who has an independent or conflicting interest in the litigation—for example, in a personal injury case—can refuse to testify on behalf of the organization. * * *

The new procedure should be viewed as an added facility for discovery, one which may be advantageous to both sides as well as an improvement in the deposition process. It will reduce the difficulties now encountered in determining, prior to the taking of a deposition, whether a particular employee or agent is a "managing agent." See Note, *Discovery Against Corporations Under the Federal Rules,* 47 Iowa L.Rev. 1006–1016 (1962). It will curb the "bandying" by which officers or managing agents of a corporation are deposed in turn but each disclaims knowledge of facts that are clearly known to persons in the organization and thereby to it. *Cf. Haney v. Woodward & Lothrop, Inc.*, 330 F.2d 940, 944 (4th Cir.1964). The provision should also assist organizations which find that an unnecessarily large number of their officers and agents are being deposed by a party uncertain of who in the organization has knowledge. Some courts have held that under the existing rules a corporation should not be burdened with choosing which person is to appear for it. *E.g., United States v. Gahagan Dredging Corp.*, 24 F.R.D. 328, 329 (S.D.N.Y.1958). This burden is not essentially different from that of answering interrogatories under Rule 33, and is in any case lighter than that of an examining party ignorant of who in the corporation has knowledge. * * *

(c) *Amendments in 1980 to Rule 30*

The Advisory Committee commented as follows on the 1980 addition of Rule 30(b)(7):

> Depositions by telephone are now authorized by Rule 29 upon stipulation of the parties. The amendment authorizes that method by order of the court. The final sentence is added to make it clear that when a deposition is taken by telephone it is taken in the district and at the place where the witness is to answer the questions rather than that where the questions are propounded.

Rule 31. Depositions Upon Written Questions

(a) Serving Questions; Notice.

(1) A party may take the testimony of any person, including a party, by deposition upon written questions without leave of court except as provided in paragraph (2). The attendance of witnesses may be compelled by the use of subpoena provided in Rule 45.

(2) A party must obtain leave of court, which shall be granted to the extent consistent with the principles stated in Rule 26(b)(2), if the person to be examined is confined in prison or if, without the written stipulation of the parties:

(A) a proposed deposition would result in more than ten depositions being taken under this rule or Rule 30 by the plaintiffs, or by the defendants, or by third-party defendants;

(B) the person to be examined has already been deposed in the case; or

(C) a party seeks to take a deposition before the time specified in Rule 26(d).

(3) A party desiring to take a deposition upon written questions shall serve them upon every other party with a notice stating (1) the name and address of the person who is to answer them, if known, and if the name is not known, a general description sufficient to identify the person or the particular class or group to which the person belongs, and (2) the name or descriptive title and address of the officer before whom the deposition is to be taken. A deposition upon written questions may be taken of a public or private corporation or a partnership or association or governmental agency in accordance with the provisions of Rule 30(b)(6).

(4) Within 14 days after the notice and written questions are served, a party may serve cross questions upon all other parties. Within 7 days after being served with the cross questions, a party may serve redirect questions upon all other parties. Within 7 days after being served with redirect questions, a party may serve recross questions upon all other parties. The court may for cause shown enlarge or shorten the time.

(b) Officer to Take Responses and Prepare Record. A copy of the notice and copies of all questions served shall be delivered by the party taking the deposition to the officer designated in the notice, who shall proceed promptly, in the manner provided by Rule 30(c), (e), and (f), to take the testimony of the witness in response to the questions and to prepare, certify, and file or mail the deposition, attaching thereto the copy of the notice and the questions received by the officer.

(c) Notice of Filing. When the deposition is filed the party taking it shall promptly give notice thereof to all other parties.

Rule 32. Use of Depositions in Court Proceedings

(a) Use of Depositions. At the trial or upon the hearing of a motion or an interlocutory proceeding, any part or all of a deposition, so far as admissible under the rules of evidence applied as though the witness were then present and testifying, may be used against any party who was present or represented at the taking of the deposition or who had reasonable notice thereof, in accordance with any of the following provisions:

(1) Any deposition may be used by any party for the purpose of contradicting or impeaching the testimony of deponent as a witness, or for any other purpose permitted by the Federal Rules of Evidence.

(2) The deposition of a party or of anyone who at the time of taking the deposition was an officer, director, or managing agent, or a person designated under Rule 30(b)(6) or 31(a) to testify on behalf of a public or private corporation, partnership or association or governmental agency which is a party may be used by an adverse party for any purpose.

(3) The deposition of a witness, whether or not a party, may be used by any party for any purpose if the court finds:

(A) that the witness is dead; or

(B) that the witness is at a greater distance than 100 miles from the place of trial or hearing, or is out of the United States, unless it appears that the absence of the witness was procured by the party offering the deposition; or

(C) that the witness is unable to attend or testify because of age, illness, infirmity, or imprisonment; or

(D) that the party offering the deposition has been unable to procure the attendance of the witness by subpoena; or

(E) upon application and notice, that such exceptional circumstance exist as to make it desirable, in the interest of justice and with due regard to the importance of presenting the testimony of witnesses orally in open court, to allow the deposition to be used.

A deposition taken without leave of court pursuant to a notice under Rule 30(a)(2)(C) shall not be used against a party who demonstrates that, when served with the notice, it was unable through the exercise of diligence to obtain counsel to represent it at the taking of the deposition; nor shall a deposition be used against a party who, having received less than 11 days notice of the deposition, has promptly upon receiving such notice filed a motion for a protective order under Rule 26(c)(2) requesting that the deposition not be held or be held at a different time or place and such motion is pending at the time the deposition is held.

(4) If only part of a deposition is offered in evidence by a party, an adverse party may require the offeror to introduce any other part which ought in fairness to be considered with the part introduced, and any party may introduce any other parts.

Substitution of parties pursuant to Rule 25 does not affect the right to use depositions previously taken; and, when an action has been brought in any court of the United States or of any State and another action involving the same subject matter is afterward brought between the same parties or their representatives or successors in interest, all depositions lawfully taken and duly filed in the former action may be used in the latter as if originally taken therefor. A deposition previously taken may also be used as permitted by the Federal Rules of Evidence.

(b) Objections to Admissibility. Subject to the provisions of Rule 28(b) and subdivision (d)(3) of this rule, objection may be made at the trial or hearing to receiving in evidence any deposition or part thereof for any reason which would require the exclusion of the evidence if the witness were then present and testifying.

(c) Form of Presentation. Except as otherwise directed by the court, a party offering deposition testimony pursuant to this rule may offer it in stenographic or nonstenographic form, but, if in nonstenographic form, the party shall also provide the court with a transcript of the portions so offered. On request of any party in a case tried before a jury, deposition testimony offered other than for impeachment purposes shall be presented in nonstenographic form, if available, unless the court for good cause orders otherwise.

(d) Effect of Errors and Irregularities in Depositions.

(1) *As to Notice.* All errors and irregularities in the notice for taking a deposition are waived unless written objection is promptly served upon the party giving the notice.

(2) *As to Disqualification of Officer.* Objection to taking a deposition because of disqualification of the officer before whom it is to be

taken is waived unless made before the taking of the deposition begins or as soon thereafter as the disqualification becomes known or could be discovered with reasonable diligence.

(3) *As to Taking of Deposition.*

(A) Objections to the competency of a witness or to the competency, relevancy, or materiality of testimony are not waived by failure to make them before or during the taking of the deposition, unless the ground of the objection is one which might have been obviated or removed if presented at that time.

(B) Errors and irregularities occurring at the oral examination in the manner of taking the deposition, in the form of the questions or answers, in the oath or affirmation, or in the conduct of parties, and errors of any kind which might be obviated, removed, or cured if promptly presented, are waived unless seasonable objection thereto is made at the taking of the deposition.

(C) Objections to the form of written questions submitted under Rule 31 are waived unless served in writing upon the party propounding them within the time allowed for serving the succeeding cross or other questions and within 5 days after service of the last questions authorized.

(4) *As to Completion and Return of Deposition.* Errors and irregularities in the manner in which the testimony is transcribed or the deposition is prepared, signed, certified, sealed, indorsed, transmitted, filed, or otherwise dealt with by the officer under Rules 30 and 31 are waived unless a motion to suppress the deposition or some part thereof is made with reasonable promptness after such defect is, or with due diligence might have been, ascertained.

Comparative State Provisions

Rule 32(a)

Michigan Court Rule 2.302(B)(4)(d)

A party may depose a witness that he or she expects to call as an expert at trial. The deposition may be taken at any time before trial on reasonable notice to the opposite party, and may be offered as evidence at trial as provided in MCR 2.308(A). The court need not adjourn the trial because of the unavailability of expert witnesses or their depositions.

Michigan Court Rule 2.308(A)

Depositions or parts thereof shall be admissible at trial or on the hearing of a motion or in an interlocutory proceeding only as provided in the Michigan Rules of Evidence.

Rule 33. Interrogatories to Parties

(a) Availability. Without leave of court or written stipulation, any party may serve upon any other party written interrogatories, not exceeding 25 in number including all discrete subparts, to be answered by the party served or, if the party served is a public or private corporation or a partnership or association or governmental agency, by any officer or agent, who shall furnish such information as is available to the party. Leave to serve additional interrogatories shall be granted to the extent consistent with the principles of Rule 26(b)(2). Without leave of court or written stipulation, interrogatories may not be served before the time specified in Rule 26(d).

(b) Answers and Objections.

(1) Each interrogatory shall be answered separately and fully in writing under oath, unless it is objected to, in which event the objecting party shall state the reasons for objection and shall answer to the extent the interrogatory is not objectionable.

(2) The answers are to be signed by the person making them, and the objections signed by the attorney making them.

(3) The party upon whom the interrogatories have been served shall serve a copy of the answers, and objections if any, within 30 days after the service of the interrogatories. A shorter or longer time may be directed by the court or, in the absence of such an order, agreed to in writing by the parties subject to Rule 29.

(4) All grounds for an objection to an interrogatory shall be stated with specificity. Any ground not stated in a timely objection is waived unless the party's failure to object is excused by the court for good cause shown.

(5) The party submitting the interrogatories may move for an order under Rule 37(a) with respect to any objection to or other failure to answer an interrogatory.

(c) Scope; Use at Trial. Interrogatories may relate to any matters which can be inquired into under Rule 26(b)(1), and the answers may be used to the extent permitted by the rules of evidence.

An interrogatory otherwise proper is not necessarily objectionable merely because an answer to the interrogatory involves an opinion or contention that relates to fact or the application of law to fact, but the court may order that such an interrogatory need not be answered until after designated discovery has been completed or until a pre-trial conference or other later time.

(d) Option to Produce Business Records. Where the answer to an interrogatory may be derived or ascertained from the business records of the party upon whom the interrogatory has been served or from an examination, audit or inspection of such business records, including a compilation, abstract or summary thereof and the burden of deriving or ascertaining the answer is substantially the same for the party serving the interrogatory as for the party served, it is a sufficient answer to such interrogatory to specify the records from which the answer may be derived or ascertained and to afford to the party serving the interrogatory reasonable opportunity to examine, audit or inspect such records and to make copies, compilations, abstracts or summaries. A specification shall be in sufficient detail to permit the interrogating party to locate and to identify, as readily as can the party served, the records from which the answer may be ascertained.

Notes on Amendments to Federal Rule 33 and Comparative Provisions

(a) *Amendments in 1970 to Rule 33*

The Advisory Committee commented on the 1970 amendments to Federal Rule 33 as follows:

*Subdivision * * * [(c)].* There are numerous and conflicting decisions on the question whether and to what extent interrogatories are limited to matters "of fact," or may elicit opinions, contentions, and legal conclusions. * * *

Rule 33 is amended to provide that an interrogatory is not objectionable merely because it calls for an opinion or contention that relates to fact or the application of law to fact. Efforts to draw sharp lines between facts and opinions have invariably been unsuccessful, and the clear trend of the cases is to permit "factual" opinions. As to requests for opinions or contentions that call for the application of law to fact, they can be most useful in narrowing and sharpening the issues, which is a major purpose of discovery. * * * On the other hand, under the new language interrogatories may not extend to issues of "pure law," i.e., legal issues unrelated to the facts of the case. * * *

*Subdivision * * * [(d)].* This is a new subdivision, adapted from Calif.Code Civ.Proc. [§ 2030(f)(2)] * * *, relating especially to interrogatories which require a party to engage in burdensome or expensive research into his own business records in order to give an answer. * * * The interrogating party is protected against abusive use of this provision through the requirement that the burden of ascertaining the answer be substantially the same for both sides. A respondent may not impose on an interrogating party a mass of records as to which research is feasible only for one familiar with the records. At the same time, the respondent unable to invoke this subdivision does not on that account lose the protection available to him under new Rule 26(c) against oppressive or unduly burdensome or expensive interrogatories. And even when the respondent successfully invokes the subdivision, the court is not deprived of its usual power, in appropriate cases, to require that the interrogating party reimburse the respondent for the expense of assembling his records and making them intelligible.

(b) *Amendments in 1980 to What Is Now Rule 33(d)*

The last sentence of Rule 33(d) * * * was added in 1980. The Advisory Committee commented as follows:

The Committee is advised that parties upon whom interrogatories are served have occasionally responded by directing the interrogating party to a mass of business records or by offering to make all of their records available, justifying the response by the option provided by this subdivision. Such practices are an abuse of the option. A party who is permitted by the terms of this subdivision to offer records for inspection in lieu of answering an interrogatory should offer them in a manner that permits the same direct and economical access that is available to the party. If the information sought exists in the form of compilations, abstracts or summaries then available to the responding party, those should be made available to the interrogating party. The final sentence is added to make it clear that a responding party has the duty to specify, by category and location, the records from which answers to interrogatories can be derived.

(c) *Amendments in 1993 to Rule 33*

Revisions to Rule 33 have been made to limit interrogatory practice. The Advisory Committee on Rules, in commenting on the changes, stated:

Because Rule 26(a)(1)(3) requires disclosure of much of the information previously obtained by this form of discovery, there should be less occasion to use [Rule 33]. Experience in over half of the district courts has confirmed that limitations on the number of interrogatories are useful and manageable.

(d) *Local Federal Rules*

United States District Court, Southern District New York, Civil Rule 33.4(a)

Federal Rule of Civil Procedure 33(a) (only insofar as it limits the number of interrogatories) is not operative in this District.

(e) *Comparative State Provisions*

1. *Scope of Usage as to Claims and Parties*

New York Civil Practice Law and Rules 3130

1. Except as otherwise provided herein, after commencement of an action, any party may serve upon any other party written interrogatories. Except in a matrimonial action, a party may not serve written interrogatories on another party and also demand a bill of particulars of the same party pursuant to section 3041. In the case of an action to recover damages for personal injury, injury to property or wrongful death predicated solely on * * * negligence, a party shall not be permitted to serve interrogatories on and conduct a deposition of the same party * * * without leave of court.

2. After commencement of a matrimonial action or proceeding, upon motion brought by either party, upon such notice to the other party and to the non-party from whom financial disclosure is sought, and given in such manner as the court shall direct, the court may order a non-party to respond under oath to written interrogatories limited to furnishing financial information concerning a party, and further provided such information is both reasonable and necessary in the prosecution or the defense of such matrimonial action or proceeding.

2. *Limitations on Detail Required in Response*

California Civil Procedure Code § 2030(f)(2)

If the answer to an interrogatory would necessitate the preparation or the making of a compilation, abstract, audit, or summary of or from the documents of the party to whom the interrogatory is directed, and if the burden or expense of preparing or making it would be substantially the same for the party propounding the interrogatory as for the responding party, it is a sufficient answer to that interrogatory to refer to this subdivision and to specify the writings from which the answer may be derived or ascertained. This specification shall be in sufficient detail to permit the propounding party to locate and to identify, as readily as the responding party can, the writings from which the answer may be ascertained. The responding party shall then afford to the propounding party a reasonable opportunity to examine, audit, or inspect these documents and to make copies, compilations, abstracts, or summaries of them.

3. *Restriction on Number of Interrogatories Allowed*

Minnesota Rule of Civil Procedure 33.01(a)

Any party may serve written interrogatories upon any other party. Interrogatories may, without leave of court, be served upon any party after service of the summons and complaint. No party may serve more than a total of 50 interrogatories upon any other party unless permitted to do so by the court upon motion, notice and a showing of a good cause. In computing the total number of interrogatories each subdivision of separate questions shall be counted as an interrogatory.

Rule 34. Production of Documents and Things and Entry Upon Land for Inspection and Other Purposes

(a) Scope. Any party may serve on any other party a request (1) to produce and permit the party making the request, or someone acting on the requestor's behalf, to inspect and copy, any designated documents (including writings, drawings, graphs, charts, photographs, phono-records, and other data compilations from which information can be obtained, translated, if necessary, by the respondent through detection devices into reasonably usable form), or to inspect and copy, test, or sample any tangible things which constitute or contain matters within the scope of Rule 26(b) and which are in the possession, custody or control of the party upon whom the request is served; or (2) to permit entry upon designated land or other property in the possession or control of the party upon whom the request is served for the purpose of inspection and measuring, surveying, photographing, testing, or sampling the property or any designated object or operation thereon, within the scope of Rule 26(b).

(b) Procedure. The request shall set forth, either by individual item or by category, the items to be inspected, and describe each with reasonable particularity. The request shall specify a reasonable time, place, and manner of making the inspection and performing the related acts. Without leave of court or written stipulation, a request may not be served before the time specified in Rule 26(d).

The party upon whom the request is served shall serve a written response within 30 days after the service of the request. A shorter or longer time may be directed by the court or, in the absence of such an order, agreed to in writing by the parties, subject to Rule 29. The response shall state, with respect to each item or category, that inspection and related activities will be permitted as requested, unless the request is objected to, in which event the reasons for the objection shall be stated. If objection is made to part of an item or category, the part shall be specified and inspection permitted of the remaining parts. The party submitting the request may move for an order under Rule 37(a) with respect to any objection to or other failure to respond to the request or any part thereof, or any failure to permit inspection as requested.

A party who produces documents for inspection shall produce them as they are kept in the usual course of business or shall organize and label them to correspond with the categories in the request.

(c) Persons Not Parties. A person not a party to the action may be compelled to produce documents and things or to submit to an inspection as provided in Rule 45.

Notes on Amendments to Federal Rule 34 and Comparative State Provisions

(a) *Amendments in 1970 to Rule 34*

The Advisory Committee commented on the 1970 amendments to Rule 34 as follows:

Rule 34 is revised to accomplish the following major changes in the existing rule: (1) to eliminate the requirement of good cause; (2) to have the rule operate extrajudicially; (3) to include testing and sampling as well as inspecting or photographing tangible things; and (4) to make clear that the rule does not preclude an independent action for analogous discovery against persons not parties.

Subdivision (a). * * * The good cause requirement was originally inserted in Rule 34 as a general protective provision in the absence of experience with the specific problems that would arise thereunder. As the note to Rule 26(b)(3) on trial preparation materials makes clear, good cause has been applied differently to varying classes of documents, though not without confusion. It has often been said in court opinions that good cause requires a consideration of need for the materials and of alternative means of obtaining them, i. e., something more than relevance and lack of privilege. But the overwhelming proportion of the cases in which the formula of good cause has been applied to require a special showing are those involving trial preparation. In practice, the courts have not treated documents as having a special immunity to discovery simply because of their being documents. Protection may be afforded to claims of privacy or secrecy or of undue burden or expense under what is now Rule 26(c) (previously Rule 30(b)). To be sure, an appraisal of "undue" burden inevitably entails consideration of the needs of the party seeking discovery. With special provisions added to govern trial preparation materials and experts, there is no longer any occasion to retain the requirement of good cause.

The revision of Rule 34 to have it operate extrajudicially, rather than by court order, is to a large extent a reflection of existing law office practice. The Columbia Survey shows that of the litigants seeking inspection of documents or things, only about 25 percent filed motions for court orders. This minor fraction nevertheless accounted for a significant number of motions. About half of these motions were uncontested and in almost all instances the party seeking production ultimately prevailed. Although an extrajudicial procedure will not drastically alter existing practice under Rule 34—it will conform to it in most cases—it has the potential of saving court time in a substantial though proportionately small number of cases tried annually. * * *

Subdivision (c). Rule 34 as revised continues to apply only to parties. Comments from the bar make clear that in the preparation of cases for trial it is occasionally necessary to enter land or inspect large tangible things in the possession of a person not a party, and that some courts have dismissed independent actions in the nature of bills in equity for such discovery on the ground that Rule 34 is preemptive. While an ideal solution to this problem is to provide for discovery against persons not parties in Rule 34, both the jurisdictional and procedural problems are very complex. For the present, this subdivision makes clear that Rule 34 does not preclude independent actions for discovery against persons not parties.

(b) *Amendment in 1980 to Rule 34(b)*

The last paragraph of Rule 34(b) was added in 1980 to proscribe the practice of some litigants of deliberately mixing critical documents with many others in order to obscure significance.

(c) *Comparative State Provisions*

New York Civil Practice Law and Rules 3120

(a) As against party:

1. After commencement of an action, any party may serve on any other party notice:

(i) to produce and permit the party seeking discovery, or someone acting on his behalf, to inspect, copy, test or photograph any specifically designated documents or any things which are in the possession, custody or control of the party served; or

(ii) to permit entry upon designated land or other property in the possession, custody or control of the party served for the purpose of inspecting, measuring, surveying, sampling, testing, photographing or recording by motion pictures or otherwise the property or any specifically designated object or operation thereon.

2. The notice shall specify the time, which shall be not less than twenty days after service of the notice, and the place and manner of making the inspection, copy, test or photograph, or of the entry upon the land or other property * * *.

(b) As against non-party. A person not a party may be directed by order to do whatever a party may be directed to do under subdivision (a). The motion for such order shall be on notice to all adverse parties; the non-party shall be served with the notice of motion in the same manner as a summons. The order shall contain, in addition to such specifications as the notice is required to contain under paragraph two of subdivision (a), provision for the defraying of the expenses of the non-party.

Rule 35.   Physical and Mental Examination of Persons

(a) Order for Examination. When the mental or physical condition (including the blood group) of a party, or of a person in the custody or under the legal control of a party, is in controversy, the court in which the action is pending may order the party to submit to a physical or mental examination by a suitably licensed or certified examiner or to produce for examination the person in the party's custody or legal control. The order may be made only on motion for good cause shown and upon notice to the person to be examined and to all parties and shall specify the time, place, manner, conditions, and scope of the examination and the person or persons by whom it is to be made.

(b) Report of Examiner.

(1) If requested by the party against whom an order is made under Rule 35(a) or the person examined, the party causing the examination to be made shall deliver to the requestor a copy of a detailed written report of the examiner setting out the examiner's findings, including results of all tests made, diagnoses and conclusions, together with like reports of all earlier examinations of the same condition. After delivery the party causing the examination shall be entitled upon request to receive from the party against whom the order is made a like report of any examination, previously or thereafter made, of the same condition, unless, in the case of a report of examination of a person not a party, the party shows that such party is unable to obtain it. The court on motion may make an order against a party requiring delivery of a report on such terms as are just, and if an examiner fails or refuses to make a report the court may exclude the examiner's testimony if offered at the trial.

(2) By requesting and obtaining a report of the examination so ordered or by taking the deposition of the examiner, the party examined waives any privilege the party may have in that action or any other involving the same controversy, regarding the testimony of every other person who has examined or may thereafter examine the party in respect of the same mental or physical condition.

(3) This subdivision applies to examinations made by agreement of the parties, unless the agreement expressly provides otherwise. This subdivision does not preclude discovery of a report of an examiner or the taking of a deposition of the examiner in accordance with the provisions of any other rule.

Notes on Amendments to Federal Rule 35 and Comparative State Provisions

(a) *Amendments in 1970 to Rule 35*

The Advisory Committee commented on the 1970 amendment to Rule 35 as follows:

Subdivision (a). Rule 35(a) has hitherto provided only for an order requiring a party to submit to an examination. It is desirable to extend the rule to provide for an order against the party for examination of a person in his custody or under his legal control. As appears from the provisions of amended Rule 37(b)(2) and the comment under that rule, an order to "produce" the third person imposes only an obligation to use good faith efforts to produce the person.

The amendment will settle beyond doubt that a parent or guardian suing to recover for injuries to a minor may be ordered to produce the minor for examination. Further, the amendment expressly includes blood examination within the kinds of examinations that can be ordered under the rule.

(b) *Amendment in 1991 to Rule 35*

The 1991 amendment eliminated the requirement that an examination be carried out by a physician, or, in the case of a mental examination, by a physician or psychologist. Instead, an order for an examination is proper if carried out "by a suitably licensed or certified examiner."

(c) *Comparative State Provisions*

1. *Rule 35(a)*

Minnesota Rule of Civil Procedure 35.01

In an action in which the physical or mental condition or the blood relationship of a party, or of an agent of a party, or of a person under control of a party, is in controversy, the court in which the action is pending may order the party to submit to, or produce such agent or person for, a mental, physical, or blood examination by a suitably licensed or certified examiner. The order may be made only on motion for good cause shown and upon notice to the party or person to be examined and to all other parties and shall specify the time, place, manner, conditions, and scope of the examination and the person or persons by whom it is made.

2. *Rule 35(b)*

New York Civil Practice Law and Rules 3121(b)

A copy of a detailed written report of the examining physician setting out his findings and conclusions shall be delivered by the party seeking the examination to any party requesting to exchange therefor a copy of each report in his control of an examination made with respect to the mental or physical condition in controversy.

Rule 36.   Requests for Admission

(a) Request for Admission. A party may serve upon any other party a written request for the admission, for purposes of the pending action only, of the truth of any matters within the scope of Rule 26(b)(1) set forth in the request that relate to statements or opinions of fact or of the application of law to fact, including the genuineness of any documents described in the request. Copies of documents shall be served with the request unless they have been or are otherwise furnished or made available for inspection and copying. Without leave of court or written stipulation, requests for admission may not be served before the time specified in Rule 26(d).

Each matter of which an admission is requested shall be separately set forth. The matter is admitted unless, within 30 days after service of the request, or within such shorter or longer time as the court may allow or the parties may agree to in writing, subject to Rule 29, the party to whom the request is directed serves upon the party requesting the admission a written answer or objection addressed to the matter, signed by the party or by the party's attorney. If objection is made, the reasons therefor shall be stated. The answer shall specifically deny the matter or set forth in detail the reasons why the answering party cannot truthfully admit or deny the matter. A denial shall fairly meet the substance of the requested admission, and when good faith requires that a party qualify an answer or deny only a part of the matter of which an admission is requested, the party shall specify so much of it as is true and qualify or deny the remainder. An answering party may not give lack of information or knowledge as a reason for failure to admit or deny unless the party states that the party has made reasonable inquiry and that the information known or readily obtainable by the party is insufficient to enable the party to admit or deny. A party who considers that a matter of which an admission has been requested presents a genuine issue for trial may not, on that ground alone, object to the request; the party may, subject to the provisions of Rule 37(c), deny the matter or set forth reasons why the party cannot admit or deny it.

The party who has requested the admissions may move to determine the sufficiency of the answers or objections. Unless the court determines that an objection is justified, it shall order that an answer be served. If the court determines that an answer does not comply with the requirements of this rule, it may order either that the matter is admitted or that an amended answer be served. The court may, in lieu of these orders, determine that final disposition of the request be made at a pre-trial conference or at a designated time prior to trial. The provisions of Rule 37(a)(4) apply to the award of expenses incurred in relation to the motion.

(b) Effect of Admission. Any matter admitted under this rule is conclusively established unless the court on motion permits withdrawal or amendment of the admission. Subject to the provisions of Rule 16 governing amendment of a pre-trial order, the court may permit withdrawal or amendment when the presentation of the merits of the action will be subserved thereby and the party who obtained the admission fails to satisfy the court that withdrawal or amendment will prejudice that party in maintaining the action or defense on the merits. Any admission made by a party under this rule is for the purpose of the pending action only and is not an admission for any other purpose nor may it be used against the party in any other proceeding.

Notes on Amendments to Federal Rule 36

The 1970 amendments made several important changes in Rule 36. The Advisory Committee commented on these changes as follows:

Subdivision (a). As revised, the subdivision provides that a request may be made to admit any matters within the scope of Rule 26(b) that relate to statements or opinions of fact or of the application of law to fact. It thereby eliminates the requirement that the matters be "of fact." This change resolves conflicts in the court decisions as to whether a request to admit matters of "opinion" and matters involving "mixed law and fact" is proper under the rule. * * *

Not only is it difficult as a practical matter to separate "fact" from "opinion," see 4 *Moore's Federal Practice* ¶ 36.04 (2d ed. 1966); *cf.* 2A Barron & Holtzoff, *Federal Practice and Procedure* 317 (Wright ed. 1961), but an admission on a matter of opinion may facilitate proof or narrow the issues or both. An admission of a matter involving the application of law to fact may, in a given case, even more clearly narrow the issues. For example, an admission that an employee acted in the scope of his employment may remove a major issue from the trial. * * *

Courts have also divided on whether an answering party may properly object to request for admission as to matters which that party regards as "in dispute." * * * The proper response in such cases is an answer. The very purpose of the request is to ascertain whether the answering party is prepared to admit or regards the matter as presenting a genuine issue for trial. In his answer, the party may deny, or he may give as his reason for inability to admit or deny the existence of a genuine issue. The party runs no risk of sanctions if the matter is genuinely in issue, since Rule 37(c) provides a sanction of costs only when there are no good reasons for a failure to admit.

* * *

Another sharp split of authority exists on the question whether a party may base his answer on lack of information or knowledge without seeking out additional information. One line of cases has held that a party may answer on the basis of such knowledge as he has at the time he answers. * * *

The rule as revised adopts the majority view, as in keeping with a basic principle of the discovery rules that a reasonable burden may be imposed on the parties when its discharge will facilitate preparation for trial and ease the trial process. It has been argued against this view that one side should not have the burden of "proving" the other side's case. The revised rule requires only that the answering party make reasonable inquiry and secure such knowledge and information as are readily obtainable by him. In most instances, the investigation will be necessary either to his own case or to preparation for rebuttal. Even when it is not, the information may be close enough at hand to be "readily obtainable." Rule 36 requires only that the party state that he has taken these steps. The sanction for failure of a party to inform himself before he answers lies in the award of costs after trial, as provided in Rule 37(c). * * *

A problem peculiar to Rule 36 arises if the responding party serves answers that are not in conformity with the requirements of the rule—for example, a denial is not "specific," or the explanation of inability to admit or deny is not "in detail." Rule 36 now makes no provision for court scrutiny of such answers before trial, and it seems to contemplate that defective answers bring about admissions just as effectively as if no answer had been served. Some cases have so held. * * *

Giving a defective answer the automatic effect of an admission may cause unfair surprise. A responding party who purported to deny or to be unable to admit or deny will for the first time at trial confront the contention that he has made a binding admission. Since it is not always easy to know whether a denial is "specific" or an explanation is "in detail," neither party can know how the court will rule at trial and whether proof must be prepared. Some courts, therefore, have entertained motions to rule on defective answers. They have at times ordered that amended answers be served, when the defects were technical, and at other times have declared that the matter was admitted. * * * The rule as revised conforms to the latter practice.

Subdivision (b). The rule does not now indicate the extent to which a party is bound by his admission. Some courts view admissions as the equivalent of sworn testimony. * * * At least in some jurisdictions a party may rebut his own testimony, e. g., *Alamo v. Del Rosario,* 98 F.2d 328 (D.C.Cir.1938), and by analogy an admission made pursuant to Rule 36 may likewise be thought rebuttable. * * * In *McSparran v. Hanigan,* 225 F.Supp. 628, 636–637 (E.D.Pa.1963), the court held that an admission is conclusively binding, though noting the confusion created by prior decisions.

The new provisions give an admission a conclusively binding effect, for purposes only of the pending action, unless the admission is withdrawn or amended. In form and substance a Rule 36 admission is comparable to an admission in pleadings or a stipulation drafted by counsel for use at trial, rather than to an evidentiary admission of a party. * * *

Rule 37. Failure to Make or Cooperate in Discovery: Sanctions

[See proposed change to Rule 37(c)(1), in Part IX, infra.]

(a) Motion for Order Compelling Disclosure or Discovery. A party, upon reasonable notice to other parties and all persons affected thereby, may apply for an order compelling disclosure or discovery as follows:

(1) *Appropriate Court.* An application for an order to a party shall be made to the court in which the action is pending. An application for an order to a person who is not a party shall be made to the court in the district where the discovery is being, or is to be, taken.

(2) *Motion.*

(A) If a party fails to make a disclosure required by Rule 26(a), any other party may move to compel disclosure and for appropriate sanctions. The motion must include a certification that the movant has in good faith conferred or attempted to confer with the party not making the disclosure in an effort to secure the disclosure without court action.

(B) If a deponent fails to answer a question propounded or submitted under Rules 30 or 31, or a corporation or other entity fails to make a designation under Rule 30(b)(6) or 31(a), or a party fails to answer an interrogatory submitted under Rule 33, or if a party, in response to a request for inspection submitted under Rule 34, fails to respond that inspection will be permitted as requested or fails to permit inspection as requested, the discovering party may move for an order compelling an answer, or a designation, or an order compelling inspection in accordance with the request. The motion must include a certification that the movant has in good faith conferred or attempted to confer with the person or party failing to make the discovery in an effort to secure the information or material without court action. When taking a deposition on oral examination, the proponent of the question may complete or adjourn the examination before applying for an order.

(3) *Evasive or Incomplete Disclosure, Answer, or Response.* For purposes of this subdivision an evasive or incomplete disclosure, answer, or response is to be treated as a failure to disclose, answer, or respond.

(4) *Expenses and Sanctions.*

(A) If the motion is granted or if the disclosure or requested discovery is provided after the motion was filed, the court shall, after affording an opportunity to be heard, require the party or deponent whose conduct necessitated the motion or the party or attorney advising such conduct or both of them to pay to the moving party the reasonable expenses incurred in making the motion, including attorney's fees, unless the court finds that the motion was filed without the movant's first making a good faith effort to obtain the disclosure or discovery without court action, or that the opposing party's nondisclosure, response, or objection was substantially justified, or that other circumstances make an award of expenses unjust.

(B) If the motion is denied, the court may enter any protective order authorized under Rule 26(c) and shall, after affording an opportunity to be heard, require the moving party or the attorney filing the motion or both of them to pay to the party or deponent who opposed the motion the reasonable expenses incurred in opposing the motion, including attorney's fees, unless the court finds that the making of the motion was substantially justified or that other circumstances make an award of expenses unjust.

(C) If the motion is granted in part and denied in part, the court may enter any protective order authorized under Rule 26(c) and may, after affording an opportunity to be heard, apportion the reasonable expenses incurred in relation to the motion among the parties and persons in a just manner.

(b) Failure to Comply With Order.

(1) *Sanctions by Court in District Where Deposition Is Taken.* If a deponent fails to be sworn or to answer a question after being directed to do so by the court in the district in which the deposition is being taken, the failure may be considered a contempt of that court.

(2) *Sanctions by Court in Which Action Is Pending.* If a party or an officer, director, or managing agent of a party or a person designated under Rule 30(b)(6) or 31(a) to testify on behalf of a party fails to obey an order to provide or permit discovery, including an order made under subdivision (a) of this rule or Rule 35, or if a party fails to obey an order entered under Rule 26(f), the court in which the action is pending may

make such orders in regard to the failure as are just, and among others the following:

(A) An order that the matters regarding which the order was made or any other designated facts shall be taken to be established for the purposes of the action in accordance with the claim of the party obtaining the order;

(B) An order refusing to allow the disobedient party to support or oppose designated claims or defenses, or prohibiting that party from introducing designated matters in evidence;

(C) An order striking out pleadings or parts thereof, or staying further proceedings until the order is obeyed, or dismissing the action or proceeding or any part thereof, or rendering a judgment by default against the disobedient party;

(D) In lieu of any of the foregoing orders or in addition thereto, an order treating as a contempt of court the failure to obey any orders except an order to submit to a physical or mental examination;

(E) Where a party has failed to comply with an order under Rule 35(a) requiring that party to produce another for examination, such orders as are listed in paragraphs (A), (B), and (C) of this subdivision, unless the party failing to comply shows that that party is unable to produce such person for examination.

In lieu of any of the foregoing orders or in addition thereto, the court shall require the party failing to obey the order or the attorney advising that party or both to pay the reasonable expenses, including attorney's fees, caused by the failure, unless the court finds that the failure was substantially justified or that other circumstances make an award of expenses unjust.

(c) Failure to Disclose; False or Misleading Disclosure; Refusal to Admit.

(1) A party that without substantial justification fails to disclose information as required by Rule 26(a) or 26(e)(1) shall not, unless such failure is harmless, be permitted to use as evidence at trial, at a hearing, or on a motion, any witness or information not so disclosed. In addition or in lieu of this sanction, the court, on motion after affording opportunity to be heard, may impose other appropriate sanctions. In addition to requiring payment of reasonable expenses, including attorney's fees, caused by the failure, these sanctions may include any actions authorized under subparagraphs (A), (B), and (C) of subdivision (b)(2) of this rule and may include informing the jury of the failure to make the disclosure.

(2) If a party fails to admit the genuineness of any document or the truth of any matter requested under Rule 36, and if the party requesting the admissions thereafter proves the genuineness of the document or the truth of the matter, the requesting party may apply to the court for an order requiring the other party to pay the party the reasonable expenses

incurred in making that proof, including reasonable attorney's fees. The court shall make the order unless it finds that (A) the request was held objectionable pursuant to Rule 36(a), or (B) the admission sought was of no substantial importance, or (C) the party failing to admit had reasonable ground to believe that the party might prevail on the matter, or (D) there was other good reason for the failure to admit.

(d) Failure of Party to Attend at Own Deposition or Serve Answers to Interrogatories or Respond to Request for Inspection. If a party or an officer, director, or managing agent of a party or a person designated under Rule 30(b)(6) or 31(a) to testify on behalf of a party fails (1) to appear before the officer who is to take the deposition, after being served with a proper notice, or (2) to serve answers or objections to interrogatories submitted under Rule 33, after proper service of the interrogatories, or (3) to serve a written response to a request for inspection submitted under Rule 34, after proper service of the request, the court in which the action is pending on motion may make such orders in regard to the failure as are just, and among others it may take any action authorized under paragraphs (A), (B), and (C) of subdivision (b)(2) of this rule. Any motion specifying a failure under clauses (2) or (3) of this subdivision shall include a certification that the movant in good faith has conferred or attempted to confer with the party failing to answer or respond in an effort to obtain such answer or response without court action. In lieu of any order or in addition thereto, the court shall require the party failing to act or the attorney advising that party or both to pay the reasonable expenses, including attorney's fees, caused by the failure, unless the court finds that the failure was substantially justified or that other circumstances make an award of expenses unjust.

The failure to act described in this subdivision may not be excused on the ground that the discovery sought is objectionable unless the party failing to act has a pending motion for a protective order as provided by Rule 26(c).

(e) [Abrogated]

(f) [Repealed. Pub.L. 96–481, Title II, § 205(a), Oct. 21, 1980, 94 Stat. 2330.]

(g) Failure to Participate in the Framing of a Discovery Plan. If a party or a party's attorney fails to participate in good faith in the development and submission of a proposed discovery plan as required by Rule 26(f), the court may, after opportunity for hearing, require such party or attorney to pay to any other party the reasonable expenses, including attorney's fees, caused by the failure.

Notes on Amendments to Federal Rule 37 and Comparative Federal and State Provisions

(a) *Amendments in 1993 to Federal Rule 37*

Rule 37 has been revised to reflect the revisions made to Rule 26(a) mandating the automatic exchange of information without formal discovery. Subdivision (a)(2)(A) has been added to provide a method for compelling disclosure where a party fails to fully comply with Rule 26(a). Under (c)(1) of the revised rule, if the information is important evidence for the non-disclosing party, the party seeking to compel disclosure may, as an alternative measure, ask the court to exclude the evidence at trial.

Language has been added to paragraph (d) and to subparagraph (a)(2)(B) which requires litigants to use informal means of resolving discovery disputes before filing a motion to compel compliance. Paragraph (a)(3), as revised, clarifies that evasive or incomplete disclosures and answers to requests for production of documents and interrogatories will be treated as failures to respond and may serve as the basis for sanctions under Rule 37(a).

Subdivision (c) provides that as a sanction for failing to automatically disclose information required by Rule 26(a) or 26(e)(1), a party will be prohibited from using such information at trial. Unlike the old version of the rule, this provision is self-executing and does not require the opposing party to make a motion. The inclusion of the requirement that the failure to disclose must be "without substantial justification" and the exception from sanctions where the failure to disclose is harmless serve to mitigate the harshness of this rule.

(b) *Comparative Provisions*

Rule 37(a)

1. *Local Federal Rule*

United States District Court, District of Columbia, Rule 7.1(m)

Before filing any nondispositive motion in a civil action, counsel shall discuss the anticipated motion with opposing counsel, either in person or by telephone, in a good-faith effort to determine whether there is any opposition to the relief sought and, if there is opposition, to narrow the areas of disagreement. A party shall include in its motion a statement that the required discussion occurred, and a statement as to whether the motion is opposed.

2. *Comparative State Provision*

California Civil Procedure Code § 2023

(a) Misuses of the discovery process include, but are not limited to, the following:

(1) Persisting, over objection and without substantial justification, in an attempt to obtain information or materials that are outside the scope of permissible discovery.

(2) Using a discovery method in a manner that does not comply with its specified procedures.

(3) Employing a discovery method in a manner or to an extent that causes unwarranted annoyance, embarrassment, or oppression, or undue burden and expense.

(4) Failing to respond or submit to an authorized method of discovery.

(5) Making, without substantial justification, an unmeritorious objection to discovery.

(6) Making an evasive response to discovery.

(7) Disobeying a court order to provide discovery.

(8) Making or opposing, unsuccessfully and without substantial justification, a motion to compel or to limit discovery.

(9) Failing to confer in person, by telephone, or by letter with an opposing party or attorney in a reasonable and good faith attempt to resolve informally any dispute concerning discovery, if the section governing a particular discovery motion requires the filing of a declaration stating facts showing

that such an attempt has been made. Notwithstanding the outcome of the particular discovery motion, the court shall impose a monetary sanction ordering that any party or attorney who fails to confer as required pay the reasonable expenses, including attorney's fees, incurred by anyone as a result of that conduct.

(b) To the extent authorized by the section governing any particular discovery method or any other provision of this article, the court, after notice to any affected party, person, or attorney, and after opportunity for hearing, may impose the following sanctions against anyone engaging in conduct that is a misuse of the discovery process.

(1) The court may impose a monetary sanction ordering that one engaging in the misuse of the discovery process, or any attorney advising that conduct, or both pay the reasonable expenses, including attorney's fees, incurred by anyone as a result of that conduct. The court may also impose this sanction on one unsuccessfully asserting that another has engaged in the misuse of the discovery process, or on any attorney who advised that assertion, or on both. If a monetary sanction is authorized by any provision of this article, the court shall impose that sanction unless it finds that the one subject to the sanction acted with substantial justification or that other circumstances make the sanction unjust.

(2) The court may impose an issue sanction ordering that designed facts shall be taken as established in the action in accordance with the claim of the party adversely affected by the misuse of the discovery process. The court may also impose an issue sanction by an order prohibiting any party engaging in the misuse of the discovery process from supporting or opposing designated claims or defenses.

(3) The court may impose an evidence sanction by an order prohibiting any party engaging in the misuse of the discovery process from introducing designated matters in evidence.

(4) The court may impose a terminating sanction by one of the following orders:

(A) An order striking out the pleadings or parts of the pleadings of any party engaging in the misuse of the discovery process.

(B) An order staying further proceedings by that party until an order for discovery is obeyed.

(C) An order dismissing the action, or any part of the action, of that party.

(D) An order rendering a judgment by default against that party.

(5) The court may impose a contempt sanction by an order treating the misuse of the discovery process as a contempt of court.

(c) A request for a sanction shall, in the notice of motion, identify every person, party, and attorney against whom the sanction is sought, and specify the type of sanction sought. The notice of motion shall be supported by a memorandum of points and authorities, and accompanied by a declaration setting forth facts supporting the amount of any monetary sanction sought.

VI. TRIALS

Rule 38. Jury Trial of Right

(a) Right Preserved. The right of trial by jury as declared by the Seventh Amendment to the Constitution or as given by a statute of the United States shall be preserved to the parties inviolate.

(b) Demand. Any party may demand a trial by jury of any issue triable of right by a jury by (1) serving upon the other parties a demand therefor in writing at any time after the commencement of the action and not later than 10 days after the service of the last pleading directed to such issue, and (2) filing the demand as required by Rule 5(d). Such demand may be indorsed upon a pleading of the party.

(c) Same: Specification of Issues. In the demand a party may specify the issues which the party wishes so tried; otherwise the party shall be deemed to have demanded trial by jury for all the issues so triable. If the party has demanded trial by jury for only some of the issues, any other party within 10 days after service of the demand or such lesser time as the court may order, may serve a demand for trial by jury of any other or all of the issues of fact in the action.

(d) Waiver. The failure of a party to serve and file a demand as required by this rule constitutes a waiver by the party of trial by jury. A demand for trial by jury made as herein provided may not be withdrawn without the consent of the parties.

(e) Admiralty and Maritime Claims. These rules shall not be construed to create a right to trial by jury of the issues in an admiralty or maritime claim within the meaning of Rule 9(h).

Federal and State Provisions Governing the Right to Jury Trial

(a) Constitutional Provisions

United States Constitution, 7th Amendment

In Suits at common law, where the value in controversy shall exceed twenty dollars, the right of trial by jury shall be preserved, and no fact tried by a jury shall be otherwise re-examined in any Court of the United States than according to the rules of the common law.

Pennsylvania Constitution Art. 1, § 6

Trial by jury shall be as heretofore, and the right thereof remain inviolate. The General Assembly may provide, however, by law, that a verdict may be rendered by not less than five-sixths of the jury in any civil case. * * *

Virginia Constitution Art. 1, § 11

* * *

That in controversies respecting property, and in suits between man and man, trial by jury is preferable to any other, and ought to be held sacred. The General Assembly may limit the number of jurors for civil cases in courts of record to not less than five.

(b) Federal Statute for Certain Title VII Cases

42 U.S.C.A. § 1981a

[This provision, enacted in 1991, provides for a jury trial in those Title VII suits in which respondent is alleged to have engaged in unlawful *intentional* discrimination.]

(c) *State Statute on Demand and Waiver*

New York Civil Practice Law and Rules 4103

When it appears in the course of a trial by the court that the relief required, although not originally demanded by a party, entitles the adverse party to a trial by jury of certain issues of fact, the court shall give the adverse party an opportunity to demand a jury trial of such issues. Failure to make such demand within the time limited by the court shall be deemed a waiver of the right to trial by jury. Upon such demand, the court shall order a jury trial of any issues of fact which are required to be tried by jury.

Rule 39. Trial by Jury or by the Court

(a) By Jury. When trial by jury has been demanded as provided in Rule 38, the action shall be designated upon the docket as a jury action. The trial of all issues so demanded shall be by jury, unless (1) the parties or their attorneys of record, by written stipulation filed with the court or by an oral stipulation made in open court and entered in the record, consent to trial by the court sitting without a jury or (2) the court upon motion or of its own initiative finds that a right of trial by jury of some or all of those issues does not exist under the Constitution or statutes of the United States.

(b) By the Court. Issues not demanded for trial by jury as provided in Rule 38 shall be tried by the court; but, notwithstanding the failure of a party to demand a jury in an action in which such a demand might have been made of right, the court in its discretion upon motion may order a trial by a jury of any or all issues.

(c) Advisory Jury and Trial by Consent. In all actions not triable of right by a jury the court upon motion or of its own initiative may try any issue with an advisory jury or, except in actions against the United States when a statute of the United States provides for trial without a jury, the court, with the consent of both parties, may order a trial with a jury whose verdict has the same effect as if trial by jury had been a matter of right.

Rule 40. Assignment of Cases for Trial

The district courts shall provide by rule for the placing of actions upon the trial calendar (1) without request of the parties or (2) upon request of a party and notice to the other parties or (3) in such other manner as the courts deem expedient. Precedence shall be given to actions entitled thereto by any statute of the United States.

Rule 41. Dismissal of Actions

(a) Voluntary Dismissal: Effect Thereof.

(1) *By Plaintiff; by Stipulation.* Subject to the provisions of Rule 23(e), of Rule 66, and of any statute of the United States, an action may be dismissed by the plaintiff without order of court (i) by filing a notice of dismissal at any time before service by the adverse party of an answer

or of a motion for summary judgment, whichever first occurs, or (ii) by filing a stipulation of dismissal signed by all parties who have appeared in the action. Unless otherwise stated in the notice of dismissal or stipulation, the dismissal is without prejudice, except that a notice of dismissal operates as an adjudication upon the merits when filed by a plaintiff who has once dismissed in any court of the United States or of any state an action based on or including the same claim.

(2) *By Order of Court.* Except as provided in paragraph (1) of this subdivision of this rule, an action shall not be dismissed at the plaintiff's instance save upon order of the court and upon such terms and conditions as the court deems proper. If a counterclaim has been pleaded by a defendant prior to the service upon the defendant of the plaintiff's motion to dismiss, the action shall not be dismissed against the defendant's objection unless the counterclaim can remain pending for independent adjudication by the court. Unless otherwise specified in the order, a dismissal under this paragraph is without prejudice.

(b) Involuntary Dismissal: Effect Thereof. For failure of the plaintiff to prosecute or to comply with these rules or any order of court, a defendant may move for dismissal of an action or of any claim against the defendant. Unless the court in its order for dismissal otherwise specifies, a dismissal under this subdivision and any dismissal not provided for in this rule, other than a dismissal for lack of jurisdiction, for improper venue, or for failure to join a party under Rule 19, operates as an adjudication upon the merits.

(c) Dismissal of Counterclaim, Cross-Claim, or Third-Party Claim. The provisions of this rule apply to the dismissal of any counterclaim, cross-claim, or third-party claim. A voluntary dismissal by the claimant alone pursuant to paragraph (1) of subdivision (a) of this rule shall be made before a responsive pleading is served or, if there is none, before the introduction of evidence at the trial or hearing.

(d) Costs of Previously-Dismissed Action. If a plaintiff who has once dismissed an action in any court commences an action based upon or including the same claim against the same defendant, the court may make such order for the payment of costs of the action previously dismissed as it may deem proper and may stay the proceedings in the action until the plaintiff has complied with the order.

Comparative Provisions and Notes on Amendments to Federal Rule 41

(a) *Rule 41(a)*

Illinois Compiled Statutes ch. 735, 5/2–1009(a), (c)

(a) The plaintiff may, at any time before trial or hearing begins, upon notice to each party who has appeared or each such party's attorney, and upon payment of costs, dismiss his or her action or any part thereof as to any defendant, without prejudice, by order filed in the cause.

(c) After trial or hearing begins, the plaintiff may dismiss, only on terms fixed by the court (1) upon filing a stipulation to that effect signed by the defendant, or (2) on motion specifying the ground for dismissal, which shall be supported by affidavit or other proof.

(b) *Rule 41(b)*

1. *Amendments in 1963 to Federal Rule 41(b)*

Prior to 1963 the second sentence of Rule 41(b) providing for a dismissal upon completion of plaintiff's presentation of evidence was not restricted to non-jury cases. The purpose of the amendment was set forth by the Advisory Committee as follows:

Under the present text of the second sentence of this subdivision, the motion for dismissal at the close of the plaintiff's evidence may be made in a case tried to a jury as well as in a case tried without a jury. But, when made in a jury-tried case, this motion overlaps the motion for a directed verdict under Rule 50(a), which is also available in the same situation. It has been held that the standard to be applied in deciding the Rule 41(b) motion at the close of the plaintiff's evidence in a jury-tried case is the same as that used upon a motion for a directed verdict made at the same stage; and, just as the court need not make findings pursuant to Rule 52(a) when it directs a verdict, so in a jury-tried case it may omit these findings in granting the Rule 41(b) motion. See generally *O'Brien v. Westinghouse Electric Corp.*, 293 F.2d 1, 5–10 (3d Cir.1961).

As indicated by the discussion in the *O'Brien* case, the overlap has caused confusion. Accordingly, the second and third sentences of Rule 41(b) are amended to provide that the motion for dismissal at the close of the plaintiff's evidence shall apply only to nonjury cases (including cases tried with an advisory jury). Hereafter the correct motion in jury-tried cases will be the motion for a directed verdict. This involves no change of substance. * * *

The first sentence of Rule 41(b), providing for dismissal for failure to prosecute or to comply with the Rules or any order of court, and the general provisions of the last sentence remain applicable in jury as well as non-jury cases.

* * *

2. *Local Federal Rule*

United States District Court, District of Connecticut, Local Rule of Civil Procedure 16(a)

In civil actions in which no action has been taken by the parties for six (6) months or in which deadlines established by the Court pursuant to Rule 11 appear not to have been met, the Clerk shall give notice of proposed dismissal to counsel of record. If such notice has been given and no action has been taken in the action in the meantime and no satisfactory explanation is submitted to the Court within twenty (20) days thereafter, the Clerk shall enter an order of dismissal. Any such order entered by the Clerk under this Rule may be suspended, altered, or rescinded by the Court for cause shown.

3. *Comparative State Provisions*

California Civil Procedure Code § 583.210

(a) The summons and complaint shall be served upon a defendant within three years after the action is commenced against the defendant. For the purpose of this subdivision an action is commenced at the time the complaint is filed.

(b) Return of summons or other proof of service shall be made within 60 days after the time the summons and complaint must be served upon a defendant.

California Civil Procedure Code § 583.310

An action shall be brought to trial within five years after the action is commenced against the defendant.

California Civil Procedure Code § 583.320

(a) If a new trial is granted in the action the action shall again be brought to trial within the following times:

(1) If a trial is commenced but no judgment is entered because of a mistrial or because a jury is unable to reach a decision, within three years after the order of the court declaring the mistrial or the disagreement of the jury is entered.

(2) If after judgment a new trial is granted and no appeal is taken, within three years after the order granting the new trial is entered.

(3) If on appeal an order granting a new trial is affirmed or a judgment is reversed and the action remanded for a new trial, within three years after the remittitur is filed by the clerk of the trial court.

(b) Nothing in this section requires that an action again be brought to trial before expiration of the time prescribed in Section 583.310.

California Civil Procedure Code § 583.330

The parties may extend the time within which an action must be brought to trial pursuant to this article by the following means:

(a) By written stipulation. The stipulation need not be filed but, if it is not filed, the stipulation shall be brought to the attention of the court if relevant to a motion for dismissal.

(b) By oral agreement made in open court, if entered in the minutes of the court or a transcript is made.

California Civil Procedure Code § 583.360

(a) An action shall be dismissed by the court on its own motion or on motion of the defendant, after notice to the parties, if the action is not brought to trial within the time prescribed in this article.

(b) The requirements of this article are mandatory and are not subject to extension, excuse, or exception except as expressly provided by statute.

California Civil Procedure Code § 583.410(a)

The court may in its discretion dismiss an action for delay in prosecution pursuant to this article on its own motion or on motion of the defendant if to do so appears to the court appropriate under the circumstances of the case.

California Civil Procedure Code § 583.420

(a) The court may not dismiss an action pursuant to this article for delay in prosecution except after one of the following conditions has occurred:

(1) Service is not made within two years after the action is commenced against the defendant.

(2) The action is not brought to trial within the following times:

(A) Three years after the action is commenced against the defendant unless otherwise prescribed by rule under subparagraph (B).

(B) Two years after the action is commenced against the defendant if the Judicial Council by rule adopted pursuant to Section 583.410 so prescribes for the court because of the condition of the court calendar or for other reasons affecting the conduct of litigation or the administration of justice.

(3) A new trial is granted and the action is not again brought to trial within the following times:

(A) If a trial is commenced but no judgment is entered because of a mistrial or because a jury is unable to reach a decision, within two years after the order of the court declaring the mistrial or the disagreement of the jury is entered.

(B) If after judgment a new trial is granted and no appeal is taken, within two years after the order granting the new trial is entered.

(C) If on appeal an order granting a new trial is affirmed or a judgment is reversed and the action remanded for a new trial, within two years after the remittitur is filed by the clerk of the trial court.

(b) The times provided in subdivision (a) shall be computed in the manner provided for computation of the comparable times under Articles 2 (commencing with Section 583.210) and 3 (commencing with Section 583.310).

Indiana Rules of Trial Procedure, Trial Rule 41(E)

Whenever there has been a failure to comply with these rules or when no action has been taken in a civil case for a period of sixty [60] days, the court, on motion of a party or on its own motion shall order a hearing for the purpose of dismissing such case. The court shall enter an order of dismissal at plaintiff's costs if the plaintiff shall not show sufficient cause at or before such hearing. Dismissal may be withheld or reinstatement of dismissal may be made subject to the condition that the plaintiff comply with these rules and diligently prosecute the action and upon such terms that the court in its discretion determines to be necessary to assure such diligent prosecution.

Rule 42. Consolidation; Separate Trials

(a) Consolidation. When actions involving a common question of law or fact are pending before the court, it may order a joint hearing or trial of any or all the matters in issue in the actions; it may order all the actions consolidated; and it may make such orders concerning proceedings therein as may tend to avoid unnecessary costs or delay.

(b) Separate Trials. The court, in furtherance of convenience or to avoid prejudice, or when separate trials will be conducive to expedition and economy, may order a separate trial of any claim, cross-claim, counterclaim, or third-party claim, or of any separate issue or of any number of claims, cross-claims, counterclaims, third-party claims, or issues, always preserving inviolate the right of trial by jury as declared by the Seventh Amendment to the Constitution or as given by a statute of the United States.

Comparative State Provisions

(a) *Rule 42(a)*

New York Civil Practice Law and Rules 602

(a) Generally. When actions involving a common question of law or fact are pending before a court, the court, upon motion, may order a joint trial of any or all the matters in issue, may order the actions consolidated, and may make such other orders concerning proceedings therein as may tend to avoid unnecessary costs or delay.

(b) Cases pending in different courts. Where an action is pending in the supreme court it may, upon motion, remove to itself an action pending in another court and consolidate it or have it tried together with that in the supreme court. Where an action is pending in the county court, it may, upon motion, remove to itself an action pending in a city, municipal, district or justice court in the county and consolidate it or have it tried together with that in the county court.

New York Civil Practice Law and Rules 1002(c)

It shall not be necessary that each plaintiff be interested in obtaining, or each defendant be interested in defending against, all the relief demanded or as to every claim included in an action; but the court may make such orders as will prevent a party from being embarrassed, delayed, or put to expense by the inclusion of a party against whom he asserts no claim and, who asserts no claim against him, and may order separate trials or make other orders to prevent prejudice.

Rule 43.   Taking of Testimony

(a) Form. In every trial the testimony of witnesses shall be taken in open court, unless a federal law, these rules, the Federal Rules of Evidence, or other rules adopted by the Supreme Court provide otherwise. The court may, for good cause show in compelling circumstances and upon appropriate safeguards, permit presentation of testimony in open court by contemporaneous transmission from a different location.

(b), (c) [Abrogated]

(d) Affirmation in Lieu of Oath. Whenever under these rules an oath is required to be taken, a solemn affirmation may be accepted in lieu thereof.

(e) Evidence on Motions. When a motion is based on facts not appearing of record the court may hear the matter on affidavits presented by the respective parties, but the court may direct that the matter be heard wholly or partly on oral testimony or deposition.

(f) Interpreters. The court may appoint an interpreter of its own selection and may fix the interpreter's reasonable compensation. The compensation shall be paid out of funds provided by law or by one or more of the parties as the court may direct, and may be taxed ultimately as costs, in the discretion of the court.

Rule 44.   Proof of Official Record

(a) Authentication.

(1) *Domestic.* An official record kept within the United States, or any state, district, or commonwealth, or within a territory subject to the administrative or judicial jurisdiction of the United States, or an entry therein, when admissible for any purpose, may be evidenced by an official publication thereof or by a copy attested by the officer having the legal custody of the record, or by the officer's deputy, and accompanied by a certificate that such officer has the custody. The certificate may be made by a judge of a court of record of the district or political subdivision in which the record is kept, authenticated by the seal of the court, or may be made by any public officer having a seal of office and having official duties in the district or political subdivision in which the record is kept, authenticated by the seal of the officer's office.

(2) *Foreign.* A foreign official record, or an entry therein, when admissible for any purpose, may be evidenced by an official publication thereof; or a copy thereof, attested by a person authorized to make the attestation, and accompanied by a final certification as to the genuineness of the signature and official position (i) of the attesting person, or (ii) of any foreign official whose certificate of genuineness of signature and official position relates to the attestation or is in a chain of certificates of genuineness of signature and official position relating to the attestation. A final certification may be made by a secretary of embassy or legation, consul general, consul, vice consul, or consular agent of the United States, or a diplomatic or consular official of the foreign country assigned or accredited to the United States. If reasonable opportunity has been given to all parties to investigate the authenticity and accuracy of the documents, the court may, for good cause shown, (i) admit an attested copy without final certification or (ii) permit the foreign official record to be evidenced by an attested summary with or without a final certification. The final certification is unnecessary if the record and the attestation are certified as provided in a treaty or convention to which the United States and the foreign country in which the official record is located are parties.

(b) Lack of Record. A written statement that after diligent search no record or entry of a specified tenor is found to exist in the records of his office, designated by the statement, authenticated as provided in subdivision (a) (1) of this rule in the case of a domestic record, or complying with the requirements of subdivision (a) (2) of this rule for a summary in the case of a foreign record, is admissible as evidence that the records contain no such record or entry.

(c) Other Proof. This rule does not prevent the proof of official records or of entry or lack of entry therein by any other method authorized by law.

Rule 44.1   Determination of Foreign Law

A party who intends to raise an issue concerning the law of a foreign country shall give notice by pleadings or other reasonable written notice. The court, in determining foreign law, may consider any relevant material or source, including testimony, whether or not submitted by a party or admissible under the Federal Rules of Evidence. The court's determination shall be treated as a ruling on a question of law.

Notes by Advisory Committee on Adoption of Federal Rule 44.1

Rule 44.1 was added by amendment to furnish Federal courts with a uniform and effective procedure for raising and determining an issue concerning the law of a foreign country.

To avoid unfair surprise, the *first sentence* of the new rule requires that a party who intends to raise an issue of foreign law shall give notice thereof. The uncertainty under Rule 8(a) about whether foreign law must be pleaded * * * is eliminated by the provision that the notice shall be "written" and "reasonable."

It may, but need not be, incorporated in the pleadings. In some situations the pertinence of foreign law is apparent from the outset; accordingly the necessary investigation of that law will have been accomplished by the party at the pleading stage, and the notice can be given conveniently in the pleadings. In other situations the pertinence of foreign law may remain doubtful until the case is further developed. A requirement that notice of foreign law be given only through the medium of the pleadings would tend in the latter instances to force the party to engage in a peculiarly burdensome type of investigation which might turn out to be unnecessary; and correspondingly the adversary would be forced into a possibly wasteful investigation. * * *

The *second sentence* of the new rule describes the materials to which the court may resort in determining an issue of foreign law. Heretofore the district courts, applying Rule 43(a), have looked in certain cases to State law to find the rules of evidence by which the content of foreign-country law is to be established. The State laws vary; some embody procedures which are inefficient, time consuming, and expensive. * * * In all events the ordinary rules of evidence are often inapposite to the problem of determining foreign law and have in the past prevented examination of material which could have provided a proper basis for the determination. * * *

The new rule refrains from imposing an obligation on the court to take "judicial notice" of foreign law because this would put an extreme burden on the court in many cases; and it avoids use of the concept of "judicial notice" in any form because of the uncertain meaning of that concept as applied to foreign law. See, *e.g.,* Stern, *Foreign Law in the Courts: Judicial Notice and Proof,* 45 Calif.L.Rev. 23, 43 (1957). Rather the rule provides flexible procedures for presenting and utilizing material on issues of foreign law by which a sound result can be achieved with fairness to the parties.

Under the *third sentence,* the court's determination of an issue of foreign law is to be treated as a ruling on a question of "law," not "fact," so that appellate review will not be narrowly confined by the "clearly erroneous" standard of Rule 52(a). * * *

Rule 45. Subpoena

(a) Form; Issuance.

(1) Every subpoena shall

(A) state the name of the court from which it is issued; and

(B) state the title of the action, the name of the court in which it is pending, and its civil action number; and

(C) command each person to whom it is directed to attend and give testimony or to produce and permit inspection and copying of designated books, documents or tangible things in the possession, custody or control of that person, or to permit the inspection of premises, at a time and place therein specified; and

(D) set forth the text of subdivisions (c) and (d) of this rule.

A command to produce evidence or to permit inspection may be joined with a command to appear at trial or hearing or at deposition, or may be issued separately.

(2) A subpoena commanding attendance at a trial or hearing shall issue from the court for the district in which the hearing or trial is to be held. A subpoena for attendance at a deposition shall issue from the court for the district designated by the notice of deposition as the district

in which the deposition is to be taken. If separate from a subpoena commanding the attendance of a person, a subpoena for production or inspection shall issue from the court for the district in which the production or inspection is to be made.

(3) The clerk shall issue a subpoena, signed but otherwise in blank, to a party requesting it, who shall complete it before service. An attorney as officer of the court may also issue and sign a subpoena on behalf of

(A) a court in which the attorney is authorized to practice; or

(B) a court for a district in which a deposition or production is compelled by the subpoena, if the deposition or production pertains to an action pending in a court in which the attorney is authorized to practice.

(b) Service.

(1) A subpoena may be served by any person who is not a party and is not less than 18 years of age. Service of a subpoena upon a person named therein shall be made by delivering a copy thereof to such person and, if the person's attendance is commanded, by tendering to that person the fees for one day's attendance and the mileage allowed by law. When the subpoena is issued on behalf of the United States or an officer or agency thereof, fees and mileage need not be tendered. Prior notice of any commanded production of documents and things or inspection of premises before trial shall be served on each party in the manner prescribed by Rule 5(b).

(2) Subject to the provisions of clause (ii) of subparagraph (c)(3)(A) of this rule, a subpoena may be served at any place within the district of the court by which it is issued, or at any place without the district that is within 100 miles of the place of the deposition, hearing, trial, production, or inspection specified in the subpoena or at any place within the state where a state statute or rule of court permits service of a subpoena issued by a state court of general jurisdiction sitting in the place of the deposition, hearing, trial, production, or inspection specified in the subpoena. When a statute of the United States provides therefor, the court upon proper application and cause shown may authorize the service of a subpoena at any other place. A subpoena directed to a witness in a foreign country who is a national or resident of the United States shall issue under the circumstances and in the manner and be served as provided in Title 28, U.S.C. § 1783.

(3) Proof of service when necessary shall be made by filing with the clerk of the court by which the subpoena is issued a statement of the date and the manner of service and of the names of the persons served, certified by the person who made the service.

(c) Protection of Persons Subject to Subpoenas.

(1) A party or an attorney responsible for the issuance and service of a subpoena shall take reasonable steps to avoid imposing undue

burden or expense on a person subject to that subpoena. The court on behalf of which the subpoena was issued shall enforce this duty and impose upon the party or attorney in breach of this duty an appropriate sanction, which may include, but is not limited to, lost earnings and a reasonable attorney's fee.

(2)(A) A person commanded to produce and permit inspection and copying of designated books, papers, documents or tangible things, or inspection of premises need not appear in person at the place of production or inspection unless commanded to appear for deposition, hearing or trial.

(B) Subject to paragraph (d)(2) of this rule, a person commanded to produce and permit inspection and copying may, within 14 days after service of the subpoena or before the time specified for compliance if such time is less than 14 days after service, serve upon the party or attorney designated in the subpoena written objection to inspection or copying of any or all of the designated materials or of the premises. If objection is made, the party serving the subpoena shall not be entitled to inspect and copy the materials or inspect the premises except pursuant to an order of the court by which the subpoena was issued. If objection has been made, the party serving the subpoena may, upon notice to the person commanded to produce, move at any time for an order to compel the production. Such an order to compel production shall protect any person who is not a party or an officer of a party from significant expense resulting from the inspection and copying commanded.

(3)(A) On timely motion, the court by which a subpoena was issued shall quash or modify the subpoena if it

(i) fails to allow reasonable time for compliance;

(ii) requires a person who is not a party or an officer of a party to travel to a place more than 100 miles from the place where that person resides, is employed or regularly transacts business in person, except that, subject to provisions of clause (c)(3)(B)(iii) of this rule, such a person may in order to attend trial be commanded to travel from any such place within the state in which the trial is held, or

(iii) requires disclosure of privileged or other protected matter and no exception or waiver applies, or

(iv) subjects a person to undue burden.

(B) If a subpoena

(i) requires disclosure of a trade secret or other confidential research, development, or commercial information, or

(ii) requires disclosure of an unretained expert's opinion or information not describing specific events or occurrences in dispute and resulting from the expert's study made not at the request of any party, or

(iii) requires a person who is not a party or an officer of a party to incur substantial expense to travel more than 100 miles to attend trial,

the court may, to protect a person subject to or affected by the subpoena, quash or modify the subpoena or, if the party in whose behalf the subpoena is issued shows a substantial need for the testimony or material that cannot be otherwise met without undue hardship and assures that the person to whom the subpoena is addressed will be reasonably compensated, the court may order appearance or production only upon specified conditions.

(d) Duties in Responding to Subpoena.

(1) A person responding to a subpoena to produce documents shall produce them as they are kept in the usual course of business or shall organize and label them to correspond with the categories in the demand.

(2) When information subject to a subpoena is withheld on a claim that it is privileged or subject to protection as trial preparation materials, the claim shall be made expressly and shall be supported by a description of the nature of the documents, communications, or things not produced that is sufficient to enable the demanding party to contest the claim.

(e) Contempt.
Failure by any person without adequate excuse to obey a subpoena served upon that person may be deemed a contempt of the court from which the subpoena is issued. An adequate cause for failure to obey exists when a subpoena purports to require a non-party to attend or produce at a place not within the limits provided by clause (ii) of subparagraph (c)(3)(A).

Notes on Amendments to Federal Rule 45 and Comparative State Provisions

(a) *Amendments in 1991 to Rule 45*

In 1991 Rule 45 was modified in a number of significant respects. Rule 45(c)(2)(A) was added to provide that a subpoena may be issued for the production of documents and other items without requiring the person in possession to be summoned to a deposition as Rule 45 previously required. Indeed current Rule 45(c) was entirely new and was added to provide protection for any person who has been served with a subpoena. The purpose of the provision is to ensure that such a person be given reasonable time to comply and not be faced with other undue burdens.

(b) *Comparative State Provisions*

Nebraska Revised Statutes § 25–1223

The clerks of the several courts and judges of the county courts shall, on application of any person having a cause or any matter pending in court, issue a subpoena for witnesses, under the seal of the court, inserting all the names required by the applicant in one subpoena, which may be served by any person not interested in the action, or by the sheriff, coroner or constable * * *.

Nebraska Revised Statutes § 25–1224

The subpoena shall be directed to the person therein named, requiring him to attend at a particular time and place, to testify as a witness; and it may contain a clause directing the witness to bring with him any book, writing or other thing under his control, which he is bound by law to produce as evidence.

Nebraska Revised Statutes § 25–1227(1)

Witnesses in civil cases cannot be compelled to attend a trial out of the state where they are served or at a distance of more than one hundred miles from the place of their residence or from the place where they are served with a subpoena, unless within the same county. Witnesses in civil cases shall not be obliged to attend a deposition outside the county of their residence, or outside the county where the subpoena is served.

Nebraska Revised Statutes § 25–1228(1)

* * * [A] witness may demand his traveling fees, and fee for one day's attendance, when the subpoena is served upon him, and if the same be not paid the witness shall not be obliged to obey the subpoena. * * *

See also New York Civil Practice Law and Rules 3120(b) as set out following Federal Rule 34, supra.

Rule 46. Exceptions Unnecessary

Formal exceptions to rulings or orders of the court are unnecessary; but for all purposes for which an exception has heretofore been necessary it is sufficient that a party, at the time the ruling or order of the court is made or sought, makes known to the court the action which the party desires the court to take or the party's objection to the action of the court and the grounds therefor; and, if a party has no opportunity to object to a ruling or order at the time it is made, the absence of an objection does not thereafter prejudice the party.

Rule 47. Jurors

(a) Examination of Jurors. The court may permit the parties or their attorneys to conduct the examination of prospective jurors or may itself conduct the examination. In the latter event, the court shall permit the parties or their attorneys to supplement the examination by such further inquiry as it deems proper or shall itself submit to the prospective jurors such additional questions of the parties or their attorneys as it deems proper.

(b) Peremptory Challenges. The court shall allow the number of peremptory challenges provided by 28 U.S.C. § 1870.

(c) Excuse. The court may for good cause excuse a juror from service during trial or deliberation.

Comparative State Provisions

California Rule of Court 228

This rule applies to all civil jury trials. To select a fair and impartial jury, the trial judge shall examine the prospective jurors orally or by written questionnaire, or by both methods. * * * Upon completion of the initial examination, the trial judge shall permit counsel for each party who so requests to submit additional questions which the judge shall put to the jurors. Upon request of counsel, the trial judge shall permit counsel to supplement the judge's examination by oral and direct questioning of any of the prospective jurors. The scope of the additional questions or supplemental examination shall be within reasonable limits prescribed by the trial judge in the judge's sound discretion.

The court may, upon stipulation by counsel for all parties appearing in the action, permit counsel to examine the prospective jurors outside a judge's presence.

South Carolina Code § 14–7–1020

The court shall, on motion of either party in the suit, examine on oath any person who is called as a juror to know whether he is related to either party, has any interest in the cause, has expressed or formed any opinion, or is sensible of any bias or prejudice therein, and the party objecting to the juror may introduce any other competent evidence in support of the objection. If it appears to the court that the juror is not indifferent in the cause, he must be placed aside as to the trial of that cause and another must be called.

Rule 48. Number of Jurors—Participation in Verdict

The court shall seat a jury of not fewer than six and not more than twelve members and all jurors shall participate in the verdict unless excused from service by the court pursuant to Rule 47(c). Unless the parties otherwise stipulate, (1) the verdict shall be unanimous and (2) no verdict shall be taken from a jury reduced in size to fewer than six members.

Comparative State Provisions

Minnesota Constitution Art. 1, § 4

The right of trial by jury shall remain inviolate, and shall extend to all cases at law without regard to the amount in controversy. A jury trial may be waived by the parties in all cases in the manner prescribed by law. The legislature may provide that the agreement of five-sixths of a jury in a civil action or proceeding, after not less than six hours' deliberation, is a sufficient verdict. The legislature may provide for the number of jurors in a civil action or proceeding, provided that the jury have at least six members.

Virginia Code § 8.01–359

A. Five persons from a panel of eleven shall constitute a jury in a civil case when the amount involved exclusive of interest and costs does not exceed [specified] jurisdictional limits. ... Seven persons from a panel of thirteen shall constitute a jury in all other civil cases except that when a special jury is allowed, twelve persons from a panel of twenty shall constitute the jury.

* * *

D. In any civil case in which the consent of the plaintiff and defendant shall be entered of record, it shall be lawful for the plaintiff to select one person who is eligible as a juror and for the defendant to select another, and for the two so selected to select a third of like qualifications, and the three so selected shall constitute a jury in the case. They shall take the oath required of jurors, and hear and determine the issue, and any two concurring shall render a verdict in like manner and with like effect as a jury of seven.

Rule 49.   Special Verdicts and Interrogatories

(a) **Special Verdicts.**   The court may require a jury to return only a special verdict in the form of a special written finding upon each issue of fact.   In that event the court may submit to the jury written questions susceptible of categorical or other brief answer or may submit written forms of the several special findings which might properly be made under the pleadings and evidence;   or it may use such other method of submitting the issues and requiring the written findings thereon as it deems most appropriate.   The court shall give to the jury such explanation and instruction concerning the matter thus submitted as may be necessary to enable the jury to make its findings upon each issue.   If in so doing the court omits any issue of fact raised by the pleadings or by the evidence, each party waives the right to a trial by jury of the issue so omitted unless before the jury retires the party demands its submission to the jury.   As to an issue omitted without such demand the court may make a finding;   or, if it fails to do so, it shall be deemed to have made a finding in accord with the judgment on the special verdict.

(b) **General Verdict Accompanied by Answer to Interrogatories.**   The court may submit to the jury, together with appropriate forms for a general verdict, written interrogatories upon one or more issues of fact the decision of which is necessary to a verdict.   The court shall give such explanation or instruction as may be necessary to enable the jury both to make answers to the interrogatories and to render a general verdict, and the court shall direct the jury both to make written answers and to render a general verdict.   When the general verdict and the answers are harmonious, the appropriate judgment upon the verdict and answers shall be entered pursuant to Rule 58.   When the answers are consistent with each other but one or more is inconsistent with the general verdict, judgment may be entered pursuant to Rule 58 in accordance with the answers, notwithstanding the general verdict, or the court may return the jury for further consideration of its answers and verdict or may order a new trial.   When the answers are inconsistent with each other and one or more is likewise inconsistent with the general verdict, judgment shall not be entered, but the court shall return the jury for further consideration of its answers and verdict or shall order a new trial.

Comparative State Provisions

Wisconsin Statutes Annotated § 805.12(1)

Unless it orders otherwise, the court shall direct the jury to return a special verdict.   The verdict shall be prepared by the court in the form of written questions relating only to material issues of ultimate fact and admitting a direct answer.   The jury shall answer in writing.   In cases founded upon negligence, the court need not submit separately any particular respect in which the party was allegedly negligent.   The court may also direct the jury to find upon particular questions of fact.

Wisconsin Statutes Annotated § 805.12(2)

When some material issue of ultimate fact not brought to the attention of the trial court but essential to sustain the judgment is omitted from the verdict, the issue shall be deemed determined by the court in conformity with its judgment and the failure to request a finding by the jury on the issue shall be deemed a waiver of jury trial on that issue.

Rule 50. Judgment as a Matter of Law in Jury Trials; Alternative Motion for New Trial; Conditional Rulings

(a) Judgment as a Matter of Law.

(1) If during a trial by jury a party has been fully heard on an issue and there is no legally sufficient evidentiary basis for a reasonable jury to find for that party on that issue, the court may determine the issue against that party and may grant a motion for judgment as a matter of law against that party with respect to a claim or defense that cannot under the controlling law be maintained or defeated without a favorable finding on that issue.

(2) Motions for judgment as a matter of law may be made at any time before submission of the case to the jury. Such a motion shall specify the judgment sought and the law and the facts on which the moving party is entitled to the judgment.

(b) Renewing Motion for Judgment After Trial; Alternative Motion for New Trial.
If, for any reason, the court does not grant a motion for judgment as a matter of law made at the close of all the evidence, the court is considered to have submitted the action to the jury subject to the court's later deciding the legal questions raised by the motion. The movant may renew its request for judgment as a matter of law by filing a motion no later than 10 days after entry of judgment—and may alternatively request a new trial or join a motion for a new trial under Rule 59. In ruling on a renewed motion, the court may:

(1) if a verdict was returned;

    (A) allow the judgment to stand,

    (B) order a new trial, or

    (C) direct entry of judgment as a matter of law;

or

(2) if no verdict was returned;

    (A) order a new trial, or

    (B) direct entry of judgment as a matter of law.

(c) Granting Renewed Motion for Judgment as a Matter of Law; Conditional Rulings; New Trial Motion.

(1) If the renewed motion for judgment as a matter of law is granted, the court shall also rule on the motion for a new trial, if any, by determining whether it should be granted if the judgment is thereafter

137

vacated or reversed, and shall specify the grounds for granting or denying the motion for the new trial. If the motion for a new trial is thus conditionally granted, the order thereon does not affect the finality of the judgment. In case the motion for a new trial has been conditionally granted and the judgment is reversed on appeal, the new trial shall proceed unless the appellate court has otherwise ordered. In case the motion for a new trial has been conditionally denied, the order thereon does not affect the finality of the judgment. In case the motion for a new trial has been conditionally granted, the appellee on appeal may assert error in that denial; and if the judgment is reversed on appeal, subsequent proceedings shall be in accordance with the order of the appellate court.

(2) Any motion for a new trial under Rule 59 by a party against whom judgment as a matter of law is rendered shall be filed no later than 10 days after entry of the judgment.

(d) Same: Denial of Motion for Judgment as a Matter of Law. If the motion for judgment as a matter of law is denied, the party who prevailed on that motion may, as appellee, assert grounds entitling the party to a new trial in the event the appellate court concludes that the trial court erred in denying the motion for judgment. If the appellate court reverses the judgment, nothing in this rule precludes it from determining that the appellee is entitled to a new trial, or from directing the trial court to determine whether a new trial shall be granted.

Comparative State Provisions and Notes on Amendments to Federal Rule 50

(a) *Rules 50(a) and (b)—Comparative State Provisions*

New York Civil Practice Law and Rules 4404(a)

After a trial of a cause of action or issue triable of right by a jury, upon the motion of any party or on its own initiative, the court may set aside a verdict or any judgment entered thereon and direct that judgment be entered in favor of a party entitled to judgment as a matter of law or it may order a new trial of a cause of action or separable issue where the verdict is contrary to the weight of the evidence, in the interest of justice or where the jury cannot agree after being kept together for as long as is deemed reasonable by the court.

Indiana Rules of Trial Procedure, Trial Rule 50

(A) Where all or some of the issues in a case tried before a jury or an advisory jury are not supported by sufficient evidence or a verdict thereon is clearly erroneous as contrary to the evidence because the evidence is insufficient to support it, the court shall withdraw such issues from the jury and enter judgment thereon or shall enter judgment thereon notwithstanding a verdict. * * *

(B) Every case tried by a jury is made subject to the right of the court, before or after the jury is discharged, to enter final judgment on the evidence, without directing a verdict thereon.

(b) *Notes on Amendments in 1963 Adding Rules 50(c) and (d)*

The Advisory Committee commented on Rules 50(c) and (d), which were added in 1963, as follows:

Subdivision (c) deals with the situation where a party joins a motion for a new trial with his motion for judgment n.o.v., or prays for a new trial in the alternative, and the motion for judgment n.o.v. is granted. The procedure to be followed in making rulings on the motion for the new trial, and the consequences of the rulings thereon, were partly set out in *Montgomery Ward & Co. v. Duncan,* 311 U.S. 243, 253, 61 S.Ct. 189, 85 L.Ed. 147 (1940), and have been further elaborated in later cases. * * * However, courts as well as counsel have often misunderstood the procedure, and it will be helpful to summarize the proper practice in the text of the rule. The amendments do not alter the effects of a jury verdict or the scope of appellate review.

In the situation mentioned, *subdivision (c)(1)* requires that the court make a "conditional" ruling on the new-trial motion, *i.e.,* a ruling which goes on the assumption that the motion for judgment n. o. v. was erroneously granted and will be reversed or vacated; and the court is required to state its grounds for the conditional ruling. Subdivision (c)(1) then spells out the consequences of a reversal of the judgment in the light of the conditional ruling on the new-trial motion.

If the motion for new trial has been conditionally granted, and the judgment is reversed, "the new trial shall proceed unless the appellate court has otherwise ordered." The party against whom the judgment n.o.v. was entered below may, as appellant, besides seeking to overthrow that judgment, also attack the conditional grant of the new trial. And the appellate court, if it reverses the judgment n. o. v., may in an appropriate case also reverse the conditional grant of the new trial and direct that judgment be entered on the verdict. * * *

If the motion for a new trial has been conditionally denied, and the judgment is reversed, "subsequent proceedings shall be in accordance with the order of the appellate court." The party in whose favor judgment n. o. v. was entered below may, as appellee, besides seeking to uphold that judgment, also urge on the appellate court that the trial court committed error in conditionally denying the new trial. The appellee may assert this error in his brief, without taking a cross-appeal. * * * If the appellate court concludes that the judgment cannot stand, but accepts the appellee's contention that there was error in the conditional denial of the new trial, it may order a new trial in lieu of directing the entry of judgment upon the verdict.

Subdivision (c)(2), which also deals with the situation where the trial court has granted the motion for judgment n. o. v., states that the verdict-winner may apply to the trial court for a new trial pursuant to Rule 59 after the judgment n. o. v. has been entered against him. In arguing to the trial court in opposition to the motion for judgment n. o. v., the verdict-winner may, and often will, contend that he is entitled, at the least, to a new trial, and the court has a range of discretion to grant a new trial or (where plaintiff won the verdict) to order a dismissal of the action without prejudice instead of granting judgment n. o. v. * * *

Subdivision (d) deals with the situation where judgment has been entered on the jury verdict, the motion for judgment n. o. v. and any motion for a new trial having been denied by the trial court. The verdict-winner, as appellee, besides seeking to uphold the judgment, may urge upon the appellate court that in case the trial court is found to have erred in entering judgment on the verdict, there are grounds for granting him a new trial instead of directing the entry of judgment for his opponent. In appropriate cases the appellate court is not precluded from itself directing that a new trial be had. * * *

Rule 51. Instructions to Jury: Objection

At the close of the evidence or at such earlier time during the trial as the court reasonably directs, any party may file written requests that the court instruct the jury on the law as set forth in the requests. The court shall inform counsel of its proposed action upon the requests prior to their arguments to the jury. The court, at its election, may instruct the jury before or after argument, or both.   No party may assign as error the giving or the failure to give an instruction unless that party objects thereto before the jury retires to consider its verdict, stating distinctly the matter objected to and the grounds of the objection.   Opportunity shall be given to make the objection out of the hearing of the jury.

critical

Notes on Amendment to Federal Rule 51 and Comparative State Provisions

(a) *1987 Amendment to Federal Rule 51*

In 1987, on recommendation of the Advisory Committee, Rule 51 was amended to give the court discretion to instruct the jury either before or after the argument.   See generally Raymond, *Merits and Demerits of the Missouri System of Instructing Juries*, 5 St. Louis U.L.J. 317 (1959).

(b) *Comparative State Provisions*

Georgia Code Annotated § 5-5-24

(a) Except as otherwise provided in this Code section, in all civil cases, no party may complain of the giving or the failure to give an instruction to the jury unless he objects thereto before the jury returns its verdict, stating distinctly the matter to which he objects and the grounds of his objection.   Opportunity shall be given to make the objection out of the hearing of the jury.   Objection need not be made with the particularity formerly required of assignments of error and need only be as reasonably definite as the circumstances will permit.   * * *

(b) In all cases, at the close of the evidence or at such earlier time during the trial as the court reasonably directs, any party may present to the court written requests that it instruct the jury on the law as set forth therein.   Copies of requests shall be given to opposing counsel for their consideration prior to the charge of the court.   The court shall inform counsel of its proposed action upon the requests prior to their arguments to the jury but shall instruct the jury after the arguments are completed.   The trial judge shall file with the clerk all requests submitted to him, whether given in charge or not.

(c) Notwithstanding any other provision of this Code section, the appellate courts shall consider and review erroneous charges where there has been a substantial error in the charge which was harmful as a matter of law, regardless of whether objection was made hereunder or not.

Minnesota Rule of Civil Procedure 51

At the close of the evidence or at such earlier time during the trial as the court reasonably directs, any party may file written requests that the court instruct the jury on the law as set forth in the requests.   The court shall inform counsel of its proposed action upon the requests prior to their arguments to the jury, and such action shall be made a part of the record.   The court shall instruct the jury before or after closing arguments of counsel except, in the discretion of the court, preliminary instructions need not be repeated.   The instructions may be in writing and, in the discretion of the court, one or more complete copies may be taken to the jury room when the jury retires to deliberate.   No party may assign as error unintentional misstatements and verbal errors or omissions in the charge, unless that party objects thereto before the jury retires to consider its verdict, stating specifically the matter to which that party objects and the ground of the objections.   An error in the instructions with respect to fundamental law or controlling principle may be assigned in a motion for a new trial although it was not otherwise called to the attention of the court.

Mississippi Code Annotated § 11-7-155

The judge in any civil cause shall not sum up or comment on the testimony, or charge the jury as to the weight of evidence.

Illinois Supreme Court Rule 239

(a) Use of IPI Instructions; Requirements of Other Instructions. Whenever Illinois Pattern Jury Instructions (IPI) contains an instruction applicable in a civil case, giving due consideration to the facts and the prevailing law, and the court determines that the jury should be instructed on the subject, the IPI instruction shall be used, unless the court determines that it does not accurately state the law. Whenever IPI does not contain an instruction on a subject on which the court determines that the jury should be instructed, the instruction given in that subject should be simple, brief, impartial, and free from argument.

(b) Court's Instructions. At any time before or during the trial, the court may direct counsel to prepare designated instructions. Counsel shall comply with the direction and copies of instructions so prepared shall be marked "Court's Instruction." Counsel may object at the conference on instructions to any instruction prepared at the court's direction, regardless of who prepared it, and the court shall rule on these objections as well as objections to other instructions. The grounds of the objections shall be particularly specified.

(c) Procedure. Each instruction shall be accompanied by a copy, and a copy shall be delivered to opposing counsel. In addition to numbering the copies and indicating who tendered them, as required by section 2–1107 of the Code of Civil Procedure, the copy shall contain a notation substantially as follows:

"IPI No. _____" or "IPI No. _____ Modified" or "Not in IPI" as the case may be. All objections made at the conference and the rulings thereon shall be shown in the report of proceedings. The original instructions given by the court to the jury shall be taken by the jury to the jury room.

* * *

Rule 52. Findings by the Court; Judgment on Partial Findings

(a) Effect. In all actions tried upon the facts without a jury or with an advisory jury, the court shall find the facts specially and state separately its conclusions of law thereon, and judgment shall be entered pursuant to Rule 58; and in granting or refusing interlocutory injunctions the court shall similarly set forth the findings of fact and conclusions of law which constitute the grounds of its action. Requests for findings are not necessary for purposes of review. Findings of fact, whether based on oral or documentary evidence, shall not be set aside unless clearly erroneous, and due regard shall be given to the opportunity of the trial court to judge of the credibility of the witnesses. The findings of a master, to the extent that the court adopts them, shall be considered as the findings of the court. It will be sufficient if the findings of fact and conclusions of law are stated orally and recorded in open court following the close of the evidence or appear in an opinion or memorandum of decision filed by the court. Findings of fact and conclusions of law are unnecessary on decisions of motions under Rules 12 or 56 or any other motion except as provided in subdivision (c) of this rule.

(b) Amendment. On a party's motion filed no later than 10 days after entry of judgment, the court may amend its findings—or make additional findings—and may amend the judgment accordingly. The motion may accompany a motion for a new trial under Rule 59. When findings of fact are made in actions tried without a jury, the sufficiency of the evidence supporting the findings may be later questioned whether or not in the district court the party raising the question objected to the findings, moved to amend them, or moved for partial findings.

(c) Judgment on Partial Findings. If during a trial without a jury a party has been fully heard on an issue and the court finds against the party on that issue, the court may enter judgment as a matter of law against that party with respect to a claim or defense that cannot under the controlling law be maintained or defeated without a favorable finding on that issue, or the court may decline to render any judgment until the close of all the evidence. Such a judgment shall be supported by findings of fact and conclusions of law as required by subdivision (a) of this rule.

Notes on Amendments to Rule 52 and Comparative State Provisions

(a) Amendment in 1985

The purpose of the 1985 amendment was to make certain that the "clearly erroneous" standard applies when the trial court's decision is based solely on documentary evidence as well as when it is based on oral testimony. Previously, appellate courts were divided on the matter, some holding that the scope of review is broader when witness credibility is not involved. The change was designed to support the integrity of the trial court's findings of fact, thus to promote judicial economy by discouraging retrial at the appellate level.

(b) Amendment in 1983

Rule 52(a) was amended to provide explicitly that the district judge may make the findings of fact and conclusions of law required in nonjury cases orally. The objective is to lighten the burden on the trial court in preparing findings in nonjury cases. It should also reduce the number of published district court opinions that embrace written findings.

(c) Comparative State Provision

Oklahoma Statutes Annotated Tit. 12, § 611

Upon the trial of questions of fact by the court, it shall not be necessary for the court to state its findings, except generally, for the plaintiff or defendant, unless one of the parties request it, with the view of excepting to the decision of the court upon the questions of law involved in the trial; in which case the court shall state, in writing, the findings of fact found, separately from the conclusions of law.

Rule 53. Masters

(a) Appointment and Compensation. The court in which any action is pending may appoint a special master therein. As used in these rules the word "master" includes a referee, an auditor, an examiner, and an assessor. The compensation to be allowed to a master shall be fixed by the court, and shall be charged upon such of the parties or paid out of any fund or subject matter of the action, which is in the custody and control of the court as the court may direct; provided that this provision for compensation shall not apply when a United States magistrate judge is designated to serve as a master. The master shall not retain the master's report as security for the master's compensation; but when the party ordered to pay the compensation allowed by the court does not pay it after notice and within the time prescribed by the court, the master is entitled to a writ of execution against the delinquent party.

(b) Reference. A reference to a master shall be the exception and not the rule. In actions to be tried by a jury, a reference shall be made only when the issues are complicated; in actions to be tried without a jury, save in matters of account and of difficult computation of damages, a reference shall be made only upon a showing that some exceptional condition requires it. Upon the consent of the parties, a magistrate judge may be designated to serve as a special master without regard to the provisions of this subdivision.

(c) Powers. The order of reference to the master may specify or limit the master's powers and may direct the master to report only upon particular issues or to do or perform particular acts or to receive and report evidence only and may fix the time and place for beginning and closing the hearings and for the filing of the master's report. Subject to the specifications and limitations stated in the order, the master has and shall exercise the power to regulate all proceedings in every hearing before the master and to do all acts and take all measures necessary or proper for the efficient performance of the master's duties under the order. The master may require the production before the master of evidence upon all matters embraced in the reference, including the production of all books, papers, vouchers, documents, and writings applicable thereto. The master may rule upon the admissibility of evidence unless otherwise directed by the order of reference and has the authority to put witnesses on oath and may examine them and may call the parties to the action and examine them upon oath. When a party so requests, the master shall make a record of the evidence offered and excluded in the same manner and subject to the same limitations as provided in the Federal Rules of Evidence for a court sitting without a jury.

(d) Proceedings.

(1) *Meetings.* When a reference is made, the clerk shall forthwith furnish the master with a copy of the order of reference. Upon receipt thereof unless the order of reference otherwise provides, the master shall forthwith set a time and place for the first meeting of the parties or their attorneys to be held within 20 days after the date of the order of reference and shall notify the parties or their attorneys. It is the duty of the master to proceed with all reasonable diligence. Either party, on notice to the parties and master, may apply to the court for an order requiring the master to speed the proceedings and to make the report. If a party fails to appear at the time and place appointed, the master may proceed ex parte or, in the master's discretion, adjourn the proceedings to a future day, giving notice to the absent party of the adjournment.

(2) *Witnesses.* The parties may procure the attendance of witnesses before the master by the issuance and service of subpoenas as provided in Rule 45. If without adequate excuse a witness fails to appear or give evidence, the witness may be punished as for a contempt and be subjected to the consequences, penalties, and remedies provided in Rules 37 and 45.

(3) *Statement of Accounts.* When matters of accounting are in issue before the master, the master may prescribe the form in which the accounts shall be submitted and in any proper case may require or receive in evidence a statement by a certified public accountant who is called as a witness. Upon objection of a party to any of the items thus submitted or upon a showing that the form of statement is insufficient, the master may require a different form of statement to be furnished, or the accounts or specific items thereof to be proved by oral examination of the accounting parties or upon written interrogatories or in such other manner as the master directs.

(e) Report.

(1) *Contents and Filing.* The master shall prepare a report upon the matters submitted to the master by the order of reference and, if required to make findings of fact and conclusions of law, the master shall set them forth in the report. The master shall file the report with the clerk of the court and serve on all parties notice of the filing. In an action to be tried without a jury, unless otherwise directed by the order of reference, the master shall file with the report a transcript of the proceedings and of the evidence and the original exhibits. Unless otherwise directed by the order of reference, the master shall serve a copy of the report on each party.

(2) *In Non-jury Actions.* In an action to be tried without a jury the court shall accept the master's findings of fact unless clearly erroneous. Within 10 days after being served with notice of the filing of the report any party may serve written objections thereto upon the other parties. Application to the court for action upon the report and upon objections thereto shall be by motion and upon notice as prescribed in Rule 6(d). The court after hearing may adopt the report or may modify it or may reject it in whole or in part or may receive further evidence or may recommit it with instructions.

(3) *In Jury Actions.* In an action to be tried by a jury the master shall not be directed to report the evidence. The master's findings upon the issues submitted to the master are admissible as evidence of the matters found and may be read to the jury, subject to the ruling of the court upon any objections in point of law which may be made to the report.

(4) *Stipulation as to Findings.* The effect of a master's report is the same whether or not the parties have consented to the reference; but, when the parties stipulate that a master's findings of fact shall be final,

only questions of law arising upon the report shall thereafter be considered.

(5) *Draft Report.* Before filing the master's report a master may submit a draft thereof to counsel for all parties for the purpose of receiving their suggestions.

(f) Application to Magistrate Judge. A magistrate judge is subject to this rule only when the order referring a matter to the magistrate judge expressly provides that the reference is made under this Rule.

Amendments to Rule 53 and Comparative State Provisions

(a) *Amendments in 1983 to Rule 53*

Because the federal courts now have full time magistrates, serving at government expense, the changes eliminated as unnecessary a clause of the first sentence in Rule 53(a) providing for "standing masters."

In addition Rule 53(b) was altered to provide that upon consent of the parties a magistrate may be appointed to serve as a special master even though "exceptional circumstances" do not exist. The latter requirement would still apply to appointment of others for whose services the parties would be required to pay.

The new subdivision (f) responded to the confusion resulting from the dual authority for references of pretrial matters to magistrates. Under the rule, the appointment of a master, without consent of the parties, to supervise discovery would require some exceptional condition (Rule 53(b)) and would subject the proceedings to the report procedures of Rule 53(e). This subdivision, therefore, establishes a presumption that the limitations of Rule 53 are not applicable unless the reference is specifically made subject to Rule 53.

(b) *Comparative State Provisions*

(1) *Rules 53(a) and (b)*

New York Civil Practice Law and Rules 4317

(a) Upon consent of the parties. The parties may stipulate that any issue shall be determined by a referee. Upon the filing of the stipulation with the clerk, the clerk shall forthwith enter an order referring the issue for trial to the referee named therein. * * *

(b) Without consent of the parties. On motion of any party or on its own initiative, the court may order a reference to determine a cause of action or an issue where the trial will require the examination of a long account, including actions to foreclose mechanic's liens; or to determine an issue of damages separately triable and not requiring a trial by jury; or where otherwise authorized by law.

(2) *Rules 53(c)(2) and (3)*

New Jersey Civil Practice Rule 4:41–5(b) & (c)

(b) In an action to be tried without a jury the court shall accept the master's findings of fact unless contrary to the weight of the evidence. * * *

(c) In an action to be tried by a jury the findings of the master upon the issues submitted to him are admissible as evidence of the matters found, and may together with the evidence taken before the master be read to the jury, subject to the ruling of the court upon objections to the report or the evidence.

VII. JUDGMENT

Rule 54. Judgments; Costs

(a) Definition; Form. "Judgment" as used in these rules includes a decree and any order from which an appeal lies. A judgment shall not contain a recital of pleadings, the report of a master, or the record of prior proceedings.

(b) Judgment Upon Multiple Claims or Involving Multiple Parties. When more than one claim for relief is presented in an action, whether as a claim, counterclaim, cross-claim, or third-party claim, or when multiple parties are involved, the court may direct the entry of a final judgment as to one or more but fewer than all of the claims or parties only upon an express determination that there is no just reason for delay and upon an express direction for the entry of judgment. In the absence of such determination and direction, any order or other form of decision, however designated, which adjudicates fewer than all the claims or the rights and liabilities of fewer than all the parties shall not terminate the action as to any of the claims or parties, and the order or other form of decision is subject to revision at any time before the entry of judgment adjudicating all the claims and the rights and liabilities of all the parties.

(c) Demand for Judgment. A judgment by default shall not be different in kind from or exceed in amount that prayed for in the demand for judgment. Except as to a party against whom a judgment is entered by default, every final judgment shall grant the relief to which the party in whose favor it is rendered is entitled, even if the party has not demanded such relief in the party's pleadings.

(d) Costs; Attorneys' Fees.

(1) *Costs Other Than Attorneys' Fees.* Except when express provision therefor is made either in a statute of the United States or in these rules, costs other than attorneys' fees shall be allowed as of course to the prevailing party unless the court otherwise directs; but costs against the United States, its officers, and agencies shall be imposed only to the extent permitted by law. Such costs may be taxed by the clerk on one day's notice. On motion served within 5 days thereafter, the action of the clerk may be reviewed by the court.

(2) *Attorneys' Fees.*

(A) Claims for attorneys' fees and related nontaxable expenses shall be made by motion unless the substantive law governing the action provides for the recovery of such fees as an element of damages to be proved at trial.

(B) Unless otherwise provided by statute or order of the court, the motion must be filed and served no later than 14 days after the entry of judgment; must specify the judgment and the statute, rule, or other grounds entitling the moving party to the award; and must state the amount or provide a fair estimate of the amount sought. If directed by the court, the motion shall also disclose the terms of any agreement with respect to fees to be paid for the services for which the claim is made.

(C) On request of a party or class member, the court shall afford an opportunity for adversary submissions with respect to the motion in accordance with Rule 43(e) or Rule 78. The court may determine issues of liability for fees before receiving submissions bearing on issues of evaluation of services for which liability is imposed by the court. The court shall find the facts and state its conclusions of law as provided in Rule 52(a), and a judgment shall be set forth in a separate document as provided in Rule 58.

(D) By local rule the court may establish special procedures by which issues relating to such fees may be resolved without extensive evidentiary hearings. In addition, the court may refer issues relating to the value of services to a special master under Rule 53 without regard to the provisions of subdivision (b) thereof and may refer a motion for attorneys' fees to a magistrate judge under Rule 72(b) as if it were a dispositive pretrial matter.

(E) The provisions of subparagraphs (A) through (D) do not apply to claims for fees and expenses as sanctions for violations of these rules or under 28 U.S.C. § 1927.

Notes on Amendments to Federal Rule 54 and Comparative State Provisions

(a) Amendments in 1948 to Rule 54(b)

Rule 54(b) originally read as follows:

When more than one claim for relief is presented in an action, the court at any stage, upon a determination of the issues material to a particular claim and all counterclaims arising out of the transaction or occurrence which is the subject matter of the claim, may enter a judgment disposing of such claim. The judgment shall terminate the action with respect to the claim so disposed of and the action shall proceed as to the remaining claims. In case a separate judgment is so entered, the court by order may stay its enforcement until the entering of a subsequent judgment or judgments and may prescribe such conditions as are necessary to secure the benefit thereof to the party in whose favor the judgment is entered.

In 1946 the Advisory Committee commented as follows on proposed amendments to the Rule which were promulgated in 1948:

The historic rule in the federal courts has always prohibited piecemeal disposal of litigation * * *. Rule 54(b) was originally adopted in view of the wide scope and possible content of the newly created "civil action" in order to avoid the possible injustice of a delay in judgment of a distinctly separate claim to await adjudication of the entire case. It was not designed to overturn the settled federal rule stated above * * *.

Unfortunately, this was not always understood, and some confusion ensued. Hence situations arose where district courts made a piecemeal disposition of an action and entered what the parties thought amounted to a judgment, although a trial remained to be had on other claims similar or identical with those disposed of. In the interim the parties did not know their ultimate rights, and accordingly took an appeal, thus putting the finality of the partial judgment in question. While most appellate courts have reached a result generally in accord with the intent of the rule, yet there have been divergent precedents and division of views which have served to render the issues more clouded to the parties appellant. It hardly seems a case where multiplicity of precedents will tend to remove the problem from debate. * * *

In view of the difficulty thus disclosed, the Advisory Committee * * * attempted to redefine the original rule with particular stress upon the interlocutory nature of partial judgments which did not adjudicate all claims arising out of a single transaction or occurrence. * * * The Committee, however, became convinced on careful study of its own proposals that the seeds of ambiguity still remained, and that it had not completely solved the problem of piecemeal appeals. After extended consideration, it concluded that a retention of the older federal rule was desirable, and that this rule needed only the exercise of a discretionary power to afford a remedy in the infrequent harsh case to provide a simple, definite, workable rule. * * *

In 1961 the Advisory Committee again commented as follows:

A serious difficulty has * * * arisen because the rule speaks of claims but nowhere mentions parties. A line of cases had developed in the circuits consistently holding the rule to be inapplicable to the dismissal, even with the requisite trial court determination, of one or more but fewer than all defendants jointly charged in an action, *i.e.,* charged with various forms of concerted or related wrongdoing or related liability. * * * For purposes of Rule 54(b) it was arguable that there were as many "claims" as there were parties defendant and that the rule in its present text applied where fewer than all of the parties were dismissed, * * * but the Courts of Appeals are now committed to an opposite view.

* * *

(b) *Comparative State Provisions*

1. *Rule 54(b)*

Texas Rule of Civil Procedure 301

* * * Only one final judgment shall be rendered in any cause except where it is otherwise specially provided by law. Judgment may, in a proper case, be given for or against one or more of several plaintiffs, and for or against one or more of several defendants or intervenors.

2. *Rule 54(c)*

Georgia Code Annotated § 9–11–54(c)(1)

A judgment by default shall not be different in kind from or exceed in amount that prayed for in the demand for judgment. Except as to a party against whom a judgment is entered by default, every final judgment shall grant the relief to which the party in whose favor it is rendered is entitled, even if the party has not demanded such relief in his pleadings; but the court shall not give the successful party relief, though he may be entitled to it, where the propriety of the relief was not litigated and the opposing party had no opportunity to assert defenses to such relief.

Rule 55.   Default

(a) Entry. When a party against whom a judgment for affirmative relief is sought has failed to plead or otherwise defend as provided by these rules and that fact is made to appear by affidavit or otherwise, the clerk shall enter the party's default.

(b) Judgment. Judgment by default may be entered as follows:

(1) *By the Clerk.* When the plaintiff's claim against a defendant is for a sum certain or for a sum which can by computation be made certain, the clerk upon request of the plaintiff and upon affidavit of the amount due shall enter judgment for that amount and costs against the defendant, if the defendant has been defaulted for failure to appear and is not an infant or incompetent person.

(2) *By the Court.* In all other cases the party entitled to a judgment by default shall apply to the court therefor; but no judgment by default shall be entered against an infant or incompetent person unless represented in the action by a general guardian, committee, conservator, or other such representative who has appeared therein. If the party against whom judgment by default is sought has appeared in the action, the party (or, if appearing by representative, the party's representative) shall be served with written notice of the application for judgment at least 3 days prior to the hearing on such application. If, in order to enable the court to enter judgment or to carry it into effect, it is necessary to take an account or to determine the amount of damages or to establish the truth of any averment by evidence or to make an investigation of any other matter, the court may conduct such hearings or order such references as it deems necessary and proper and shall accord a right of trial by jury to the parties when and as required by any statute of the United States.

(c) Setting Aside Default. For good cause shown the court may set aside an entry of default and, if a judgment by default has been entered, may likewise set it aside in accordance with Rule 60(b).

(d) Plaintiffs, Counterclaimants, Cross-Claimants. The provisions of this rule apply whether the party entitled to the judgment by default is a plaintiff, a third-party plaintiff, or a party who has pleaded a cross-claim or counterclaim. In all cases a judgment by default is subject to the limitations of Rule 54(c).

(e) Judgment Against the United States. No judgment by default shall be entered against the United States or an officer or agency thereof unless the claimant establishes a claim or right to relief by evidence satisfactory to the court.

Comparative State Provision

Florida Rule of Civil Procedure 1.500

(a) By the Clerk. When a party against whom affirmative relief is sought has failed to file or serve any paper in the action, the party seeking relief may have the clerk enter a default against the party failing to serve or file such paper.

(b) By the Court. When a party against whom affirmative relief is sought has failed to plead or otherwise defend as provided by these rules or any applicable statute or any order of court, the court may enter a default against such party; provided that if such party has filed or served any paper in the action, he shall be served with notice of the application for default.

(c) Right to Plead. A party may plead or otherwise defend at any time before default is entered. If a party in default files any paper after the default is entered, the clerk shall notify the party of the entry of the default. * * *

(d) Setting Aside Default. The court may set aside a default and if a final judgment consequent thereon has been entered, the court may set it aside in accordance with Rule 1.540(b).

(e) Final Judgment. Final judgments after default may be entered by the court at any time but no judgment may be entered against an infant or incompetent person unless represented in the action by a general guardian, committee, conservator or other representative who has appeared * * *. If it is necessary to take an account or to determine the amount of damages or to establish the truth of any averment by evidence or to make an investigation of any other matter to enable the court to enter judgment or to effectuate it, the court may receive affidavits, make references or conduct hearings as it deems necessary and shall accord a right of trial by jury to the parties when required by the Constitution or any statute.

Rule 56. Summary Judgment

(a) For Claimant. A party seeking to recover upon a claim, counterclaim, or cross-claim or to obtain a declaratory judgment may, at any time after the expiration of 20 days from the commencement of the action or after service of a motion for summary judgment by the adverse party, move with or without supporting affidavits for a summary judgment in the party's favor upon all or any part thereof.

(b) For Defending Party. A party against whom a claim, counterclaim, or cross-claim is asserted or a declaratory judgment is sought may, at any time, move with or without supporting affidavits for a summary judgment in the party's favor as to all or any part thereof.

(c) Motion and Proceedings Thereon. The motion shall be served at least 10 days before the time fixed for the hearing. The adverse party prior to the day of hearing may serve opposing affidavits. The judgment sought shall be rendered forthwith if the pleadings, depositions, answers to interrogatories, and admissions on file, together with the affidavits, if any, show that there is no genuine issue as to any material fact and that the moving party is entitled to a judgment as a matter of law. A summary judgment, interlocutory in character, may be rendered on the issue of liability alone although there is a genuine issue as to the amount of damages.

(d) Case Not Fully Adjudicated on Motion. If on motion under this rule judgment is not rendered upon the whole case or for all the relief asked and a trial is necessary, the court at the hearing of the motion, by examining the pleadings and the evidence before it and by interrogating counsel, shall if practicable ascertain what material facts exist without substantial controversy and what material facts are actually and in good faith controverted. It shall thereupon make an order specifying the facts that appear without substantial controversy, including the extent to which the amount of damages or other relief is not in controversy, and directing such further proceedings in the action as are just. Upon the trial of the action the facts so specified shall be deemed established, and the trial shall be conducted accordingly.

(e) Form of Affidavits; Further Testimony; Defense Required. Supporting and opposing affidavits shall be made on personal knowledge, shall set forth such facts as would be admissible in evidence, and shall show affirmatively that the affiant is competent to testify to the matters stated therein. Sworn or certified copies of all papers or parts thereof referred to in an affidavit shall be attached thereto or served therewith. The court may permit affidavits to be supplemented or opposed by depositions, answers to interrogatories, or further affidavits. When a motion for summary judgment is made and supported as provided in this rule, an adverse party may not rest upon the mere allegations or denials of the adverse party's pleading, but the adverse party's response, by affidavits or as otherwise provided in this rule, must set forth specific facts showing that there is a genuine issue for trial. If the adverse party does not so respond, summary judgment, if appropriate, shall be entered against the adverse party.

(f) When Affidavits Are Unavailable. Should it appear from the affidavits of a party opposing the motion that the party cannot for reasons stated present by affidavit facts essential to justify the party's opposition, the court may refuse the application for judgment or may order a continuance to permit affidavits to be obtained or depositions to be taken or discovery to be had or may make such other order as is just.

(g) Affidavits Made in Bad Faith. Should it appear to the satisfaction of the court at any time that any of the affidavits presented pursuant to this rule are presented in bad faith or solely for the purpose of delay, the court shall forthwith order the party employing them to pay to the other party the amount of the reasonable expenses which the filing of the affidavits caused the other party to incur, including reasonable attorney's fees, and any offending party or attorney may be adjudged guilty of contempt.

**Comparative State Provisions and Notes on Amendments
and Proposed Amendments to Federal Rule 56**

(a) *Comparative State Provisions*

California Civil Procedure Code § 437c

(a) Any party may move for summary judgment in any action or proceeding if it is contended that the action has no merit or that there is no defense to the action or proceeding. The motion may be made at any time after 60 days have elapsed since the general appearance in the action or proceeding of each party against whom the motion is directed or at such earlier time after the general appearance as the court * * * may direct. Notice of the motion and supporting papers shall be served on all other parties to the action at least 28 days before the time appointed for hearing. However, if the notice is served by mail, the required 28-day period of notice shall be increased by five days if the place of address is within the State of California, 10 days if the place of address is outside the State of California but within the United States, and 20 days if the place of address is outside the United States and if the notice is served by facsimile transmission,

151

Express Mail, or another method of delivery providing for overnight delivery, the required 28–day period of notice shall be increased by two court days. The motion shall be heard no later than 30 days before the date of trial, unless the court for good cause orders otherwise. The filing of such motion shall not extend the time within which a party must otherwise file a responsive pleading.

(b) The motion shall be supported by affidavits, declarations, admissions, answers to interrogatories, depositions and matters of which judicial notice shall or may be taken. The supporting papers shall include a separate statement setting forth plainly and concisely all material facts which the moving party contends are undisputed. Each of the material facts stated shall be followed by a reference to the supporting evidence. The failure to comply with this requirement of a separate statement may in the court's discretion constitute a sufficient ground for denial of the motion.

Any opposition to the motion shall be served and filed not less than 14 days preceding the noticed or continued date of hearing, unless the court for good cause orders otherwise. The opposition, where appropriate, shall consist of affidavits, declarations, admissions, answers to interrogatories, depositions and matters of which judicial notice shall or may be taken. The opposition papers shall include a separate statement which responds to each of the material facts contended by the moving party to be undisputed, indicating whether the opposing party agrees or disagrees that those facts are undisputed. The statement also shall set forth plainly and concisely any other material facts which the opposing party contends are disputed. Each material fact contended by the opposing party to be disputed shall be followed by a reference to the supporting evidence. Failure to comply with this requirement of a separate statement may constitute a sufficient ground, in the court's discretion, for granting the motion.

Any reply to the opposition shall be served and filed by the moving party not less than five days preceding the noticed or continued date of hearing, unless the court for good cause orders otherwise.

Evidentiary objections not made at the hearing shall be deemed waived.

Sections 1005 and 1013, extending the time within which a right may be exercised or an act may be done, do not apply to this section.

Any incorporation by reference of matter in the court's file shall set forth with specificity the exact matter to which reference is being made and shall not incorporate the entire file.

(c) The motion for summary judgment shall be granted if all the papers submitted show that there is no triable issue as to any material fact and that the moving party is entitled to a judgment as a matter of law. In determining whether the papers show that there is no triable issue as to any material fact the court shall consider all of the evidence set forth in the papers, except that to which objections have been made and sustained by the court, and all inferences reasonably deducible from the evidence, except summary judgment shall not be granted by the court based on inferences reasonably deducible from the evidence, if contradicted by other inferences or evidence, which raise a triable issue as to any material fact.

(d) Supporting and opposing affidavits or declarations shall be made by any person on personal knowledge, shall set forth admissible evidence, and shall show affirmatively that the affiant is competent to testify to the matters stated therein. Any objections based on the failure to comply with the requirements of this subdivision shall be made at the hearing or shall be deemed waived.

(e) If a party is otherwise entitled to a summary judgment pursuant to this section, summary judgment shall not be denied on grounds of credibility or for want of cross-examination of witnesses furnishing affidavits or declarations in support of the summary judgment, except that summary judgment may be denied in the discretion of the court, where the only proof of a material fact offered in support of the summary judgment is an affidavit or declaration made by an individual who was the sole witness to that fact; or where a material fact is an individual's state of mind, or lack thereof, and that fact is sought to be established solely by the individual's affirmation thereof.

(f)(1) A party may move for summary judgment as to one or more causes of action within an action, one or more affirmative defenses, one or more claims for damages, or one or more issues of duty, if that party contends that the cause of action has no merit or that there is no merit to an affirmative defense as to any cause of action, or both, or that there is no merit to a claim for damages, as specified in Section 3294 of the Civil Code, or that one or more defendants either owed or did not owe a duty to the plaintiff or plaintiffs. A motion for summary adjudication shall be granted only if it completely disposes of a cause of action, an affirmative defense, a claim for damages, or an issue of duty.

(2) A motion for summary adjudication may be made by itself or as an alternative to a motion for summary judgment and shall proceed in all procedural respects as a motion for summary judgment. However, a party may not move for summary judgment based on issues asserted in a prior motion for summary adjudication and denied by the court, unless that party establishes to the satisfaction of the court, newly discovered facts or circumstances supporting the issues reasserted in the summary judgment motion.

(g) Upon the denial of a motion for summary judgment, on the ground that there is a triable issue as to one or more material facts, the court shall, by written or oral order, specify one or more material facts raised by the motion as to which the court has determined there exists a triable controversy. This determination shall specifically refer to the evidence proffered in support of and in opposition to the motion which indicates that a triable controversy exists. Upon the grant of a motion for summary judgment, on the ground that there is no triable issue of material fact, the court shall, by written or oral order, specify the reasons for its determination. The order shall specifically refer to the evidence proffered in support of, and if applicable in opposition to, the motion which indicates that no triable issue exists. The court shall also state its reasons for any other determination. The court shall record its determination by court reporter or written order.

(h) If it appears from the affidavits submitted in opposition to a motion for summary judgment or summary adjudication or both that facts essential to justify opposition may exist but cannot, for reasons stated, then be presented, the court shall deny the motion, or order a continuance to permit affidavits to be obtained or discovery to be had or may make any other order as may be just.

(i) If the court determines at any time that any of the affidavits are presented in bad faith or solely for purposes of delay, the court shall order the party presenting the affidavits to pay the other party the amount of the reasonable expenses which the filing of the affidavits caused the other party to incur. Sanctions shall not be imposed pursuant to this subdivision except on notice contained in a party's papers, or on the court's own noticed motion, and after an opportunity to be heard.

(j) Except where a separate judgment may properly be awarded in the action, no final judgment shall be entered on a motion for summary judgment prior to the termination of such action, but the final judgment shall, in addition to any matters determined in the action, award judgment as established by the summary proceeding herein provided for.

(k) In actions which arise out of an injury to the person or to property, when a motion for summary judgment was granted on the basis that the defendant was without fault, no other defendant during trial, over plaintiff's objection, may attempt to attribute fault to or comment on the absence or involvement of the defendant who was granted the motion.

(l) A summary judgment entered under this section is an appealable judgment as in other cases. Upon entry of any order pursuant to this section except the entry of summary judgment, a party may, within 20 days after service upon him or her of a written notice of entry of the order, petition an appropriate reviewing court for a peremptory writ. If the notice is served by mail, the initial period within which to file the petition shall be increased by five days if the place of address is within the State of California, 10 days if the place of address is outside the State of California but within the United States, and 20 days if the place of address is outside the United States. If the notice is served by facsimile transmission, Express Mail, or another method of delivery, providing for overnight delivery, the initial period within which to file the petition shall be increased by two court days. The superior court may, for good cause, and prior to the expiration of the initial period, extend the time for one additional period not to exceed 10 days.

* * *

(p) Nothing in this section shall be construed to extend the period for trial provided by Section 1170.5.

California Civil Procedure Code § 436

The court may, upon a motion made pursuant to Section 435, or at any time in its discretion, and upon terms it deems proper:

(a) Strike out any irrelevant, false, or improper matter inserted in any pleading.

(b) Strike out all or any part of any pleading not drawn or filed in conformity with the laws of this State, a court rule, or an order of the court.

(b) *Notes on Amendments in 1963 to Rule 56(e)*

The 1963 amendment added the last two sentences to present Rule 56(e). The Advisory Committee's Notes on the alteration read as follows:

The last two sentences are added to overcome a line of cases, chiefly in the Third Circuit, which has impaired the utility of the summary judgment device. A typical case is as follows: A party supports his motion for summary judgment by affidavits or other evidentiary matter sufficient to show that there is no genuine issue as to a material fact. The adverse party, in opposing the motion, does not produce any evidentiary matter, or produces some but not enough to establish that there is a genuine issue for trial. Instead, the adverse party rests on averments of his pleadings which on their face present an issue. In this situation Third Circuit cases have taken the view that summary judgment must be denied, at least if the averments are "well-pleaded," and not supposititious, conclusory, or ultimate. * * *

The very mission of the summary judgment procedure is to pierce the pleadings and to assess the proof in order to see whether there is a genuine need for trial. The Third Circuit doctrine, which permits the pleadings themselves to stand in the way of granting an otherwise justified summary judgment, is incompatible with the basic purpose of the rule. * * *

It is hoped that the amendment will contribute to the more effective utilization of the salutary device of summary judgment.

The amendment is not intended to derogate from the solemnity of the pleadings. Rather it recognizes that, despite the best efforts of counsel to make his pleadings accurate, they may be overwhelmingly contradicted by the proof available to his adversary.

Nor is the amendment designed to affect the ordinary standards applicable to the summary judgment motion. So, for example: Where an issue as to a material fact cannot be resolved without observation of the demeanor of witnesses in order to evaluate their credibility, summary judgment is not appropriate. Where the evidentiary matter in support of the motion does not establish the absence of a genuine issue, summary judgment must be denied even if no opposing evidentiary matter is presented. And summary judgment may be inappropriate where the party opposing it shows under subdivision (f) that he cannot at the time present facts essential to justify his opposition.

(c) *Proposed Amendments in 1991 to Rule 56*

The proposal involved an extensive rewriting of Rule 56, but generally did not change its basic substance. One significant alteration would have allowed the trial court to "summarily establish as a matter of law any facts that are not genuinely controverted or it may establish law to control further proceedings in an action." At present a court, pursuant to Rule 56(d), may establish the existence of facts, but only if a motion for summary judgment has been made and the court is unable to render judgment on the entire case. There is no current provision with respect to the establishment of law.

A second significant provision would specifically have permitted a party seeking relief, in addition to producing material to support the existence of facts to be established, to make "reference to any absence of probative evidence enabling an opposing party to satisfy a burden of producing evidence or proof." The ability of a party to rely upon the absence of probative evidence by which an opposing party could meet his or her burden of proof was the subject of controversy in the Supreme Court case of Celotex Corp. v. Catrett, 477 U.S. 317, 106 S.Ct. 2548, 91 L.Ed.2d 265 (1986), in which none of the opinions commanded a majority of the Court.

Rule 57. Declaratory Judgments

The procedure for obtaining a declaratory judgment pursuant to Title 28 U.S.C. § 2201, shall be in accordance with these rules, and the right to trial by jury may be demanded under the circumstances and in the manner provided in Rules 38 and 39. The existence of another adequate remedy does not preclude a judgment for declaratory relief in cases where it is appropriate. The court may order a speedy hearing of an action for a declaratory judgment and may advance it on the calendar.

Rule 58. Entry of Judgment

Subject to the provisions of Rule 54(b): (1) upon a general verdict of a jury, or upon a decision by the court that a party shall recover only a sum certain or costs or that all relief shall be denied, the clerk, unless the court otherwise orders, shall forthwith prepare, sign, and enter the judgment without awaiting any direction by the court; (2) upon a decision by the court granting other relief, or upon a special verdict or a general verdict accompanied by answers to interrogatories, the court shall promptly approve the form of the judgment, and the clerk shall thereupon enter it. Every judgment shall be set forth on a separate document. A judgment is effective only when so set forth and when entered as provided in Rule 79(a). Entry of the judgment shall not be delayed, nor the time for appeal extended, in order to tax costs or award fees, except that, when a timely motion for attorneys' fees is made under Rule 54(d)(2), the court, before a notice of appeal has been filed and become effective, may order that the motion have the same effect under 4(a)(4) of the Federal Rules of Appellate Procedure as a timely motion under Rule 59. Attorneys shall not submit forms of judgment except upon direction of the court, and these directions shall not be given as a matter of course.

Notes on 1963 Amendments to Federal Rule 58

Rule 58 as originally promulgated read as follows:

Unless the court otherwise directs and subject to the provisions of Rule 54(b), judgment upon the verdict of a jury shall be entered forthwith by the clerk; but the court shall direct the appropriate judgment to be entered upon a special verdict or upon a general verdict accompanied by answers to interrogatories returned by a jury pursuant to Rule 49. When the court directs that a party recover only money or costs or that all relief be denied, the clerk shall enter judgment forthwith upon receipt by him of the directions; but when the court directs entry of judgment for other relief, the judge shall promptly settle or approve the form of the judgment and direct that it be entered by the clerk. The notation of a judgment in the civil docket as provided by Rule 79(a) constitutes the entry of the judgment; and the judgment is not effective before such entry. The entry of the judgment shall not be delayed for the taxing of costs.

The Advisory Committee commented on the 1963 amendments as follows:

Under the present rule a distinction has sometimes been made between judgments on general jury verdicts, on the one hand, and, on the other, judgments upon decisions of the court that a party shall recover only money or costs or that all relief shall be denied. In the first situation, it is clear that the clerk should enter the judgment without awaiting a direction by the court unless the court otherwise orders. In the second situation it was intended that the clerk should similarly enter the judgment forthwith upon the court's decision; but because of the separate listing in the rule, and the use of the phrase "upon receipt * * * of the direction," the rule has sometimes been interpreted as requiring the clerk to await a separate direction of the court. All these judgments are usually uncomplicated, and should be handled in the same way. The amended rule accordingly deals with them as a single group in clause (1) (substituting the expression "only a sum certain" for the present expression "only money"), and requires the clerk to prepare, sign, and enter them forthwith, without awaiting court direction, unless the court makes a contrary order. * * * The more complicated judgments described in clause (2) must be approved by the court before they are entered.

    * * *

Hitherto some difficulty has arisen, chiefly where the court has written an opinion or memorandum containing some apparently directive or dispositive words * * *. Clerks on occasion have viewed these opinions or memoranda as being in themselves a sufficient basis for entering judgment in the civil docket as provided by Rule 79(a). However, where the opinion or memoranda has not contained all the elements of a judgment, or where the judge has later signed a formal judgment, it has become a matter of doubt whether the purported entry of judgment was effective, starting the time running for postverdict motions and for the purpose of appeal. * * *

The amended rule eliminates these uncertainties by requiring that there be a judgment set out on a separate document—distinct from any opinion or memorandum—which provides the basis for the entry of judgment. That judgments shall be on separate documents is also indicated in Rule 79(b) * * *.

Rule 59. New Trials; Amendment of Judgments

(a) Grounds. A new trial may be granted to all or any of the parties and on all or part of the issues (1) in an action in which there has been a trial by jury, for any of the reasons for which new trials have heretofore been granted in actions at law in the courts of the United States; and (2) in an action tried without a jury, for any of the reasons for which rehearings have heretofore been granted in suits in equity in the courts of the United States. On a motion for a new trial in an action tried without a jury, the court may open the judgment if one has been entered, take additional testimony, amend findings of fact and conclusions of law or make new findings and conclusions, and direct the entry of a new judgment.

(b) Time for Motion. A motion for a new trial shall be filed no later than 10 days after the entry of the judgment.

(c) Time for Serving Affidavits. When a motion for new trial is based upon affidavits they shall be filed with the motion. The opposing party has 10 days after service to file opposing affidavits, but that period may be extended for up to 20 days, either by the court for good cause or by the parties' written stipulation. The court may permit reply affidavits.

(d) On Initiative of Court. No later than 10 days after entry of judgment the court, on its own, may order a new trial for any reason that would justify granting one on a party's motion. After giving the parties notice and an opportunity to be heard, the court may grant a timely motion for a new trial for a reason not stated in the motion. When granting a new trial on its own initiative or for a reason not stated in the motion, the court shall specify the grounds in its order.

(e) Motion to Alter or Amend a Judgment. A motion to alter or amend a judgment shall be filed no later than 10 days after entry of the judgment.

Comparative State Provisions

(a) *Rule 59(a)*

Minnesota Rule of Civil Procedure 59.01

A new trial may be granted to all or any of the parties and on all or part of the issues for any of the following causes:

(a) Irregularity in the proceedings of the court, referee, jury, or prevailing party, or any order or abuse of discretion, whereby the moving party was deprived of a fair trial;

(b) Misconduct of the jury or prevailing party;

(c) Accident or surprise which could not have been prevented by ordinary prudence;

(d) Material evidence, newly discovered, which with reasonable diligence could not have been found and produced at the trial;

(e) Excessive or insufficient damages, appearing to have been given under the influence of passion or prejudice;

(f) Errors of law occurring at the trial, and objected to at the time or, if no objection need have been made under Rules 46 and 51, plainly assigned in the notice of motion;

(g) The verdict, decision, or report is not justified by the evidence, or is contrary to law; but, unless it be so expressly stated in the order granting a new trial, it shall not be presumed, on appeal, to have been made on the ground that the verdict, decision, or report was not justified by the evidence.

On a motion for a new trial in an action tried without a jury, the court may open the judgment if one has been entered, take additional testimony, amend findings of fact and conclusions of law or make new findings and conclusions, and direct entry of a new judgment.

Missouri Statutes Annotated § 510.330

A new trial may be granted for any of the reasons for which new trials have heretofore been granted. A new trial may be granted to all or any of the parties and on all or part of the issues after trial by jury, court or referee. On a motion for a new trial in an action tried without a jury, the court may open the judgment if one has been entered, take additional testimony, amend findings of fact or make new findings, and direct the entry of a new judgment. Only one new trial shall be allowed on the ground that the verdict is against the weight of the evidence. Every order allowing a new trial shall specify of record the ground or grounds on which said new trial is granted.

(b) *Rule 59(b)*

Minnesota Rule of Civil Procedure 59.03

A notice of motion for a new trial shall be served within 15 days after a general verdict or service of notice by a party of the filing of the decision or order; and the motion shall be heard within 30 days after such general verdict or notice of filing, unless the time for hearing be extended by the court within the 30 days period for good cause shown.

Rule 60.   Relief From Judgment or Order

(a) Clerical Mistakes. Clerical mistakes in judgments, orders or other parts of the record and errors therein arising from oversight or omission may be corrected by the court at any time of its own initiative or on the motion of any party and after such notice, if any, as the court orders. During the pendency of an appeal, such mistakes may be so corrected before the appeal is docketed in the appellate court, and thereafter while the appeal is pending may be so corrected with leave of the appellate court.

(b) Mistakes; Inadvertence; Excusable Neglect; Newly Discovered Evidence; Fraud, etc. On motion and upon such terms as are just, the court may relieve a party or a party's legal representative from a final judgment, order, or proceeding for the following reasons: (1) mistake, inadvertence, surprise, or excusable neglect; (2) newly discovered evidence which by due diligence could not have been discovered in time to move for a new trial under Rule 59(b); (3) fraud (whether heretofore denominated intrinsic or extrinsic), misrepresentation, or other misconduct of an adverse party; (4) the judgment is void; (5) the judgment has been satisfied, released, or discharged, or a prior judgment upon which it is based has been reversed or otherwise vacated, or it is no longer equitable that the judgment should have prospective application; or (6) any other reason justifying relief from the operation of the judgment. The motion shall be made within a reasonable time, and for reasons (1), (2), and (3) not more than one year after the judgment, order, or proceeding was entered or taken. A motion under this subdivision (b) does not affect the finality of a judgment or suspend its operation. This rule does not limit the power of a court to entertain an independent action to relieve a party from a judgment, order, or proceeding, or to grant relief to a defendant not actually personally notified as provided in Title 28, U.S.C., § 1655, or to set aside a judgment for fraud upon the court. Writs of coram nobis, coram vobis, audita querela, and bills of review and bills in the nature of a bill of review, are abolished, and the procedure for obtaining any relief from a judgment shall be by motion as prescribed in these rules or by an independent action.

Comparative State Provisions

(a) In General

Georgia Code Annotated § 9–11–60

(a) * * *

(b) Methods of direct attack. A judgment may be attacked by motion for a new trial or motion to set aside. Judgments may be attacked by motion only in the court of rendition.

(c) Motion for new trial. A motion for new trial must be predicated upon some intrinsic defect which does not appear upon the face of the record or pleadings.

(d) Motion to set aside. A motion may be brought to set aside a judgment based upon:

(1) Lack of jurisdiction over the person or the subject matter;

(2) Fraud, accident, or mistake or the acts of the adverse party unmixed with the negligence or fault of the movant; or

(3) A nonamendable defect which appears upon the face of the record or pleadings. Under this paragraph, it is not sufficient that the complaint or other pleading fails to state a claim upon which relief can be granted, but the pleadings must affirmatively show no claim in fact existed.

(e) Complaint in equity. The use of a complaint in equity to set aside a judgment is prohibited.

(f) Procedure; time of relief. * * * Motions for new trial must be brought within the time prescribed by law. In all other instances, all motions to set aside judgments shall be brought within three years from entry of the judgment complained of.

(g) Clerical mistakes. Clerical mistakes in judgments, orders, or other parts of the record and errors therein arising from oversight or omission may be corrected by the court at any time of its own initiative or on the motion of any party and after such notice, if any, as the court orders.

(h) Law of the case rule. The law of the case rule is abolished; but generally judgments and orders shall not be set aside or modified without just cause and, in setting aside or otherwise modifying judgments and orders, the court shall consider whether rights have vested thereunder and whether or not innocent parties would be injured thereby; provided, however, that any ruling by the Supreme Court or the Court of Appeals in a case shall be binding in all subsequent proceedings in that case in the lower court and in the Supreme Court or the Court of Appeals as the case may be.

(b) Perjury as a Ground for Relief

Missouri Rule of Civil Procedure 78.01

[On January 1, 1975, Rule 78.01 was revised to eliminate all references to specific grounds for a new trial. The legislative note makes clear that the revision was not intended to alter or eliminate any ground upon which new trials previously were permitted. Prior to the change Rule 78.01 read in part as follows:] * * * The court may award a new trial of any issue upon good cause shown and in any case where there has been * * * a fraud or deceit practiced by one party on the other or the court is satisfied that perjury or mistake has been committed by a witness, and is also satisfied that an improper verdict or finding was occasioned by any such matters * * *, it shall, on motion of the proper party, grant a new trial * * *.

Rule 61.   Harmless Error

No error in either the admission or the exclusion of evidence and no error or defect in any ruling or order or in anything done or omitted by the court or by any of the parties is ground for granting a new trial or for setting aside a verdict or for vacating, modifying or otherwise disturbing a judgment or order, unless refusal to take such action appears to the court inconsistent with substantial justice. The court at every stage of the proceeding must disregard any error or defect in the proceeding which does not affect the substantial rights of the parties.

Rule 62.   Stay of Proceedings to Enforce a Judgment

(a) Automatic Stay; Exceptions—Injunctions, Receiverships, and Patent Accountings. Except as stated herein, no execution shall issue upon a judgment nor shall proceedings be taken for its enforcement until the expiration of 10 days after its entry. Unless otherwise ordered by the court, an interlocutory or final judgment in an action for an injunction or in a receivership action, or a judgment or order directing an accounting in an action for infringement of letters patent, shall not be stayed during the period after its entry and until an appeal is taken or during the pendency of an appeal. The provisions of subdivision (c) of this rule govern the suspending, modifying, restoring, or granting of an injunction during the pendency of an appeal.

(b) Stay on Motion for New Trial or for Judgment. In its discretion and on such conditions for the security of the adverse party as are proper, the court may stay the execution of or any proceedings to enforce a judgment pending the disposition of a motion for a new trial or to alter or amend a judgment made pursuant to Rule 59, or of a motion for relief from a judgment or order made pursuant to Rule 60, or of a motion for judgment in accordance with a motion for a directed verdict made pursuant to Rule 50, or of a motion for amendment to the findings or for additional findings made pursuant to Rule 52(b).

(c) Injunction Pending Appeal. When an appeal is taken from an interlocutory or final judgment granting, dissolving, or denying an injunction, the court in its discretion may suspend, modify, restore, or grant an injunction during the pendency of the appeal upon such terms as to bond or otherwise as it considers proper for the security of the rights of the adverse party. If the judgment appealed from is rendered by a district court of three judges specially constituted pursuant to a statute of the United States, no such order shall be made except (1) by such court sitting in open court or (2) by the assent of all the judges of such court evidenced by their signatures to the order.

(d) Stay Upon Appeal. When an appeal is taken the appellant by giving a supersedeas bond may obtain a stay subject to the exceptions contained in subdivision (a) of this rule. The bond may be given at or after the time of filing the notice of appeal or of procuring the order allowing the appeal, as the case may be. The stay is effective when the supersedeas bond is approved by the court.

(e) Stay in Favor of the United States or Agency Thereof. When an appeal is taken by the United States or an officer or agency thereof or by direction of any department of the Government of the United States and the operation or enforcement of the judgment is stayed, no bond, obligation, or other security shall be required from the appellant.

(f) Stay According to State Law. In any state in which a judgment is a lien upon the property of the judgment debtor and in which the judgment debtor is entitled to a stay of execution, a judgment debtor is entitled, in the district court held therein, to such stay as would be accorded the judgment debtor had the action been maintained in the courts of that state.

(g) Power of Appellate Court Not Limited. The provisions in this rule do not limit any power of an appellate court or of a judge or justice thereof to stay proceedings during the pendency of an appeal or to suspend, modify, restore, or grant an injunction during the pendency of an appeal or to make any order appropriate to preserve the status quo or the effectiveness of the judgment subsequently to be entered.

(h) Stay of Judgment as to Multiple Claims or Multiple Parties. When a court has ordered a final judgment under the conditions stated in Rule 54(b), the court may stay enforcement of that judgment until the entering of a subsequent judgment or judgments and may prescribe such conditions as are necessary to secure the benefit thereof to the party in whose favor the judgment is entered.

Rule 63. Inability of a Judge to Proceed

If a trial or hearing has been commenced and the judge is unable to proceed, any other judge may proceed with it upon certifying familiarity with the record and determining that the proceedings in the case may be completed without prejudice to the parties. In a hearing or trial without a jury, the successor judge shall at the request of a party recall any witness whose testimony is material and disputed and who is available to testify again without undue burden. The successor judge may also recall any other witness.

VIII. PROVISIONAL AND FINAL REMEDIES

Rule 64. Seizure of Person or Property

At the commencement of and during the course of an action, all remedies providing for seizure of person or property for the purpose of securing satisfaction of the judgment ultimately to be entered in the action are available under the circumstances and in the manner provided by the law of the state in which the district court is held, existing at the time the remedy is sought, subject to the following qualifications: (1) any existing statute of the United States governs to the extent to which it is applicable; (2) the action in which any of the foregoing remedies is used shall be commenced and prosecuted or, if removed from a state court, shall be prosecuted after removal, pursuant to these rules. The remedies thus available include arrest, attachment, garnishment, replevin, sequestration, and other corresponding or equivalent remedies, however designated and regardless of whether by state procedure the remedy is ancillary to an action or must be obtained by an independent action.

Comparative State Provisions

New York Civil Practice Law and Rules 6201

An order of attachment may be granted in any action, except a matrimonial action, where the plaintiff has demanded and would be entitled, in whole or in part, or in the alternative, to a money judgment against one or more defendants, when:

1. the defendant is a nondomiciliary residing within the state, or is a foreign corporation not qualified to do business in the state; or

2. the defendant resides or is domiciled in the state and cannot be personally served despite diligent efforts to do so; or

3. the defendant, with intent to defraud his creditors or frustrate the enforcement of a judgment that might be rendered in plaintiff's favor, has assigned, disposed of, encumbered or secreted property, or removed it from the state or is about to do any of these acts; or

4. the action is brought by the victim * * * of a crime * * * to recover damages sustained as a result of such crime * * *.

5. the cause of action is based on a judgment, decree or order of a court of the United States or of any other court which is entitled to full faith and credit in this state, or on a [recognized foreign] judgment * * *.

Rule 65. Injunctions

[See proposed addition of Rule 65(f), in Part IX, infra.]

(a) Preliminary Injunction.

(1) *Notice.* No preliminary injunction shall be issued without notice to the adverse party.

(2) *Consolidation of Hearing With Trial on Merits.* Before or after the commencement of the hearing of an application for a preliminary injunction, the court may order the trial of the action on the merits to be advanced and consolidated with the hearing of the application. Even when this consolidation is not ordered, any evidence received upon an application for a preliminary injunction which would be admissible upon the trial on the merits becomes part of the record on the trial and need not be repeated upon the trial. This subdivision (a)(2) shall be so construed and applied as to save to the parties any rights they may have to trial by jury.

(b) Temporary Restraining Order; Notice; Hearing; Duration. A temporary restraining order may be granted without written or oral notice to the adverse party or that party's attorney only if (1) it clearly appears from specific facts shown by affidavit or by the verified complaint that immediate and irreparable injury, loss, or damage will result to the applicant before the adverse party or that party's attorney can be heard in opposition, and (2) the applicant's attorney certifies to the court in writing the efforts, if any, which have been made to give the notice and the reasons supporting the claim that notice should not be required. Every temporary restraining order granted without notice shall be indorsed with the date and hour of issuance; shall be filed forthwith in the clerk's office and entered of record; shall define the injury and state why it is irreparable and why the order was granted without notice; and shall expire by its terms within such time after entry, not to exceed 10 days, as the court fixes, unless within the time so fixed the order, for good cause shown, is extended for a like period or unless the party against whom the order is directed consents that it may be extended for a longer period. The reasons for the extension shall be entered of record. In case a temporary restraining order is granted without notice, the motion for a preliminary injunction shall be set down for hearing at the earliest possible time and takes precedence of all matters except older matters of the same character; and when the motion comes on for hearing the party who obtained the temporary restraining order shall proceed with the application for a preliminary injunction and, if the party does not do so, the court shall dissolve the temporary restraining order. On 2 days' notice to the party who obtained the temporary restraining order without notice or on such shorter notice to that party as the court may prescribe, the adverse party may appear and move its dissolution or modification and in that event the court shall proceed to hear and determine such motion as expeditiously as the ends of justice require.

(c) Security. No restraining order or preliminary injunction shall issue except upon the giving of security by the applicant, in such sum as the court deems proper, for the payment of such costs and damages as may be incurred or suffered by any party who is found to have been wrongfully enjoined or restrained. No such security shall be required of the United States or of an officer or agency thereof.

The provisions of Rule 65.1 apply to a surety upon a bond or undertaking under this rule.

(d) Form and Scope of Injunction or Restraining Order. Every order granting an injunction and every restraining order shall set forth the reasons for its issuance; shall be specific in terms; shall describe in reasonable detail, and not by reference to the complaint or other document, the act or acts sought to be restrained; and is binding only upon the parties to the action, their officers, agents, servants, employees, and attorneys, and upon those persons in active concert or participation with them who receive actual notice of the order by personal service or otherwise.

(e) Employer and Employee; Interpleader; Constitutional Cases. These rules do not modify any statute of the United States relating to temporary restraining orders and preliminary injunctions in actions affecting employer and employee; or the provisions of Title 28, U.S.C. § 2361, relating to preliminary injunctions in actions of interpleader or in the nature of interpleader; or Title 28, U.S.C. § 2284, relating to actions required by Act of Congress to be heard and determined by a district court of three judges.

Notes on Amendments to Federal Rule 65 and Comparative State Provision

(a) *Notes on Amendments in 1966 to Federal Rules 65(a) and (b)*

The 1966 amendments added Rule 65(a)(2) and clause (2) in Rule 65(b). The Advisory Committee's Notes on these amendments read as follows:

Subdivision (a)(2). This new subdivision provides express authority for consolidating the hearing of an application for a preliminary injunction with the trial on the merits. The authority can be exercised with particular profit when it appears that a substantial part of the evidence offered on the application will be relevant to the merits and will be presented in such form as to qualify for admission on the trial proper. Repetition of evidence is thereby avoided. The fact that the proceedings have been consolidated should cause no delay in the disposition of the application for the preliminary injunction, for the evidence will be directed in the first instance to that relief, and the preliminary injunction, if justified by the proof, may be issued in the course of the consolidated proceedings. Furthermore, to consolidate the proceedings will tend to expedite the final disposition of the action. It is believed that consolidation can be usefully availed of in many cases.

The subdivision further provides that even when consolidation is not ordered, evidence received in connection with an application for a preliminary injunction which would be admissible on the trial on the merits forms part of the trial record. This evidence need not be repeated on the trial. On the other hand, repetition is not altogether prohibited. That would be impractical and unwise. For example, a witness testifying comprehensively on the trial who has previously testified upon the application for a preliminary injunction might sometimes be hamstrung in telling his story if he could not go over some part of his prior testimony to connect it with his present testimony. So also, some repetition of testimony may be called for where the trial is conducted by a judge who did not hear the application for the preliminary injunction. In general, however, repetition can be avoided with an increase of efficiency in the conduct of the case and without any distortion of the presentation of evidence by the parties.

Since an application for a preliminary injunction may be made in an action in which, with respect to all or part of the merits, there is a right to trial by jury, it is appropriate to add the caution appearing in the last sentence of the subdivision. In such a case the jury will have to hear all the evidence bearing on its verdict, even if some part of the evidence has already been heard by the judge alone on the application for the preliminary injunction.

The subdivision is believed to reflect the substance of the best current practice and introduces no novel conception.

Subdivision (b). In view of the possibly drastic consequences of a temporary restraining order, the opposition should be heard, if feasible, before the order is granted. Many judges have properly insisted that, when time does not permit of formal notice of the application to the adverse party, some expedient, such as telephonic notice to the attorney for the adverse party, be resorted to if this can reasonably be done. On occasion, however, temporary restraining orders have been issued without any notice when it was feasible for some fair, although informal, notice to be given. * * *

Heretofore the first sentence of subdivision (b), in referring to a notice "served" on the "adverse party" on which a "hearing" could be held, perhaps invited the interpretation that the order might be granted without notice if the circumstances did not permit of a formal hearing on the basis of a formal notice. The subdivision is amended to make it plain that informal notice, which may be communicated to the attorney rather than the adverse party, is to be preferred to no notice at all.

Before notice can be dispensed with, the applicant's counsel must give his certificate as to any efforts made to give notice and the reasons why notice should not be required. This certificate is in addition to the requirement of an affidavit or verified complaint setting forth the facts as to the irreparable injury which would result before the opposition could be heard.

* * *

(b) *Comparative State Provision*

New York Civil Practice Law and Rules 6301

A preliminary injunction may be granted in any action where it appears that the defendant threatens or is about to do, or is doing or procuring or suffering to be done, an act in violation of the plaintiff's rights respecting the subject of the action, and tending to render the judgment ineffectual, or in any action where the plaintiff has demanded and would be entitled to a judgment restraining the defendant from the commission or continuance of an act, which, if committed or continued during the pendency of the action, would produce injury to the plaintiff. A temporary restraining order may be granted pending a hearing for a preliminary injunction where it appears that immediate and irreparable injury, loss or damage will result unless the defendant is restrained before the hearing can be had.

Rule 65.1 Security: Proceedings Against Sureties

Whenever these rules, including the Supplemental Rules for Certain Admiralty and Maritime Claims, require or permit the giving of security by a party, and security is given in the form of a bond or stipulation or other undertaking with one or more sureties, each surety submits to the jurisdiction of the court and irrevocably appoints the clerk of the court as the surety's agent upon whom any papers affecting the surety's liability on the bond or undertaking may be served. The surety's liability may be enforced on motion without the necessity of an independent action. The motion and such notice of the motion as the court prescribes may be served on the clerk of the court, who shall forthwith mail copies to the sureties if their addresses are known.

Rule 66. Receivers Appointed by Federal Courts

An action wherein a receiver has been appointed shall not be dismissed except by order of the court. The practice in the administration of estates by receivers or by other similar officers appointed by the court shall be in accordance with the practice heretofore followed in the courts of the United States or as provided in rules promulgated by the district courts. In all other respects the action in which the appointment of a receiver is sought or which is brought by or against a receiver is governed by these rules.

Rule 66 RULES OF CIVIL PROCEDURE

Comparative State Provision

New York Civil Practice Law and Rules 6401

(a) Upon motion of a person having an apparent interest in property which is the subject of an action in the supreme or a county court, a temporary receiver of the property may be appointed, before or after service of summons and at any time prior to judgment, or during the pendency of an appeal, where there is danger that the property will be removed from the state, or lost, materially injured or destroyed. * * *

(b) The court appointing a receiver may authorize him to take and hold real and personal property, and sue for, collect and sell debts or claims, upon such conditions and for such purposes as the court shall direct. A receiver shall have no power to employ counsel unless expressly so authorized by order of the court. Upon motion of the receiver or a party, powers granted to a temporary receiver may be extended or limited or the receivership may be extended to another action involving the property.

Rule 67. Deposit in Court

In an action in which any part of the relief sought is a judgment for a sum of money or the disposition of a sum of money or the disposition of any other thing capable of delivery, a party, upon notice to every other party, and by leave of court, may deposit with the court all or any part of such sum or thing, whether or not that party claims all or any part of the sum or thing. The party making the deposit shall serve the order permitting deposit on the clerk of the court. Money paid into court under this rule shall be deposited and withdrawn in accordance with the provisions of Title 28, U.S.C. §§ 2041, and 2042; the Act of June 26, 1934, c. 756, § 23, as amended (48 Stat. 1236, 58 Stat. 845), U.S.C., Title 31, § 725v; or any like statute. The fund shall be deposited in an interest-bearing account or invested in an interest-bearing instrument approved by the court.

Amendments in 1983 to Federal Rule 67

The first alteration to Rule 67 made clear that a litigant could deposit money or other property with the court even though that litigant continues to claim an interest in such property. The second alteration provided that money so deposited shall be invested in an interest bearing account or instrument approved by the court.

Rule 68. Offer of Judgment

At any time more than 10 days before the trial begins, a party defending against a claim may serve upon the adverse party an offer to allow judgment to be taken against the defending party for the money or property or to the effect specified in the offer, with costs then accrued. If within 10 days after the service of the offer the adverse party serves written notice that the offer is accepted, either party may then file the offer and notice of acceptance together with proof of service thereof and thereupon the clerk shall enter judgment. An offer not accepted shall be deemed withdrawn and evidence thereof is not admissible except in a proceeding to determine costs. If the judgment finally obtained by the offeree is not more favorable than the offer, the offeree must pay the costs incurred after the making of the offer. The fact that an offer is made but not accepted does not preclude a subsequent offer. When the liability of one party to another has been determined by verdict or order or judgment, but the amount or extent of the liability remains to be determined by further proceedings, the party adjudged liable may make an offer of judgment, which shall have the same effect as an offer made before trial if it is served within a reasonable time not less than 10 days prior to the commencement of hearings to determine the amount or extent of liability.

Proposed Amendments to Federal Rule 68 and Comparative State Provisions

(a) Proposed Amendments

The Advisory Committee on the Federal Rules once circulated a draft proposal that would have altered the rule dramatically. In the main, the suggested rule provided for sanctions against any party who unreasonably refuses an offer to settle whether or not that party ultimately prevails in the action. The trial judge would be permitted to impose any "appropriate sanction" in light of all of the circumstances of the case.

(b) Comparative State Provisions

New York Civil Practice Law and Rules 3219

At any time not later than ten days before trial, any party against whom a cause of action based upon contract, expressed or implied, is asserted, and against whom a separate judgment may be taken, may, without court order, deposit with the clerk of the court for safekeeping, an amount deemed by him to be sufficient to satisfy the claim asserted against him, and serve upon the claimant a written tender of payment to satisfy such claim. * * * Within ten days after such deposit the claimant may withdraw the amount deposited upon filing a duly acknowledged statement that the withdrawal is in satisfaction of the claim. The clerk shall thereupon enter judgment dismissing the pleading setting forth the claim, without costs.

* * * If the tender is not accepted and the claimant fails to obtain a more favorable judgment, he shall not recover interest or costs from the time of the offer, but shall pay costs for defending against the claim from that time. A tender shall not be made known to the jury.

* * *

New York Civil Practice Law and Rules 3220

At any time not later than ten days before trial, any party against whom a cause of action based upon contract, express or implied, is asserted may serve upon the claimant a written offer to allow judgment to be taken against him for a sum therein specified, with costs then accrued, if the party against whom the claim is asserted fails in his defense. If within ten days thereafter the claimant serves a written notice that he accepts the offer, and damages are awarded to him on the trial, they shall be assessed in the sum specified in the offer. If the offer is not so accepted and the claimant fails to obtain a more favorable judgment, he shall pay the expenses necessarily incurred by the party against whom the claim is asserted, for trying the issue of damages from the time of the offer. The expenses shall be ascertained by the judge or referee before whom the case is tried. An offer under this rule shall not be made known to the jury.

New York Civil Practice Law and Rules 3221

Except in a matrimonial action, at any time not later than ten days before trial, any party against whom a claim is asserted, and against whom a separate judgment may be taken, may serve upon the claimant a written offer to allow judgment to be taken against him for a sum or property or to the effect therein specified, with costs then accrued. If within ten days thereafter the claimant serves a written notice that he accepts the offer, either party may file the summons, complaint and offer, with proof of acceptance, and thereupon the clerk shall enter judgment accordingly. If the offer is not accepted and the claimant fails to obtain a more favorable judgment, he shall not recover costs from the time of the offer, but shall pay costs from that time. An offer of judgment shall not be made known to the jury.

Rule 69. Execution

(a) In General. Process to enforce a judgment for the payment of money shall be a writ of execution, unless the court directs otherwise. The procedure on execution, in proceedings supplementary to and in aid of a judgment, and in proceedings on and in aid of execution shall be in accordance with the practice and procedure of the state in which the district court is held, existing at the time the remedy is sought, except that any statute of the United States governs to the extent that it is applicable. In aid of the judgment or execution, the judgment creditor or a successor in interest when that interest appears of record, may obtain discovery from any person, including the judgment debtor, in the manner provided in these rules or in the manner provided by the practice of the state in which the district court is held.

(b) Against Certain Public Officers. When a judgment has been entered against a collector or other officer of revenue under the circumstances stated in Title 28, U.S.C. § 2006, or against an officer of Congress in an action mentioned in the Act of March 3, 1875, ch. 130, § 8 (18 Stat. 401), U.S.C. Title 2, § 118, and when the court has given the certificate of probable cause for the officer's act as provided in those statutes, execution shall not issue against the officer or the officer's property but the final judgment shall be satisfied as provided in such statutes.

State Provisions Exempting Property from Execution

New York Civil Practice Law and Rules 5205

(a) **Exemption for personal property.** The following personal property when owned by any person is exempt from application to the satisfaction of a money judgment except where the judgment is for the purchase price of the exempt property or was recovered by a domestic, laboring person or mechanic for work performed by that person in such capacity:

    1. all stoves kept for use in the judgment debtor's dwelling house and necessary fuel therefor for sixty days; one sewing machine with its appurtenances;

    2. the family bible, family pictures, and school books used by the judgment debtor or in the family; and other books, not exceeding fifty dollars in value, kept and used as part of the family or judgment debtor's library;

3. a seat or pew occupied by the judgment debtor or the family in a place of public worship;

4. domestic animals with the necessary food for those animals for sixty days, provided that the total value of such animals and food does not exceed four hundred fifty dollars; all necessary food actually provided for the use of the judgment debtor or his family for sixty days;

5. all wearing apparel, household furniture, one mechanical, gas or electric refrigerator, one radio receiver, one television set, crockery, tableware and cooking utensils necessary for the judgment debtor and the family;

6. a wedding ring; a watch not exceeding thirty-five dollars in value; and

7. necessary working tools and implements, including those of a mechanic, farm machinery, team, professional instruments, furniture and library, not exceeding six hundred dollars in value, together with the necessary food for the team for sixty days, provided, however, that the articles specified in this paragraph are necessary to the carrying on of the judgment debtor's profession or calling.

(b) Exemption of cause of action and damages for taking or injuring exempt personal property. A cause of action, to recover damages for taking or injuring personal property exempt from application to the satisfaction of a money judgment, is exempt from application to the satisfaction of a money judgment. A money judgment and its proceeds arising out of such a cause of action is exempt, for one year after the collection thereof, from application to the satisfaction of a money judgment.

(c) Trust exemption. 1. * * * [A]ll property while held in trust for a judgment debtor, where the trust has been created by, or the fund so held in trust has proceeded from, a person other than the judgment debtor, is exempt from application to the satisfaction of a money judgment. * * *

(d) Income exemptions. The following personal property is exempt from application to the satisfaction of a money judgment, except such part as a court determines to be unnecessary for the reasonable requirements of the judgment debtor and his dependents:

1. ninety per cent of the income or other payments from a trust the principal of which is exempt under subdivision (c) [and one hundred per cent of income from keogh and other retirement plans];

2. ninety per cent of the earnings of the judgment debtor for his personal services rendered within sixty days before, and at any time after, an income execution is delivered to the sheriff or a motion is made to secure the application of the judgment debtor's earnings to the satisfaction of the judgment; and

3. payments pursuant to an award in a matrimonial action, for the support of a wife, where the wife is the judgment debtor, or for the support of a child, where the child is the judgment debtor; where the award was made by a court of the state, determination of the extent to which it is unnecessary shall be made by that court.

(e) Exemptions to members of armed forces. The pay and bounty of a non-commissioned officer, musician or private in the armed forces of the United States or the state of New York; a land warrant, pension or other reward granted by the United States, or by a state, for services in the armed forces; a sword, horse, medal, emblem or device of any kind presented as a testimonial for services rendered in the armed forces of the United States or a state; and the uniform, arms and equipments which were used by a person in the service, are exempt from application to the satisfaction of a money judgment; provided, however, that the provisions of this subdivision shall not apply to the satisfaction of any order or money judgment for the support of a person's child, spouse, or former spouse.

(f) Exemption for unpaid milk proceeds. Ninety per cent of any money or debt due or to become due to the judgment debtor for the sale of milk produced on a farm operated by him and delivered for his account to a milk dealer licensed pursuant to article twenty-one of the agriculture and markets law is exempt from application to the satisfaction of a money judgment.

(g) Security deposit exemption. Money deposited as security for the rental of real property to be used as the residence of the judgment debtor or the judgment debtor's family; and money deposited as security with a gas, electric, water, steam, telegraph or telephone corporation, or a municipality rendering equivalent utility services, for services to judgment debtor's residence or the residence of judgment debtor's family, are exempt from application to the satisfaction of a money judgment.

(h) The following personal property is exempt from application to the satisfaction of money judgment, except such part as a court determines to be unnecessary for the reasonable requirements of the judgment debtor and his dependents:

1. any and all medical and dental accessions to the human body and all personal property or equipment that is necessary or proper to maintain or assist in sustaining or maintaining one or more major life activities or is utilized to provide mobility for a person with a permanent disability; and

2. any guide dog, service dog or hearing dog, as those terms are defined in section one hundred eight of the agriculture and markets law, or any animal trained to aid or assist a person with a permanent disability and actually being so used by such person, together with any and all food or feed for any such dog or other animal.

(i) * * *

(j) * * *

New York Civil Practice Law and Rules 5206

(a) Exemption of homestead. Property of one of the following types, not exceeding ten thousand dollars in value above liens and encumbrances, owned and occupied as a principal residence, is exempt from application to the satisfaction of a money judgment, unless the judgment was recovered wholly for the purchase price thereof:

1. a lot of land with a dwelling thereon,

2. shares of stock in a cooperative apartment corporation,

3. units of a condominium apartment, or

4. a mobile home.

But no exempt homestead shall be exempt from taxation or from sale for nonpayment of taxes or assessments.

(b) Homestead exemption after owner's death. The homestead exemption continues after the death of the person in whose favor the property was exempted for the benefit of the surviving spouse and surviving children until the majority of the youngest surviving child and until the death of the surviving spouse.

(c) Suspension of occupation as affecting homestead. The homestead exemption ceases if the property ceases to be occupied as a residence by a person for whose benefit it may so continue, except where the suspension of occupation is for a period not exceeding one year, and occurs in consequence of injury to, or destruction of, the dwelling house upon the premises.

(d) Exemption of homestead exceeding ten thousand dollars in value. The exemption of a homestead is not void because the value of the property exceeds ten thousand dollars but the lien of a judgment attaches to the surplus.

(e) Sale of homestead exceeding ten thousand dollars in value. A judgment creditor may commence a special proceeding in the county in which the homestead is located against the judgment debtor for the sale, by a sheriff or receiver, of a homestead exceeding ten thousand dollars in value. The court may direct that the notice of petition be served upon any other person. The court, if it directs such a sale, shall so marshal the proceeds of the sale that the right and interest of each person in the proceeds shall correspond as nearly as may be to his right and interest in the property sold.   Money, not exceeding ten thousand dollars, paid to a judgment debtor, as representing his interest in the proceeds, is exempt for one year after the payment, unless, before the expiration of the year, he acquires an exempt homestead, in which case, the exemption ceases with respect to so much of the money as was not expended for the purchase of that property; and the exemption of the property so acquired extends to every debt against which the property sold was exempt.   Where the exemption of property sold as prescribed in this subdivision has been continued after the judgment debtor's death, or where he dies after the sale and before payment to him of his portion of the proceeds of the sale, the court may direct that portion of the proceeds which represents his interest be invested for the benefit of the person or persons entitled to the benefit of the exemption, or be otherwise disposed of as justice requires.

(f) **Exemption of burying ground.**   Land, set apart as a family or private burying ground, is exempt from application to the satisfaction of a money judgment, upon the following conditions only:

1.   a portion of it must have been actually used for that purpose;

2.   it must not exceed in extent one-fourth of an acre;   and

3.   it must not contain any building or structure, except one or more vaults or other places of deposit for the dead, or mortuary monuments.

Rule 70.   Judgment for Specific Acts;   Vesting Title

If a judgment directs a party to execute a conveyance of land or to deliver deeds or other documents or to perform any other specific act and the party fails to comply within the time specified, the court may direct the act to be done at the cost of the disobedient party by some other person appointed by the court and the act when so done has like effect as if done by the party.   On application of the party entitled to performance, the clerk shall issue a writ of attachment or sequestration against the property of the disobedient party to compel obedience to the judgment.   The court may also in proper cases adjudge the party in contempt.   If real or personal property is within the district, the court in lieu of directing a conveyance thereof may enter a judgment divesting the title of any party and vesting it in others and such judgment has the effect of a conveyance executed in due form of law.   When any order or judgment is for the delivery of possession, the party in whose favor it is entered is entitled to a writ of execution or assistance upon application to the clerk.

Rule 71.   Process in Behalf of and Against Persons Not Parties

When an order is made in favor of a person who is not a party to the action, that person may enforce obedience to the order by the same process as if a party;   and, when obedience to an order may be lawfully enforced against a person who is not a party, that person is liable to the same process for enforcing obedience to the order as if a party.

IX.   SPECIAL PROCEEDINGS

Rule 71A.   Condemnation of Property

(a) Applicability of Other Rules. The Rules of Civil Procedure for the United States District Courts govern the procedure for the condemnation of real and personal property under the power of eminent domain, except as otherwise provided in this rule.

(b) Joinder of Properties. The plaintiff may join in the same action one or more separate pieces of property, whether in the same or different ownership and whether or not sought for the same use.

(c) Complaint.

(1) *Caption.* The complaint shall contain a caption as provided in Rule 10(a), except that the plaintiff shall name as defendants the property, designated generally by kind, quantity, and location, and at least one of the owners of some part of or interest in the property.

(2) *Contents.* The complaint shall contain a short and plain statement of the authority for the taking, the use for which the property is to be taken, a description of the property sufficient for its identification, the interests to be acquired, and as to each separate piece of property a designation of the defendants who have been joined as owners thereof or of some interest therein. Upon the commencement of the action, the plaintiff need join as defendants only the persons having or claiming an interest in the property whose names are then known, but prior to any hearing involving the compensation to be paid for a piece of property, the plaintiff shall add as defendants all persons having or claiming an interest in that property whose names can be ascertained by a reasonably diligent search of the records, considering the character and value of the property involved and the interests to be acquired, and also those whose names have otherwise been learned. All others may be made defendants under the designation "Unknown Owners." Process shall be served as provided in subdivision (d) of this rule upon all defendants, whether named as defendants at the time of the commencement of the action or subsequently added, and a defendant may answer as provided in subdivision (e) of this rule. The court meanwhile may order such distribution of a deposit as the facts warrant.

(3) *Filing.* In addition to filing the complaint with the court, the plaintiff shall furnish to the clerk at least one copy thereof for the use of the defendants and additional copies at the request of the clerk or of a defendant.

(d) Process.

(1) *Notice; Delivery.* Upon the filing of the complaint the plaintiff shall forthwith deliver to the clerk joint or several notices directed to the defendants named or designated in the complaint. Additional notices

directed to defendants subsequently added shall be so delivered. The delivery of the notice and its service have the same effect as the delivery and service of the summons under Rule 4.

(2) *Same; Form.* Each notice shall state the court, the title of the action, the name of the defendant to whom it is directed, that the action is to condemn property, a description of the defendant's property sufficient for its identification, the interest to be taken, the authority for the taking, the uses for which the property is to be taken, that the defendant may serve upon the plaintiff's attorney an answer within 20 days after service of the notice, and that the failure so to serve an answer constitutes a consent to the taking and to the authority of the court to proceed to hear the action and to fix the compensation. The notice shall conclude with the name of the plaintiff's attorney and an address within the district in which action is brought where the attorney may be served. The notice need contain a description of no other property than that to be taken from the defendants to whom it is directed.

(3) *Service of Notice.*

A. Personal Service. Personal service of the notice (but without copies of the complaint) shall be made in accordance with Rule 4 upon a defendant whose residence is known and who resides within the United States or a territory subject to the administration or judicial jurisdiction of the United States.

B. Service by Publication. Upon the filing of a certificate of the plaintiff's attorney stating that the attorney believes a defendant cannot be personally served, because after diligent inquiry within the state in which the complaint is filed the defendant's place of residence cannot be ascertained by the plaintiff or, if ascertained, that it is beyond the territorial limits of personal service as provided in this rule, service of the notice shall be made on this defendant by publication in a newspaper published in the county where the property is located, or if there is no such newspaper, then in a newspaper having a general circulation where the property is located, once a week for not less than three successive weeks. Prior to the last publication, a copy of the notice shall also be mailed to a defendant who cannot be personally served as provided in this rule but whose place of residence is then known. Unknown owners may be served by publication in like manner by a notice addressed to "Unknown Owners."

Service by publication is complete upon the date of the last publication. Proof of publication and mailing shall be made by certificate of the plaintiff's attorney, to which shall be attached a printed copy of the published notice with the name and dates of the newspaper marked thereon.

(4) *Return; Amendment.* Proof of service of the notice shall be made and amendment of the notice or proof of its service allowed in the

manner provided for the return and amendment of the summons under Rule 4.

(e) Appearance or Answer. If a defendant has no objection or defense to the taking of the defendant's property, the defendant may serve a notice of appearance designating the property in which the defendant claims to be interested. Thereafter, the defendant shall receive notice of all proceedings affecting it. If a defendant has any objection or defense to the taking of the property, the defendant shall serve an answer within 20 days after the service of notice upon the defendant. The answer shall identify the property in which the defendant claims to have an interest, state the nature and extent of the interest claimed, and state all the defendant's objections and defenses to the taking of the property. A defendant waives all defenses and objections not so presented, but at the trial of the issue of just compensation, whether or not the defendant has previously appeared or answered, the defendant may present evidence as to the amount of the compensation to be paid for the property, and the defendant may share in the distribution of the award. No other pleading or motion asserting any additional defense or objection shall be allowed.

(f) Amendment of Pleadings. Without leave of court, the plaintiff may amend the complaint at any time before the trial of the issue of compensation and as many times as desired, but no amendment shall be made which will result in a dismissal forbidden by subdivision (i) of this rule. The plaintiff need not serve a copy of an amendment, but shall serve notice of the filing, as provided in Rule 5(b), upon any party affected thereby who has appeared and, in the manner provided in subdivision (d) of this rule, upon any party affected thereby who has not appeared. The plaintiff shall furnish to the clerk of the court for the use of the defendants at least one copy of each amendment, and shall furnish additional copies on the request of the clerk or of a defendant. Within the time allowed by subdivision (e) of this rule a defendant may serve an answer to the amended pleading, in the form and manner and with the same effect as there provided.

(g) Substitution of Parties. If a defendant dies or becomes incompetent or transfers an interest after the defendant's joinder, the court may order substitution of the proper party upon motion and notice of hearing. If the motion and notice of hearing are to be served upon a person not already a party, service shall be made as provided in subdivision (d)(3) of this rule.

(h) Trial. If the action involves the exercise of the power of eminent domain under the law of the United States, any tribunal specially constituted by an Act of Congress governing the case for the trial of the issue of just compensation shall be the tribunal for the determination of that issue; but if there is no such specially constituted tribunal any party may have a trial by jury of the issue of just compensation by filing a demand therefor within the time allowed for answer or within such further time as the court may fix, unless the court in its discretion orders that, because of the character, location, or quantity of the property to be condemned, or for other reasons in the interest of justice, the issue of compensation shall be determined by a commission of three persons appointed by it.

In the event that a commission is appointed the court may direct that not more than two additional persons serve as alternate commissioners to hear the case and replace commissioners who, prior to the time when a decision is filed, are found by the court to be unable or disqualified to perform their duties. An alternate who does not replace a regular commissioner shall be discharged after the commission renders its final decision. Before appointing the members of the commission and alternates the court shall advise the parties of the identity and qualifications of each prospective commissioner and alternate and may permit the parties to examine each such designee. The parties shall not be permitted or required by the court to suggest nominees. Each party shall have the right to object for valid cause to the appointment of any person as a commissioner or alternate. If a commission is appointed it shall have the powers of a master provided in subdivision (c) of Rule 53 and proceedings before it shall be governed by the provisions of paragraphs (1) and (2) of subdivision (d) of Rule 53. Its action and report shall be determined by a majority and its findings and report shall have the effect, and be dealt with by the court in accordance with the practice, prescribed in paragraph (2) of subdivision (e) of Rule 53. Trial of all issues shall otherwise be by the court.

(i) Dismissal of Action.

(1) *As of Right.* If no hearing has begun to determine the compensation to be paid for a piece of property and the plaintiff has not acquired the title or a lesser interest in or taken possession, the plaintiff may dismiss the action as to that property, without an order of the court, by filing a notice of dismissal setting forth a brief description of the property as to which the action is dismissed.

(2) *By Stipulation.* Before the entry of any judgment vesting the plaintiff with title or a lesser interest in or possession of property, the action may be dismissed in whole or in part, without an order of the court, as to any property by filing a stipulation of dismissal by the plaintiff and the defendant affected thereby; and, if the parties so stipulate, the court may vacate any judgment that has been entered.

(3) *By Order of the Court.* At any time before compensation for a piece of property has been determined and paid and after motion and hearing, the court may dismiss the action as to that property, except that it shall not dismiss the action as to any part of the property of which the plaintiff has taken possession or in which the plaintiff has taken title or a lesser interest, but shall award just compensation for the possession,

175

title or lesser interest so taken.   The court at any time may drop a defendant unnecessarily or improperly joined.

(4) *Effect.*   Except as otherwise provided in the notice, or stipulation of dismissal, or order of the court, any dismissal is without prejudice.

(j) Deposit and Its Distribution.   The plaintiff shall deposit with the court any money required by law as a condition to the exercise of the power of eminent domain; and, although not so required, may make a deposit when permitted by statute.   In such cases the court and attorneys shall expedite the proceedings for the distribution of the money so deposited and for the ascertainment and payment of just compensation. If the compensation finally awarded to any defendant exceeds the amount which has been paid to that defendant on distribution of the deposit, the court shall enter judgment against the plaintiff and in favor of that defendant for the deficiency. If the compensation finally awarded to any defendant is less than the amount which has been paid to that defendant, the court shall enter judgment against that defendant and in favor of the plaintiff for the overpayment.

(k) Condemnation Under a State's Power of Eminent Domain.   The practice as herein prescribed governs in actions involving the exercise of the power of eminent domain under the law of a state, provided that if the state law makes provision for trial of any issue by jury, or for trial of the issue of compensation by jury or commission or both, that provision shall be followed.

(*l*) Costs.   Costs are not subject to Rule 54(d).

Rule 72.   Magistrates; Pretrial Matters

(a) Nondispositive Matters.   A magistrate judge to whom a pretrial matter not dispositive of a claim or defense of a party is referred to hear and determine shall promptly conduct such proceedings as are required and when appropriate enter into the record a written order setting forth the disposition of the matter.   Within 10 days after being served with a copy of the magistrate judge's order, a party may serve and file objections to the order; a party may not thereafter assign as error a defect in the magistrate judge's order to which objection was not timely made.   The district judge to whom the case is assigned shall consider such objections and shall modify or set aside any portion of the magistrate judge's order found to be clearly erroneous or contrary to law.

(b) Dispositive Motions and Prisoner Petitions.   A magistrate judge assigned without consent of the parties to hear a pretrial matter dispositive of a claim or defense of a party or a prisoner petition challenging the conditions of confinement shall promptly conduct such proceedings as are required.   A record shall be made of all evidentiary proceedings before the magistrate judge, and a record may be made of such other proceedings as the magistrate judge deems necessary.   The magistrate judge shall enter into the record a recommendation for disposition of the matter, including proposed findings of fact when appropriate. The clerk shall forthwith mail copies to all parties.

A party objecting to the recommended disposition of the matter shall promptly arrange for the transcription of the record, or portions of it as all parties may agree upon or the magistrate judge deems sufficient, unless the district judge otherwise directs. Within 10 days after being served with a copy of the recommended disposition, a party may serve and file specific, written objections to the proposed findings and recommendations. A party may respond to another party's objections within 10 days after being served with a copy thereof. The district judge to whom the case is assigned shall make a de novo determination upon the record, or after additional evidence, of any portion of the magistrate judge's disposition to which specific written objection has been made in accordance with this rule. The district judge may accept, reject, or modify the recommended decision, receive further evidence, or recommit the matter to the magistrate judge with instructions.

Rule 73. Magistrate Judges; Trial by Consent and Appeal Options

(a) Powers; Procedure. When specially designated to exercise such jurisdiction by local rule or order of the district court and when all parties consent thereto, a magistrate judge may exercise the authority provided by Title 28, U.S.C. § 636(c) and may conduct any or all proceedings, including a jury or nonjury trial, in a civil case. A record of the proceedings shall be made in accordance with the requirements of Title 28, U.S.C. § 636(c)(5).

(b) Consent. When a magistrate judge has been designated to exercise civil trial jurisdiction, the clerk shall give written notice to the parties of their opportunity to consent to the exercise by a magistrate of civil jurisdiction over the case, as authorized by Title 28, U.S.C. § 636(c). If, within the period specified by local rule, the parties agree to a magistrate judge's exercise of such authority, they shall execute and file a joint form of consent or separate forms of consent setting forth such election.

A district judge, magistrate judge, or other court official may again advise the parties of the availability of the magistrate judge, but, in so doing, shall also advise the parties that they are free to withhold consent without adverse substantive consequences. A district judge or magistrate judge shall not be informed of a party's response to the clerk's notification, unless all parties have consented to the referral of the matter to a magistrate judge.

The district judge, for good cause shown on the judge's own initiative, or under extraordinary circumstances shown by a party, may vacate a reference of a civil matter to a magistrate judge under this subdivision.

(c) Appeal. In accordance with Title 28, U.S.C. § 636(c)(3), appeal from a judgment entered upon direction of a magistrate judge in proceedings under this rule will lie to the court of appeals as it would from a judgment of the district court.

Rule 74–76. (Abrogated, eff. Dec. 1, 1997)

X. DISTRICT COURTS AND CLERKS

Rule 77. District Courts and Clerks

[See proposed changes to Rule 77(d), in Part IX, infra.

(a) District Courts Always Open. The district courts shall be deemed always open for the purpose of filing any pleading or other proper paper, of issuing and returning mesne and final process, and of making and directing all interlocutory motions, orders, and rules.

(b) Trials and Hearings; Orders in Chambers. All trials upon the merits shall be conducted in open court and so far as convenient in a regular court room. All other acts or proceedings may be done or conducted by a judge in chambers, without the attendance of the clerk or other court officials and at any place either within or without the district; but no hearing, other than one ex parte, shall be conducted outside the district without the consent of all parties affected thereby.

(c) Clerk's Office and Orders by Clerk. The clerk's office with the clerk or a deputy in attendance shall be open during business hours on all days except Saturdays, Sundays, and legal holidays, but a district court may provide by local rule or order that its clerk's office shall be open for specified hours on Saturdays or particular legal holidays other than New Year's Day, Washington's Birthday, Memorial Day, Independence Day, Labor Day, Columbus Day, Veterans Day, Thanksgiving Day, and Christmas Day. All motions and applications in the clerk's office for issuing mesne process, for issuing final process to enforce and execute judgments, for entering defaults or judgments by default, and for other proceedings which do not require allowance or order of the court are grantable of course by the clerk; but the clerk's action may be suspended or altered or rescinded by the court upon cause shown.

(d) Notice of Orders or Judgments. Immediately upon the entry of an order or judgment the clerk shall serve a notice of the entry by mail in the manner provided for in Rule 5 upon each party who is not in default for failure to appear, and shall make a note in the docket of the mailing. Any party may in addition serve a notice of such entry in the manner provided in Rule 5 for the service of papers. Lack of notice of the entry by the clerk does not affect the time to appeal or relieve or authorize the court to relieve a party for failure to appeal within the time allowed, except as permitted in Rule 4(a) of the Federal Rules of Appellate Procedure.

Rule 78. Motion Day

Unless local conditions make it impracticable, each district court shall establish regular times and places, at intervals sufficiently frequent for the prompt dispatch of business, at which motions requiring notice and hearing may be heard and disposed of; but the judge at any time or place and on such notice, if any, as the judge considers reasonable may make orders for the advancement, conduct, and hearing of actions.

To expedite its business, the court may make provision by rule or order for the submission and determination of motions without oral hearing upon brief written statements of reasons in support and opposition.

Rule 79. Books and Records Kept by the Clerk and Entries Therein

(a) Civil Docket. The clerk shall keep a book known as "civil docket" of such form and style as may be prescribed by the Director of the Administrative Office of the United States Courts with the approval of the Judicial Conference of the United States, and shall enter therein each civil action to which these rules are made applicable. Actions shall be assigned consecutive file numbers. The file number of each action shall be noted on the folio of the docket whereon the first entry of the action is made. All papers filed with the clerk, all process issued and returns made thereon, all appearances, orders, verdicts, and judgments shall be entered chronologically in the civil docket on the folio assigned to the action and shall be marked with its file number. These entries shall be brief but shall show the nature of each paper filed or writ issued and the substance of each order or judgment of the court and of the returns showing execution of process. The entry of an order or judgment shall show the date the entry is made. When in an action trial by jury has been properly demanded or ordered the clerk shall enter the word "jury" on the folio assigned to that action.

(b) Civil Judgments and Orders. The clerk shall keep, in such form and manner as the Director of the Administrative Office of the United States Courts with the approval of the Judicial Conference of the United States may prescribe, a correct copy of every final judgment or appealable order, or order affecting title to or lien upon real or personal property, and any other order which the court may direct to be kept.

(c) Indices; Calendars. Suitable indices of the civil docket and of every civil judgment and order referred to in subdivision (b) of this rule shall be kept by the clerk under the direction of the court. There shall be prepared under the direction of the court calendars of all actions ready for trial, which shall distinguish "jury actions" from "court actions."

(d) Other Books and Records of the Clerk. The clerk shall also keep such other books and records as may be required from time to time by the Director of the Administrative Office of the United States Courts with the approval of the Judicial Conference of the United States.

Rule 80. Stenographer; Stenographic Report or Transcript as Evidence

(a), (b) [Abrogated]

(c) Stenographic Report or Transcript as Evidence. Whenever the testimony of a witness at a trial or hearing which was stenographically reported is admissible in evidence at a later trial, it may be proved by the transcript thereof duly certified by the person who reported the testimony.

XI. GENERAL PROVISIONS

Rule 81. Applicability in General

[See proposed changes to Rule 81(a), in Part IX, infra.]

(a) To What Proceedings Applicable.

(1) These rules do not apply to prize proceedings in admiralty governed by Title 10, U.S.C. §§ 7651–7681. They do not apply to proceedings in bankruptcy or proceedings in copyright under Title 17, U.S.C., except in so far as they may be made applicable thereto by rules promulgated by Supreme Court of the United States. They do not apply to mental health proceedings in the United States District Court for the District of Columbia.

(2) These rules are applicable to proceedings for admission to citizenship, habeas corpus, and quo warranto, to the extent that the practice in such proceedings is not set forth in statutes of the United States and has heretofore conformed to the practice in civil actions. The writ of habeas corpus, or order to show cause, shall be directed to the person having custody of the person detained. It shall be returned within 3 days unless for good cause shown additional time is allowed which in cases brought under 28 U.S.C. § 2254 shall not exceed 40 days, and in all other cases shall not exceed 20 days.

(3) In proceedings under Title 9, U.S.C., relating to arbitration, or under the Act of May 20, 1926, ch. 347, § 9 (44 Stat. 585), U.S.C., Title 45, § 159, relating to boards of arbitration of railway labor disputes, these rules apply only to the extent that matters of procedure are not provided for in those statutes. These rules apply to proceedings to compel the giving of testimony or production of documents in accordance with a subpoena issued by an officer or agency of the United States under any statute of the United States except as otherwise provided by statute or by rules of the district court or by order of the court in the proceedings.

(4) These rules do not alter the method prescribed by the Act of February 18, 1922, c. 57, § 2 (42 Stat. 388), U.S.C., Title 7, § 292; or by the Act of June 10, 1930, c. 436, § 7 (46 Stat. 534), as amended, U.S.C., Title 7, § 499g(c), for instituting proceedings in the United States district courts to review orders of the Secretary of Agriculture; or prescribed by the Act of June 25, 1934, c. 742, § 2 (48 Stat. 1214), U.S.C., Title 15, § 522, for instituting proceedings to review orders of the Secretary of the Interior; or prescribed by the Act of February 22, 1935, c. 18, § 5 (49 Stat. 31), U.S.C., Title 15, § 715d(c), as extended, for instituting proceedings to review orders of petroleum control boards; but the conduct of such proceedings in the district courts shall be made to conform to these rules as far as applicable.

(5) These rules do not alter the practice in the United States district courts prescribed in the Act of July 5, 1935, c. 372, §§ 9 and 10 (49 Stat. 453), as amended, U.S.C., Title 29, §§ 159 and 160, for beginning and conducting proceedings to enforce orders of the National Labor Relations Board; and in respects not covered by those statutes, the practice in the district courts shall conform to these rules so far as applicable.

(6) These rules apply to proceedings for enforcement or review of compensation orders under the Longshoremen's and Harbor Workers' Compensation Act, Act of March 4, 1927, c. 509, §§ 18, 21 (44 Stat. 1434, 1436), as amended, U.S.C., Title 33, §§ 918, 921, except to the extent that matters of procedure are provided for in that Act. The provisions for service by publication and for answer in proceedings to cancel certificates of citizenship under the Act of June 27, 1952, c. 477, Title III, c. 2, § 340 (66 Stat. 260), U.S.C., Title 8, § 1451, remain in effect.

(7) [Abrogated]

(b) Scire Facias and Mandamus. The writs of scire facias and mandamus are abolished. Relief heretofore available by mandamus or scire facias may be obtained by appropriate action or by appropriate motion under the practice prescribed in these rules.

(c) Removed Actions. These rules apply to civil actions removed to the United States district courts from the state courts and govern procedure after removal. Repleading is not necessary unless the court so orders. In a removed action in which the defendant has not an- swered, the defendant shall answer or present the other defenses or objections available under these rules within 20 days after the receipt through service or otherwise of a copy of the initial pleading setting forth the claim for relief upon which the action or proceeding is based, or within 20 days after the service of summons upon such initial pleading, then filed, or within 5 days after the filing of the petition for removal, whichever period is longest. If at the time of removal all necessary pleadings have been served, a party entitled to trial by jury under Rule 38 shall be accorded it, if the party's demand therefor is served within 10 days after the petition for removal is filed if the party is the petitioner, or if not the petitioner within 10 days after service on the party of the notice of filing the petition. A party who, prior to removal, has made an express demand for trial by jury in accordance with state law, need not make a demand after removal. If state law applicable in the court from which the case is removed does not require the parties to make express demands in order to claim trial by jury, they need not make demands after removal unless the court directs that they do so within a specified time if they desire to claim trial by jury. The court may make this direction on its own motion and shall do so as a matter of course at the request of any party. The failure of a party to make demand as directed constitutes a waiver by that party of trial by jury.

(d) [Abrogated]

(e) Law Applicable. Whenever in these rules the law of the state in which the district court is held is made applicable, the law applied in the District of Columbia governs proceedings in the United States District Court for the District of Columbia. When the word "state" is used, it includes, if appropriate, the District of Columbia. When the term "statute of the United States" is used, it includes, so far as concerns proceedings in the United States District Court for the District of Columbia, any Act of Congress locally applicable to and in force in the District of Columbia. When the law of a state is referred to, the word "law" includes the statutes of that state and the state judicial decisions construing them.

(f) References to Officer of the United States. Under any rule in which reference is made to an officer or agency of the United States, the term "officer" includes a district director of internal revenue, a former district director or collector of internal revenue, or the personal representative of a deceased district director or collector of internal revenue.

Rule 82. Jurisdiction and Venue Unaffected

These rules shall not be construed to extend or limit the jurisdiction of the United States district courts or the venue of actions therein. An admiralty or maritime claim within the meaning of Rule 9(h) shall not be treated as a civil action for the purposes of Title 28, U.S.C. §§ 1391–93.

Rule 83. Rules by District Courts; Judge's Directives

(a) Local Rules.

(1) Each district court, acting by a majority of its district judges, may, after giving appropriate public notice and an opportunity for comment, make and amend rules governing its practice. A local rule shall be consistent with—but not duplicative of—Acts of Congress and rules adopted under 28 U.S.C. §§ 2072 and 2075, and shall conform to any uniform numbering system prescribed by the Judicial Conference of

the United States. A local rule takes effect on the date specified by the district court and remains in effect unless amended by the court or abrogated by the judicial council of the circuit. Copies of rules and amendments shall, upon their promulgation, be furnished to the judicial council and the Administrative Office of the United States Courts and be made available to the public.

(2) A local rule imposing a requirement of form shall not be enforced in a manner that causes a party to lose rights because of a nonwillful failure to comply with the requirement.

(b) Procedures When There Is No Controlling Law. A judge may regulate practice in any manner consistent with federal law, rules adopted under 28 U.S.C. §§ 2072 and 2075, and local rules of the district. No sanction or other disadvantage may be imposed for noncompliance with any requirement not in federal law, federal rules, or the local district rules unless the alleged violator has been furnished in the particular case with actual notice of the requirement.

1985 Amendment to Rule 83

The 1985 alteration enhances the local rulemaking process by requiring appropriate public notice of proposed rules and an opportunity to comment on them. It attempts to assure that the expert advice of practitioners and scholars is made available to the district court before local rules are promulgated.

Rule 84. Forms

The forms contained in the Appendix of Forms are sufficient under the rules and are intended to indicate the simplicity and brevity of statement which the rules contemplate.

Notes on the 1946 Amendment to Federal Rule 84

In 1946 Rule 84 was amended to state that the forms were sufficient under the rules. The Advisory Committee commented as follows:

The amendment serves to emphasize that the forms contained in the Appendix of Forms are sufficient to withstand attack under the rules under which they are drawn, and that the practitioner using them may rely on them to that extent. The circuit courts of appeals generally have upheld the use of the forms as promoting desirable simplicity and brevity of statement. Sierocinski v. E. I. DuPont DeNemours & Co. (CCA3d, 1939) 103 F.2d 843; Swift & Co. v. Young (CCA4th, 1939) 107 F.2d 170; Sparks v. England (CCA8th, 1940) 113 F.2d 579; Ramsouer v. Midland Valley R. Co. (CCA8th, 1943) 135 F.2d 101. And the forms as a whole have met with widespread approval in the courts. See cases cited in 1 Moore's Federal Practice (1938), Cum.Supplement § 8.07, under "Page 554"; see also Commentary, The Official Forms, 1941, 4 Fed. Rules Serv. 954. In Cook, "Facts" and "Statements of Fact", 1937, 4 U.Chi.L.Rev. 233, 245–246, it is said with reference to what is now Rule 84: "... pleaders in the federal courts are not to be left to guess as to the meaning of [the] language" in Rule 8(a) regarding the form of the complaint. "All of which is as it should be. In no other way can useless litigation be avoided." Ibid. The amended rule will operate to discourage isolated results such as those found in Washburn v. Moorman Mfg. Co. (S.D.Cal. 1938) 25 F.Supp. 546; Employers Mutual Liability Ins. Co. of Wisconsin v. Blue Line Transfer Co. (W.D.Mo.1941) 5 Fed.Rules Serv. 12e.235, Case 2.

Rule 85. Title

These rules may be known and cited as the Federal Rules of Civil Procedure.

Rule 86.   Effective Date

(a) **[Effective Date of Original Rules].** These rules will take effect on the day which is 3 months subsequent to the adjournment of the second regular session of the 75th Congress, but if that day is prior to September 1, 1938, then these rules will take effect on September 1, 1938. They govern all proceedings in actions brought after they take effect and also all further proceedings in actions then pending, except to the extent that in the opinion of the court their application in a particular action pending when the rules take effect would not be feasible or would work injustice, in which event the former procedure applies.

(b) **Effective Date of Amendments.** The amendments adopted by the Supreme Court on December 27, 1946, and transmitted to the Attorney General on January 2, 1947, shall take effect on the day which is three months subsequent to the adjournment of the first regular session of the 80th Congress, but, if that day is prior to September 1, 1947, then these amendments shall take effect on September 1, 1947. They govern all proceedings in actions brought after they take effect and also all further proceedings in actions then pending, except to the extent that in the opinion of the court their application in a particular action pending when the amendments take effect would not be feasible or would work injustice, in which event the former procedure applies.

(c) **Effective Date of Amendments.** The amendments adopted by the Supreme Court on December 29, 1948, and transmitted to the Attorney General on December 31, 1948, shall take effect on the day following the adjournment of the first regular session of the 81st Congress.

(d) **Effective Date of Amendments.** The amendments adopted by the Supreme Court on April 17, 1961, and transmitted to the Congress on April 18, 1961, shall take effect on July 19, 1961. They govern all proceedings in actions brought after they take effect and also all further proceedings in actions then pending, except to the extent that in the opinion of the court their application in a particular action pending when the amendments take effect would not be feasible or would work injustice, in which event the former procedure applies.

(e) **Effective Date of Amendments.** The amendments adopted by the Supreme Court on January 21, 1963, and transmitted to the Congress on January 21, 1963, shall take effect on July 1, 1963. They govern all proceedings in actions brought after they take effect and also all further proceedings in actions then pending, except to the extent that in the opinion of the court their application in a particular action pending when the amendments take effect would not be feasible or would work injustice, in which event the former procedure applies.

APPENDIX OF FORMS

(See Rule 84)

Introductory Statement

1. The following forms are intended for illustration only. They are limited in number. No attempt is made to furnish a manual of forms. Each form assumes the action to be brought in the Southern District of New York. If the district in which an action is brought has divisions, the division should be indicated in the caption.

2. Except where otherwise indicated each pleading, motion, and other paper should have a caption similar to that of the summons, with the designation of the particular paper substituted for the word "Summons". In the caption of the summons and in the caption of the complaint all parties must be named but in other pleadings and papers, it is sufficient to state the name of the first party on either side, with an appropriate indication of other parties. See Rules 4(b), 7(b)(2), and 10(a).

3. In Form 3 and the forms following, the words, "Allegation of jurisdiction," are used to indicate the appropriate allegation in Form 2.

4. Each pleading, motion, and other paper is to be signed in his individual name by at least one attorney of record (Rule 11). The attorney's name is to be followed by his address as indicated in Form 3. In forms following Form 3 the signature and address are not indicated.

5. If a party is not represented by an attorney, the signature and address of the party are required in place of those of the attorney.

Form 1.

SUMMONS

UNITED STATES DISTRICT COURT FOR THE SOUTHERN DISTRICT OF NEW YORK

Civil Action, File Number _____

A. B., Plaintiff)
)
v.) *Summons*
)
C. D., Defendant)

To the above-named Defendant:

You are hereby summoned and required to serve upon _____, plaintiff's attorney, whose address is _____, an answer to the complaint which is herewith served upon you, within 20 [1] days after service of this summons upon you, exclusive of the day of service. If you fail to do so, judgment by default will be taken against you for the relief demanded in the complaint.

—————————————————————,
Clerk of Court.

[Seal of the U. S. District Court]

Dated _____

(This summons is issued pursuant to Rule 4
  of the Federal Rules of Civil Procedure)

Form 1–A.

NOTICE OF LAWSUIT AND REQUEST FOR WAIVER OF SERVICE OF SUMMONS

TO: _____(A)_____ [as _____(B)_____ of _____(C)_____]

A lawsuit has been commenced against you (or the entity on whose behalf you are addressed). A copy of the complaint is attached to this notice. It has been filed in the United States District Court for the (D)_____ and has been assigned docket number _____(E)_____.

This is not a formal summons or notification from the court, but rather my request that you sign and return the enclosed waiver of service in order to save the cost of serving you with a judicial summons and an additional copy of the complaint. The cost of service will be avoided if I receive a signed copy of the waiver within _____(F) days after the date designated below as the date on which this Notice and Request is sent. I enclose a stamped and addressed envelope (or other means of cost-free return) for your use. An extra copy of the waiver is also attached for your records.

If you comply with this request and return the signed waiver, it will be filed with the court and no summons will be served on you. The action will then proceed as if you had been served on the date the waiver is filed, except that you will not be obligated to answer the complaint before 60 days from the date designated below as the date on which this notice is sent (or before 90 days from that date if your address is not in any judicial district of the United States).

If you do not return the signed waiver within the time indicated, I will take appropriate steps to effect formal service in a manner authorized by the Federal Rules of Civil Procedure and will then, to the extent authorized by those Rules, ask the court to require you (or the party on

[1] If the United States or an officer or agency thereof is a defendant, the time to [answer] * * * is 60 days.

whose behalf you are addressed) to pay the full costs of such service. In that connection, please read the statement concerning the duty of parties to waive the service of the summons, which is set forth on the reverse side (or at the foot) of the waiver form.

I affirm that this request is being sent to you on behalf of the plaintiff, this ___ day of _____, ___.

Signature of Plaintiff's Attorney
or Unrepresented Plaintiff

Notes:

A—Name of individual defendant (or name of officer or agent of corporate defendant)

B—Title, or other relationship of individual to corporate defendant

C—Name of corporate defendant, if any

D—District

E—Docket number of action

F—Addressee must be given at least 30 days (60 days if located in foreign country) in which to return waiver

Form 1–B.

WAIVER OF SERVICE OF SUMMONS

TO: (name of plaintiff's attorney or unrepresented plaintiff)

I acknowledge receipt of your request that I waive service of a summons in the action of   (caption of action)   , which is case number   (docket number)   in the United States District Court for the   (district)   . I have also received a copy of the complaint in the action, two copies of this instrument, and a means by which I can return the signed waiver to you without cost to me.

I agree to save the cost of service of a summons and an additional copy of the complaint in this lawsuit by not requiring that I (or the entity on whose behalf I am acting) be served with judicial process in the manner provided by Rule 4.

I (or the entity on whose behalf I am acting) will retain all defenses or objections to the lawsuit or to the jurisdiction or venue of the court except for objections based on a defect in the summons or in the service of the summons.

I understand that a judgment may be entered against me (or the party on whose behalf I am acting) if an answer or motion under Rule 12 is not served upon you within 60 days after   (date request was sent)   , or within 90 days after that date if the request was sent outside the United States.

Date   Signature
            Printed/typed name: _____
             [as _____]
             [of _____]

*To be printed on reverse side of the waiver form
or set forth at the foot of the form:*

Duty to Avoid Unnecessary Costs of Service of Summons

Rule 4 of the Federal Rules of Civil Procedure requires certain parties to cooperate in saving unnecessary costs of service of the summons and complaint. A defendant located in the United States who, after being notified of an action and asked by a plaintiff located in the United States to waive service of a summons, fails to do so will be required to bear the cost of such service unless good cause be shown for its failure to sign and return the waiver.

It is not good cause for a failure to waive service that a party believes that the complaint is unfounded, or that the action has been brought in an improper place or in a court that lacks jurisdiction over the subject matter of the action or over its person or property. A party who waives service of the summons retains all defenses and objections (except any relating to the summons or to the service of the summons), and may later object to the jurisdiction of the court or to the place where the action has been brought.

A defendant who waives service must within the time specified on the waiver form serve on the plaintiff's attorney (or unrepresented plaintiff) a response to the complaint and must also file a signed copy of the response with the court. If the answer or motion is not served within this time, a default judgment may be taken against that defendant. By waiving service, a defendant is allowed more time to answer than if the summons had been actually served when the request for waiver of service was received.

Form 2.

ALLEGATION OF JURISDICTION

(a) Jurisdiction founded on diversity of citizenship and amount.

[Note: A proposed amendment to Form 2(a), to take effect in December 1999, would eliminate the words "of fifty thousand dollars" and substitute "specified by 28 U.S.C. § 1332." The statute currently requires a sum in excess of $75,000.]

Plaintiff is a [citizen of the State of Connecticut] [corporation incorporated under the laws of the State of Connecticut having its principal place of business in the State of Connecticut] and defendant is a corporation incorporated under the laws of the State of New York having its principal place of business in a State other than the State of Connecticut. The matter in controversy exceeds, exclusive of interest and costs, the sum of fifty thousand dollars.

(b) Jurisdiction founded on the existence of a Federal question.

The action arises under [the Constitution of the United States, Article ___, Section ___]; [the ___ Amendment to the Constitution of the United States, Section ___]; [the Act of ___, ___ Stat. ___; U.S.C., Title ___, § ___]; [the Treaty of the United States (here describe the treaty)], as hereinafter more fully appears.

(c) Jurisdiction founded on the existence of a question arising under particular statutes.

The action arises under the Act of ___, ___ Stat. ___; U.S.C., Title ___, § ___, as hereinafter more fully appears.

(d) Jurisdiction founded on the admiralty or maritime character of the claim.

This is a case of admiralty and maritime jurisdiction, as hereinafter more fully appears. [If the pleader wishes to invoke the distinctively maritime procedures referred to in Rule 9(h), add the following or its substantial equivalent: This is an admiralty or maritime claim within the meaning of Rule 9(h).]

Form 3.

COMPLAINT ON A PROMISSORY NOTE

1. Allegation of jurisdiction.

2. Defendant on or about June 1, 1935, executed and delivered to plaintiff a promissory note [in the following words and figures: (here set out the note verbatim)]; [a copy of which is hereto annexed as Exhibit A]; [whereby defendant promised to pay to plaintiff or order on June 1, 1936 the sum of _____ dollars with interest thereon at the rate of six percent * * * per annum].

3. Defendant owes to plaintiff the amount of said note and interest.

Wherefore plaintiff demands judgment against defendant for the sum of _____ dollars, interest, and costs.

Signed: _____
                Attorney for Plaintiff

Address: _____

Form 4.

COMPLAINT ON AN ACCOUNT

1. Allegation of jurisdiction.

2. Defendant owes plaintiff _____ dollars according to the account hereto annexed as Exhibit A.

Wherefore (etc. as in Form 3).

Form 5.

COMPLAINT FOR GOODS SOLD AND DELIVERED

1. Allegation of jurisdiction.

2. Defendant owes plaintiff _____ dollars for goods sold and delivered by plaintiff to defendant between June 1, 1936 and December 1, 1936.

Wherefore (etc. as in Form 3).

Form 6.

COMPLAINT FOR MONEY LENT

1. Allegation of jurisdiction.

2. Defendant owes plaintiff _____ dollars for money lent by plaintiff to defendant on June 1, 1936.

Wherefore (etc. as in Form 3).

Form 7.

COMPLAINT FOR MONEY PAID BY MISTAKE

1. Allegation of jurisdiction.

2. Defendant owes plaintiff _____ dollars for money paid by plaintiff to defendant by mistake on June 1, 1936, under the following circumstances: [here state the circumstances with particularity—see Rule 9(b)].

Wherefore (etc. as in Form 3).

Form 8.

COMPLAINT FOR MONEY HAD AND RECEIVED

1. Allegation of jurisdiction.

2. Defendant owes plaintiff _____ dollars for money had and received from one G. H. on June 1, 1936, to be paid by defendant to plaintiff.

Wherefore (etc. as in Form 3).

Form 9.

COMPLAINT FOR NEGLIGENCE

1. Allegation of jurisdiction.

2. On June 1, 1936, in a public highway called Boylston Street in Boston, Massachusetts, defendant negligently drove a motor vehicle against plaintiff who was then crossing said highway.

3. As a result plaintiff was thrown down and had his leg broken and was otherwise injured, was prevented from transacting his business, suffered great pain of body and mind, and incurred expenses for medical attention and hospitalization in the sum of one thousand dollars.

Wherefore plaintiff demands judgment against defendant in the sum of _____ dollars and costs.

Comparative State Provision

North Carolina Rules of Civil Procedure—[Form] (3) Complaint for Negligence

1. On _____, 19__, at [name of place where accident occurred], defendant negligently drove a motor vehicle against plaintiff who was then crossing said street.

2. Defendant was negligent in that:

(a) Defendant drove at an excessive speed.

(b) Defendant drove through a red light.

(c) Defendant failed to yield the right-of-way to plaintiff in a marked crosswalk.

3. As a result plaintiff was thrown down and had his leg broken and was otherwise injured, was prevented from transacting his business, suffered great pain of body and mind, and incurred expenses for medical attention and hospitalization [in the sum of one thousand dollars] (or) [in an amount not yet determined].

Wherefore, plaintiff demands judgment against defendant in the sum of _____ dollars and costs.

See also New York Civil Practice Law and Rules 3041, 3043, as set out in connection with Federal Rule 8(a), supra.

Form 10.

COMPLAINT FOR NEGLIGENCE WHERE PLAINTIFF IS UNABLE TO DETERMINE DEFINITELY WHETHER THE PERSON RESPONSIBLE IS C. D. OR E. F. OR WHETHER BOTH ARE RESPONSIBLE AND WHERE HIS EVIDENCE MAY JUSTIFY A FINDING OF WILFULNESS OR OF RECKLESSNESS OR OF NEGLIGENCE

A. B., Plaintiff   )

)

     v.   ) *Complaint*

)

C. D. and E. F., Defendants)

1. Allegation of jurisdiction.

2. On June 1, 1936, in a public highway called Boylston Street in Boston, Massachusetts, defendant C. D. or defendant E. F., or both defendants C. D. and E. F. wilfully or recklessly or negligently drove or caused to be driven a motor vehicle against plaintiff who was then crossing said highway.

3. As a result plaintiff was thrown down and had his leg broken and was otherwise injured, was prevented from transacting his business, suffered great pain of body and mind, and incurred expenses for medical attention and hospitalization in the sum of one thousand dollars.

Wherefore plaintiff demands judgment against C. D. or against E. F. or against both in the sum of _____ dollars and costs.

Form 11.

COMPLAINT FOR CONVERSION

1. Allegation of jurisdiction.

2. On or about December 1, 1936, defendant converted to his own use ten bonds of the _____ Company (here insert brief identification as by number and issue) of the value of _____ dollars, the property of plaintiff.

Wherefore plaintiff demands judgment against defendant in the sum of _____ dollars, interest, and costs.

Form 12.

COMPLAINT FOR SPECIFIC PERFORMANCE
OF CONTRACT TO CONVEY LAND

1. Allegation of jurisdiction.

2. On or about December 1, 1936, plaintiff and defendant entered into an agreement in writing a copy of which is hereto annexed as Exhibit A.

3. In accord with the provisions of said agreement plaintiff tendered to defendant the purchase price and requested a conveyance of the land, but defendant refused to accept the tender and refused to make the conveyance.

4. Plaintiff now offers to pay the purchase price.

Wherefore plaintiff demands (1) that defendant be required specifically to perform said agreement, (2) damages in the sum of one thousand dollars, and (3) that if specific performance is not granted plaintiff have judgment against defendant in the sum of _____ dollars.

Form 13.

COMPLAINT ON CLAIM FOR DEBT AND TO SET ASIDE
FRAUDULENT CONVEYANCE UNDER RULE 18(b)

A.B., Plaintiff)
)
      v.) *Complaint*
)
C.D. and E.F., Defendants)

1. Allegation of jurisdiction.

2. Defendant C.D. on or about ___ executed and delivered to plaintiff a promissory note [in the following words and figures: (here set out the note verbatim)]; [a copy of which is hereto annexed as Exhibit A]; [whereby defendant C.D. promised to pay to plaintiff or order on ___ the sum of five thousand dollars with interest thereon at the rate of ___ percent. per annum].

3. Defendant C.D. owes to plaintiff the amount of said note and interest.

4. Defendant C.D. on or about ___ conveyed all his property, real and personal [or specify and describe] to defendant E.F. for the purpose of defrauding plaintiff and hindering and delaying the collection of the indebtedness evidenced by the note above referred to.

Wherefore plaintiff demands:

(1) That plaintiff have judgment against defendant C.D. for ___ dollars and interest; (2) that the aforesaid conveyance to defendant E.F.

be declared void and the judgment herein be declared a lien on said property; (3) that plaintiff have judgment against the defendants for costs.

Form 14.

COMPLAINT FOR NEGLIGENCE UNDER FEDERAL EMPLOYER'S LIABILITY ACT

1. Allegation of jurisdiction.

2. During all the times herein mentioned defendant owned and operated in interstate commerce a railroad which passed through a tunnel located at ___ and known as Tunnel No. ___.

3. On or about June 1, 1936, defendant was repairing and enlarging the tunnel in order to protect interstate trains and passengers and freight from injury and in order to make the tunnel more conveniently usable for interstate commerce.

4. In the course of thus repairing and enlarging the tunnel on said day defendant employed plaintiff as one of its workmen, and negligently put plaintiff to work in a portion of the tunnel which defendant had left unprotected and unsupported.

5. By reason of defendant's negligence in thus putting plaintiff to work in that portion of the tunnel, plaintiff was, while so working pursuant to defendant's orders, struck and crushed by a rock, which fell from the unsupported portion of the tunnel, and was (here describe plaintiff's injuries).

6. Prior to these injuries, plaintiff was a strong, able-bodied man, capable of earning and actually earning ___ dollars per day. By these injuries he has been made incapable of any gainful activity, has suffered great physical and mental pain, and has incurred expense in the amount of ___ dollars for medicine, medical attendance, and hospitalization.

Wherefore plaintiff demands judgment against defendant in the sum of ___ dollars and costs.

Form 15.

COMPLAINT FOR DAMAGES UNDER MERCHANT MARINE ACT

1. Allegation of jurisdiction. [If the pleader wishes to invoke the distinctively maritime procedures referred to in Rule 9(h), add the following or its substantial equivalent: This is an admiralty or maritime claim within the meaning of Rule 9(h).]

2. During all the times herein mentioned defendant was the owner of the steamship _____ and used it in the transportation of freight for hire by water in interstate and foreign commerce.

194

3. During the first part of (month and year) at _____ plaintiff entered the employ of defendant as an able seaman on said steamship under seamen's articles of customary form for a voyage from _____ ports to the Orient and return at a wage of _____ dollars per month and found, which is equal to a wage of _____ dollars per month as a shore worker.

4. On June 1, 1936, said steamship was about _____ days out of the port of _____ and was being navigated by the master and crew on the return voyage to _____ ports. (Here describe weather conditions and the condition of the ship and state as in an ordinary complaint for personal injuries the negligent conduct of defendant.)

5. By reason of defendant's negligence in thus (brief statement of defendant's negligent conduct) and the unseaworthiness of said steamship, plaintiff was (here describe plaintiff's injuries).

6. Prior to these injuries, plaintiff was a strong, able-bodied man, capable of earning and actually earning _____ dollars per day. By these injuries he has been made incapable of any gainful activity; has suffered great physical and mental pain, and has incurred expense in the amount of _____ dollars for medicine, medical attendance, and hospitalization.

Wherefore plaintiff demands judgment against defendant in the sum of _____ dollars and costs.

Form 16.

COMPLAINT FOR INFRINGEMENT OF PATENT

1. Allegation of jurisdiction.

2. On May 16, 1934, United States Letters Patent No. __ were duly and legally issued to plaintiff for an invention in an electric motor; and since that date plaintiff has been and still is the owner of those Letters Patent.

3. Defendant has for a long time past been and still is infringing those Letters Patent by making, selling, and using electric motors embodying the patented invention, and will continue to do so unless enjoined by this court.

4. Plaintiff has placed the required statutory notice on all electric motors manufactured and sold by him under said Letters Patent, and has given written notice to defendant of his said infringement.

Wherefore plaintiff demands a preliminary and final injunction against continued infringement, an accounting for damages, and an assessment of interest and costs against defendant.

Form 17.

COMPLAINT FOR INFRINGEMENT OF COPYRIGHT AND UNFAIR COMPETITION

1. Allegation of jurisdiction.

2. Prior to March, 1936, plaintiff, who then was and ever since has been a citizen of the United States, created and wrote an original book, entitled _____.

3. This book contains a large amount of material wholly original with plaintiff and is copyrightable subject matter under the laws of the United States.

4. Between March 2, 1936, and March 10, 1936, plaintiff complied in all respects with the Act of (give citation) and all other laws governing copyright, and secured the exclusive rights and privileges in and to the copyright of said book, and received from the Register of Copyrights a certificate of registration, dated and identified as follows: "March 10, 1936, Class _____, No. _____."

5. Since March 10, 1936, said book has been published by plaintiff and all copies of it made by plaintiff or under his authority or license have been printed, bound, and published in strict conformity with the provisions of the Act of _____ and all other laws governing copyright.

6. Since March 10, 1936, plaintiff has been and still is the sole proprietor of all rights, title, and interest in and to the copyright in said book.

7. After March 10, 1936, defendant infringed said copyright by publishing and placing upon the market a book entitled _____, which was copied largely from plaintiff's copyrighted book, entitled _____.

8. A copy of plaintiff's copyrighted book is hereto attached as "Exhibit 1"; and a copy of defendant's infringing book is hereto attached as "Exhibit 2."

9. Plaintiff has notified defendant that defendant has infringed the copyright of plaintiff, and defendant has continued to infringe the copyright.

10. After March 10, 1936, and continuously since about _____, defendant has been publishing, selling and otherwise marketing the book entitled _____, and has thereby been engaging in unfair trade practices and unfair competition against plaintiff's irreparable damage.

Wherefore plaintiff demands:

(1) That defendant, his agents, and servants be enjoined during the pendency of this action and permanently from infringing said copyright of said plaintiff in any manner, and from publishing, selling, marketing or otherwise disposing of any copies of the book entitled _____.

(2) That defendant be required to pay to plaintiff such damages as plaintiff has sustained in consequence of defendant's infringement of said copyright and said unfair trade practices and unfair competition and to account for

(a) all gains, profits and advantages derived by defendant by said trade practices and unfair competition and

(b) all gains, profits, and advantages derived by defendant by his infringement of plaintiff's copyright or such damages as to the court shall appear proper within the provisions of the copyright statutes, but not less than two hundred and fifty dollars.

(3) That defendant be required to deliver up to be impounded during the pendency of this action all copies of said book entitled _____ in his possession or under his control and to deliver up for destruction all infringing copies and all plates, molds, and other matter for making such infringing copies.

(4) That defendant pay to plaintiff the costs of this action and reasonable attorney's fees to be allowed to the plaintiff by the court.

(5) That plaintiff have such other and further relief as is just.

Form 18.

COMPLAINT FOR INTERPLEADER
AND DECLARATORY RELIEF

1. Allegation of jurisdiction.

2. On or about June 1, 1935, plaintiff issued to G.H. a policy of life insurance whereby plaintiff promised to pay to K.L. as beneficiary the sum of _____ dollars upon the death of G.H. The policy required the payment by G.H. of a stipulated premium on June 1, 1936, and annually thereafter as a condition precedent to its continuance in force.

3. No part of the premium due June 1, 1936, was ever paid and the policy ceased to have any force or effect on July 1, 1936.

4. Thereafter, on September 1, 1936, G.H. and K.L. died as the result of a collision between a locomotive and the automobile in which G.H. and K.L. were riding.

5. Defendant C.D. is the duly appointed and acting executor of the will of G.H.; defendant E.F. is the duly appointed and acting executor of the will of K.L.; defendant X.Y. claims to have been duly designated as beneficiary of said policy in place of K.L.

6. Each of defendants, C.D., E.F., and X.Y. is claiming that the above-mentioned policy was in full force and effect at the time of the death of G.H.; each of them is claiming to be the only person entitled to receive payment of the amount of the policy and has made demand for payment thereof.

7. By reason of these conflicting claims of the defendants, plaintiff is in great doubt as to which defendant is entitled to be paid the amount of the policy, if it was in force at the death of G.H.

Wherefore plaintiff demands that the court adjudge:

(1) That none of the defendants is entitled to recover from plaintiff the amount of said policy or any part thereof.

(2) That each of the defendants be restrained from instituting any action against plaintiff for the recovery of the amount of said policy or any part thereof.

(3) That, if the court shall determine that said policy was in force at the death of G.H., the defendants be required to interplead and settle between themselves their rights to the money due under said policy, and that plaintiff be discharged from all liability in the premises except to the person whom the court shall adjudge entitled to the amount of said policy.

(4) That plaintiff recover its costs.

Form 18–A. [Abrogated]

Form 19.

MOTION TO DISMISS, PRESENTING DEFENSES OF FAILURE TO STATE A CLAIM, OF LACK OF SERVICE OF PROCESS, OF IMPROPER VENUE, AND OF LACK OF JURISDICTION UNDER RULE 12(b)

The defendant moves the court as follows:

1. To dismiss the action because the complaint fails to state a claim against defendant upon which relief can be granted.

2. To dismiss the action or in lieu thereof to quash the return of service of summons on the grounds (a) that the defendant is a corporation organized under the laws of Delaware and was not and is not subject to service of process within the Southern District of New York, and (b) that the defendant has not been properly served with process in this action, all of which more clearly appears in the affidavits of M.N. and X.Y. hereto annexed as Exhibit A and Exhibit B respectively.

3. To dismiss the action on the ground that it is in the wrong district because (a) the jurisdiction of this court is invoked solely on the ground that the action arises under the Constitution and laws of the United States and (b) the defendant is a corporation incorporated under the laws of the State of Delaware and is not licensed to do or doing business in the Southern District of New York, all of which more clearly appears in the affidavits of K.L. and V.W. hereto annexed as Exhibits C and D respectively.

4. To dismiss the action on the ground that the court lacks jurisdiction because the amount actually in controversy is less than ten thousand dollars exclusive of interest and costs.

Signed: _____,
Attorney for Defendant.

Address: _____

Notice of Motion

To: _____
Attorney for Plaintiff.

_____

Please take notice, that the undersigned will bring the above motion on for hearing before this Court at Room ___, United States Court House, Foley Square, City of New York, on the ___ day of _____, 193__, at 10 o'clock in the forenoon of that day or as soon thereafter as counsel can be heard.

Signed: _____,
Attorney for Defendant.

Address: _____

Form 20.

ANSWER PRESENTING DEFENSES UNDER RULE 12(b)

First Defense

The complaint fails to state a claim against defendant upon which relief can be granted.

Second Defense

If defendant is indebted to plaintiffs for the goods mentioned in the complaint, he is indebted to them jointly with G.H. G.H. is alive; is a citizen of the State of New York and a resident of this district, is subject to the jurisdiction of this court, as to both service of process and venue; can be made a party without depriving this court of jurisdiction of the present parties, and has not been made a party.

Third Defense

Defendant admits the allegation contained in paragraphs 1 and 4 of the complaint; alleges that he is without knowledge or information sufficient to form a belief as to the truth of the allegations contained in paragraph 2 of the complaint; and denies each and every other allegation contained in the complaint.

Fourth Defense

The right of action set forth in the complaint did not accrue within six years next before the commencement of this action.

Counterclaim

(Here set forth any claim as a counterclaim in the manner in which a claim is pleaded in a complaint. No statement of the grounds on which the court's jurisdiction depends need be made unless the counterclaim requires independent grounds of jurisdiction.)

Cross-Claim Against Defendant M.N.

(Here set forth the claim constituting a cross-claim against defendant M.N. in the manner in which a claim is pleaded in a complaint. The statement of grounds upon which the court's jurisdiction depends need not be made unless the cross-claim requires independent grounds of jurisdiction.)

Form 21.

ANSWER TO COMPLAINT SET FORTH IN FORM 8, WITH COUNTERCLAIM FOR INTERPLEADER

Defense

Defendant admits the allegations stated in paragraph 1 of the complaint; and denies the allegations stated in paragraph 2 to the extent set forth in the counterclaim herein.

Counterclaim for Interpleader

1. Defendant received the sum of _____ dollars as a deposit from E.F.

2. Plaintiff has demanded the payment of such deposit to him by virtue of an assignment of it which he claims to have received from E.F.

3. E.F. has notified the defendant that he claims such deposit, that the purported assignment is not valid, and that he holds the defendant responsible for the deposit.

Wherefore defendant demands:

(1) That the court order E.F. to be made a party defendant to respond to the complaint and to this counterclaim.[1]

(2) That the court order the plaintiff and E.F. to interplead their respective claims.

(3) That the court adjudge whether the plaintiff or E.F. is entitled to the sum of money.

---

[1] Rule 13(h) provides for the court ordering parties to a counterclaim, but who are not parties to the original action, to be brought in as defendants.

(4) That the court discharge defendant from all liability in the premises except to the person it shall adjudge entitled to the sum of money.

(5) That the court award to the defendant its costs and attorney's fees.

Form 22.

MOTION TO BRING IN THIRD–PARTY DEFENDANT

[The contents of Form 22 are eliminated; they are adequately covered by Forms 22–A and 22–B.]

Form 22–A.

SUMMONS AND COMPLAINT AGAINST THIRD-PARTY DEFENDANT

UNITED STATES DISTRICT COURT FOR THE SOUTHERN DISTRICT OF NEW YORK

Civil Action, File Number _____

A.B., Plaintiff	)	
	)	
v.	)	
	)	
C.D., Defendant and Third-Party Plaintiff	))	Summons
	)	
v.	)	
	)	
E.F., Third-Party Defendant	))	

To the above-named Third-Party Defendant:

You are hereby summoned and required to serve upon _____, plaintiff's attorney whose address is _____, and upon _____, who is attorney for C.D., defendant and third-party plaintiff, and whose address is _____, and answer to the third-party complaint which is herewith served upon you within 20 days after the service of this summons upon you exclusive of the day of service. If you fail to do so, judgment by default will be taken against you for the relief demanded in the third-party complaint. There is also served upon you herewith a copy of the complaint of the plaintiff which you may but are not required to answer.

_____,
Clerk of Court.

Form 22–A RULES OF CIVIL PROCEDURE

[Seal of District Court]

Dated _____

UNITED STATES DISTRICT COURT FOR THE SOUTHERN DISTRICT OF NEW YORK

Civil Action, File Number _____

A.B., Plaintiff)		
)		
v.)		
)		
C.D., Defendant and)		
Third-Party Plaintiff)	Third-Party Complaint	
)		
v.)		
)		
E.F., Third-Party)		
Defendant)		

1. Plaintiff A.B. has filed against defendant C.D. a complaint, a copy of which is hereto attached as "Exhibit A."

2. (Here state the grounds upon which C.D. is entitled to recover from E.F., all or part of what A.B. may recover from C.D. The statement should be framed as in an original complaint.)

Wherefore C.D. demands judgment against third-party defendant E.F. for all sums [1] that may be adjudged against defendant C.D. in favor of plaintiff A.B.

Signed: _____

Attorney for C.D.,
Third-Party Plaintiff

Address: _____

Form 22–B.

MOTION TO BRING IN THIRD–PARTY DEFENDANT

Defendant moves for leave, as third-party plaintiff, to cause to be served upon E.F. a summons and third-party complaint, copies of which are hereto attached as Exhibit X.

---

[1] Make appropriate change where C.D. is entitled to only partial recovery-over against E.F.

Signed: _____
               Attorney for Defendant
               C.D.

Address: _____

Notice of Motion

(Contents the same as in Form 19. The notice should be addressed to all parties to the action.)

Exhibit X

(Contents the same as in Form 22–A.)

Form 23.

MOTION TO INTERVENE AS A DEFENDANT UNDER RULE 24

(Based upon the complaint, Form 16)

United States District Court for the Southern District of New York

Civil Action, File Number _____

A.B., plaintiff	)
	)
v.	) *Motion to intervene as*
	) *a defendant*
C.D., defendant	)
E.F., applicant for intervention	)

E.F. moves for leave to intervene as a defendant in this action, in order to assert the defenses set forth in his proposed answer, of which a copy is hereto attached, on the ground that he is the manufacturer and vendor to the defendant, as well as to others, of the articles alleged in the complaint to be an infringement of plaintiff's patent, and as such has a defense to plaintiff's claim presenting both questions of law and of fact which are common to the main action.*

Signed: _____,
               Attorney for E.F., Applicant
               for Intervention.
Address: _____

Notice of Motion

(Contents the same as in Form 19)

United States District Court for the Southern District of New York

Civil Action, File Number _____

---

* For other grounds of intervention, either of right or in the discretion of the court, see Rule 24(a) and (b).

```
A.B., plaintiff     )
                    )
        v.          )  Intervener's Answer
                    )
C.D., defendant     )
E.F., intervener    )
```

First Defense

Intervener admits the allegations stated in paragraphs 1 and 4 of the complaint; denies the allegations in paragraph 3, and denies the allegations in paragraph 2 in so far as they assert the legality of the issuance of the Letters Patent to plaintiff.

Second Defense

Plaintiff is not the first inventor of the articles covered by the Letters Patent specified in his complaint, since articles substantially identical in character were previously patented in Letters Patent granted to intervener on January 5, 1920.

Signed: _____,

Attorney for E.F., Intervener

Address: _____

Form 24.

REQUEST FOR PRODUCTION OF DOCUMENTS, ETC., UNDER RULE 34

Plaintiff A.B. requests defendant C.D. to respond within _____ days to the following requests:

(1) That defendant produce and permit plaintiff to inspect and to copy each of the following documents:

(Here list the documents either individually or by category and describe each of them.)

(Here state the time, place, and manner of making the inspection and performance of any related acts.)

(2) That defendant produce and permit plaintiff to inspect and to copy, test, or sample each of the following objects:

(Here list the objects either individually or by category and describe each of them.)

(Here state the time, place, and manner of making the inspection and performance of any related acts.)

(3) That defendant permit plaintiff to enter (here describe property to be entered) and to inspect and to photograph, test or sample (here describe the portion of the real property and the objects to be inspected).

(Here state the time, place, and manner of making the inspection and performance of any related acts.)

Signed: _____

Attorney for Plaintiff.

Address: _____

Form 25.

REQUEST FOR ADMISSION UNDER RULE 36

Plaintiff A.B. requests defendant C.D. within _____ days after service of this request to make the following admissions for the purpose of this action only and subject to all pertinent objections to admissibility which may be interposed at the trial:

1. That each of the following documents, exhibited with this request, is genuine.

(Here list the documents and describe each document.)

2. That each of the following statements is true.

(Here list the statements.)

Signed: _____,

Attorney for Plaintiff.

Address: _____

Form 26.

ALLEGATION OF REASON FOR OMITTING PARTY

When it is necessary, under Rule 19(c), for the pleader to set forth in his pleading the names of persons who ought to be made parties, but who are not so made, there should be an allegation such as the one set out below:

John Doe named in this complaint is not made a party to this action [because he is not subject to the jurisdiction of this court]; [because he cannot be made a party to this action without depriving this court of jurisdiction].

Form 27.

NOTICE OF APPEAL TO COURT OF APPEALS UNDER RULE 73(b)

Abrogated Dec. 4, 1967, eff. July 1, 1968

Form 28.

NOTICE: CONDEMNATION

United States District Court for the Southern District of New York

Civil Action, File Number _____

UNITED STATES OF AMERICA, PLAINTIFF	)	
	)	
v.	)	
	)	
1,000 ACRES OF LAND IN [here insert	)	Notice.
a general location as "City of	)	
. . . ." or "County of	)	
. . . ."], JOHN DOE ET AL., AND	)	
UNKNOWN OWNERS, DEFENDANTS	)	

To (here insert the names of the defendants to whom the notice is directed):

You are hereby notified that a complaint in condemnation has heretofore been filed in the office of the clerk of the United States District Court for the Southern District of New York, in the United States Court House in New York City, New York, for the taking (here state the interest to be acquired, as "an estate in fee simple") for use (here state briefly the use, "as a site for a postoffice building") of the following described property in which you have or claim an interest.

(Here insert brief description of the property in which the defendants, to whom the notice is directed, have or claim an interest.)

The authority for the taking is (here state briefly, as "the Act of _____, _____ Stat. _____, U.S.C.A., Title _____ § _____".)[1]

You are further notified that if you desire to present any objection or defense to the taking of your property you are required to serve your answer on the plaintiff's attorney at the address herein designated within twenty days after _____

_____.[2]

---

[1] And where appropriate add a citation to any applicable Executive Order.

[2] Here insert the words "personal service of this notice upon you," if personal service

Your answer shall identify the property in which you claim to have an interest, state the nature and extent of the interest you claim, and state all of your objections and defenses to the taking of your property. All defenses and objections not so presented are waived. And in case of your failure so to answer the complaint, judgment of condemnation of that part of the above-described property in which you have or claim an interest will be rendered.

But without answering, you may serve on the plaintiff's attorney a notice of appearance designating the property in which you claim to be interested. Thereafter you will receive notice of all proceedings affecting it. At the trial of the issue of just compensation, whether or not you have previously appeared or answered, you may present evidence as to the amount of the compensation to be paid for your property, and you may share in the distribution of the award.

United States Attorney.

Address _____

(Here state an address within the district where the United States Attorney may be served as "United States Court House, New York, N.Y.")

Dated _____

Form 29.

COMPLAINT: CONDEMNATION

United States District Court for the Southern District of New York

Civil Action, File Number _____

UNITED STATES OF AMERICA, PLAINTIFF) *v.*) 1,000 ACRES OF LAND IN [here insert) a general location as "City of) ...." or "County of) ...."], JOHN DOE ET AL., AND) UNKNOWN OWNERS, DEFENDANTS)	Complaint.

1. This is an action of a civil nature brought by the United States of America for the taking of property under the power of eminent domain and for the ascertainment and award of just compensation to the

is to be made pursuant to subdivision (d)(3)(i) of this rule [Rule 71A]; or, insert the date of the last publication of notice, if service by publication is to be made pursuant to subdivision (d)(3)(ii) of this rule.

owners and parties in interest.[1]

2. The authority for the taking is (here state briefly, as "the Act of _____, _____ Stat. _____, U.S.C.A., Title _____, § _____").[2]

3. The use for which the property is to be taken is (here state briefly the use, "as a site for a post-office building").

4. The interest to be acquired in the property is (here state the interest as "an estate in fee simple").

5. The property so to be taken is (here set forth a description of the property sufficient for its identification) or (described in Exhibit A hereto attached and made a part hereof).

6. The persons known to the plaintiff to have or claim an interest in the property[3] are:

(Here set forth the names of such persons and the interests claimed.)[4]

7. In addition to the persons named, there are or may be others who have or may claim some interest in the property to be taken, whose names are unknown to the plaintiff and on diligent inquiry have not been ascertained. They are made parties to the action under the designation "Unknown Owners."

Wherefore the plaintiff demands judgment that the property be condemned and that just compensation for the taking be ascertained and awarded and for such other relief as may be lawful and proper.

_____

United States Attorney.

Address _____

(Here state an address within the district where the United States Attorney may be served, as "United States Court House, New York, N.Y.").

---

[1] If the plaintiff is not the United States, but is, for example, a corporation invoking the power of eminent domain delegated to it by the state, then this paragraph 1 of the complaint should be appropriately modified and should be preceded by a paragraph appropriately alleging federal jurisdiction for the action, such as diversity. See Form 2.

[2] And where appropriate add a citation to any applicable Executive Order.

[3] At the commencement of the action the plaintiff need name as defendants only the persons having or claiming an interest in the property whose names are then known, but prior to any hearing involving the compensation to be paid for a particular piece of property the plaintiff must add as defendants all persons having or claiming an interest in that property whose names can be ascertained by an appropriate search of the records and also those whose names have otherwise been learned. See Rule 71A(c)(2).

[4] The plaintiff should designate, as to each separate piece of property, the defendants who have been joined as owners thereof or of some interest therein. See Rule 71A(c)(2).

Form 30.

SUGGESTION OF DEATH UPON THE RECORD UNDER RULE 25(a)(1)

A.B. [describe as a party, or as executor, administrator, or other representative or successor of C.D., the deceased party] suggests upon the record, pursuant to Rule 25(a)(1), the death of C.D. [describe as party] during the pendency of this action.

Form 31.

JUDGMENT ON JURY VERDICT

United States District Court for the Southern District of New York

Civil Action, File Number _____

A.B., Plaintiff	)	
	)	
v.	)	Judgment
	)	
C.D., Defendant	)	

This action came on for trial before the Court and a jury, Honorable John Marshall, District Judge, presiding, and the issues having been duly tried and the jury having duly rendered its verdict,

It is Ordered and Adjudged

[that the plaintiff A.B. recover of the defendant C.D. the sum of _____, with interest thereon at the rate of _____ per cent as provided by law, and his costs of action.]

[that the plaintiff take nothing, and that the action be dismissed on the merits, and that the defendant C.D. recover of the plaintiff A.B. his costs of action.]

Dated at New York, New York, this _____ day of _____, 19__.

_____

Clerk of Court

Form 32.

JUDGMENT ON DECISION BY THE COURT

UNITED STATES DISTRICT COURT FOR THE SOUTHERN DISTRICT OF NEW YORK

Civil Action, File Number _____

A.B., Plaintiff)	
)	
v.)	Judgment
)	
C.D., Defendant)	

This action came on for [trial] [hearing] before the Court, Honorable John Marshall, District Judge, presiding, and the issues having been duly [tried] [heard] and a decision having been duly rendered,

It is Ordered and Adjudged

[that the plaintiff A.B. recover of the defendant C.D. the sum of _____, with interest thereon at the rate of _____ per cent as provided by law, and his costs of action.]

[that the plaintiff take nothing, that the action be dismissed on the merits, and that the defendant C.D. recover of the plaintiff A.B. his costs of action.]

Dated at New York, New York, this _____ day of _____, 19__.

_____
Clerk of Court

Form 33.

NOTICE OF AVAILABILITY OF A MAGISTRATE JUDGE TO EXERCISE JURISDICTION AND APPEAL OPTION

In accordance with the provisions of Title 28, U.S.C. § 636(c), you are hereby notified that a United States magistrate judge of this district court is available to exercise the court's jurisdiction and to conduct any or all proceedings in this case including a jury or nonjury trial, and entry of a final judgment. Exercise of this jurisdiction by a magistrate judge is, however, permitted only if all parties voluntarily consent.

You may, without adverse substantive consequences, withhold your consent, but this will prevent the court's jurisdiction from being exercised by a magistrate judge. If any party withholds consent, the identity of the parties consenting or withholding consent will not be communicated to any magistrate judge or to the district judge to whom the case has been assigned.

An appeal from a judgment entered by a magistrate judge may be taken directly to the United States court of appeals for this judicial circuit in the same manner as an appeal from any other judgment of a district court.

Copies of the Form for the "Consent to Jurisdiction by a United States Magistrate Judge" are available from the clerk of the court.

Form 34.

CONSENT TO EXERCISE OF JURISDICTION BY A UNITED STATES MAGISTRATE JUDGE, ELECTION OF APPEAL TO DISTRICT JUDGE

UNITED STATES DISTRICT COURT
_____ DISTRICT OF _____

Plaintiff,)
)
vs.   ) Docket No. _____
)
Defendant.)

CONSENT TO JURISDICTION BY A UNITED STATES MAGISTRATE JUDGE

In accordance with the provisions of Title 28, U.S.C. § 636(c), the undersigned party or parties to the above-captioned civil matter hereby voluntarily consent to have a United States magistrate judge conduct any and all further proceedings in the case, including trial, and order the entry of a final judgment.

_____   _____
            Date   Signature

Note: Return this form to the Clerk of the Court if you consent to jurisdiction by a magistrate judge. Do not send a copy of this form to any district judge or magistrate judge.

Form 34A.

ORDER OF REFERENCE

UNITED STATES DISTRICT COURT
_____ DISTRICT OF _____

Plaintiff,)
)
vs.   ) Docket No. _____
)
Defendant.)

211

ORDER OF REFERENCE

IT IS HEREBY ORDERED that the above-captioned matter be referred to United States Magistrate Judge _____ for all further proceedings and entry of judgment in accordance with Title 28, U.S.C. § 636(c) and the consent of the parties.

_____

U.S. District Judge

Form 35.

REPORT OF PARTIES' PLANNING MEETING

[Caption and Names of Parties]

1. Pursuant to Fed.R.Civ.P. 26(f), a meeting was held on ___(date)___ at ___(place)___ and was attended by:

   ___(name)___ for plaintiff(s)

   ___(name)___ for defendant(s) ___(party name)___

   ___(name)___ for defendant(s) ___(party name)___

2. Pre–Discovery Disclosures. The parties [have exchanged] [will exchange by ___(date)___] the information required by [Fed.R.Civ.P. 26(a)(1)] [local rule __].

3. Discovery Plan. The parties jointly propose to the court the following discovery plan: [Use separate paragraphs or subparagraphs as necessary if parties disagree.]

   Discovery will be needed on the following subjects: ___(brief description of subjects on which discovery will be needed)___

   All discovery commenced in time to be completed by ___(date)___. [Discovery on ___(issue for early discovery)___ to be completed by ___(date)___.]

   Maximum of __ interrogatories by each party to any other party. [Responses due __ days after service.]

   Maximum of __ requests for admission by each party to any other party. [Responses due __ days after service.]

   Maximum of __ depositions by plaintiff(s) and __ by defendant(s).

   Each deposition [other than of _____] limited to maximum of __ hours unless extended by agreement of parties.

   Reports from retained experts under Rule 26(a)(2) due:

   from plaintiff(s) by ___(date)___

   from defendant(s) by ___(date)___

Supplementations under Rule 26(e) due _____(time(s) or interval(s))_____ .

4. Other Items. [Use separate paragraphs or subparagraphs as necessary if parties disagree.]

The parties [request] [do not request] a conference with the court before entry of the scheduling order.

The parties request a pretrial conference in _____(month and year)_____ .

Plaintiff(s) should be allowed until _____(date)_____ to join additional parties and until _____(date)_____ to amend the pleadings.

Defendant(s) should be allowed until _____(date)_____ to join additional parties and until _____(date)_____ to amend the pleadings.

All potentially dispositive motions should be filed by _____(date)_____ .

Settlement [is likely] [is unlikely] [cannot be evaluated prior to (date)] [may be enhanced by use of the following alternative dispute resolution procedure: [_____]].

SUPPLEMENTAL RULES

For Certain Admiralty and Maritime Claims

The former Rules of Practice in Admiralty and Maritime Cases, promulgated by the Supreme Court on December 6, 1920, effective March 7, 1921, as revised, amended and supplemented, were rescinded, effective July 1, 1966.

Rule A. Scope of Rules

These Supplemental Rules apply to the procedure in admiralty and maritime claims within the meaning of Rule 9(h) with respect to the following remedies:

(1) Maritime attachment and garnishment;

(2) Actions in rem;

(3) Possessory, petitory, and partition actions;

(4) Actions for exoneration from or limitation of liability.

These rules also apply to the procedure in statutory condemnation proceedings analogous to maritime actions in rem, whether within the admiralty and maritime jurisdiction or not. Except as otherwise provided, references in these Supplemental Rules to actions in rem include such analogous statutory condemnation proceedings.

The general Rules of Civil Procedure for the United States District Courts are also applicable to the foregoing proceedings except to the extent that they are inconsistent with these Supplemental Rules.

Rule B. Attachment and Garnishment: Special Provisions

[See proposed changes to Supplemental Rule B (1) and (2), in Part IX, infra.]

(1) When Available: Complaint, Affidavit, Judicial Authorization, and Process. With respect to any admiralty or maritime claim in personam a verified complaint may contain a prayer for process to attach the defendant's goods and chattels, or credits and effects in the hands of garnishees to be named in the process to the amount sued for, if the defendant shall not be found within the district. Such a complaint shall be accompanied by an affidavit signed by the plaintiff or the plaintiff's attorney that, to the affiant's knowledge, or to the best of the affiant's information and belief, the defendant cannot be found within the district. The verified complaint and affidavit shall be reviewed by the court and, if the conditions set forth in this rule appear to exist, an order so stating and authorizing process of attachment and garnishment shall issue. Supplemental process enforcing the court's order may be issued by the clerk upon application without further order of the court.

If the plaintiff or the plaintiff's attorney certifies that exigent circumstances make review by the court impracticable, the clerk shall issue a summons and process of attachment and garnishment and the plaintiff shall have the burden on a post-attachment hearing under Rule E(4)(f) to show that exigent circumstances existed. In addition, or in the alternative, the plaintiff may, pursuant to Rule 4(e), invoke the remedies provided by state law for attachment and garnishment or similar seizure of the defendant's property. Except for Rule E(8) these Supplemental Rules do not apply to state remedies so invoked.

(2) Notice to Defendant. No judgment by default shall be entered except upon proof, which may be by affidavit, (a) that the plaintiff or the garnishee has given notice of the action to the defendant by mailing to the defendant a copy of the complaint, summons, and process of attachment or garnishment, using any form of mail requiring a return receipt, or (b) that the complaint, summons, and process of attachment or garnishment have been served on the defendant in a manner authorized by Rule 4(d) or (i), or (c) that the plaintiff or the garnishee has made diligent efforts to give notice of the action to the defendant and has been unable to do so.

(3) Answer.

(a) By Garnishee. The garnishee shall serve an answer, together with answers to any interrogatories served with the complaint, within 20 days after service of process upon the garnishee. Interrogatories to the garnishee may be served with the complaint without leave of court. If the garnishee refuses or neglects to answer on oath as to the debts, credits, or effects of the defendant in the garnishee's hands, or any interrogatories concerning such debts, credits, and effects that may be propounded by the plaintiff, the court may award compulsory process against the garnishee. If the garnishee admits any debts, credits, or effects, they shall be held in the garnishee's hands or paid into the registry of the court, and shall be held in either case subject to the further order of the court.

(b) By Defendant. The defendant shall serve an answer within 30 days after process has been executed, whether by attachment of property or service on the garnishee.

1985 Amendment to Rule B(1)

The 1985 alterations were designed to ensure that the rule is consistent with the principles of procedural due process enunciated by the Supreme Court in *Sniadach v. Family Finance Corp.,* 395 U.S. 337 (1969), and later developed in *Fuentes v. Shevin,* 407 U.S. 67 (1972), *Mitchell v. W.T. Grant Co.,* 416 U.S. 600 (1974), and *North Georgia Finishing, Inc. v. Di-Chem, Inc.,* 419 U.S. 601 (1975).

Rule C. Actions in Rem: Special Provisions

[See proposed changes to Supplemental Rule C (2), (3), (4), and (6), in Part IX, infra.]

(1) When Available. An action in rem may be brought:

(a) To enforce any maritime lien;

(b) Whenever a statute of the United States provides for a maritime action in rem or a proceeding analogous thereto.

Except as otherwise provided by law a party who may proceed in rem may also, or in the alternative, proceed in personam against any person who may be liable.

Statutory provisions exempting vessels or other property owned or possessed by or operated by or for the United States from arrest or seizure are not affected by this rule. When a statute so provides, an action against the United States or an instrumentality thereof may proceed on in rem principles.

(2) Complaint. In actions in rem the complaint shall be verified on oath or solemn affirmation. It shall describe with reasonable particularity the property that is the subject of the action and state that it is within the district or will be during the pendency of the action. In actions for the enforcement of forfeitures for violation of any statute of the United States the complaint shall state the place of seizure and whether it was on land or on navigable waters, and shall contain such allegations as may be required by the statute pursuant to which the action is brought.

(3) Judicial Authorization and Process. Except in actions by the United States for forfeitures for federal statutory violations, the verified complaint and any supporting papers shall be reviewed by the court and, if the conditions for an action in rem appear to exist, an order so stating and authorizing a warrant for the arrest of the vessel or other property that is the subject of the action shall issue and be delivered to the clerk who shall prepare the warrant. If the property is a vessel or a vessel and tangible property on board the vessel, the warrant shall be delivered to the marshal for service. If other property, tangible or intangible is the subject of the action, the warrant shall be delivered by the clerk to a person or organization authorized to enforce it, who may be a marshal, a person or organization contracted with by the United States, a person specially appointed for that purpose, or, if the action is brought by the United States, any officer or employee of the United States. If the property that is the subject of the action consists in whole or in part of freight, or the proceeds of property sold, or other intangible property, the clerk shall issue a summons directing any person having control of the funds to show cause why they should not be paid into court to abide the judgment. Supplemental process enforcing the court's order may be issued by the clerk upon application without further order of the court. If the plaintiff or the plaintiff's attorney certifies that exigent circumstances make review by the court impracticable, the clerk shall issue a summons and warrant for the arrest and the plaintiff shall have the burden on a post-arrest hearing under Rule E(4)(f) to show that exigent circumstances existed. In actions by the United States for forfeitures for federal statutory violations the clerk, upon filing of the complaint, shall forthwith issue a summons and warrant for the arrest of the vessel or other property without requiring a certification of exigent circumstances.

(4) Notice. No notice other than the execution of the process is required when the property that is the subject of the action has been released in accordance with Rule E(5). If the property is not released within 10 days after execution of process, the plaintiff shall promptly or within such time as may be allowed by the court cause public notice of the action and arrest to be given in a newspaper of general circulation in the district, designated by order of the court. Such notice shall specify the time within which the answer is required to be filed as provided by subdivision (6) of this rule. This rule does not affect the requirements of notice in actions to foreclose a preferred ship mortgage pursuant to the Act of June 5, 1920, ch. 250, § 30, as amended.

(5) Ancillary Process. In any action in rem in which process has been served as provided by this rule, if any part of the property that is the subject of the action has not been brought within the control of the court because it has been removed or sold, or because it is intangible property in the hands of a person who has not been served with process, the court may, on motion, order any person having possession or control of such property or its proceeds to show cause why it should not be delivered into the custody of the marshal or other person or organization having a warrant for the arrest of the property, or paid into court to abide the judgment; and, after hearing, the court may enter such judgment as law and justice may require.

(6) Claim and Answer; Interrogatories. The claimant of property that is the subject of an action in rem shall file a claim within 30 days after process has been executed, or within such additional time as may be allowed by the court, and shall serve an answer within 20 days after the filing of the claim. The claim shall be verified on oath or solemn affirmation, and shall state the interest in the property by virtue of which the claimant demands its restitution and the right to defend the action. If the claim is made on behalf of the person entitled to possession by an agent, bailee, or attorney, it shall state that the agent, bailee, or attorney is duly authorized to make the claim. At the time of answering the claimant shall also serve answers to any interrogatories served with the complaint. In actions in rem interrogatories may be so served without leave of court.

1985 Amendment to Rule C(3)

The 1985 amendments provide for judicial scrutiny before the issuance of any warrant of arrest. Their purpose is to eliminate any doubt as to the rule's constitutionality under the *Sniadach* line of cases. See 1985 Amendment to Rule B(1), following Rule B, supra.

Rule D.　Possessory, Petitory, and Partition Actions

In all actions for possession, partition, and to try title maintainable according to the course of the admiralty practice with respect to a vessel, in all actions so maintainable with respect to the possession of cargo or other maritime property, and in all actions by one or more part owners against the others to obtain security for the return of the vessel from any voyage undertaken without their consent, or by one or more part owners against the others to obtain possession of the vessel for any voyage on giving security for its safe return, the process shall be by a warrant of arrest of the vessel, cargo, or other property, and by notice in the manner provided by Rule B(2) to the adverse party or parties.

Rule E.　Actions in Rem and Quasi in Rem: General Provisions

[See proposals to change Supplemental Rule E (3), (7), (8), and (9), and to add a section (10), in Part IX, infra.]

(1) Applicability.　Except as otherwise provided, this rule applies to actions in personam with process of maritime attachment and garnishment, actions in rem, and petitory, possessory, and partition actions, supplementing Rules B, C, and D.

(2) Complaint; Security.

(a) Complaint.　In actions to which this rule is applicable the complaint shall state the circumstances from which the claim arises with such particularity that the defendant or claimant will be able, without moving for a more definite statement, to commence an investigation of the facts and to frame a responsive pleading.

(b) Security for Costs.　Subject to the provisions of Rule 54(d) and of relevant statutes, the court may, on the filing of the complaint or on the appearance of any defendant, claimant, or any other party, or at any later time, require the plaintiff, defendant, claimant, or other party to give security, or additional security, in such sum as the court shall direct to pay all costs and expenses that shall be awarded against the party by any interlocutory order or by the final judgment, or on appeal by any appellate court.

(3) Process.

(a) Territorial Limits of Effective Service.　Process in rem and of maritime attachment and garnishment shall be served only within the district.

(b) Issuance and Delivery.　Issuance and delivery of process in rem, or of maritime attachment and garnishment, shall be held in abeyance if the plaintiff so requests.

(4) Execution of Process; Marshal's Return; Custody of Property; Procedures for Release.

(a) In General.　Upon issuance and delivery of the process, or, in the case of summons with process of attachment and garnishment, when

it appears that the defendant cannot be found within the district, the marshal or other person or organization having a warrant shall forthwith execute the process in accordance with this subdivision (4), making due and prompt return.

(b) Tangible Property. If tangible property is to be attached or arrested, the marshal or other person or organization having the warrant shall take it into the marshal's possession for safe custody. If the character or situation of the property is such that the taking of actual possession is impracticable, the marshal or other person executing the process shall affix a copy thereof to the property in a conspicuous place and leave a copy of the complaint and process with the person having possession or the person's agent. In furtherance of the marshal's custody of any vessel the marshal is authorized to make a written request to the collector of customs not to grant clearance to such vessel until notified by the marshal or a deputy marshal or by the clerk that the vessel has been released in accordance with these rules.

(c) Intangible Property. If intangible property is to be attached or arrested the marshal or other person or organization having the warrant shall execute the process by leaving with the garnishee or other obligor a copy of the complaint and process requiring the garnishee or other obligor to answer as provided in Rules B(3)(a) and C(6); or the marshal may accept for payment into the registry of the court the amount owed to the extent of the amount claimed by the plaintiff with interest and costs, in which event the garnishee or other obligor shall not be required to answer unless alias process shall be served.

(d) Directions with Respect to Property in Custody. The marshal or other person or organization having the warrant may at any time apply to the court for directions with respect to property that has been attached or arrested, and shall give notice of such application to any or all of the parties as the court may direct.

(e) Expenses of Seizing and Keeping Property; Deposit. These rules do not alter the provisions of Title 28, U.S.C., § 1921, as amended, relative to the expenses of seizing and keeping property attached or arrested and to the requirement of deposits to cover such expenses.

(f) Procedure for Release from Arrest or Attachment. Whenever property is arrested or attached, any person claiming an interest in it shall be entitled to a prompt hearing at which the plaintiff shall be required to show why the arrest or attachment should not be vacated or other relief granted consistent with these rules. This subdivision shall have no application to suits for seamen's wages when process is issued upon a certification of sufficient cause filed pursuant to Title 46, U.S.C. §§ 603 and 604 or to actions by the United States for forfeitures for violation of any statute of the United States.

(5) Release of Property.

(a) Special Bond. Except in cases of seizures for forfeiture under any law of the United States, whenever process of maritime attachment and garnishment or process in rem is issued the execution of such process shall be stayed, or the property released, on the giving of security, to be approved by the court or clerk, or by stipulation of the parties, conditioned to answer the judgment of the court or of any appellate court. The parties may stipulate the amount and nature of such security. In the event of the inability or refusal of the parties so to stipulate the court shall fix the principal sum of the bond or stipulation at an amount sufficient to cover the amount of the plaintiff's claim fairly stated with accrued interest and costs; but the principal sum shall in no event exceed (i) twice the amount of the plaintiff's claim or (ii) the value of the property on due appraisement, whichever is smaller. The bond or stipulation shall be conditioned for the payment of the principal sum and interest thereon at 6 per cent per annum.

(b) General Bond. The owner of any vessel may file a general bond or stipulation, with sufficient surety, to be approved by the court, conditioned to answer the judgment of such court in all or any actions that may be brought thereafter in such court in which the vessel is attached or arrested. Thereupon the execution of all such process against such vessel shall be stayed so long as the amount secured by such bond or stipulation is at least double the aggregate amount claimed by plaintiffs in all actions begun and pending in which such vessel has been attached or arrested. Judgments and remedies may be had on such bond or stipulation as if a special bond or stipulation had been filed in each of such actions. The district court may make necessary orders to carry this rule into effect, particularly as to the giving of proper notice of any action against or attachment of a vessel for which a general bond has been filed. Such bond or stipulation shall be indorsed by the clerk with a minute of the actions wherein process is so stayed. Further security may be required by the court at any time.

If a special bond or stipulation is given in a particular case, the liability on the general bond or stipulation shall cease as to that case.

(c) Release by Consent or Stipulation; Order of Court or Clerk; Costs. Any vessel, cargo, or other property in the custody of the marshal or other person or organization having the warrant may be released forthwith upon the marshal's acceptance and approval of a stipulation, bond, or other security, signed by the party on whose behalf the property is detained or the party's attorney and expressly authorizing such release, if all costs and charges of the court and its officers shall have first been paid. Otherwise no property in the custody of the marshal, other person or organization having the warrant, or other officer of the court shall be released without an order of the court; but such order may be entered as of course by the clerk, upon the giving of approved

security as provided by law and these rules, or upon the dismissal or discontinuance of the action; but the marshal or other person or organization having the warrant shall not deliver any property so released until the costs and charges of the officers of the court shall first have been paid.

(d) Possessory, Petitory, and Partition Actions. The foregoing provisions of this subdivision (5) do not apply to petitory, possessory, and partition actions. In such cases the property arrested shall be released only by order of the court, on such terms and conditions and on the giving of such security as the court may require.

(6) Reduction or Impairment of Security. Whenever security is taken the court may, on motion and hearing, for good cause shown, reduce the amount of security given; and if the surety shall be or become insufficient, new or additional sureties may be required on motion and hearing.

(7) Security on Counterclaim. Whenever there is asserted a counterclaim arising out of the same transaction or occurrence with respect to which the action was originally filed, and the defendant or claimant in the original action has given security to respond in damages, any plaintiff for whose benefit such security has been given shall give security in the usual amount and form to respond in damages to the claims set forth in such counterclaim, unless the court, for cause shown, shall otherwise direct; and proceedings on the original claim shall be stayed until such security is given, unless the court otherwise directs. When the United States or a corporate instrumentality thereof as defendant is relieved by law of the requirement of giving security to respond in damages it shall nevertheless be treated for the purposes of this subdivision E(7) as if it had given such security if a private person so situated would have been required to give it.

(8) Restricted Appearance. An appearance to defend against an admiralty and maritime claim with respect to which there has issued process in rem, or process of attachment and garnishment whether pursuant to these Supplemental Rules or to Rule 4(e), may be expressly restricted to the defense of such claim, and in that event shall not constitute an appearance for the purposes of any other claim with respect to which such process is not available or has not been served.

(9) Disposition of Property; Sales.

(a) Actions for Forfeitures. In any action in rem to enforce a forfeiture for violation of a statute of the United States the property shall be disposed of as provided by statute.

(b) Interlocutory Sales. If property that has been attached or arrested is perishable, or liable to deterioration, decay, or injury by being detained in custody pending the action, or if the expense of keeping the property is excessive or disproportionate, or if there is unreasonable

delay in securing the release of property, the court, on application of any party or of the marshal, or other person or organization having the warrant may order the property or any portion thereof to be sold; and the proceeds, or so much thereof as shall be adequate to satisfy any judgment, may be ordered brought into court to abide the event of the action; or the court may, on motion of the defendant or claimant, order delivery of the property to the defendant or claimant, upon the giving of security in accordance with these rules.

(c) Sales; Proceeds. All sales of property shall be made by the marshal or a deputy marshal, or by other person or organization having the warrant, or by any other person assigned by the court where the marshal or other person or organization having the warrant is a party in interest; and the proceeds of sale shall be forthwith paid into the registry of the court to be disposed of according to law.

1985 Amendments to Rule E

New Rule E(4)(f), effective August 1, 1985, makes available the type of prompt post-seizure hearing in proceedings under Supplemental Rules B and C that the Supreme Court has called for in a number of cases arising in other contexts. Rule E(4)(f) is based on a proposal by the Maritime Law Association of the United States and on local admiralty rules in the Eastern and Southern Districts of New York.

Rule E(4)(f) will be triggered by the defendant or any other person with an interest in the property seized. Upon an oral or written application similar to that used in seeking a temporary restraining order, see Rule 65(b), the court will be required to hold a hearing as promptly as possible to determine whether to allow the arrest or attachment to stand. The plaintiff has the burden of showing why the seizure should not be vacated.

Rule F. Limitation of Liability

(1) Time for Filing Complaint; Security. Not later than six months after receipt of a claim in writing, any vessel owner may file a complaint in the appropriate district court, as provided in subdivision (9) of this rule, for limitation of liability pursuant to statute. The owner (a) shall deposit with the court, for the benefit of claimants, a sum equal to the amount or value of the owner's interest in the vessel and pending freight, or approved security therefor, and in addition such sums, or approved security therefor, as the court may from time to time fix as necessary to carry out the provisions of the statutes as amended; or (b) at the owner's option shall transfer to a trustee to be appointed by the court, for the benefit of claimants, the owner's interest in the vessel and pending freight, together with such sums, or approved security therefor, as the court may from time to time fix as necessary to carry out the provisions of the statutes as amended. The plaintiff shall also give security for costs and, if the plaintiff elects to give security, for interest at the rate of 6 percent per annum from the date of the security.

(2) Complaint. The complaint shall set forth the facts on the basis of which the right to limit liability is asserted, and all facts necessary to enable the court to determine the amount to which the owner's liability shall be limited. The complaint may demand exoneration from as well as limitation of liability. It shall state the voyage, if any, on which the demands sought to be limited arose, with the date and place of its termination; the amount of all demands including all unsatisfied liens or claims of lien, in contract or in tort or otherwise, arising on that voyage, so far as known to the plaintiff, and what actions and proceedings, if any, are pending thereon; whether the vessel was damaged, lost, or abandoned, and, if so, when and where; the value of the vessel at the close of the voyage or, in case of wreck, the value of her wreckage, strippings, or proceeds, if any, and where and in whose possession they are; and the amount of any pending freight recovered or recoverable. If the plaintiff elects to transfer the plaintiff's interest in the vessel to a trustee, the complaint must further show any prior paramount liens thereon, and what voyages or trips, if any, she has made since the voyage or trip on which the claims sought to be limited arose, and any existing liens arising upon any such subsequent voyage or trip, with the amounts and causes thereof, and the names and addresses of the lienors, so far as known; and whether the vessel sustained any injury upon or by reason of such subsequent voyage or trip.

(3) Claims Against Owner; Injunction. Upon compliance by the owner with the requirements of subdivision (1) of this rule all claims and proceedings against the owner or the owner's property with respect to the matter in question shall cease. On application of the plaintiff the court shall enjoin the further prosecution of any action or proceeding against the plaintiff or the plaintiff's property with respect to any claim subject to limitation in the action.

(4) Notice to Claimants. Upon the owner's compliance with subdivision (1) of this rule the court shall issue a notice to all persons asserting claims with respect to which the complaint seeks limitation, admonishing them to file their respective claims with the clerk of the court and to serve on the attorneys for the plaintiff a copy thereof on or before a date to be named in the notice. The date so fixed shall not be less than 30 days after issuance of the notice. For cause shown, the court may enlarge the time within which claims may be filed. The notice shall be published in such newspaper or newspapers as the court may direct once a week for four successive weeks prior to the date fixed for the filing of claims. The plaintiff not later than the day of second publication shall also mail a copy of the notice to every person known to have made any claim against the vessel or the plaintiff arising out of the voyage or trip on which the claims sought to be limited arose. In cases involving death a copy of such notice shall be mailed to the decedent at the decedent's last known address, and also to any person who shall be known to have made any claim on account of such death.

(5) Claims and Answer. Claims shall be filed and served on or before the date specified in the notice provided for in subdivision (4) of this rule. Each claim shall specify the facts upon which the claimant relies in support of the claim, the items thereof, and the dates on which the same accrued. If a claimant desires to contest either the right to exoneration from or the right to limitation of liability the claimant shall file and serve an answer to the complaint unless the claim has included an answer.

(6) Information to Be Given Claimants. Within 30 days after the date specified in the notice for filing claims, or within such time as the court thereafter may allow, the plaintiff shall mail to the attorney for each claimant (or if the claimant has no attorney to the claimant) a list setting forth (a) the name of each claimant, (b) the name and address of the claimant's attorney (if the claimant is known to have one), (c) the nature of the claim, i.e., whether property loss, property damage, death, personal injury, etc., and (d) the amount thereof.

(7) Insufficiency of Fund or Security. Any claimant may by motion demand that the funds deposited in court or the security given by the plaintiff be increased on the ground that they are less than the value of the plaintiff's interest in the vessel and pending freight. Thereupon the court shall cause due appraisement to be made of the value of the plaintiff's interest in the vessel and pending freight; and if the court finds that the deposit or security is either insufficient or excessive it shall order its increase or reduction. In like manner any claimant may demand that the deposit or security be increased on the ground that it is insufficient to carry out the provisions of the statutes relating to claims in respect of loss of life or bodily injury; and, after notice and hearing, the court may similarly order that the deposit or security be increased or reduced.

(8) Objections to Claims: Distribution of Fund. Any interested party may question or controvert any claim without filing an objection thereto. Upon determination of liability the fund deposited or secured, or the proceeds of the vessel and pending freight, shall be divided pro rata, subject to all relevant provisions of law, among the several claimants in proportion to the amounts of their respective claims, duly proved, saving, however, to all parties any priority to which they may be legally entitled.

(9) Venue; Transfer. The complaint shall be filed in any district in which the vessel has been attached or arrested to answer for any claim with respect to which the plaintiff seeks to limit liability; or, if the vessel has not been attached or arrested, then in any district in which the owner has been sued with respect to any such claim. When the vessel has not been attached or arrested to answer the matters aforesaid, and suit has not been commenced against the owner, the proceedings may be had in the district in which the vessel may be, but if the vessel is not within any district and no suit has been commenced in any district, then the complaint may be filed in any district. For the convenience of parties and witnesses, in the interest of justice, the court may transfer the action to any district; if venue is wrongly laid the court shall dismiss or, if it be in the interest of justice, transfer the action to any district in which it could have been brought. If the vessel shall have been sold, the proceeds shall represent the vessel for the purposes of these rules.

Part II

Selected Provisions of The Constitution of the United States and of Titles 28 and 42, United States Code *plus* Comparative Federal and State Provisions

---

TABLE OF CONTENTS

Selected Provisions of the Constitution of the United States

	Page
Article I	227
Article III	228
Article IV	229
Article VI	229
Amendment I	229
Amendment IV	229
Amendment V	229
Amendment VII	230
Amendment IX	230
Amendment X	230
Amendment XI	230
Amendment XIV	230

Selected Provisions of Title 28, United States Code—Judiciary and Judicial Procedure

Section		Page
471.	Requirement for a district court civil justice expense and delay reduction plan	231
472.	Development and implementation of a civil justice expense and delay reduction plan	231
473.	Content of civil justice expense and delay reduction plans	232
474.	Review of district court action	234
475.	Periodic district court assessment	235
476.	Enhancement of judicial information dissemination	235
477.	Model civil justice expense and delay reduction plan	235
478.	Advisory groups	236
479.	Information on litigation management and cost and delay reduction	236

(b) *Other Selected Provisions*

Section		Page
1251.	Original jurisdiction	237

Section		Page
1253.	Direct appeals from decisions of three-judge courts	237
1254.	Courts of appeals; certiorari; appeal; certified questions	238
1257.	State courts; appeal; certiorari	242
1291.	Final decisions of district courts	242
1292.	Interlocutory decisions	242
1331.	Federal question	246
1332.	Diversity of citizenship; amount in controversy; costs	246
1333.	Admiralty, maritime and prize cases	247
1334.	Bankruptcy cases and proceedings	247
1335.	Interpleader	248
1337.	Commerce and antitrust regulations	249
1338.	Patents, plant variety protection, copyrights, mask works, trademarks and unfair competition	250
1343.	Civil rights and elective franchise	250
1345.	United States as plaintiff	250
1346.	United States as defendant	251
1359.	Parties collusively joined or made	252
1361.	Action to compel an officer of the United States to perform his duty	252
1367.	Supplemental jurisdiction	252
1391.	Venue generally	253
1392.	Defendants or property in different districts in same State	254
1397.	Interpleader	255
1400.	Patents and copyrights	255
1401.	Stockholder's derivative action	255
1402.	United States as defendant	255
1404.	Change of venue	256
1406.	Cure or waiver of defects	257
1407.	Multidistrict litigation	257
1441.	Actions removable generally	259
1442.	Federal officers sued or prosecuted	260
1443.	Civil rights cases	261
1445.	Nonremovable actions	261
1446.	Procedure for removal	261
1447.	Procedure after removal generally	262
1631.	Transfer to cure want of jurisdiction	263
1651.	Writs	263
1652.	State laws as rules of decision	263
1653.	Amendment of pleadings to show jurisdiction	264
1655.	Lien enforcement; absent defendants	264
1658.	Time limitations on the commencement of civil actions arising under Acts of Congress	264
1693.	Place of arrest in civil action	264
1694.	Patent infringement action	265
1695.	Stockholder's derivative action	265
1738.	State and Territorial statutes and judicial proceedings; full faith and credit	265
1781.	Transmittal of letter rogatory or request	265
1782.	Assistance to foreign and international tribunals and to litigants before such tribunals	266
1783.	Subpoena of person in foreign country	266
1861.	Declaration of policy	267
1862.	Exemptions	267
1863.	Plan for random jury selection	267
1864.	Drawing of names from the master jury wheel; completion of juror qualification form	270
1865.	Qualifications for jury service	271

Section		Page
1866.	Selection and summoning of jury panels	272
1867.	Challenging compliance with selection procedures	274
1868.	Maintenance and inspection of records	275
1869.	Definitions	275
1870.	Challenges	278
1919.	Dismissal for lack of jurisdiction	278
1920.	Taxation of costs	278
1927.	Counsel's liability for excessive costs	278
1963.	Registration of judgments of the district courts and the Court of International Trade	278
2071.	Rule-making power generally	279
2072.	Rules of procedure and evidence; power to prescribe	280
2111.	Harmless error	280
2201.	Creation of remedy	280
2202.	Further relief	281
2283.	Stay of State court proceedings	281
2284.	Three-judge court; when required; composition; procedure	281
2361.	Process and procedure	282
2403.	Intervention by United States or a State; constitutional question	282

Selected Provision of Title 42, United States Code—The Public Health and Welfare

Section		Page
1983.	Civil action for deprivation of rights	282

Comparative Federal and State Provisions

(See Index to Comparative Provisions, Part X, infra.)

Selected Provisions of the Constitution of the United States

ARTICLE I.

Section 8. The Congress shall have Power To lay and collect Taxes, Duties, Imposts and Excises, to pay the Debts and provide for the common Defence and general Welfare of the United States; but all Duties, Imposts and Excises shall be uniform throughout the United States;

To borrow Money on the credit of the United States;

To regulate Commerce with foreign Nations, and among the several States, and with the Indian Tribes;

To establish an uniform Rule of Naturalization, and uniform Laws on the subject of Bankruptcies throughout the United States;

* * *

To promote the Progress of Science and useful Arts, by securing for limited Times to Authors and Inventors the exclusive Right to their respective Writings and Discoveries;

227

To constitute Tribunals inferior to the supreme Court;

* * *

To declare War, grant Letters of Marque and Reprisal, and make Rules concerning Captures on Land and Water;

To raise and support Armies, but no Appropriation of Money to that Use shall be for a longer Term than two Years;

To provide and maintain a Navy;

* * *

To exercise exclusive Legislation in all Cases whatsoever, over such District (not exceeding ten Miles square) as may, by Cession of particular States, and the Acceptance of Congress, become the Seat of the Government of the United States, and to exercise like Authority over all Places purchased by the Consent of the Legislature of the State in which the Same shall be, for the Erection of Forts, Magazines, Arsenals, dock-Yards, and other needful Buildings;—And

To make all Laws which shall be necessary and proper for carrying into Execution the foregoing Powers, and all other Powers vested by this Constitution in the Government of the United States, or in any Department or Officer thereof.

ARTICLE III.

Section 1. The judicial Power of the United States, shall be vested in one supreme Court, and in such inferior Courts as the Congress may from time to time ordain and establish. The Judges, both of the supreme and inferior Courts, shall hold their Offices during good Behaviour, and shall, at stated Times, receive for their Services, a Compensation, which shall not be diminished during their Continuance in Office.

Section 2. The judicial Power shall extend to all Cases, in Law and Equity, arising under this Constitution, the Laws of the United States, and Treaties made, or which shall be made, under their Authority;—to all Cases affecting Ambassadors, other public Ministers and Consuls;—to all Cases of admiralty and maritime Jurisdiction;—to Controversies to which the United States shall be a Party;—to Controversies between two or more States;—between a State and Citizens of another State;—between Citizens of different States;—between Citizens of the same State claiming Lands under Grants of different States, and between a State, or the Citizens thereof, and foreign States, Citizens or Subjects.

In all Cases affecting Ambassadors, other public Ministers and Consuls, and those in which a State shall be Party, the supreme Court shall have original Jurisdiction. In all the other Cases before mentioned, the supreme Court shall have appellate Jurisdiction, both as to Law and Fact, with such Exceptions, and under such Regulations as the Congress shall make.

The Trial of all Crimes, except in Cases of Impeachment, shall be by Jury; and such Trial shall be held in the State where the said Crimes shall have been committed; but when not committed within any State, the Trial shall be at such Place or Places as the Congress may by Law have directed.

* * *

ARTICLE IV.

Section 1. Full Faith and Credit shall be given in each State to the public Acts, Records, and judicial Proceedings of every other State. And the Congress may by general Laws prescribe the Manner in which such Acts, Records and Proceedings shall be proved, and the Effect thereof.

Section 2. The Citizens of each State shall be entitled to all Privileges and Immunities of Citizens in the several States.

* * *

ARTICLE VI.

* * *

This Constitution, and the Laws of the United States which shall be made in Pursuance thereof; and all Treaties made, or which shall be made, under the Authority of the United States, shall be the supreme Law of the Land; and the Judges in every State shall be bound thereby, any Thing in the Constitution or Laws of any State to the Contrary notwithstanding.

* * *

AMENDMENT I.

Congress shall make no law respecting an establishment of religion, or prohibiting the free exercise thereof; or abridging the freedom of speech, or of the press; or the right of the people peaceably to assemble, and to petition the Government for a redress of grievances.

AMENDMENT IV.

The right of the people to be secure in their persons, houses, papers, and effects, against unreasonable searches and seizures, shall not be violated, and no Warrants shall issue, but upon probable cause, supported by Oath or affirmation, and particularly describing the place to be searched, and the persons or things to be seized.

AMENDMENT V.

No person shall be held to answer for a capital, or otherwise infamous crime, unless on a presentment or indictment of a Grand Jury, except in cases arising in the land or naval forces, or in the Militia, when in actual service in time of War or public danger; nor shall any person be subject for the same offence to be twice put in jeopardy of life or limb; nor shall be compelled in any criminal case to be a witness against himself, nor be deprived of life, liberty, or property, without due process of law; nor shall private property be taken for public use, without just compensation.

AMENDMENT VII.

In Suits at common law, where the value in controversy shall exceed twenty dollars, the right of trial by jury shall be preserved, and no fact tried by a jury, shall be otherwise re-examined in any Court of the United States, than according to the rules of the common law.

Comparative State Provisions

See the state provisions as set out following Federal Rule of Civil Procedure 38, supra.

AMENDMENT IX.

The enumeration in the Constitution, of certain rights, shall not be construed to deny or disparage others retained by the people.

AMENDMENT X.

The powers not delegated to the United States by the Constitution, nor prohibited by it to the States, are reserved to the States respectively, or to the people.

AMENDMENT XI.

The Judicial power of the United States shall not be construed to extend to any suit in law or equity, commenced or prosecuted against one of the United States by Citizens of another State, or by Citizens or Subjects of any Foreign State.

AMENDMENT XIV.

Section 1. All persons born or naturalized in the United States, and subject to the jurisdiction thereof, are citizens of the United States and of the State wherein they reside. No State shall make or enforce any law which shall abridge the privileges or immunities of citizens of the United States; nor shall any State deprive any person of life, liberty, or property, without due process of law; nor deny to any person within its jurisdiction the equal protection of the laws.

* * *

Section 5. The Congress shall have power to enforce, by appropriate legislation, the provisions of this article.

Selected Provisions of Title 28, United States Code—Judiciary and Judicial Procedure

§ 471. Requirement for a district court civil justice expense and delay reduction plan

There shall be implemented by each United States district court, in accordance with this chapter, a civil justice expense and delay reduction plan. The plan may be a plan developed by such district court or a model plan developed by the Judicial Conference of the United States. The purposes of each plan are to facilitate deliberate adjudication of civil cases on the merits, monitor discovery, improve litigation management, and ensure just, speedy, and inexpensive resolutions of civil disputes.

§ 472. Development and implementation of a civil justice expense and delay reduction plan

(a) The civil justice expense and delay reduction plan implemented by a district court shall be developed or selected, as the case may be, after consideration of the recommendations of an advisory group appointed in accordance with section 478 of this title.

(b) The advisory group of a United States district court shall submit to the court a report, which shall be made available to the public and which shall include—

(1) an assessment of the matters referred to in subsection (c)(1);

(2) the basis for its recommendation that the district court develop a plan or select a model plan;

(3) recommended measures, rules and programs; and

(4) an explanation of the manner in which the recommended plan complies with section 473 of this title.

(c)(1) In developing its recommendations, the advisory group of a district court shall promptly complete a thorough assessment of the state of the court's civil and criminal dockets. In performing the assessment for a district court, the advisory group shall—

(A) determine the condition of the civil and criminal dockets;

(B) identify trends in case filings and in the demands being placed on the court's resources;

(C) identify the principal causes of cost and delay in civil litigation, giving consideration to such potential causes as court procedures and the ways in which litigants and their attorneys approach and conduct litigation; and

(D) examine the extent to which costs and delays could be reduced by a better assessment of the impact of new legislation on the courts.

(2) In developing its recommendations, the advisory group of a district court shall take into account the particular needs and circumstances of the district court, litigants in such court, and the litigants' attorneys.

(3) The advisory group of a district court shall ensure that its recommended actions include significant contributions to be made by the court, the litigants, and the litigants' attorneys toward reducing cost and delay and thereby facilitating access to the courts.

(d) The chief judge of the district court shall transmit a copy of the plan implemented in accordance with subsection (a) and the report prepared in accordance with subsection (b) of this section to—

(1) the Director of the Administrative Office of the United States Courts;

(2) the judicial council of the circuit in which the district court is located; and

(3) the chief judge of each of the other United States district courts located in such circuit.

§ 473. Content of civil justice expense and delay reduction plans

(a) In formulating the provisions of its civil justice expense and delay reduction plan, each United States district court, in consultation with an advisory group appointed under section 478 of this title, shall consider and may include the following principles and guidelines of litigation management and cost and delay reduction:

(1) systematic, differential treatment of civil cases that tailors the level of individualized and case specific management to such criteria as case complexity, the amount of time reasonably needed to prepare the case for trial, and the judicial and other resources required and available for the preparation and disposition of the case;

(2) early and ongoing control of the pretrial process through involvement of a judicial officer in—

(A) assessing and planning the progress of a case;

(B) setting early, firm trial dates, such that the trial is scheduled to occur within eighteen months after the filing of the complaint, unless a judicial officer certifies that—

(i) the demands of the case and its complexity make such a trial date incompatible with serving the ends of justice; or

(ii) the trial court cannot reasonably be held within such time because of the complexity of the case or the number or complexity of pending criminal cases;

(C) controlling the extent of discovery and the time for completion of discovery, and ensuring compliance with appropriate requested discovery in a timely fashion; and

(D) setting, at the earliest practicable time, deadlines for filing motions and a time framework for their disposition;

(3) for all cases that the court or an individual judicial officer determines are complex and any other appropriate cases, careful and deliberate monitoring through a discovery-case management conference or a series of such conferences at which the presiding judicial officer—

(A) explores the parties' receptivity to, and the propriety of, settlement or proceeding with the litigation;

(B) identifies or formulates the principal issues in contention and, in appropriate cases, provides for the staged resolution or bifurcation of issues for trial consistent with Rule 42(b) of the Federal Rules of Civil Procedure;

(C) prepares a discovery schedule and plan consistent with any presumptive time limits that a district court may set for the completion of discovery and with any procedures a district court may develop to—

(i) identify and limit the volume of discovery available to avoid unnecessary or unduly burdensome or expensive discovery; and

(ii) phase discovery into two or more stages; and

(D) sets, at the earliest practicable time, deadlines for filing motions and a time framework for their disposition;

(4) encouragement of cost-effective discovery through voluntary exchange of information among litigants and their attorneys and through the use of cooperative discovery devices;

(5) conservation of judicial resources by prohibiting the consideration of discovery motions unless accompanied by a certification that the moving party has made a reasonable and good faith effort to reach agreement with opposing counsel on the matters set forth in the motion; and

(6) authorization to refer appropriate cases to alternative dispute resolution programs that—

(A) have been designated for use in a district court; or

(B) the court may make available, including mediation, minitrial, and summary jury trial.

(b) In formulating the provisions of its civil justice expense and delay reduction plan, each United States district court, in consultation with an advisory group appointed under section 478 of this title, shall consider and may include the following litigation management and cost and delay reduction techniques:

(1) a requirement that counsel for each party to a case jointly present a discovery-case management plan for the case at the initial pretrial conference, or explain the reasons for their failure to do so;

(2) a requirement that each party be represented at each pretrial conference by an attorney who has the authority to bind that party regarding all matters previously identified by the court for discussion at the conference and all reasonably related matters;

(3) a requirement that all requests for extensions of deadlines for completion of discovery or for postponement of the trial be signed by the attorney and the party making the request;

(4) a neutral evaluation program for the presentation of the legal and factual basis of a case to a neutral court representative selected by the court at a nonbinding conference conducted early in the litigation;

(5) a requirement that, upon notice by the court, representatives of the parties with authority to bind them in settlement discussions be present or available by telephone during any settlement conference; and

(6) such other features as the district court considers appropriate after considering the recommendations of the advisory group referred to in section 472(a) of this title.

(c) Nothing in a civil justice expense and delay reduction plan relating to the settlement authority provisions of this section shall alter or conflict with the authority of the Attorney General to conduct litigation on behalf of the United States, or any delegation of the Attorney General.

§ 474. Review of district court action

(a)(1) The chief judge of each district court in a circuit and the chief judge of the circuit shall, as a committee—

(A) review each plan and report submitted pursuant to section 472(d) of this title; and

(B) make such suggestions for additional actions or modified actions of that district court as the committee considers appropriate for reducing cost and delay in civil litigation in the district court.

(2) The chief judge of a circuit may designate another judge of the court of appeals of that circuit, and the chief judge of a district court may designate another judge of such court, to perform that chief judge's responsibilities under paragraph (1) of this subsection.

(b) The Judicial Conference of the United States—

(1) shall review each plan and report submitted by a district court pursuant to section 472(d) of this title; and

(2) may request the district court to take additional action if the Judicial Conference determines that such court has not adequately responded to the conditions relevant to the civil and criminal dockets of the court or to the recommendations of the district court's advisory group.

§ 475. Periodic district court assessment

After developing or selecting a civil justice expense and delay reduction plan, each United States district court shall assess annually the condition of the court's civil and criminal dockets with a view to determining appropriate additional actions that may be taken by the court to reduce cost and delay in civil litigation and to improve the litigation management practices of the court. In performing such assessment, the court shall consult with an advisory group appointed in accordance with section 478 of this title.

§ 476. Enhancement of judicial information dissemination

(a) The Director of the Administrative Office of the United States Courts shall prepare a semiannual report, available to the public, that discloses for each judicial officer—

(1) the number of motions that have been pending for more than six months and the name of each case in which such motion has been pending;

(2) the number of bench trials that have been submitted for more than six months and the name of each case in which such trials are under submission; and

(3) the number and names of cases that have not been terminated within three years after filing.

(b) To ensure uniformity of reporting, the standards for categorization or characterization of judicial actions to be prescribed in accordance with section 481 of this title shall apply to the semiannual report prepared under subsection (a).

§ 477. Model civil justice expense and delay reduction plan

(a)(1) Based on the plans developed and implemented by the United States district courts designated as Early Implementation District Courts pursuant to section 103(c) of the Civil Justice Reform Act of 1990, the Judicial Conference of the United States may develop one or more model civil justice expense and delay reduction plans. Any such model plan shall be accompanied by a report explaining the manner in which the plan complies with section 473 of this title.

(2) The Director of the Federal Judicial Center and the Director of the Administrative Office of the United States Courts may make recommendations to the Judicial Conference regarding the development of any model civil justice expense and delay reduction plan.

(b) The Director of the Administrative Office of the United States Courts shall transmit to the United States district courts and to the Committees on the Judiciary of the Senate and the House of Representatives copies of any model plan and accompanying report.

§ 478. Advisory groups

(a) Within ninety days after the date of the enactment of this chapter, the advisory group required in each United States district court in accordance with section 472 of this title shall be appointed by the chief judge of each district court, after consultation with the other judges of such court.

(b) The advisory group of a district court shall be balanced and include attorneys and other persons who are representative of major categories of litigants in such court, as determined by the chief judge of such court.

(c) Subject to subsection (d), in no event shall any member of the advisory group serve longer than four years.

(d) Notwithstanding subsection (c), the United States Attorney for a judicial district, or his or her designee, shall be a permanent member of the advisory group for that district court.

(e) The chief judge of a United States district court may designate a reporter for each advisory group, who may be compensated in accordance with guidelines established by the Judicial Conference of the United States.

(f) The members of an advisory group of a United States district court and any person designated as a reporter for such group shall be considered as independent contractors of such court when in the performance of official duties of the advisory group and may not, solely by reason of service on or for the advisory group, be prohibited from practicing law before such court.

§ 479. Information on litigation management and cost and delay reduction

(a) Within four years after the date of the enactment of this chapter, the Judicial Conference of the United States shall prepare a comprehensive report on all plans received pursuant to section 472(d) of this title. The Director of the Federal Judicial Center and the Director of the Administrative Office of the United States Courts may make recommendations regarding such report to the Judicial Conference during the preparation of the report. The Judicial Conference shall transmit copies of the report to the United States district courts and to the Committees on the Judiciary of the Senate and the House of Representatives.

(b) The Judicial Conference of the United States shall, on a continuing basis—

(1) study ways to improve litigation management and dispute resolution services in the district courts; and

(2) make recommendations to the district courts on ways to improve such services.

(c)(1) The Judicial Conference of the United States shall prepare, periodically revise, and transmit to the United States district courts a Manual for Litigation Management and Cost and Delay Reduction. The Director of the Federal Judicial Center and the Director of the Administrative Office of the United States Courts may make recommendations regarding the preparation of and any subsequent revisions to the Manual.

(2) The Manual shall be developed after careful evaluation of the plans implemented under section 472 of this title, the demonstration program conducted under section 104 of the Civil Justice Reform Act of 1990, and the pilot program conducted under section 105 of the Civil Justice Reform Act of 1990.

(3) The Manual shall contain a description and analysis of the litigation management, cost and delay reduction principles and techniques, and alternative dispute resolution programs considered most effective by the Judicial Conference, the Director of the Federal Judicial Center, and the Director of the Administrative Office of the United States Courts.

§ 1251. Original jurisdiction

(a) The Supreme Court shall have original and exclusive jurisdiction of all controversies between two or more States.

(b) The Supreme Court shall have original but not exclusive jurisdiction of:

(1) All actions or proceedings to which ambassadors, other public ministers, consuls, or vice consuls of foreign states are parties;

(2) All controversies between the United States and a State;

(3) All actions or proceedings by a State against the citizens of another State or against aliens.

§ 1253. Direct appeals from decisions of three-judge courts

Except as otherwise provided by law, any party may appeal to the Supreme Court from an order granting or denying, after notice and hearing, an interlocutory or permanent injunction in any civil action, suit or proceeding required by any Act of Congress to be heard and determined by a district court of three judges.

§ 1254. Courts of appeals; certiorari; appeal; certified questions

Cases in the courts of appeals may be reviewed by the Supreme Court by the following methods:

(1) By writ of certiorari granted upon the petition of any party to any civil or criminal case, before or after rendition of judgment or decree;

(2) By certification at any time by a court of appeals of any question of law in any civil or criminal case as to which instructions are desired, and upon such certification the Supreme Court may give binding instructions or require the entire record to be sent up for decision of the entire matter in controversy.

Related Provisions Regarding Appeals to the Highest Court in a Jurisdiction

(a) *Discretionary Review*

1. *Comparative state provisions*

California Constitution Art. 6, § 11

The Supreme Court has appellate jurisdiction when judgment of death has been pronounced. With that exception courts of appeal have appellate jurisdiction when superior courts have original jurisdiction and in other causes prescribed by statute.

* * *

California Constitution Art. 6, § 12

(a) The Supreme Court may, before decision, transfer to itself a cause in a court of appeal. It may, before decision, transfer a cause from itself to a court of appeal or from one court of appeal or division to another. The court to which a cause is transferred has jurisdiction.

(b) The Supreme Court may review the decision of a court of appeal in any cause.

(c) The Judicial Council shall provide, by rules of court, for the time and procedure for transfer and for review, including, among other things, provisions for the time and procedure for transfer with instructions, for review of all or part of a decision, and for remand as improvidently granted.

(d) This section shall not apply to an appeal involving a judgment of death.

California Rule of Court 28

(a) [Time within which court may order review]

(1) [*On own motion*] If no petition for review is filed, within 30 days after a decision of a Court of Appeal becomes final as to that court the Supreme Court, on its own motion, may order review of the Court of Appeal decision. Within the original 30-day period or any extension of it, the Supreme Court may for good cause extend the time for one or more additional periods amounting to not more than an additional 60 days in the aggregate. The total time, including extensions shall not exceed 90 days after the decision becomes final as to the Court of Appeal.

If any period in this subdivision ends on a day the clerk's office is closed, the Supreme Court may on its own motion order review of the Court of Appeal decision on the next day the clerk's office is open.

(2) [*On petition*] Within 60 days after the filing, as provided in subdivision (b), of the last timely petition for review, the Supreme Court may order review of a Court of Appeal decision. Within the original 60-day period or any extension of it the Supreme Court may, for good cause, extend the time for one or more additional periods amounting to not more than an additional 30 days in the aggregate. The total time, including extensions, shall not exceed 90 days after the filing of the last timely petition for review.

(b) [Time for filing petition] A party seeking review must serve and file a petition within 10 days after the decision of the Court of Appeal becomes final as to that court, but a petition may not be filed after denial of a transfer to a Court of Appeal in a case within the original jurisdiction of a municipal court * * *. Proof shall be filed of the delivery or mailing of one copy of the petition to the clerk of the Court of Appeal which rendered the decision. The clerk of that court shall transmit to the Clerk of the Supreme Court the original record, briefs, and all original papers and exhibits on file in the cause * * *. If the petition is denied, the Clerk of the Supreme Court shall return them to the clerk of the proper Court of Appeal. If the petition is granted, they shall be retained and properly numbered by the clerk of the Supreme Court.

* * *

New York Civil Practice Law and Rules 5602

(a) Permission of appellate division or court of appeals. An appeal may be taken to the court of appeals by permission of the appellate division granted before application to the court of appeals, or by permission of the court of appeals upon refusal by the appellate division or upon direct application. * * * Permission by the court of appeals for leave to appeal shall be pursuant to rules * * * which shall provide that leave to appeal be granted upon the approval of two judges of the court of appeals. Such appeal may be taken:

1. in an action originating in the supreme court, a county court, a surrogate's court, the family court, the court of claims or an administrative agency or an arbitration,

(i) from an order of the appellate division which finally determines the action and which is not appealable as of right, or

(ii) from a final judgment of such court or final determination of such agency or final arbitration award where the appellate division has made an order on a prior appeal in the action which necessarily affects the final judgment, determination or award and the final judgment or determination or award is not appealable as of right pursuant to subdivision (d) of section 5601 of this article; and

2. in a proceeding instituted by or against one or more public officers or a board, commission or other body of public officers or a court or tribunal, from an order of the appellate division which does not finally determine such proceeding, except that the appellate division shall not grant permission to appeal from an order granting or affirming the granting of a new trial or hearing.

(b) Permission of appellate division. An appeal may be taken to the court of appeals by permission of the appellate division:

1. from an order of the appellate division which does not finally determine an action, except an order described in paragraph two of subdivision (a) or subparagraph (iii) of paragraph two of subdivision (b) of this section or in subdivision (c) of section 5601;

2. in an action originating in a court other than the supreme court, a county court, a surrogate's court, the family court, the court of claims or an administrative agency,

(i) from an order of the appellate division which finally determines the action, and which is not appealable as of right pursuant to paragraph one of subdivision (b) of section 5601, or

(ii) from a final judgment of such court or a final determination of such agency where the appellate division has made an order on a prior appeal in the action which necessarily affects the final judgment or determination and the final judgment or determination is not appealable as of right pursuant to subdivision (d) of section 5601, or

(iii) from an order of the appellate division granting or affirming the granting of a new trial or hearing where the appellant stipulates that, upon affirmance, judgment absolute shall be entered against him.

2. *Basis for exercise of discretion*

United States Supreme Court Rule 10 (Former Rule 17.1)

Review on a writ of certiorari is not a matter of right, but of judicial discretion. A petition for a writ of certiorari will be granted only for compelling reasons. The following, although neither controlling nor fully measuring the Court's discretion, indicate the character of the reasons the Court considers:

(a) a United States court of appeals has entered a decision in conflict with the decision of another United States court of appeals on the same important matter; or has decided an important federal question in a way that conflicts with the decision of a state court of last resort; or has so far departed from the accepted and usual course of judicial proceedings, or sanctioned such a departure by a lower court, as to call for an exercise of this Court's supervisory power;

(b) a state court of last resort has decided an important federal question in a way that conflicts with the decision of another state court of last resort or of a United States court of appeals;

(c) a state court or a United States court of appeals has decided an important question of federal law that has not been, but should be, settled by this Court, or has decided an important federal question in a way that conflicts with relevant decisions of this Court.

A petition for certiorari is rarely granted when the asserted error consists of erroneous factual findings or the misapplication of a properly stated rule of law.

California Rule of Court 29

(a) [Grounds]   Review by the Supreme Court of a decision of a Court of Appeal will be ordered (1) where it appears necessary to secure uniformity of decision or the settlement of important questions of law; (2) where the Court of Appeal was without jurisdiction of the cause; or (3) where, because of disqualification or other reason, the decision of the Court of Appeal lacks the concurrence of the required majority of qualified judges.

(b) [Limitations]   As a matter of policy, on petition for review the Supreme Court normally will not consider: (1) any issue that could have been but was not timely raised in the briefs filed in the Court of Appeal; (2) any issue or any material fact that was omitted from or misstated in the opinion of the Court of Appeal, unless the omission or misstatement was called to the attention of the Court of Appeal in a petition for rehearing. All other issues and facts may be presented in the petition for review without the necessity of filing a petition for rehearing.

(b) *Mandatory Review*

Georgia Constitution Art. VI, § 1, ¶ 8

Any court shall transfer to the appropriate court in the state any civil case in which it determines that jurisdiction or venue lies elsewhere.

Georgia Constitution Art. VI, § 5, ¶ 5

In the event of an equal division of the Judges when sitting as a body, the case shall be immediately transmitted to the Supreme Court.

Georgia Constitution Art. VI, § 6, ¶ 2

The Supreme Court shall be a court of review and shall exercise exclusive appellate jurisdiction in the following cases:

(1) All cases involving the construction of a treaty or of the Constitution of the State of Georgia or of the United States and all cases in which the constitutionality of a law, ordinance, or constitutional provision has been drawn in question; and

(2) All cases of election contest.

Georgia Constitution Art. VI, § 6, ¶ 3

Unless otherwise provided by law, the Supreme Court shall have appellate jurisdiction of the following classes of cases:

(1) Cases involving title to land;

(2) All equity cases;

(3) All cases involving wills;

(4) All habeas corpus cases;

(5) All cases involving extraordinary remedies;

(6) All divorce and alimony cases;

(7) All cases certified to it by the Court of Appeals; and

(8) All cases in which a sentence of death was imposed or could be imposed.

Review of all cases shall be as provided by law.

Georgia Constitution, Art. VI, § 6, ¶ 5

The Supreme Court may review by certiorari cases in the Court of Appeals which are of gravity or great public importance.

New York Civil Practice Law and Rules 5601

(a) Dissent. An appeal may be taken to the court of appeals as of right in an action originating in the supreme court, a county court, a surrogate's court, the family court, the court of claims or an administrative agency, from an order of the appellate division which finally determines the action, where there is a dissent by at least two justices on a question of law in favor of the party taking such appeal.

(b) Constitutional grounds. An appeal may be taken to the court of appeals as of right:

1. from an order of the appellate division which finally determines an action where there is directly involved the construction of the constitution of the state or of the United States; and

2. from a judgment of a court of record of original instance which finally determines an action where the only question involved on the appeal is the validity of a statutory provision of the state or of the United States under the constitution of the state or of the United States.

(c) From order granting new trial or hearing, upon stipulation for judgment absolute. An appeal may be taken to the court of appeals as of right in an action originating in the supreme court, a county court, a surrogate's court, the family court, the court of claims or an administrative agency, from an order of the appellate division granting or affirming the granting of a new trial or hearing where the appellant stipulates that, upon affirmance, judgment absolute shall be entered against him.

(d) Based upon non-final determination of appellate division. An appeal may be taken to the court of appeals as of right from a final judgment entered in a court of original instance or from a final determination of an administrative agency or from a final arbitration award, or from an order of the appellate division which finally determines an appeal from such a judgment or determination, where the appellate division has made an order on a prior appeal in the action which necessarily affects the judgment, determination or award and which satisfies the requirements of subdivision (a) or of paragraph one of subdivision (b) except that of finality.

§ 1257. State courts; appeal; certiorari

(a) Final judgments or decrees rendered by the highest court of a State in which a decision could be had, may be reviewed by the Supreme Court by writ of certiorari, where the validity of a treaty or statute of the United States is drawn in question or where the validity of a statute of any State is drawn in question on the ground of its being repugnant to the Constitution, treaties, or laws of the United States, or where any title, right, privilege or immunity is specially set up or claimed under the Constitution or the treaties or statutes of, or any commission held or authority exercised under, the United States.

(b) For purposes of this section, the term "highest court of a State" includes the District of Columbia Court of Appeals.

Related Provision

See United States Supreme Court Rule 10 as set out following 28 U.S.C. § 1254, supra.

§ 1291. Final decisions of district courts

The courts of appeals (other than the United States Court of Appeals for the Federal Circuit) shall have jurisdiction of appeals from all final decisions of the district courts of the United States, the United States District Court for the District of the Canal Zone, the District Court of Guam, and the District Court of the Virgin Islands, except where a direct review may be had in the Supreme Court * * *.

Comparative State Provision

See New York Civil Practice Law and Rules 5701 as set out following 28 U.S.C. § 1292, infra.

§ 1292. Interlocutory decisions

(a) Except as provided in subsections (c) and (d) of this section, the courts of appeals shall have jurisdiction of appeals from:

(1) Interlocutory orders of the district courts of the United States, the United States District Court for the District of the Canal Zone, the District Court of Guam, and the District Court of the Virgin Islands, or of the judges thereof, granting, continuing, modifying, refusing or dissolving injunctions, or refusing to dissolve or modify injunctions, except where a direct review may be had in the Supreme Court;

(2) Interlocutory orders appointing receivers, or refusing orders to wind up receiverships or to take steps to accomplish the purposes thereof, such as directing sales or other disposals of property;

(3) Interlocutory decrees of such district courts or the judges thereof determining the rights and liabilities of the parties to admiralty cases in which appeals from final decrees are allowed.

(b) When a district judge, in making in a civil action an order not otherwise appealable under this section, shall be of the opinion that such order involves a controlling question of law as to which there is substantial ground for difference of opinion and that an immediate appeal from the order may materially advance the ultimate termination of the litigation, he shall so state in writing in such order. The Court of Appeals which would have jurisdiction of an appeal of such action may thereupon, in its discretion, permit an appeal to be taken from such order, if application is made to it within ten days after the entry of the order: *Provided, however,* That application for an appeal hereunder shall not stay proceedings in the district court unless the district judge or the Court of Appeals or a judge thereof shall so order.

(c) The United States Court of Appeals for the Federal Circuit shall have exclusive jurisdiction—

(1) of an appeal from an interlocutory order or decree described in subsection (a) or (b) of this section in any case over which the court would have jurisdiction of an appeal under section 1295 of this title; and

(2) of an appeal from a judgment in a civil action for patent infringement which would otherwise be appealable to the United States Court of Appeals for the Federal Circuit and is final except for an accounting.

(d)(1) When the chief judge of the Court of International Trade issues an order under the provisions of section 256(b) of this title, or when any judge of the Court of International Trade, in issuing any other interlocutory order, includes in the order a statement that a controlling question of law is involved with respect to which there is a substantial ground for difference of opinion and that an immediate appeal from that order may materially advance the ultimate termination of the litigation, the United States Court of Appeals for the Federal Circuit may, in its discretion, permit an appeal to be taken from such order, if application is made to that Court within ten days after the entry of such order.

(2) When the chief judge of the United States Court of Federal Claims issues an order under section 798(b) of this title, or when any judge of the United States Court of Federal Claims, in issuing an interlocutory order, includes in the order a statement that a controlling question of law is involved with respect to which there is a substantial ground for difference of opinion and that an immediate appeal from that order may materially advance the ultimate termination of the litigation, the United States Court of Appeals for the Federal Circuit may, in its discretion, permit an appeal to be taken from such order, if application is made to that Court within ten days after the entry of such order.

(3) Neither the application for nor the granting of an appeal under this subsection shall stay proceedings in the Court of International Trade or in the Court of Federal Claims, as the case may be, unless a stay is ordered by a judge of the Court of International Trade or of the Court of Federal Claims or by the United States Court of Appeals for the Federal Circuit or a judge of that court.

(4)(A) The United States Court of Appeals for the Federal Circuit shall have exclusive jurisdiction of an appeal from an interlocutory order of a district court of the United States, the District Court of Guam, the District Court of the Virgin Islands, or the District Court for the Northern Mariana Islands, granting or denying, in whole or in part, a motion to transfer an action to the United States Court of Federal Claims under section 1631 of this title.

(B) When a motion to transfer an action to the Court of Federal Claims is filed in a district court, no further proceedings shall be taken in the district court until 60 days after the court has ruled upon the motion. If an appeal is taken from the district court's grant or denial of the motion, proceedings shall be further stayed until the appeal has been decided by the Court of Appeals for the Federal Circuit. The stay of proceedings in the district court shall not bar the granting of preliminary or injunctive relief, where appropriate and where expedition is reasonably necessary. However, during the period in which proceedings are stayed as provided in this subparagraph, no transfer to the Court of Federal Claims pursuant to the motion shall be carried out.

(e) The Supreme Court may prescribe rules, in accordance with section 2072 of this title, to provide for an appeal of an interlocutory decision to the courts of appeals that is not otherwise provided for under subsection (a), (b), (c), or (d).

Comparative Federal and State Provisions

(a) *Related Federal Rules*

See Federal Rule of Civil Procedure 23(f), Part I, supra, and Federal Rule of Appellate Procedure 5, Part IV, infra.

(b) *Comparative State Provisions*

Minnesota Rules of Civil Appellate Procedure 103.03

An appeal may be taken to the Court of Appeals:

(a) from a final judgment or from a partial judgment entered pursuant to Minn.R.Civ.P. 54.02;

(b) from an order which grants, refuses, dissolves or refuses to dissolve, an injunction;

(c) from an order vacating or sustaining an attachment;

(d) from an order denying a new trial, or from an order granting a new trial if the trial court expressly states therein, or in a memorandum attached thereto, that the order is based exclusively upon errors of law occurring at the trial, and upon no other ground; and the trial court shall specify such errors in its order or memorandum, but upon appeal, such order granting a new trial may be sustained for errors of law prejudicial to respondent other than those specified by the trial court;

(e) from an order which, in effect, determines the action and prevents a judgment from which an appeal might be taken;

(f) from a final order or judgment made or rendered in proceedings supplementary to execution;

(g) * * *

(h) if the trial court certifies that the question presented is important and doubtful, from an order which denies a motion to dismiss for failure to state a claim upon which relief can be granted or from an order which denies a motion for summary judgment.

(i) from such other orders or decisions as may be appealable by statute or under the decisions of the Minnesota appellate courts.

New York Civil Practice Law and Rules 5701

(a) Appeals as of right. An appeal may be taken to the appellate division as of right in an action, originating in the supreme court or a county court:

1. from any final or interlocutory judgment except one entered subsequent to an order of the appellate division which disposes of all the issues in the action; or

2. from an order not specified in subdivision (b), where the motion it decided was made upon notice and it:

> (i) grants, refuses, continues or modifies a provisional remedy; or

> (ii) settles, grants or refuses an application to resettle a transcript or statement on appeal; or

> (iii) grants or refuses a new trial; except where specific questions of fact arising upon the issues in an action triable by the court have been tried by a jury, pursuant to an order for that purpose, and the order grants or refuses a new trial upon the merits; or

> (iv) involves some part of the merits; or

> (v) affects a substantial right; or

> (vi) in effect determines the action and prevents a judgment from which an appeal might be taken; or

> (vii) determines a statutory provision of the state to be unconstitutional, and the determination appears from the reasons given for the decision or is necessarily implied in the decision; or

> (viii) grants a motion for leave to reargue ... or determines a motion for leave to renew ... [an earlier motion that resulted in an order].

3. from an order, where the motion it decided was made upon notice, refusing to vacate or modify a prior order, if the prior order would have been appealable as of right under paragraph two had it decided a motion made upon notice.

(b) Orders not appealable as of right. An order is not appealable to the appellate division as of right where it:

1. is made in a proceeding against a body or officer pursuant to article 78; or

2. requires or refuses to require a more definite statement in a pleading; or

3. orders or refuses to order that scandalous or prejudicial matter be stricken from a pleading.

(c) Appeals by permission. An appeal may be taken to the appellate division from any order which is not appealable as of right in an action originating in the supreme court or a county court by permission of the judge who made the order granted before application to a justice of the appellate division; or by permission of a justice of the appellate division in the department to which the appeal could be taken, upon refusal by the judge who made the order or upon direct application.

§ 1331. Federal question

The district courts shall have original jurisdiction of all civil actions arising under the Constitution, laws, or treaties of the United States.

§ 1332. Diversity of citizenship; amount in controversy; costs

[See proposed congressional legislation to amend § 1332 and to add a new § 1369, in Part IX, infra.]

(a) The district courts shall have original jurisdiction of all civil actions where the matter in controversy exceeds the sum or value of $75,000, exclusive of interest and costs, and is between—

(1) citizens of different States;

(2) citizens of a State and citizens or subjects of a foreign state;

(3) citizens of different States and in which citizens or subjects of a foreign state are additional parties; and

(4) a foreign state, * * * as plaintiff and citizens of a State or of different States.

For the purposes of this section, section 1335, and section 1441, an alien admitted to the United States for permanent residence shall be deemed a citizen of the State in which such alien is domiciled.

(b) Except when express provision therefor is otherwise made in a statute of the United States, where the plaintiff who files the case originally in the Federal courts is finally adjudged to be entitled to recover less than the sum or value of $75,000, computed without regard to any setoff or counterclaim to which the defendant may be adjudged to be entitled, and exclusive of interest and costs, the district court may deny costs to the plaintiff and, in addition, may impose costs on the plaintiff.

(c) For the purposes of this section and section 1441 of this title—

(1) a corporation shall be deemed to be a citizen of any State by which it has been incorporated and of the State where it has its principal place of business, except that in any direct action against the insurer of a policy or contract of liability insurance, whether incorporated or unincorporated, to which action the insured is not joined as a party-defendant, such insurer shall be deemed a citizen of the State of which the insured is a citizen, as well as of any State by which the insurer has been incorporated and of the State where it has its principal place of business; and

(2) the legal representative of the estate of a decedent shall be deemed to be a citizen only of the same State as the decedent, and the legal representative of an infant or incompetent shall be deemed to be a citizen only of the same State as the infant or incompetent.

(d) The word "States", as used in this section, includes the Territories, the District of Columbia, and the Commonwealth of Puerto Rico.

§ 1333. Admiralty, maritime and prize cases

The district courts shall have original jurisdiction, exclusive of the courts of the States, of:

(1) Any civil case of admiralty or maritime jurisdiction, saving to suitors in all cases all other remedies to which they are otherwise entitled.

(2) Any prize brought into the United States and all proceedings for the condemnation of property taken as prize.

§ 1334. Bankruptcy cases and proceedings

(a) Except as provided in subsection (b) of this section, the district courts shall have original and exclusive jurisdiction of all cases under title 11.

(b) Notwithstanding any Act of Congress that confers exclusive jurisdiction on a court or courts other than the district courts, the district courts shall have original but not exclusive jurisdiction of all civil proceedings arising under title 11, or arising in or related to cases under title 11.

(c)(1) Nothing in this section prevents a district court in the interest of justice, or in the interest of comity with State courts or respect for State law, from abstaining from hearing a particular proceeding arising under title 11 or arising in or related to a case under title 11.

(2) Upon timely motion of a party in a proceeding based upon a State law claim or State law cause of action, related to a case under title 11 but not arising under title 11 or arising in a case under title 11, with respect to which an action could not have been commenced in a court of

the United States absent jurisdiction under this section, the district court shall abstain from hearing such proceeding if an action is commenced, and can be timely adjudicated, in a State forum of appropriate jurisdiction.

(d) Any decision to abstain or not to abstain made under this subsection (other than a decision not to abstain in a proceeding described in subsection (c)(2)) is not reviewable by appeal or otherwise by the court of appeals under section 158(d), 1291, or 1292 of this title or by the Supreme Court of the United States under section 1254 of this title. This subsection shall not be construed to limit the applicability of the stay provided for by section 362 of title 11, United States Code, as such section applies to an action affecting the property of the estate in bankruptcy.

(e) The district court in which a case under title 11 is commenced or is pending shall have exclusive jurisdiction of all of the property, wherever located, of the debtor as of the commencement of such case, and of property of the estate.

§ 1335. Interpleader

(a) The district courts shall have original jurisdiction of any civil action of interpleader or in the nature of interpleader filed by any person, firm, or corporation, association, or society having in his or its custody or possession money or property of the value of $500 or more, or having issued a note, bond, certificate, policy of insurance, or other instrument of value or amount of $500 or more, or providing for the delivery or payment or the loan of money or property of such amount or value, or being under any obligation written or unwritten to the amount of $500 or more, if

(1) Two or more adverse claimants, of diverse citizenship as defined in section 1332 of this title, are claiming or may claim to be entitled to such money or property, or to any one or more of the benefits arising by virtue of any note, bond, certificate, policy or other instrument, or arising by virtue of any such obligation; and if (2) the plaintiff has deposited such money or property or has paid the amount of or the loan or other value of such instrument or the amount due under such obligation into the registry of the court, there to abide the judgment of the court, or has given bond payable to the clerk of the court in such amount and with such surety as the court or judge may deem proper, conditioned upon the compliance by the plaintiff with the future order or judgment of the court with respect to the subject matter of the controversy.

(b) Such an action may be entertained although the titles or claims of the conflicting claimants do not have a common origin, or are not identical, but are adverse to and independent of one another.

§ 1337. Commerce and antitrust regulations

(a) The district courts shall have original jurisdiction of any civil action or proceeding arising under any Act of Congress regulating commerce or protecting trade and commerce against restraints and monopolies * * *.

Related Federal Provisions

United States Code Tit. 15, § 15(a)

Except as provided in subsection (b) [regarding suits by foreign states], any person who shall be injured in his business or property by reason of anything forbidden in the antitrust laws may sue therefor in any district court of the United States in the district in which the defendant resides or is found or has an agent, without respect to the amount in controversy, and shall recover threefold the damages by him sustained, and the cost of suit, including a reasonable attorney's fee. * * *

Proposed Consumer Class Action Act [House of Representatives Bill 839, January 3, 1973]

Sec. 2. Section 5 of the Federal Trade Commission Act (15 U.S.C. 45) is amended by adding at the end thereof the following:

"(m) Consumers who have been damaged by unfair or deceptive acts or practices in commerce are hereby authorized to bring consumer class actions for redress of such damages. Such actions shall be brought as consumer class actions in accordance with section 4 of the Consumer Class Action Act." * * *

Sec. 4. (a)(1) An Act in defraud of consumers which affects commerce is unlawful and the district courts of the United States shall have original jurisdiction without regard to the amount in controversy to entertain civil class actions for redress of such unlawful acts.

(2) For the purposes of this section an "act in defraud of consumers" is—

(A) an unfair or deceptive act or practice which is unlawful within the meaning of section 5(a)(1) of the Federal Trade Commission Act, or

(B) an act that gives rise to a civil action by a consumer or consumers under State, statutory or decisional law for the benefit of consumers. * * *

(c) In the case of any class action brought upon the basis of a violation of consumers' rights under any State law the court shall, in deciding such action, apply the following criteria:

(1) State law relating to the consumers' rights under State statutory or decisional law is adopted as Federal law.

(2) Federal law applicable to each class shall be fashioned upon the law of the State and the State statutory and decisional construction shall be applied as if jurisdiction of the Federal court were based on diversity of citizenship.

(3) In cases of conflict between State statutory and decisional construction and Federal law the latter shall prevail, and Federal law governing the case shall be fashioned from State law not in conflict, as near as may be, and from Federal law.

(4) If, prior to the date of enactment of this Act, a cause was not subject to removal under section 1441 of title 28, United States Code, the adoption of State law as Federal law by this Act shall not authorize the removal of such a cause on the jurisdictional basis of a Federal question.

(d) Whenever a class of consumers prevails in a class action under this Act, including the amendments made by this Act, the court shall award to the attorneys representing such class a reasonable fee based on the value of their services to the class. An award of attorney's fees is to be made in addition to the damages or relief recovered by the class except that attorney's fees may be awarded from money damages or financial penalties which the defendant owes to members of the class who cannot be located with due diligence. Such attorneys' fees awarded by the court shall not exceed 10 percent of the total judgment unless failure to award a greater amount would be manifestly unjust and not commensurate with the efforts of counsel.

§ 1338. Patents, plant variety protection, copyrights, mask works, trademarks and unfair competition

(a) The district courts shall have original jurisdiction of any civil action arising under any Act of Congress relating to patents, plant variety protection, copyrights and trademarks. Such jurisdiction shall be exclusive of the courts of the states in patent, plant variety protection and copyright cases.

(b) The district courts shall have original jurisdiction of any civil action asserting a claim of unfair competition when joined with a substantial and related claim under the copyright, patent, plant variety protection or trademark laws.

(c) Subsections (a) and (b) apply to exclusive rights in mask works under chapter 9 of title 17, and to exclusive rights in designs under chapter 13 of title 17, to the same extent as such subsections apply to copyrights.

§ 1343. Civil rights and elective franchise

(a) The district courts shall have original jurisdiction of any civil action authorized by law to be commenced by any person:

(1) To recover damages for injury to his person or property, or because of the deprivation of any right or privilege of a citizen of the United States, by any act done in furtherance of any conspiracy mentioned in section 1985 of Title 42;

(2) To recover damages from any person who fails to prevent or to aid in preventing any wrongs mentioned in section 1985 of Title 42 which he had knowledge were about to occur and power to prevent;

(3) To redress the deprivation, under color of any State law, statute, ordinance, regulation, custom or usage, of any right, privilege or immunity secured by the Constitution of the United States or by any Act of Congress providing for equal rights of citizens or of all persons within the jurisdiction of the United States;

(4) To recover damages or to secure equitable or other relief under any Act of Congress providing for the protection of civil rights, including the right to vote.

* * *

§ 1345. United States as plaintiff

Except as otherwise provided by Act of Congress, the district courts shall have original jurisdiction of all civil actions, suits or proceedings commenced by the United States, or by any agency or officer thereof expressly authorized to sue by Act of Congress.

§ 1346.   United States as defendant

(a) The district courts shall have original jurisdiction, concurrent with the United States Court of Federal Claims, of:

(1) Any civil action against the United States for the recovery of any internal-revenue tax alleged to have been erroneously or illegally assessed or collected, or any penalty claimed to have been collected without authority or any sum alleged to have been excessive or in any manner wrongfully collected under the internal-revenue laws;

(2) Any other civil action or claim against the United States, not exceeding $10,000 in amount, founded either upon the Constitution, or any Act of Congress, or any regulation of an executive department, or upon any express or implied contract with the United States, or for liquidated or unliquidated damages in cases not sounding in tort * * *. For the purpose of this paragraph, an express or implied contract with the Army and Air Force Exchange Service, Navy Exchanges, Marine Corps Exchanges, Coast Guard Exchanges, or Exchange Councils of the National Aeronautics and Space Administration shall be considered an express or implied contract with the United States.

(b)(1) Subject to the provisions of chapter 171 of this title, the district courts, together with the United States District Court for the District of the Canal Zone and the District Court of the Virgin Islands, shall have exclusive jurisdiction of civil actions on claims against the United States for money damages, accruing on and after January 1, 1945, for injury or loss of property, or personal injury or death caused by the negligent or wrongful act of omission of any employee of the Government while acting within the scope of his office or employment, under circumstances where the United States, if a private person, would be liable to the claimant in accordance with the law of the place where the act or omission occurred.

(2) No person convicted of a felony who is incarcerated * * * may bring a civil action against the United States or an agency, officer, or employee of the Government, for mental or emotional injury suffered while in custody without a prior showing of physical injury.

(c) The jurisdiction conferred by this section includes jurisdiction of any set-off, counterclaim, or other claim or demand whatever on the part of the United States against any plaintiff commencing an action under this section.

(d) The district courts shall not have jurisdiction under this section of any civil action or claim for a pension.

(e) The district courts shall have original jurisdiction of any civil action against the United States provided in section 6226, 6228(a), 7426, or 7428 * * * or section 7429 of the Internal Revenue Code of 1954.

(f) The district courts shall have exclusive original jurisdiction of civil actions under section 2409a to quiet title to an estate or interest in real property in which an interest is claimed by the United States.

(g) * * *

§ 1359. Parties collusively joined or made

A district court shall not have jurisdiction of a civil action in which any party, by assignment or otherwise, has been improperly or collusively made or joined to invoke the jurisdiction of such court.

§ 1361. Action to compel an officer of the United States to perform his duty

The district courts shall have original jurisdiction of any action in the nature of mandamus to compel an officer or employee of the United States or any agency thereof to perform a duty owed to the plaintiff.

§ 1367. Supplemental jurisdiction

(a) Except as provided in subsections (b) and (c) or as expressly provided otherwise by Federal statute, in any civil action of which the district courts have original jurisdiction, the district courts shall have supplemental jurisdiction over all other claims that are so related to claims in the action within such original jurisdiction that they form part of the same case or controversy under Article III of the United States Constitution. Such supplemental jurisdiction shall include claims that involve the joinder or intervention of additional parties.

(b) In any civil action of which the district courts have original jurisdiction founded solely on section 1332 of this title, the district courts shall not have supplemental jurisdiction under subsection (a) over claims by plaintiffs against persons made parties under Rule 14, 19, 20, or 24 of the Federal Rules of Civil Procedure; or over claims by persons proposed to be joined as plaintiffs under Rule 19 of such rules, or seeking to intervene as plaintiffs under Rule 24 of such rules, when exercising supplemental jurisdiction over such claims would be inconsistent with the jurisdictional requirements of section 1332.

(c) The district courts may decline to exercise supplemental jurisdiction over a claim under subsection (a) if—

(1) the claim raises a novel or complex issue of State law,

(2) the claim substantially predominates over the claim or claims over which the district court has original jurisdiction,

(3) the district court has dismissed all claims over which it has original jurisdiction, or

(4) in exceptional circumstances there are other compelling reasons for declining jurisdiction.

(d) The period of limitations for any claim asserted under subsection (a), and for any other claim in the same action that is voluntarily dismissed at the same time as or after the dismissal of the claim under subsection (a), shall be tolled while the claim is pending and for a period of 30 days after it is dismissed unless State law provides for a longer tolling period.

[handwritten margin note: tolling § still allows π a ct. it kicked out of fed. ct. gives 30 days more]

(e) As used in this section, the term "State" includes the District of Columbia, the Commonwealth of Puerto Rico, and any territory or possession of the United States.

§ 1391. Venue generally

[See proposed congressional legislation to add a new § 1369, in Part IX, infra.]

(a) A civil action wherein jurisdiction is founded only on diversity of citizenship may, except as otherwise provided by law, be brought only in (1) a judicial district where any defendant resides, if all defendants reside in the same State, (2) a judicial district in which a substantial part of the events or omissions giving rise to the claim occurred, or a substantial part of property that is the subject of the action is situated, or (3) a judicial district in which any defendant is subject to personal jurisdiction at the time the action is commenced, if there is no district in which the action may otherwise be brought.

[handwritten margin note: founded only on diversity. 1) where any Δ resides (all Δs in same state) 2) substantial part of events or COA occurred 3) Δ subject to per jld at time action begun]

(b) A civil action wherein jurisdiction is not founded solely on diversity of citizenship may, except as otherwise provided by law, be brought only in (1) a judicial district where any defendant resides, if all defendants reside in the same State, (2) a judicial district in which a substantial part of the events or omissions giving rise to the claim occurred, or a substantial part of property that is the subject of the action is situated, or (3) a judicial district in which any defendant may be found, if there is no district in which the action may otherwise be brought.

[handwritten margin note: — Bates]

[handwritten note below brought: Meaning diff than (a)(3) — hotly debated, Maybe not on purpose]

(c) For purposes of venue under this chapter, a defendant that is a corporation shall be deemed to reside in any judicial district in which it is subject to personal jurisdiction at the time the action is commenced. In a State which has more than one judicial district and in which a defendant that is a corporation is subject to personal jurisdiction at the time an action is commenced, such corporation shall be deemed to reside in any district in that State within which its contacts would be sufficient to subject it to personal jurisdiction if that district were a separate State, and, if there is no such district, the corporation shall be deemed to reside in the district within which it has the most significant contacts.

(d) An alien may be sued in any district. *after have j/d 1st*

(e) A civil action in which a defendant is an officer or employee of the United States or any agency thereof acting in his official capacity or under color of legal authority, or an agency of the United States, or the United States, may, except as otherwise provided by law, be brought in any judicial district in which (1) a defendant in the action resides, (2) a substantial part of the events or omissions giving rise to the claim occurred, or a substantial part of property that is the subject of the action is situated, or (3) the plaintiff resides if no real property is involved in the action. Additional persons may be joined as parties to any such action in accordance with the Federal Rules of Civil Procedure and with such other venue requirements as would be applicable if the United States or one of its officers, employees, or agencies were not a party.

The summons and complaint in such an action shall be served as provided by the Federal Rules of Civil Procedure except that the delivery of the summons and complaint to the officer or agency as required by the rules may be made by certified mail beyond the territorial limits of the district in which the action is brought.

(f) A civil action against a foreign state as defined in section 1603(a) of this title may be brought—

(1) in any judicial district in which a substantial part of the events or omissions giving rise to the claim occurred, or a substantial part of property that is the subject of the action is situated;

(2) in any judicial district in which the vessel or cargo of a foreign state is situated, if the claim is asserted under section 1605(b) of this title;

(3) in any judicial district in which the agency or instrumentality is licensed to do business or is doing business, if the action is brought against an agency or instrumentality of a foreign state as defined in section 1603(b) of this title; or

(4) in the United States District Court for the District of Columbia if the action is brought against a foreign state or political subdivision thereof.

§ 1392. Defendants or property in different districts in same State

Any civil action, of a local nature, involving property located in different districts in the same State, may be brought in any of such districts.

§ 1397. Interpleader

Any civil action of interpleader or in the nature of interpleader under section 1335 of this title may be brought in the judicial district in which one or more of the claimants reside.

§ 1400. Patents and copyrights, mask works and designs

(a) Civil actions, suits, or proceedings arising under any Act of Congress relating to copyrights or exclusive rights in mask works or designs may be instituted in the district in which the defendant or his agent resides or may be found.

(b) Any civil action for patent infringement may be brought in the 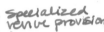 judicial district where the defendant resides, or where the defendant has committed acts of infringement and has a regular and established place of business.

§ 1401. Stockholder's derivative action

Any civil action by a stockholder on behalf of his corporation may be prosecuted in any judicial district where the corporation might have sued the same defendants.

§ 1402. United States as defendant

(a) Any civil action in a district court against the United States under subsection (a) of section 1346 of this title may be prosecuted only:

(1) Except as provided in paragraph (2), in the judicial district where the plaintiff resides;

(2) In the case of a civil action by a corporation under paragraph (1) of subsection (a) of section 1346, in the judicial district in which is located the principal place of business or principal office or agency of the corporation; or if it has no principal place of business or principal office or agency in any judicial district (A) in the judicial district in which is located the office to which was made the return of the tax in respect of which the claim is made, or (B) if no return was made, in the judicial district in which lies the District of Columbia. Notwithstanding the foregoing provisions of this paragraph a district court, for the convenience of the parties and witnesses, in the interest of justice, may transfer any such action to any other district or division.

(b) Any civil action on a tort claim against the United States under subsection (b) of section 1346 of this title may be prosecuted only in the judicial district where the plaintiff resides or wherein the act or omission complained of occurred.

(c) Any civil action against the United States under subsection (e) of section 1346 of this title may be prosecuted only in the judicial district where the property is situated at the time of levy, or if no levy is made, in the judicial district in which the event occurred which gave rise to the cause of action.

(d) Any civil action under section 2409a to quiet title to an estate or interest in real property in which an interest is claimed by the United States shall be brought in the district court of the district where the property is located or, if located in different districts, in any of such districts.

§ 1404.   Change of venue   *Brought in proper forum*

(a) For the convenience of parties and witnesses, in the interest of justice, a district court may transfer any civil action to any other district or division where it might have been brought.

* * *

Comparative State Provision

Wisconsin Statutes Annotated § 801.63

(1) **Stay on initiative of parties.** If a court of this state, on motion of any party, finds that trial of an action pending before it should as a matter of substantial justice be tried in a forum outside this state, the court may in conformity with sub. (3) enter an order to stay further proceedings on the action in this state. A moving party under this subsection must stipulate consent to suit in the alternative forum and waive right to rely on statutes of limitation which may have run in the alternative forum after commencement of the action in this state. A stay order may be granted although the action could not have been commenced in the alternative forum without consent of the moving party.

(2) **Time for filing and hearing motion.** The motion to stay the proceedings shall be filed prior to or with the answer unless the motion is to stay proceedings on a cause raised by counterclaim, in which instance the motion shall be filed prior to or with the reply. The issues raised by this motion shall be tried to the court in advance of any issue going to the merits of the action and shall be joined with objections, if any, raised by answer or motion pursuant to S. 802.06(2). The court shall find separately on each issue so tried and these findings shall be set forth in a single order.

(3) **Scope of trial court discretion on motion to stay proceedings.** The decision on any timely motion to stay proceedings pursuant to sub. (1) is within the discretion of the court in which the action is pending. In the exercise of that discretion the court may appropriately consider such factors as:

(a) Amenability to personal jurisdiction in this state and in any alternative forum of the parties to the action;

(b) Convenience to the parties and witnesses of trial in this state and in any alternative forum;

(c) Differences in conflict of law rules applicable in this state and in any alternative forum; or

(d) Any other factors having substantial bearing upon the selection of a convenient, reasonable and fair place of trial.

(4) **Subsequent modification of order to stay proceedings.** Jurisdiction of the court continues over the parties to a proceeding in which a stay has been ordered under this section until a period of 5 years has elapsed since the last order affecting the stay was entered in the court. At any time during which jurisdiction of the court continues over the parties to the proceedings, the court may, on motion and notice to the parties, subsequently modify the stay order and

take any further action in the proceeding as the interests of justice require. When jurisdiction of the court over the parties and the proceeding terminates by reason of the lapse of 5 years following the last court order in the action, the clerk of the court in which the stay was granted shall without notice enter an order dismissing the action.

* * *

§ 1406. Cure or waiver of defects

[handwritten: Brought in improper forum]

(a) The district court of a district in which is filed a case laying venue in the <u>wrong division or district</u> shall dismiss, or if it be in the interest of justice, transfer such case to any district or division in which it could have been brought.

[handwritten: Can waive w/o making motion]

(b) Nothing in this chapter shall impair the jurisdiction of a district court of any matter involving a party who does not interpose timely and sufficient objection to the venue.

* * *

Comparative State Provisions

Illinois Compiled Statutes ch. 735, 5/2–104(a), (b)

(a) No order or judgment is void because rendered in the wrong venue, except in case of judgment by confession as provided in subsection (c) of Section 2–1301 of this Act. No action shall abate or be dismissed because commenced in the wrong venue if there is a proper venue to which the cause may be transferred. (Footnote omitted.)

(b) All objections of improper venue are waived by a defendant unless a motion to transfer to a proper venue is made by the defendant on or before the date upon which he or she is required to appear or within any further time that may be granted him or her to answer or move with respect to the complaint, except that if a defendant upon whose residence venue depends is dismissed upon motion of plaintiff, a remaining defendant may promptly move for transfer as though the dismissed defendant had not been a party.

See also California Civil Procedure Code § 396 as set out in connection with Federal Rule 12(b), supra.

§ 1407. Multidistrict litigation

[See proposed congressional legislation to add a new § 1369, in Part IX, infra.]

(a) When civil actions involving one or more common questions of fact are pending in different districts, such actions may be transferred to any district for coordinated or consolidated pretrial proceedings. Such transfers shall be made by the judicial panel on multidistrict litigation authorized by this section upon its determination that transfers for such proceedings will be for the convenience of parties and witnesses and will promote the just and efficient conduct of such actions. Each action so transferred shall be remanded by the panel at or before the conclusion of such pretrial proceedings to the district from which it was transferred unless it shall have been previously terminated: *Provided, however,* That the panel may separate any claim, cross-claim, counter-claim, or third-party claim and remand any of such claims before the remainder of the action is remanded.

(b) Such coordinated or consolidated pretrial proceedings shall be conducted by a judge or judges to whom such actions are assigned by the judicial panel on multidistrict litigation. For this purpose, upon request of the panel, a circuit judge or a district judge may be designated and assigned temporarily for service in the transferee district by the Chief Justice of the United States or the chief judge of the circuit, as may be required, in accordance with the provisions of chapter 13 of this title. With the consent of the transferee district court, such actions may be assigned by the panel to a judge or judges of such district. The judge or judges to whom such actions are assigned, the members of the judicial panel on multidistrict litigation, and other circuit and district judges designated when needed by the panel may exercise the powers of a district judge in any district for the purpose of conducting pretrial depositions in such coordinated or consolidated pretrial proceedings.

(c) Proceedings for the transfer of an action under this section may be initiated by—

(i) the judicial panel on multidistrict litigation upon its own initiative, or

(ii) motion filed with the panel by a party in any action in which transfer for coordinated or consolidated pretrial proceedings under this section may be appropriate. A copy of such motion shall be filed in the district court in which the moving party's action is pending.

The panel shall give notice to the parties in all actions in which transfers for coordinated or consolidated pretrial proceedings are contemplated, and such notice shall specify the time and place of any hearing to determine whether such transfer shall be made. Orders of the panel to set a hearing and other orders of the panel issued prior to the order either directing or denying transfer shall be filed in the office of the clerk of the district court in which a transfer hearing is to be or has been held. The panel's order of transfer shall be based upon a record of such hearing at which material evidence may be offered by any party to an action pending in any district that would be affected by the proceedings under this section, and shall be supported by findings of fact and conclusions of law based upon such record. Orders of transfer and such other orders as the panel may make thereafter shall be filed in the office of the clerk of the district court of the transferee district and shall be effective when thus filed. The clerk of the transferee district court shall forthwith transmit a certified copy of the panel's order to transfer to the clerk of the district court from which the action is being transferred. An order denying transfer shall be filed in each district wherein there is a case pending in which the motion for transfer has been made.

(d) The judicial panel on multidistrict litigation shall consist of seven circuit and district judges designated from time to time by the Chief Justice of the United States, no two of whom shall be from the same circuit. The concurrence of four members shall be necessary to any action by the panel.

(e) No proceedings for review of any order of the panel may be permitted except by extraordinary writ pursuant to the provisions of title 28, section 1651, United States Code. Petitions for an extraordinary writ to review an order of the panel to set a transfer hearing and other orders of the panel issued prior to the order either directing or denying transfer shall be filed only in the court of appeals having jurisdiction over the district in which a hearing is to be or has been held. Petitions for an extraordinary writ to review an order to transfer or orders subsequent to transfer shall be filed only in the court of appeals having jurisdiction over the transferee district. There shall be no appeal or review of an order of the panel denying a motion to transfer for consolidated or coordinated proceedings.

(f) The panel may prescribe rules for the conduct of its business not inconsistent with Acts of Congress and the Federal Rules of Civil Procedure.

(g) Nothing in this section shall apply to any action in which the United States is a complainant arising under the antitrust laws. "Antitrust laws" as used herein include those acts referred to in the Act of October 15, 1914, as amended (38 Stat. 730; 15 U.S.C. 12), and also include the Act of June 19, 1936 (49 Stat. 1526; 15 U.S.C. 13, 13a, and 13b) and the Act of September 26, 1914, as added March 21, 1938 (52 Stat. 116, 117; 15 U.S.C. 56); but shall not include section 4A of the Act of October 15, 1914, as added July 7, 1955 (69 Stat. 282; 15 U.S.C. 15a).

(h) Notwithstanding the provisions of section 1404 or subsection (f) of this section, the judicial panel on multidistrict litigation may consolidate and transfer with or without the consent of the parties, for both pretrial purposes and for trial, any action brought under section 4C of the Clayton Act.

§ 1441. Actions removable generally

[See proposed congressional legislation to amend § 1441 and to add a new § 1453, in Part IX, infra.]

(a) Except as otherwise expressly provided by Act of Congress, any civil action brought in a State court of which the district courts of the United States have original jurisdiction, may be removed by the defendant or the defendants, to the district court of the United States for the district and division embracing the place where such action is pending. For purposes of removal under this chapter, the citizenship of defendants sued under fictitious names shall be disregarded.

venue rule

(b) Any civil action of which the district courts have original jurisdiction founded on a claim or right arising under the Constitution, treaties or laws of the United States shall be removable without regard to the citizenship or residence of the parties. Any other such action shall be removable only if none of the parties in interest properly joined and served as defendants is a citizen of the State in which such action is brought.

(c) Whenever a separate and independent claim or cause of action within the jurisdiction conferred by section 1331 of this title is joined with one or more otherwise non-removable claims or causes of action, the entire case may be removed and the district court may determine all issues therein, or, in its discretion, may remand all matters in which State law predominates.

(d) Any civil action brought in a State court against a foreign state as defined in section 1603(a) of this title may be removed by the foreign state to the district court of the United States for the district and division embracing the place where such action is pending. Upon removal the action shall be tried by the court without jury. Where removal is based upon this subsection, the time limitations of section 1446(b) of this chapter may be enlarged at any time for cause shown.

(e) The court to which such civil action is removed is not precluded from hearing and determining any claim in such civil action because the State court from which such civil action is removed did not have jurisdiction over that claim.

§ 1442. Federal officers sued or prosecuted

(a) A civil action or criminal prosecution commenced in a State court against any of the following persons may be removed by them to the district court of the United States for the district and division embracing the place wherein it is pending:

(1) The United States or any agency thereof or any officer (or any person acting under that officer) of the United States or of any agency thereof, sued in an official on individual capacity for any act under color of such office or on account of any right, title or authority claimed under any Act of Congress for the apprehension or punishment of criminals or the collection of the revenue.

(2) A property holder whose title is derived from any such officer, where such action or prosecution affects the validity of any law of the United States.

(3) Any officer of the courts of the United States, for any Act under color of office or in the performance of his duties.

(4) Any officer of either House of Congress, for any act in the discharge of his official duty under an order of such House.

260

(b) A personal action commenced in any State court by an alien against any citizen of a State who is, or at the time the alleged action accrued was, a civil officer of the United States and is a nonresident of such State, wherein jurisdiction is obtained by the State court by personal service of process, may be removed by the defendant to the district court of the United States for the district and division in which the defendant was served with process.

§ 1443. Civil rights cases

Any of the following civil actions or criminal prosecutions, commenced in a State court may be removed by the defendant to the district court of the United States for the district and division embracing the place wherein it is pending:

(1) Against any person who is denied or cannot enforce in the courts of such State a right under any law providing for the equal civil rights of citizens of the United States, or of all persons within the jurisdiction thereof;

(2) For any act under color of authority derived from any law providing for equal rights, or for refusing to do any act on the ground that it would be inconsistent with such law.

§ 1445. Nonremovable actions

(a) A civil action in any State court against a railroad or its receivers or trustees, arising under * * * [the Federal Employers' Liability Act, 45 U.S.C. §§ 51–60], may not be removed to any district court of the United States.

* * *

(c) A civil action in any State court arising under the workmen's compensation laws of such State may not be removed to any district court of the United States.

(d) A civil action in any State court arising under section 40302 of the Violence Against Women Act of 1994 may not be removed to any district court of the United States.

§ 1446. Procedure for removal

(a) A defendant or defendants desiring to remove any civil action or criminal prosecution from a State court shall file in the district court of the United States for the district and division within which such action is pending a notice of removal signed pursuant to Rule 11 of the Federal Rules of Civil Procedure and containing a short and plain statement of the grounds for removal, together with a copy of all process, pleadings, and orders served upon such defendant or defendants in such action.

(b) The notice of removal of a civil action or proceeding shall be filed within thirty days after the receipt by the defendant, through service or otherwise, of a copy of the initial pleading setting forth the claim for relief upon which such action or proceeding is based, or within thirty days after the service of summons upon the defendant if such initial pleading has then been filed in court and is not required to be served on the defendant, whichever period is shorter.

If the case stated by the initial pleading is not removable, a notice of removal may be filed within thirty days after receipt by the defendant, through service or otherwise, of a copy of an amended pleading, motion, order or other paper from which it may first be ascertained that the case is one which is or has become removable, except that a case may not be removed on the basis of jurisdiction conferred by section 1332 of this title more than 1 year after commencement of the action.

(c) * * * [This section refers solely to criminal matters.]

(d) Promptly after the filing of such notice of removal of a civil action the defendant or defendants shall give written notice thereof to all adverse parties and shall file a copy of the notice with the clerk of such State court, which shall effect removal and the State court shall proceed no further unless and until the case is remanded.

(e) If the defendant or defendants are in actual custody on process issued by the State court, the district court shall issue its writ of habeas corpus, and the marshal shall thereupon take such defendant or defendants into his custody and deliver a copy of the writ to the clerk of such State court.

(f) * * *

§ 1447. Procedure after removal generally

(a) In any case removed from a State court, the district court may issue all necessary orders and process to bring before it all proper parties whether served by process issued by the State court or otherwise.

(b) It may require the removing party to file with its clerk copies of all records and proceedings in such State court or may cause the same to be brought before it by writ of certiorari issued to such State court.

(c) A motion to remand the case on the basis of any defect other than lack of subject matter jurisdiction must be made within 30 days after the filing of the notice of removal under section 1446(a). If at any time before final judgment it appears that the district court lacks subject matter jurisdiction, the case shall be remanded. An order remanding the case may require payment of just costs and any actual expenses, including attorney fees, incurred as a result of the removal. A certified copy of the order of remand shall be mailed by the clerk to the clerk of the State court. The State court may thereupon proceed with such case.

(d) An order remanding a case to the State court from which it was removed is not reviewable on appeal or otherwise, except that an order remanding a case to the State court from which it was removed pursuant to section 1443 of this title shall be reviewable by appeal or otherwise.

(e) If after removal the plaintiff seeks to join additional defendants whose joinder would destroy subject matter jurisdiction, the court may deny joinder, or permit joinder and remand the action to the State court.

§ 1631.   Transfer to cure want of jurisdiction

Whenever a civil action is filed in a court as defined in section 610 of this title or an appeal, including a petition for review of administrative action, is noticed for or filed with such a court and that court finds that there is a want of jurisdiction, the court shall, if it is in the interest of justice, transfer such action or appeal to any other such court in which the action or appeal could have been brought at the time it was filed or noticed, and the action or appeal shall proceed as if it had been filed in or noticed for the court to which it is transferred on the date upon which it was actually filed in or noticed for the court from which it is transferred.

§ 1651.   Writs

(a) The Supreme Court and all courts established by Act of Congress may issue all writs necessary or appropriate in aid of their respective jurisdictions and agreeable to the usages and principles of law.

(b) An alternative writ or rule nisi may be issued by a justice or judge of a court which has jurisdiction.

§ 1652.   State laws as rules of decision

The laws of the several states, except where the Constitution or treaties of the United States or Acts of Congress otherwise require or provide, shall be regarded as rules of decision in civil actions in the courts of the United States, in cases where they apply.

Illinois Supreme Court Rule 20

(a) **Certification.** When it shall appear to the Supreme Court of the United States, or to the United States Court of Appeals for the Seventh Circuit, that there are involved in any proceeding before it questions as to the law of this State, which may be determinative of the said cause, and there are no controlling precedents in the decisions of this court, such court may certify such questions of the laws of this State to this court for instructions concerning such questions of State law, which certificate this court, by written opinion, may answer.

(b) **Contents of Certification Order.** A certification order shall contain:

(1) the questions of law to be answered; and

(2) a statement of all facts relevant to the questions certified and showing fully the nature of the controversy in which the questions arose.

(c) **Record Before Certifying Court.** This court may require the original or copies of all or of any portion of the record before the certifying court to be filed with it, if, in the opinion of this court, the record or a portion thereof may be necessary in answering the questions.

* * *

§ 1653. Amendment of pleadings to show jurisdiction

Defective allegations of jurisdiction may be amended, upon terms, in the trial or appellate courts.

§ 1655. Lien enforcement; absent defendants

In an action in a district court to enforce any lien upon or claim to, or to remove any incumbrance or lien or cloud upon the title to, real or personal property within the district, where any defendant cannot be served within the State, or does not voluntarily appear, the court may order the absent defendant to appear or plead by a day certain.

Such order shall be served on the absent defendant personally if practicable, wherever found, and also upon the person or persons in possession or charge of such property, if any. Where personal service is not practicable, the order shall be published as the court may direct, not less than once a week for six consecutive weeks.

If an absent defendant does not appear or plead within the time allowed, the court may proceed as if the absent defendant had been served with process within the State, but any adjudication shall, as regards the absent defendant without appearance, affect only the property which is the subject of the action. When a part of the property is within another district, but within the same state, such action may be brought in either district.

Any defendant not so personally notified may, at any time within one year after final judgment, enter his appearance, and thereupon the court shall set aside the judgment and permit such defendant to plead on payment of such costs as the court deems just.

§ 1658. Time limitations on the commencement of civil actions arising under Acts of Congress

Except as otherwise provided by law, a civil action arising under an Act of Congress enacted after the date of the enactment of this section may not be commenced later than 4 years after the cause of action accrues.

§ 1693. Place of arrest in civil action

Except as otherwise provided by Act of Congress, no person shall be arrested in one district for trial in another in any civil action in a district court.

§ 1694. Patent infringement action

In a patent infringement action commenced in a district where the defendant is not a resident but has a regular and established place of business, service of process, summons or subpoena upon such defendant may be made upon his agent or agents conducting such business.

§ 1695. Stockholder's derivative action

Process in a stockholder's action in behalf of his corporation may be served upon such corporation in any district where it is organized or licensed to do business or is doing business.

§ 1738. State and Territorial statutes and judicial proceedings; full faith and credit

The Acts of the legislature of any State, Territory, or Possession of the United States, or copies thereof, shall be authenticated by affixing the seal of such State, Territory or Possession thereto.

The records and judicial proceedings of any court of any such State, Territory or Possession, or copies thereof, shall be proved or admitted in other courts within the United States and its Territories and Possessions by the attestation of the clerk and seal of the court annexed, if a seal exists, together with a certificate of a judge of the court that the said attestation is in proper form.

Such Acts, records and judicial proceedings or copies thereof, so authenticated, shall have the same full faith and credit in every court within the United States and its Territories and Possessions as they have by law or usage in the courts of such State, Territory or Possession from which they are taken.

§ 1781. Transmittal of letter rogatory or request

(a) The Department of State has power, directly, or through suitable channels—

(1) to receive a letter rogatory issued, or request made, by a foreign or international tribunal, to transmit it to the tribunal, officer, or agency in the United States to whom it is addressed, and to receive and return it after execution; and

(2) to receive a letter rogatory issued, or request made, by a tribunal in the United States, to transmit it to the foreign or international tribunal, officer, or agency to whom it is addressed, and to receive and return it after execution.

(b) This section does not preclude—

(1) the transmittal of a letter rogatory or request directly from a foreign or international tribunal to the tribunal, officer, or agency

in the United States to whom it is addressed and its return in the same manner; or

(2) the transmittal of a letter rogatory or request directly from a tribunal in the United States to the foreign or international tribunal, officer, or agency to whom it is addressed and its return in the same manner.

§ 1782.   Assistance to foreign and international tribunals and to litigants before such tribunals

(a) [Subject to any legally applicable privilege] the district court of the district in which a person resides or is found may order him to give his testimony or statement or to produce a document or other thing for use in a proceeding in a foreign or international tribunal * * *.   The order may be made pursuant to a letter rogatory issued, or request made, by a foreign or international tribunal or upon the application of any interested person and may direct that the testimony or statement be given, or the document or other thing be produced, before a person appointed by the court.   By virtue of his appointment, the person appointed has power to administer any necessary oath and take the testimony or statement.   The order may prescribe the practice and procedure, which may be in whole or part the practice and procedure of the foreign country or the international tribunal, for taking the testimony or statement or producing the document or other thing.   To the extent that the order does not prescribe otherwise, the testimony or statement shall be taken, and the document or other thing produced, in accordance with the Federal Rules of Civil Procedure.

* * *

Comparative State Provision

Massachusetts General Laws Annotated c. 233, § 45

A person may be summoned and compelled, in like manner and under the same penalties as are provided for a witness before a court, to give his deposition in a cause pending in a court of any other state or government.   Such deposition may be taken before a justice of the peace or a notary public in the commonwealth, or before a commissioner appointed under the authority of the state or government in which the action is pending.   If the deposition is taken before such commissioner, the witness may be summoned and compelled to appear before him by process from a justice of the peace or a notary public in the commonwealth.

§ 1783.   Subpoena of person in foreign country

(a) A court of the United States may order the issuance of a subpoena requiring the appearance as a witness before it, or before a person or body designated by it, of a national or resident of the United States who is in a foreign country, or requiring the production of a specified document or other thing by him, if the court finds that particular testimony or the production of the document or other thing by him is necessary in the interest of justice, and, in other than a criminal action or proceeding, if the court finds, in addition, that it is not possible to obtain his testimony in admissible form without his personal appearance or to obtain the production of the document or other thing in any other manner.

* * *

§ 1861. Declaration of policy

It is the policy of the United States that all litigants in Federal courts entitled to trial by jury shall have the right to grand and petit juries selected at random from a fair cross section of the community in the district or division wherein the court convenes. It is further the policy of the United States that all citizens shall have the opportunity to be considered for service on grand and petit juries in the district courts of the United States, and shall have an obligation to serve as jurors when summoned for that purpose.

§ 1862. Exemptions

No citizen shall be excluded from service as a grand or petit juror in the district courts of the United States or in the Court of International Trade on account of race, color, religion, sex, national origin, or economic status.

§ 1863. Plan for random jury selection

(a) Each United States district court shall devise and place into operation a written plan for random selection of grand and petit jurors that shall be designed to achieve the objectives of sections 1861 and 1862 of this title, and that shall otherwise comply with the provisions of this title. The plan shall be placed into operation after approval by a reviewing panel consisting of the members of the judicial council of the circuit and either the chief judge of the district whose plan is being reviewed or such other active district judge of that district as the chief judge of the district may designate. The panel shall examine the plan to ascertain that it complies with the provisions of this title. If the reviewing panel finds that the plan does not comply, the panel shall state the particulars in which the plan fails to comply and direct the district court to present within a reasonable time an alternative plan remedying the defect or defects. Separate plans may be adopted for each division or combination of divisions within a judicial district. The district court may modify a plan at any time and it shall modify the plan when so directed by the reviewing panel. The district court shall promptly notify the panel, the Administrative Office of the United States Courts, and the Attorney General of the United States, of the initial adoption and future modifications of the plan by filing copies therewith. Modifications of the plan made at the instance of the district court shall become effective after approval by the panel. Each district court shall submit a report on the jury selection process within its jurisdiction to the Administrative Office of the United States Courts in such form and at such times as the Judicial Conference of the United States may specify. The Judicial Conference of the United States may, from time to time, adopt rules and regulations governing the provisions and the operation of the plans formulated under this title.

(b) Among other things, such plan shall—

(1) either establish a jury commission, or authorize the clerk of the court, to manage the jury selection process. If the plan establishes a jury commission, the district court shall appoint one citizen to serve with the clerk of the court as the jury commission: *Provided, however*, That the plan for the District of Columbia may establish a jury commission consisting of three citizens. The citizen jury commissioner shall not belong to the same political party as the clerk serving with him. The clerk or the jury commission, as the case may be, shall act under the supervision and control of the chief judge of the district court or such other judge of the district court as the plan may provide. Each jury commissioner shall, during his tenure in office, reside in the judicial district or division for which he is appointed. Each citizen jury commissioner shall receive compensation to be fixed by the district court plan at a rate not to exceed $50 per day for each day necessarily employed in the performance of his duties, plus reimbursement for travel, subsistence, and other necessary expenses * * *.

(2) specify whether the names of prospective jurors shall be selected from the voter registration lists or the lists of actual voters of the political subdivisions within the district or division. The plan shall prescribe some other source or sources of names in addition to voter lists where necessary to foster the policy and protect the rights secured by sections 1861 and 1862 of this title.   * * *

(3) specify detailed procedures to be followed by the jury commission or clerk in selecting names from the sources specified in paragraph (2) of this subsection. These procedures shall be designed to ensure the random selection of a fair cross section of the persons residing in the community in the district or division wherein the court convenes. They shall ensure that names of persons residing in each of the counties, parishes, or similar political subdivisions within the judicial district or division are placed in a master jury wheel; and shall insure that each county, parish, or similar political subdivision within the district or division is substantially proportionally represented in the master jury wheel for that judicial district, division, or combination of divisions. For the purposes of determining proportional representation in the master jury wheel, either the number of actual voters at the last general election in each county, parish, or similar political subdivision, or the number

of registered voters if registration of voters is uniformly required throughout the district or division, may be used.

(4) provide for a master jury wheel (or a device similar in purpose and function) into which the names of those randomly selected shall be placed. The plan shall fix a minimum number of names to be placed initially in the master jury wheel, which shall be at least one-half of 1 per centum of the total number of persons on the lists used as a source of names for the district or division; but if this number of names is believed to be cumbersome and unnecessary, the plan may fix a smaller number of names to be placed in the master wheel, but in no event less than one thousand. The chief judge of the district court, or such other district court judge as the plan may provide, may order additional names to be placed in the master jury wheel from time to time as necessary. The plan shall provide for periodic emptying and refilling of the master jury wheel at specified times, the interval for which shall not exceed four years.

(5)(A) except as provided in subparagraph (B), specify those groups of persons or occupational classes whose members shall, on individual request therefor, be excused from jury service. Such groups or classes shall be excused only if the district court finds, and the plan states, that jury service by such class or group would entail undue hardship or extreme inconvenience to the members thereof, and excuse of members thereof would not be inconsistent with sections 1861 and 1862 of this title.

(B) specify that volunteer safety personnel, upon individual request, shall be excused from jury service. For purposes of this subparagraph, the term "volunteer safety personnel" means individuals serving a public agency (as defined in section 1203(6) of title I of the Omnibus Crime Control and Safe Streets Act of 1968) in an official capacity, without compensation, as firefighters or members of a rescue squad or ambulance crew.

(6) specify that the following persons are barred from jury service on the ground that they are exempt: [A] members in active service in the Armed Forces of the United States; [B] members of the fire or police departments of any State, the District of Columbia, any territory or possession of the United States, or any subdivision of a State, the District of Columbia, or such territory or possession; [C] public officers in the executive, legislative, or judicial branches of the Government of the United States, or of any State, the District of Columbia, any territory or possession of the United States, or any subdivision of a State, the District of Columbia, or such territory or possession, who are actively engaged in the performance of official duties.

(7) fix the time when the names drawn from the qualified jury wheel shall be disclosed to parties and to the public. If the plan

permits these names to be made public, it may nevertheless permit the chief judge of the district court, or such other district court judge as the plan may provide, to keep these names confidential in any case where the interests of justice so require.

(8) specify the procedures to be followed by the clerk or jury commission in assigning persons whose names have been drawn from the qualified jury wheel to grand and petit jury panels.

(c) The initial plan shall be devised by each district court and transmitted to the reviewing panel specified in subsection (a) of this section within one hundred and twenty days of the date of enactment of the Jury Selection and Service Act of 1968. The panel shall approve or direct the modification of each plan so submitted within sixty days thereafter. Each plan or modification made at the direction of the panel shall become effective after approval at such time thereafter as the panel directs, in no event to exceed ninety days from the date of approval. Modifications made at the instance of the district court under subsection (a) of this section shall be effective at such time thereafter as the panel directs, in no event to exceed ninety days from the date of modification.

(d) State, local and Federal officials having custody, possession, or control of voter registration lists, lists of actual voters, or other appropriate records shall make such lists and records available to the jury commission or clerks for inspection, reproduction, and copying at all reasonable times as the commission or clerk may deem necessary and proper for the performance of duties under this title. The district courts shall have jurisdiction upon application by the Attorney General of the United States to compel compliance with this subsection by appropriate process.

§ 1864. Drawing of names from the master jury wheel; completion of juror qualification form

(a) From time to time as directed by the district court, the clerk or a district judge shall publicly draw at random from the master jury wheel the names of as many persons as may be required for jury service. The clerk or jury commission may upon order of the court prepare an alphabetical list of the names drawn from the master jury wheel. Any list so prepared shall not be disclosed to any person except pursuant to the district court plan or pursuant to section 1867 or 1868 of this title. The clerk or jury commission shall mail to every person whose name is drawn from the master wheel a juror qualification form accompanied by instructions to fill out and return the form, duly signed and sworn, to the clerk or jury commission by mail within ten days. If the person is unable to fill out the form, another shall do it for him, and shall indicate that he has done so and the reason therefor. In any case in which it appears that there is an omission, ambiguity, or error in a form, the clerk or jury commission shall return the form with instructions to the person to make such additions or corrections as may be necessary and to return the form to the clerk or jury commission within ten days. Any person who fails to return a completed juror qualification form as instructed may be summoned by the clerk or jury commission forthwith to appear before the clerk or jury commission to fill out a juror qualification form. A person summoned to appear because of failure to return a juror qualification form as instructed who personally appears and executes a juror qualification form before the clerk or jury commission may, at the discretion of the district court, except where his prior failure to execute and mail such form was willful, be entitled to receive for such appearance the same fees and travel allowances paid to jurors under section 1871 of this title. At the time of his appearance for jury service, any person may be required to fill out another juror qualification form in the presence of the jury commission or the clerk or the court, at which time, in such cases as it appears warranted, the person may be questioned, but only with regard to his responses to questions contained on the form. Any information thus acquired by the clerk or jury commission may be noted on the juror qualification form and transmitted to the chief judge or such district court judge as the plan may provide.

(b) Any person summoned pursuant to subsection (a) of this section who fails to appear as directed shall be ordered by the district court forthwith to appear and show cause for his failure to comply with the summons. Any person who fails to appear pursuant to such order or who fails to show good cause for noncompliance with the summons may be fined not more than $100 or imprisoned not more than three days, or both. Any person who willfully misrepresents a material fact on a juror qualification form for the purpose of avoiding or securing service as a juror may be fined not more than $100 or imprisoned not more than three days, or both.

§ 1865. Qualifications for jury service

(a) The chief judge of the district court, or such other district court judge as the plan may provide, on his initiative or upon recommendation of the clerk or jury commission, shall determine solely on the basis of information provided on the juror qualification form and other competent evidence whether a person is unqualified for, or exempt, or to be excused from jury service. The clerk shall enter such determination in the space provided on the juror qualification form and in any alphabetical list of names drawn from the master jury wheel. If a person did not appear in response to a summons, such fact shall be noted on said list.

(b) In making such determination the chief judge of the district court, or such other district court judge as the plan may provide, shall deem any person qualified to serve on grand and petit juries in the district court unless he—

(1) is not a citizen of the United States eighteen years old who has resided for a period of one year within the judicial district;

(2) is unable to read, write, and understand the English language with a degree of proficiency sufficient to fill out satisfactorily the juror qualification form;

(3) is unable to speak the English language;

(4) is incapable, by reason of mental or physical infirmity, to render satisfactory jury service; or

(5) has a charge pending against him for the commission of, or has been convicted in a State or Federal court of record of, a crime punishable by imprisonment for more than one year and his civil rights have not been restored.

§ 1866. Selection and summoning of jury panels

(a) The jury commission, or in the absence thereof the clerk, shall maintain a qualified jury wheel and shall place in such wheel names of all persons drawn from the master jury wheel who are determined to be qualified as jurors and not exempt or excused pursuant to the district court plan. From time to time, the jury commission or the clerk shall publicly draw at random from the qualified jury wheel such number of names of persons as may be required for assignment to grand and petit jury panels. The jury commission or the clerk shall prepare a separate list of names of persons assigned to each grand and petit jury panel.

(b) When the court orders a grand or petit jury to be drawn the clerk or jury commission or their duly designated deputies shall issue summonses for the required number of jurors.

Each person drawn for jury service may be served personally, or by registered, certified, or first-class mail addressed to such person at his usual residence or business address.

If such service is made personally, the summons shall be delivered by the clerk or the jury commission or their duly designated deputies to the marshal who shall make such service.

If such service is made by mail, the summons may be served by the marshal or by the clerk, the jury commission or their duly designated deputies, who shall make affidavit of service and shall attach thereto any receipt from the addressee for a registered or certified summons.

(c) Except as provided in section 1865 of this title or in any jury selection plan provision adopted pursuant to paragraph (5) or (6) of section 1863(b) of this title, no person or class of persons shall be disqualified, excluded, excused, or exempt from service as jurors: *Provided*, That any person summoned for jury service may be (1) excused by the court, or by the clerk under supervision of the court if the court's jury selection plan so authorizes, upon a showing of undue hardship or extreme inconvenience, for such period as the court deems necessary, at the conclusion of which such person either shall be summoned again for jury service under subsections (b) and (c) of this section, or if the court's jury selection plan so provides, the name of such person shall be reinserted into the qualified jury wheel for selection pursuant to subsection (a) of this section, or (2) excluded by the court on the ground that such person may be unable to render impartial jury service or that his service as a juror would be likely to disrupt the proceedings, or (3) excluded upon peremptory challenge as provided by law, or (4) excluded pursuant to the procedure specified by law upon a challenge by any party for good cause shown, or (5) excluded upon determination by the court that his service as a juror would be likely to threaten the secrecy of the proceedings, or otherwise adversely affect the integrity of jury deliberations. No person shall be excluded under clause (5) of this subsection unless the judge, in open court, determines that such is warranted and that exclusion of the person will not be inconsistent with sections 1861 and 1862 of this title. The number of persons excluded under clause (5) of this subsection shall not exceed one per centum of the number of persons who return executed jury qualification forms during the period, specified in the plan, between two consecutive fillings of the master jury wheel. The names of persons excluded under clause (5) of this subsection, together with detailed explanations for the exclusions, shall be forwarded immediately to the judicial council of the circuit, which shall have the power to make any appropriate order, prospective or retroactive, to redress any misapplication of clause (5) of this subsection, but otherwise exclusions effectuated under such clause shall not be subject to challenge under the provisions of this title. Any person excluded from a particular jury under clause (2), (3), or (4) of this subsection shall be eligible to sit on another jury if the basis for his initial exclusion would not be relevant to his ability to serve on such other jury.

(d) Whenever a person is disqualified, excused, exempt, or excluded from jury service, the jury commission or clerk shall note in the space provided on his juror qualification form or on the juror's card drawn from the qualified jury wheel the specific reason therefor.

(e) In any two-year period, no person shall be required to (1) serve or attend court for prospective service as a petit juror for a total of more than thirty days, except when necessary to complete service in a particular case, or (2) serve on more than one grand jury, or (3) serve as both a grand and petit juror.

(f) When there is an unanticipated shortage of available petit jurors drawn from the qualified jury wheel, the court may require the marshal to summon a sufficient number of petit jurors selected at random from the voter registration lists, lists of actual voters, or other lists specified in the plan, in a manner ordered by the court consistent with sections 1861 and 1862 of this title.

(g) Any person summoned for jury service who fails to appear as directed shall be ordered by the district court to appear forthwith and show cause for his failure to comply with the summons. Any person who fails to show good cause for noncompliance with a summons may be fined not more than $100 or imprisoned not more than three days, or both.

§ 1867.   Challenging compliance with selection procedures

(a) In criminal cases, before the voir dire examination begins, or within seven days after the defendant discovered or could have discovered, by the exercise of diligence, the grounds therefor, whichever is earlier, the defendant may move to dismiss the indictment or stay the proceedings against him on the ground of substantial failure to comply with the provisions of this title in selecting the grand or petit jury.

(b) In criminal cases, before the voir dire examination begins, or within seven days after the Attorney General of the United States discovered or could have discovered, by the exercise of diligence, the grounds therefor, whichever is earlier, the Attorney General may move to dismiss the indictment or stay the proceedings on the ground of substantial failure to comply with the provisions of this title in selecting the grand or petit jury.

(c) In civil cases, before the voir dire examination begins, or within seven days after the party discovered or could have discovered, by the exercise of diligence, the grounds therefor, whichever is earlier, any party may move to stay the proceedings on the ground of substantial failure to comply with the provisions of this title in selecting the petit jury.

(d) Upon motion filed under subsection (a), (b), or (c) of this section, containing a sworn statement of facts which, if true, would constitute a substantial failure to comply with the provisions of this title, the moving party shall be entitled to present in support of such motion the testimony of the jury commission or clerk, if available, any relevant records and papers not public or otherwise available used by the jury commissioner or clerk, and any other relevant evidence. If the court determines that there has been a substantial failure to comply with the provisions of this title in selecting a grand jury, the court shall stay the proceedings pending the selection of a grand jury in conformity with this title or dismiss the indictment, whichever is appropriate. If the court determines that there has been a substantial failure to comply with the provisions of this title in selecting the petit jury, the court shall stay the proceedings pending the selection of a petit jury in conformity with this title.

(e) The procedures prescribed by this section shall be the exclusive means by which a person accused of a Federal crime, the Attorney General of the United States or a party in a civil case may challenge any jury on the ground that such jury was not selected in conformity with the provisions of this title. Nothing in this section shall preclude any person or the United States from pursuing any other remedy, civil or criminal, which may be available for the vindication or enforcement of any law prohibiting discrimination on account of race, color, religion, sex, national origin or economic status in the selection of persons for service on grand or petit juries.

(f) The contents of records or papers used by the jury commission or clerk in connection with the jury selection process shall not be disclosed, except pursuant to the district court plan or as may be necessary in the preparation or presentation of a motion under subsection (a), (b), or (c) of this section, until after the master jury wheel has been emptied and refilled pursuant to section 1863(b)(4) of this title and all persons selected to serve as jurors before the master wheel was emptied have completed such service. The parties in a case shall be allowed to inspect, reproduce, and copy such records or papers at all reasonable times during the preparation and pendency of such a motion. Any person who discloses the contents of any record or paper in violation of this subsection may be fined not more than $1,000 or imprisoned not more than one year, or both.

§ 1868. Maintenance and inspection of records

After the master jury wheel is emptied and refilled pursuant to section 1863(b)(4) of this title, and after all persons selected to serve as jurors before the master wheel was emptied have completed such service, all records and papers compiled and maintained by the jury commission or clerk before the master wheel was emptied shall be preserved in the custody of the clerk for four years or for such longer period as may be ordered by a court, and shall be available for public inspection for the purpose of determining the validity of the selection of any jury.

§ 1869. Definitions

For purposes of this chapter—

(a) "clerk" and "clerk of the court" shall mean the clerk of the district court of the United States, any authorized deputy clerk, and any other person authorized by the court to assist the clerk in the performance of functions under this chapter;

(b) "chief judge" shall mean the chief judge of any district court of the United States;

(c) "voter registration lists" shall mean the official records maintained by State or local election officials of persons registered to vote in either the most recent State or the most recent Federal general election, or, in the case of a State or political subdivision thereof that does not require registration as a prerequisite to voting, other official lists of persons qualified to vote in such election. The term shall also include the list of eligible voters maintained by any Federal examiner pursuant to the Voting Rights Act of 1965 where the names on such list have not been included on the official registration lists or other official lists maintained by the appropriate State or local officials. With respect to the districts of Guam and the Virgin Islands, "voter registration lists" shall mean the official records maintained by territorial election officials of persons registered to vote in the most recent territorial general election;

(d) "lists of actual voters" shall mean the official lists of persons actually voting in either the most recent State or the most recent Federal general election;

(e) "division" shall mean: (1) one or more statutory divisions of a judicial district; or (2) in statutory divisions that contain more than one place of holding court, or in judicial districts where there are no statutory divisions, such counties, parishes, or similar political subdivisions surrounding the places where court is held as the district court plan shall determine: *Provided*, That each county, parish, or similar political subdivision shall be included in some such division;

(f) "district court of the United States", "district court", and "court" shall mean any district court established by chapter 5 of this title, and any court which is created by Act of Congress in a territory and is invested with any jurisdiction of a district court established by chapter 5 of this title;

(g) "jury wheel" shall include any device or system similar in purpose or function, such as a properly programmed electronic data processing system or device;

(h) "juror qualification form" shall mean a form prescribed by the Administrative Office of the United States Courts and approved by the Judicial Conference of the United States, which shall elicit the name, address, age, race, occupation, education, length of residence within the judicial district, distance from residence to place of holding court, prior jury service, and citizenship of a potential juror, and whether he should be excused or exempted from jury service, has any physical or mental infirmity impairing his capacity to serve as juror, is able to read, write, speak and understand the English language, has pending against him any charge for the commission of a State or Federal criminal offense punishable by imprisonment for more than one year, or has been convicted in any State or Federal Court of record of a crime punishable by imprisonment for more than one year and has not had his civil rights restored. The form shall request, but not require, any other information not inconsistent with the provisions of this title and required by the district court plan in the interests of the sound administration of justice. The form also shall elicit the sworn statement that his responses are true to the best of his knowledge. Notarization shall not be required. The form shall contain words clearly informing the person that the furnishing of any information with respect to his religion, national origin, or economic status is not a prerequisite to his qualification for jury service, that such information need not be furnished if the person finds it objectionable to do so, and that information concerning race is required solely to enforce nondiscrimination in jury selection and has no bearing on an individual's qualification for jury service.

(i) "public officer" shall mean a person who is either elected to public office or who is directly appointed by a person elected to public office;

(j) "undue hardship or extreme inconvenience", as a basis for excuse from immediate jury service under section 1866(c)(1) of this chapter, shall mean great distance, either in miles or travel-time, from the place of holding court, grave illness in the family or any other emergency which outweighs in immediacy and urgency the obligation to serve as a juror when summoned, or any other factor which the court determines to constitute an undue hardship or to create an extreme inconvenience to the juror; and in addition, in situations where it is anticipated that a trial or grand jury proceeding may require more than thirty days of service, the court may consider, as a further basis for temporary excuse, severe economic hardship to an employer which would result from the absence of a key employee during the period of such service;

(k) "publicly draw", as referred to in sections 1864 and 1866 of this chapter, shall mean a drawing which is conducted within the district after a reasonable public notice and which is open to the public at large under the supervision of the clerk or jury commission, except that when a drawing is made by means of electronic data processing, "publicly draw" shall mean a drawing which is conducted at a data processing center located in or out of the district, after reasonable public notice given in the district for which juror names are being drawn, and which is open to the public at large under such supervision of the clerk or jury commission as the Judicial Conference of the United States shall by regulation require; and

(l) "jury summons" shall mean a summons issued by a clerk of court, jury commission, or their duly designated deputies, containing either a preprinted or stamped seal of court, and containing the name of the issuing clerk imprinted in preprinted, type, or facsimile manner on the summons or the envelopes transmitting the summons.

§ 1870. Challenges

In civil cases, each party shall be entitled to three peremptory challenges. Several defendants or several plaintiffs may be considered as a single party for the purposes of making challenges, or the court may allow additional peremptory challenges and permit them to be exercised separately or jointly.

All challenges for cause or favor, whether to the array or panel or to individual jurors, shall be determined by the court.

2-15-01 ✓

§ 1919. Dismissal for lack of jurisdiction

Whenever any action or suit is dismissed in any district court, the Court of International Trade, or the Court of Federal Claims for want of jurisdiction, such court may order the payment of just costs.

§ 1920. Taxation of costs

A judge or clerk of any court of the United States may tax as costs the following:

(1) Fees of the clerk and marshal;

(2) Fees of the court reporter for all or any part of the stenographic transcript necessarily obtained for use in the case;

(3) Fees and disbursements for printing and witnesses;

(4) Fees for exemplification and copies of papers necessarily obtained for use in the case;

(5) Docket fees under section 1923 of this title;

(6) Compensation of court appointed experts, compensation of interpreters, and salaries, fees, expenses, and costs of special interpretation services under section 1828 of this title.

A bill of costs shall be filed in the case and, upon allowance, included in the judgment or decree.

§ 1927. Counsel's liability for excessive costs

Any attorney or other person admitted to conduct cases in any court of the United States or any Territory thereof who so multiplies the proceedings in any case unreasonably and vexatiously may be required by the court to satisfy personally the excess costs, expenses, and attorneys' fees reasonably incurred because of such conduct.

§ 1963. Registration of judgments of the district courts and the Court of International Trade

A judgment in an action for the recovery of money or property entered in any court of appeals, district court, bankruptcy court, or in the Court of International Trade may be registered by filing a certified copy of such judgment in any other district or, with respect to the Court of International Trade, in any judicial district, when the judgment has become final by appeal or expiration of the time for appeal or when ordered by the court that entered the judgment for good cause shown. Such a judgment entered in favor of the United States may be so registered any time after judgment is entered. A judgment so registered shall have the same effect as a judgment of the district court of the district where registered and may be enforced in like manner.

A certified copy of the satisfaction of any judgment in whole or in part may be registered in like manner in any district in which the judgment is a lien.

The procedure prescribed under this section is in addition to other procedures provided by law for the enforcement of judgments.

Comparative State Provisions

Uniform Enforcement of Foreign Judgments Act (1964 Revision) § 2

A copy of any foreign judgment authenticated in accordance with the act of Congress or the statutes of this state may be filed in the office of the Clerk of any [District Court of any city or county] of this state. The Clerk shall treat the foreign judgment in the same manner as a judgment of the [District Court of any city or county] of this state. A judgment so filed has the same effect and is subject to the same procedures, defenses and proceedings for reopening, vacating, or staying as a judgment of a [District Court of any city or county] of this state and may be enforced or satisfied in like manner.

Uniform Enforcement of Foreign Judgments Act (1964 Revision) § 6

The right of a judgment creditor to bring an action to enforce his judgment instead of proceeding under this Act remains unimpaired.

§ 2071. Rule-making power generally

(a) The Supreme Court and all courts established by Act of Congress may from time to time prescribe rules for the conduct of their business. Such rules shall be consistent with Acts of Congress and rules of practice and procedure prescribed under section 2072 of this title.

(b) Any rule prescribed by a court, other than the Supreme Court, under subsection (a) shall be prescribed only after giving appropriate public notice and an opportunity for comment. Such rule shall take effect upon the date specified by the prescribing court and shall have such effect on pending proceedings as the prescribing court may order.

(c)(1) A rule of a district court prescribed under subsection (a) shall remain in effect unless modified or abrogated by the judicial council of the relevant circuit.

(2) Any other rule prescribed by a court other than the Supreme Court under subsection (a) shall remain in effect unless modified or abrogated by the Judicial Conference.

(d) Copies of rules prescribed under subsection (a) by a district court shall be furnished to the judicial council, and copies of all rules prescribed by a court other than the Supreme Court under subsection (a) shall be furnished to the director of the Administrative Office of the United States Courts and made available to the public.

(e) If the prescribing court determines that there is an immediate need for a rule, such court may proceed under this section without public notice and opportunity for comment, but such court shall promptly thereafter afford such notice and opportunity for comment.

(f) No rule may be prescribed by a district court other than under this section.

§ 2072. Rules of procedure and evidence; power to prescribe

(a) The Supreme Court shall have the power to prescribe general rules of practice and procedure and rules of evidence for cases in the United States district courts (including proceedings before magistrates thereof) and courts of appeals.

(b) Such rules shall not abridge, enlarge or modify any substantive right. All laws in conflict with such rules shall be of no further force or effect after such rules have taken effect.

(c) Such rules may define when a ruling of a district court is final for the purposes of appeal under section 1291 of this title.

§ 2111. Harmless error

On the hearing of any appeal or writ of certiorari in any case, the court shall give judgment after an examination of the record without regard to errors or defects which do not affect the substantial rights of the parties.

§ 2201. Creation of remedy

(a) In a case of actual controversy within its jurisdiction, except with respect to Federal taxes other than actions brought under section 7428 of the Internal Revenue Code of 1986 * * *, any court of the United States, upon the filing of an appropriate pleading, may declare the rights and other legal relations of any interested party seeking such declaration, whether or not further relief is or could be sought. Any such declaration shall have the force and effect of a final judgment or decree and shall be reviewable as such.

* * *

Comparative State Provisions

Connecticut Superior Court Rules of Civil Procedure § 17–55

A declaratory judgment action may be maintained if all of the following conditions have been met:

(1) The party seeking the declaratory judgment has an interest, legal or equitable, by reason of danger of loss or of uncertainty as to the party's rights or other jural relations; or

(2) There is an actual bona fide and substantial question or issue in dispute or substantial uncertainty of legal relations which requires settlement between the parties; and

(3) In the event that there is another form of proceeding that can provide the party seeking the declaratory judgment immediate redress, the court is of the opinion that such party should be allowed to proceed with the claim for declaratory judgment despite the existence of such alternate procedure.

Uniform Declaratory Judgments Act § 6

The court may refuse to render or enter a declaratory judgment or decree where such judgment or decree, if rendered or entered, would not terminate the uncertainty or controversy giving rise to the proceeding.

§ 2202. Further relief

Further necessary or proper relief based on a declaratory judgment or decree may be granted, after reasonable notice and hearing, against any adverse party whose rights have been determined by such judgment.

§ 2283. Stay of State court proceedings

A court of the United States may not grant an injunction to stay proceedings in a State court except as expressly authorized by Act of Congress, or where necessary in aid of its jurisdiction, or to protect or effectuate its judgments.

§ 2284. Three-judge court; when required; composition; procedure

(a) A district court of three judges shall be convened when otherwise required by Act of Congress, or when an action is filed challenging the constitutionality of the apportionment of congressional districts or the apportionment of any statewide legislative body.

(b) In any action required to be heard and determined by a district court of three judges under subsection (a) of this section, the composition and procedure of the court shall be as follows:

(1) Upon the filing of a request for three judges, the judge to whom the request is presented shall, unless he determines that three judges are not required, immediately notify the chief judge of the circuit, who shall designate two other judges, at least one of whom shall be a circuit judge. The judges so designated, and the judge to whom the request was presented, shall serve as members of the court to hear and determine the action or proceeding.

* * *

§ 2361. Process and procedure

In any civil action of interpleader or in the nature of interpleader under section 1335 of this title, a district court may issue its process for all claimants and enter its order restraining them from instituting or prosecuting any proceeding in any State or United States court affecting the property, instrument or obligation involved in the interpleader action until further order of the court. Such process and order shall be returnable at such time as the court or judge thereof directs, and shall be addressed to and served by the United States marshals for the respective districts where the claimants reside or may be found.

Such district court shall hear and determine the case, and may discharge the plaintiff from further liability, make the injunction permanent, and make all appropriate orders to enforce its judgment.

§ 2403. Intervention by United States or a State; constitutional question

(a) In any action, suit or proceeding in a court of the United States to which the United States or any agency, officer or employee thereof is not a party, wherein the constitutionality of any Act of Congress affecting the public interest is drawn in question, the court shall certify such fact to the Attorney General, and shall permit the United States to intervene for presentation of evidence, if evidence is otherwise admissible in the case, and for argument on the question of constitutionality. The United States shall, subject to the applicable provisions of law, have all the rights of a party and be subject to all liabilities of a party as to court costs to the extent necessary for a proper presentation of the facts and law relating to the question of constitutionality.

(b) In any action, suit, or proceeding in a court of the United States to which a State or any agency, officer, or employee thereof is not a party, wherein the constitutionality of any statute of that State affecting the public interest is drawn in question, the court shall certify such fact to the attorney general of the State, and shall permit the State to intervene for presentation of evidence, if evidence is otherwise admissible in the case, and for argument on the question of constitutionality. The State shall, subject to the applicable provisions of law, have all the rights of a party and be subject to all liabilities of a party as to court costs to the extent necessary for a proper presentation of the facts and law relating to the question of constitutionality.

Selected Provision of Title 42, United States Code—The Public Health and Welfare

§ 1983. Civil action for deprivation of rights

Every person who, under color of any statute, ordinance, regulation, custom, or usage, of any State or Territory or the District of Columbia, subjects, or causes to be subjected, any citizen of the United States or other person within the jurisdiction thereof to the deprivation of any rights, privileges, or immunities secured by the Constitution and laws, shall be liable to the party injured in an action at law, suit in equity, or other proper proceeding for redress, except that in any action brought against a judicial officer for an act or omission taken in such officer's judicial capacity, injunctive relief shall not be granted unless a declaratory decree was violated or declaratory relief was unavailable. For the purposes of this section, any Act of Congress applicable exclusively to the District of Columbia shall be considered to be a statute of the District of Columbia.

Part III

Selected State Jurisdictional Statutes
and
Selected State Statutes Governing the Powers of Appellate Courts

---

TABLE OF CONTENTS

Selected State Jurisdictional Statutes

Statute		Page
New York Civil Practice Law and Rules 302(a)		284
North Carolina General Statutes	§ 1–75.2	285
	§ 1–75.4	285
	§ 1–75.7	288
	§ 1–75.8	288
Rhode Island General Laws Annotated	§ 9–5–33(a)	288
Uniform Interstate and International Procedure Act	§ 1.02	289
	§ 1.03	289
	§ 1.05	289
Uniform Parentage Act	§ 8(b)	289

Selected State Statutes Governing the Powers of the Appellate Courts

Statute	Page
Alabama Code § 12–2–13	290
California Civil Procedure Code § 909	290

Selected State Jurisdictional Statutes

New York Civil Practice Law and Rules 302(a)

As to a cause of action arising from any of the acts enumerated in this section, a court may exercise personal jurisdiction over any non-domiciliary, or his executor or administrator, who in person or through an agent:

1. transacts any business within the state or contracts anywhere to supply goods or services in the state; or

2. commits a tortious act within the state, except as to a cause of action for defamation of character arising from the act; or

3. commits a tortious act without the state causing injury to person or property within the state, except as to a cause of action for defamation of character arising from the act, if he

(i) regularly does or solicits business, or engages in any other persistent course of conduct, or derives substantial revenue from goods used or consumed or services rendered, in the state, or

(ii) expects or should reasonably expect the act to have consequences in the state and derives substantial revenue from interstate or international commerce; or

4. owns, uses or possesses any real property situated within the state.

North Carolina General Statutes § 1-75.2

Definitions.—In this article the following words have the designated meanings:

(1) "Person" means any natural person, partnership, corporation, body politic, and any unincorporated association, organization, or society which may sue or be sued under a common name.
 * * *

North Carolina General Statutes § 1-75.4

Personal jurisdiction, grounds for generally.—A court of this State having jurisdiction of the subject matter has jurisdiction over a person served in an action pursuant to Rule 4(j) or Rule 4(j1) or 4(j3) of the Rules of Civil Procedure under any of the following circumstances:

(1) Local Presence or Status.—In any action, whether the claim arises within or without this State, in which a claim is asserted against a party who when service of process is made upon such party:

 a. Is a natural person present within this State; or

 b. Is a natural person domiciled within this State; or

 c. Is a domestic corporation; or

 d. Is engaged in substantial activity within this State, whether such activity is wholly interstate, intrastate, or otherwise.

(2) Special Jurisdiction Statutes.—In any action which may be brought under statutes of this State that specifically confer grounds for personal jurisdiction.

(3) Local Act or Omission.—In any action claiming injury to person or property or for wrongful death within or without this State arising out of an act or omission within this State by the defendant.

(4) Local Injury; Foreign Act.—In any action for wrongful death occurring within this State or in any action claiming injury to person or property within this State arising out of an act or omission outside this State by the defendant, provided in addition that at or about the time of the injury either:

a. Solicitation or services activities were carried on within this State by or on behalf of the defendant; or

b. Products, materials or things processed, serviced or manufactured by the defendant were used or consumed within this State in the ordinary course of trade.

(5) Local Services, Goods or Contracts.—In any action which:

a. Arises out of a promise, made anywhere to the plaintiff or to some third party for the plaintiff's benefit, by the defendant to perform services within this State or to pay for services to be performed in this State by the plaintiff; or

b. Arises out of services actually performed for the plaintiff by the defendant within this State, or services actually performed for the defendant by the plaintiff within this State if such performance within this State was authorized or ratified by the defendant; or

c. Arises out of a promise, made anywhere to the plaintiff or to some third party for the plaintiff's benefit, by the defendant to deliver or receive within this State, or to ship from this State goods, documents of title, or other things of value; or

d. Relates to goods, documents of title, or other things of value shipped from this State by the plaintiff to the defendant on his order or direction; or

e. Relates to goods, documents of title, or other things of value actually received by the plaintiff in this State from the defendant through a carrier without regard to where delivery to the carrier occurred.

(6) Local Property.—In any action which arises out of:

a. A promise, made anywhere to the plaintiff or to some third party for the plaintiff's benefit, by the defendant to create in either party an interest in, or protect, acquire, dispose of, use, rent, own, control or possess by either party real property situated in this State; or

b. A claim to recover for any benefit derived by the defendant through the use, ownership, control or possession by the defendant of tangible property situated within this State either at the time of the first use, ownership, control or possession or at the time the action is commenced; or

c. A claim that the defendant return, restore, or account to the plaintiff for any asset or thing of value which was within this State at the time the defendant acquired possession or control over it.

(7) Deficiency Judgment on Local Foreclosure or Resale.—In any action to recover a deficiency judgment upon an obligation

secured by a mortgage, deed of trust, conditional sale, or other security instrument executed by the defendant or his predecessor to whose obligation the defendant has succeeded and the deficiency is claimed either:

    a.   In an action in this State to foreclose such security instrument upon real property, tangible personal property, or an intangible represented by an indispensable instrument, situated in this State; or

    b.   Following sale of real or tangible personal property or an intangible represented by an indispensable instrument in this State under a power of sale contained in any security instrument.

(8) Director or Officer of a Domestic Corporation.—In any action against a defendant who is or was an officer or director of a domestic corporation where the action arises out of the defendant's conduct as such officer or director or out of the activities of such corporation while the defendant held office as a director or officer.

(9) Taxes or Assessments.—In any action for the collection of taxes or assessments levied, assessed or otherwise imposed by a taxing authority of this State after the date of ratification of this act.

(10) Insurance or Insurers.—In any action which arises out of a contract of insurance as defined in G.S. 58-3 made anywhere between the plaintiff or some third party and the defendant and in addition either:

    a.   The plaintiff was a resident of this State when the event occurred out of which the claim arose; or

    b.   The event out of which the claim arose occurred within this State, regardless of where the plaintiff resided.

(11) Personal Representative.—In any action against a personal representative to enforce a claim against the deceased person represented, whether or not the action was commenced during the lifetime of the deceased, where one or more of the grounds stated in subdivisions (2) to (10) of this section would have furnished a basis for jurisdiction over the deceased had he been living.

(12) Marital Relationship.—In any action under Chapter 50 that arises out of the marital relationship within this State, notwithstanding subsequent departure from the State, if the other party to the marital relationship continues to reside in this State.

North Carolina General Statutes § 1–75.7

Personal jurisdiction—Grounds for without service of summons.—A court of this State having jurisdiction of the subject matter may, without serving a summons upon him, exercise jurisdiction in an action over a person:

(1) Who makes a general appearance in an action; * * * or

(2) With respect to any counterclaim asserted against that person in an action which he has commenced in this State.

North Carolina General Statutes § 1–75.8

Jurisdiction in rem or quasi in rem—Grounds for generally.—A court of this State having jurisdiction of the subject matter may exercise jurisdiction in rem or quasi in rem on the grounds stated in this section. A judgment in rem or quasi in rem may affect the interests of a defendant in a status, property or thing acted upon only if process has been served upon the defendant pursuant to Rule 4(k) of the Rules of Civil Procedure. Jurisdiction in rem or quasi in rem may be invoked in any of the following cases:

(1) When the subject of the action is real or personal property in this State and the defendant has or claims any lien or interest therein, or the relief demanded consists wholly or partially in excluding the defendant from any interest or lien therein. This subdivision shall apply whether any such defendant is known or unknown.

(2) When the action is to foreclose, redeem from or satisfy a deed of trust, mortgage, claim or lien upon real or personal property in this State.

(3) When the action is for a divorce or for annulment of marriage of a resident of this State.

(4) When the defendant has property within this State which has been attached or has a debtor within the State who has been garnished. Jurisdiction under this subdivision may be independent of or supplementary to jurisdiction acquired under subdivisions (1), (2) and (3) of this section.

[In Balcon, Inc. v. Sadler, 36 N.C.App. 322, 244 S.E.2d 164 (1978), the court held that subdivision (4) fails to meet standards set forth in Shaffer v. Heitner, 433 U.S. 186, 97 S.Ct. 2569, 53 L.Ed.2d 683 (1977), and is therefor unconstitutional.]

(5) In any other action in which in rem or quasi in rem jurisdiction may be constitutionally exercised.

Rhode Island General Laws Annotated § 9–5–33(a)

Every foreign corporation, every individual not a resident of this state or his executor or administrator, and every partnership or association, composed of any person or persons, not such residents, that shall have the necessary minimum contacts with the state of Rhode Island, shall be subject to the jurisdiction of the state of Rhode Island, and the courts of this state shall hold such foreign corporations and such nonresident individuals or their executors or administrators, and such partnerships or associations amenable to suit in Rhode Island in every case not contrary to the provisions of the constitution or laws of the United States.

Uniform Interstate and International Procedure Act § 1.02

A court may exercise personal jurisdiction over a person domiciled in, organized under the laws of, or maintaining his or its principal place of business in, this state as to any [cause of action] [claim for relief].

Uniform Interstate and International Procedure Act § 1.03

(a) A court may exercise personal jurisdiction over a person, who acts directly or by an agent, as to a [cause of action] [claim for relief] arising from the person's

(1) transacting any business in this state;

(2) contracting to supply services or things in this state;

(3) causing tortious injury by an act or omission in this state;

(4) causing tortious injury in this state by an act or omission outside this state if he regularly does or solicits business, or engages in any other persistent course of conduct, or derives substantial revenue from goods used or consumed or services rendered, in this state; [or]

(5) having an interest in, using, or possessing real property in this state[; or

(6) contracting to insure any person, property, or risk located within this state at the time of contracting].

(b) When jurisdiction over a person is based solely upon this section, only a [cause of action] [claim for relief] arising from acts enumerated in this section may be asserted against him.

Uniform Interstate and International Procedure Act § 1.05

When the court finds that in the interest of substantial justice the action should be heard in another forum, the court may stay or dismiss the action in whole or in part on any conditions that may be just.

Uniform Parentage Act § 8(b)

A person who has sexual intercourse in this State thereby submits to the jurisdiction of the courts of this State as to an action brought under this Act [to establish parentage] with respect to a child who may have been conceived by that act of intercourse. * * *

289

Selected State Statutes Governing the
Powers of the Appellate Courts

Alabama Code § 12-2-13

The supreme court, in deciding each case when there is a conflict between its existing opinion and any former ruling in the case, must be governed by what, in its opinion, at that time is law, without any regard to such former ruling on the law by it; but the right of third persons, acquired on the faith of the former ruling, shall not be defeated or interfered with by or on account of any subsequent ruling.

Comparative Provision

See Georgia Code Annotated § 9-11-60(h) as set out following Federal Rule of Civil Procedure 60, supra.

California Civil Procedure Code § 909

In all cases where trial by jury is not a matter of right or where trial by jury has been waived, the reviewing court may make factual determinations contrary to or in addition to those made by the trial court. The factual determinations may be based on the evidence adduced before the trial court either with or without the taking of evidence by the reviewing court. The reviewing court may for the purpose of making the factual determinations or for any other purpose in the interests of justice, take additional evidence of or concerning facts occurring at any time prior to the decision of the appeal, and may give or direct the entry of any judgment or order and may make any further or other order as the case may require. This section shall be liberally construed to the end among others that, where feasible, causes may be finally disposed of by a single appeal and without further proceedings in the trial court except where in the interests of justice a new trial is required on some or all of the issues.

Part IV

Selected Portions of the Federal Rules of Appellate Procedure

---

TABLE OF RULES

Title I. Applicability of Rules

Rule		Page
1.	Scope of Rules; Title	293
2.	Suspension of Rules	293

Title II. Appeal From a Judgment or Order of a District Court

3.	Appeal as of Right—How Taken	293
4.	Appeal as of Right—When Taken	295
5.	Appeal by Permission	297
6.	Appeals by Allowance in Bankruptcy Proceedings	[Omitted]
7.	Bond for Costs on Appeal in a Civil Case	298
8.	Stay or Injunction Pending Appeal	298
9.	Release in a Criminal Case	[Omitted]
10.	The Record on Appeal	300
11.	Forwarding the Record	301
12.	Docketing the Appeal; Filing a Representation Statement; Filing the Record	303

Title III. Review of a Decision of the United States Tax Court

13.	Review of a Decision of the Tax Court	[Omitted]
14.	Applicability of Other Rules to the Review of a Tax Court Decision	[Omitted]

Title IV. Review and Enforcement of an Order of an Administrative Agency, Board, Commission or Officer

15.	Review or Enforcement of an Agency Order—How Obtained; Intervention	304
15.1	Briefs and Oral Argument in a National Labor Relations Board Proceeding	[Omitted]
16.	The Board on Review or Enforcement	[Omitted]
17.	Filing of the Record	[Omitted]
18.	Stay Pending Review	305
19.	Settlement of a Judgment Enforcing an Agency Order in Part	306
20.	Applicability of Rules to the Review or Enforcement of an Agency Order	[Omitted]

Rule   **Page**

Title V.   Extraordinary Writs

21. Writs of Mandamus and Prohibition, and Other Extraordinary Writs 306

Title VI.   Habeas Corpus; Proceedings in Forma Pauperis

22. Habeas Corpus and Section 2255 Proceedings .... [Omitted]
23. Custody or Release of a Prisoner in a Habeas Corpus
        Proceeding .... [Omitted]
24. Proceeding in Forma Pauperis 307

Title VII.   General Provisions

25.   Filing and Service 308
26.   Computing and Extending Time 310
26.1. Corporate Disclosure Statement 311
27.   Motions 311
28.   Briefs 313
29.   Brief of an Amicus Curiae 316
30.   Appendix to the Briefs 317
31.   Serving and Filing Briefs 319
32.   Form of Briefs, Appendices, and Other Papers 319
33.   Appeal Conferences 322
34.   Oral Argument 322
35.   En Banc Determination 323
36.   Entry of Judgment; Notice 324
37.   Interest on Judgment 324
38.   Frivolous Appeal—Damages and Costs 324
39.   Costs 325
40.   Petition for Panel Rehearing 325
41.   Mandate: Contents; Issuance and Effective Date; Stay 326
42.   Voluntary Dismissal 327
43.   Substitution of Parties 327
44.   Case Involving a Constitutional Question When the United States Is
        Not a Party 328
45.   Clerk's Duties 328
46.   Attorneys 329
47.   Local Rules by Courts of Appeals 330
48.   Masters 331

Forms

Form 1. Notice of Appeal to a Court of Appeals from a
            Judgment or Order of a District Court   [Omitted]
Form 2. Notice of Appeal to a Court of Appeals from a
            Decision of the Tax Court .... [Omitted]
Form 3. Petition for Review of Order of an Agency,
            Board, Commission or Officer .... [Omitted]
Form 4. Affidavit to Accompany Motion for Leave to
            Appeal in Forma Pauperis .... [Omitted]

TITLE I. APPLICABILITY OF RULES

Rule 1. Scope of Rules; Title

(a) Scope of Rules.

(1) These rules govern procedure in the United States courts of appeals.

(2) When these rules provide for filing a motion or other document in the district court, the procedure must comply with the practice of the district court.

(b) Rules Do Not Affect Jurisdiction. These rules do not extend or limit the jurisdiction of the courts of appeals.

(c) Title. These rules are to be known as the Federal Rules of Appellate Procedure.

Rule 2. Suspension of Rules

On its own or a party's motion, a court of appeals may—to expedite its decision or for other good cause—suspend any provision of these rules in a particular case and order proceedings as it directs, except as otherwise provided in Rule 26(b).

TITLE II. APPEAL FROM A JUDGMENT OR ORDER OF A DISTRICT COURT

Rule 3. Appeal as of Right—How Taken

(a) Filing the Notice of Appeal.

(1) An appeal permitted by law as of right from a district court to a court of appeals may be taken only by filing a notice of appeal with the district clerk within the time allowed by Rule 4. At the time of filing, the appellant must furnish the clerk with enough copies of the notice to enable the clerk to comply with Rule 3(d).

(2) An appellant's failure to take any step other than the timely filing of a notice of appeal does not affect the validity of the appeal, but is ground only for the court of appeals to act as it considers appropriate, including dismissing the appeal.

(3) An appeal from a judgment by a magistrate judge in a civil case is taken in the same way as an appeal from any other district court judgment.

(4) An appeal by permission under 28 U.S.C. § 1292(b) or an appeal in a bankruptcy case may be taken only in the manner prescribed by Rules 5 and 6, respectively.

(b) Joint or Consolidated Appeals.

(1) When two or more parties are entitled to appeal from a district-court judgment or order, and their interests make joinder practicable,

they may file a joint notice of appeal. They may then proceed on appeal as a single appellant.

(2) When the parties have filed separate timely notices of appeal, the appeals may be joined or consolidated by the court of appeals.

(c) Contents of the Notice of Appeal.

(1) The notice of appeal must:

(A) specify the party or parties taking the appeal by naming each one in the caption or body of the notice, but an attorney representing more than one party may describe those parties with such terms as "all plaintiffs," "the defendants," "the plaintiffs A, B, et al.," or "all defendants except X";

(B) designate the judgment, order, or part thereof being appealed; and

(C) name the court to which the appeal is taken.

(2) A pro se notice of appeal is considered filed on behalf of the signer and the signer's spouse and minor children (if they are parties), unless the notice clearly indicates otherwise.

(3) In a class action, whether or not the class has been certified, the notice of appeal is sufficient if it names one person qualified to bring the appeal as representative of the class.

(4) An appeal must not be dismissed for informality of form or title of the notice of appeal, or for failure to name a party whose intent to appeal is otherwise clear from the notice.

(5) Form 1 in the Appendix of Forms is a suggested form of a notice of appeal.

(d) Serving the Notice of Appeal.

(1) The district clerk must serve notice of the filing of a notice of appeal by mailing a copy to each party's counsel of record—excluding the appellant's—or, if a party is proceeding pro se, to the party's last known address. When a defendant in a criminal case appeals, the clerk must also serve a copy of the notice of appeal on the defendant, either by personal service or by mail addressed to the defendant. The clerk must promptly send a copy of the notice of appeal and of the docket entries— and any later docket entries—to the clerk of the court of appeals named in the notice. The district clerk must note, on each copy, the date when the notice of appeal was filed.

(2) If an inmate confined in an institution files a notice of appeal in the manner provided by Rule 4(c), the district clerk must also note the date when the clerk docketed the notice.

(3) The district clerk's failure to serve notice does not affect the validity of the appeal. The clerk must note on the docket the names of

the parties to whom the clerk mails copies, with the date of mailing. Service is sufficient despite the death of a party or the party's counsel.

(e) Payment of Fees. Upon filing a notice of appeal, the appellant must pay the district clerk all required fees. The district clerk receives the appellate docket fee on behalf of the court of appeals.

Rule 4.   Appeal as of Right—When Taken

(a) Appeal in a Civil Case.

(1) *Time for Filing a Notice of Appeal.*

(A) In a civil case, except as provided in Rules 4(a)(1)(B), 4(a)(4), and 4(c), the notice of appeal required by Rule 3 must be filed with the district clerk within 30 days after the judgment or order appealed from is entered.

(B) When the United States or its officer or agency is a party, the notice of appeal may be filed by any party within 60 days after the judgment or order appealed from is entered.

(2) *Filing Before Entry of Judgment.* A notice of appeal filed after the court announces a decision or order—but before the entry of the judgment or order—is treated as filed on the date of and after the entry.

(3) *Multiple Appeals.* If one party timely files a notice of appeal, any other party may file a notice of appeal within 14 days after the date when the first notice was filed, or within the time otherwise prescribed by this Rule 4(a), whichever period ends later.

(4) *Effect of a Motion on a Notice of Appeal.*

(A) If a party timely files in the district court any of the following motions under the Federal Rules of Civil Procedure, the time to file an appeal runs for all parties from the entry of the order disposing of the last such remaining motion:

(i) for judgment under Rule 50(b);

(ii) to amend or make additional factual findings under Rule 52(b), whether or not granting the motion would alter the judgment;

(iii) for attorney's fees under Rule 54 if the district court extends the time to appeal under Rule 58;

(iv) to alter or amend the judgment under Rule 59;

(v) for a new trial under Rule 59; or

(vi) for relief under Rule 60 if the motion is filed no later than 10 days (computed using Federal Rule of Civil Procedure 6(a)) after the judgment is entered.

(B)(i) If a party files a notice of appeal after the court announces or enters a judgment—but before it disposes of any motion listed in Rule 4(a)(4)(A)—the notice becomes effective to appeal a judgment or order, in whole or in part, when the order disposing of the last such remaining motion is entered.

(ii) A party intending to challenge an order disposing of any motion listed in Rule 4(a)(4)(A), or a judgment altered or amended upon such a motion, must file a notice of appeal, or an amended notice of appeal—in compliance with Rule 3(c)—within the time prescribed by this Rule measured from the entry of the order disposing of the last such remaining motion.

(iii) No additional fee is required to file an amended notice.

(5) *Motion for Extension of Time.*

(A) The district court may extend the time to file a notice of appeal if:

(i) a party so moves no later than 30 days after the time prescribed by this Rule 4(a) expires; and

(ii) that party shows excusable neglect or good cause.

(B) A motion filed before the expiration of the time prescribed in Rule 4(a)(1) or (3) may be ex parte unless the court requires otherwise. If the motion is filed after the expiration of the prescribed time, notice must be given to the other parties in accordance with local rules.

(C) No extension under this Rule 4(a)(5) may exceed 30 days after the prescribed time or 10 days after the date when the order granting the motion is entered, whichever is later.

(6) *Reopening the Time to File an Appeal.* The district court may reopen the time to file an appeal for a period of 14 days after the date when its order to reopen is entered, but only if all the following conditions are satisfied:

(A) the motion is filed within 180 days after the judgment or order is entered or within 7 days after the moving party receives notice of the entry, whichever is earlier;

(B) the court finds that the moving party was entitled to notice of the entry of the judgment or order sought to be appealed but did not receive the notice from the district court or any party within 21 days after entry; and

(C) the court finds that no party would be prejudiced.

(7) *Entry Defined.* A judgment or order is entered for purposes of this Rule 4(a) when it is entered in compliance with Rules 58 and 79(a) of the Federal Rules of Civil Procedure.

(b) Appeal in a Criminal Case.

(1) *Time for Filing a Notice of Appeal.* * * *

(c) Appeal by an Inmate Confined in an Institution.

(1) If an inmate confined in an institution files a notice of appeal in either a civil or a criminal case, the notice is timely if it is deposited in the institution's internal mail system on or before the last day for filing. If an institution has a system designed for legal mail, the inmate must use that system to receive the benefit of this rule. Timely filing may be shown by a declaration in compliance with 28 U.S.C. § 1746 or by a notarized statement, either of which must set forth the date of deposit and state that first-class postage has been prepaid.

(2) If an inmate files the first notice of appeal in a civil case under this Rule 4(c), the 14–day period provided in Rule 4(a)(3) for another party to file a notice of appeal runs from the date when the district court dockets the first notice.

(3) When a defendant in a criminal case files a notice of appeal under this Rule 4(c), the 30–day period for the government to file its notice of appeal runs from the entry of the judgment or order appealed from or from the district court's docketing of the defendant's notice of appeal, whichever is later.

(d) Mistaken Filing in the Court of Appeals. If a notice of appeal in either a civil or a criminal case is mistakenly filed in the court of appeals, the clerk of that court must note on the notice the date when it was received and send it to the district clerk. The notice is then considered filed in the district court on the date so noted.

Rule 5. Appeal by Permission

(a) Petition for Permission to Appeal.

(1) To request permission to appeal when an appeal is within the court of appeals' discretion, a party must file a petition for permission to appeal. The petition must be filed with the circuit clerk with proof of service on all other parties to the district-court action.

(2) The petition must be filed within the time specified by the statute or rule authorizing the appeal or, if no such time is specified, within the time provided by Rule 4(a) for filing a notice of appeal.

(3) If a party cannot petition for appeal unless the district court first enters an order granting permission to do so or stating that the necessary conditions are met, the district court may amend its order, either on its own or in response to a party's motion, to include the required permission or statement. In that event, the time to petition runs from entry of the amended order.

(b) Contents of the Petition; Answer or Cross–Petition; Oral Argument.

(1) The petition must include the following:

(A) the facts necessary to understand the question presented;

(B) the question itself;

(C) the relief sought;

(D) the reasons why the appeal should be allowed and is authorized by a statute or rule; and

(E) an attached copy of:

(i) the order, decree, or judgment complained of and any related opinion or memorandum, and

(ii) any order stating the district court's permission to appeal or finding that the necessary conditions are met.

(2) A party may file an answer in opposition or a cross-petition within 7 days after the petition is served.

(3) The petition and answer will be submitted without oral argument unless the court of appeals orders otherwise.

(c) Form of Papers; Number of Copies. All papers must conform to Rule 32(a)(1). An original and 3 copies must be filed unless the court requires a different number by local rule or by order in a particular case.

(d) Grant of Permission; Fees; Cost Bond; Filing the Record.

(1) Within 10 days after the entry of the order granting permission to appeal, the appellant must:

(A) pay the district clerk all required fees; and

(B) file a cost bond if required under Rule 7.

(2) A notice of appeal need not be filed. The date when the order granting permission to appeal is entered serves as the date of the notice of appeal for calculating time under these rules.

(3) The district clerk must notify the circuit clerk once the petitioner has paid the fees. Upon receiving this notice, the circuit clerk must enter the appeal on the docket. The record must be forwarded and filed in accordance with Rules 11 and 12(c).

Rule 7.   Bond for Costs on Appeal in a Civil Case

In a civil case, the district court may require an appellant to file a bond or provide other security in any form and amount necessary to ensure payment of costs on appeal. Rule 8(b) applies to a surety on a bond given under this rule.

Rule 8.   Stay or Injunction Pending Appeal

(a) Motion for Stay.

(1) *Initial Motion in the District Court.* A party must ordinarily move first in the district court for the following relief:

(A) a stay of the judgment or order of a district court pending appeal;

(B) approval of a supersedeas bond; or

(C) an order suspending, modifying, restoring, or granting an injunction while an appeal is pending.

(2) *Motion in the Court of Appeals; Conditions on Relief.* A motion for the relief mentioned in Rule 8(a)(1) may be made to the court of appeals or to one of its judges.

(A) The motion must:

(i) show that moving first in the district court would be impracticable; or

(ii) state that, a motion having been made, the district court denied the motion or failed to afford the relief requested and state any reasons given by the district court for its action.

(B) The motion must also include:

(i) the reasons for granting the relief requested and the facts relied on;

(ii) originals or copies of affidavits or other sworn statements supporting facts subject to dispute; and

(iii) relevant parts of the record.

(C) The moving party must give reasonable notice of the motion to all parties.

(D) A motion under this Rule 8(a)(2) must be filed with the circuit clerk and normally will be considered by a panel of the court. But in an exceptional case in which time requirements make that procedure impracticable, the motion may be made to and considered by a single judge.

(E) The court may condition relief on a party's filing a bond or other appropriate security in the district court.

(b) Proceeding Against a Surety. If a party gives security in the form of a bond or stipulation or other undertaking with one or more sureties, each surety submits to the jurisdiction of the district court and irrevocably appoints the district clerk as the surety's agent on whom any papers affecting the surety's liability on the bond or undertaking may be served. On motion, a surety's liability may be enforced in the district court without the necessity of an independent action. The motion and any notice that the district court prescribes may be served on the district clerk, who must promptly mail a copy to each surety whose address is known.

(c) Stay in a Criminal Case. * * *

Rule 10. The Record on Appeal

(a) Composition of the Record on Appeal. The following items constitute the record on appeal:

(1) the original papers and exhibits filed in the district court;

(2) the transcript of proceedings, if any; and

(3) a certified copy of the docket entries prepared by the district clerk.

(b) The Transcript of Proceedings.

(1) *Appellant's Duty to Order.* Within 10 days after filing the notice of appeal or entry of an order disposing of the last timely remaining motion of a type specified in Rule 4(a)(4)(A), whichever is later, the appellant must do either of the following:

> (A) order from the reporter a transcript of such parts of the proceedings not already on file as the appellant considers necessary, subject to a local rule of the court of appeals and with the following qualifications:

>> (i) the order must be in writing;

>> (ii) if the cost of the transcript is to be paid by the United States under the Criminal Justice Act, the order must so state; and

>> (iii) the appellant must, within the same period, file a copy of the order with the district clerk; or

> (B) file a certificate stating that no transcript will be ordered.

(2) *Unsupported Finding or Conclusion.* If the appellant intends to urge on appeal that a finding or conclusion is unsupported by the evidence or is contrary to the evidence, the appellant must include in the record a transcript of all evidence relevant to that finding or conclusion.

(3) *Partial Transcript.* Unless the entire transcript is ordered:

> (A) the appellant must—within the 10 days provided in Rule 10(b)(1)—file a statement of the issues that the appellant intends to present on the appeal and must serve on the appellee a copy of both the order or certificate and the statement;

> (B) if the appellee considers it necessary to have a transcript of other parts of the proceedings, the appellee must, within 10 days after the service of the order or certificate and the statement of the issues, file and serve on the appellant a designation of additional parts to be ordered; and

> (C) unless within 10 days after service of that designation the appellant has ordered all such parts, and has so notified the appellee, the appellee may within the following 10 days either order the

parts or move in the district court for an order requiring the appellant to do so.

(4) *Payment.* At the time of ordering, a party must make satisfactory arrangements with the reporter for paying the cost of the transcript.

(c) Statement of the Evidence When the Proceedings Were Not Recorded or When a Transcript Is Unavailable. If the transcript of a hearing or trial is unavailable, the appellant may prepare a statement of the evidence or proceedings from the best available means, including the appellant's recollection. The statement must be served on the appellee, who may serve objections or proposed amendments within 10 days after being served. The statement and any objections or proposed amendments must then be submitted to the district court for settlement and approval. As settled and approved, the statement must be included by the district clerk in the record on appeal.

(d) Agreed Statement as the Record on Appeal. In place of the record on appeal as defined in Rule 10(a), the parties may prepare, sign, and submit to the district court a statement of the case showing how the issues presented by the appeal arose and were decided in the district court. The statement must set forth only those facts averred and proved or sought to be proved that are essential to the court's resolution of the issues. If the statement is truthful, it—together with any additions that the district court may consider necessary to a full presentation of the issues on appeal—must be approved by the district court and must then be certified to the court of appeals as the record on appeal. The district clerk must then send it to the circuit clerk within the time provided by Rule 11. A copy of the agreed statement may be filed in place of the appendix required by Rule 30.

(e) Correction or Modification of the Record.

(1) If any difference arises about whether the record truly discloses what occurred in the district court, the difference must be submitted to and settled by that court and the record conformed accordingly.

(2) If anything material to either party is omitted from or misstated in the record by error or accident, the omission or misstatement may be corrected and a supplemental record may be certified and forwarded:

(A) on stipulation of the parties;

(B) by the district court before or after the record has been forwarded; or

(C) by the court of appeals.

(3) All other questions as to the form and content of the record must be presented to the court of appeals.

Rule 11. Forwarding the Record

(a) Appellant's Duty. An appellant filing a notice of appeal must comply with Rule 10(b) and must do whatever else is necessary to enable the clerk to assemble and forward the record. If there are multiple appeals from a judgment or order, the clerk must forward a single record.

(b) Duties of Reporter and District Clerk.

(1) *Reporter's Duty to Prepare and File a Transcript.* The reporter must prepare and file a transcript as follows:

(A) Upon receiving an order for a transcript, the reporter must enter at the foot of the order the date of its receipt and the expected completion date and send a copy, so endorsed, to the circuit clerk.

(B) If the transcript cannot be completed within 30 days of the reporter's receipt of the order, the reporter may request the circuit clerk to grant additional time to complete it. The clerk must note on the docket the action taken and notify the parties.

(C) When a transcript is complete, the reporter must file it with the district clerk and notify the circuit clerk of the filing.

(D) If the reporter fails to file the transcript on time, the circuit clerk must notify the district judge and do whatever else the court of appeals directs.

(2) *District Clerk's Duty to Forward.* When the record is complete, the district clerk must number the documents constituting the record and send them promptly to the circuit clerk together with a list of the documents correspondingly numbered and reasonably identified. Unless directed to do so by a party or the circuit clerk, the district clerk will not send to the court of appeals documents of unusual bulk or weight, physical exhibits other than documents, or other parts of the record designated for omission by local rule of the court of appeals. If the exhibits are unusually bulky or heavy, a party must arrange with the clerks in advance for their transportation and receipt.

(c) Retaining the Record Temporarily in the District Court for Use in Preparing the Appeal.

The parties may stipulate, or the district court on motion may order, that the district clerk retain the record temporarily for the parties to use in preparing the papers on appeal. In that event the district clerk must certify to the circuit clerk that the record on appeal is complete. Upon receipt of the appellee's brief, or earlier if the court orders or the parties agree, the appellant must request the district clerk to forward the record.

(d) [Abrogated.]

(e) Retaining the Record by Court Order.

(1) The court of appeals may, by order or local rule, provide that a certified copy of the docket entries be forwarded instead of the entire record. But a party may at any time during the appeal request that designated parts of the record be forwarded.

(2) The district court may order the record or some part of it retained if the court needs it while the appeal is pending, subject, however, to call by the court of appeals.

(3) If part or all of the record is ordered retained, the district clerk must send to the court of appeals a copy of the order and the docket entries together with the parts of the original record allowed by the district court and copies of any parts of the record designated by the parties.

(f) Retaining Parts of the Record in the District Court by Stipulation of the Parties. The parties may agree by written stipulation filed in the district court that designated parts of the record be retained in the district court subject to call by the court of appeals or request by a party. The parts of the record so designated remain a part of the record on appeal.

(g) Record for a Preliminary Motion in the Court of Appeals. If, before the record is forwarded, a party makes any of the following motions in the court of appeals:

- for dismissal;

- for release;

- for a stay pending appeal;

- for additional security on the bond on appeal or on a supersedeas bond; or

- for any other intermediate order—

the district clerk must send the court of appeals any parts of the record designated by any party.

Rule 12. Docketing the Appeal; Filing a Representation Statement; Filing the Record

(a) Docketing the Appeal. Upon receiving the copy of the notice of appeal and the docket entries from the district clerk under Rule 3(d), the circuit clerk must docket the appeal under the title of the district-court action and must identify the appellant, adding the appellant's name if necessary.

(b) Filing a Representation Statement. Unless the court of appeals designates another time, the attorney who filed the notice of appeal must, within 10 days after filing the notice, file a statement with the circuit clerk naming the parties that the attorney represents on appeal.

(c) Filing the Record, Partial Record, or Certificate. Upon receiving the record, partial record, or district clerk's certificate as provided in Rule 11, the circuit clerk must file it and immediately notify all parties of the filing date.

TITLE IV. REVIEW OR ENFORCEMENT OF AN ORDER OF AN ADMINISTRATIVE AGENCY, BOARD, COMMISSION, OR OFFICER

Rule 15. Review or Enforcement of an Agency Order—How Obtained; Intervention

(a) Petition for Review; Joint Petition.

(1) Review of an agency order is commenced by filing, within the time prescribed by law, a petition for review with the clerk of a court of appeals authorized to review the agency order. If their interests make joinder practicable, two or more persons may join in a petition to the same court to review the same order.

(2) The petition must:

(A) name each party seeking review either in the caption or the body of the petition—using such terms as "et al.," "petitioners," or "respondents" does not effectively name the parties;

(B) name the agency as a respondent (even though not named in the petition, the United States is a respondent if required by statute); and

(C) specify the order or part thereof to be reviewed.

(3) Form 3 in the Appendix of Forms is a suggested form of a petition for review.

(4) In this rule "agency" includes an agency, board, commission, or officer; "petition for review" includes a petition to enjoin, suspend, modify, or otherwise review, or a notice of appeal, whichever form is indicated by the applicable statute.

(b) Application or Cross–Application to Enforce an Order; Answer; Default.

(1) An application to enforce an agency order must be filed with the clerk of a court of appeals authorized to enforce the order. If a petition is filed to review an agency order that the court may enforce, a party opposing the petition may file a cross-application for enforcement.

(2) Within 20 days after the application for enforcement is filed, the respondent must serve on the applicant an answer to the application and file it with the clerk. If the respondent fails to answer in time, the court will enter judgment for the relief requested.

(3) The application must contain a concise statement of the proceedings in which the order was entered, the facts upon which venue is based, and the relief requested.

(c) Service of the Petition or Application. The circuit clerk must serve a copy of the petition for review, or an application or cross-application to enforce an agency order, on each respondent as prescribed by Rule 3(d), unless a different manner of service is prescribed by statute. At the time of filing, the petitioner must:

(1) serve, or have served, a copy on each party admitted to participate in the agency proceedings, except for the respondents;

(2) file with the clerk a list of those so served; and

(3) give the clerk enough copies of the petition or application to serve each respondent.

(d) Intervention. Unless a statute provides another method, a person who wants to intervene in a proceeding under this rule must file a motion for leave to intervene with the circuit clerk and serve a copy on all parties. The motion—or other notice of intervention authorized by statute—must be filed within 30 days after the petition for review is filed and must contain a concise statement of the interest of the moving party and the grounds for intervention.

(e) Payment of Fees. When filing any separate or joint petition for review in a court of appeals, the petitioner must pay the circuit clerk all required fees.

Rule 18. Stay Pending Review

(a) Motion for a Stay.

(1) *Initial Motion Before the Agency.* A petitioner must ordinarily move first before the agency for a stay pending review of its decision or order.

(2) *Motion in the Court of Appeals.* A motion for a stay may be made to the court of appeals or one of its judges.

(A) The motion must:

(i) show that moving first before the agency would be impracticable; or

(ii) state that, a motion having been made, the agency denied the motion or failed to afford the relief requested and state any reasons given by the agency for its action.

(B) The motion must also include:

(i) the reasons for granting the relief requested and the facts relied on;

(ii) originals or copies of affidavits or other sworn statements supporting facts subject to dispute; and

(iii) relevant parts of the record.

(C) The moving party must give reasonable notice of the motion to all parties.

(D) The motion must be filed with the circuit clerk and normally will be considered by a panel of the court. But in an exceptional case in which time requirements make that procedure impracticable, the motion may be made to and considered by a single judge.

(b) Bond. The court may condition relief on the filing of a bond or other appropriate security.

Rule 19. Settlement of a Judgment Enforcing an Agency Order in Part

When the court files an opinion directing entry of judgment enforcing the agency's order in part, the agency must within 14 days file with the clerk and serve on each other party a proposed judgment conforming to the opinion. A party who disagrees with the agency's proposed judgment must within 7 days file with the clerk and serve the agency with a proposed judgment that the party believes conforms to the opinion. The court will settle the judgment and direct entry without further hearing or argument.

TITLE V.   EXTRAORDINARY WRITS

Rule 21. Writs of Mandamus and Prohibition, and Other Extraordinary Writs

(a) Mandamus or Prohibition to a Court: Petition, Filing, Service, and Docketing.

(1) A party petitioning for a writ of mandamus or prohibition directed to a court must file a petition with the circuit clerk with proof of service on all parties to the proceeding in the trial court. The party must also provide a copy to the trial-court judge. All parties to the proceeding in the trial court other than the petitioner are respondents for all purposes.

(2)(A) The petition must be titled "In re [name of petitioner]."

(B) The petition must state:

(i) the relief sought;

(ii) the issues presented;

(iii) the facts necessary to understand the issue presented by the petition; and

(iv) the reasons why the writ should issue.

(C) The petition must include a copy of any order or opinion or parts of the record that may be essential to understand the matters set forth in the petition.

(3) Upon receiving the prescribed docket fee, the clerk must docket the petition and submit it to the court.

(b) Denial; Order Directing Answer; Briefs; Precedence.

(1) The court may deny the petition without an answer. Otherwise, it must order the respondent, if any, to answer within a fixed time.

(2) The clerk must serve the order to respond on all persons directed to respond.

(3) Two or more respondents may answer jointly.

(4) The court of appeals may invite or order the trial-court judge to address the petition or may invite an amicus curiae to do so. The trial-court judge may request permission to address the petition but may not do so unless invited or ordered to do so by the court of appeals.

(5) If briefing or oral argument is required, the clerk must advise the parties, and when appropriate, the trial-court judge or amicus curiae.

(6) The proceeding must be given preference over ordinary civil cases.

(7) The circuit clerk must send a copy of the final disposition to the trial-court judge.

(c) Other Extraordinary Writs. An application for an extraordinary writ other than one provided for in Rule 21(a) must be made by filing a petition with the circuit clerk with proof of service on the respondents. Proceedings on the application must conform, so far as is practicable, to the procedures prescribed in Rule 21(a) and (b).

(d) Form of Papers; Number of Copies. All papers must conform to Rule 32(a)(1). An original and 3 copies must be filed unless the court requires the filing of a different number by local rule or by order in a particular case.

TITLE VI. HABEAS CORPUS; PROCEEDINGS IN FORMA PAUPERIS

Rule 24. Proceeding in Forma Pauperis

(a) Leave to Proceed in Forma Pauperis.

(1) *Motion in the District Court.* Except as stated in Rule 24(a)(3), a party to a district-court action who desires to appeal in forma pauperis must file a motion in the district court. The party must attach an affidavit that:

    (A) shows in the detail prescribed by Form 4 of the Appendix of Forms, the party's inability to pay or to give security for fees and costs;

    (B) claims an entitlement to redress; and

    (C) states the issues that the party intends to present on appeal.

(2) *Action on the Motion.* If the district court grants the motion, the party may proceed on appeal without prepaying or giving security for fees and costs. If the district court denies the motion, it must state its reasons in writing.

(3) *Prior Approval.* A party who was permitted to proceed in forma pauperis in the district-court action, or who was determined to be financially unable to obtain an adequate defense in a criminal case, may proceed on appeal in forma pauperis without further authorization, unless the district court—before or after the notice of appeal is filed— certifies that the appeal is not taken in good faith or finds that the party is not otherwise entitled to proceed in forma pauperis. In that event, the district court must state in writing its reasons for the certification or finding.

(4) *Notice of District Court's Denial.* The district clerk must immediately notify the parties and the court of appeals when the district court does any of the following:

(A) denies a motion to proceed on appeal in forma pauperis;

(B) certifies that the appeal is not taken in good faith; or

(C) finds that the party is not otherwise entitled to proceed in forma pauperis.

(5) *Motion in the Court of Appeals.* A party may file a motion to proceed on appeal in forma pauperis in the court of appeals within 30 days after service of the notice prescribed in Rule 24(a)(4). The motion must include a copy of the affidavit filed in the district court and the district court's statement of reasons for its action. If no affidavit was filed in the district court, the party must include the affidavit prescribed by Rule 24(a)(1).

(b) Leave to Proceed in Forma Pauperis on Appeal or Review of an Administrative–Agency Proceeding. When an appeal or review of a proceeding before an administrative agency, board, commission, or officer (including for the purpose of this rule the United States Tax Court) proceeds directly in a court of appeals, a party may file in the court of appeals a motion for leave to proceed on appeal in forma pauperis with an affidavit prescribed by Rule 24(a)(1).

(c) Leave to Use Original Record. A party allowed to proceed on appeal in forma pauperis may request that the appeal be heard on the original record without reproducing any part.

TITLE VII. GENERAL PROVISIONS

Rule 25. Filing and Service

(a) Filing.

(1) *Filing with the Clerk.* A paper required or permitted to be filed in a court of appeals must be filed with the clerk.

(2) *Filing: Method and Timeliness.*

(A) In General. Filing may be accomplished by mail addressed to the clerk, but filing is not timely unless the clerk receives the papers within the time fixed for filing.

(B) A Brief or Appendix. A brief or appendix is timely filed, however, if on or before the last day for filing, it is:

(i) mailed to the clerk by First–Class Mail, or other class of mail that is at least as expeditious, postage prepaid; or

(ii) dispatched to a third-party commercial carrier for delivery to the clerk within 3 calendar days.

(C) Inmate Filing. A paper filed by an inmate confined in an institution is timely if deposited in the institution's internal mailing system on or before the last day for filing. If an institution has a system designed for legal mail, the inmate must use that system to receive the benefit of this rule. Timely filing may be shown by a declaration in compliance with 28 U.S.C. § 1746 or by a notarized statement, either of which must set forth the date of deposit and state that first-class postage has been prepaid.

(D) Electronic Filing. A court of appeals may by local rule permit papers to be filed, signed, or verified by electronic means that are consistent with technical standards, if any, that the Judicial Conference of the United States establishes. A paper filed by electronic means in compliance with a local rule constitutes a written paper for the purpose of applying these rules.

(3) *Filing a Motion with a Judge.* If a motion requests relief that may be granted by a single judge, the judge may permit the motion to be filed with the judge; the judge must note the filing date on the motion and give it to the clerk.

(4) *Clerk's Refusal of Documents.* The clerk must not refuse to accept for filing any paper presented for that purpose solely because it is not presented in proper form as required by these rules or by any local rule or practice.

(b) Service of All Papers Required. Unless a rule requires service by the clerk, a party must, at or before the time of filing a paper, serve a copy on the other parties to the appeal or review. Service on a party represented by counsel must be made on the party's counsel.

(c) Manner of Service. Service may be personal, by mail, or by third-party commercial carrier for delivery within 3 calendar days. When reasonable considering such factors as the immediacy of the relief sought, distance, and cost, service on a party must be by a manner at least as expeditious as the manner used to file the paper with the court. Personal service includes delivery of the copy to a responsible person at the office of counsel. Service by mail or by commercial carrier is complete on mailing or delivery to the carrier.

(d) Proof of Service.

(1) A paper presented for filing must contain either of the following:

(A) an acknowledgment of service by the person served; or

(B) proof of service consisting of a statement by the person who made service certifying:

(i) the date and manner of service;

(ii) the names of the persons served; and

(iii) their mailing addresses or the addresses of the places of delivery.

(2) When a brief or appendix is filed by mailing or dispatch in accordance with Rule 25(a)(2)(B), the proof of service must also state the date and manner by which the document was mailed or dispatched to the clerk.

(3) Proof of service may appear on or be affixed to the papers filed.

(e) Number of Copies. When these rules require the filing or furnishing of a number of copies, a court may require a different number by local rule or by order in a particular case.

Rule 26. Computing and Extending Time

(a) Computing Time. The following rules apply in computing any period of time specified in these rules or in any local rule, court order, or applicable statute:

(1) Exclude the day of the act, event, or default that begins the period.

(2) Exclude intermediate Saturdays, Sundays, and legal holidays when the period is less than 7 days, unless stated in calendar days.

(3) Include the last day of the period unless it is a Saturday, Sunday, legal holiday, or—if the act to be done is filing a paper in court—a day on which the weather or other conditions make the clerk's office inaccessible.

(4) As used in this rule, "legal holiday" means New Year's Day, Martin Luther King, Jr.'s Birthday, Presidents' Day, Memorial Day, Independence Day, Labor Day, Columbus Day, Veterans' Day, Thanksgiving Day, Christmas Day, and any other day declared a holiday by the President, Congress, or the state in which is located either the district court that rendered the challenged judgment or order, or the circuit clerk's principal office.

(b) Extending Time. For good cause, the court may extend the time prescribed by these rules or by its order to perform any act, or may permit an act to be done after that time expires. But the court may not extend the time to file:

(1) a notice of appeal (except as authorized in Rule 4) or a petition for permission to appeal; or

(2) a notice of appeal from or a petition to enjoin, set aside, suspend, modify, enforce, or otherwise review an order of an administrative agency, board, commission, or officer of the United States, unless specifically authorized by law.

(c) Additional Time after Service. When a party is required or permitted to act within a prescribed period after a paper is served on that party, 3 calendar days are added to the prescribed period unless the paper is delivered on the date of service stated in the proof of service.

Rule 26.1. Corporate Disclosure Statement

(a) Who Must File. Any nongovernmental corporate party to a proceeding in a court of appeals must file a statement identifying all its parent corporations and listing any publicly held company that owns 10% or more of the party's stock.

(b) Time for Filing. A party must file the statement with the principal brief or upon filing a motion, response, petition, or answer in the court of appeals, whichever occurs first, unless a local rule requires earlier filing. Even if the statement has already been filed, the party's principal brief must include the statement before the table of contents.

(c) Number of Copies. If the statement is filed before the principal brief, the party must file an original and 3 copies unless the court requires a different number by local rule or by order in a particular case.

Rule 27. Motions

(a) In General.

(1) *Application for Relief.* An application for an order or other relief is made by motion unless these rules prescribe another form. A motion must be in writing unless the court permits otherwise.

(2) *Contents of a Motion.*

(A) Grounds and Relief Sought. A motion must state with particularity the grounds for the motion, the relief sought, and the legal argument necessary to support it.

(B) Accompanying Documents.

(i) Any affidavit or other paper necessary to support a motion must be served and filed with the motion.

(ii) An affidavit must contain only factual information, not legal argument.

(iii) A motion seeking substantive relief must include a copy of the trial court's opinion or agency's decision as a separate exhibit.

(C) Documents Barred or not Required.

(i) A separate brief supporting or responding to a motion must not be filed.

(ii) A notice of motion is not required.

(iii) A proposed order is not required.

(3) *Response.*

(A) Time to File. Any party may file a response to a motion; Rule 27(a)(2) governs its contents. The response must be filed within 10 days after service of the motion unless the court shortens or extends the time. A motion authorized by Rules 8, 9, 18, or 41 may be granted before the 10–day period runs only if the court gives reasonable notice to the parties that it intends to act sooner.

(B) Request for Affirmative Relief. A response may include a motion for affirmative relief. The time to respond to the new motion, and to reply to that response, are governed by Rule 27(a)(3)(A) and (a)(4). The title of the response must alert the court to the request for relief.

(4) *Reply to Response.* Any reply to a response must be filed within 7 days after service of the response. A reply must not present matters that do not relate to the response.

(b) Disposition of a Motion for a Procedural Order. The court may act on a motion for a procedural order—including a motion under Rule 26(b)—at any time without awaiting a response, and may, by rule or by order in a particular case, authorize its clerk to act on specified types of procedural motions. A party adversely affected by the court's, or the clerk's, action may file a motion to reconsider, vacate, or modify that action. Timely opposition filed after the motion is granted in whole or in part does not constitute a request to reconsider, vacate, or modify the disposition; a motion requesting that relief must be filed.

(c) Power of a Single Judge to Entertain a Motion. A circuit judge may act alone on any motion, but may not dismiss or otherwise determine an appeal or other proceeding. A court of appeals may provide by rule or by order in a particular case that only the court may act on any motion or class of motions. The court may review the action of a single judge.

(d) Form of Papers; Page Limits; and Number of Copies.

(1) *Format.*

(A) Reproduction. A motion, response, or reply may be reproduced by any process that yields a clear black image on light paper.

The paper must be opaque and unglazed. Only one side of the paper may be used.

(B) Cover. A cover is not required but there must be a caption that includes the case number, the name of the court, the title of the case, and a brief descriptive title indicating the purpose of the motion and identifying the party or parties for whom it is filed.

(C) Binding. The document must be bound in any manner that is secure, does not obscure the text, and permits the document to lie reasonably flat when open.

(D) Paper Size, Line Spacing, and Margins. The document must be on 8½ by 11 inch paper. The text must be double-spaced, but quotations more than two lines long may be indented and single-spaced. Headings and footnotes may be single-spaced. Margins must be at least one inch on all four sides. Page numbers may be placed in the margins, but no text may appear there.

(2) *Page Limits.* A motion or a response to a motion must not exceed 20 pages, exclusive of the corporate disclosure statement and accompanying documents authorized by Rule 27(a)(2)(B), unless the court permits or directs otherwise. A reply to a response must not exceed 10 pages.

(3) *Number of Copies.* An original and 3 copies must be filed unless the court requires a different number by local rule or by order in a particular case.

(e) Oral Argument. A motion will be decided without oral argument unless the court orders otherwise.

Rule 28. Briefs

(a) Appellant's Brief. The appellant's brief must contain, under appropriate headings and in the order indicated:

(1) a corporate disclosure statement if required by Rule 26.1;

(2) a table of contents, with page references;

(3) a table of authorities—cases (alphabetically arranged), statutes, and other authorities—with references to the pages of the brief where they are cited;

(4) a jurisdictional statement, including:

(A) the basis for the district court's or agency's subject-matter jurisdiction, with citations to applicable statutory provisions and stating relevant facts establishing jurisdiction;

(B) the basis for the court of appeals' jurisdiction, with citations to applicable statutory provisions and stating relevant facts establishing jurisdiction;

(C) the filing dates establishing the timeliness of the appeal or petition for review; and

(D) an assertion that the appeal is from a final order or judgment that disposes of all parties' claims, or information establishing the court of appeals' jurisdiction on some other basis;

(5) a statement of the issues presented for review;

(6) a statement of the case briefly indicating the nature of the case, the course of proceedings, and the disposition below;

(7) a statement of facts relevant to the issues submitted for review with appropriate references to the record (see Rule 28(e));

(8) a summary of the argument, which must contain a succinct, clear, and accurate statement of the arguments made in the body of the brief, and which must not merely repeat the argument headings;

(9) the argument, which must contain:

(A) appellant's contentions and the reasons for them, with citations to the authorities and parts of the record on which the appellant relies; and

(B) for each issue, a concise statement of the applicable standard of review (which may appear in the discussion of the issue or under a separate heading placed before the discussion of the issues);

(10) a short conclusion stating the precise relief sought; and

(11) the certificate of compliance, if required by Rule 32(a)(7).

(b) Appellee's Brief.   The appellee's brief must conform to the requirements of Rule 28(a)(1)–(9) and (11), except that none of the following need appear unless the appellee is dissatisfied with the appellant's statement:

(1) the jurisdictional statement;

(2) the statement of the issues;

(3) the statement of the case;

(4) the statement of the facts; and

(5) the statement of the standard of review.

(c) Reply Brief.   The appellant may file a brief in reply to the appellee's brief. An appellee who has cross-appealed may file a brief in reply to the appellant's response to the issues presented by the cross-appeal. Unless the court permits, no further briefs may be filed. A reply brief must contain a table of contents, with page references, and a table of authorities—cases (alphabetically arranged), statutes, and other authorities—with references to the pages of the reply brief where they are cited.

(d) References to Parties.   In briefs and at oral argument, counsel should minimize use of the terms "appellant" and "appellee."

To make briefs clear, counsel should use the parties' actual names or the designations used in the lower court or agency proceeding, or such descriptive terms as "the employee," "the injured person," "the taxpayer," "the ship," "the stevedore."

(e) References to the Record. References to the parts of the record contained in the appendix filed with the appellant's brief must be to the pages of the appendix. If the appendix is prepared after the briefs are filed, a party referring to the record must follow one of the methods detailed in Rule 30(c). If the original record is used under Rule 30(f) and is not consecutively paginated, or if the brief refers to an unreproduced part of the record, any reference must be to the page of the original document. For example:

- Answer p. 7;
- Motion for Judgment p. 2;
- Transcript p. 231.

Only clear abbreviations may be used. A party referring to evidence whose admissibility is in controversy must cite the pages of the appendix or of the transcript at which the evidence was identified, offered, and received or rejected.

(f) Reproduction of Statutes, Rules, Regulations, etc. If the court's determination of the issues presented requires the study of statutes, rules, regulations, etc., the relevant parts must be set out in the brief or in an addendum at the end, or may be supplied to the court in pamphlet form.

(g) [Reserved]

(h) Briefs in a Case Involving a Cross–Appeal. If a cross-appeal is filed, the party who files a notice of appeal first is the appellant for the purposes of this rule and Rules 30, 31, and 34. If notices are filed on the same day, the plaintiff in the proceeding below is the appellant. These designations may be modified by agreement of the parties or by court order. With respect to appellee's cross-appeal and response to appellant's brief, appellee's brief must conform to the requirements of Rule 28(a)(1)–(11). But an appellee who is satisfied with appellant's statement need not include a statement of the case or of the facts.

(i) Briefs in a Case Involving Multiple Appellants or Appellees. In a case involving more than one appellant or appellee, including consolidated cases, any number of appellants or appellees may join in a brief, and any party may adopt by reference a part of another's brief. Parties may also join in reply briefs.

(j) Citation of Supplemental Authorities. If pertinent and significant authorities come to a party's attention after the party's brief has been filed—or after oral argument but before decision—a party may promptly advise the circuit clerk by letter, with a copy to all other parties, setting forth the citations. The letter must state without argument the reasons for the supplemental citations, referring either to the page of the brief or to a point argued orally. Any response must be made promptly and must be similarly limited.

Rule 29. Brief of an Amicus Curiae

(a) When Permitted. The United States or its officer or agency, or a State, Territory, Commonwealth, or the District of Columbia may file an amicus-curiae brief without the consent of the parties or leave of court. Any other amicus curiae may file a brief only by leave of court or if the brief states that all parties have consented to its filing.

(b) Motion for Leave to File. The motion must be accompanied by the proposed brief and state:

(1) the movant's interest; and

(2) the reason why an amicus brief is desirable and why the matters asserted are relevant to the disposition of the case.

(c) Contents and Form. An amicus brief must comply with Rule 32. In addition to the requirements of Rule 32, the cover must identify the party or parties supported and indicate whether the brief supports affirmance or reversal. If an amicus curiae is a corporation, the brief must include a disclosure statement like that required of parties by Rule 26.1. An amicus brief need not comply with Rule 28, but must include the following:

(1) a table of contents, with page references;

(2) a table of authorities—cases (alphabetically arranged), statutes and other authorities—with references to the pages of the brief where they are cited;

(3) a concise statement of the identity of the amicus curiae, its interest in the case, and the source of its authority to file;

(4) an argument, which may be preceded by a summary and which need not include a statement of the applicable standard of review; and

(5) a certificate of compliance, if required by Rule 32(a)(7).

(d) Length. Except by the court's permission, an amicus brief may be no more than one-half the maximum length authorized by these rules for a party's principal brief. If the court grants a party permission to file a longer brief, that extension does not affect the length of an amicus brief.

(e) Time for Filing. An amicus curiae must file its brief, accompanied by a motion for filing when necessary, no later than 7 days after the principal brief of the party being supported is filed. An amicus curiae that does not support either party must file its brief no later than 7 days after the appellant's or petitioner's principal brief is filed. A court may grant leave for later filing, specifying the time within which an opposing party may answer.

(f) Reply Brief. Except by the court's permission, an amicus curiae may not file a reply brief.

(g) Oral Argument. An amicus curiae may participate in oral argument only with the court's permission.

Rule 30. Appendix to the Briefs

(a) Appellant's Responsibility.

(1) *Contents of the Appendix.* The appellant must prepare and file an appendix to the briefs containing:

(A) the relevant docket entries in the proceeding below;

(B) the relevant portions of the pleadings, charge, findings, or opinion;

(C) the judgment, order, or decision in question; and

(D) other parts of the record to which the parties wish to direct the court's attention.

(2) *Excluded Material.* Memoranda of law in the district court should not be included in the appendix unless they have independent relevance. Parts of the record may be relied on by the court or the parties even though not included in the appendix.

(3) *Time to File; Number of Copies.* Unless filing is deferred under Rule 30(c), the appellant must file 10 copies of the appendix with the brief and must serve one copy on counsel for each party separately represented. An unrepresented party proceeding in forma pauperis must file 4 legible copies with the clerk, and one copy must be served on counsel for each separately represented party. The court may by local rule or by order in a particular case require the filing or service of a different number.

(b) All Parties' Responsibilities.

(1) *Determining the Contents of the Appendix.* The parties are encouraged to agree on the contents of the appendix. In the absence of an agreement, the appellant must, within 10 days after the record is filed, serve on the appellee a designation of the parts of the record the appellant intends to include in the appendix and a statement of the issues the appellant intends to present for review. The appellee may, within 10 days after receiving the designation, serve on the appellant a designation of additional parts to which it wishes to direct the court's attention. The appellant must include the designated parts in the appendix. The parties must not engage in unnecessary designation of parts of the record, because the entire record is available to the court. This paragraph applies also to a cross-appellant and a cross-appellee.

(2) *Costs of Appendix.*   Unless the parties agree otherwise, the appellant must pay the cost of the appendix.   If the appellant considers parts of the record designated by the appellee to be unnecessary, the appellant may advise the appellee, who must then advance the cost of including those parts.   The cost of the appendix is a taxable cost.   But if any party causes unnecessary parts of the record to be included in the appendix, the court may impose the cost of those parts on that party.   Each circuit must, by local rule, provide for sanctions against attorneys who unreasonably and vexatiously increase litigation costs by including unnecessary material in the appendix.

(c) Deferred Appendix.

(1) *Deferral Until After Briefs Are Filed.*   The court may provide by rule for classes of cases or by order in a particular case that preparation of the appendix may be deferred until after the briefs have been filed and that the appendix may be filed 21 days after the appellee's brief is served.   Even though the filing of the appendix may be deferred, Rule 30(b) applies; except that a party must designate the parts of the record it wants included in the appendix when it serves its brief, and need not include a statement of the issues presented.

(2) *References to the Record.*

(A) If the deferred appendix is used, the parties may cite in their briefs the pertinent pages of the record.   When the appendix is prepared, the record pages cited in the briefs must be indicated by inserting record page numbers, in brackets, at places in the appendix where those pages of the record appear.

(B) A party who wants to refer directly to pages of the appendix may serve and file copies of the brief within the time required by Rule 31(a), containing appropriate references to pertinent pages of the record.   In that event, within 14 days after the appendix is filed, the party must serve and file copies of the brief, containing references to the pages of the appendix in place of or in addition to the references to the pertinent pages of the record.   Except for the correction of typographical errors, no other changes may be made to the brief.

(d) Format of the Appendix.   The appendix must begin with a table of contents identifying the page at which each part begins.   The relevant docket entries must follow the table of contents.   Other parts of the record must follow chronologically.   When pages from the transcript of proceedings are placed in the appendix, the transcript page numbers must be shown in brackets immediately before the included pages.   Omissions in the text of papers or of the transcript must be indicated by asterisks.   Immaterial formal matters (captions, subscriptions, acknowledgments, etc.) should be omitted.

(e) Reproduction of Exhibits. Exhibits designated for inclusion in the appendix may be reproduced in a separate volume, or volumes, suitably indexed. Four copies must be filed with the appendix, and one copy must be served on counsel for each separately represented party. If a transcript of a proceeding before an administrative agency, board, commission, or officer was used in a district-court action and has been designated for inclusion in the appendix, the transcript must be placed in the appendix as an exhibit.

(f) Appeal on the Original Record Without an Appendix. The court may, either by rule for all cases or classes of cases or by order in a particular case, dispense with the appendix and permit an appeal to proceed on the original record with any copies of the record, or relevant parts, that the court may order the parties to file.

Rule 31. Serving and Filing Briefs

(a) Time to Serve and File a Brief.

(1) The appellant must serve and file a brief within 40 days after the record is filed. The appellee must serve and file a brief within 30 days after the appellant's brief is served. The appellant may serve and file a reply brief within 14 days after service of the appellee's brief but a reply brief must be filed at least 3 days before argument, unless the court, for good cause, allows a later filing.

(2) A court of appeals that routinely considers cases on the merits promptly after the briefs are filed may shorten the time to serve and file briefs, either by local rule or by order in a particular case.

(b) Number of Copies. Twenty-five copies of each brief must be filed with the clerk and 2 copies must be served on counsel for each separately represented party. An unrepresented party proceeding in forma pauperis must file 4 legible copies with the clerk, and one copy must be served on counsel for each separately represented party. The court may by local rule or by order in a particular case require the filing or service of a different number.

(c) Consequence of Failure to File. If an appellant fails to file a brief within the time provided by this rule, or within an extended time, an appellee may move to dismiss the appeal. An appellee who fails to file a brief will not be heard at oral argument unless the court grants permission.

Rule 32. Form of Briefs, Appendices, and Other Papers

(a) Form of a Brief.

(1) *Reproduction.*

(A) A brief may be reproduced by any process that yields a clear black image on light paper. The paper must be opaque and unglazed. Only one side of the paper may be used.

(B) Text must be reproduced with a clarity that equals or exceeds the output of a laser printer.

(C) Photographs, illustrations, and tables may be reproduced by any method that results in a good copy of the original; a glossy finish is acceptable if the original is glossy.

(2) *Cover.*   Except for filings by unrepresented parties, the cover of the appellant's brief must be blue; the appellee's, red; an intervenor's or amicus curiae's, green; and any reply brief, gray. The front cover of a brief must contain:

(A) the number of the case centered at the top;

(B) the name of the court;

(C) the title of the case (see Rule 12(a));

(D) the nature of the proceeding (e.g., Appeal, Petition for Review) and the name of the court, agency, or board below;

(E) the title of the brief, identifying the party or parties for whom the brief is filed; and

(F) the name, office address, and telephone number of counsel representing the party for whom the brief is filed.

(3) *Binding.*   The brief must be bound in any manner that is secure, does not obscure the text, and permits the brief to lie reasonably flat when open.

(4) *Paper Size, Line Spacing, and Margins.*   The brief must be on 8½ by 11 inch paper.   The text must be double-spaced, but quotations more than two lines long may be indented and single-spaced.   Headings and footnotes may be single-spaced.   Margins must be at least one inch on all four sides.   Page numbers may be placed in the margins, but no text may appear there.

(5) *Typeface.*   Either a proportionally spaced or a monospaced face may be used.

(A) A proportionally spaced face must include serifs, but sans-serif type may be used in headings and captions.   A proportionally spaced face must be 14–point or larger.

(B) A monospaced face may not contain more than 10½ characters per inch.

(6) *Type Styles.*   A brief must be set in a plain, roman style, although italics or boldface may be used for emphasis.   Case names must be italicized or underlined.

(7) *Length.*

(A) Page limitation.   A principal brief may not exceed 30 pages, or a reply brief 15 pages, unless it complies with Rule 32(a)(7)(B) and (C).

(B) Type-volume limitation.

(i) A principal brief is acceptable if:

- it contains no more than 14,000 words; or

- it uses a monospaced face and contains no more than 1,300 lines of text.

(ii) A reply brief is acceptable if it contains no more than half of the type volume specified in Rule 32(a)(7)(B)(i).

(iii) Headings, footnotes, and quotations count toward the word and line limitations. The corporate disclosure statement, table of contents, table of citations, statement with respect to oral argument, any addendum containing statutes, rules or regulations, and any certificates of counsel do not count toward the limitation.

(C) Certificate of Compliance. A brief submitted under Rule 32(a)(7)(B) must include a certificate by the attorney, or an unrepresented party, that the brief complies with the type-volume limitation. The person preparing the certificate may rely on the word or line count of the word-processing system used to prepare the brief. The certificate must state either:

(i) the number of words in the brief; or

(ii) the number of lines of monospaced type in the brief.

(b) Form of an Appendix. An appendix must comply with Rule 32(a)(1), (2), (3), and (4), with the following exceptions:

(1) The cover of a separately bound appendix must be white.

(2) An appendix may include a legible photocopy of any document found in the record or of a printed judicial or agency decision.

(3) When necessary to facilitate inclusion of odd-sized documents such as technical drawings, an appendix may be a size other than 8½ by 11 inches, and need not lie reasonably flat when opened.

(c) Form of Other Papers.

(1) *Motion.* The form of a motion is governed by Rule 27(d).

(2) *Other Papers.* Any other paper, including a petition for rehearing and a petition for rehearing en banc, and any response to such a petition, must be reproduced in the manner prescribed by Rule 32(a), with the following exceptions:

(A) a cover is not necessary if the caption and signature page of the paper together contain the information required by Rule 32(a)(2); and

(B) Rule 32(a)(7) does not apply.

(d) Local Variation. Every court of appeals must accept documents that comply with the form requirements of this rule. By local rule or order in a particular case a court of appeals may accept documents that do not meet all of the form requirements of this rule.

Rule 33. Appeal Conferences

The court may direct the attorneys—and, when appropriate, the parties—to participate in one or more conferences to address any matter that may aid in disposing of the proceedings, including simplifying the issues and discussing settlement. A judge or other person designated by the court may preside over the conference, which may be conducted in person or by telephone. Before a settlement conference, the attorneys must consult with their clients and obtain as much authority as feasible to settle the case. The court may, as a result of the conference, enter an order controlling the course of the proceedings or implementing any settlement agreement.

Rule 34. Oral Argument

(a) In General.

(1) *Party's Statement.* Any party may file, or a court may require by local rule, a statement explaining why oral argument should, or need not, be permitted.

(2) *Standards.* Oral argument must be allowed in every case unless a panel of three judges who have examined the briefs and record unanimously agrees that oral argument is unnecessary for any of the following reasons:

(A) the appeal is frivolous;

(B) the dispositive issue or issues have been authoritatively decided; or

(C) the facts and legal arguments are adequately presented in the briefs and record, and the decisional process would not be significantly aided by oral argument.

(b) Notice of Argument; Postponement. The clerk must advise all parties whether oral argument will be scheduled, and, if so, the date, time, and place for it, and the time allowed for each side. A motion to postpone the argument or to allow longer argument must be filed reasonably in advance of the hearing date.

(c) Order and Contents of Argument. The appellant opens and concludes the argument. Counsel must not read at length from briefs, records, or authorities.

(d) Cross–Appeals and Separate Appeals. If there is a cross-appeal, Rule 28(h) determines which party is the appellant and which is the appellee for purposes of oral argument. Unless the court directs otherwise, a cross-appeal or separate appeal must be argued when the initial appeal is argued. Separate parties should avoid duplicative argument.

(e) Nonappearance of a Party. If the appellee fails to appear for argument, the court must hear appellant's argument. If the appellant fails to appear for argument, the court may hear the appellee's argument. If neither party appears, the case will be decided on the briefs, unless the court orders otherwise.

(f) Submission on Briefs. The parties may agree to submit a case for decision on the briefs, but the court may direct that the case be argued.

(g) Use of Physical Exhibits at Argument; Removal. Counsel intending to use physical exhibits other than documents at the argument must arrange to place them in the courtroom on the day of the argument before the court convenes. After the argument, counsel must remove the exhibits from the courtroom, unless the court directs otherwise. The clerk may destroy or dispose of the exhibits if counsel does not reclaim them within a reasonable time after the clerk gives notice to remove them.

Rule 35. En Banc Determination

(a) When Hearing or Rehearing En Banc May Be Ordered. A majority of the circuit judges who are in regular active service may order that an appeal or other proceeding be heard or reheard by the court of appeals en banc. An en banc hearing or rehearing is not favored and ordinarily will not be ordered unless:

(1) en banc consideration is necessary to secure or maintain uniformity of the court's decisions; or

(2) the proceeding involves a question of exceptional importance.

(b) Petition for Hearing or Rehearing En Banc. A party may petition for a hearing or rehearing en banc.

(1) The petition must begin with a statement that either:

(A) the panel decision conflicts with a decision of the United States Supreme Court or of the court to which the petition is addressed (with citation to the conflicting case or cases) and consideration by the full court is therefore necessary to secure and maintain uniformity of the court's decisions; or

(B) the proceeding involves one or more questions of exceptional importance, each of which must be concisely stated; for example, a petition may assert that a proceeding presents a question of exceptional importance if it involves an issue on which the panel decision conflicts with the authoritative decisions of other United States Courts of Appeals that have addressed the issue.

(2) Except by the court's permission, a petition for an en banc hearing or rehearing must not exceed 15 pages, excluding material not counted under Rule 32.

(3) For purposes of the page limit in Rule 35(b)(2), if a party files both a petition for panel rehearing and a petition for rehearing en banc, they are considered a single document even if they are filed separately, unless separate filing is required by local rule.

(c) Time for Petition for Hearing or Rehearing En Banc. A petition that an appeal be heard initially en banc must be filed by the date when the appellee's brief is due. A petition for a rehearing en banc must be filed within the time prescribed by Rule 40 for filing a petition for rehearing.

(d) Number of Copies. The number of copies to be filed must be prescribed by local rule and may be altered by order in a particular case.

(e) Response. No response may be filed to a petition for an en banc consideration unless the court orders a response.

(f) Call for a Vote. A vote need not be taken to determine whether the case will be heard or reheard en banc unless a judge calls for a vote.

Rule 36. Entry of Judgment; Notice

(a) Entry. A judgment is entered when it is noted on the docket. The clerk must prepare, sign, and enter the judgment:

(1) after receiving the court's opinion—but if settlement of the judgment's form is required, after final settlement; or

(2) if a judgment is rendered without an opinion, as the court instructs.

(b) Notice. On the date when judgment is entered, the clerk must mail to all parties a copy of the opinion—or the judgment, if no opinion was written—and a notice of the date when the judgment was entered.

Rule 37. Interest on Judgment

(a) When the Court Affirms. Unless the law provides otherwise, if a money judgment in a civil case is affirmed, whatever interest is allowed by law is payable from the date when the district court's judgment was entered.

(b) When the Court Reverses. If the court modifies or reverses a judgment with a direction that a money judgment be entered in the district court, the mandate must contain instructions about the allowance of interest.

Rule 38. Frivolous Appeal—Damages and Costs

If a court of appeals determines that an appeal is frivolous, it may, after a separately filed motion or notice from the court and reasonable opportunity to respond, award just damages and single or double costs to the appellee.

Rule 39. Costs

   (a) Against Whom Assessed. The following rules apply unless the law provides or the court orders otherwise:

   (1) if an appeal is dismissed, costs are taxed against the appellant, unless the parties agree otherwise;

   (2) if a judgment is affirmed, costs are taxed against the appellant;

   (3) if a judgment is reversed, costs are taxed against the appellee;

   (4) if a judgment is affirmed in part, reversed in part, modified, or vacated, costs are taxed only as the court orders.

   (b) Costs For and Against the United States. Costs for or against the United States, its agency, or officer will be assessed under Rule 39(a) only if authorized by law.

   (c) Costs of Copies. Each court of appeals must, by local rule, fix the maximum rate for taxing the cost of producing necessary copies of a brief or appendix, or copies of records authorized by Rule 30(f). The rate must not exceed that generally charged for such work in the area where the clerk's office is located and should encourage economical methods of copying.

   (d) Bill of Costs: Objections; Insertion in Mandate.

   (1) A party who wants costs taxed must—within 14 days after entry of judgment—file with the circuit clerk, with proof of service, an itemized and verified bill of costs.

   (2) Objections must be filed within 10 days after service of the bill of costs, unless the court extends the time.

   (3) The clerk must prepare and certify an itemized statement of costs for insertion in the mandate, but issuance of the mandate must not be delayed for taxing costs. If the mandate issues before costs are finally determined, the district clerk must—upon the circuit clerk's request—add the statement of costs, or any amendment of it, to the mandate.

   (e) Costs on Appeal Taxable in the District Court. The following costs on appeal are taxable in the district court for the benefit of the party entitled to costs under this rule:

   (1) the preparation and transmission of the record;

   (2) the reporter's transcript, if needed to determine the appeal;

   (3) premiums paid for a supersedeas bond or other bond to preserve rights pending appeal; and

   (4) the fee for filing the notice of appeal.

Rule 40. Petition for Panel Rehearing

   (a) Time to File; Contents; Answer; Action by the Court if Granted.

   (1) *Time.* Unless the time is shortened or extended by order or local rule, a petition for panel rehearing may be filed within 14 days

after entry of judgment. But in a civil case, if the United States or its officer or agency is a party, the time within which any party may seek rehearing is 45 days after entry of judgment, unless an order shortens or extends the time.

(2) *Contents.* The petition must state with particularity each point of law or fact that the petitioner believes the court has overlooked or misapprehended and must argue in support of the petition. Oral argument is not permitted.

(3) *Answer.* Unless the court requests, no answer to a petition for panel rehearing is permitted. But ordinarily rehearing will not be granted in the absence of such a request.

(4) *Action by the Court.* If a petition for panel rehearing is granted, the court may do any of the following:

    (A) make a final disposition of the case without reargument;

    (B) restore the case to the calendar for reargument or resubmission; or

    (C) issue any other appropriate order.

(b) Form of Petition; Length. The petition must comply in form with Rule 32. Copies must be served and filed as Rule 31 prescribes. Unless the court permits or a local rule provides otherwise, a petition for panel rehearing must not exceed 15 pages.

Rule 41. Mandate: Contents; Issuance and Effective Date; Stay

(a) Contents. Unless the court directs that a formal mandate issue, the mandate consists of a certified copy of the judgment, a copy of the court's opinion, if any, and any direction about costs.

(b) When Issued. The court's mandate must issue 7 days after the time to file a petition for rehearing expires, or 7 days after entry of an order denying a timely petition for panel rehearing, rehearing en banc, or motion for stay of mandate, whichever is later. The court may shorten or extend the time.

(c) Effective Date. The mandate is effective when issued.

(d) Staying the Mandate.

(1) *On Petition for Rehearing or Motion.* The timely filing of a petition for panel rehearing, petition for rehearing en banc, or motion for stay of mandate, stays the mandate until disposition of the petition or motion, unless the court orders otherwise.

(2) *Pending Petition for Certiorari.*

    (A) A party may move to stay the mandate pending the filing of a petition for a writ of certiorari in the Supreme Court. The motion must be served on all parties and must show that the certiorari petition would present a substantial question and that there is good cause for a stay.

(B) The stay must not exceed 90 days, unless the period is extended for good cause or unless the party who obtained the stay files a petition for the writ and so notifies the circuit clerk in writing within the period of the stay. In that case, the stay continues until the Supreme Court's final disposition.

(C) The court may require a bond or other security as a condition to granting or continuing a stay of the mandate.

(D) The court of appeals must issue the mandate immediately when a copy of a Supreme Court order denying the petition for writ of certiorari is filed.

Rule 42. Voluntary Dismissal

(a) Dismissal in the District Court. Before an appeal has been docketed by the circuit clerk, the district court may dismiss the appeal on the filing of a stipulation signed by all parties or on the appellant's motion with notice to all parties.

(b) Dismissal in the Court of Appeals. The circuit clerk may dismiss a docketed appeal if the parties file a signed dismissal agreement specifying how costs are to be paid and pay any fees that are due. But no mandate or other process may issue without a court order. An appeal may be dismissed on the appellant's motion on terms agreed to by the parties or fixed by the court.

Rule 43. Substitution of Parties

(a) Death of a Party.

(1) *After Notice of Appeal Is Filed.* If a party dies after a notice of appeal has been filed or while a proceeding is pending in the court of appeals, the decedent's personal representative may be substituted as a party on motion filed with the circuit clerk by the representative or by any party. A party's motion must be served on the representative in accordance with Rule 25. If the decedent has no representative, any party may suggest the death on the record, and the court of appeals may then direct appropriate proceedings.

(2) *Before Notice of Appeal Is Filed—Potential Appellant.* If a party entitled to appeal dies before filing a notice of appeal, the decedent's personal representative—or, if there is no personal representative, the decedent's attorney of record—may file a notice of appeal within the time prescribed by these rules. After the notice of appeal is filed, substitution must be in accordance with Rule 43(a)(1).

(3) *Before Notice of Appeal Is Filed—Potential Appellee.* If a party against whom an appeal may be taken dies after entry of a judgment or order in the district court, but before a notice of appeal is filed, an

appellant may proceed as if the death had not occurred. After the notice of appeal is filed, substitution must be in accordance with Rule 43(a)(1).

(b) Substitution for a Reason Other Than Death. If a party needs to be substituted for any reason other than death, the procedure prescribed in Rule 43(a) applies.

(c) Public Officer: Identification; Substitution.

(1) *Identification of Party.* A public officer who is a party to an appeal or other proceeding in an official capacity may be described as a party by the public officer's official title rather than by name. But the court may require the public officer's name to be added.

(2) *Automatic Substitution of Officeholder.* When a public officer who is a party to an appeal or other proceeding in an official capacity dies, resigns, or otherwise ceases to hold office, the action does not abate. The public officer's successor is automatically substituted as a party. Proceedings following the substitution are to be in the name of the substituted party, but any misnomer that does not affect the substantial rights of the parties may be disregarded. An order of substitution may be entered at any time, but failure to enter an order does not affect the substitution.

Rule 44. Case Involving a Constitutional Question When the United States Is Not a Party

If a party questions the constitutionality of an Act of Congress in a proceeding in which the United States or its agency, officer, or employee is not a party in an official capacity, the questioning party must give written notice to the circuit clerk immediately upon the filing of the record or as soon as the question is raised in the court of appeals. The clerk must then certify that fact to the Attorney General.

Rule 45. Clerk's Duties

(a) General Provisions.

(1) *Qualifications.* The circuit clerk must take the oath and post any bond required by law. Neither the clerk nor any deputy clerk may practice as an attorney or counselor in any court while in office.

(2) *When Court Is Open.* The court of appeals is always open for filing any paper, issuing and returning process, making a motion, and entering an order. The clerk's office with the clerk or a deputy in attendance must be open during business hours on all days except Saturdays, Sundays, and legal holidays. A court may provide by local rule or by order that the clerk's office be open for specified hours on Saturdays or on legal holidays other than New Year's Day, Martin Luther King, Jr.'s Birthday, Presidents' Day, Memorial Day, Independence Day, Labor Day, Columbus Day, Veterans' Day, Thanksgiving Day, and Christmas Day.

(b) Records.

(1) *The Docket.* The circuit clerk must maintain a docket and an index of all docketed cases in the manner prescribed by the Director of the Administrative Office of the United States Courts. The clerk must record all papers filed with the clerk and all process, orders, and judgments.

(2) *Calendar.* Under the court's direction, the clerk must prepare a calendar of cases awaiting argument. In placing cases on the calendar for argument, the clerk must give preference to appeals in criminal cases and to other proceedings and appeals entitled to preference by law.

(3) *Other Records.* The clerk must keep other books and records required by the Director of the Administrative Office of the United States Courts, with the approval of the Judicial Conference of the United States, or by the court.

(c) Notice of an Order or Judgment. Upon the entry of an order or judgment, the circuit clerk must immediately serve by mail a notice of entry on each party to the proceeding, with a copy of any opinion, and must note the mailing on the docket. Service on a party represented by counsel must be made on counsel.

(d) Custody of Records and Papers. The circuit clerk has custody of the court's records and papers. Unless the court orders or instructs otherwise, the clerk must not permit an original record or paper to be taken from the clerk's office. Upon disposition of the case, original papers constituting the record on appeal or review must be returned to the court or agency from which they were received. The clerk must preserve a copy of any brief, appendix, or other paper that has been filed.

Rule 46. Attorneys

(a) Admission to the Bar.

(1) *Eligibility.* An attorney is eligible for admission to the bar of a court of appeals if that attorney is of good moral and professional character and is admitted to practice before the Supreme Court of the United States, the highest court of a state, another United States court of appeals, or a United States district court (including the district courts for Guam, the Northern Mariana Islands, and the Virgin Islands).

(2) *Application.* An applicant must file an application for admission, on a form approved by the court that contains the applicant's personal statement showing eligibility for membership. The applicant must subscribe to the following oath or affirmation:

> "I, _____, do solemnly swear [or affirm] that I will conduct myself as an attorney and counselor of this court, uprightly and according to law; and that I will support the Constitution of the United States."

(3) *Admission Procedures.*   On written or oral motion of a member of the court's bar, the court will act on the application.   An applicant may be admitted by oral motion in open court.   But, unless the court orders otherwise, an applicant need not appear before the court to be admitted.   Upon admission, an applicant must pay the clerk the fee prescribed by local rule or court order.

(b) Suspension or Disbarment.

(1) *Standard.*   A member of the court's bar is subject to suspension or disbarment by the court if the member:

(A) has been suspended or disbarred from practice in any other court; or

(B) is guilty of conduct unbecoming a member of the court's bar.

(2) *Procedure.*   The member must be given an opportunity to show good cause, within the time prescribed by the court, why the member should not be suspended or disbarred.

(3) *Order.*   The court must enter an appropriate order after the member responds and a hearing is held, if requested, or after the time prescribed for a response expires, if no response is made.

(c) Discipline.   A court of appeals may discipline an attorney who practices before it for conduct unbecoming a member of the bar or for failure to comply with any court rule.   First, however, the court must afford the attorney reasonable notice, an opportunity to show cause to the contrary, and, if requested, a hearing.

Rule 47.   Local Rules by Courts of Appeals

(a) Local Rules.

(1) Each court of appeals acting by a majority of its judges in regular active service may, after giving appropriate public notice and opportunity for comment, make and amend rules governing its practice. A generally applicable direction to parties or lawyers regarding practice before a court must be in a local rule rather than an internal operating procedure or standing order.   A local rule must be consistent with—but not duplicative of—Acts of Congress and rules adopted under 28 U.S.C. § 2072 and must conform to any uniform numbering system prescribed by the Judicial Conference of the United States.   Each circuit clerk must send the Administrative Office of the United States Courts a copy of each local rule and internal operating procedure when it is promulgated or amended.

(2) A local rule imposing a requirement of form must not be enforced in a manner that causes a party to lose rights because of a nonwillful failure to comply with the requirement.

RULES OF APPELLATE PROCEDURE **Rule 48**

(b) Procedure When There Is No Controlling Law. A court of appeals may regulate practice in a particular case in any manner consistent with federal law, these rules, and local rules of the circuit. No sanction or other disadvantage may be imposed for noncompliance with any requirement not in federal law, federal rules, or the local circuit rules unless the alleged violator has been furnished in the particular case with actual notice of the requirement.

Rule 48. Masters

(a) Appointment; Powers. A court of appeals may appoint a special master to hold hearings, if necessary, and to recommend factual findings and disposition in matters ancillary to proceedings in the court. Unless the order referring a matter to a master specifies or limits the master's powers, those powers include, but are not limited to, the following:

(1) regulating all aspects of a hearing;

(2) taking all appropriate action for the efficient performance of the master's duties under the order;

(3) requiring the production of evidence on all matters embraced in the reference; and

(4) administering oaths and examining witnesses and parties.

(b) Compensation. If the master is not a judge or court employee, the court must determine the master's compensation and whether the cost is to be charged to any party.

Part V

Selected Sample Court Orders and Notices for Controlling Discovery, Pretrial Conferences, and Settlement of Class Action

TABLE OF CONTENTS

	Page
Stipulation and Order Governing Discovery and the Protection and Exchange of Confidential Information	332
Pretrial Order Establishing Schedules for Completion of All Subsequent Steps in a Case	334
Final Pretrial Order	341
Notice of Settlement of Class Action With Proof of Claim Form	344

Stipulation and Order Governing Discovery and the Protection and Exchange of Confidential Information [1]

It is hereby stipulated and agreed by and between the undersigned parties to this action that the following restrictions and procedures shall apply to all documents, testimony, interrogatories, and other information produced, given or exchanged by any party or non-party in the course of pretrial discovery in this action (hereinafter collectively referred to as "Pre-trial Information").

1. All Pre-trial Information shall be treated and deemed as confidential and protected within the meaning of Chancery Court Rule 26(c). In addition to the foregoing, any party or non-party may designate any Pre-trial Information that reflects sensitive internal business or competitive information not relating to proposed transactions or negotiations between or among the parties as "Confidential—Attorneys Only."

2. Unless otherwise ordered by the Court in this proceeding, all Pre-trial Information will be held by the receiving party solely for use in connection with the above-captioned action.

3. Pre-trial Information shall not be disclosed to any person, except:

---

[1] Sussman & Sussman, "Confidentiality Agreements Help Protect Clients," Legal Times of New York, September 1984, p. 6, 36 (reproducing protective order entered in Pennzoil Co. v. Getty Oil Co., No. 7425 (Del. Ch. Jan. 24, 1984)).

(a) outside counsel and to house counsel for the parties;

(b) employees of such counsel assigned to and necessary to assist such counsel in the preparation of this litigation;

(c) officers, directors, or employees of the parties, to the extent deemed necessary by counsel for the prosecution or defense of this litigation;

(d) consultants or experts, to the extent deemed necessary by counsel for the prosecution or defense of the litigation; and

(e) the Court.

4. Pre-trial Information designated "Confidential–Attorneys Only" shall not be disclosed to any person other than those persons included in paragraphs 3(a), 3(b) and 3(c) above.

5. Any person given access to Pre-trial Information pursuant to the terms hereof shall be advised that the documents, material or information are being disclosed pursuant to and subject to the terms of this Stipulation and Order and may not be disclosed other than pursuant to the terms hereof.

6. Pre-trial Information used in connection with any pleading, motion, hearing or trial or otherwise submitted to the Court shall be filed under seal.

7. Inadvertent production of any document or other information during discovery in this action shall be without prejudice to any claim that such material is privileged or protected from discovery as work product within the meaning of Chancery Court Rule 26, and no party shall be held to have waived any rights under Rule 26 by such inadvertent production. Any document or information so produced and subject to a claim of privilege or work product subsequently made shall immediately be returned to the producing party, or expunged, and, in either event, such document or information shall not be introduced into evidence in this or any other proceeding by any person without the consent of the producing party or by order of the Court, nor will such document or information be subject to production in any proceeding by virtue of the fact that it was inadvertently produced in this proceeding.

8. Nothing herein shall preclude any of the parties from, upon twenty-four (24) hours notice to the other parties, making application to the Court for an order modifying any of the terms hereof or contesting or seeking designation of any information as "Confidential—Attorneys Only."

9. The parties agree forthwith to submit this Stipulation and Order to the Court to be "So Ordered" and further agree that, prior to approval by the Court, this Stipulation and Order shall be effective as if approved and, specifically, that any violation of its terms shall be subject to the same sanctions and penalties, including those under Chancery

Court Rule 37 as if this Stipulation and Order had been entered by the Court.

10. At the conclusion of the litigation, all Pre-trial Information and all copies thereof, and all documents designated "Confidential–Attorneys Only" and all copies thereof, shall be promptly returned to the producing parties or, at their written request, destroyed. The return or destruction of such documents shall be certified by the receiving persons.

11. This Stipulation and Order shall inure to the benefit of and be enforceable by non-parties with respect to information produced, given, or exchanged by them in the course of pre-trial discovery.

Pretrial Order Establishing Schedules for Completion of All Subsequent Steps in a Case

Part I. Second Wave and Completion of Discovery [2]

Part II. Designation of Deposition Evidence and Documents for Objections Thereto

Part III. Final Pretrial Briefs, Written Offers of Proof, Written Narrative Summaries of Expert Testimony, and Statements of Uncontroverted Facts

Part IV. Listing of Trial Witnesses

Part V. Filing of Proposed Voir Dire Questions

Part VI. Scheduling Final Pretrial Conference

Part VII. Setting Trial Date

A pretrial conference was held in the above-captioned cause on the _____ day of _____, 19__, wherein or as a result of which the following proceedings were had:

Part I. Second Wave and Completion of Discovery

A. The following interrogatories on behalf of plaintiffs were approved and ordered answered on or before the _____ day of _____, 19__ [list interrogatories].

B. The following requests for production of documents on behalf of plaintiffs were granted and the documents were ordered produced at [insert location] on or before the _____ day of _____, 19__ [list motions approved].

C. Depositions on behalf of plaintiffs of the following persons, at the places and times designated, were approved:

[2] Pretrial Order, except for Part VII, taken from "Manual for Complex Litigation," Fifth Edition, For Use With Federal Practice and Procedure by Charles Alan Wright and Arthur R. Miller (West Publishing Co.).

Witness	Company	Location	Date

D. The following interrogatories on behalf of defendants were approved and ordered answered on or before the _____ day of _____, 19__ [*list interrogatories*].

E. The following requests for production of documents on behalf of defendants were granted and the documents were ordered produced at [*insert location*] on or before the _____ day of _____, 19__ [*list motions approved*].

F. Depositions on behalf of defendants of the following persons, at the places and times designated, were approved:

Witness	Company	Location	Date

G. Except as may hereafter be ordered by the Court for good cause shown and in the interest of the just determination of this cause, no discovery in addition to the discovery heretofore ordered shall be taken in this cause.

Part II. Designation of Deposition Testimony,
Documents, and Objections Thereto

H. On or before the _____ day of _____, 19__, plaintiffs shall designate those portions of deposition testimony that plaintiffs desire to offer in evidence at the trial.

I. On or before the _____ day of _____, 19__, defendants (1) shall designate the parts of the depositions designated by plaintiffs that defendants seek to require plaintiffs to introduce under Federal Rule of Civil Procedure 32(a)(4), and (2) shall designate such portions of depositions as defendants desire to offer in evidence at the trial.

J. On or before the _____ day of _____, 19__, plaintiffs (1) shall designate the part of the depositions designated by defendants that plaintiffs seek to require defendants to introduce under Federal Rule of Civil Procedure 32(a)(4), and (2) shall counter-designate such portions of the depositions designated by defendants as plaintiffs desire to offer in evidence at the trial.

K. On or before the _____ day of _____, 19__, plaintiffs shall designate those documents they desire to introduce at trial and shall provide each defendant with a copy of each such document.

L.   On or before the _____ day of _____, 19__, defendants shall designate those documents they desire to introduce at trial and shall provide each plaintiff with a copy of each such document.

M.   On or before the _____ day of _____, 19__, plaintiffs and defendants shall file all objections to designated deposition testimony and exhibits.

Part III.   Final Pretrial Briefs, Written Offers of Proof,
Written Narrative Summaries of Expert Testimony,
and Statements of Uncontroverted Facts

N.[3]   Plaintiffs and defendants shall each file two detailed, written pretrial briefs constructed as hereinafter provided. The first such brief shall be filed by the plaintiffs on or before the _____ day of _____, 19__, and shall relate to the claims for relief by plaintiffs against defendants. The second such brief shall be filed by the defendants on or before the _____ day of _____, 19__, and shall relate to the defenses, including affirmative defenses, of the defendants to plaintiffs' claims for relief, and, in a separate section, to the defendants' claims for relief on their counterclaims herein. The third such brief shall be filed by the plaintiffs on or before the _____ day of _____, 19__, and shall relate to plaintiffs' reply to the affirmative matter in the defenses of defendants to plaintiffs' claims for relief, and to plaintiffs' defenses, including affirmative defenses, to defendants' counterclaims for relief. The fourth such brief shall be filed by the defendants on or before the _____ day of _____, 19__, and shall relate to the reply of the defendants to any affirmative matter in the defenses of plaintiffs to the counterclaims of defendants.

Each of the four briefs required to be filed as hereinafter provided shall consist of (1) a detailed narrative statement of the facts proposed to be proved by the party filing the brief, and (2) concise statements of legal contentions of the party filing the brief in support of any affirmative matter contained in the brief and in response to legal contentions made by the adverse party in the next preceding brief. In sections of the pretrial brief there shall be a narrative statement or statement of facts and statements of legal contentions. Neither shall be commingled with the other, and they shall be in the following form:

(1) In support of each claim for relief, whether contained in the complaint or the counterclaim, the party or parties asserting the claim for relief shall set forth in simple declarative sentences, separately numbered, the narration of all facts relied upon in support of the claim or claims for relief herein. Each narrative statement of facts shall be in a separate section and shall be

[3] This paragraph of Part III is based upon a pretrial order entered by Chief Judge William H. Becker on June 21, 1967, in Johnson v. Tri-State Motor Transit Co., Civil Action No. 15974–3 (W.D.Mo.), in which both a complaint and a counterclaim were filed.

complete in itself and shall contain no recitation of what any witness testified to, or what the adverse party or parties stated or admitted in these or other proceedings, and no reference to the pleadings or other documents or schedules as such; provided, however, that at the option of a party or parties, any narrative statement of facts may contain references in parentheses to the names of witnesses, depositions, pleadings, exhibits, or other documents, but no party or parties shall be required to admit or deny the accuracy of such references. No narrative statement of facts shall, so far as possible, contain any color words, labels, or legal conclusions; and in no event shall any color word, label, or legal conclusion be commingled with any statement of fact in any sentence or paragraph. Each narrative statement of facts shall be constructed, to the best of the ability of plaintiffs' counsel, so that the opposite party will be able to admit or deny each separate sentence of the statement of facts. Each separate sentence of the statement of facts shall be separately and consecutively numbered.

(2) In each separate section of the pretrial brief containing the statement of legal contentions and authorities in support thereof, all legal contentions and authorities in support of the claim or claims for relief that are the subject for the foregoing narrative statement of facts, necessary to demonstrate the liability of the adverse party or parties to the party or parties filing the brief, shall be separately, clearly, and concisely stated in separately numbered paragraphs. Each such paragraph shall be followed by a citation of authorities in support thereof without quotations therefrom.

(3) The party or parties filing a pretrial brief in defense of a claim or claims for relief shall set forth in a separate section, in separate simple declarative sentences, factual statements admitting or denying each separate sentence contained in the narrative statement of facts of the adverse party in support of its claim for relief, except in instances where a portion of a sentence can be admitted and a portion denied. In those instances the brief shall state clearly the portion of the sentence admitted and the portion denied. Each separate sentence of a brief in response to a narrative statement of facts in support of a claim for relief shall bear the same number as the corresponding sentence in the narrative statement of facts in support of the claim for relief. In a separate portion of the narrative fact statement in response to a narrative fact brief in support of a claim for relief, the responding party shall set forth in a separate narrative statement all affirmative matters of a factual nature relied upon by it in defense (in whole or in part) against the claim or claims for relief. This separate narrative statement of affirmative

337

matters shall be contained in a narrative statement of facts constructed in the same manner as hereinabove provided for a narrative statement of facts in support of a claim for relief.

(4) In response to a brief in support of a claim for relief, the party or parties responding shall, in a separate section of the pretrial brief, set forth a statement of legal contentions and authorities in defense (in whole or in part) against the claim for relief to which the response is made. In this separate section the party or parties shall set forth its legal contentions and authorities in support thereof, directly responding to the legal contentions of the adverse party in support of the claim for relief, and shall separately set forth such additional contentions of the party or parties as may be necessary to demonstrate the nonliability (in whole or in part) of the party or parties filing the brief or briefs. The statement of legal contentions in a brief responding to a brief in support of a claim for relief shall be constructed in the same manner as provided in subparagraph (2) hereinabove for the statement of legal contentions of a party or parties in support of a claim for relief.

(5) Within _____ days after the service of defendant's pretrial brief containing statements of affirmative matter, the plaintiff shall file a reply pretrial brief containing factual statements admitting or denying each separate sentence of the separate narrative statement of affirmative matters of the defendant. This portion of the plaintiff's reply brief shall be constructed in the same manner provided in subparagraph (3) above for defendant's factual statements responding to plaintiff's narrative statement of facts, and shall be in a separate portion of the reply brief.

(6) Within _____ days after the service of defendant's statement of additional legal contentions and authorities in support thereof, plaintiff shall file, in a separate part of its reply brief, its separate statement of additional legal contentions and authorities in support thereof, which shall directly respond to the additional legal contentions of defendant. The statement of legal contentions and authorities in support thereof shall be constructed in the same manner provided in subparagraph (4) above for defendant's pretrial brief, and shall be in a separate portion of the reply brief.

(7) Any factual contention, any legal contention, any claim for relief or defense (in whole or in part), or any affirmative matter not set forth in detail as provided hereinabove shall be deemed abandoned, uncontroverted, or withdrawn in future proceedings, notwithstanding the contents of any pleadings or other papers on file herein, except for factual contentions, legal contentions,

338

claims for relief or defenses thereto, and affirmative matters of which a party may not be aware and could not be aware in the exercise of reasonable diligence at the time of filing the briefs hereinabove provided for. Any matters of which a party was not aware at the time of filing and of which he could not have been aware in the exercise of diligence at the time of the filing of a brief may be supplemented by a supplemental brief by leave of Court for good cause shown on timely motion therefor.

O. On or before the _____ day of _____, 19__, each plaintiff and each defendant herein shall serve and file written offers of proof on the following issues: (list)

P. On or before the _____ day of _____, 19__, each plaintiff and each defendant herein shall serve and file written narrative summaries setting forth in detail the testimony of each expert whom the party so filing will employ at trial, including a complete listing of all documents, data, and authorities studied by each such expert.

Q. On or before the _____ day of _____, 19__, the parties shall confer and attempt to agree on a joint statement of those factual issues that are without substantial controversy, and agree upon forms of statements of factual issues that are controverted. If the parties are unable to agree upon the uncontroverted factual issues or upon the forms of statements of the controverted factual issues, each party shall separately prepare on or before the _____ day of _____, 19__, a proposed statement thereof.

Part IV. Listing of Trial Witnesses

R. On or before the _____ day of _____, 19__, each plaintiff shall identify each witness it intends to call at trial in its case in chief and state whether such witness will appear in person or by deposition.

S. On or before the _____ day of _____, 19__, each defendant shall identify each witness it intends to call at trial in its case in chief and state whether such witness will appear in person or by deposition.

Part V. Filing of Proposed Voir Dire Questions

T. On or before the _____ day of _____, 19__, all parties shall file in writing (1) proposed topics for questions for voir dire examination of the jury, and (2) separate written requests for instructions to the jury and for special interrogatories. On each request for an instruction to the jury, there shall be noted the source of authorities from which it is derived or on which it is based.

Part VI. Scheduling Final Pretrial Conference

U. A final pretrial conference is set for the _____ day of _____, 19__, beginning at the hour of _____ o'clock, __.m.

V. At the pretrial conference set in paragraph U, final trial plans will be developed and, among other things, the following matters will be considered:

    (1) The then undetermined issues of fact and law will be delineated and, to the extent feasible, simplified;

    (2) The reception in evidence of documentary matters not precluded by stipulation of fact, subject to such objections, if any, as may be reserved for the trial;

    (3) The identity and scope of testimony of witnesses to be called at time of trial and their possible limitation will be considered;

    (4) An agreement upon a trial schedule;

    (5) The handling of documentary evidence;

    (6) Authentication of documents;

    (7) Witness lists;

    (8) Spokesmen;

    (9) Examination of witnesses;

    (10) Use of written narrative statements of expert witnesses;

    (11) Use of depositions, including the possible use of narrative summaries or verbatim extracts;

    (12) Final pretrial briefs filed pursuant to this pretrial order;

    (13) Limitation of opening statements;

    (14) Current index of the record;

    (15) Daily transcripts;

    (16) Instructions;

    (17) Separation of issues;

    (18) Use of and mechanics for special jury verdict, or general verdict with interrogatories;

    (19) Possibility of settlement.

Part VII. Setting Trial Date

W. Trial of the above-captioned case shall begin on the _____ day of _____, 19__, at _____ o'clock, __.m.

Dated this _____ day of _____, 19__.

_____

JUDGE

Final Pretrial Order [4]

A final pretrial conference was held in this cause on the _____ day of _____, 19__, wherein the following proceedings were had:

A. The following counsel were present representing the plaintiffs: (list).

B. The following counsel were present representing the defendants: (list).

C. The following issues of fact and law were framed, and the following witnesses who may be called at trial and exhibits that may be offered at trial were identified (list):

    (1) Jurisdiction and venue
    (2) Admitted facts
    (3) Plaintiffs' contentions on disputed facts
    (4) Defendants' contentions on disputed facts
    (5) Plaintiffs' contentions on the principal issues of law
    (6) Defendants' contentions on the principal issues of law
    (7) Plaintiffs' exhibits

Exhibit No.	Identification (Description)
_____	_____
_____	_____

    (8) Defendants' exhibits

Exhibit No.	Identification (Description)
_____	_____
_____	_____

    (9) Plaintiffs' witness list

Name	Live or Deposition Testimony
_____	_____
_____	_____

    (10) Defendants' witness list

Name	Live or Deposition Testimony
_____	_____
_____	_____

D. Trial in this cause shall commence on the _____ day of _____, 19__. Court sessions will be held from _____ o'clock a.m. to _____ o'clock p.m. on _____.

[4] Taken from "Manual for Complex Litigation," Fifth Edition, For Use With Federal Practice and Procedure by Charles Alan Wright and Arthur R. Miller (West Publishing Co.). This order is based on a final pretrial order developed by Judge George H. Boldt for use in Public Utility District No. 2 v. General Elec. Co., Civil Action No. 5380 (W.D.Wash.).

(1) Plaintiffs shall, to the extent possible, present separately the evidence regarding each issue following the order set forth below: (list).

(2) When plaintiffs' case is completed, defendants shall, to the extent possible, present separately the evidence regarding each issue following the order set forth below: (list).

(3) Each defendant shall present its evidence in the order in which defendants are named in the caption of this case.

(4) When defendants' case is completed, plaintiffs shall present their rebuttal evidence.

(5) None of the provisions herein shall require witnesses to make multiple appearances to maintain the order of presentation set forth above.

(6) The Court will not receive evidence relating to the period prior to _____ or subsequent to _____.

(7) _____, of counsel for plaintiffs, and _____, of counsel for defendants, are designated to represent all counsel of the parties as liaison counsel to receive notifications and act as spokesmen for co-counsel.

(8) Each motion by any defendant (or any plaintiff) on each objection shall be considered as made by each defendant (or plaintiff) in the same manner and to the same extent as though made separately by each such party, unless otherwise stated.

(9) Unless otherwise authorized by the Court, only one counsel for each party shall examine any witness. Counsel for the respective defendants shall attempt to designate one of their number to handle the cross-examination of any witness. Cross-examination of witnesses shall follow the direct examination, unless otherwise authorized by the Court.

(10) Plaintiffs' opening statements shall be limited to _____. Defendants' opening statements shall be limited to _____. Plaintiffs' and defendants' counsel respectively shall agree on the division of time. If necessary, the Court will make the division.

(11) Daily transcript shall be delivered after adjournment of the Court each day. Corrections shall be suggested at the opening of Court on the second following morning.

(12) (Jury Case) A jury of twelve jurors and _____ alternates shall be selected. Each plaintiff is permitted _____ peremptory challenges. Each defendant is permitted _____ peremptory challenges. The voir dire examination initially shall be conducted on the basis of the following questions:

(Questions (a)–(o) to be asked of the entire panel as a group.)

(a) This trial in all probability will be a lengthy one. While it is not possible to make a precise estimate, it may last as long as _____ months or more. Is there any reason why you cannot serve as a juror for that duration? What is it?

(b) Are you or any of your immediate family (spouse, children, parents, or brothers and sisters) or have you or any of your immediate family ever been employed by or represented any of the following: (list plaintiffs)?

(c) Are you or are any of your immediate family (spouse, children, parents, or brothers and sisters) or have you or any of your immediate family ever been employed by or represented any of the following: (list defendants)?

(d) Are you or any of your immediate family stockholders or holders of any other securities or obligations, or have you or any of your immediate family ever been stockholders or holders of any other securities or obligations, of any of the above companies?

(e) Do you or any of your immediate family have any business connections or dealings, or have you or any of your immediate family ever had any business connections or dealings, with any of the above companies? (If so, elicit details.)

(f) Have you or any of your immediate family or any organization you have been associated with ever had any dispute or unpleasantness with any of the above-named companies? If so, was it resolved to your satisfaction?

(g) Do you know any lawyers who are or ever have been associated with any of the following firms: (list)?

(h) Do you have any relatives or friends who are lawyers? (If so, elicit details.)

(i) Have you ever worked for a lawyer or law firm? (If so, elicit details.)

(j) Have you ever served on a federal jury in the past year?

(k) Have you or any of your immediate family ever been involved in a lawsuit as a plaintiff or a defendant? (If so, elicit details.)

(l) Has any one among you ever heard or read anything concerning any proceeding in this cause?

(m) Have you ever discussed this case with anyone?

(n) Would the fact that the defendant (or defendants) in a prior federal criminal proceeding entered a plea of guilty make it difficult or impossible for you to find for the defendants if the evidence shows that plaintiffs were not injured?

(*o*) Have you formed or expressed an opinion who should prevail in this controversy?

(Questions (p)–(u) to be asked of each juror individually.)

(p) What is your name?

(q) What is your home address?

(r) Are you married? If so: (a) How many children do you have? How old are they? What are the occupations of each of your adult children, and by whom are they employed? What is the occupation of your spouse? Who is his (her) employer?

(s) Who is your employer?

(t) Briefly describe the work you do.

(u) How long have you been with your present employer? (a) (If less than 10 years:) Would you describe what jobs you have had since 19__?

It is hereby so ORDERED.

Dated this _____ day of _____, 19__.

_____

JUDGE

Notice of Settlement of Class Action
With Proof of Claim Form [5]

NOTICE OF CLASS ACTION DETERMINATION AND SETTLEMENT HEARING TO PURCHASERS OF THE FOLLOWING SECURITIES OF THE SINGER COMPANY BETWEEN JANUARY 20, 1973 AND DECEMBER 29, 1975 (INCLUSIVE): (i) SINGER'S COMMON STOCK, PAR VALUE $10 PER SHARE, (ii) SINGER'S $3.50 CUMULATIVE PREFERRED STOCK, STATED VALUE $13 PER SHARE AND (iii) SINGER'S 8% SINKING FUND DEBENTURES DUE JANUARY 15, 1999

AND

PROOF OF CLAIM
UNITED STATES DISTRICT COURT FOR THE DISTRICT
OF NEW JERSEY

THIS NOTICE IS GIVEN pursuant to Rule 23 of the Federal Rules of Civil Procedure and pursuant to an Order of the United States District Court for the District of New Jersey (hereinafter sometimes called the

---

[5] Taken from "Manual for Complex Litigation," Fifth Edition, For Use With Federal Practice and Procedure, by Charles Alan Wright and Arthur R. Miller (West Publishing Co.). This notice and proof of claim form were used by the Honorable Stanley S. Brotman in Bullock v. Kircher, Civil Action No. 76–1173 (D.N.J.), and published in the *Wall Street Journal* (Jan. 8, 1979).

"Court") entered November 14, 1978, to all persons who, during the period from January 20, 1973 through December 29, 1975 purchased (i) shares of Common Stock, par value $10 per share of The Singer Company (hereinafter called the "Company"), or (ii) shares of the Company's $3.50 Cumulative Preferred Stock, stated value $13 per share, or (iii) any of the Company's 8% Sinking Fund Debentures due January 15, 1999 (hereinafter sometimes called the "Class Securities"). Such persons who are not employees of the Company purchasing their shares pursuant to a stock option plan, stock purchase plan or executive incentive plan sponsored or adopted by the Company, and who are not individual defendants in the action or a spouse, child, parent, brother or sister of such defendants, are herein collectively called the "Class."

NATURE OF THE ACTION

The above action entitled Thomas Bullock v. Donald P. Kircher, et al., asserts a claim on behalf of the Class against the Company and certain of its officers and directors. The consolidated complaint, which is brought under the provisions of the Securities Exchange Act of 1934 and Rule 10b–5 adopted by the Securities and Exchange Commission thereunder, alleges, *inter alia*, that the defendants conspired to and did cause certain of the Company's financial statements and other publicly disseminated information to contain material untrue statements and omissions concerning the assets and net worth of the Company and the Company's business generally. Damages are sought on behalf of the members of the Class.

FURTHER PROCEEDINGS

The defendants have filed answers denying, and continue to deny, any liability or any wrongdoing whatever in connection with claims in the action and have asserted various defenses. The Court has not yet passed on the merits of the claims or of any defenses thereto. The giving of this notice is not meant to imply that there has been any violation of the law, or that a recovery after a trial could be had if the action is not settled. Following the joinder of issues in the action, the attorneys for plaintiff engaged in extensive pre-trial discovery, including the review and analysis of tens of thousands of documents produced by defendants and third parties and the taking of in excess of twenty depositions. On the basis of their detailed investigation of the facts and the law relating to the issues involved in this action, they have concluded that the proposed settlement described below is fair to the members of the Class.

THE CLASS

The Court has ruled that the action may, pursuant to Rule 23 of the Federal Rules of Civil Procedure, proceed and be maintained as a class action on behalf of all persons who purchased any of the Class Securities described in the first paragraph of this Notice during the period January 20, 1973 through December 29, 1975.

If you purchased shares of the Company's Common Stock or $3.50 Cumulative Preferred Stock or any of the Company's 8% Sinking Fund Debentures due January 15, 1999 during the period January 20, 1973 through December 29, 1975 and are not related to or affiliated with any of the defendants, and are not an employee of the Company who purchased securities through a plan sponsored or adopted by the Company, you are a member of the Class. Any Class member may, however, request the Court to exclude him from the Class, provided that such request is made in writing, postmarked on or before March 15, 1979, addressed to:

Singer Settlement Administration Committee
c/o Heffler & Company
P.O. Box 30
Philadelphia, Pennsylvania 19105

setting forth the name and number of this case (Bullock v. Kircher, Civ. 76–1173); your name and present address; the number of shares, and/or amount of debentures, included in the Class Securities which were purchased by you between January 20, 1973 and December 29, 1975, inclusive; the date(s) of purchase; your address on the date of purchase if the Class Securities were registered in your own name; if the Class Securities were not so registered, the name and address on the date of purchase of the person who was the registered holder of such Class Securities on such date; and your request to be excluded from the Class (all joint owners must sign this request and provide such information). A Class member who has excluded himself from the Class in the manner above specified will not share in the benefits of any favorable judgment or settlement and will not be affected by the proposed settlement described below or bound by any adverse judgment which may be rendered. Any judgment, whether or not favorable to the members of the Class, will include all Class members who have not requested exclusion, whether or not they join or intervene in the action. Any Class member who does not request exclusion may, if he desires, enter an appearance in the action through counsel of his own choice. If he does so, he may be responsible for the fees, costs and disbursements resulting therefrom or relating thereto. Any Class member who does not request exclusion and who does not enter an appearance through his own counsel will be represented by Mssrs. Barrack, Rodos & McMahon, 2000 Market Street, Philadelphia, Pennsylvania 19103, counsel for plaintiff Thomas Bullock in this action.

THE PROPOSED SETTLEMENT

An agreement of settlement has been reached in the action between counsel for the plaintiff and counsel for the defendants, which is embodied in a Stipulation and Agreement of Compromise and Settlement dated

November 10, 1978 (the "Settlement Agreement") on file with the Court. As noted above, the attorneys for plaintiff, on the basis of an extensive investigation of the facts and the law relating to the matters complained of, have concluded that the proposed settlement is fair to, and in the best interests of, the Class. While defendants deny all charges of wrongdoing and do not concede liability, they desire to settle the action on the basis proposed in order to put to rest all further controversy, and to avoid substantial expenses and the inconvenience and distraction of burdensome and protracted litigation. The following description of the proposed settlement is a summary only, and reference is made to the text of the Settlement Agreement for a full statement of the provisions thereof:

1. The Company has established a Settlement Fund of $4,400,000 which has been invested in interest bearing obligations. Such interest will, if the settlement is approved by the Court, inure to the benefit of the Class.

2. The Company has established an Administration Fund of $175,-000.

3. The Administration Fund will be used to pay the costs of administering the settlement provided for in the Settlement Agreement, including costs of compiling lists of holders of Class Securities, costs of identifying through informal requests or judicial proceedings beneficial owners of Class Securities, expenses of publishing and mailing notices of the settlement and hearings thereon, and the fees and disbursements of accountants and disbursing agents retained to administer claims of, and payments to, holders of Class Securities.

4. The Settlement Fund and all interest earned thereon will be distributed under the Court's direction and supervision, as follows: (i) in payment of all expenses in excess of $175,000 incurred in the administration of the settlement; (ii) to the extent approved by Order of the Court in payment of the fees, allowances and disbursements of counsel for plaintiff; (iii) the balance (the "Net Settlement Fund") to the members of the Class who file valid Proofs of Claim in accordance with the procedure set forth below in proportion to the Recognized Loss incurred by each such member.

5. *The Recognized Loss* of a member of the Class shall be measured as follows: the actual cost of all shares of the Company's Common Stock, par value $10 per share, and the actual cost of all shares of the Company's $3.50 Cumulative Preferred Stock, stated value $13 per share, and the actual cost of all of the Company's 8% Sinking Fund Debentures due January 15, 1999 purchased by him during the period from January 20, 1973 through December 29, 1975 less the total of: (i) the actual sales price received for such shares or debentures sold on or prior to October 16, 1978, and (ii) as to any such shares or debentures still held after October 16, 1978, (a) the number of such shares of

Common Stock multiplied by $18.375 (the closing price for such Common Stock of the Company on October 16, 1978), (b) the number of such shares of Cumulative Preferred Stock multiplied by $35.50 (the closing price for such Cumulative Preferred Stock of the Company on October 16, 1978), and (c) the number of $1,000 multiples of such Sinking Fund Debentures multiplied by $852.50 (the closing price for each $1,000 of such Sinking Fund Debentures on October 16, 1978). The terms "actual cost" and "actual sales price" shall be deemed to include brokerage commissions, stock transfer taxes and other miscellaneous charges (excepting accrued interest) usually incurred in connection with a purchase or sale. The date of purchase or sale shall be the "contract" or "trade" date, as distinguished from the "settlement" date. Any member of the Class who acquired shares of such Common Stock or shares of such Cumulative Preferred Stock or any such Sinking Fund Debentures by gift or bequest or operation of law shall assume the actual cost of his transferor for the purpose of this paragraph.

6. Any Class member who excludes himself from the Class by following the procedure described above shall not be entitled to any distribution from the Net Settlement Fund.

7. If the proposed settlement is approved by the Court, there will be a dismissal on the merits of all claims, demands and causes of action, without limitation and whether or not heretofore asserted, which plaintiff and each member of the Class (except those who exclude themselves from the Class as provided above) have or may have, or which have been or might have been asserted on their behalf, against the defendants, or any of them, or which have been or might have been asserted against the officers, directors, employees, agents, attorneys, and representatives of the Company and/or the individual defendants, or any of them, in connection with or arising out of any of the matters, transactions and occurrences recited, described or referred to in the pleadings and proceedings herein, and with prejudice to all members of the Class except those Class members who exclude themselves from the Class as provided above.

8. By filing a Proof of Claim, a member of the Class will thereby submit himself to the jurisdiction of the Court, and each Proof of Claim shall be subject to investigation and discovery if deemed necessary by the Settlement Administration Committee pursuant to the Federal Rules of Civil Procedure.

9. Plaintiff or defendants may withdraw from the Settlement Agreement under certain circumstances described in the Settlement Agreement, in which event the Settlement Fund and all interest thereon and the Administration Fund and all interest therein, less any amounts incurred for administering the settlement, shall be returned to the Company.

NOTICE TO BROKERS AND OTHER NOMINEES

The Court has directed each brokerage house, bank and other institutional nominee which purchased Class Securities to forward a copy of the Notice and Proof of Claim to all persons who were the beneficial owners of any Class Securities purchased in your record name during the period January 20, 1973 through January 15, 1976. Adequate quantities of the Notice and Proof of Claim will be mailed to you by the Settlement Administration Committee upon your request.

ATTORNEYS' FEES AND COSTS

Messrs. Barrack, Rodos & McMahon, attorneys for plaintiff Thomas Bullock, and other associated plaintiff's counsel, will apply to the Court, at the hearing described below, for an award of counsel fees not to exceed 25% of the total of the Settlement Fund and the Administration Fund and all interest earned on those funds, plus litigation expenses and disbursements actually incurred. Such award as may be granted by the Court will be paid from the Settlement Fund.

THE HEARING

Pursuant to an order of the Court filed November 14, 1978, a hearing will be held before The Honorable Stanley S. Brotman, or Magistrate Stephen M. Oriofsky to whom this matter may be referred, United States Court House, Fourth and Market Streets, Camden, New Jersey 08101 at 10 a.m. on April 9, 1979 for the purpose of determining whether the proposed settlement is fair, reasonable and adequate and whether it should be approved by the Court and the action dismissed on the merits and with prejudice as provided above and for the purpose of considering plaintiff's counsel's application for fees, allowances and disbursements. The hearing may be adjourned from time to time by the Court at the hearing or at any adjourned session thereof without further notice.

Any member of the Class who has not requested exclusion therefrom may appear at the hearing and show cause, if any he has, why the proposed settlement should not be approved and the action should not be dismissed on the merits and with prejudice and/or present any opposition to the application of plaintiff's counsel for fees, allowances and disbursements, provided that no such person shall be heard, except by special permission of the Court, unless his objection or opposition is made in writing and is filed together with copies of all other papers and briefs to be submitted by him to the Court at the hearing with the Court on or before March 15, 1979, and showing due proof of service on Barrack, Rodos & McMahon, 2000 Market Street, Philadelphia, Pennsylvania 19103; Riker, Danzig, Scherer, Debevoise & Hyland, 744 Broad Street, Newark, New Jersey 07102; and Pitney, Hardin & Kipp, 163 Madison Avenue, Morristown, New Jersey 07960. Any member of the Class who does not make his objection in the manner provided above shall be deemed to have waived such objection and shall be forever foreclosed from making any objection to the fairness or adequacy of the proposed settlement or to the request of plaintiff's counsel for fees, allowances and disbursements.

EXAMINATION OF PAPERS AND INQUIRIES

For a more detailed statement of the matters involved in the above-entitled action, reference is made to the pleadings, to the Stipulation and Agreement of Compromise and Settlement, and to the other papers filed in this action, all of which may be inspected at the Office of the Clerk of the United States District Court for the District of New Jersey, Fourth and Market Streets, Camden, New Jersey 08101, during the hours of each business day.

The Court has appointed a settlement administration committee consisting of Leonard Barrack, Dickinson R. Debevoise and William D. Hardin. Any contact by members of the Class should be with the Committee through the office of Heffler & Company, P.O. Box 30, Philadelphia, Pennsylvania 19105 (Tel. 215–665–8870). No inquiry should be directed to the Clerk of the Court or to Judge Stanley S. Brotman.

PROOF OF CLAIM

1. TO RECEIVE ANY PAYMENTS FROM THIS SETTLEMENT, YOU MUST SIGN AND HAVE NOTARIZED THE ATTACHED PROOF OF CLAIM FORM, AND SUBMIT PROPER DOCUMENTATION SUPPORTING YOUR CLAIM.

2. Distribution of the proceeds of any settlement or of any judgment is subject to Court Approval.

3. You must file your completed and signed Proof of Claim on or before March 15, 1979 addressed as follows:

Singer Settlement Administration Committee
c/o Heffler & Company
P.O. Box 30
Philadelphia, Pennsylvania 19105
Tel. 215–665–8870

Your Proof of Claim form shall be deemed to have been filed when posted, if mailed by registered or certified mail, postage prepaid, addressed in accordance with the instructions given therein. A Proof of Claim filed otherwise shall be deemed to be filed at the time it is actually received by the person or office designated to receive it in the Proof of Claim.

4. The claim must be filed in the name, or names, of the actual beneficial owner, or owners, of the securities upon which the claim is based. All joint owners must sign this Proof of Claim. Executors, administrators, guardians, and trustees may complete and sign the form

on behalf of persons represented by them, but must identify the beneficial owners. Proof of their authority need not accompany the Proof of Claim but their titles or capacities must be stated.

5. You must list all acquisitions of any Class Securities on or after January 20, 1973 through December 29, 1975 and all dispositions of any Class Securities at any time.

6. If you acquired any Class Securities by gift, inheritance or operation of law, you are to report them as if you acquired them at the actual cost of your transferor.

7. Brokerage commissions, stock transfer taxes or other miscellaneous charges (excepting accrued interest) usually incurred in connection with either a purchase or a sale of the Class Securities shall be included in the cost and the sales price of such Class Securities.

8. Your Proof of Claim must be under oath, and must be accompanied by the documents called for therein.

Dated this _____ day of _____, _____.

_____

JUDGE

THIS ENTIRE FORM (OTHER THAN SIGNATURES)
MUST BE TYPED OR PRINTED

UNITED STATES DISTRICT COURT

FOR THE DISTRICT OF NEW JERSEY

_____

THOMAS BULLOCK, on behalf of himself and all others similarly situated,

Plaintiff,

vs.

DONALD P. KIRCHER, JOSEPH B. FLAVIN, GILBERT W. FITZHUGH, ARTHUR H. FREDSTON, EDWIN J. GRAF, WILLIAM G. HAMILTON, JR., LLOYD L. KELLEY, IAN K. MacGREGOR, JAMES W. McKEE, JR., DONALD E. MEADS, WILLIAM H. MORTON, DONALD G. ROBBINS, JR., ARTHUR J. SANTRY, JR., F. WAYNE VALLEY, THE SINGER COMPANY,

Defendants.

_____

Herein designated as the "Claimant"

The undersigned, being duly sworn, deposes and says that the following is true, correct and complete to the best of his knowledge, information and belief.

I. IDENTITY OF CLAIMANT:
    A. Claimant's name,* mailing address and telephone number are as follows:

    _____

    _____

    B. Claimant is (check one)—
        _____ An Individual
        _____ Two or more persons holding stock or debentures jointly
        _____ Partnership
        _____ Corporation
        _____ Executor or Administrator
        _____ Trustee
        _____ Other (specify)_____

II. STATEMENT OF CLAIM:
    A. Claimant (or person from whom Claimant acquired shares by gifts or inheritance, or deceased person for whom Claimant is acting as executor or administrator) made the following purchases of (i) Common Stock of The Singer Company, par value $10 per share, (ii) $3.50 Cumulative Preferred Stock of The Singer Company, stated value $13 per share and (iii) The Singer Company's 8% Sinking Fund Debentures due January 15, 1999, during the period January 20, 1973 through December 29, 1975. *Claimant has included information as to all such purchases made during such period.*

Number of shares and amount of debentures purchased (list each type of security separately)	Date of purchase (trade date)	Price for the purchases, shares or debentures (including commissions)
	Type of Security	
Name in which shares or debentures registered	Common Preferred Debenture	

B. Claimant sold the following (i) Common Stock of The Singer Company, par value $10 per share, (ii) $3.50 Cumulative Preferred Stock of The Singer Company, stated value $13 per share and (iii) The Singer Company's 8% Sinking Fund Debentures due January 15, 1999, referred to Paragraph II A above. *Claimant has included information with*

* If stock or debentures are held jointly, the stock or debentures.
give the names of all persons interested in

*respect to all such sales, and such shares and debentures are still held by
the Claimant to the extent that their sale is not listed below.*

Number of shares and amount of debentures sold (list each type of security separately)	Date of sale (trade date)	Price for the sold shares or debentures (including commissions and expenses)
Name in which shares or debentures registered at time of sale		Type of Security

		Common	Preferred	Debenture

III. ADDITIONAL PROOF REQUIRED:

CLAIMANT MUST ANNEX TO THIS PROOF OF CLAIM COPIES
OF BROKER'S CONFIRMATION, MONTHLY ACCOUNT STATE-
MENTS, DELIVERY RECEIPTS, OR OTHER DOCUMENTATION ES-
TABLISHING EVIDENCE OF ALL PURCHASES AND SALES IN-
CLUDED IN PARAGRAPH II OF THIS PROOF OF CLAIM.

IV. THE FOLLOWING PARAGRAPHS APPLY TO ALL CLAIMANTS:

A. By the filing of this Proof of Claim, Claimant hereby submits to
the jurisdiction of the United States District Court for the District of
New Jersey.

B. Claimant understands that the information contained in this
Proof of Claim is subject to investigation and discovery pursuant to the
Federal Rules of Civil Procedure and that Claimant may be required to
furnish additional information to support this Proof of Claim.

C. Claimant hereby certifies that neither he (it) nor any purchaser
of shares or debentures of The Singer Company which are the subject of
this Proof of Claim was (i) an employee of The Singer Company who
purchased his shares pursuant to a stock option plan, stock purchase
plan or executive incentive plan sponsored or adopted by Singer, or (ii)
an individual defendant in this action, or (iii) a spouse, child, parent,
brother, sister, officer, director, partner, or controlling person of any
named defendant or a subsidiary or affiliate of a named defendant, or
(iv) an underwriter, purchasing for its own beneficial account, with
respect to any of the securities which are the subject of this Proof of
Claim.

D. By the filing of this Proof of Claim, and in consideration of the
right to participate in the distribution of the Settlement Fund, Claimant
hereby waives and releases all claims and demands which he (it) may
have against any defendant in the Action, or against the officers,
directors, employees, agents, attorneys and representatives of any of
such defendants, or against any other person or business entity, arising
from or related to the matters complained of in the above-entitled action

or the consummation of the terms of the Stipulation and Agreement of Compromise and Settlement entered into in said action.

Sworn to before me this
———— day of 19—.

Signed ————————————
(Name(s)—all reg-
istered joint own-
ers must sign)

————————————
Notary Public

————————————
(Address)

THIS PROOF OF CLAIM MUST BE FILED NO LATER THAN MARCH 15, 19— AND MUST BE MAILED TO:

Singer Settlement Administration Committee

c/o Heffler & Company

P.O. Box 30

Philadelphia, Pennsylvania 19105 **

1.45 Additional Sample Sections That May Be Used in Settlement Notices

In addition to the sections contained in the sample notices of settlement set out above, the Court may desire to use one or more of the following sections:

(a) Section on reasons for settlement [6]

REASONS FOR SETTLEMENT: Defendants disclaim any liability and any wrongdoing of any kind whatsoever and have denied the allegations in both actions and have asserted defenses that they believe are meritorious, but they consider it desirable that this action and the claims alleged therein be settled upon the terms and conditions set forth in the Settlement Agreement, in order to avoid further expenses, and burdensome, protracted litigation, and to put at rest all claims that have been or might be asserted by any member of either class arising from the subject matter of the complaints herein. The proposed settlements and this Notice are not to be construed as admissions of liability of any kind whatsoever by any of the defendants.

Counsel for plaintiffs and the classes represented by them have thoroughly investigated the facts and circumstances underlying the issues raised by the pleadings herein and the law applicable thereto, have conducted extensive discovery, and have concluded that, taking into account the risks involved in establishing, in whole or in part, a right to

---

** A Proof of Claim shall be deemed to have been filed when posted, if mailed by registered or certified mail, postage prepaid. A Proof of Claim filed otherwise shall be deemed to be filed at the time it is actually received by the Singer Settlement Adminis-tration Committee at the address set forth above.

[6] From an order used in Weisberg v. APL Corp., Civil Action No. 74–C–1794 (E.D.N.Y.).

recovery on behalf of the named plaintiffs and the classes they represent against the defendants and the likelihood that this litigation will be further protracted and expensive, it would be in the best interests of the named plaintiffs and the classes they represent to settle these actions upon the terms and conditions set forth in the Settlement Agreement and that such terms are fair, adequate, and reasonable.

Once again, the Court has not expressed any opinion concerning the merits of the claims or defenses herein.

(b) Section on effect of failure to file proof of claim form [7]

If you do not exclude yourself and also do not file a valid Claim Form, you will be included in the Class, but you will not receive any portion of the Net Settlement Fund, and you will be bound by the Final Judgment in this Litigation, the Settlement Stipulation, and the releases therein, and you will be barred from any further assertion of released and settled claims. To receive a portion of the Settlement Fund you must file a Claim Form in a proper manner and mail it so that it is received on or before _____ _____, 19__.

(c) Section on effect of failure to file proof of claim form and filing objections to settlement [8]

TO ALL PERSONS WHO PURCHASED COMMON STOCK OF GIANT STORES CORP. DURING THE PERIOD APRIL 16, 1971 THROUGH AND INCLUDING MAY 23, 1973.

PLEASE TAKE NOTICE that a hearing will be held on May 9, 1979 at 9:30 a. m. before the Honorable Charles M. Metzner, Judge of the United States District Court for the Southern District of New York, at the United States Courthouse, Foley Square, New York, New York in Room 519. The purpose of the hearing is to determine whether the two proposed settlements of the above-entitled Consolidated Class Action for sums aggregating $4,750,000, which will constitute the entire recovery to the class members, pursuant to two Stipulations of Settlement, should be approved by the Court as fair, reasonable, and adequate, and to consider the application of plaintiffs for the award of counsel fees and expenses. If you have not excluded yourself from the class, you may be entitled to share in the distribution of the settlement fund. TO SHARE IN THE DISTRIBUTION OF THE SETTLEMENT FUND, YOU MUST FILE A PROOF OF CLAIM ON OR BEFORE JUNE 15, 1979, establishing that you purchased common stock of Giant Stores Corp. during the period April 16, 1971 through and including May 23, 1973.

Objections to the settlement or the award of counsel fees, expenses, and disbursements must be filed no later than April 27, 1979 as provided in the detailed notice referred to below.

[7] From an order used in Friedman v. Zale Corp., Civil Action No. 3–77–0850–C (N.D.Tex.).

[8] From an order used in Goldberg v. Touche Ross & Co., Civil Action No. 74 Civ. 1483 (S.D.N.Y.).

A more detailed notice describing the proposed settlements of this consolidated class action, the fees and expenses requested, the hearing thereon, and the requirement that a proof of claim be filed, has been mailed to all persons appearing on the transfer records of Giant Stores Corp. as record purchasers during the period April 16, 1971 through and including May 23, 1973. If you have not received a copy of that notice, *you may obtain one and a Proof of Claim form by making a written request to* Clerk of the Court, P.O. Box 1220, General Post Office, New York, New York 10001.

Re: Giant Stores Corp., *or* Attorneys for Plaintiffs,

One Pennsylvania Plaza, New York, New York 10001

Attention: Jared Specthrie, Esq.

Part VI

Illustrative Litigation Problem
with
Sample Documents

Introduction

The purpose of the illustrative problem is three-fold: to give a general picture of the flow of litigation; to present a series of sample documents in the context of a factual setting; and, finally, to demonstrate how specific procedural matters may arise during the course of an actual case. The problem is broken into four sections: Jurisdiction, Pleadings, Pretrial Discovery and Motions, and Trial, Verdict, and Attacks on Verdict. Each section contains a number of questions to focus attention on the problems raised.

Stage I. Jurisdiction

Plaintiff Thomas A———, filed an action in a state court. His complaint read as follows:

IN THE SUPERIOR COURT, DELTA COUNTY, STATE OF ARVADA

Thomas A———,	)	
Plaintiff	)	
	)	
vs.	)	Civil P 15163
	)	COMPLAINT
Reginald B———, Daniel C———,	)	
and D——— Corporation,	)	
Defendants	)	

COUNT ONE

I

On or about June 1, 1999, plaintiff Thomas A——— was involved in a motor vehicle collision with an automobile driven by defendant Reginald B——— and with a bulldozer operated by defendant Daniel C——— who was acting within the scope of his employment with defendant D_____ Corporation. The collision occurred on Public Highway 10 in the state of Arvada, approximately twenty miles east of the City of Diego.

II

Defendants and each of them have informed plaintiff that they suffered injuries to persons and property in a total amount of $100,000 and have demanded that plaintiff remit the amount of such damages or face institution of legal action against him for their recovery.

III

Defendants have informed plaintiff that their injuries are proximately due to the plaintiff's negligence in that at the time of the collision, plaintiff was operating his vehicle in excess of the speed limit.

IV

Plaintiff is an agent of the Federal Bureau of Investigation. At the time of the collision he was proceeding at a speed of 80 miles per hour along Public Highway 10 pursuant to orders, duly issued, to assist in the apprehension of escaped federal prisoners. Plaintiff's speed, although in excess of the state speed limit, was necessary in order for him to carry out his assigned duties.

WHEREFORE, Plaintiff prays for a declaration:

(1) That he was not negligent at the time of the collision.

(2) That he is immune from liability because his acts were required within the scope of his federal duties.

(3) Awarding him such other relief to which he is entitled.

James L. W_____
Attorney for Plaintiff

_____

Question:

On the basis of facts stated in the complaint could plaintiff have maintained suit in a federal district court?

_____

Plaintiff A_____ is a citizen of the State of Mindon, defendant B_____ is a citizen of the State of Arvada, defendant C_____ is a citizen of the State of Lamar, and the D_____ Corporation, which does considerable business in all three states is incorporated in Lamar where its equipment is housed and where all of its 2000 workmen reside. Its administrative offices, however, are located in Mindon, which is the residence of its 10 executive officers and 25 office workers.

Questions:

1. How does the information regarding the citizenship and activities of the parties affect the ability of plaintiff to bring his action in a federal court? In the federal court of Arvada?

2. Assuming that Arvada has enacted the broadest possible statutes permitting service of process on out-of-state residents, can the courts of Arvada constitutionally assert personal jurisdiction over all the defendants in this action by personally serving them where they reside? Is the extension of jurisdiction to cover such a case a wise policy?

After filing his action, but prior to attempting service of process, plaintiff's attorney called defendant C_____ at his house, informed him of the pending suit, and requested a meeting in Arvada in order to arrange a settlement. The attorney promised that C_____ would be paid a substantial sum but only if he tacitly agreed to take a job in another part of the country and to resist all efforts by his codefendants to induce him to testify against plaintiff. C_____ agreed to the meeting. Immediately upon his arrival in Arvada, however, he was greeted by a process server who handed him a summons to appear in plaintiff's action. (For a form summons see Federal Rules of Civil Procedure Form 1, in Part I, supra.) When C_____ arrived at the attorney's office, he was told by the secretary there that the scheduled meeting was canceled and would be rescheduled. C_____, justifiably angry, stormed out of the office to return home. Before leaving Arvada, however, he tarried long enough to look at 100 acres of unimproved real estate that was for sale. Several days after returning home, he purchased the property for $5,000 in a transaction handled through the mail.

Questions:

1. Is the service made on C_____ in Arvada sufficient to bring him before the state courts? What arguments might he make if he wishes to avoid being sued in Arvada?

2. May C_____'s purchase of the property in any way assist plaintiff in bringing his action against C_____?

The original complaint was served on all defendants on June 30, 1999. On July 31, 1999, prior to the filing of any response by defendants, and without leave of court, plaintiff filed a "First Amended Complaint" containing all the information in the original complaint and adding the following new counts:

COUNT TWO

I

Plaintiff incorporates herein the allegations contained in paragraphs I and IV of Count One.

II

Defendant C_____ negligently stopped the bulldozer along the side of Public Highway 10. As a direct and proximate result thereof, plaintiff was unable to avoid striking the vehicle driven by defendant B_____ which in turn caused plaintiff to strike the bulldozer.

III

As a direct and proximate result of defendant C_____'s negligence, plaintiff suffered severe physical injuries involving his head and right shoulder. Plaintiff has endured great pain and suffering and will have large hospital and doctor bills in an amount as yet unascertained.

WHEREFORE, Plaintiff prays for damages in the amount of $160,-000 against defendant C_____ and such other relief to which plaintiff is entitled.

COUNT THREE

I

On July 15, 1999, plaintiff deposited the sum of $2,500 cash with the Efficiency Bank of Mindon as trustee, to deliver said sum to defendant B_____ upon his execution of a release form provided by plaintiff.

II

On July 17, 1999, the Efficiency Bank paid B_____ $2,500 cash. The Bank did not receive the executed form from defendant B_____ then or at any subsequent time.

WHEREFORE, Plaintiff prays that the court order defendant B_____ to execute such release form or in the alternative to hold the $2,500 as a constructive trustee for plaintiff or for any other relief to which plaintiff is entitled.

Attached to the amended complaint and labeled "Exhibit" was the following document:

RELEASE FORM

Whereas B_____ is alleging a claim for personal injury and property damage against A_____ arising from an automobile collision, and whereas both parties wish to avoid litigation,

B_____ hereby acknowledges receipt of $2,500 from A_____ and in consideration therefor, forever releases A_____ from any and all liability to B_____ arising from any cause whatsoever occurring on or before the date of this instrument.

_____   _____

Date   Signature

_____

Question:

May defendants, or any one of them, when served with the amended complaint have the entire case removed to the federal court in Arvada?

_____

Stage II. Pleadings

Five days after receiving the amended complaint, defendant B_____'s attorney filed the following document and sent a copy to each of the parties through their attorneys:

IN THE SUPERIOR COURT, DELTA COUNTY STATE OF ARVADA

Thomas A_____,
                      Plaintiff)
) Civil P 15163

         vs.   )

Reginald B_____, Daniel C_____   ) NOTICE OF MOTION
  and D_____ Corporation,   ) TO STRIKE
                   Defendants)

To Thomas A_____, plaintiff, and to his attorneys, W_____ and B_____.

You and each of you will please take notice that on August 10, 1999, at the hour of 9:00 A.M. in the above entitled court, defendant Reginald

B_____ will move to strike the First Amended Complaint. The motion is made on the ground that the said Amended Complaint was filed without leave of court as required by Rule 15 of the Arvada Rules of Civil Procedure.

In the alternative, defendant B_____ will move to strike Count Three of the First Amended Complaint on the ground that it is improperly joined with Counts One and Two in violation of section 20 of the Arvada Civil Practice Act.

> Louis F_____
> Attorney for Defendant B_____

Attached to the motion was the following supporting document which is required of all motions to strike in Arvada courts:

STATEMENT OF POINTS AND AUTHORITIES
SUPPORTING MOTION TO STRIKE

I

1. Rule 15(a) of the Arvada Rules of Civil Procedure provides that a complaint cannot be amended without leave of court "after defendant's answer has been filed."

2. This rule should logically be interpreted to prohibit amendment without leave of court if the normal time for answer has elapsed, whether or not such answer is filed.

3. Under Rule 12(a) of the Arvada Rules of Civil Procedure the time for answer is twenty days after service. Plaintiff's First Amended Complaint was filed on July 30, 1999, whereas the original complaint was served on June 29, 1999.

II

1. Section 20 of the Arvada Civil Practice Act permits joinder of causes all of which fall within one of the following classes:

    (1) Contracts, express or implied

    (2) Physical injury to person

    (3) Injury to property

    (4) Injury to character

    (5) Matters arising out of the same transactions or occurrences.

2. Count Three of plaintiff's First Amended Complaint does not appear in any of the statutory categories in which Counts One and Two appear.

Questions:

1. How likely is it that the court will grant the motion to strike the entire complaint? See Federal Rule 15(a) and the comparative state materials, supra.

2. What chance does defendant have on his motion to strike Count Three? See Federal Rule 18(a) and the comparative state materials, supra.

At the same time that he filed his notice of motion, defendant B_____'s attorney filed and served on all parties the following:

IN THE SUPERIOR COURT, DELTA COUNTY, STATE OF ARVADA

Thomas A_____,	)
Plaintiff	)
	) Civil P 15163
vs.	)
	) DEMURRER
Reginald B_____, Daniel C_____	)
and D_____ Corporation,	)
Defendants	)

Defendant B_____ demurs to the First Amended Complaint on file herein as follows:

I

Count One does not state facts sufficient to constitute a cause of action.

II

Count Three does not state facts sufficient to constitute a cause of action.

III

There is a defect of parties in plaintiff's Count Three.

IV

The court has no jurisdiction over the matters in Count Three because an Indispensable Party has not been joined.

Louis F_____

Attorney for Defendant B_____

Under Arvada rules, defendant need not set the date for the demurrer; instead the clerk of the court must notify all parties as to the time the hearing will be held.

Questions:

1. **Assuming that this case, if properly pleaded, would justify declaratory relief under Arvada law, and further assuming that Arvada follows the classic rules of code pleading, what chance does defendant B_____ have on his challenge to the sufficiency of Counts One and Three? What possible defects may he point to in arguing that the demurrer should be sustained? Would the result be different if the court was operating under the Federal Rules of Civil Procedure?**

2. **How successful will B_____ be regarding his challenges as to joinder of parties? Does anything turn on whether or not the Efficiency Bank is subject to personal jurisdiction in Arvada? See Federal Rule 19, supra.**

After hearing arguments on both the motion to strike and the demurrer, the trial judge issued the following order, which was prepared at his direction by defendant B_____'s attorney:

IN THE SUPERIOR COURT, DELTA COUNTY STATE OF ARVADA

Thomas A_____,	)
Plaintiff	)
	) Civil P 15163
vs.	)
	) ORDER
Reginald B_____, Daniel C_____	)
and D_____ Corporation,	)
Defendants	)

The motion of defendant Reginald B_____ to strike the First Amended Complaint or in the alternative to strike parts therefrom and his demurrer to counts One and Three having come on regularly for hearing before the undersigned this 10th day of August, 1999, at the hour of 10 A.M., upon notice duly and regularly served and plaintiff Thomas A_____ appearing by his counsel James. L. W_____ and defendant Reginald B_____, appearing by his counsel, Louis F_____, and no appearance having been made on behalf of the other named defendants and the matter having been argued and submitted and good cause appearing therefore,

IT IS HEREBY ORDERED, AS FOLLOWS:

(1) That defendant's motion to strike be denied in all particulars.

(2) That defendant's demurrer to Count One be denied.

(3) That defendant's demurrer to Count Three be sustained on the ground that it fails to state facts constituting a cause of action.

(4) That the demurrer otherwise be denied in all particulars.

(5) That plaintiff has leave to file an amended complaint in ten days from the date hereof and that defendant is granted twenty days from the date hereof to file his Answer.

Dated: August 10, 1999

Learned W_____
Judge of the Superior Court

Questions:

1. **What choices does plaintiff now have with regard to the Court's ruling on Count Three of his complaint? What will be the consequences of an amendment if he later wishes to claim that the trial court erred? If he fails to amend, will he be prohibited from bringing any new action against B_____ for the same damages?**

2. **What chance does plaintiff have to appeal immediately the ruling as to Count Three? If it is within the trial or appellate court's discretion to permit an amendment, should it be allowed?**

On August 20, 1999, plaintiff filed a Second Amended Complaint changing only the allegations of Count Three as follows:

COUNT THREE

I

On July 15, 1999, plaintiff deposited the sum of $2,500 cash with the Efficiency Bank of Mindon. The money was held in trust to deliver said sum to defendant B_____ upon his execution of a specific release form provided by plaintiff. The release form is attached to this complaint as an "Exhibit" and is made a part hereof as if set forth in full herein.

II

On July 17, 1999, the Efficiency Bank paid the $2,500 held in trust to defendant B_____. The Bank did not receive the executed form from defendant B_____ then or at any subsequent time.

WHEREFORE, Plaintiff prays that the court order defendant B_____ to execute such release form or in the alternative to hold the $2,500 as a constructive trustee for plaintiff or for any other relief to which plaintiff is entitled.

———————

Once again defendant B_____ demurred to the complaint on the ground that Count Three failed to state a cause of action. The demurrer was overruled.

———————

Questions:

1. **To what extent does this amendment cure any defects in the prior complaint?**

2. **What choices does B_____ have with regard to the court's ruling on Count Three? If he answers does he waive the defense that Count Three doesn't state a valid cause of action? What if he fails to answer? See Federal Rule 8(d).**

3. **What opportunity does B_____ have to appeal immediately the overruling of his demurrer to Count Three? Should a trial or appellate court in its discretion permit the appeal?**

———————

On August 23, 1999, defendant C_____ filed and served on all other parties the following Answer and Cross-Claim:

IN THE SUPERIOR COURT, DELTA COUNTY STATE OF ARVADA

Thomas A——————,	)	
Plaintiff	)	
	)	Civil P 15163
vs.	)	
	)	ANSWER AND
Reginald B——————, Daniel C——————	)	CROSS–CLAIM
and D—————— Corporation,	)	
Defendants	)	

Defendant Daniel C—————— Answers and alleges as follows:

I

Admits the allegations of paragraph I of Count One of plaintiff's complaint.

II

Admits the allegations of paragraphs II and III of Count One of plaintiff's complaint and alleges the truth of those facts in paragraph III of Count One of which plaintiff alleges defendant C—————— informed him and further alleges that defendant C—————— was severely injured, endured great pain and suffering and medical expenses, none of which can presently be ascertained with certainty but which will amount at a minimum to $25,000.

III

Admits so much of paragraph IV of Count One of plaintiff's complaint that alleges that plaintiff drove in excess of the state speed limit; has no information as to plaintiff's employment at the time of the collision and on that ground denies the allegation relating to plaintiff's employment as an FBI agent; and denies that a speed of 80 miles per hour was required by defendant's duties or was in any way reasonable or non-negligent.

IV

Refuses to admit or deny each and every allegation of paragraph II of Count Two of plaintiff's complaint and demands that plaintiff be put to his proof.

V

Has no information or belief as to the allegations of paragraph III of Count Two of plaintiff's complaint, and on that ground denies the allegations of said paragraph III.

CROSS–CLAIM

Defendant C_____ as a Cross-Claim alleges as follows:

I

At the time of the collision which is the subject of plaintiff's action, defendant Daniel C_____ was stopping his bulldozer on the shoulder of Public Highway 10 in the State of Arvada, to assist defendant Reginald B_____ whose vehicle had stalled on the highway.

II

Defendant B_____ was instructing and directing defendant C_____ in parking the bulldozer in order that it would not be a hazard to vehicles approaching along the highway. Defendant C_____ followed such instructions as given by defendant B_____. C_____'s reliance on such instructions was reasonable.

III

Plaintiff in this action seeks damages from defendant C_____ on the grounds that said bulldozer was improperly stopped so as to create an unreasonable risk to passing traffic. The position of the bulldozer when stopped was the direct and proximate result of defendant B_____'s negligence in giving the aforesaid instructions.

WHEREFORE, Defendant C_____ prays as follows:

1. That plaintiff take nothing by his action.

2. That defendant B_____ be held liable to indemnify defendant C_____ for all amounts, if any, which defendant C_____ is ordered to pay plaintiff on the basis of his complaint herein.

3. That defendant C_____ be awarded such damages and other relief to which he is entitled.

Samuel R_____

Attorney for Defendant C_____

Questions:

1. **Could plaintiff successfully move for a judgment on the pleadings against defendant C_____? What arguments does plaintiff have that all of the essential elements of his case have been admitted?**

2. **Suppose the case had been brought in a federal court and that B_____ had not been named as a codefendant by plaintiff. Could the cross-claim still have been maintained by defendant C_____? See Federal**

Rule 14. How would your answer be affected if the Arvada law, on the basis of the facts alleged, clearly prohibited C_____'s claim against B_____ for indemnity but permitted C_____ to recover damages for his own personal injuries from B_____? Could C_____ sue for such injuries on a cross-complaint? See Federal Rules 13(g) and (h).

Shortly after defendant C_____ filed his Answer and Cross-Claim, defendants B_____ and D_____ Corporation filed separate answers to Counts One and Two of plaintiff's complaint, asserting that the sole cause of the accident was plaintiff's negligence. Both B_____ and D_____ Corporation demanded, by way of counterclaim, payment for the damages they suffered. In addition defendant B_____ generally denied allegations in Count Three of the complaint.

B_____ then filed an answer to defendant C_____'s Cross-Claim as follows:

IN THE SUPERIOR COURT, DELTA COUNTY STATE OF ARVADA

Thomas A_____, Plaintiff	))) Civil P 15163))) ANSWER TO CROSS–) CLAIM))
vs.	
Reginald B_____, Daniel C_____ and D_____ Corporation, Defendants	

Defendant B_____ for an Answer to the Cross-Claim filed by Defendant C_____:

I

Denies each and every allegation therein stated.

II

Alleges that defendant C_____ was negligent in stopping the bulldozer and that said negligence was a direct and proximate cause of plaintiff's injuries.

WHEREFORE, Defendant B_____ prays that defendant C_____ take nothing from defendant B_____ on his cross-action.

Louis F_____
Attorney for Defendant B_____

Question:

Should any of the parties file further pleadings? To what extent are they permitted to do so? See Federal Rule 7(a) and the accompanying state materials, supra.

Stage III. Pretrial Discovery and Motions

On September 1, 1999, defendant B_____ filed and served on all parties the following document:

IN THE SUPERIOR COURT, DELTA COUNTY STATE OF ARVADA

Thomas A_____,	)	
Plaintiff	)	
	)	Civil P 15163
vs.	)	
	)	NOTICE OF MOTION
Reginald B_____, Daniel C_____	)	
and D_____ Corporation,	)	
Defendants	)	

To plaintiff Thomas A_____ and his attorney, James L. W_____:

You are hereby notified that on September 6, 1999, at the hour of 10 A.M. in the courtroom of the above entitled court, defendant Reginald B_____ will move this court for an order directing plaintiff to submit to a physical examination by Dr. William M_____, whose office is at 420 D_____ Avenue, in the City of Diego, State of Arvada. The purpose of the examination is to determine the state of plaintiff's mental health at the time of the collision described in the Complaint herein. The motion is based upon Rule 35 of the Arvada Rules of Civil Procedure. The examination is necessary to determine whether plaintiff was mentally capable of safely operating a motor vehicle at a speed of 80 miles per hour; whether he was aware of his ability or inability to do so; and whether he is capable of truthful testimony. The motion is made upon the affidavit of Louis F_____, Attorney for defendant Reginald B_____, and upon evidence, oral and documentary, to be presented at the hearing of this motion.

Louis F_____

Attorney for Defendant B_____

AFFIDAVIT

STATE OF ARVADA   )

                     ss.   ) Civil P 15163

COUNTY OF DELTA   )

Louis F_____, being first duly sworn, states that he is attorney for defendant Reginald B_____ herein and is familiar with the issues to be tried.

In this action plaintiff seeks a declaration that he was not negligent in operating a vehicle although he was traveling at a high rate of speed in excess of the state speed laws. The ability of an individual to control a motor vehicle at high speeds depends upon his individual psychological make-up which determines his reaction time. Defendant is without expert information as to these matters regarding plaintiff.

Plaintiff further alleges that his speeding was reasonable. This will in part depend on whether plaintiff knew he created an unreasonable risk by driving much faster than was necessary under the circumstances. Defendant B_____ can ascertain such knowledge on the part of plaintiff only through an examination by an expert.

The undersigned is informed and believes that plaintiff will testify during trial on his own behalf. Defendant B_____ is unable without the examination here requested, to obtain evidence as to whether plaintiff is a pathological liar or is otherwise psychologically unable or unlikely to tell the truth.

Dr. M_____ is a practicing clinical psychologist, with a Ph.D. degree from Midwestern University. He is licensed to practice under the laws of the State of Arvada and has been practicing in the State for the past 12 years and enjoys an excellent reputation in his field.

                                          Louis F_____

Subscribed and sworn to before me this First day of September, 1999

      [Signed] Rita N_____   [Notary Seal
      Notary Public In and For the   of the State
      State of Arvada, Delta County   of Arvada]

Questions:

How likely is the court to grant the motion? Assuming that Federal Rule 35 is applicable, what arguments could be made by A_____ to avoid such examination?

Defendant B_____'s attorney subsequently learned that the lawyer for defendant D_____ Corporation has done considerable investigation of every aspect of the case. B_____'s attorney therefore sent the following interrogatories to D_____ Corporation (Assume that Arvada has not as yet adopted amended Federal Rule 26(a) requiring automatic disclosure of potential witnesses.):

IN THE SUPERIOR COURT, DELTA COUNTY STATE OF ARVADA

Thomas A_____,	)
Plaintiff	)
	) Civil P 15163
vs.	)
	) INTERROGATORIES
Reginald B_____, Daniel C_____	)
and D_____ Corporation,	)
Defendants	)

To D_____ Corporation:

Please take notice that the following interrogatories are submitted pursuant to Rule 33 of the Arvada Rules of Civil Procedure; answers are required by said Rule 33 within 30 days of the receipt hereof:

1. What are the names and addresses of persons, if any, other than the named parties to this action, whom you are aware witnessed the activities of plaintiff and defendant C_____ just prior to, at the time of, and immediately subsequent to the collision which is the subject of plaintiff's action?

2. What are the names and addresses of those persons, if any, other than the parties named in this action, whom you are aware witnessed the activities of defendant B_____ just prior to, at the time of, and immediately subsequent to the collision which is the subject of plaintiff's action and defendant C_____'s counterclaim?

3. What information concerning the events in this action has D_____ Corporation or its attorneys voluntarily turned over to defendant C_____ or his attorneys?

4. What is the nature of the conspiracy, if any, between defendant C_____ and defendant D_____ Corporation or their attorneys regarding a concerted effort to avoid liability by placing all blame for the accident on plaintiff and defendant B_____?

5. It is true that two days after the collision defendant C_____ told an investigating attorney for D_____ Corporation that the only instruction given by him by B_____ just prior to the accident was "Get the hell off of the road!"?

6. What is the substance of the reports of any experts hired by defendant D_____ Corporation regarding the speed and exact location of the vehicles involved in the accident just prior to and at the time of the collision?

7. What are the names and addresses of any experts referred to in Interrogatory 6 above?

Louis F_____
Attorney for Defendant B_____

D_____ Corporation responded to these interrogatories as follows:

IN THE SUPERIOR COURT, DELTA COUNTY STATE OF ARVADA

Thomas A_____,
               Plaintiff
 	
       vs.
 	
Reginald B_____, Daniel C_____
  and D_____ Corporation,
              Defendants
	)
	)
	) Civil P 15163
	)
	) OBJECTIONS TO
	) INTERROGATORIES
	)
	)

To defendant Reginald B_____ and Louis F_____, his attorney:

Please take notice that defendant D_____ Corporation, objects to the interrogatories which were served by you on September 8, 1999, and said defendant will on September 16, 1999, at the hour of 10 A.M. in the above entitled Court, move for an order striking said interrogatories for the following reasons:

1. Interrogatories may not be served by one defendant on a codefendant in an action.

2. Interrogatory Number 2 is irrelevant as to matters between D_____ Corporation and B_____.

3. Interrogatories Numbers 3, 4, 5, 6 and 7 request information within the work-product privilege.

Paul Y_____
Attorney for Defendant
D_____ Corporation

Question:

Assume that the Arvada discovery rule regarding interrogatories is the same as the federal rule. What are

defendant D_____ Corporation's chances on its motion?
See Federal Rule 33(a) and (b), supra.

On September 10, 1999, defendant B_____ moved for summary
judgment on the cross-claim filed by defendant C_____. The motion
was supported by an affidavit of one William G_____, which read as
follows:

AFFIDAVIT

STATE OF ARVADA	)	
	ss.)	Civil P 15163
COUNTY OF DELTA	)	

William G_____, being first duly sworn deposes and says:

That on June 1, 1999, he was a passenger in a vehicle driven by
Reginald B_____; that said vehicle was involved in a collision on
Public Highway 10, East of the City of Diego; that just prior to the
collision, the vehicle driven by B_____ was required to stop on the
highway because the pavement was blocked by a bulldozer crossing over
the road; that B_____ had shouted a few words to the bulldozer
operator; that said operator had shouted back and waved his fist in an
angry manner; that B_____ had then said, "I told him to get the hell
out of the middle of the road"; that thereupon another vehicle approaching from the opposite direction at a high rate of speed struck the
bulldozer and careened into the car driven by B_____.

William G_____

Subscribed and sworn to before me this First day of September,
1999

[Signed] Rita N_____   [Notary Seal
Notary Public In and For the   of the State of
State of Arvada, Delta County   Arvada]

Defendant C_____ filed no answering affidavits; at the hearing his
attorney argued that the affidavit was insufficient to justify summary
judgment, that the failure of B_____ to file his own affidavit was in
itself sufficient reason to deny the motion, and that C_____'s pleadings
clearly contradicted the statements in the affidavit. The court took the
matter under advisement and one week later signed an order granting
the motion in favor of B_____.

Questions:

Was the decision of the trial judge appropriate? Should it be reversed on appeal?

The filing of G_____'s affidavit was the first notice to defendant D_____ Corporation that he had been a witness to the collision. The Corporation's attorney sent copies of the following document to all other parties:

IN THE SUPERIOR COURT, DELTA COUNTY STATE OF ARVADA

Thomas A_____,	)	
Plaintiff	)	Civil P 15163
	)	
vs.	)	NOTICE OF TIME
	)	AND PLACE OF
Reginald B_____, Daniel C_____	)	DEPOSITION
and D_____ Corporation,	)	
Defendants	)	

To Thomas A_____, plaintiff, and to James W_____, his Attorney; to Reginald B_____, defendant and Louis F_____, his Attorney; to Daniel C_____, defendant, and Samuel R_____, his Attorney:

YOU AND EACH OF YOU will please take notice that on September 17, 1999, at the hour of 9 a.m., at the office of Irma W_____, Notary Public, whose address is 13 W_____ Drive, City of Diego, State of Arvada, defendant D_____ Corporation will take the deposition of William G_____, whose address is 280 F_____ Street, City of Diego, State of Arvada, upon oral examination before the above named Irma W_____, Notary Public said deposition to continue from day to day until completed.

Paul Y_____

Attorney for Defendant
D_____ Corporation

The following document was prepared by D_____ Corporation's attorney for service on William G_____:

IN THE SUPERIOR COURT, DELTA COUNTY STATE OF ARVADA

Thomas A_____,	)
Plaintiff	)
	) Civil P 15163
vs.	)
	) SUBPOENA
Reginald B_____, Daniel C_____	)
and D_____ Corporation,	)
Defendants	)

The People of the State of Arvada to

William G_____

280 F_____ Street

Diego, Arvada

GREETING:

You are commanded to appear and attend proceedings of the above entitled Court to be held on September 17, 1999, at the hour of 9 A.M. at the office of Irma W_____, Notary Public, whose address is 13 W_____ Drive, City of Diego, State of Arvada, then and there to give testimony on deposition as a witness produced by defendant D_____ Corporation in said action now pending in said Court.

And you are advised that disobedience of said subpoena may be punished as acontempt by the above entitled Court and for such disobedience you will also forfeit to any party or parties aggrieved thereby the sum of all damages suffered due to your failure so to attend.

September 13, 1999

Angus B_____
(Clerk)

By Solomon D_____
(Deputy Clerk)

Questions:

Is it necessary to subpoena every witness for deposition? Is it wise to do so? See Federal Rule 30(g)(2).

Stage IV. Trial, Verdict, and Attacks on Verdict

After all of the parties engaged in and completed their discovery and defendants B_____ and C_____ submitted voluntarily to physical examinations by plaintiff's doctor, defendant B_____ filed the following document on October 12, 1999:

Thomas A_____,	)
Plaintiff	) Civil P 15163
	)
vs.	) MEMORANDUM TO
	) SET FOR TRIAL AND
Reginald B_____, Daniel C_____	) DEMAND FOR JURY
and D_____ Corporation,	) TRIAL
Defendant	)

The Court is requested to set the above entitled case for trial. Jury is hereby demanded on all factual issues.

I hereby represent to the Court that this cause is at issue; that all affirmative pleadings have been answered; that to my knowledge no new parties will be served with summons prior to time of trial, and I know of no further pleading to be filed and know of no reason why the cause should not be tried as soon as the calendar of the Court will permit. I certify that the party filing this memorandum has completed all discovery proceedings.

October 12, 1999

                         Louis F_____
                         Attorney for Defendant B_____

Plaintiff then filed a special memorandum taking the position that a jury trial was not appropriate on the issued involved in Count Three of his complaint. The trial court, on October 18, 1999, issued an order setting the case for trial by jury on January 20, 2000. The order specified that jury trial was denied as to the issues contained in Count Three.

Questions:

If the case had been brought in a federal court would the Constitutional right to trial by jury extend to the issues in Count Three? Would the demand for jury trial have been adequate?

At the trial testimony was given by A_____, B_____, C_____ and their medical experts, the highway patrolmen who arrived at the scene shortly after the accident, and G_____. The evidence, in addition to bearing on the question of which of the parties was at fault and the purported settlement agreement between A_____ and B_____, showed that all three participants, A_____, B_____, and C_____ had suffered serious personal injuries and that both the bulldozer and B_____'s car had been badly damaged. In addition, on cross-examination, A_____'s attorney adduced the following testimony from one of the highway patrolmen who had been called as a witness by C_____'s attorney:

Q. Now you say that plaintiff's car struck the bulldozer head-on?

A. Yes.

Q. Are you certain that the car didn't hit the side of the bulldozer which was projecting out toward the roadway?

A. I don't think it did.

Q. How do you know?

A. Well, plaintiff's car appeared to have struck something head-on; the impact was directly in front. I looked at the wreck.

Q. Did you see evidence of a second impact?

A. No.

Q. You mean to say that you disagree with the testimony of every participant in the collision that plaintiff's car hit the bulldozer and bounced into the automobile driven by B_____?

A. I guess so. The car was in awful shape. Really too bad. It was a brand new model. I have one just like it myself. Worth $13,800. Total wreck.

Court: Just answer the questions please.

Q. Then you really couldn't tell where the initial impact was?

A. I guess not.

After all parties had rested and the final arguments were about to begin, defendant B_____ requested that the court reopen the case to take additional testimony from witnesses on a "new" point. On the promise that the new presentation would take no more than one hour, the court granted permission, subject to a motion to strike if the evidence was unfair to any of the other parties. B_____'s attorney first called to the stand the owner of the largest construction company in Arvada who testified that the custom of every local construction company was to plant flares to warn approaching traffic when a piece of heavy equipment was crossing the road. Then three people testified. Each was the driver of a vehicle that had preceded plaintiff's car by a few minutes on Highway 10 on the day of the accident. Each remembered passing the site where the accident subsequently took place. They remembered seeing a huge bulldozer as it was moving along the road. The testimony of witness H_____ is typical.

Q. As you approached the area where the bulldozer was located did you see a warning flare?

A. No. Not that I recall. I don't remember seeing it.

Cross-examination by C_____'s attorney.

Q. How far had you driven?

A. 200 miles.

Q. Had you passed other construction sites?

A. Sure.

Q. Did you see flares there?

A. I may have. I guess I did.

Q. Were you looking to see if flares were or were not present at construction sites?

A. No, of course not. If a flare was present, I'd slow down.

Q. Was there anything unusual about the construction site in question here?

A. No.

Q. How much farther did you drive after you passed the site?

A. About 150 miles.

Q. When did you realize that an accident occurred there shortly after you passed?

A. Not until a few days ago when one of the lawyers here tracked us down. I'll never know how he did it!

After this evidence was presented, defendant C_____'s attorney moved to strike on the ground that it raised a new issue regarding the use of flares, that he was unable, because of such short notice, to "scour the countryside" for other witnesses to rebut the testimony given, and that since none of the parties had mentioned the seeing of or the setting of flares in their testimony, the new evidence was all improper. He rejected the judge's offer to grant a two-day continuance on the ground that it would be "futile."

The trial court denied the motion. Each of the parties then made final arguments, and moved for directed verdicts, which were denied; and the court then gave its instructions. The instructions on negligence, causation, and respondeat superior were general in form but correct, and no specific instructions were requested. After instructing on how to compute damages the court added the following as Instruction 46:

Ladies and gentlemen of the jury. You will be given a number of verdict forms. One asks whether or not plaintiff should collect from defendant C_____, and if so how much. Another does the same regarding defendant D_____ Corporation. Then you have three other forms asking whether any of the three defendants should collect on counterclaims against plaintiff. You must answer each of these. If you find liability, there is a place where you set down the amount of damages. You are required to decide how much is for personal injury and how much for property damage. These forms are to aid you in making a proper verdict; you may write additional information on them as you wish.

Defendant C_____ objected to the instruction insofar as it permitted plaintiff to collect damages for his vehicle on the ground that such damages had never been pleaded or proved. Plaintiff objected to that part of the instruction permitting defendant C_____ to collect any damages whatsoever against plaintiff on the ground that defendant C_____ had failed to file a counterclaim therefor.

Defendant B_____ objected on the ground that the court should have left to the jury those issues involved in Count Three of plaintiff's complaint.

The Court denied the objections of C_____ and B_____, but granted plaintiff's motion and ordered the jury to find that in no event would plaintiff A_____ be liable to Defendant C_____.

While the jury was debating the court said: "I find for plaintiff on Count Three of his complaint. However, the equitable relief sought by plaintiff is totally inappropriate. There is clearly an adequate remedy at law. Defendant B_____ never intended to sign a release of liability. Therefore I find that defendant B_____ has been unjustly enriched by the amount of $2,500 and I hereby award plaintiff that sum against defendant B_____."

The jury then returned with its verdict. It found for plaintiff on all points, awarding $150,000 for physical injuries and $13,800 for property damage against C_____ and D_____ Corporation. The jury foreman wrote on the verdict sheet, "We find defendant C_____ negligent because of his failure to set out warning flares. Since defendant C_____ was operating within the scope of his employment with D_____ Corporation, we find against D_____ Corporation too. Everybody else seemed reasonable to us."

Defendant C_____ then filed the following motion:

IN THE SUPERIOR COURT, DELTA COUNTY STATE OF ARVADA

Thomas A_____,	)	
Plaintiff	)	Civil P 15163
	)	
vs.	)	NOTICE OF MOTION
	)	FOR JUDGMENT
Reginald B_____, Daniel C_____	)	N.O.V. AND FOR
and D_____ Corporation,	)	NEW TRIAL
Defendants	)	

To plaintiff A_____, and his Attorney James W_____:

YOU AND EACH OF YOU ARE NOTIFIED that on the 31st day of January, 2000, at the hour of 10 A.M. in the above entitled Court, defendant Daniel C_____ will move for an order for judgment notwithstanding the verdict on Counts One and Two of the Complaint, and if the same be denied, for a new trial. In addition defendant C_____ will move for a new trial for the purposes of collecting damages for his injuries as alleged in his Answer and Cross-Claim. Said motions are based on the insufficiency of the evidence to sustain or legally justify a ruling that defendant was negligent on the ground specified by the jury in its special verdict, that it was error for the court at the end of trial to admit and not to strike the evidence pertaining to the use of flares, that it was error to instruct the jury that plaintiff could collect damages for his vehicle, and that the Court erred in instructing the jury that defendant C_____ failed to state a valid claim for damages against plaintiff.

Samuel R_____
Attorney for Defendant C_____

Defendant B_____ filed his own motion for new trial as to Count Three on the ground that he was denied his constitutional right to a trial by jury.

Defendant D_____ Corporation filed a motion to dismiss the action for failure of the complaint to state a cause of action for collection of damages against the corporation. In the alternative it requested a new trial on the same ground.

All of the motions were consolidated for hearing.

Questions:

1. **What argument does defendant C_____ have to support his motion for a judgment as a matter of law? Is**

he likely to be successful? Has C_____ failed to include any significant error in the trial as a basis for seeking a new trial?

2. **What arguments will the various parties make regarding the other motions? In considering defendant B_____'s motion assume that the right to jury trial in Arvada is identical to that in the federal courts.**

Shortly after arguments on these motions the court made the following order:

IN THE SUPERIOR COURT, DELTA COUNTY STATE OF ARVADA

Thomas A_____,	)
Plaintiff	)
	) Civil P 15163
vs.	)
	) ORDER
Reginald B_____, Daniel C_____	)
and D_____ Corporation,	)
Defendants	)

The motion of defendant C_____ for a judgment N.O.V. and for a new trial and the motions of defendants B_____ and D_____ Corporation for a new trial and dismissal having come on regularly for hearing before the undersigned on the 31st day of January, 2000, at the hour of 10 A.M., upon notice duly and regularly served and plaintiff A_____ appearing by James L. W_____, his counsel, and defendant C_____ appearing by Samuel R_____, his counsel, and defendant B_____ appearing by Louis F_____, his counsel, and defendant D_____ Corporation appearing by Paul Y_____, its counsel, and the matter having been argued and submitted and good cause appearing therefor,

IT IS HEREBY ORDERED that defendant C_____'s motion for judgment notwithstanding the verdict be denied, and that defendant C_____'s motion and defendant B_____'s motion for new trial be denied.

IT IS FURTHER ORDERED that defendant D_____ Corporation's motion to dismiss plaintiff's complaint for failure of plaintiff to allege a claim for damages against D_____ Corporation is granted without leave to amend.

Dated: January 31, 2000

Learned W_____
Judge of the Superior
Court

The Court then rendered the following judgment:

IN THE SUPERIOR COURT, DELTA COUNTY STATE OF ARVADA

Thomas A_____,	)
Plaintiff	)
	) Civil P 15163
vs.	)
	) JUDGMENT
Reginald B_____, Daniel C_____,	)
and D_____ Corporation,	)
Defendants	)

The above entitled cause came on regularly for trial before the undersigned sitting with a jury on January 20, 2000. Upon the jury being duly sworn and impaneled, evidence was presented, the matter argued and the jury instructed by the undersigned.

The Court, after deliberation, rendered the following verdict on issues not triable to a jury: that plaintiff recover the sum of $2,500 from defendant B_____.

The jury, after deliberation, rendered the following verdict: We the jury find for the plaintiff and against defendants Reginald B_____, Daniel C_____ and D_____ Corporation, and declare that plaintiff was not negligent. We further find that plaintiff suffered damages against defendants C_____ and D_____ Corporation in the amount of $150,000 for personal injuries and $13,800 for property damage.

The Court then dismissed plaintiff's claim for damages against defendant D_____ Corporation on the ground that the complaint failed to state a claim for such relief.

IT IS HEREBY ORDERED ADJUDGED AND DECREED that plaintiff have judgment as follows:

1. Plaintiff is declared to have been not negligent in his conduct toward defendants B_____, C_____ and D_____ Corporation.

2. Plaintiff is entitled to damages against defendant B_____ in the amount of $2,500, plus interest thereon, from the 28th day of January, 2000, until paid, at the rate of 7% per annum, and for his costs of action.

3. Plaintiff is entitled to damages against defendant C_____ in the amount of $163,800 plus interest thereon from the 28th day of January, 2000, until paid, at the rate of 7% per annum, and for his costs of suit.

Dated: February 10, 2000

Learned W_____

Judge of the Superior
Court

_____

Defendants C_____ and D_____ Corporation decided to appeal this decision. Their attorneys filed the following documents which were duly served on plaintiff:

IN THE SUPERIOR COURT, DELTA COUNTY STATE OF ARVADA

Thomas A_____,	)	
Plaintiff	)	
	)	Civil P 15163
vs.	)	
	)	NOTICE OF APPEAL
Reginald B_____, Daniel C_____,	)	
D_____ Corporation,	)	
Defendants	)	

To Angus B_____, County Clerk;

Notice is hereby given that defendants Daniel C_____ and D_____ Corporation appeal from that part of the judgment relating to Counts One and Two of plaintiff's Complaint and also to that part of the judgment denying to said defendants Daniel C_____ and D_____ Corporation damages for their injuries to person and property.

Dated: February 25, 2000.

Samuel R_____

Attorney for Defendant Daniel C_____

Paul Y_____

Attorney for Defendant
D_____ Corporation

IN THE SUPERIOR COURT, DELTA COUNTY STATE OF ARVADA

Thomas A_____,	)	Civil P 15163
Plaintiff	)	
	)	
vs.	)	NOTICE TO PREPARE
Reginald B_____, Daniel C_____,	)	TRANSCRIPT
and D_____ Corporation,	)	
Defendants	)	

To Angus B_____, Clerk of the above entitled Court:

Please take notice that defendants Daniel C_____ and D_____ Corporation have commenced an appeal and in connection therewith require a reporter's transcript of the proceedings and testimony in the above entitled case which transcript shall also include the instructions to the jury which were given and those which were refused, all statements, orders, requests, rulings and remarks of the court, counsel, the parties or any witnesses, and all exhibits introduced into evidence during the course of trial.

Samuel R _____
    Attorney for Defendant
    Appellant Daniel C_____
Paul Y_____
    Attorney for Defendant
    Appellant D_____
    Corporation

While the appeal was pending plaintiff brought a new action against D_____ Corporation for damages of $163,800, alleging the negligence of C_____ and the fact that C_____ had been acting within the scope of his employment. The Corporation filed an answer denying both these allegations, alleging that plaintiff had been contributorily negligent, and that the action was barred by res judicata. Both parties then moved for summary judgment in their favor on the entire case or as to those issues which could be so decided. Each party supported its case solely with a certified copy of the entire record in the first suit.

Question:

Should the court grant a full summary judgment to either party? If not, to what extent, if any, is a partial summary judgment appropriate?

The trial court, after a hearing, rendered a decision granting summary judgment for the plaintiff. Shortly thereafter the appeal in the first action was argued and submitted. Within two weeks the appellate court handed down a decision setting aside the verdict in the first action and ordering a new trial on all issues.

Question:

What steps should D_____ Corporation's lawyer now take with regard to the summary judgment rendered in the second action? See Federal Rule 60(b)(5).

Part VII

Local (Civil) Rules for the United States District Courts for the Eastern and Southern Districts of New York

Effective April 15, 1997
(as amended March 26, 1998)

Table of Contents

Rule		Page
1.1.	Application of Rules	389
1.2.	Clerk's Office	389
1.3.	Admission to the Bar	389
1.4.	Withdrawal or Displacement of Attorney of Record	390
1.5.	Discipline of Attorneys	391
1.6.	Duty of Attorneys in Related Cases	394
1.7.	Fees of Clerks and Reporters	394
1.8.	Photographs, Radio, Recordings, Television	394
1.9.	Disclosure of Interested Parties	395
1.10.	Acceptable Substitutes for Affidavits	395
5.1.	Filing of Discovery Materials	395
6.1.	Service and Filing of Motion Papers	395
6.2.	Orders on Motions	396
6.3.	Motions for Reconsideration or Reargument	396
6.4.	Computation of Time	397
7.1.	Memoranda of Law	397
7.2.	Specification of Statutes or Rules	397
11.1.	Form of Pleadings, Motions, and Other Papers	397
16.1.	Exemptions from Mandatory Scheduling Order	397
16.2.	Entry and Modification of Mandatory Scheduling Orders by Magistrate Judges	397
23.1.	Fees in Stockholder and Class Actions	398
24.1.	Notice of Claim of Unconstitutionality	398
26.1.	Address of Party and Original Owner of Claim to Be Furnished	398
26.2.	Assertion of Claim of Privilege	398
26.3.	Uniform Definitions in Discovery Requests	399
26.4.	Opt–Out From Certain Provisions of Federal Rule of Civil Procedure 26 (Southern District Only)	401
26.5.	Cooperation Among Counsel in Discovery (Eastern District Only)	401
26.6.	Form Discovery Requests (Eastern District Only)	401
26.7.	Discovery Requests to Be Read Reasonably (Eastern District Only)	401
30.1.	Counsel Fees on Taking Depositions More Than 100 Miles From Courthouse	401
30.2.	Opt–Out From Certain Provisions of Federal Rule of Civil Procedure 30 (Southern District Only)	401
30.3.	Telephone Depositions (Eastern District Only)	402

Rule		Page
30.4.	Persons Attending Depositions (Eastern District Only)	402
30.5.	Depositions of Witnesses Who Have No Knowledge of the Facts (Eastern District Only)	402
30.6.	Conferences Between Deponent and Defending Attorney (Eastern District Only)	402
30.7.	Document Production at Depositions (Eastern District Only)	402
31.1.	Opt–Out From Certain Provisions of Federal Rule of Civil Procedure 31 (Southern District Only)	403
33.1.	Answering Interrogatory by Reference to Records	403
33.2.	Standard Discovery in Prisoner Pro Se Actions	403
33.3.	Interrogatories (Southern District Only)	405
33.4.	Opt–Out From Certain Provisions of Federal Rule of Civil Procedure 33 (Southern District Only)	405
34.1.	Opt–Out From Certain Provisions of Federal Rule of Civil Procedure 34 (Southern District Only)	405
36.1.	Opt–Out From Certain Provisions of Federal Rule of Civil Procedure 36 (Southern District Only)	405
37.1.	Verbatim Quotation of Interrogatories, Requests for Admissions, and Objections or Exceptions	405
37.2.	Mode of Raising Discovery Disputes With the Court (Southern District Only)	406
37.3.	Mode of Raising Discovery and Other Non–Dispositive Pretrial Disputes With the Court (Eastern District Only)	406
39.1.	Custody of Exhibits	407
39.2.	Order of Summation	407
47.1.	Assessment of Jury Costs	407
53.1.	Masters	408
54.1.	Taxable Costs	408
54.2.	Security for Costs	410
54.3.	Entering Satisfaction of Money Judgment	410
55.1.	Certificate of Default	411
55.2.	Default Judgment	411
56.1.	Statements of Material Facts on Motion for Summary Judgment ..	411
56.2.	Notice to Pro Se Litigants Opposing Summary Judgment	412
58.1.	Remand by an Appellate Court	412
65.1.1.	Sureties	413
67.1.	Order for Deposit in Interest–Bearing Account	413
72.1.	Powers of Magistrate Judges	414
72.2.	Reference to Magistrate Judge (Eastern District Only)	414
73.1.	Consent Jurisdiction Procedure	415
77.1.	Submission of Orders, Judgments and Decrees	415
81.1.	Removal of Cases from State Courts	415
83.1.	Transfer of Cases to Another District	416
83.2.	Settlement of Actions by or on Behalf of Infants or Incompetents and Wrongful Death Actions	416
83.3.	Habeas Corpus	417
83.4.	Proceedings to Stay the Deportation of Aliens in Deportation and Exclusion Cases	417
83.5.	Three–Judge Court	419
83.6.	Publication of Advertisements	419
83.7.	Notice of Sale	419
83.8.	Filing of Notice of Appeal	420
83.9.	Contempt Proceedings in Civil Cases	420
83.10.	Court-Annexed Arbitration (Eastern District Only)	421
83.11.	Court-Annexed Mediation (Eastern District Only)	426
83.12.	Alternative Dispute Resolution (Southern District Only)	428

Rule 1.1. Application of Rules

These Local Civil Rules apply in civil actions as defined in Federal Rules of Civil Procedure 1 and 2.

Rule 1.2. Clerk's Office

The offices of the clerk are open from 8:30 a.m. to 5:00 p.m. Monday through Friday and closed on Saturdays, Sundays, and legal holidays. A night depository with an automatic time and date stamp shall be maintained by the clerk of the Southern District in the Pearl Street Courthouse and by the clerk of the Eastern District in the Brooklyn Courthouse. After regular business hours, papers for the district court only may be deposited in the night depository. Such papers will be considered as having been filed in the district court as of the time and date stamped thereon, which shall be deemed presumptively correct.

Rule 1.3. Admission to the Bar

(a) A member in good standing of the bar of the state of New York, or a member in good standing of the bar of the United States District Court in New Jersey, Connecticut or Vermont and of the bar of the State in which such district court is located, provided such district court by its rule extends a corresponding privilege to members of the bar of this court, may be admitted to practice in this court on compliance with the following provisions:

Each applicant for admission shall file with the clerk, at least ten (10) days prior to hearing (unless, for good cause shown, the judge shall shorten the time), a verified written petition for admission on a form supplied by the clerk stating: (1) applicant's residence and office address; (2) the time when, and courts where, admitted; (3) applicant's legal training and experience; (4) whether applicant has ever been held in contempt of court, and, if so, the nature of the contempt and the final disposition thereof; (5) whether applicant has ever been censured, suspended or disbarred by any court, and, if so, the facts and circumstances connected therewith; (6) that applicant has read and is familiar with (a) the provisions of the Judicial Code (Title 28, U.S.C.) which pertain to the jurisdiction of, and practice in, the United States District Courts; (b) the Federal Rules of Civil Procedure; (c) the Federal Rules of Criminal Procedure; (d) the Federal Rules of Evidence; (e) the Local Rules of the United States District Court for the Southern and Eastern Districts of New York; and (f) the New York State Lawyer's Code of Professional Responsibility as adopted from time to time by the Appellate Divisions of the State of New York; and (7) that applicant will faithfully adhere to all rules applicable to applicant's conduct in connection with any activities in this court.

The petition shall be accompanied by a certificate of the clerk of the court for each of the states in which the applicant is a member of the bar, which has been issued within thirty (30) days and states that the applicant is a member in good standing of the bar of that state court. The petition shall also be accompanied by an affidavit of an attorney of this court who has known the applicant for at least one year, stating when the affiant was admitted to practice in this court, how long and under what circumstances the attorney has known the applicant, and what the attorney knows of the applicant's character and experience at the bar. Such petition shall be placed at the head of the calendar and, on the call thereof, the attorney whose affidavit accompanied the petition shall personally move the admission of the applicant. If the petition is granted, the applicant shall take the oath of office and sign the roll of attorneys.

(b) A member in good standing of the bar of either the Southern or Eastern District of New York may be admitted to the bar of the other district without formal application (1) upon filing in that district a certificate of the Clerk of the United States District Court for the district in which the applicant is a member of the bar, which has been issued within thirty (30) days and states that the applicant is a member in good standing of the bar of that court and (2) upon taking the oath of office, signing the roll of attorneys of that district, and paying the fee required in that district.

(c) A member in good standing of the bar of any state or of any United States District Court may be permitted to argue or try a particular case in whole or in part as counsel or advocate, upon motion and upon filing with the Clerk of the District Court a certificate of the court for each of the states in which the applicant is a member of the bar, which has been issued within thirty (30) days and states that the applicant is a member in good standing of the bar of that state court. Only an attorney who has been so admitted or who is a member of the bar of this court may enter appearances for parties, sign stipulations or receive payments upon judgments, decrees or orders.

(d) If an attorney who is a member of the bar of this court, or who has been authorized to appear in a case in this court, changes his or her residence or office address, the attorney shall immediately notify the clerk of the court, in addition to serving and filing a notice of change of address in each pending case in which the attorney has appeared.

Rule 1.4.   Withdrawal or Displacement of Attorney of Record

An attorney who has appeared as attorney of record for a party may be relieved or displaced only by order of the court and may not withdraw from a case without leave of the court granted by order. Such an order may be granted only upon a showing by affidavit or otherwise of satisfactory reasons for withdrawal or displacement and the posture of the case, including its position, if any, on the calendar.

Rule 1.5. Discipline of Attorneys

(a) Committee on Grievances. The chief judge shall appoint a committee of the board of judges known as the Committee on Grievances, which under the direction of the chief judge shall have charge of all matters relating to the discipline of attorneys. The chief judge shall appoint a panel of attorneys who are members of the bar of this court to advise or assist the Committee on Grievances. At the direction of the Committee on Grievances or its chair, members of this panel of attorneys may investigate complaints, may prepare and support statements of charges, or may serve as members of hearing panels.

(b) Grounds for Discipline or Other Relief. Discipline or other relief, of the types set forth in paragraph (c) below, may be imposed, by the Committee on Grievances, after notice and opportunity to respond as set forth in paragraph (d) below, if any of the following grounds is found by clear and convincing evidence:

(1) Any member of the bar of this court has been convicted of a felony or misdemeanor in any federal court, or in a court of any state or territory.

(2) Any member of the bar of this court has been disciplined by any federal court or by a court of any state or territory.

(3) Any member of the bar of this court has resigned from the bar of any federal court or of a court of any state or territory while an investigation into allegations of misconduct by the attorney was pending.

(4) Any member of the bar of this court has an infirmity which prevents the attorney from engaging in the practice of law.

(5) In connection with activities in this court, any attorney is found to have engaged in conduct violative of the New York State Lawyer's Code of Professional Responsibility as adopted from time to time by the Appellate Divisions of the State of New York, and as interpreted and applied by the United States Supreme Court, the United States Court of Appeals for the Second Circuit, and this court.

(6) Any attorney not a member of the bar of this court has appeared at the bar of this court without permission to do so.

(c) Types of Discipline or Other Relief.

(1) In the case of an attorney admitted to the bar of this court, discipline imposed pursuant to paragraph (b)(1), (b)(2), (b)(3), or (b)(5) above may consist of a letter of reprimand or admonition,

censure, suspension, or an order striking the name of the attorney from the roll of attorneys admitted to the bar of this court.

(2) In the case of an attorney not admitted to the bar of this court, discipline imposed pursuant to paragraph (b)(5) or (b)(6) above may consist of a letter of reprimand or admonition, censure, or an order precluding the attorney from again appearing at the bar of this court.

(3) Relief required pursuant to paragraph (b)(4) above shall consist of suspending the attorney from practice before this court.

(d) Procedure.

(1) If it appears that there exists a ground for discipline set forth in paragraph (b)(1), (b)(2), or (b)(3), notice thereof shall be served by the Committee on Grievances upon the attorney concerned by first class mail, directed to the address of the attorney as shown on the rolls of this court and to the last known address of the attorney (if any) as shown in the complaint and any materials submitted therewith, together with an order by the Committee on Grievances directing the attorney to show cause in writing why discipline should not be imposed. If the attorney fails to respond in writing to the order to show cause, or if the response fails to show good cause to hold an evidentiary hearing, the Committee on Grievances may proceed to impose discipline or to take such other action as justice and this rule may require. If good cause is shown to hold an evidentiary hearing, the Committee on Grievances may direct such a hearing pursuant to paragraph (d)(4) below.

(2) In the case of a ground for discipline set forth in paragraph (b)(2) or (b)(3) above, discipline may be imposed unless the attorney concerned establishes by clear and convincing evidence (i) that there was such an infirmity of proof of misconduct by the attorney as to give rise to the clear conviction that this court could not consistent with its duty accept as final the conclusion of the other court, or (ii) that the procedure resulting in the investigation or discipline of the attorney by the other court was so lacking in notice or opportunity to be heard as to constitute a deprivation of due process, or (iii) that the imposition of discipline by this court would result in grave injustice.

(3) Complaints in writing alleging any ground for discipline or other relief set forth in paragraph (b) above shall be directed to the chief judge, who shall refer such complaints to the Committee on Grievances. The Committee on Grievances, by its chair, may designate an attorney, who may be selected from the panel of attorneys established pursuant to paragraph (a) above, to investigate the complaint, if it deems investigation necessary or warranted, and to prepare a statement of charges, if the Committee deems that necessary or warranted. Complaints, and any files based on them, shall

be treated as confidential unless otherwise ordered by the chief judge for good cause shown.

(4) A statement of charges alleging a ground for discipline or other relief set forth in paragraph (b)(4), (b)(5), or (b)(6) shall be served upon the attorney concerned by certified mail, return receipt requested, directed to the address of the attorney as shown on the rolls of this court and to the last known address of the attorney (if any) as shown in the complaint and any materials submitted therewith, together with an order by the Committee on Grievances directing the attorney to show cause in writing why discipline or other relief should not be imposed. Upon the respondent attorney's answer to the charges the matter will be designated by the Committee on Grievances for a prompt evidentiary hearing before a magistrate judge of the court or before a panel of three attorneys, who may be selected from the panel of attorneys established pursuant to paragraph (a) above. The magistrate judge or panel of attorneys conducting the hearing may grant such pre-hearing discovery as they determine to be necessary, shall hear witnesses called by the attorney supporting the charges and by the respondent attorney, and may consider such other evidence included in the record of the hearing as they deem relevant and material. The magistrate judge or panel of attorneys conducting the hearing shall report their findings and recommendations in writing to the Committee on Grievances and shall serve them upon the respondent attorney and the attorney supporting the charges. After affording the respondent attorney and the attorney supporting the charges an opportunity to respond in writing to such report, or if no timely answer is made by the respondent attorney, or if the Committee on Grievances determines that the answer raises no issue requiring a hearing, the Committee on Grievances may proceed to impose discipline or to take such action as justice and this rule may require.

(e) Reinstatement. Any attorney who has been suspended or precluded from appearing in this court or whose name has been struck from the roll of the members of the bar of this court may apply in writing to the chief judge, for good cause shown, for the lifting of the suspension or preclusion or for reinstatement to the rolls. The chief judge shall refer such application to the Committee on Grievances. The Committee on Grievances may refer the application to a magistrate judge or hearing panel of attorneys (who may be the same magistrate judge or panel of attorneys who previously heard the matter) for findings and recommendations, or may act upon the application without making such a referral.

(f) Remedies for Misconduct. The remedies provided by this rule are in addition to the remedies available to individual judges and magistrate judges under applicable law with respect to lawyers appearing before them. Individual judges and magistrate judges may also refer any matter to the chief judge for referral to the Committee on Grievances to consider the imposition of discipline or other relief pursuant to this rule.

(g) Notice to Other Courts. When an attorney is known to be admitted to practice in the court of any state or territory, or in any other federal court, and has been convicted of any crime or disbarred, precluded from appearing, suspended or censured in this court, the clerk shall send to such other court or courts a certified copy of the judgment of conviction or order of disbarment, preclusion, suspension or censure, a certified copy of the court's opinion, if any, and a statement of the attorney's last known office and residence address.

Rule 1.6.   Duty of Attorneys in Related Cases

(a) It shall be the continuing duty of each attorney appearing in any civil or criminal case to bring promptly to the attention of the clerk all facts which said attorney believes are relevant to a determination that said case and one or more pending civil or criminal cases should be heard by the same judge, in order to avoid unnecessary duplication of judicial effort. As soon as the attorney becomes aware of such relationship, said attorney shall notify the clerk in writing, who shall transmit that notification to the judges to whom the cases have been assigned.

(b) If counsel fails to comply with Local Civil Rule 1.6(a), the court may assess reasonable costs directly against counsel whose action has obstructed the effective administration of the court's business.

Rule 1.7.   Fees of Clerks and Reporters

(a) The clerk shall not be required to render any service for which a fee is prescribed by statute or by the Judicial Conference of the United States unless the fee for the particular service is paid to the clerk in advance or the court orders otherwise.

(b) Every attorney appearing in any proceeding who orders a transcript of any trial, hearing, or any other proceeding, is obligated to pay the cost thereof to the court reporters of the court upon rendition of the invoice unless at the time of such order, the attorney, in writing, advises the court reporter that only the client is obligated to pay.

Rule 1.8.   Photographs, Radio, Recordings, Television

No one other than court officials engaged in the conduct of court business shall bring any camera, transmitter, receiver, portable telephone or recording device into any courthouse or its environs without written permission of a judge of that court.

Environs as used in this rule shall include the entire United States Courthouse property, including all entrances to and exits from the buildings.

Rule 1.9. Disclosure of Interested Parties

To enable judges and magistrate judges of the court to evaluate possible disqualification or recusal, counsel for a private (non-governmental) party shall submit at the time of filing the initial pleading or other court paper on behalf of that party a certificate of identification of any corporate or other parents, subsidiaries, or affiliates of that party, securities or other interests in which are publicly held.

Rule 1.10. Acceptable Substitutes for Affidavits

In situations in which any local rule provides for an affidavit or a verified statement, the following are acceptable substitutes: (a) a statement subscribed under penalty of perjury as prescribed in 28 U.S.C. § 1746; or (b) if accepted by the court as a substitute for an affidavit or a verified statement, (1) a statement signed by an attorney or by a party not represented by an attorney pursuant to Federal Rule of Civil Procedure 11, or (2) an oral representation on the record in open court.

Rule 5.1. Filing of Discovery Materials

(a) Depositions and notices of deposition, subpoenas, interrogatories, requests for documents, requests for admissions, and answers and responses thereto, and other discovery requests and materials produced in pretrial disclosure and discovery, shall not be filed with the clerk's office except by order of the court.

(b) A party seeking relief under Rules 26 through 37 inclusive of the Federal Rules of Civil Procedure shall quote or attach only those portions of the depositions, interrogatories, requests for documents, requests for admissions, or other discovery or disclosure materials that are the subject of the motion, together with the objections there to.

(c) When discovery or disclosure material not on file is needed for an appeal, upon an order of the court, the necessary portion of that material shall be filed with the clerk.

Rule 6.1. Service and Filing of Motion Papers

Unless otherwise provided by statute or rule, or unless otherwise ordered by the court in an individual rule or in a direction in a particular case, upon any motion, the notice of motion, supporting affidavits, and memoranda shall be served and filed as follows:

(a) On all motions and exceptions under Rules 26 through 37 inclusive and Rule 45(c)(3) of the Federal Rules of Civil Procedure, (1) the notice of motion, supporting affidavits, and memoranda of law shall be served by the moving party on all other parties that have appeared in the action, (2) any opposing affidavits and answering memoranda of law shall be served within four business days after service of the moving papers, and (3) any reply affidavits and reply memoranda of law shall be served within one business day after service of the answering papers.

(b) On all civil motions, petitions, applications, and exceptions other than those described in Rule 6.1(a), and other than petitions for writs of habeas corpus, (1) the notice of motion, supporting affidavits, and memoranda of law shall be served by the moving party on all other parties that have appeared in the action, (2) any opposing affidavits and answering memoranda shall be served within ten business days after service of the moving papers, and (3) any reply affidavits and memoranda of law shall be served within five business days after service of the answering papers.

(c) The parties and their attorneys shall only appear to argue the motion if so directed by the court by order or by individual rule or upon application.

(d) No ex parte order, or order to show cause to bring on a motion, will be granted except upon a clear and specific showing by affidavit of good and sufficient reasons why a procedure other than by notice of motion is necessary, and stating whether a previous application for similar relief has been made.

Rule 6.2.   Orders on Motions

A memorandum signed by the court of the decision on a motion that does not finally determine all claims for relief, or an oral decision on such a motion, shall constitute the order unless the memorandum or oral decision directs the submission or settlement of an order in more extended form.   The notation in the docket of a memorandum or oral decision that does not direct the submission or settlement of an order in more extended form shall constitute the entry of the order.   Where an order in more extended form is required to be submitted or settled, the notation in the docket of such order shall constitute the entry of the order.

Rule 6.3.   Motions for Reconsideration or Reargument

A notice of motion for reconsideration or reargument shall be served within ten (10) days after the docketing of the court's determination of the original motion.   There shall be served with the notice of motion a memorandum setting forth concisely the matters or controlling decisions which counsel believes the court has overlooked.   The time periods for the service of answering and reply memoranda, if any, shall be governed by Local Civil Rule 6.1(a) or (b), as in the case of the original motion. No oral argument shall be heard unless the court directs that the matter shall be reargued orally.   No affidavits shall be filed by any party unless directed by the court.

Rule 6.4. Computation of Time

In computing any period of time prescribed or allowed by the Local Civil Rules or the Local Admiralty and Maritime Rules, the provisions of Federal Rule of Civil Procedure 6(a) and 6(e) shall apply unless otherwise stated.

Rule 7.1. Memoranda of Law

Except as otherwise permitted by the court, all motions and all oppositions thereto shall be supported by a memorandum of law, setting forth the points and authorities relied upon in support of or in opposition to the motion, and divided, under appropriate headings, into as many parts as there are points to be determined. Willful failure to comply with this rule may be deemed sufficient cause for the denial of a motion or for the granting of a motion by default.

Rule 7.2. Specification of Statutes or Rules

Upon any motion based upon rules or statutes, the notice of motion or order to show cause shall specify the rules or statutes upon which the motion is predicated.

Rule 11.1. Forum of Pleadings, Motions, and Other Papers

(a) Every pleading, written motion, and other paper must (1) be plainly written, typed, printed, or copied without erasures or interlineations which materially de face it, (2) bear the docket number and the initials of the judge and any magistrate judge before whom the action or proceeding is pending, and (3) have the name of each person signing it clearly printed or typed directly below the signature.

(b) Every pleading, written motion, and other paper that is signed by an attorney must show directly after the typed name of the attorney (1) the initials of the attorney's first and last name, and (2) the last four digits of the attorney's social security number, or any other four-digit number registered by the attorney with the clerk of the court.

Rule 16.1. Exemptions from Mandatory Scheduling Order

Matters involving habeas corpus petitions, social security disability cases, motions to vacate sentences, forfeitures, and reviews from administrative agencies are exempted from the mandatory scheduling order required by Federal Rule of Civil Procedure 16(b).

Rule 16.2. Entry and Modification of Mandatory Scheduling Orders by Magistrate Judges

In any case referred to a magistrate judge by a district judge, the magistrate judge may make scheduling orders pursuant to Federal Rule of Civil Procedure 16(b), and may modify for good cause shown scheduling orders previously entered.

Rule 23.1. Fees in Stockholder and Class Actions

Fees for attorneys or others shall not be paid upon recovery or compromise in a derivative or class action on behalf of a corporation or class except as allowed by the court after a hearing upon such notice as the court may direct. The notice shall include a statement of the names and addresses of the applicants for such fees and the amounts requested respectively and shall disclose any fee sharing agreements with anyone. Where the court directs notice of a hearing upon a proposed voluntary dismissal or settlement of a derivative or class action, the above information as to the applications shall be included in the notice.

Rule 24.1. Notice of Claim of Unconstitutionality

(a) If, in any action to which neither the United States nor any agency, officer or employee thereof is a party, a party draws in question the constitutionality of an act of Congress affecting the public interest, such party shall notify the court in writing of the existence of such question so as to enable the court to comply with 28 U.S.C. § 2403(a).

(b) If, in any action to which neither a State nor any agency, officer or employee thereof is a party, a party draws in question the constitutionality of a statute of such State affecting the public interest, such party shall notify the court in writing of the existence of such question so as to enable the court to comply with 28 U.S.C. § 2403(b).

Rule 26.1. Address of Party and Original Owner of Claim to Be Furnished

A party shall furnish to any other party, within five (5) days after a demand, a verified statement setting forth that party's post office address and residence, and like information as to partners if a partnership is involved and, if a corporation or an unincorporated association, the name, post office addresses and residences of its principal officers. In the case of an assigned claim, the statement shall include the post office address and residence of the original owner of the claim and of any assignee.

Rule 26.2. Assertion of Claim of Privilege

(a) Where a claim of privilege is asserted in objecting to any means of discovery or disclosure, including but not limited to a deposition, and an answer is not provided on the basis of such assertion.

(1) the attorney asserting the privilege shall identify the nature of the privilege (including work product) which is being claimed and, if the privilege is governed by state law, indicate the state's privilege rule being invoked; and

(2) the following information shall be provided in the objection, unless divulgence of such information would cause disclosure of the allegedly privileged information:

(A) for documents: (i) the type of document, e.g., letter or memorandum; (ii) the general subject matter of the document; (iii) the date of the document; and (iv) such other information as is sufficient to identify the document for a subpoena duces tecum, including, where appropriate, the author of the document, the addressees of the document, and any other recipients shown in the document, and, where not apparent, the relationship of the author, addressees, and recipients to each other;

(B) for oral communications: (i) the name of the person making the communication and the names of persons present while the communication was made and, where not apparent, the relationship of the persons present to the person making the communication; (ii) the date and place of communication; and (iii) the general subject matter of the communication.

(b) Where a claim of privilege is asserted during a deposition, and information is not provided on the basis of such assertion, the information set forth in paragraph (a) above shall be furnished (1) at the deposition, to the extent it is readily available from the witness being deposed or otherwise, and (2) to the extent the information is not readily available at the deposition, in writing within ten business days after the deposition session at which the privilege is asserted, unless otherwise ordered by the court.

(c) Where a claim of privilege is asserted in response to discovery or disclosure other than a deposition, and information is not provided on the basis of such assertion, the information set forth in paragraph (a) above shall be furnished in writing at the time of the response to such discovery or disclosure, unless otherwise ordered by the court.

Rule 26.3. Uniform Definitions in Discovery Requests

(a) The full text of the definitions and rules of construction set forth in paragraphs (c) and (d) is deemed incorporated by reference into all discovery requests. No discovery request shall use broader definitions or rules of construction than those set forth in paragraphs (c) and (d). This rule shall not preclude (1) the definition of other terms specific to the particular litigation, (2) the use of abbreviations, or (3) a more narrow definition of a term defined in paragraph (c).

(b) This rule is not intended to broaden or narrow the scope of discovery permitted by the Federal Rules of Civil Procedure.

(c) The following definitions apply to all discovery requests:

(1) *Communication.* The term "communication" means the transmittal of information (in the form of facts, ideas, inquiries or otherwise)

(2) *Document.* The term "document" is defined to be synonymous in meaning and equal in scope to the usage of this term in Federal Rule of Civil Procedure 34(a), including, without limitation, electronic or computerized data compilations. A draft or nonidentical copy is a separate document within the meaning of this term.

(3) *Identify (with respect to persons).* When referring to a person, "to identify" means to give, to the extent known, the person's full name, present or last known address, and when referring to a natural person, additionally, the present or last known place of employment. Once a person has been identified in accordance with this subparagraph, only the name of that person need be listed in response to subsequent discovery requesting the identification of that person.

(4) *Identify (with respect to documents).* When referring to documents, "to identify" means to give, to the extent known, the (i) type of document; (ii) general subject matter; (iii) date of the document; and (iv) author(s), addressee(s) and recipient(s).

(5) *Parties.* The terms "plaintiff" and "defendant" as well as a party's full or abbreviated name or a pronoun referring to a party mean the party and, where applicable, its officers, directors, employees, partners, corporate parent, subsidiaries or affiliates. This definition is not intended to impose a discovery obligation on any person who is not a party to the litigation.

(6) *Person.* The term "person" is defined as any natural person or any business, legal or governmental entity or association.

(7) *Concerning.* The term "concerning" means relating to, referring to, describing, evidencing or constituting.

(d) The following rules of construction apply to all discovery requests:

(1) *All/Each.* The terms "all" and "each" shall be construed as all and each.

(2) *And/Or.* The connectives "and" and "or" shall be construed either disjunctively or conjunctively as necessary to bring within the scope of the discovery request all responses that might otherwise be construed to be outside of its scope.

(3) *Number.* The use of the singular form of any word includes the plural and vice versa.

Rule 26.4. Opt–Out From Certain Provisions of Federal Rule of Civil Procedure 26 (Southern District Only)

(a) Federal Rules of Civil Procedure 26(a)(1) and 26(d) (first sentence only) are not operative in this District.

(b) Since Federal Rule of Civil Procedure 26(d) (first sentence only) is not operative in this District, Rules 26(f) (insofar only as it relates to disclosures under Rule 26(a)(1)) and 26(g)(1) (insofar only as it relates to disclosures under Rule 26(a)(1)) are not applicable in this District.

Rule 26.5. Cooperation Among Counsel in Discovery (Eastern District Only)

Counsel are expected to cooperate with each other, consistent with the interests of their clients, in all phases of the discovery process and to be courteous in their dealings with each other, including in matters relating to scheduling and timing of various discovery procedures.

Rule 26.6. Form Discovery Requests (Eastern District Only)

Attorneys using form discovery requests shall review them to ascertain that they are relevant to the subject matter involved in the particular case. Discovery requests which are not relevant to the subject matter involved in the particular case shall not be used.

Rule 26.7. Discovery Requests to Be Read Reasonably (Eastern District Only)

Discovery requests shall be read reasonably in the recognition that the attorney serving them generally does not have the information being sought and the attorney receiving them generally does have such information or can obtain it from the client.

Rule 30.1. Counsel Fees on Taking Depositions More Than 100 Miles From Courthouse

When a proposed deposition upon oral examination, including a deposition before action or pending appeal, is sought to be taken at a place more than one hundred (100) miles from the courthouse, the court may by order provide that prior to the examination, the applicant pay the expense (including a reasonable counsel fee) of the attendance of one attorney for each adversary party at the place where the deposition is to be taken. The amounts so paid, unless otherwise directed by the court, shall be a taxable cost in the event that the applicant recovers costs of the action or proceeding.

Rule 30.2. Opt–Out From Certain Provisions of Federal Rule of Civil Procedure 30 (Southern District Only)

(a) Federal Rule of Civil Procedure 30(a)(2)(A) is not operative in this District.

(b) Since Federal Rule of Civil Procedure 26(d) (first sentence only) is not operative in this District, Rule 30(a)(2)(C) is not applicable in this District.

Rule 30.3. Telephonic Depositions (Eastern District Only)

The motion of a party to take the deposition of an adverse party by telephone will presumptively be granted. Where the opposing party is a corporation, the term "adverse party" means an officer, director, managing agent or corporate designee pursuant to Federal Rule of Civil Procedure 30(b)(6).

Rule 30.4. Persons Attending Depositions (Eastern District Only)

A person who is a party in the action may attend the deposition of a party or witness. A witness or potential witness in the action may attend the deposition of a party or witness unless otherwise ordered by the court.

Rule 30.5. Depositions of Witnesses Who Have No Knowledge of the Facts (Eastern District Only)

(a) Where an officer, director or managing agent of a corporation or a governmental official is served with a notice of deposition or subpoena regarding a matter about which he or she has no knowledge, he or she may submit reasonably before the date noticed for the deposition an affidavit to the noticing party so stating and identifying a person within the corporation or government entity having knowledge of the subject matter involved in the pending action.

(b) The noticing party may, notwithstanding such affidavit of the noticed witness, proceed with the deposition, subject to the witness's right to seek a protective order.

Rule 30.6. Conferences Between Deponent and Defending Attorney (Eastern District Only)

An attorney for a deponent shall not initiate a private conference with the deponent during the actual taking of a deposition, except for the purpose of determining whether a privilege should be asserted.

Rule 30.7. Document Production at Depositions (Eastern District Only)

Consistent with the requirements of Federal Rules of Civil Procedure 30 and 34, a party seeking production of documents of another party in connection with a deposition should schedule the deposition to allow for the production of the documents in advance of the deposition. If documents which have been so requested are not produced prior to the deposition, the party noticing the deposition may either adjourn the deposition until after such documents are produced or, without waiving the right to have access to the documents, may proceed with the deposition.

Rule 31.1. Opt–Out From Certain Provisions of Federal Rule of Civil Procedure 31 (Southern District Only)

(a) Federal Rule of Civil Procedure 31(a)(2)(A) is not operative in this District.

(b) Since Federal Rule of Civil Procedure 26(d) (first sentence only) is not operative in this District, Rule 31(a)(2)(C) is not applicable in this District.

Rule 33.1. Answering Interrogatory by Reference to Records

Whenever a party answers any interrogatory by reference to records from which the answer may be derived or ascertained, as permitted in Federal Rule of Civil Procedure 33(d):

(a) The specifications of documents to be produced shall be in sufficient detail to permit the interrogating party to locate and identify the records and to ascertain the answer as readily as could the party from whom discovery is sought.

(b) The producing party shall also make available any computerized information or summaries thereof that it either has, or can adduce by a relatively simple procedure, unless these materials are privileged or otherwise immune from discovery.

(c) The producing party shall also provide any relevant compilations, abstracts or summaries in its custody or readily obtainable by it, unless these materials are privileged or otherwise immune from discovery.

(d) Unless otherwise ordered by the court, the documents shall be made available for inspection and copying within ten days after service of the answers to interrogatories or at a date agreed upon by the parties.

Rule 33.2. Standard Discovery in Prisoner Pro Se Actions

(a) This rule shall apply in any action commenced pro se in which the plaintiff's complaint includes any claim described in paragraph (b) of this rule and in which the named defendants include one or more current or former employees of New York State or New York City sued in matters arising out of events alleged to have occurred while the plaintiff was in the custody of either the Department of Corrections of the City of New York or the New York State Department of Correctional Services. In each such action in the Southern District of New York, such defendants shall, except as otherwise set forth herein, respond to the standing discovery requests adopted by the court, in accordance with the instructions and definitions set forth in the standing requests, unless otherwise ordered by the court. In each such action in the Eastern District of New York, such defendants shall respond to the standing discovery requests if so ordered by the court.

(b) The claims to which the standard discovery requests shall apply are Use of Force Cases, Inmate Against Inmate Assault Cases and Disciplinary Due Process Cases, as defined below, in which the events alleged in the complaint have occurred while the plaintiff was in the custody of either the Department of Corrections of the City of New York or the New York State Department of Correctional Services.

(1) "Use of Force Case" refers to an action in which the complaint alleges that any employee of the Department used physical force against the plaintiff in violation of the plaintiff's rights.

(2) "Inmate against Inmate Assault Case" refers to an action in which the complaint alleges that any defendant was responsible for the plaintiff's injury resulting from physical contact with another inmate.

(3) "Disciplinary Due Process Case" refers to an action in which (i) the complaint alleges that a defendant violated or permitted the violation of a right or rights in a disciplinary proceeding against plaintiff, and (ii) the punishment imposed upon plaintiff as a result of that proceeding was placement in a special housing unit for more than thirty days.

(c) Responses to the requests shall be made on behalf of the individual defendants, but shall be made on the basis of information and documents within the possession, custody or control of the City or State of New York in accordance with the instructions contained in the requests. If no defendant is represented by the Office of Corporation Counsel of the City of New York or the New York State Department of Law, responses based upon such information need not be made pursuant to this local rule, without prejudice to such other discovery procedures as the plaintiff shall initiate.

(d) The two requests, denominated Plaintiff's First and Second Set of Interrogatories and Requests for Production of Documents, shall be answered within 90 and 150 days of service of the complaint respectively except (i) as otherwise ordered by the court for good cause shown, which shall be based upon the facts and procedural status of the particular case and not upon a generalized claim of burden, expense or relevance or (ii) as otherwise provided in the instructions to the requests. The responses to the requests shall be served upon the plaintiff and shall be filed with the Pro Se Office of the court. Copies of the requests are available through the Pro Se Office of the court.

(e) Except upon permission of the court, for good cause shown, the requests shall constitute the sole form of discovery available to plaintiff during the 150 day period as designated above.

(f) If the Pro Se Office determines that this rule applies, it shall provide copies of the standard requests to those pro se plaintiffs for service upon defendants together with the summons and complaint.

Rule 33.3. Interrogatories (Southern District Only)

(a) Unless otherwise ordered by the court, at the commencement of discovery, interrogatories will be restricted to those seeking names of witnesses with knowledge of information relevant to the subject matter of the action, the computation of each category of damage alleged, and the existence, custodian, location and general description of relevant documents, including pertinent insurance agreements, and other physical evidence, or information of a similar nature.

(b) During discovery, interrogatories other than those seeking information described in paragraph (a) above may only be served (1) if they are a more practical method of obtaining the information sought than a request for production or a deposition, or (2) if ordered by the court.

(c) At the conclusion of other discovery, and at least 30 days prior to the discovery cut-off date, interrogatories seeking the claims and contentions of the opposing party may be served unless the court has ordered otherwise.

Rule 33.4. Opt–Out From Certain Provisions of Federal Rule of Civil Procedure 33 (Southern District Only)

(a) Federal Rule of Civil Procedure 33(a) (only insofar as it limits the number of interrogatories) is not operative in this District.

(b) Since Federal Rule of Civil Procedure 26(d) (first sentence only) is not operative in this District, Rule 33(a) (third sentence only) is not applicable in this District.

Rule 34.1. Opt–Out From Certain Provisions of Federal Rule of Civil Procedure 34 (Southern District Only)

Since Federal Rule of Civil Procedure 26(d) (first sentence only) is not operative in this District, Rule 34(b) (third sentence only) is not applicable in this District.

Rule 36.1. Opt–Out From Certain Provisions of Federal Rule of Civil Procedure 36 (Southern District Only)

Since Federal Rule of Civil Procedure 26(d) (first sentence only) is not operative in this District, Rule 36(a) (third sentence only) is not applicable in this District.

Rule 37.1. Verbatim Quotation of Interrogatories, Requests for Admissions, and Objections or Exceptions

Upon any motion involving objections or exceptions addressed to interrogatories, answers to interrogatories or requests for admissions, under Rule 37(a) of the Federal Rules of Civil Procedure, the moving party shall specify and quote or set forth verbatim in the motion papers (a) each interrogatory, answer or request to which the objection or exception is taken, and, immediately thereafter, (b) the objection or exception to such interrogatory, answer or request. The motion shall also set forth the grounds upon which the moving party is entitled to prevail as to each interrogatory, answer or request to which the objection or exception is taken.

Rule 37.2. Mode of Raising Discovery Disputes With the Court (Southern District Only)

No motion under Rules 26 through 37 inclusive of the Federal Rules of Civil Procedure shall be heard unless counsel for the moving party has first requested an informal conference with the court and such request has either been denied or the discovery dispute has not been resolved as a consequence of such a conference.

Rule 37.3. Mode of Raising Discovery and Other Non–Dispositive Pretrial Disputes With the Court (Eastern District Only)

(a) Premotion Conference. Prior to seeking judicial resolution of a discovery or non-dispositive pretrial dispute, the attorneys for the affected parties or non-party witness shall attempt to confer in good faith in person or by telephone in an effort to resolve the dispute.

(b) Disputes Arising During Depositions. Where the attorneys for the affected parties or a non-party witness cannot agree on a resolution of a discovery dispute that arises during a deposition, they shall, to the extent practicable, notify the court by telephone and seek a ruling while the deposition is in progress. If a prompt ruling cannot be obtained, and the dispute involves an instruction to the witness not to answer a question, the instruction not to answer may stand and the deposition shall continue until a ruling is obtained pursuant to the procedure set forth in paragraph (c) below.

(c) Other Discovery and Non–Dispositive Pretrial Disputes. Where the attorneys for the affected parties or non-party witness cannot agree on a resolution of any other discovery dispute or non-dispositive pretrial dispute, or if they are unable to obtain a telephonic ruling on a discovery dispute that arises during a deposition as provided in paragraph (b) above, they shall notify the court, at the option of the attorney for any affected party or non-party witness, either by telephone conference with all affected parties on the line or by letter not exceeding three pages in length outlining the nature of the dispute and attaching relevant materials. Within three days of receiving such a letter, any opposing affected party or non-party witness may submit a responsive letter not exceeding three pages attaching relevant materials. Except for the letters and attachments authorized herein, or where a ruling which was made exclusively as a result of a telephone conference is the subject of de novo review pursuant to paragraph (d) hereof, papers shall not be submitted with respect to a dispute governed by this rule unless the court has so directed.

(d) Motion for Reconsideration. A ruling made exclusively as a result of a telephone conference may be the subject of de novo reconsideration by a letter not exceeding five pages in length attaching relevant materials submitted by any affected party or non-party witness. Within three days of receiving such a letter, any other affected party or non-party witness may submit a responsive letter not exceeding five pages in length attaching relevant materials.

(e) Decision of the Court. The court shall record or arrange for the recording of the court's decision in writing. Such written order may take the form of an oral order read into the record of a deposition or other proceeding, a handwritten memorandum, a handwritten marginal notation on a letter or other document, or any other form the court deems appropriate.

Rule 39.1. Custody of Exhibits

(a) Except in proceedings before a master or commissioner, and unless the court orders otherwise, exhibits shall not be filed with the clerk, but shall be retained in the custody of the respective attorneys who produced them in court.

(b) Exhibits which have been filed with the clerk shall be removed by the party responsible for them (1) if no appeal is taken, within ninety (90) days after a final decision is rendered, or (2) if an appeal has been taken, within thirty (30) days after the final disposition of the appeal. Parties failing to comply with this rule shall be notified by the clerk to remove their exhibits and upon their failure to do so within thirty (30) days, the clerk may dispose of them as the clerk may see fit.

Rule 39.2. Order of Summation

After the close of evidence in civil trials, the order of summation shall be determined in the discretion of the court.

Rule 47.1. Assessment of Jury Costs

All counsel in civil cases shall seriously discuss the possibility of settlement a reasonable time prior to trial. The court may, in its discretion, assess the parties or counsel with the cost of one day's attendance of the jurors if a case is settled after the jury has been summoned or during trial, the amount to be paid to the clerk of the court. For purposes of this rule, a civil jury is considered summoned for a trial as of Noon of the business day prior to the designated date of the trial.

Rule 53.1.   Masters

(a) Oath. Every person appointed master, special master, commissioner, special commissioner, assessor or appraiser shall before entering upon those duties take and subscribe an oath, which, except as otherwise prescribed by statute or rule, shall be the same as the oath prescribed for judges pursuant to 28 U.S.C. § 453, with the addition of the words "in conformance with the order of appointment" after the words "administer justice." Such an oath may be taken before any federal or state officer authorized by federal law to administer oaths, and shall be filed in the office of the clerk.

(b) Agreement on a Master. Upon a stipulation by the parties to a civil action, either in writing or upon the record in open court, the court may appoint a master to report on particular issues, or upon all the issues. The stipulation may suggest the master, in which case the court may appoint the person named. The procedure covering such a reference shall be the same as that governing any other reference to a master.

(c) May Sit Outside District. A master may sit within or outside the district. When the master is requested to sit outside the district for the convenience of a party and there is opposition by another party, the master may make an order for the holding of the hearing, or a part thereof, outside the district, upon such terms and conditions as shall be just. Such order may be reviewed by the court upon motion of any party, served within ten (10) days after service on all parties by the master of the order.

Rule 54.1.   Taxable Costs

(a) Request to Tax Costs. Within thirty (30) days after the entry of final judgment, or, in the case of an appeal by any party, within thirty (30) days after the final disposition of the appeal, unless this period is extended by the court for good cause shown, any party seeking to recover costs shall file with the clerk a request to tax costs annexing a bill of costs and indicating the date and time of taxation. Costs will not be taxed during the pendency of any appeal. Any party failing to file a request to tax costs within this thirty (30) day period will be deemed to have waived costs. The request to tax costs shall be served upon each other party not less than three (3) days (if service is made by hand delivery) or six (6) days (if service is made by any means other than hand delivery) before the date and time fixed for taxation. The bill of costs shall include an affidavit that the costs claimed are allowable by law, are correctly stated and were necessarily incurred. Bills for the costs claimed shall be attached as exhibits.

(b) Objections to Bill of Costs. A party objecting to any cost item shall serve objections in writing prior to or at the time for taxation. The clerk will proceed to tax costs at the time noticed and allow such items as are properly taxable. In the absence of written objection, any item listed may be taxed within the discretion of the clerk.

(c) Items Taxable as Costs.

(1) *Transcripts.* The cost of any part of the original trial transcript that was necessarily obtained for use in this court or on appeal is taxable. The cost of a transcript of court proceedings prior to or subsequent to trial is taxable only when authorized in advance or ordered by the court.

(2) *Depositions.* Unless otherwise ordered by the court, the original transcript of a deposition, plus one copy, is taxable if the deposition was used or received in evidence at the trial, whether or not it was read in its entirety. Costs for depositions are also taxable if they were used by the court in ruling on a motion for summary judgment or other dispositive substantive motion. Costs for depositions taken solely for discovery are not taxable. Counsel's fees and expenses in attending the taking of a deposition are not taxable except as provided by statute, rule (including Local Civil Rule 30.1), or order of the court. Fees, mileage, and subsistence for the witness at the deposition are taxable at the same rates as for attendance at trial if the deposition taken was used or received in evidence at the trial.

(3) *Witness Fees, Mileage and Subsistence.* Witness fees and mileage pursuant to 28 U.S.C. § 1821 are taxable if the witness testifies. Subsistence pursuant to 28 U.S.C. § 1821 is taxable if the witness testifies and it is not practical for the witness to return to his or her residence from day to day. No party to the action may receive witness fees, mileage, or subsistence. Fees for expert witnesses are taxable only to the extent of fees for ordinary witnesses unless prior court approval was obtained.

(4) *Interpreting Costs.* The reasonable fee of a competent interpreter, and the reasonable cost of special interpretation services pursuant to 28 U.S.C. § 1828, are taxable if the fee of the witness involved is taxable. The reasonable fee of a translator is also taxable if the document translated is used or received in evidence.

(5) *Exemplifications and Copies of Papers.* A copy of an exhibit is taxable if the original was not available and the copy was used or received in evidence. The cost of copies used for the convenience of counsel or the court are not taxable. The fees for a search and certification or proof of the non-existence of a document in a public office is taxable.

(6) *Maps, Charts, Models, Photographs and Summaries.* The cost of photographs, 8″ × 10″ in size or less, is taxable if used or received in evidence. Enlargements greater than 8″ × 10″ are not taxable except by order of court. Costs of maps, charts, and models,

including computer generated models, are not taxable except by order of court. The cost of compiling summaries, statistical comparisons and reports is not taxable.

(7) *Attorney Fees and Related Costs.* Attorney fees and disbursements and other related fees and paralegal expenses are not taxable except by order of the court.

(8) *Fees of Masters, Receivers, Commissioners and Court Appointed Experts.* Fees of masters, receivers, commissioners, and court appointed experts are taxable as costs, unless otherwise ordered by the court.

(9) *Costs for Title Searches.* A party is entitled to tax necessary disbursements for the expenses of searches made by title insurance, abstract or searching companies, or by any public officer authorized to make official searches and certify to the same, taxable at rates not exceeding the cost of similar official searches.

(10) *Docket and Miscellaneous Fees.* Docket fees, and the reasonable and actual fees of the clerk and of a marshal, sheriff, and process server, are taxable unless otherwise ordered by the court.

Rule 54.2.   Security for Costs

The court, on motion or on its own initiative, may order any party to file an original bond for costs or additional security for costs in such an amount and so conditioned as it may designate. For failure to comply with the order the court may make such orders in regard to noncompliance as are just, and among others the following: an order striking out pleadings or staying further proceedings until the bond is filed or dismissing the action or rendering a judgment by default against the non-complying party.

Rule 54.3.   Entering Satisfaction of Money Judgment

Satisfaction of a money judgment recovered or registered in this district shall be entered by the clerk as follows:

(a) upon the payment into the court of the amount thereof, plus interest, and the payment of the clerk's and marshal's fees, if any;

(b) upon the filing of a satisfaction executed and acknowledged by: (1) the judgment creditor; or (2) the judgment creditor's legal representatives or assigns, with evidence of their authority; or (3) the judgment creditor's attorney if within ten (10) years of the entry of the judgment or decree;

(c) if the judgment creditor is the United States, upon the filing of a satisfaction executed by the United States Attorney;

(d) pursuant to an order of satisfaction entered by the court; or

(e) upon the registration of a certified copy of a satisfaction entered in another district.

Rule 55.1. Certificate of Default

A party applying for a certificate of default by the clerk pursuant to Federal Rule of Civil Procedure 55(a) shall submit an affidavit showing (1) that the party against whom a notation of default is sought is not an infant, in the military, or an incompetent person; (2) that the party has failed to plead or otherwise defend the action; and (3) that the pleading to which no response has been made was properly served.

Rule 55.2. Default Judgment

(a) By the Clerk. Upon issuance of a clerk's certificate of default, if the claim to which no response has been made only sought payment of a sum certain, and does not include a request for attorney's fees or other substantive relief, and if a default judgment is sought against all remaining parties to the action, the moving party may request the clerk to enter a default judgment, by submitting an affidavit showing the principal amount due and owing, not exceeding the amount sought in the claim to which no response has been made, plus interest, if any, computed by the party, with credit for all payments received to date clearly set forth, and costs, if any, pursuant to 28 U.S.C. § 1920.

(b) By the Court. In all other cases the party seeking a judgment by default shall apply to the court as described in Federal Rule of Civil Procedure 55(b)(2), and shall append to the application (1) the clerk's certificate of default, (2) a copy of the claim to which no response has been made, and (3) a proposed form of default judgment.

Rule 56.1. Statements of Material Facts on Motion for Summary Judgment

(a) Upon any motion for summary judgment pursuant to Rule 56 of the Federal Rules of Civil Procedure, there shall be annexed to the notice of motion a separate, short and concise statement of the material facts as to which the moving party contends there is no genuine issue to be tried. Failure to submit such a statement may constitute grounds for denial of the motion.

(b) The papers opposing a motion for summary judgment shall include a separate, short and concise statement of the material facts as to which it is contended that there exists a genuine issue to be tried.

(c) All material facts set forth in the statement required to be served by the moving party will be deemed to be admitted unless controverted by the statement required to be served by the opposing party.

(d) Each statement of material fact by a movant or opponent must be followed by citation to evidence which would be admissible, set forth as required by Federal Rule of Civil Procedure 56(e).

Local Civil Rule 56.2. Notice to Pro Se Litigants Opposing Summary Judgment

Any represented party moving for summary judgment against a party proceeding *pro se* shall serve and file as a separate document, together with the papers in support of the motion, a "Notice To Pro Se Litigant Opposing Motion For Summary Judgment" in the form indicated below. Where the pro se party is not the plaintiff, the movant shall amend the form notice as necessary to reflect that fact.

Notice To Pro Se Litigant Opposing Motion For Summary Judgment

The defendant in this case has moved for summary judgment pursuant to Rule 56 of the Federal Rules of Civil Procedure. This means that the defendant has asked the court to decide this case without a trial, based on written materials, including affidavits, submitted in support of the motion. THE CLAIMS YOU ASSERT IN YOUR COMPLAINT MAY BE DISMISSED WITHOUT A TRIAL IF YOU DO NOT RESPOND TO THIS MOTION by filing your own sworn affidavits or other papers as required by Rule 56(e). An affidavit is a sworn statement of fact based on personal knowledge that would be admissible in evidence at trial. The full text of Rule 56 is attached.

In short, Rule 56 provides that you may NOT oppose summary judgment simply by relying upon the allegations in your complaint. Rather, you must submit evidence, such as witness statements or documents, countering the facts asserted by the defendant and raising issues of fact for trial. Any witness statements, which may include your own statements, must be in the form of affidavits. You may submit affidavits that were prepared specifically in response to defendant's motion for summary judgment.

Any issue of fact that you wish to raise in opposition to the motion for summary judgment must be supported by affidavits or by other documentary evidence contradicting the facts asserted by the defendant. If you do not respond to the motion for summary judgment on time with affidavits or documentary evidence contradicting the facts asserted by the defendant, the court may accept defendant's factual assertions as true. Judgment may then be entered in defendant's favor without a trial.

If you have any questions, you may direct them to the Pro Se Office.

Rule 58.1. Remand by an Appellate Court

Any order or judgment of an appellate court, when filed in the office of the clerk of the district court, shall automatically become the order or judgment of the district court and be entered as such by the clerk without further order, except if such order or judgment of the appellate court requires further proceedings in the district court other than a new trial, an order shall be entered making the order or judgment of the appellate court the order or judgment of the district court.

Rule 65.1.1. Sureties

(a) Whenever a bond, undertaking or stipulation is required, it shall be sufficient, except as otherwise prescribed by law, if the instrument is executed by the surety or sureties only.

(b) Except as otherwise provided by law, every bond, undertaking or stipulation must be secured by: (1) the deposit of cash or government bonds in the amount of the bond, undertaking or stipulation; or (2) the undertaking or guaranty of a corporate surety holding a certificate of authority from the Secretary of the Treasury; or (3) the undertaking or guaranty of two individual residents of the district in which the case is pending, each of whom owns real or personal property within the district worth double the amount of the bond, undertaking or stipulation, over all his or her debts and liabilities, and over all obligations assumed by said surety on other bonds, undertakings or stipulations, and exclusive of all legal exemptions.

(c) Except as otherwise provided by law, all bonds, undertakings and stipulations of corporate sureties holding certificates of authority from the Secretary of the Treasury, where the amount of such bonds or undertakings has been fixed by a judge or by court rule or statute, may be approved by the clerk.

(d) In the case of a bond, or undertaking, or stipulation executed by individual sureties, each surety shall attach the surety's affidavit of justification, giving the surety's full name, occupation, residence and business addresses, and showing that the surety is qualified as an individual surety under paragraph (b) of this rule.

(e) Members of the bar who have appeared in the case, administrative officers and employees of the court, the marshal, and the marshal's deputies and assistants, shall not act as a surety in any suit, action or proceeding pending in this court.

(f) Whenever a notice of motion to enforce the liability of a surety upon an appeal or a supersedeas bond is served upon the clerk pursuant to Federal Rule of Appellate Procedure 8(b), the party making such motion shall deposit with the clerk the original, three copies, and one additional copy for each surety to be served.

Rule 67.1. Order for Deposit in Interest–Bearing Account

(a) Whenever a party seeks a court order for money to be deposited by the clerk in an interest-bearing account, the party shall personally deliver the order to the clerk or financial deputy who will inspect the proposed order for proper form and content and compliance with this rule prior to signature by the judge for whom the order is prepared. After the judge has signed the order, the person who obtained the order shall serve the clerk and the financial deputy with a copy of the order signed by the judge.

(b) Proposed orders directing the clerk to invest such funds in an interest-bearing account or other instrument shall include the following:

(1) the exact United States dollar amount of the principal sum to be invested; and

(2) wording which directs the clerk to deduct from the income on the investment a fee equal to ten percent (10%) of the income earned, but not exceeding the fee authorized by the Judicial Conference of the United States and set by the Director of the Administrative Office.

Rule 72.1. Powers of Magistrate Judges

In addition to other powers of magistrate judges:

(a) Full-time magistrate judges are hereby specially designated to exercise the jurisdiction set forth in 28 U.S.C. § 636(c).

(b) Magistrate judges are authorized to entertain ex parte applications by appropriate representatives of the United States government for the issuance of administrative inspection orders or warrants.

(c) Magistrate judges may issue subpoenas, writs of habeas corpus ad testificandum or ad prosequendum or other orders necessary to obtain the presence of parties or witnesses or evidence needed for court proceedings, and may sign in forma pauperis orders.

(d) Matters arising under 28 U.S.C. §§ 2254 and 2255 or challenging the conditions of the confinement of prisoners may be referred to a magistrate judge by the judge to whom the case has been assigned. A magistrate judge may perform any or all of the duties imposed upon a judge by the rules governing such proceedings in the United States district courts. In so doing, a magistrate judge may issue any preliminary orders and conduct any necessary evidentiary hearing or other appropriate proceeding and shall submit to a judge a report containing proposed findings of fact and recommendations for disposition of the matter by the judge. Any order disposing of the petition may only be made by a judge.

Rule 72.2. Reference to Magistrate Judge (Eastern District Only)

(a) **Selection of Magistrate Judge.** A magistrate judge shall be assigned to each case upon the commencement of the action, except in those categories of actions set forth in Local Civil Rule 16.1. In any courthouse in this District in which there is more than one magistrate judge such assignment shall be at random on a rotating basis. Except in multi-district cases and antitrust cases, a magistrate judge so assigned is empowered to act with respect to all non-dispositive pretrial matters unless the assigned district judge orders otherwise.

(b) Orders Affecting Reference. The attorneys for the parties shall be provided with copies of all orders affecting the scope of the reference to the magistrate judge.

Rule 73.1. Consent Jurisdiction Procedure

(a) When a civil action is filed with the clerk, the clerk shall give the filing party notice of the magistrate judge's consent jurisdiction in a form approved by the court, with sufficient copies to be served with the complaint on adversary parties. A copy of such notice shall be attached to any third-party complaint served by a defendant.

(b) When a completed consent form has been filed, the clerk shall forward the form for final approval to the district judge to whom the case was originally assigned. Once the district judge has approved the transfer and returned the consent form to the clerk for filing, the clerk shall reassign the case for all purposes to the magistrate judge previously designated to receive any referrals or to whom the case has previously been referred for any purpose. If no designation or referral has been made, or in the Eastern District upon application of the parties, the clerk shall select a new magistrate judge at random.

Rule 77.1. Submission of Orders, Judgments and Decrees

(a) Proposed orders, judgments and decrees shall be presented to the clerk, and not presented directly to the judge. Unless the form of order, judgment or decree is consented to in writing, or unless the court otherwise directs, three (3) days' notice of settlement is required. One (1) day's notice is required of all counter-proposals. Unless adopted by the court or submitted for docketing by a party in connection with an anticipated appeal, such proposed orders, judgments or decrees shall not form any part of the record of this action.

(b) The party who obtains entry of an order or judgment shall append to or endorse upon it a list of the names of the parties entitled to be notified of the entry thereof and the names and addresses of their respective attorneys.

Rule 81.1. Removal of Cases from State Courts

(a) If the court's jurisdiction is based upon diversity of citizenship, and regardless of whether or not service of process has been effected on all parties, the notice of removal shall set forth (1) in the case of each individual named as a party, the states of citizenship and residence and the address of that party, (2) in the case of each corporation named as a party, the state of incorporation and of its principal place of business, and (3) the date on which each party that has been served was served. If such information or a designated part is unknown to the removing party, the removing party may so state, and in that case plaintiff within twenty (20) days after removal shall file in the office of the clerk a statement of the omitted information.

(b) Unless otherwise ordered by the court, within twenty (20) days after filing the notice of removal, the removing party shall file with the clerk a copy of all records and proceedings in the state court.

Rule 83.1. Transfer of Cases to Another District

In a case ordered transferred from this district, the clerk, unless otherwise ordered, shall upon the expiration of five (5) days mail to the clerk of the court to which the case is transferred (1) certified copies of the court's opinion ordering the transfer, of its order, and of the docket entries in the case, and (2) the originals of all other papers on file in the case.

Rule 83.2. Settlement of Actions by or on Behalf of Infants or Incompetents and Wrongful Death Actions*

(a) Settlement of Actions by or on Behalf of Infants or Incompetents.

(1) An action by or on behalf of an infant or incompetent shall not be settled or compromised, or voluntarily discontinued, dismissed or terminated, without leave of the court embodied in an order, judgment or decree. The proceeding upon an application to settle or compromise such an action shall conform, as nearly as may be, to the New York State statutes and rules, but the court, for cause shown, may dispense with any New York State requirement.

(2) The court shall authorize payment to counsel for the infant or incompetent of a reasonable attorney's fee and proper disbursements from the amount recovered in such an action, whether realized by settlement, execution or otherwise and shall determine the said fee and disbursements, after due inquiry as to all charges against the fund.

(3) The court shall order the balance of the proceeds of the recovery or settlement to be distributed as it deems may best protect the interest of the infant or incompetent.

(b) Settlement of Wrongful Death Actions. In an action for wrongful death:

---

* In the Eastern District only, language has been added to expand both (a) and (b) to cover actions for conscious pain and suffering.

(1) Where required by statute or otherwise, the court shall apportion the avails of the action, and shall approve the terms of any settlement.

(2) The court shall approve an attorney's fee only upon application in accordance with the provisions of the New York State statutes and rules.

Rule 83.3. Habeas Corpus

Unless otherwise provided by statute, applications for a writ of habeas corpus made by persons under the judgment and sentence of a court of the State of New York shall be filed, heard and determined in the district court for the district within which they were convicted and sentenced; provided, however, that if the convenience of the parties and witnesses requires a hearing in a different district, such application may be transferred to any district which is found by the assigned judge to be more convenient. The clerks of the Southern and Eastern District Courts are authorized and directed to transfer such applications to the District herein designated for filing, hearing and determination.

Rule 83.4. Proceedings to Stay the Deportation of Aliens in Deportation and Exclusion Cases

(a) The Petition or Complaint.

(1) Any application to stay an alien's deportation must be verified and, if made by someone other than the alien, must show either that the applicant has been authorized by the alien to make the application, or that the applicant is the parent, child, spouse, brother, sister, attorney or next friend of the alien.

(2) The application must state in detail why the alien's deportation is invalid. This shall include a statement setting forth the reasons why a stay is warranted, including a description of the irreparable harm that the alien will suffer if the application is not granted. The application shall also state in what manner the applicable administrative remedies have been exhausted or why such exhaustion is not required and whether any prior application to the court for the same or similar relief has been made.

(3) The application shall recite the source of the factual allegations it contains. If the Immigration and Naturalization Service has been requested to grant the alien, the alien's attorney or the alien's representative access to the alien's records and access has been refused, the application shall state who made the request to review the records, when and to whom it was made, and by whom access was refused. In the event it is claimed that insufficient time was available to examine the alien's records, the application shall state when the alien was informed of his deportation and why he has been unable to examine the records since that time.

(4) Every application to stay the alien's deportation shall contain the alien's immigration file number or other identifying information supplied to the applicant, and the decision, if any, the alien seeks the court to review. In the event this decision was oral, the application shall state the nature of the relief requested, who denied the request, the reasons for the denial and the date the request was denied.

(5) The application shall also state the basis upon which the applicant believes that this court has jurisdiction over the custodian of the alien.

(b) Commencement of the Proceeding. In any proceeding to stay the deportation of an alien, the original verified petition or complaint shall be filed with the clerk. In addition to service pursuant to Federal Rule of Civil Procedure 4, a copy of the petition or complaint, and application for a writ of habeas corpus or order to show cause shall be delivered to the United States attorney prior to the issuance of any writ or order staying the deportation; if the United States attorney's office is closed, delivery shall be made before 10:00 A.M. the following business day, unless the court otherwise directs.

(c) Procedure for Issuance of an Order or Writ.

(1) In the event the court determines to stay temporarily an alien's deportation, it shall briefly set forth why the order or writ was issued, endorse upon the order or writ the date and time it was issued, and set the matter for prompt hearing on the merits.

(2) All orders or writs temporarily enjoining an alien's expulsion shall expire by their terms within such time after entry, not to exceed ten (10) days, as the court fixes, unless within the time so fixed the order, for good cause shown, is extended for a like period or unless the government consents to an extension for a longer period.

(d) Service of the writ or order upon the United States attorney's office within the time specified by the court shall be sufficient service to stay an alien's deportation.

(e) After delivery of an alien for deportation to the master of a ship or the commanding officer of an airplane, the writ or order staying the alien's deportation shall be addressed to and served upon only such master or commanding officer. Notice to the respondent, or the United States attorney's office, of the allowance of the writ or issuance of the order shall not operate to stay an alien's deportation if the alien is no longer in the government's custody. Service of the writ or order may not be made upon a master after the ship has left on her voyage or upon a commanding officer once the airplane has closed its doors and left the terminal.

Rule 83.5.   Three–Judge Court

Whenever upon an application for injunctive relief counsel is of opinion that the relief is such as may be granted only by a three-judge court, the petition shall so state, and the proposed order to show cause (whether or not containing a stay), or the notice of motion, shall include a request for a hearing before a three-judge court. Upon the convening of a three-judge court, in addition to the original papers on file, there shall be submitted three additional copies of all papers filed with the court.

Rule 83.6.   Publication of Advertisements

(a) All advertisements except notices of sale of real estate or of any interest in land shall be published in a newspaper which has a general circulation in this district or a circulation reasonably calculated to give public notice of a legal publication. The court may direct the publication of such additional advertisement as it may deem advisable.

(b) Unless otherwise ordered, notices for the sale of real estate or of any interest in land shall be published in a newspaper of general circulation in the county in which the real estate or the land in question is located.

Rule 83.7.   Notice of Sale

In any civil action, the notice of any proposed sale of property directed to be made by any order or judgment of the court, unless otherwise ordered by the court, need not set out the terms of sale specified in the order or judgment, and the notice will be sufficient if in substantially the following form:

UNITED STATES DISTRICT COURT
.... **District of New York**

[CAPTION]   [Docket No. and Judge's Initials]

NOTICE OF SALE

Pursuant to .... of the United
(Order of Judgement)
States Court for the .... District of New York, filed in the office of the clerk on
.... in the
(Date)
case entitled ....
(Name and Docket Number)
.... the undersigned will sell at ....

(Place of Sale)

on ....

(Date and Hour of Sale)

the property in said

....

(Order of Judgment)

described and therein directed to be sold, to which

....

(Order or Judgment)

reference is made for the terms of sale and for a description of the property which may be briefly described as follows:

Dated:

_____

Signature and Official Title

The notice need not describe the property by metes and bounds or otherwise in detail and will be sufficient if in general terms it identifies the property by specifying its nature and location. However, it shall state: the approximate acreage of any real estate outside the limits of any town or city; the street, lot and block number of any real estate within any town or city; and a general statement of the character of any improvements upon the property.

Rule 83.8. Filing of Notice of Appeal

A notice of appeal shall state the names of the several parties to the judgment, and the names and addresses of their respective attorneys of record. Upon the filing of the notice of appeal the appellant shall furnish the clerk with three additional copies thereof, as well as a sufficient number of further copies thereof to enable the clerk to comply with the provisions of Federal Rule of Appellate Procedure 3(a).

Rule 83.9. Contempt Proceedings in Civil Cases

(a) A proceeding to adjudicate a person in civil contempt, including a case provided for in Federal Rules of Civil Procedure 37(b)(1) and 37(b)(2)(D), shall be commenced by the service of a notice of motion or order to show cause. The affidavit upon which such notice of motion or order to show cause is based shall set out with particularity the misconduct complained of, the claim, if any, for damages occasioned thereby and such evidence as to the amount of damages as may be available to the moving party. A reasonable counsel fee, necessitated by the contempt proceedings, may be included as an item of damage. Where the alleged contemnor has appeared in the action by an attorney, the notice of motion or order to show cause and the papers upon which it is based may be served upon said attorney; otherwise service shall be made personally, in the manner provided for by the Federal Rules of Civil Procedure for the service of a summons. If an order to show cause is sought, such order may, upon necessity shown, embody a direction to the United States marshal to arrest the alleged contemnor and hold such person unless bail is posted in an amount fixed by the order, conditioned on the appearance of such person in all further proceedings on the motion, and further conditioned that the alleged contemnor will hold himself or herself amenable to all orders of the court for surrender.

(b) If the alleged contemnor puts in issue his or her alleged misconduct or the damages thereby occasioned, said person shall upon demand be entitled to have oral evidence taken, either before the court or before a master appointed by the court. When by law such alleged contemnor is entitled to a trial by jury, said person shall make written demand before the beginning of the hearing on the application; otherwise the alleged contemnor will be deemed to have waived a trial by jury.

(c) If the alleged contemnor is found to be in contempt of court, an order shall be entered (1) reciting or referring to the verdict or findings of fact upon which the adjudication is based; (2) setting forth the amount of damages, if any, to which the complainant is entitled; (3) fixing the fine, if any, imposed by the court, which fine shall include the damages found and naming the person to whom such fine shall be payable; (4) stating any other conditions, the performance of which will operate to purge the contempt; and (5) directing, where appropriate, the arrest of the contemnor by the United States marshal and confinement until the performance of the condition fixed in the order and the payment of the fine, or until the contemnor be otherwise discharged pursuant to law. Upon such an order, no person shall be detained in prison by reason of the non-payment of the fine for a period exceeding six months. A certified copy of the order committing the contemnor shall be sufficient warrant to the marshal for the arrest and confinement of the contemnor. The complainant shall also have the same remedies against the property of the contemnor as if the order awarding the fine were a final judgment.

(d) If the alleged contemnor is found not guilty of the charges, said person shall be discharged from the proceedings and, in the discretion of the court, may have judgment against the complainant for costs and disbursements and a reasonable counsel fee.

Rule 83.10. Court–Annexed Arbitration (Eastern District Only)

* * * [Parts (a), (b), and (c) refer to the selection and compensation of arbitrators.]

(d) Civil Cases Eligible for Compulsory Arbitration.

(1) The Clerk of Court shall, as to all cases filed after January 1, 1986, designate and process for compulsory arbitration all civil cases

(excluding social security cases, tax matters, prisoners' civil rights cases and any action based on an alleged violation of a right secured by the Constitution of the United States or if jurisdiction is based in whole or in part on Title 28, U.S.C. § 1343) wherein money damages only are being sought in an amount not in excess of $150,000.00 exclusive of interest and costs.

(2) The parties may by written stipulation agree that the Clerk of Court shall designate and process for court-annexed arbitration any civil case that is not subject to compulsory arbitration hereunder.

(3) For purposes of this Rule only, in all civil cases damages shall be presumed to be not in excess of $150,000.00 exclusive of interest and costs, unless:

(A) Counsel for plaintiff, at the time of filing the complaint, or in the event of the removal of a case from state court or transfer of a case from another district to this court, within thirty (30) days of the docketing of the case in this district, files a certification with the court that the damages sought exceed $150,000.00, exclusive of interest and costs; or

(B) Counsel for a defendant, at the time of filing a counterclaim or cross-claim files a certification with the court that the damages sought by the counter-claim or cross-claim exceed $150,000.00 exclusive of interest and costs.

(e) Referral to Arbitration.

(1) After an answer is filed in a case determined eligible for arbitration, the arbitration clerk shall send a notice to counsel setting the date and time for the arbitration hearing. The date of the arbitration hearing set forth in the notice shall be approximately four months but in no event later than 120 days from the date the answer was filed, except that the arbitration proceeding shall not, in the absence of the consent of the parties, commence until 30 days after the disposition by the district court of any motion to dismiss the complaint, motion for judgment on the pleadings, motion to join necessary parties, or motion for summary judgment, if the motion was filed during a time period specified by the district court. The 120–day and 30–day periods specified in the preceding sentence may be modified by the court for good cause shown. The notice shall also advise counsel that they may agree to an earlier date for the arbitration hearing provided the arbitration clerk is notified within 30 days of the date of the notice. The notice shall also advise counsel that they have 90 days to complete discovery unless the judge to whom the case has been assigned orders a shorter or longer period for discovery. The judge may refer the case to a magistrate for purposes of discovery. In the event a third party has been brought into the action, this notice shall not be sent until an answer has been filed by the third party.

(2) The court shall, *sua sponte,* or on motion of a party exempt any case from arbitration in which the objectives of arbitration would not be realized

     (A) because the case involve complex or novel issues,

     (B) because legal issues predominate over factual issues, or

     (C) for other good cause.

Application by a party for an exemption from compulsory arbitration shall be made by written letter to the court not exceeding three pages in length, outlining the basis for the request and attaching relevant materials, which shall be submitted no later than 20 days after receipt of the notice to counsel setting forth the date and time for the arbitration hearing. Within three days of receiving such a letter, any opposing affected party may submit a responsive letter not exceeding three pages attaching relevant materials.

(3) Cases not originally designated as eligible for compulsory arbitration, but which in the discretion of the assigned judge, are later found to qualify, may be referred to arbitration. A U.S. District Judge or a U.S. Magistrate Judge, in cases that exceed the arbitration ceiling of $150,000 exclusive of interest and costs, in their discretion, may suggest that the parties should consider arbitration. If the parties are agreeable, an appropriate consent form signed by all parties or their representatives may be entered and filed in the case prior to scheduling an arbitration hearing.

(4) The arbitration shall be held before one arbitrator unless a panel of three arbitrators is requested by a party, in which case one of them shall be designated as chairperson of the panel. If the amount of controversy, exclusive of interest and costs, if $5,000 or less, the arbitration shall be held before a single arbitrator. The arbitration panel shall be chosen at random by the Clerk of the Court from the lawyers who have been duly certified as arbitrators. The arbitration panel shall be scheduled to hear not more than three cases.

(5) The judge to whom the case has been assigned shall, 30 days prior to the date scheduled for the arbitration hearing, sign an order setting forth the date and time of the arbitration hearing and the names of the arbitrators designated to hear the case. If a party has filed a motion for judgment on the pleadings, summary judgment or similar relief, the judge shall not sign the order before ruling on the motion, but the filing of such a motion on or after the date of the order shall not stay the arbitration unless the judge so orders.

(6) Upon entry of the order designating the arbitrators, the arbitration clerk shall send to each arbitrator a copy of all pleadings, including the order designating the arbitrators, and the guidelines for arbitrators.

(7) Persons selected to be arbitrators shall be disqualified for bias or prejudice as provided in Title 28, U.S.C. § 144, and shall disqualify

themselves in any action which they would be required under title 28, U.S.C. § 455 to disqualify themselves if they were a justice, judge, or magistrate.

(f) Arbitration Hearing.

(1) The arbitration hearing shall take place in the United States Courthouse in a courtroom assigned by the arbitration clerk on the date and at the time set forth in the order of the Court. The arbitrators are authorized to change the date and time of the hearing provided the hearing is commenced within 30 days of the hearing date set forth in the order of the Court. Any continuance beyond this 30 day period must be approved by the judge to whom the case has been assigned. The arbitration clerk must be notified immediately of any continuance.

(2) Counsel for the parties shall report settlement of the case to the arbitration clerk and all members of the arbitration panel assigned to the case.

(3) The arbitration hearing may proceed in the absence of any party who, after notice, fails to be present. In the event, however, that a party fails to participate in the arbitration process in a meaningful manner, the Court may impose appropriate sanctions, including, but not limited to, the striking of any demand for a trial de novo filed by that party.

(4) Rule 45 of the Federal Rules of Civil Procedure shall apply to subpoenas for attendance of witnesses and the production of documentary evidence at an arbitration hearing under this Rule. Testimony at an arbitration hearing shall be under oath or affirmation.

(5) The Federal Rules of Evidence shall be used as guides to the admissibility of evidence. Copies or photographs of all exhibits, except those intended solely for impeachment, must be marked for identification and delivered to adverse parties at least ten (10) days prior to the hearing. The arbitrators shall receive exhibits in evidence without formal proof unless counsel has been notified at least five (5) days prior to the hearing that the adverse party intends to raise an issue concerning the authenticity of the exhibit. The arbitrators may refuse to receive in evidence any exhibit, a copy or photograph of which has not been delivered to the adverse party as provided herein.

(6) A party may have a recording and transcript made of the arbitration hearing, but that party shall make all necessary arrangements and bear all expenses thereof.

(g) Arbitration Award and Judgment.

(1) The arbitration award shall be filed with the court promptly after the hearing is concluded and shall be entered as the judgment of the court after the 30 day period for requesting a trial de novo pursuant to Section (g) has expired, unless a party has demanded a trial de novo. The judgment so entered shall be subject to the same provisions of law and shall have the same force and effect as a judgment of the court in a

civil action, except that it shall not be appealable. In a case involving multiple claims and parties, any segregable part of an arbitration award as to which an aggrieved party has not timely demanded a trial de novo shall become part of the final judgment with the same force and effect as a judgment of the court in a civil action, except that it shall not be appealable.

(2) The contents of any arbitration award shall not be made known to any judge who might be assigned the case,

(A) except as necessary for the court to determine whether to assess costs or attorneys fees,

(B) until the district court has entered final judgment in the action or the action has been otherwise terminated, or

(C) except for purposes of preparing the report required by section 903(b) of the Judicial Improvement and Access to Justice Act.

(3) Costs may be taxed as part of any arbitration award pursuant to Title 28, U.S.C. § 1920.

(b) Trial De Novo.

(1) Within 30 days after the arbitration award is entered on the docket, any party may demand in writing a trial de novo in the district court. Such demand shall be filed with the arbitration clerk, and served by the moving party upon all counsel of record or other parties. Withdrawal of a demand for a trial de novo shall not reinstate the arbitrators' award and the case shall proceed as if it had not been arbitrated.

(2) Upon demand for a trial de novo and the payment to the clerk required by paragraph (4) of this section, the action shall be placed on the calendar of the court and treated for all purposes as if it had not been referred to arbitration, and any right of trial by jury that a party would otherwise have shall be preserved inviolate.

(3) At the trial de novo, the court shall not admit evidence that there had been an arbitration proceeding, the nature or amount of the award, or any other matter concerning the conduct of the arbitration proceeding.

(4) Upon making a demand for trial de novo the moving party shall, unless permitted to proceed in forma pauperis, deposit with the clerk of the court an amount equal to the arbitration fees of the arbitrators as provided in Section (b). The sum so deposited shall be returned to the party demanding a trial de novo in the event that party obtains a final judgment, exclusive of interest and costs, more favorable than the arbitration award. If the party demanding a trial de novo does not obtain a more favorable result after trial or if the court determines that the party's conduct in seeking a trial de novo was in bad faith, the sum so deposited shall be paid by the Clerk to the Treasury of the United States.

Rule 83.11. Court–Annexed Mediation (Eastern District Only)

(a) Description. Mediation is a process in which parties and counsel agree to meet with a neutral mediator trained to assist them in settling disputes. The mediator improves communication across party lines, helps parties articulate their interests and understand those of the other party, probes the strengths and weaknesses of each party's legal positions, and identifies areas of agreement and helps generate options for a mutually agreeable resolution to the dispute. In all cases, mediation provides an opportunity to explore a wide range of potential solutions and to address interests that may be outside the scope of the stated controversy or which could not be addressed by judicial action. A hallmark of mediation is its capacity to expand traditional settlement discussions and broaden resolution options, often by exploring litigant needs and interests that may be formally independent of the legal issues in controversy.

(b) Mediation Procedures.

(1) *Eligible cases.* Judges and Magistrate Judges may designate civil cases for inclusion in the mediation program, and when doing so shall prepare an order to that effect. Alternatively, and subject to the availability of qualified mediators, the parties may consent to participation in the mediation program by preparing and executing a stipulation signed by all parties to the action and so-ordered by the Court.

(A) Mediation deadline. Any court order designating a case for inclusion in the mediation program, however arrived at, may contain a deadline not to exceed six months from the date of entry on the docket of that order. This deadline may be extended upon motion to the Court for good cause shown.

(2) *Mediators.* Parties whose case has been designated for inclusion in the mediation program shall be offered the options of (a) using a mediator from the Court's panel, a listing of which is available in the Clerk's Office; (b) selecting a mediator on their own; or (c) seeking the assistance of a reputable neutral ADR organization in the selection of a mediator. * * *

(3) *Scheduling the mediation.* The mediator, however chosen, will contact all attorneys to fix the date and place of the first mediation session, which shall be held within thirty days of the date the mediator was appointed or at such other time as the Court may establish.

(A) The Clerk's Office will provide counsel with copies of the Judge's order referring the case to the mediation program, the Clerk's Office notice of appointment of mediator (if applicable), and a copy of the program procedures.

(4) *Written mediation statements.* No less than seven days prior to the first mediation session, each party shall submit directly to the mediator a mediation statement not to exceed ten pages double-spaced,

not including exhibits, outlining the key facts and legal issues in the case. The statement will also include a description of motions filed and their status, and any other information that will advance settlement prospects or make the mediation more productive. Mediation statements are not briefs and are not filed with the Court, nor shall the assigned Judge or Magistrate Judge have access to them.

(5) *Mediation session(s).* The mediator meets initially with all parties to the dispute and their counsel in a joint session. The mediator may hold mediation sessions in his/her office, or at the Court, or at such other place as the parties and the mediator shall agree. At this meeting, the mediator explains the mediation process and gives each party an opportunity to explain his or her views about the matters in dispute. There is then likely to be discussion and questioning among the parties as well as between the mediator and the parties.

(A) Separate caucuses. At the conclusion of the joint session, the mediator will typically caucus individually with each party. Caucuses permit the mediator and the parties to explore more fully the needs and interests underlying the stated positions. In caucuses the mediator strives to facilitate settlement on matters in dispute and the possibilities for settlement. in some cases the mmy offer specific suggestions for settlement; in other Cases the mediator may help the parties generate creative settlement proposals.

(B) Additional sessions. The mediator may conduct additional joint sessions to promote further direct discussion between the parties, or she/he may continue to work with the parties in private caucuses.

(C) Conclusion. The mediation concludes when the parties reach a mutually acceptable resolution, when the parties fail to reach an agreement, on the date the Judge or Magistrate Judge specified as the mediation deadline in their designation order, or in the event no such date has been specified by the Court, at such other time as the parties and/or the mediator may determine. The mediator has no power to impose settlement and the mediation process is confidential, whether or not a settlement is reached.

(6) *Settlement.* If settlement is reached, in whole or in part, the agreement, which shall be binding upon all parties, will be put into writing and counsel will file a stipulation of dismissal or such other document as may be appropriate. If the case does not settle, the mediator will immediately notify the Clerk's Office, and the case or the portion of the case that has not settled will continue in the litigation process.

(c) Attendance at Mediation Sessions.

(1) In all civil cases designated by the Court for inclusion in the mediation program, attendance at one mediation session shall be mandatory: thereafter, attendance shall be voluntary. The Court requires of

each party that the attorney who has primary responsibility for handling the trial of the matter attend the mediation sessions.

(2) In addition, the Court may require, and if it does not, the mediator may require the attendance at the mediation session of a party or its representative in the case of a business or governmental entity or a minor, with authority to settle the matter and to bind the party. This requirement reflects the Court's view that the principal values of mediation include affording litigants with an opportunity to articulate their positions and interests directly to the other parties and to a mediator and to hear, first hand, the other party's version of the matters in dispute. Mediation also enables parties to search directly with the other party for mutually agreeable solutions.

(d) Confidentiality.

(1) The parties will be asked to sign an agreement of confidentiality at the beginning of the first mediation session to the following effect:

(A) Unless the parties otherwise agree, all written and oral communications made by the parties and the mediator in connection with or during any mediation session are confidential and may not be disclosed or used for any purpose unrelated to the mediation.

(B) The mediator shall not be called by any party as a witness in any court proceeding related to the subject matter of the mediation unless related to the alleged misconduct of the mediator.

(2) Mediators will maintain the confidentiality of all information provided to, or discussed with, them. The Clerk of Court and the ADR Administrator are responsible for program administration, evaluation, and liaison between mediators, and the Court and will maintain strict confidentiality.

(3) No papers generated by the mediation process will be included in Court files, nor shall the Judge or Magistrate Judge assigned to the case have access to them. Information about what transpires during mediation sessions will not at any time be made known to the Court, except to the extent required to resolve issues of noncompliance with the mediation procedures. However, communications made in connection with or during a mediation may be disclosed if all parties and, if appropriate as determined by the mediator, the mediator so agree. Nothing in this section shall be construed to prohibit parties from entering into written agreements resolving some or all of the case or entering and filing with the Court procedural or factual stipulations based on suggestions or agreements made in connection with a mediation. * * *

Rule 83.12. Alternative Dispute Resolution (Southern District Only)

Introduction

The Court's existing alternative dispute resolution ("ADR") program of mediation shall continue as set forth below.

(a) Definition

Mediation is a confidential ADR process in which a disinterested third party directs settlement discussions but does not evaluate the merits of either side's position or render any judgments. By holding meetings, defining issues, diffusing emotions and suggesting possibilities of resolution, the mediator assists the parties in reaching their own negotiated settlement. The main benefit of mediation is that it can produce creative solutions to complex disputes often unavailable in traditional litigation.

(b) Administration

Staff counsel, appointed by the Clerk of the Court, shall administer the Court's mediation program. The Chief Judge shall appoint one or more judicial officers to oversee the program.

(c) Service as a Mediator

An individual may serve as a mediator if he or she: 1) has been a member of the Bar of any state or the District of Columbia for at least five years; 2) is admitted to practice in this Court; and 3) is certified by the Chief Judge or the Judicial Officer appointed by the Chief Judge pursuant to paragraph (b) above to be competent to perform the duties of a mediator. Each individual certified as a mediator shall take the oath or affirmation prescribed by 28 U.S.C. § 453 and complete the training program provided by the Court before serving as a mediator.

(d) Consideration of Mediation

In all civil cases eligible for mediation pursuant to paragraph (e), each party shall consider the use of mediation and shall report to the assigned Judge at the initial case management conference whether the party believes mediation may facilitate the resolution of the lawsuit.

(e) Entry into the Program

All civil cases other than social security, tax, prisoner civil rights and *pro se* matters are eligible for mediation, whether assigned to Foley Square or White Plains.

The assigned Judge or Magistrate Judge may determine that a case is appropriate for mediation and may order that case to mediation with or without the consent of the parties. Alternatively, the parties may notify the assigned Judge and Staff Counsel at any time of their desire to mediate by filing a stipulation to that effect signed by all parties. Notification of the date, time and place will be forwarded by Staff Counsel to the parties.

(f) Scheduling Orders

In no event is the scheduling of mediation to interfere with any scheduling order of the court.

(g) Assignment of the Mediator

Staff Counsel shall assign a mediator from the individuals certified as mediators and notify the mediator and the parties of the assignment.

(h) Disqualification

The mediator shall disqualify himself or herself in any action in which he or she would be required under 28 U.S.C. § 455 to be disqualified if a Justice, Judge or Magistrate Judge. Any party may submit a written request to Staff Counsel within ten days from the date of the notification of the name of the mediator for the disqualification of the mediator for bias or prejudice as provided in 28 U.S.C. § 144. A denial of such a request by Staff Counsel is subject to review by the assigned Judge upon motion filed within ten days of the date of Staff Counsel's denial.

(i) Submission

Unless otherwise agreed, upon notification of the scheduled date of the mediation session but in no event less than seven days before the mediation, each party shall prepare and forward to the mediator (but not to the adversary) a memorandum presenting in concise form, not exceeding ten double-spaced pages, the party's contentions as to both liability and damages and the status of any settlement negotiations.

(j) Mediation Sessions

The attorney primarily responsible for each party's case shall personally attend the first mediation session and shall be fully authorized to resolve the matter and prepared to discuss all liability issues, damage issues, and the party's settlement position in detail and in good faith. At the discretion of the mediator, the party, if an individual, or a representative of the party, if a corporation, partnership or governmental entity, with knowledge of the facts and full settlement authority, may be required to attend.

The mediation will conclude when the parties reach a resolution of some or all issues in the case or where the mediator concludes that resolution (or further resolution) is impossible. If resolution is reached, a binding agreement shall be signed by all the parties, and a stipulation of discontinuance or other appropriate document filed promptly. Where resolution is not reached, the assigned judge shall be notified promptly.

(k) Confidentiality

The entire mediation process shall be confidential. The parties and the mediator shall not disclose information regarding the process, including settlement terms, to the Court or to third persons unless all parties agree. The identity of the mediator shall not be disclosed, including to the Court. However, persons authorized by the Court to administer or evaluate the program shall have access to information and documents necessary to do so, and the parties, counsel and mediators may respond to confidential inquiries or surveys by such persons.

The mediation process shall be treated as a compromise negotiation for purposes of the Federal Rules of Evidence and state rules of evidence. The mediator is disqualified as a witness, consultant, attorney, or expert in any pending or future action relating to the dispute, including actions between persons not parties to the mediation process.

(*l*) **Compensation of Mediators and Locations of Sessions**

All mediators shall serve without compensation and be eligible for credit for pro bono service. All ADR sessions will take place at the "ADR Center" in the Federal Courthouses in Manhattan or White Plains, as designated.

Part VIII

Recent U.S. Supreme Court Cases

      Page

Amchem Products, Inc. v. Windsor, 521 U.S. 591, 117 S.Ct. 2231, 138 L.Ed.2d 689 (1997) (class-action certification) 432

Free v. Abbott Laboratories, Inc., ___ U.S. ___, ___ S.Ct. ___, ___ L.Ed.2d ___, 68 U.S. Law Week 4254 (April 3, 2000) (supplemental federal court jurisdiction over a non-named member of a class who does not meet usual amount-in- controversy requirement) 451

Lexecon Inc. v. Milberg Weiss Bershad Hynes and Lerach, 523 U.S. 26, 118 S.Ct. 956, 140 L.Ed.2d 62 (1998) (lack of power of a transferee court under 28 U.S.C. 1407 to transfer a portion of the case to itself under 28 U.S.C. 1404(a)) 451

Feltner v. Columbia Pictures Television, Inc., 523 U.S. 340, 118 S.Ct. 1279, 140 L.Ed.2d 438 (1998) (Seventh Amendment right to trial by jury in cases under the Copyright Act) 457

Markman v. Westview Instruments, Inc., 517 U.S. 370, 116 S.Ct.1384, 134 L.Ed.2d 577 (1996) (lack of a Seventh Amendment right to jury trial on an issue of interpretation of a patent claim in a patent infringement action) 464

Ortiz v. Fibreboard Corp., 527 U.S. 815, 119 S.Ct. 2295, 144 L.Ed.2d 715 (1999) (certification of "mandatory" class actions) 472

Ruhrgas Ag v. Marathon Oil Co., 526 U.S. 574, 119 S.Ct. 1563, 143 L.Ed.2d 760 (1999) (power of federal court to dismiss for lack of personal jurisdiction without deciding disputed existence of subject-matter juris-diction) 492

AMCHEM PRODUCTS, INC. v. WINDSOR

Supreme Court of the United States, 1997.
521 U.S. 591, 117 S.Ct. 2231, 138 L.Ed.2d 689.

JUSTICE GINSBURG delivered the opinion of the Court.

This case concerns the legitimacy under Rule 23 of the Federal Rules of Civil Procedure of a class-action certification sought to achieve global settlement of current and future asbestos-related claims. The class proposed for certification potentially encompasses hundreds of thousands, perhaps millions, of individuals tied together by this commonality: each was, or some day may be, adversely affected by past exposure to asbestos products manufactured by one or more of 20 companies. Those companies, defendants in the lower courts, are petitioners here.

The United States District Court for the Eastern District of Pennsylvania certified the class for settlement only, finding that the proposed settlement was fair and that representation and notice had been adequate. That court enjoined class members from separately pursuing asbestos-related personal-injury suits in any court, federal or state, pending the issuance of a final order. The Court of Appeals for the Third Circuit vacated the District Court's orders, holding that the class certification failed to satisfy Rule 23's requirements in several critical respects. We affirm the Court of Appeals' judgment.

I

A

[The Panel on Multidistrict Litigation] * * * transferred all asbestos cases then filed, but not yet on trial in federal courts to a single district * * * for pretrial proceedings * * *. The order aggregated pending cases only; no authority resides in the MDL Panel to license for consolidated proceedings claims not yet filed.

B

After the consolidation, attorneys for plaintiffs and defendants formed separate steering committees and began settlement negotiations. [The negotiations included efforts to resolve future as well as pending cases.] * * * Settlement talks thus concentrated on devising an administrative scheme for disposition of asbestos cases not yet in litigation. In these negotiations, counsel for masses of [plaintiffs who had filed suit also] * * * endeavored to represent the interests of the anticipated future claimants, although those lawyers then had no attorney-client relationship with those claimants. * * * [An agreement was then reached with regard to the claims that had been filed and the lawyers then] launched this case, exclusively involving persons outside the MDL Panel's province—plaintiffs without already pending lawsuits.

C

The class action thus instituted was not intended to be litigated. Rather, within the space of a single day, January 15, 1993, the settling parties * * * presented to the District Court a complaint, an answer, a proposed settlement agreement, and a joint motion for conditional class certification.

The complaint identified nine lead plaintiffs, designating them and members of their families as representatives of a class comprising all persons who had not filed an asbestos-related lawsuit against a * * * [member of the defendant group (hereinafter referred to as a CCR defendant)] as of the date the class action commenced, but who (1) had been exposed—occupationally or through the occupational exposure of a spouse or household member—to asbestos or products containing asbestos attributable to a CCR defendant, or (2) whose spouse or family member had been so exposed. Untold numbers of individuals may fall within this description. All named plaintiffs alleged that they or a member of their family had been exposed to asbestos-containing products of CCR defendants. More than half of the named plaintiffs alleged that they or their family members had already suffered various physical injuries as a result of the exposure. The others alleged that they had not yet manifested any asbestos-related condition. The complaint delineated no subclasses; all named plaintiffs were designated as representatives of the class as a whole.

The complaint invoked the District Court's diversity jurisdiction and asserted various state-law claims for relief, including (1) negligent failure to warn, (2) strict liability, (3) breach of express and implied warranty, (4) negligent infliction of emotional distress, (5) enhanced risk of disease, (6) medical monitoring, and (7) civil conspiracy. Each plaintiff requested unspecified damages in excess of $100,000. CCR defendants' answer denied the principal allegations of the complaint and asserted 11 affirmative defenses.

A stipulation of settlement accompanied the pleadings; it proposed to settle, and to preclude nearly all class members from litigating against CCR companies, all claims not filed before January 15, 1993, involving compensation for present and future asbestos-related personal injury or death. An exhaustive document exceeding 100 pages, the stipulation presents in detail an administrative mechanism and a schedule of payments to compensate class members who meet defined asbestos-exposure and medical requirements. * * *

For each qualifying disease category, the stipulation specifies the range of damages CCR will pay to qualifying claimants. Payments under the settlement are not adjustable for inflation. * * * Compensation above the fixed ranges may be obtained for "extraordinary" claims. But the settlement places both numerical caps and dollar limits on such claims. The settlement also imposes "case flow maximums," which cap the number of claims payable for each disease in a given year.

Class members are to receive no compensation for certain kinds of claims, even if otherwise applicable state law recognizes such claims. Claims that garner no compensation under the settlement include claims by family members of asbestos-exposed individuals for loss of consortium, and claims by so-called "exposure-only" plaintiffs for increased risk of cancer, fear of future asbestos-related injury, and medical monitoring. "Pleural" claims, which might be asserted by persons with asbestos-related plaques on their lungs but no accompanying physical impairment, are also excluded. Although not entitled to present compensation, exposure-only claimants and pleural claimants may qualify for benefits when and if they develop a compensable disease and meet the relevant exposure and medical criteria. Defendants forgo defenses to liability, including statute of limitations pleas.

Class members, in the main, are bound by the settlement in perpetuity, while CCR defendants may choose to withdraw from the settlement after ten years. A small number of class members—only a few per year—may reject the settlement and pursue their claims in court. Those permitted to exercise this option, however, may not assert any punitive damages claim or any claim for increased risk of cancer. Aspects of the administration of the settlement are to be monitored by the AFL–CIO and class counsel. Class counsel are to receive attorneys' fees in an amount to be approved by the District Court.

D

On January 29, 1993, as requested by the settling parties, the District Court conditionally certified, under Federal Rule of Civil Procedure 23(b)(3), an encompassing opt-out class. The certified class included persons occupationally exposed to defendants' asbestos products, and members of their families, who had not filed suit as of January 15. * * * Record, Doc. 11, p. 3 (Class Certification Order). * * * [The class was never divided into subclasses.]. In a separate order, Judge Weiner assigned to Judge Reed, also of the Eastern District of Pennsylvania, "the task of conducting fairness proceedings and of determining whether the proposed settlement is fair to the class." See 157 F.R.D., at 258. Various class members raised objections to the settlement stipulation, and Judge Weiner granted the objectors full rights to participate in the subsequent proceedings. * * *

Objectors raised numerous challenges to the settlement. They urged that the settlement unfairly disadvantaged those without currently compensable conditions in that it failed to adjust for inflation or to account for changes, over time, in medical understanding. They maintained that compensation levels were intolerably low in comparison to awards available in tort litigation or payments received by the inventory plaintiffs. And they objected to the absence of any compensation for certain claims, for example, medical monitoring, compensable under the tort law of several States. Rejecting these and all other objections, Judge Reed concluded that the settlement terms were fair and had been negotiated without collusion. * * * He also found that adequate notice had been given to class members, and that final class certification under Rule 23(b)(3) was appropriate * * *.

Strenuous objections had been asserted regarding the adequacy of representation, a Rule 23(a)(4) requirement. Objectors maintained that class counsel and class representatives had disqualifying conflicts of interests. In particular, objectors urged, claimants whose injuries had become manifest and claimants without manifest injuries should not have common counsel and should not be aggregated in a single class. Furthermore, objectors argued, lawyers representing inventory plaintiffs should not represent the newly-formed class.

Satisfied that class counsel had ably negotiated the settlement in the best interests of all concerned, and that the named parties served as adequate representatives, the District Court rejected these objections.

* * * Subclasses were unnecessary, the District Court held, bearing in mind the added cost and confusion they would entail and the ability of class members to exclude themselves from the class during the three-month opt-out period. * * *

E

* * * [The Court of Appeals initially held] that the requirements of Rule 23(a) and (b)(3) must be met "without taking into account the settlement," [However, the court] in fact closely considered the terms of the settlement as it examined aspects of the case under Rule 23 criteria. * * * The Third Circuit recognized that Rule 23(a)(2)'s "commonality" requirement is subsumed under, or superseded by, the more stringent Rule 23(b)(3) requirement that questions common to the class "predominate over" other questions. The court therefore trained its attention on the "predominance" inquiry. * * * The harmfulness of asbestos exposure was indeed a prime factor common to the class, the Third Circuit observed. But uncommon questions abounded.

In contrast to mass torts involving a single accident, class members in this case were exposed to different asbestos-containing products, in different ways, over different periods, and for different amounts of time; some suffered no physical injury, others suffered disabling or deadly diseases. "These factual differences," the Third Circuit explained, "translate [d] into significant legal differences." * * * State law governed and varied widely on such critical issues as "viability of [exposure-only] claims [and] availability of causes of action for medical monitoring, increased risk of cancer, and fear of future injury." * * * "[T]he number of uncommon issues in this humongous class action," the Third Circuit concluded, * * * barred a determination, under existing tort law, that common questions predominated * * *.

The Court of Appeals next found that "serious intra-class conflicts preclude[d] the class from meeting the adequacy of representation requirement" of Rule 23(a)(4). Adverting to, but not resolving charges of attorney conflict of interests, the Third Circuit addressed the question whether the named plaintiffs could adequately advance the interests of all class members. The Court of Appeals acknowledged that the District Court was certainly correct to this extent: " '[T]he members of the class are united in seeking the maximum possible recovery for their asbestos-related claims.' " * * * "But the settlement does more than simply provide a general recovery fund," the Court of Appeals immediately added; "[r]ather, it makes important judgments on how recovery is to be allocated among different kinds of plaintiffs, decisions that necessarily favor some claimants over others." 83 F.3d, at 630.

In the Third Circuit's view, the "most salient" divergence of interests separated plaintiffs already afflicted with an asbestos-related disease from plaintiffs without manifest injury (exposure-only plaintiffs). The latter would rationally want protection against inflation for distant recoveries. * * * They would also seek sturdy back-end opt-out rights and "causation provisions that can keep pace with changing science and medicine, rather than freezing in place the science of 1993." * * *. Already injured parties, in contrast, would care little about such provisions and would rationally trade them for higher current payouts. * * * These and other adverse interests, the Court of Appeals carefully explained, strongly suggested that an undivided set of representatives could not adequately protect the discrete interests of both currently afflicted and exposure-only claimants.

The Third Circuit next rejected the District Court's determination that the named plaintiffs were "typical" of the class, noting that this Rule 23(a)(3) inquiry overlaps the adequacy of representation question: "both look to the potential for conflicts in the class." * * * Evident conflict problems, the court said, led it to hold that "no set of representatives can be 'typical' of this class." * * *

The Court of Appeals similarly rejected the District Court's assessment of the superiority of the class action. The Third Circuit initially noted that a class action so large and complex "could not be tried." * * * The court elaborated most particularly, however, on the unfairness of binding exposure-only plaintiffs who might be unaware of the class action or lack sufficient information about their exposure to make a reasoned decision whether to stay in or opt out. "A series of statewide or more narrowly defined adjudications, either through consolidation under Rule 42(a) or as class actions under Rule 23, would seem preferable," the Court of Appeals said. * * *.

The Third Circuit, after intensive review, ultimately ordered decertification of the class and vacation of the District Court's anti-suit injunction. * * *

We granted certiorari, 519 U.S. ___, 117 S.Ct. 379, 136 L.Ed.2d 297 (1996), and now affirm.

II

Objectors assert in this Court, as they did in the District Court and Court of Appeals, an array of jurisdictional barriers. Most fundamentally, they maintain that the settlement proceeding instituted by class counsel and CCR is not a justiciable case or controversy within the confines of Article III of the Federal Constitution. In the main, they say, the proceeding is a nonadversarial endeavor to impose on countless individuals without currently ripe claims an administrative compensation regime binding on those individuals if and when they manifest injuries. * * *

We * * * follow the path taken by the Court of Appeals [that it is unnecessary to reach these issues if we find that certification of the class is improper.] * * *

III

* * * In the 1966 class-action amendments, Rule 23(b)(3), the category at issue here, was "the most adventuresome" innovation. See Kaplan, A Prefatory Note, 10 B.C. Ind. & Com. L.Rev. 497, 497 (1969) (hereinafter Kaplan, Prefatory Note). Rule 23(b)(3) added to the complex-litigation arsenal class actions for damages designed to secure judgments binding all class members save those who affirmatively elected to be excluded. See 7A Charles Alan Wright, Arthur R. Miller, & Mary Kay Kane, Federal Practice and Procedure § 1777, p. 517 (2d ed.1986) (hereinafter Wright, Miller, & Kane) * * *. Rule 23(b)(3) "opt out" class actions superseded the former "spurious" class action, so characterized because it generally functioned as a permissive joinder ("opt in") device. See 7A Wright, Miller, & Kane § 1753, at 28–31, 42–44 * * *.

Framed for situations in which "class-action treatment is not as clearly called for" as it is in Rule 23(b)(1) and (b)(2) situations, Rule 23(b)(3) permits certification where class suit "may nevertheless be convenient and desirable." Adv. Comm. Notes, 28 U.S.C.App., p. 697. To qualify for certification under Rule 23(b)(3), a class must meet two requirements beyond the Rule 23(a) prerequisites: Common questions must "predominate over any questions affecting only individual members"; and class resolution must be "superior to other available methods for the fair and efficient adjudication of the controversy." In adding "predominance" and "superiority" to the qualification-for-certification list, the Advisory Committee sought to cover cases "in which a class action would achieve economies of time, effort, and expense, and promote ... uniformity of decision as to persons similarly situated, without sacrificing procedural fairness or bringing about other undesirable results." [Those who drafted the provision were] * * * sensitive to the competing tugs of individual autonomy for those who might prefer to go it alone or in a smaller unit, on the one hand, and systemic efficiency on the other * * * .

Rule 23(b)(3) includes a nonexhaustive list of factors pertinent to a court's "close look" at the predominance and superiority criteria * * *.

While the text of Rule 23(b)(3) does not exclude from certification cases in which individual damages run high, the Advisory Committee had dominantly in mind vindication of "the rights of groups of people who individually would be without effective strength to bring their opponents into court at all." Kaplan, Prefatory Note 497. As concisely recalled in a recent Seventh Circuit opinion:

"The policy at the very core of the class action mechanism is to overcome the problem that small recoveries do not provide the incentive for any individual to bring a solo action prosecuting his or her rights. A class action solves this problem by aggregating the relatively paltry potential recoveries into something worth someone's (usually an attorney's) labor." Mace v. Van Ru Credit Corp., 109 F.3d 338, 344 (1997).

[To protect the rights of individuals, they must be sent notice of their right to opt out and, if they choose to remain within the class, the action may not be dismissed or compromised without notice to them and subsequent court approval.] * * *

In the decades since the 1966 revision of Rule 23, class action practice has become ever more "adventuresome" as a means of coping with claims too numerous to secure their "just, speedy, and inexpensive determination" one by one. See Fed. Rule Civ. Proc. 1. The development reflects concerns about the efficient use of court resources and the conservation of funds to compensate claimants who do not line up early in a litigation queue. See generally J. Weinstein, Individual Justice in Mass Tort Litigation: The Effect of Class Actions, Consolidations, and Other Multiparty Devices (1995); Schwarzer, Settlement of Mass Tort Class Actions: Order out of Chaos, 80 Cornell L.Rev. 837 (1995). * * *

IV

We granted review to decide the role settlement may play, under existing Rule 23, in determining the propriety of class certification. The Third Circuit's opinion stated that each of the requirements of Rule 23(a) and (b)(3) "must be satisfied without taking into account the settlement." 83 F.3d, at 626. * * *. That statement, petitioners urge, is incorrect.

We agree with petitioners to this limited extent: settlement is relevant to a class certification. The Third Circuit's opinion bears modification in that respect. But, as we earlier observed, * * * the Court of Appeals in fact did not ignore the settlement; instead, that court homed in on settlement terms in explaining why it found the absentees' interests inadequately represented. See 83 F.3d, at 630–631. The Third Circuit's close inspection of the settlement in that regard was altogether proper.

Confronted with a request for settlement-only class certification, a district court need not inquire whether the case, if tried, would present intractable management problems, see Fed. Rule Civ. Proc. 23(b)(3)(D), for the proposal is that there be no trial. But other specifications of the rule—those designed to protect absentees by blocking unwarranted or overbroad class definitions—demand undiluted, even heightened, attention in the settlement context. Such attention is of vital importance, for a court asked to certify a settlement class will lack the opportunity, present when a case is litigated, to adjust the class, informed by the proceedings as they unfold. See Fed. Rule Civ. Proc. 23(c), (d).

* * * Subdivisions (a) and (b) [of Rule 23] focus court attention on whether a proposed class has sufficient unity so that absent members can fairly be bound by decisions of class representatives. That dominant concern persists when settlement, rather than trial, is proposed.

The safeguards provided by the Rule 23(a) and (b) class-qualifying criteria, we emphasize, are not impractical impediments—checks shorn of utility—in the settlement class context. First, the standards set for the protection of absent class members serve to inhibit appraisals of the chancellor's foot kind—class certifications dependent upon the court's gestalt judgment or overarching impression of the settlement's fairness.

Second, if a fairness inquiry under Rule 23(e) controlled certification, eclipsing Rule 23(a) and (b), and permitting class designation despite the impossibility of litigation, both class counsel and court would be disarmed. Class counsel confined to settlement negotiations could not use the threat of litigation to press for a better offer, see Coffee, Class Wars: The Dilemma of the Mass Tort Class Action, 95 Colum. L.Rev. 1343, 1379–1380 (1995), and the court would face a bargain proffered for its approval without benefit of adversarial investigation, see, e.g., Kamilewicz v. Bank of Boston Corp., 100 F.3d 1348, 1352 (C.A.7 1996) (Easterbrook, J., dissenting from denial of rehearing en banc) (parties "may even put one over on the court, in a staged performance"), cert. denied, 520 U.S. ___, 117 S.Ct. 1569, ___ L.Ed.2d ___ (1997).

Federal courts, in any case, lack authority to substitute for Rule 23's certification criteria a standard never adopted—that if a settlement is "fair," then certification is proper. Applying to this case criteria the rulemakers set, we conclude that the Third Circuit's appraisal is essentially correct. Although that court should have acknowledged that settlement is a factor in the calculus, a remand is not warranted on that account. The Court of Appeals' opinion amply demonstrates why—with or without a settlement on the table—the sprawling class the District Court certified does not satisfy Rule 23's requirements.

A

We address first the requirement of Rule 23(b)(3) that "[common] questions of law or fact ... predominate over any questions affecting only individual members." The District Court concluded that predominance was satisfied based on two factors: class members' shared experience of asbestos exposure and their common "interest in receiving prompt and fair compensation for their claims, while minimizing the risks and transaction costs inherent in the asbestos litigation process as it occurs presently in the tort system." 157 F.R.D., at 316. The settling parties also contend that the settlement's fairness is a common question, predominating over disparate legal issues that might be pivotal in litigation but become irrelevant under the settlement.

The predominance requirement stated in Rule 23(b)(3), we hold, is not met by the factors on which the District Court relied. The benefits asbestos-exposed persons might gain from the establishment of a grand-scale compensation scheme is a matter fit for legislative consideration, * * * but it is not pertinent to the predominance inquiry. That inquiry trains on the legal or factual questions that qualify each class member's case as a genuine controversy, questions that preexist any settlement.

In this respect, the predominance requirement of Rule 23(b)(3) is similar to the requirement of Rule 23(a)(3) that "claims or defenses" of the named representatives must be "typical of the claims or defenses of the class." The words "claims or defenses" in this context—just as in the context of Rule 24(b)(2) governing permissive intervention—"manifestly refer to the kinds of claims or defenses that can be raised in courts of law as part of an actual or impending law suit." Diamond v. Charles, 476 U.S. 54, 76–77, 106 S.Ct. 1697, 1711, 90 L.Ed.2d 48 (1986) (O'CONNOR, J., concurring in part and concurring in judgment).

The Rule 23(b)(3) predominance inquiry tests whether proposed classes are sufficiently cohesive to warrant adjudication by representation. See 7A Wright, Miller, & Kane 518–519. The inquiry appropriate under Rule 23(e), on the other hand, protects unnamed class members "from unjust or unfair settlements affecting their rights when the representatives become fainthearted before the action is adjudicated or are able to secure satisfaction of their individual claims by a compromise." See 7B Wright, Miller, & Kane § 1797, at 340–341. But it is not the mission of Rule 23(e) to assure the class cohesion that legitimizes representative action in the first place. If a common interest in a fair compromise could satisfy the predominance requirement of Rule 23(b)(3), that vital prescription would be stripped of any meaning in the settlement context.

The District Court also relied upon this commonality: "The members of the class have all been exposed to asbestos products supplied by the defendants...." 157 F.R.D., at 316. Even if Rule 23(a)'s commonality requirement may be satisfied by that shared experience, the predominance criterion is far more demanding. See 83 F.3d, at 626–627. Given the greater number of questions peculiar to the several categories of class members, and to individuals within each category, and the significance of those uncommon questions, any overarching dispute about the health consequences of asbestos exposure cannot satisfy the Rule 23(b)(3) predominance standard.

"The [exposure-only] plaintiffs especially share little in common, either with each other or with the presently injured class members. It is unclear whether they will contract asbestos-related disease and, if so, what disease each will suffer. They will also incur different medical expenses because their monitoring and treatment will depend on singular circumstances and individual medical histories." [83 F.3d at 626.] * * * Differences in state law, the Court of Appeals observed, compound these disparities. * * *

No settlement class called to our attention is as sprawling as this one. * * * Predominance is a test readily met in certain cases alleging consumer or securities fraud or violations of the antitrust laws. * * *

Even mass tort cases arising from a common cause or disaster may, depending upon the circumstances, satisfy the predominance requirement. The Advisory Committee for the 1966 revision of Rule 23, it is true, noted that "mass accident" cases are likely to present "significant questions, not only of damages but of liability and defenses of liability, ... affecting the individuals in different ways." Ibid. And the Committee advised that such cases are "ordinarily not appropriate" for class treatment. Ibid. But the text of the rule does not categorically exclude mass tort cases from class certification, and district courts, since the late 1970s, have been certifying such cases in increasing number. See Resnik, From "Cases" to "Litigation," 54 Law & Contemp.Prob. 5, 17–19 (Summer 1991) (describing trend). The Committee's warning, however, continues to call for caution when individual stakes are high and disparities among class members great. As the Third Circuit's opinion makes plain, the certification in this case does not follow the counsel of caution. That certification cannot be upheld, for it rests on a conception of Rule 23(b)(3)'s predominance requirement irreconcilable with the rule's design.

B

Nor can the class approved by the District Court satisfy Rule 23(a)(4)'s requirement that the named parties "will fairly and adequately protect the interests of the class." The adequacy inquiry under Rule 23(a)(4) serves to uncover conflicts of interest between named parties and the class they seek to represent. * * *

As the Third Circuit pointed out, named parties with diverse medical conditions sought to act on behalf of a single giant class rather than on behalf of discrete subclasses. In significant respects, the interests of those within the single class are not aligned. Most saliently, for the currently injured, the critical goal is generous immediate payments. That goal tugs against the interest of exposure-only plaintiffs in ensuring an ample, inflation-protected fund for the future. * * *

The disparity between the currently injured and exposure-only categories of plaintiffs, and the diversity within each category are not made insignificant by the District Court's finding that petitioners' assets suffice to pay claims under the settlement. See 157 F.R.D., at 291. Although this is not a "limited fund" case certified under Rule 23(b)(1)(B), the terms of the settlement reflect essential allocation decisions designed to confine compensation and to limit defendants' liability. For example, as earlier described, * * * the settlement includes no adjustment for inflation; only a few claimants per year can opt out at the back end; and loss-of-consortium claims are extinguished with no compensation.

The settling parties, in sum, achieved a global compromise with no structural assurance of fair and adequate representation for the diverse groups and individuals affected. Although the named parties alleged a range of complaints, each served generally as representative for the whole, not for a separate constituency. * * *

The Third Circuit found no assurance here—either in the terms of the settlement or in the structure of the negotiations—that the named plaintiffs operated under a proper understanding of their representational responsibilities. See 83 F.3d, at 630–631. That assessment, we conclude, is on the mark.

C

Impediments to the provision of adequate notice, the Third Circuit emphasized, rendered highly problematic any endeavor to tie to a settlement class persons with no perceptible asbestos-related disease at the time of the settlement. Id., at 633; cf. In re Asbestos Litigation, 90 F.3d, at 999–1000 (Smith, J., dissenting). Many persons in the exposure-only category, the Court of Appeals stressed, may not even know of their exposure, or realize the extent of the harm they may incur. Even if they fully appreciate the significance of class notice, those without current afflictions may not have the information or foresight needed to decide, intelligently, whether to stay in or opt out.

Family members of asbestos-exposed individuals may themselves fall prey to disease or may ultimately have ripe claims for loss of consortium. Yet large numbers of people in this category—future spouses and children of asbestos victims—could not be alerted to their class membership. And current spouses and children of the occupationally exposed may know nothing of that exposure.

Because we have concluded that the class in this case cannot satisfy the requirements of common issue predominance and adequacy of representation, we need not rule, definitively, on the notice given here. In accord with the Third Circuit, however, see 83 F.3d, at 633–634, we recognize the gravity of the question whether class action notice sufficient under the Constitution and Rule 23 could ever be given to legions so unselfconscious and amorphous.

V

The argument is sensibly made that a nationwide administrative claims processing regime would provide the most secure, fair, and efficient means of compensating victims of asbestos exposure. Congress, however, has not adopted such a solution. And Rule 23, which must be interpreted with fidelity to the Rules Enabling Act and applied with the interests of absent class members in close view, cannot carry the large load CCR, class counsel, and the District Court heaped upon it. As this case exemplifies, the rulemakers' prescriptions for class actions may be endangered by "those who embrace [Rule 23] too enthusiastically just as [they are by] those who approach [the rule] with distaste." C. Wright, Law of Federal Courts 508 (5th ed.1994); cf. 83 F.3d, at 634 (suggesting resort to less bold aggregation techniques, including more narrowly defined class certifications).

* * *

For the reasons stated, the judgment of the Court of Appeals for the Third Circuit is

Affirmed.

JUSTICE O'CONNOR took no part in the consideration or decision of this case.

JUSTICE BREYER, with whom JUSTICE STEVENS joins, concurring in part and dissenting in part.

Although I agree with the Court's basic holding that "settlement is relevant to a class certification," * * * I find several problems in its approach that lead me to a different conclusion. First, I believe that the need for settlement in this mass tort case, with hundreds of thousands of lawsuits, is greater than the Court's opinion suggests. Second, I would give more weight than would the majority to settlement-related issues for purposes of determining whether common issues predominate. Third, I am uncertain about the Court's determination of adequacy of representation, and do not believe it appropriate for this Court to second-guess the District Court on the matter without first having the Court of Appeals consider it. Fourth, I am uncertain about the tenor of an opinion that seems to suggest the settlement is unfair. And fifth, in the absence of further review by the Court of Appeals, I cannot accept the majority's suggestions that "notice" is inadequate.

These difficulties flow from the majority's review of what are highly fact-based, complex, and difficult matters, matters that are inappropriate for initial review before this Court. The law gives broad leeway to district courts in making class certification decisions, and their judgments are to be reviewed by the Court of Appeals only for abuse of discretion. See Califano v. Yamasaki, 442 U.S. 682, 703, 99 S.Ct. 2545, 2558–2559, 61 L.Ed.2d 176 (1979). Indeed, the District Court's certification decision rests upon more than 300 findings of fact reached after five weeks of comprehensive hearings. Accordingly, I do not believe that we should in effect set aside the findings of the District Court. That court is far more familiar with the issues and litigants than is a court of appeals or are we, and therefore has "broad power and discretion ... with respect to matters involving the certification" of class actions. Reiter v. Sonotone Corp., 442 U.S. 330, 345, 99 S.Ct. 2326, 2334, 60 L.Ed.2d 931 (1979); cf. Cooter & Gell v. Hartmarx Corp., 496 U.S. 384, 402, 110 S.Ct. 2447, 2459, 110 L.Ed.2d 359 (1990) (district court better situated to make fact-dependent legal determinations in Rule 11 context).

I do not believe that we can rely upon the Court of Appeals' review of the District Court record, for that review, and its ultimate conclusions, are infected by a legal error. E.g., Georgine v. Amchem Products,

Inc., 83 F.3d 610, 626 (C.A.3 1996) (holding that "considered as a litigation class," the class cannot meet Rule 23's requirements) (emphasis added). There is no evidence that the Court of Appeals at any point considered the settlement as something that would help the class meet Rule 23. I find, moreover, the fact-related issues presented here sufficiently close to warrant further detailed appellate court review under the correct legal standard. * * * And I shall briefly explain why this is so.

I

First, I believe the majority understates the importance of settlement in this case. Between 13 and 21 million workers have been exposed to asbestos in the workplace—over the past 40 or 50 years—but the most severe instances of such exposure probably occurred three or four decades ago. See Report of The Judicial Conference Ad Hoc Committee on Asbestos Litigation, pp. 6–7 (Mar.1991) (Judicial Conference Report); App. 781–782, 801; B. Castleman, Asbestos: Medical and Legal Aspects 787–788 (4th ed.1996). This exposure has led to several hundred thousand lawsuits, about 15% of which involved claims for cancer and about 30% for asbestosis. See In re Joint Eastern and Southern Dist. Asbestos Litigation, 129 B.R. 710, 936–937 (E. and S.D.N.Y.1991) (Joint Litigation). About half of the suits have involved claims for pleural thickening and plaques—the harmfulness of which is apparently controversial. (One expert below testified that they "don't transform into cancer" and are not "predictor[s] of future disease," App. 781.) Some of those who suffer from the most serious injuries, however, have received little or no compensation. In re School Asbestos Litigation, 789 F.2d 996, 1000 (C.A.3 1986); see also Edley & Weiler, Asbestos: A Multi–Billion–Dollar Crisis, 30 Harv. J. Legis. 383, 384, 393 (1993) ("[U]p to one-half of asbestos claims are now being filed by people who have little or no physical impairment. Many of these claims produce substantial payments (and substantial costs) even though the individual litigants will never become impaired"). These lawsuits have taken up more than 6% of all federal civil filings in one recent year, and are subject to a delay that is twice that of other civil suits. Judicial Conference Report 7, 10–11.

Delays, high costs, and a random pattern of noncompensation led the Judicial Conference Ad Hoc Committee on Asbestos Litigation to transfer all federal asbestos personal-injury cases to the Eastern District of Pennsylvania in an effort to bring about a fair and comprehensive settlement. It is worth considering a few of the Committee's comments. See Judicial Conference Report 2 (" 'Decisions concerning thousands of deaths, millions of injuries, and billions of dollars are entangled in a litigation system whose strengths have increasingly been overshadowed by its weaknesses.' The ensuing five years have seen the picture worsen: increased filings, larger backlogs, higher costs, more bankruptcies and poorer prospects that judgments—if ever obtained—can be collected' ") (quoting Rand Corporation Institute for Civil Justice); id., at 13 ("The

transaction costs associated with asbestos litigation are an unconsciona-
ble burden on the victims of asbestos disease," and citing Rand finding
that "of each asbestos litigation dollar, 61 cents is consumed in transaction costs.... Only 39 cents were paid to the asbestos victims"); id., at
12 ("Delays also can increase transaction costs, especially the attorneys'
fees paid by defendants at hourly rates. These costs reduce either the
insurance fund or the company's assets, thereby reducing the funds
available to pay pending and future claimants. By the end of the trial
phase in [one case], at least seven defendants had declared bankruptcy
(as a result of asbestos claims generally)"); see also J. Weinstein,
Individual Justice in Mass Tort Litigation 155 (1995); Edley & Weiler,
supra, at 389–395.

Although the transfer of the federal asbestos cases did not produce a
general settlement, it was intertwined with and led to a lengthy year-
long negotiation between the co-chairs of the Plaintiff's Multi–District
Litigation Steering Committee (elected by the Plaintiff's Committee
Members and approved by the District Court) and the 20 asbestos
defendants who are before us here. Georgine v. Amchem Products, Inc.,
157 F.R.D. 246, 266–267, (E.D.Pa.1994); App. 660–662. These "protracted and vigorous" negotiations led to the present partial settlement,
which will pay an estimated $1.3 billion and compensate perhaps 100,000
class members in the first 10 years. 157 F.R.D., at 268, 287. "The
negotiations included a substantial exchange of information" between
class counsel and the 20 defendant companies, including "confidential
data" showing the defendants' historical settlement averages, numbers
of claims filed and settled, and insurance resources. Id., at 267. "Virtually no provision" of the settlement "was not the subject of significant
negotiation," and the settlement terms "changed substantially" during
the negotiations. Ibid. In the end, the negotiations produced a settlement
that, the District Court determined based on its detailed review of the
process, was "the result of arms-length adversarial negotiations by
extraordinarily competent and experienced attorneys." Id., at 335.

The District Court, when approving the settlement, concluded that
it improved the plaintiffs' chances of compensation and reduced total
legal fees and other transaction costs by a significant amount. Under the
previous system, according to the court, "[t]he sickest of victims often go
uncompensated for years while valuable funds go to others who remain
unimpaired by their mild asbestos disease." Ibid. The court believed the
settlement would create a compensation system that would make more
money available for plaintiffs who later develop serious illnesses.

I mention this matter because it suggests that the settlement before
us is unusual in terms of its importance, both to many potential
plaintiffs and to defendants, and with respect to the time, effort, and
expenditure that it reflects. All of which leads me to be reluctant to set
aside the District Court's findings without more assurance than I have
that they are wrong. I cannot obtain that assurance through comprehen-

sive review of the record because that is properly the job of the Court of Appeals and that court, understandably, but as we now hold, mistakenly, believed that settlement was not a relevant (and, as I would say, important) consideration.

Second, the majority, in reviewing the District Court's determination that common "issues of fact and law predominate," says that the predominance "inquiry trains on the legal or factual questions that qualify each class member's case as a genuine controversy, questions that preexist any settlement." * * * I find it difficult to interpret this sentence in a way that could lead me to the majority's conclusion. If the majority means that these pre-settlement questions are what matters, then how does it reconcile its statement with its basic conclusion that "settlement is relevant" to class certification, or with the numerous lower court authority that says that settlement is not only relevant, but important?

Nor do I understand how one could decide whether common questions "predominate" in the abstract—without looking at what is likely to be at issue in the proceedings that will ensue, namely, the settlement. Every group of human beings, after all, has some features in common, and some that differ. How can a court make a contextual judgment of the sort that Rule 23 requires without looking to what proceedings will follow? * * * I am not saying that the "settlement counts only one way." * * * Rather, the settlement may simply "add a great deal of information to the court's inquiry and will often expose diverging interests or common issues that were not evident or clear from the complaint" and courts "can and should" look to it to enhance the "ability ... to make informed certification decisions." In re Asbestos, 90 F.3d 963, 975 (C.A.5 1996).

The majority may mean that the District Court gave too much weight to the settlement. But I am not certain how it can reach that conclusion. It cannot rely upon the Court of Appeals, for that court gave no positive weight at all to the settlement. * * * The settlement is relevant because it means that these common features and interests are likely to be important in the proceeding that would ensue—a proceeding that would focus primarily upon whether or not the proposed settlement fairly and properly satisfied the interests class members had in common. That is to say, the settlement underscored the importance of (a) the common fact of exposure, (b) the common interest in receiving some compensation for certain rather than running a strong risk of no compensation, and (c) the common interest in avoiding large legal fees, other transaction costs, and delays. * * *

Of course, as the majority points out, there are also important differences among class members. Different plaintiffs were exposed to different products for different times; each has a distinct medical history and a different history of smoking; and many cases arise under the laws of different States. The relevant question, however, is how much these differences matter in respect to the legal proceedings that lie ahead. Many, if not all, toxic tort class actions involve plaintiffs with such differences. And the differences in state law are of diminished importance in respect to a proposed settlement in which the defendants have waived all defenses and agreed to compensate all those who were injured. * * *

These differences might warrant subclasses * * *. Or these differences may be too serious to permit an effort at group settlement. This kind of determination, as I have said, is one that the law commits to the discretion of the district court—reviewable for abuse of discretion by a court of appeals. I believe that we are far too distant from the litigation itself to reweigh the fact-specific Rule 23 determinations and to find them erroneous without the benefit of the Court of Appeals first having restudied the matter with today's legal standard in mind.

Third, the majority concludes that the "representative parties" will not "fairly and adequately protect the interests of the class." Rule 23(a)(4). It finds a serious conflict between plaintiffs who are now injured and those who may be injured in the future because "for the currently injured, the critical goal is generous immediate payments," a goal that "tugs against the interest of exposure-only plaintiffs in ensuring an ample, inflation-protected fund for the future." * * *

I agree that there is a serious problem, but it is a problem that often exists in toxic tort cases. * * * And it is a problem that potentially exists whenever a single defendant injures several plaintiffs, for a settling plaintiff leaves fewer assets available for the others. With class actions, at least, plaintiffs have the consolation that a district court, thoroughly familiar with the facts, is charged with the responsibility of ensuring that the interests of no class members are sacrificed.

But this Court cannot easily safeguard such interests through review of a cold record. "What constitutes adequate representation is a question of fact that depends on the circumstances of each case." Wright, Miller, & Kane, 7A Federal Practice and Procedure, § 1765, at 271. * * * The majority's use of the lack of an inflation adjustment as evidence of inadequacy of representation for future plaintiffs, * * * is one example of this difficulty. An inflation adjustment might not be as valuable as the majority assumes if most plaintiffs are old and not worried about receiving compensation decades from now. There are, of course, strong arguments as to its value. But that disagreement is one that this Court is poorly situated to resolve.

Further, certain details of the settlement that are not discussed in the majority opinion suggest that the settlement may be of greater benefit to future plaintiffs than the majority suggests. The District Court concluded that future plaintiffs receive a "significant value" from the settlement due to variety of its items that benefit future plaintiffs, such as: (1) tolling the statute of limitations so that class members "will no longer be forced to file premature lawsuits or risk their claims being time-barred"; (2) waiver of defenses to liability; (3) payment of claims, if and when members become sick, pursuant to the settlement's compensation standards, which avoids "the uncertainties, long delays and high transaction costs [including attorney's fees] of the tort system"; (4) "some assurance that there will be funds available if and when they get sick," based on the finding that each defendant "has shown an ability to fund the payment of all qualifying claims" under the settlement; and (5) the right to additional compensation if cancer develops (many settlements for plaintiffs with noncancerous conditions bar such additional claims). 157 F.R.D., at 292. For these reasons, and others, the District Court found that the distinction between present and future plaintiffs was "illusory." 157 F.R.D., at 317–318.

I do not know whether or not the benefits are more or less valuable than an inflation adjustment. But I can certainly recognize an argument that they are. (To choose one more brief illustration, the majority chastises the settlement for extinguishing loss-of-consortium claims, * * * but does not note that, as the District Court found, the "defendants' historical [settlement] averages, upon which the compensation values are based, include payments for loss of consortium claims, and, accordingly, the Compensation Schedule is not unfair for this ascribed reason," 157 F.R.D., at 278.) The difficulties inherent in both knowing and understanding the vast number of relevant individual fact-based determinations here counsel heavily in favor of deference to district court decisionmaking in Rule 23 decisions. Or, at the least, making certain that appellate court review has taken place with the correct standard in mind.

Fourth, I am more agnostic than is the majority about the basic fairness of the settlement. * * * . The District Court's conclusions rested upon complicated factual findings that are not easily cast aside. It is helpful to consider some of them, such as its determination that the settlement provided "fair compensation ... while reducing the delays and transaction costs endemic to the asbestos litigation process" and that "the proposed class action settlement is superior to other available methods for the fair and efficient resolution of the asbestos-related personal injury claims of class members." 157 F.R.D., at 316 (citation omitted); see also id., at 335 ("The inadequate tort system has demonstrated that the lawyers are well paid for their services but the victims are not receiving speedy and reasonably inexpensive resolution of their claims. Rather, the victims' recoveries are delayed, excessively reduced by transaction costs and relegated to the impersonal group trials and mass consolidations. The sickest of victims often go uncompensated for years while valuable funds go to others who remain unimpaired by their mild asbestos disease. Indeed, [these] unimpaired victims have, in many states, been forced to assert their claims prematurely or risk giving up

449

all rights to future compensation for any future lung cancer or mesothe-
lioma. The plan which this Court approves today will correct that unfair
result for the class members and the ... defendants"); id., at 279, 280
(settlement "will result in less delay for asbestos claimants than that
experienced in the present tort system" and will "result in the CCR
defendants paying more claims, at a faster rate, than they have ever paid
before"); id., at 292; Edley & Weiler, 30 Harv. J. Legis., at 405, 407
(finding that "[t]here are several reasons to believe that this settlement
secures important gains for both sides" and that they "firmly endorse
the fairness and adequacy of this settlement"). Indeed, the settlement
has been endorsed as fair and reasonable by the AFL–CIO (and its
Building and Construction Trades Department), which represents a
" 'substantial percentage' " of class members, 157 F.R.D., at 325, and
which has a role in monitoring implementation of the settlement, id., at
285. I do not intend to pass judgment upon the settlement's fairness, but
I do believe that these matters would have to be explored in far greater
depth before I could reach a conclusion about fairness. And that task, as
I have said, is one for the Court of Appeals.

Finally, I believe it is up to the District Court, rather than this
Court, to review the legal sufficiency of notice to members of the class.
The District Court found that the plan to provide notice was implemented at a cost of millions of dollars and included hundreds of thousands of
individual notices, a wide-ranging television and print campaign, and
significant additional efforts by 35 international and national unions to
notify their members. 157 F.R.D., at 312–313, 336. Every notice emphasized that an individual did not currently have to be sick to be a class
member. And in the end, the District Court was "confident" that Rule
23 and due process requirements were satisfied because, as a result of
this "extensive and expensive notice procedure," "over six million"
individuals "received actual notice materials," and "millions more" were
reached by the media campaign. Id., at 312, 333, 336. Although the
majority, in principle, is reviewing a Court of Appeals' conclusion, it
seems to me that its opinion might call into question the fact-related
determinations of the District Court. * * * To the extent that it does so,
I disagree, for such findings cannot be so quickly disregarded. And I do
not think that our precedents permit this Court to do so. See Reiter, 442
U.S., at 345, 99 S.Ct., at 2334; Yamasaki, 442 U.S., at 703, 99 S.Ct., at
2558–2559.

II

The issues in this case are complicated and difficult. The District
Court might have been correct. Or not. Subclasses might be appropriate.
Or not. I cannot tell. And I do not believe that this Court should be in
the business of trying to make these fact-based determinations. That is a
job suited to the district courts in the first instance, and the courts of
appeal on review. But there is no reason in this case to believe that the

Court of Appeals conducted its prior review with an understanding that the settlement could have constituted a reasonably strong factor in favor of class certification. For this reason, I would provide the courts below with an opportunity to analyze the factual questions involved in certification by vacating the judgment, and remanding the case for further proceedings.

FREE v. ABBOTT LABORATORIES, INC.

Supreme Court of the United States, 2000.
___ U.S. ___, ___ S.Ct. ___, ___ L.Ed.2d ___, 68 U.S. Law Week 4254.

[This case was on certiorari to the 5th Circuit Court of Appeals that held that Zahn v. International Paper Co., 414 U.S. 291, 94 S.Ct. 505, 38 L.Ed.2d 511 (1973), has been overturned by enactment in 1990 of 28 U.S.C. § 1367. In re Abbott Laboratories, 51 F.3d 524, rehearing denied, 65 F.3d 33 (1995). The issue was whether federal courts can exercise subject-matter jurisdiction over any non-named members of a class who do not individually meet the amount-in-controversy requirement of 28 U.S.C. § 1332(a) even though that requirement is met by the representative parties. The appellate court held that § 1367 provides supplemental jurisdiction over the non-representative parties in such case.

By an equally divided Court, the Supreme Court affirmed the decision, with Justice O'Connor not participating.]

LEXECON INC. v. MILBERG WEISS BERSHAD HYNES & LERACH

Supreme Court of the United States, 1998.
523 U.S. 26, 118 S.Ct. 956, 140 L.Ed.2d 62.

[Defendant Milberg, a law firm, originally filed a class action suit against a number of defendants, including Plaintiff Lexecon, arising from the failure of Lincoln Savings and Loan. That action, along with others, was transferred for pretrial proceedings to the District of Arizona under 28 U.S.C. 1407(a). During the pretrial phase, the claims against Lexecon were dismissed. Subsequently, plaintiff brought the current tort action against defendant, arising from defendant's conduct as counsel in the class-action suit. The latter suit was filed in the Northern District of Illinois. On defendant's motion, the Panel on Multidistrict Litigation transferred the action to the Arizona District Court. After the class action and related suits were settled, leaving only plaintiff's current suit, plaintiff moved the Arizona court to transfer its case back to the Northern District of Illinois. Instead the Arizona court invoked 28 U.S.C. 1404(a) to transfer the case to itself for trial. Defendant won a judgment and plaintiff's appeal to the Ninth Circuit, based on the fact that the Arizona court erred in transferring the case to itself, was unsuccessful. The Supreme Court granted certiorari to decide whether

§ 1407(a) permits a transferee court to entertain a § 1404(a) transfer motion to retain a case for trial.]

Justice SOUTER delivered the opinion of the Court. [Justice SCALIA joined the opinion except for part IIC.]

* * *

II

A

In defending the Ninth Circuit majority, Milberg may claim ostensible support from two quarters. First, the Panel has itself sanctioned such assignments in a rule issued in reliance on its rulemaking authority under *28 U.S.C. § 1407* (f). The Panel's Rule 14(b) provides that "each transferred action that has not been terminated in the transferee district court shall be remanded by the Panel to the transferor district for trial, unless ordered transferred by the transferee judge to the transferee or other district under *28 U.S.C. § 1404* (a) or *28 U.S.C. § 1406.*" Thus, out of the 39,228 cases transferred under § 1407 and terminated as of September 30, 1995, 279 of the 3,787 ultimately requiring trial were retained by the courts to which the Panel had transferred them. Administrative Office of the United States, L. Mecham, Judicial Business of the United States Courts: 1995 Report of the Director, 32. Although the Panel's rule and the practice of self-assignment have not gone without challenge, see, e.g., 15 C. Wright, A. Miller, & E. Cooper, Federal Practice and Procedure § 3866, p. 619 (2d ed. 1986) (hereinafter Wright, Miller, & Cooper); Transgrud, Joinder Alternatives in Mass Tort Litigation, *70 Cornell L.Rev. 779, 809 (1985);* Levy, Complex Multidistrict Litigation and the Federal Courts, *40 Ford.L.Rev. 41, 64–65 (1972),* federal courts have treated such transfers with approval, beginning with the Second Circuit's decision in Pfizer, Inc. v. Lord, *447 F.2d 122, 124–125 (CA2 1971)* (per curiam) (upholding MDL Rule 15(d), the precursor to Rule 14(b)). * * *

[Second,] although the statute limits a transferee court's authority to the conduct of "coordinated or consolidated" proceedings and to those that are "pretrial," these limitations alone raise no obvious bar to a transferee's retention of a case under § 1404. If "consolidated" proceedings alone were authorized, there would be an argument that self-assignment of one or some cases out of many was not contemplated, but because the proceedings need only be "coordinated," no such narrow limitation is apparent. * * *

Likewise, at first blush, the statutory limitation to "pretrial" proceedings suggests no reason that a § 1407 transferor court could not entertain a § 1404(a) motion. Section 1404(a) authorizes a district court to transfer a case in the interest of justice and for the convenience of the parties and witnesses. See § 1404(a). Such transfer requests are typically resolved prior to discovery, see Wright, Miller, & Cooper § 3866, at 620, and thus are classic "pretrial" motions.

Beyond this point, however, the textual pointers reverse direction, for § 1407 not only authorizes the Panel to transfer for coordinated or consolidated pretrial proceedings, but obligates the Panel to remand any pending case to its originating court when, at the latest, those pretrial proceedings have run their course.

"Each action so transferred shall be remanded by the panel at or before the conclusion of such pretrial proceedings to the district from which it was transferred unless it shall have been previously terminated." § 1407(a) (proviso without application here omitted).

The Panel's instruction comes in terms of the mandatory "shall," which normally creates an obligation impervious to judicial discretion. *Anderson v. Yungkau, 329 U.S. 482, 485, 91 L.Ed. 436, 67 S.Ct. 428 (1947)*. In the absence of any indication that there might be circumstances in which a transferred case would be neither "terminated" nor subject to the remand obligation, then, the statutory instruction stands flatly at odds with reading the phrase "coordinated or consolidated pretrial proceedings" so broadly as to reach its literal limits, allowing a transferee court's self-assignment to trump the provision imposing the Panel's remand duty. If we do our job of reading the statute whole, we have to give effect to this plain command, see *Estate of Cowart v. Nicklos Drilling Co., 505 U.S. 469, 476, 120 L.Ed.2d 379, 112 S.Ct. 2589 (1992)*, even if doing that will reverse the longstanding practice under the statute and the rule, see *Metropolitan Stevedore Co. v. Rambo (1995)* ("'Age is no antidote to clear inconsistency with a statute.'" (quoting *Brown v. Gardner, 513 U.S. 115, 122, 130 L.Ed.2d 462, 115 S.Ct. 552 (1994)*))).

* * *

A * * * use of blinders underlies the Circuit majority's conclusion that the Panel was not even authorized to remand the case under its Rule 14(c), the terms of which condition the remand responsibility on a suggestion of the transferee court, a motion filed directly with the Panel, or the Panel's sua sponte decision to remand. None of these conditions was fulfilled, according to the Court of Appeals, which particularly faulted Lexecon for failing to file a remand motion directly with the Panel, as distinct from the transferee court. This analysis, too, is unpersuasive; it just ignores the fact that the statute places an obligation on the Panel to remand no later than the conclusion of pretrial proceedings in the transferee court, and no exercise in rulemaking can read that obligation out of the statute. See *28 U.S.C. § 1407* (f) (express requirement that rules be consistent with statute).

B

Milberg proffers two further arguments for overlooking the tension between a broad reading of a court's pretrial authority and the Panel's remand obligation. First, it relies on a subtle reading of the provision of

§ 1407(a) limiting the Panel's remand obligation to cases not "previously terminated" during the pretrial period. To be sure, this exception to the Panel's remand obligation indicates that the Panel is not meant to issue ceremonial remand orders in cases already concluded by summary judgment, say, or dismissal. But according to Milberg, the imperative to remand is also inapplicable to cases self-assigned under § 1404, because the self-assignment "terminates" the case insofar as its venue depends on § 1407. When the § 1407 character of the action disappears, Milberg argues, the strictures of § 1407 fall away as well, relieving the Panel of any further duty in the case. The trouble with this creative argument, though, is that the statute manifests no such subtlety. Section 1407(a) speaks not in terms of imbuing transferred actions with some new and distinctive venue character, but simply in terms of "civil actions" or "actions." It says that such an action, not its acquired personality, must be terminated before the Panel is excused from ordering remand. The language is straightforward, and with a straightforward application ready to hand, statutory interpretation has no business getting metaphysical.

Second, Milberg tries to draw an inference in its favor from the one subsection of § 1407 that does authorize the Panel to transfer a case for trial as well as pretrial proceedings. Subsection (h) provides that,

"notwithstanding the provisions of section 1404 or subsection (f) of this section, the judicial panel on multidistrict litigation may consolidate and transfer with or without the consent of the parties, for both pretrial purposes and for trial, any action brought under section 4C of the Clayton Act."

Milberg fastens on the introductory language explicitly overriding the "provisions of section 1404 or subsection (f)," which would otherwise, respectively, limit a district court to transferring a case "to any other district or division where it might have been brought," § 1404(a), and limit the Panel to prescribing rules "not inconsistent with Acts of Congress," § 1407(f). On Milberg's reasoning, these overrides are required because the cited provisions would otherwise conflict with the remainder of subsection (h) authorizing the Panel to order trial of certain Clayton Act cases in the transferee court. The argument then runs that since there is no override of subsection (a) of § 1407, subsection (a) must be consistent with a transfer for trial as well as pretrial matters. This reasoning is fallacious, however. Subsections (a) and (h) are independent sources of transfer authority in the Panel; each is apparently written to stand on its own feet. Subsection (h) need not exclude the application of subsection (a), because nothing in (a) would by its terms limit any provision of (h).

Subsection (h) is not merely valueless to Milberg, however; it is ammunition for Lexecon. For the one point that subsection (h) does demonstrate is that Congress knew how to distinguish between trial assignments and pretrial proceedings in cases subject to § 1407. Although the enactment of subsection (a), Act of Apr. 29, 1968, 82 Stat. 109, preceded the enactment of subsection (h), Act of Sept. 30, 1976, § 303, 90 Stat. 1394, 1396, the fact that the later section distinguishes trial assignments from pretrial proceedings generally is certainly some confirmation for our conclusion, on independent grounds, that the subjects of pretrial proceedings in subsections (a) and (b) do not include self-assignment orders.

C

There is, finally, nothing left of Milberg's position beyond an appeal to legislative history, some of which turns out to ignore the question before us, and some of which may support Lexecon. Milberg cites a House Report on the bill that became § 1407, which addresses the question of trial transfer in multidistrict litigation cases by saying that "of course, *28 U.S.C. 1404*, providing for changes of venue generally, is available in those instances where transfer of a case for all purposes is desirable." H.R.Rep. No. 1130, 90th Cong., 2d Sess., p. 4 (1968) (hereinafter H.R.Rep.), cited in Brief for Respondents Milberg et al. 25. But the question is not whether a change of venue may be ordered in a case consolidated under § 1407(a); on any view of § 1407(a), if an order may be made under § 1404(a), it may be made after remand of the case to the originating district court. The relevant question for our purposes is whether a transferee court, and not a transferor court, may grant such a motion, and on this point, the language cited by Milberg provides no guidance.

If it has anything to say to us here, the legislative history tends to confirm that self-assignment is beyond the scope of the transferee court's authority. The same House Report that spoke of the continued vitality of § 1404 in § 1407 cases also said this:

"The proposed statute affects only the pretrial stages in multidistrict litigation. It would not affect the place of trial in any case or exclude the possibility of transfer under other Federal statutes.

The subsection requires that transferred cases be remanded to the originating district at the close of coordinated pretrial proceedings. The bill does not, therefore, include the trial of cases in the consolidated proceedings." H.R.Rep., at 3–4.

* * *

III

The remaining question goes to the remedy, which Milberg argues may be omitted under the harmless error doctrine. Milberg posits a distinction between a first category of cases erroneously litigated in a district in which (absent waiver) venue may never be laid under the governing statute, see *Olberding v. Illinois Central R. Co., 346 U.S. 338, 340, 98 L.Ed. 39, 74 S.Ct. 83 (1953),* and a second category, in which the plaintiff might originally have chosen to litigate in the trial forum to which it was unwillingly and erroneously carried, as by a transfer under § 1404. In the first, reversal is necessary; in the second affirmance is possible if no independent and substantial right was violated in a trial whose venue was determined by a discretionary decision. Since Lexecon could have brought suit in the Arizona district consistently with the general venue requirements of *28 U.S.C. § 1391,* and since the transfer for trial was made on the authority of § 1404(a), Milberg argues, this case falls within the second category and should escape reversal because none of Lexecon's substantial rights was prejudicially affected, see § 2111. Assuming the distinction may be drawn, however, we think this case bears closer analogy to those in the first category, in which reversal with new trial is required because venue is precluded by the governing statute.

Milberg's argument assumes the only kind of statute entitled to respect in accordance with its uncompromising terms is a statute that categorically limits a plaintiff's initial choice of forum. But there is no apparent reason why courts should not be equally bound by a venue statute that just as categorically limits the authority of courts (and special panels) to override a plaintiff's choice. If the former statute creates interests too substantial to be denied without a remedy, the latter statute ought to be recognized as creating interests equally substantial. In each instance the substantiality of the protected interest is attested by a congressional judgment that in the circumstances described in the statute no discretion is to be left to a court faced with an objection to a statutory violation. To render relief discretionary in either instance would be to allow uncorrected defiance of a categorical congressional judgment to become its own justification. * * *

Nor is Milberg correct that our recent decision in *Caterpillar v. Lewis, 519 U.S. 61, 136 L.Ed.2d 437, 117 S.Ct. 467 (1996),* is to the contrary. In that case, which got no new trial, the jurisdictional defect (a lack of complete diversity) had been cured by subsequent events. * * * After Caterpillar, therefore, since removal is permissible only where original jurisdiction exists at the time of removal or at the time of the entry of final judgment, the condition contained in the removal statute retains significance. But the § 1407(a) mandate would lose all meaning if a party who continuously objected to an uncorrected categorical violation of the mandate could obtain no relief at the end of the day.

Accordingly, the judgment of the Court of Appeals is reversed, and the case is remanded for further proceedings consistent with this opinion.

So ordered.

FELTNER v. COLUMBIA PICTURES TELEVISION, INC.

Supreme Court of the United States, 1998.
523 U.S. 340, 118 S.Ct. 1279, 140 L.Ed.2d 438.

Justice THOMAS delivered the opinion of the Court.

Section 504(c) of the Copyright Act permits a copyright owner "to recover, instead of actual damages and profits, an award of statutory damages . . ., in a sum of not less than $500 or more than $20,000 as the court considers just." 90 Stat. 2585, as amended, *17 U.S.C. § 504*(c)(1). In this case, we consider whether § 504(c) or the Seventh Amendment grants a right to a jury trial when a copyright owner elects to recover statutory damages. We hold that although the statute is silent on the point, the Seventh Amendment provides a right to a jury trial, which includes a right to a jury determination of the amount of statutory damages. We therefore reverse.

7th Amend. right to jury even for statutory damages

I

Petitioner C. Elvin Feltner owns Krypton International Corporation, which in 1990 acquired three television stations in the southeastern United States. Respondent Columbia Pictures Television, Inc., had licensed several television series to these stations, including "Who's the Boss," "Silver Spoons," "Hart to Hart," and "T.J. Hooker." After the stations became delinquent in making their royalty payments to Columbia, Krypton and Columbia entered into negotiations to restructure the stations' debt. These discussions were unavailing, and Columbia terminated the stations' license agreements in October 1991. Despite Columbia's termination, the stations continued broadcasting the programs.

Columbia sued Feltner, Krypton, the stations, various Krypton subsidiaries, and certain Krypton officers in federal district court alleging, inter alia, copyright infringement arising from the stations' unauthorized broadcasting of the programs. Columbia sought various forms of relief under the Copyright Act of 1976 (Copyright Act), *17 U.S.C. § 101* et seq., including a permanent injunction, § 502; impoundment of all copies of the programs, § 503; actual damages or, in the alternative, statutory damages, § 504; and costs and attorney's fees, § 505. On Columbia's motion, the District Court entered partial summary judgment as to liability for Columbia on its copyright infringement claims.

Columbia exercised the option afforded by § 504(c) of the Copyright Act to recover "Statutory Damages" in lieu of actual damages. In relevant part, § 504(c) provides:

"STATUTORY DAMAGES—

"(1) Except as provided by clause (2) of this subsection, the copyright owner may elect, at any time before final judgment is rendered, to recover, instead of actual damages and profits, an award of statutory damages for all infringements involved in the action, with respect to any one work, ... in a sum of not less than $500 or more than $20,000 as the court considers just...."

"(2) In a case where the copyright owner sustains the burden of proving, and the court finds, that infringement was committed willfully, the court [in] its discretion may increase the award of statutory damages to a sum of not more than $100,000. In a case where the infringer sustains the burden of proving, and the court finds, that such infringer was not aware and had no reason to believe that his or her acts constituted an infringement of copyright, the court in its discretion may reduce the award of statutory damages to a sum of not less than $200...." *17 U.S.C. § 504* (c).

The District Court denied Feltner's request for a jury trial on statutory damages, ruling instead that such issues would be determined at a bench trial. After two days of trial, the trial judge held that each episode of each series constituted a separate work and that the airing of the same episode by different stations controlled by Feltner constituted separate violations; accordingly, the trial judge determined that there had been a total of 440 acts of infringement. The trial judge further found that Feltner's infringement was willful and fixed statutory damages at $20,000 per act of infringement. Applying that amount to the number of acts of infringement, the trial judge determined that Columbia was entitled to $8,800,000 in statutory damages, plus costs and attorney's fees.

The Court of Appeals for the Ninth Circuit affirmed in all relevant respects. *Columbia Pictures Television v. Krypton Broadcasting of Birmingham, Inc., 106 F.3d 284 (1997).* Most importantly for present purposes, the court rejected Feltner's argument that he was entitled to have a jury determine statutory damages. Relying on *Sid & Marty Krofft Television Productions, Inc. v. McDonald's Corp., 562 F.2d 1157 (CA9 1977)*—which held that § 25(b) of the Copyright Act of 1909, the statutory predecessor of § 504(c), required the trial judge to assess statutory damages—the Court of Appeals held that § 504(c) does not grant a right to a jury determination of statutory damages. The Court reasoned that "if Congress intended to overrule *Krofft* by having the jury determine the proper award of statutory damages, it would have altered" the language "as the court considers just" in § 504(c). *106 F.3d at 293.* The Court of Appeals further concluded that the "Seventh Amendment does not provide a right to a jury trial on the issue of statutory damages because an award of such damages is equitable in nature." Ibid. We granted certiorari.

II

Before inquiring into the applicability of the Seventh Amendment, we must " 'first ascertain whether a construction of the statute is fairly possible by which the [constitutional] question may be avoided.' " *Tull v. United States, 481 U.S. 412, 417, n. 3, 95 L.Ed.2d 365, 107 S.Ct. 1831 (1987)* (quoting *Curtis v. Loether, 415 U.S. 189, 192, n. 6, 39 L.Ed.2d 260, 94 S.Ct. 1005 (1974)).* Such a construction is not possible here, for we cannot discern "any congressional intent to grant . . . the right to a jury trial," *481 U.S. at 417, n. 3,* on an award of statutory damages.

The language of § 504(c) does not grant a right to have a jury assess statutory damages. Statutory damages are to be assessed in an amount that "the court considers just." § 504(c)(1). Further, in the event that "the court finds" the infringement was willful or innocent, "the court in its discretion" may, within limits, increase or decrease the amount of statutory damages. § 504(c)(2). These phrases, like the entire statutory provision, make no mention of a right to a jury trial or, for that matter, to juries at all.

The word "court" in this context appears to mean judge, not jury. Cf. *F.W. Woolworth Co. v. Contemporary Arts, Inc., 344 U.S. 228, 232, 97 L.Ed. 276, 73 S.Ct. 222 (1952)* (referring to the "judicial discretion" necessary for "the court's choice between a computed measure of damage and that imputed by" the Copyright Act of 1909) (emphasis added). In fact, the other remedies provisions of the Copyright Act use the term "court" in contexts generally thought to confer authority on a judge, rather than a jury. * * *

Feltner relies on *Lorillard v. Pons, 434 U.S. 575, 585, 55 L.Ed.2d 40, 98 S.Ct. 866 (1978),* in which we held that the Age Discrimination in Employment Act of 1967 (ADEA), 81 Stat. 602, *29 U.S.C. § 621* et seq., provides a statutory right to a jury trial in an action for unpaid wages even though the statute authorizes "the court . . . to grant such legal or equitable relief as may be appropriate," § 626(b). That holding, however, turned on two crucial factors: The ADEA's remedial provisions were expressly to be enforced in accordance with the Fair Labor Standards Act of 1938, as amended, *29 U.S.C. § 101* et seq., which had been uniformly interpreted to provide a right to a jury trial, *Lorillard v. Pons, 434 U.S. at 580–581;* and the statute used the word "legal," which we found to be a "term of art" used in cases "in which legal relief is available and legal rights are determined" by juries, *id., at 583.* Section 504(c), in contrast, does not make explicit reference to another statute that has been uniformly interpreted to provide a right to jury trial and does not use the word "legal" or other language denoting legal relief or rights.

We thus discern no statutory right to a jury trial when a copyright owner elects to recover statutory damages. Accordingly, we must reach the constitutional question.

III

The Seventh Amendment provides that "in Suits at common law, where the value in controversy shall exceed twenty dollars, the right of trial by jury shall be preserved...." U.S. Const., Amdt. 7. Since Justice Story's time, the Court has understood "Suits at common law" to refer "not merely [to] suits, which the common law recognized among its old and settled proceedings, but [to] suits in which legal rights were to be ascertained and determined, in contradistinction to those where equitable rights alone were recognized, and equitable remedies were administered." *Parsons v. Bedford, 3 Pet. 433, 447 (1830)* (emphasis in original). The Seventh Amendment thus applies not only to common-law causes of action, but also to "actions brought to enforce statutory rights that are analogous to common-law causes of action ordinarily decided in English law courts in the late 18th century, as opposed to those customarily heard by courts of equity or admiralty." *Granfinanciera, S.A. v. Nordberg, 492 U.S. 33, 42, 106 L.Ed.2d 26, 109 S.Ct. 2782 (1989)* (citing *Curtis v. Loether, 415 U.S. at 193*). To determine whether a statutory action is more analogous to cases tried in courts of law than to suits tried in courts of equity or admiralty, we examine both the nature of the statutory action and the remedy sought. See *492 U.S. at 42.*

Unlike many of our recent Seventh Amendment cases, which have involved modern statutory rights unknown to 18th-century England, see, e.g., *Wooddell v. Electrical Workers, 502 U.S. 93, 116 L.Ed.2d 419, 112 S.Ct. 494 (1991)* (alleged violations of union's duties under Labor Management Relations Act, 1947, and Labor–Management Reporting and Disclosure Act of 1959); *Granfinanciera v. Nordberg, supra* (action to rescind fraudulent preference under Bankruptcy Act); *Tull v. United States, supra* (government's claim for civil penalties under Clean Water Act); *Curtis v. Loether, supra* (claim under Title VIII of Civil Rights Act of 1968), in this case there are close analogues to actions seeking statutory damages under § 504(c). Before the adoption of the Seventh Amendment, the common law and statutes in England and this country granted copyright owners causes of action for infringement. More importantly, copyright suits for monetary damages were tried in courts of law, and thus before juries.

* * * Actions seeking damages for infringement of common-law copyright, like actions seeking damages for invasions of other property rights, were tried in courts of law in actions on the case. See *Millar v. Taylor, supra, 2396–2397, 98 Eng.Rep., at 251.* Actions on the case, like other actions at law, were tried before juries. See *M'Clenachan v. [*18] M'Carty, 1 U.S. 375, 1 Dall. 375, 378, 1 L.Ed. 183 (C.P.Phila.Cty.1788);* 5 J. Moore, Moore's Federal Practice P 8.11[5] (2d ed. 1996); 1 J. Chitty, Treatise on Pleading and Parties to Actions, at 164 (1892).

In 1710, the first English copyright statute, the Statute of Anne, was enacted to protect published books. * * * Like the earlier practice with regard to common-law copyright claims for damages, actions seeking damages under the Statute of Anne were tried in courts of law. See *Beckford v. Hood, 7 T.R. 621, 627, 101 Eng.Rep. 1164, 1167 (K.B.1798)*

("The statute having vested that right in the author, the common law gives the remedy by action on the case for the violation of it") (Kenyon, C.J.).

The practice of trying copyright damages actions at law before juries was followed in this country, where statutory copyright protections were enacted even before adoption of the Constitution. In 1783, the Continental Congress passed a resolution recommending that the States secure copyright protections for authors. * * * Twelve States (all except Delaware) responded by enacting copyright statutes, each of which provided a cause of action for damages, and none of which made any reference to equity jurisdiction. * * * Although these statutes were short-lived, and hence few courts had occasion to interpret them, the available evidence suggests that the practice was for copyright actions seeking damages to be tried to a jury. See *Hudson & Goodwin v. Patten, 1 Root 133, 134 (Conn.Super.Ct.1789)* (jury awarded copyright owner L 100 under Connecticut copyright statute).

　　　* * *

In 1790, Congress passed the first federal copyright statute, the Copyright Act of 1790, which similarly authorized the awarding of damages for copyright infringements. Act of May 31, 1790, ch. 15, §§ 2, 6, 1 Stat. 124, 125. The Copyright Act of 1790 provided that damages for copyright infringement of published works would be "the sum of fifty cents for every sheet which shall be found in [the infringer's] possession, ... to be recovered by action of debt in any court of record in the United States, wherein the same is cognizable." § 2. Like the Statute of Anne, the Copyright Act of 1790 provided that half ("one moiety") of such damages were to go to the copyright owner and half to the United States. For infringement of an unpublished manuscript, the statute entitled a copyright owner to "all damages occasioned by such injury, to be recovered by a special action on the case founded upon this act, in any court having cognizance thereof." § 6.

There is no evidence that the Copyright Act of 1790 changed the practice of trying copyright actions for damages in courts of law before juries. As we have noted, actions on the case and actions of debt were actions at law for which a jury was required. * * * Moreover, actions to recover damages under the Copyright Act of 1831—which differed from the Copyright Act of 1790 only in the amount (increased to $1 from 50 cents) authorized to be recovered for certain infringing sheets—were consistently tried to juries. See, e.g., *Backus v. Gould, 48 U.S. 798, 7 How. 798, 802, 12 L.Ed. 919 (1849)* (jury awarded damages of $2,069.75); Reed v. Carusi, 1 Taney 72, *20 F.Cas. 431, 432* (No. 11, 642) (CCMd.1845) (jury awarded damages of $200); *Millett v. Snowden, 17 F.Cas. 374, 375 (SDNY 1844)* (jury awarded damages of $625); *Dwight v. Appleton, 8 F.Cas. 183, 185 (SDNY 1843)* (jury awarded damages of $2,000).

Columbia does not dispute this historical evidence. In fact, Columbia makes no attempt to draw an analogy between an action for statutory damages under § 504(c) and any historical cause of action— including those actions for monetary relief that we have characterized as equitable, such as actions for disgorgement of improper profits. See *Teamsters v. Terry, 494 U.S. 558, 570–571, 108 L.Ed.2d 519, 110 S.Ct. 1339 (1990); Tull v. United States, 481 U.S. at 424.* Rather, Columbia merely contends that statutory damages are clearly equitable in nature.

We are not persuaded. We have recognized the "general rule" that monetary relief is legal, *Teamsters v. Terry, supra, at 570,* and an award of statutory damages may serve purposes traditionally associated with legal relief, such as compensation and punishment. See *Curtis v. Loether, 415 U.S. at 196* (actual damages are "traditional form of relief offered in the courts of law"); *Tull v. United States, supra, at 422* ("Remedies intended to punish culpable individuals . . . were issued by courts of law, not courts of equity"). Nor, as we have previously stated, is a monetary remedy rendered equitable simply because it is "not fixed or readily calculable from a fixed formula." *Id, at 422, n. 7.* And there is historical evidence that cases involving discretionary monetary relief were tried before juries. See, e.g., *Coryell v. Colbaugh, 1 N.J.L. 77 (1791)* (jury award of "exemplary damages" in an action on a promise of marriage). Accordingly, we must conclude that the Seventh Amendment provides a right to a jury trial where the copyright owner elects to recover statutory damages.

The right to a jury trial includes the right to have a jury determine the amount of statutory damages, if any, awarded to the copyright owner. It has long been recognized that "by the law the jury are judges of the damages." *Lord Townshend v. Hughes, 2 Mod. 150, 151, 86 Eng.Rep. 994, 994–995 (C.P.1677).* Thus in *Dimick v. Schiedt, 293 U.S. 474, 79 L.Ed. 603, 55 S.Ct. 296 (1935),* the Court stated that "the common law rule as it existed at the time of the adoption of the Constitution" was that "in cases where the amount of damages was uncertain[,] their assessment was a matter so peculiarly within the province of the jury that the Court should not alter it." *Id., at 480* (internal quotation marks and citations omitted). And there is overwhelming evidence that the consistent practice at common law was for juries to award damages. * * *

More specifically, this was the consistent practice in copyright cases. In *Hudson & Goodwin v. Patten, 1 Root at 134,* for example, a jury awarded a copyright owner L 100 under the Connecticut copyright statute, which permitted damages in an amount double the value of the infringed copy. In addition, juries assessed the amount of damages under the Copyright Act of 1831, even though that statute, like the Copyright Act of 1790, fixed damages at a set amount per infringing sheet. See *Backus v. Gould, supra, at 802* (jury awarded damages of $2,069.75); *Reed v. Carusi, supra, at 432* (same, but $200); *Dwight v.*

Appleton, supra, at 185 (same, but $2,000); *Millett v. Snowden, supra, at 375* (same, but $625).

Relying on *Tull v. United States, supra,* Columbia contends that the Seventh Amendment does not provide a right to a jury determination of the amount of the award. In Tull, we held that the Seventh Amendment grants a right to a jury trial on all issues relating to liability for civil penalties under the Clean Water Act, *33 U.S.C. §§ 1251,* 1319(d), see *481 U.S. at 425,* but then went on to decide that Congress could constitutionally authorize trial judges to assess the amount of the civil penalties, see *id., at 426–427.* According to Columbia, Tull demonstrates that a jury determination of the amount of statutory damages is not necessary "to preserve 'the substance of the common-law right of trial by jury.' " *Id., at 426* (quoting *Colgrove v. Battin, 413 U.S. 149, 157, 37 L.Ed.2d 522, 93 S.Ct. 2448 (1973)).*

In Tull, however, we were presented with no evidence that juries historically had determined the amount of civil penalties to be paid to the Government. Moreover, the awarding of civil penalties to the Government could be viewed as analogous to sentencing in a criminal proceeding. See *481 U.S. at 428* (SCALIA, J., concurring in part an dissenting in part). Here, of course, there is no similar analogy, and there is clear and direct historical evidence that juries, both as a general matter and in copyright cases, set the amount of damages awarded to a successful plaintiff. Tull is thus inapposite. As a result, if a party so demands, a jury must determine the actual amount of statutory damages under § 504(c) in order "to preserve 'the substance of the common-law right of trial by jury.' " *Id., at 426.*

For the foregoing reasons, we hold that the Seventh Amendment provides a right to a jury trial on all issues pertinent to an award of statutory damages under § 504(c) of the Copyright Act, including the amount itself. The judgment below is reversed, and we remand the case for proceedings consistent with this opinion.

It is so ordered.

JUSTICE SCALIA, concurring in the judgment.

It is often enough that we must hold an enactment of Congress to be unconstitutional. I see no reason to do so here—not because I believe that jury trial is not constitutionally required (I do not reach that issue), but because the statute can and therefore should be read to provide jury trial.

* * *

That is at least so in light of contradictory evidence from the statutory history, which the Court chooses to ignore. Section 504(c) is the direct descendant of a remedy created for unauthorized performance of dramatic compositions in an 1856 copyright statute. That statute provided for damages "not less than one hundred dollars for the first, and fifty dollars for every subsequent performance, as to the court having cognizance thereof shall appear to be just," enforced through an "action on the case or other equivalent remedy." Act of Aug. 18, 1856, ch. 169, 11 Stat. 138, 139. Because actions on the case were historically tried at law, it seems clear that this original statute permitted juries to assess such damages. * * *If a right to jury trial was consistent with the meaning of the phrase "as to the court ... shall appear to be just" in the 1856 statutory damages provision, I see no reason to insist that the phrase "as the court considers just" has a different meaning in that provision's latest reenactment. "Where, as here, Congress adopts a new law incorporating sections of a prior law, Congress normally can be presumed to have had knowledge of the interpretation given to the incorporated law, at least insofar as it affects the new statute." *Lorillard, 434 U.S. at 581.*

I do not contend that reading "court" to include "jury" is necessarily the best interpretation of this statutory text. The Court is perhaps correct that the indications pointing to a change in meaning from the 1856 statute predominate. As I have written elsewhere, however:

"The doctrine of constitutional doubt does not require that the problem-avoiding construction be the preferable one—the one the Court would adopt in any event. Such a standard would deprive the doctrine of all function. 'Adopt the interpretation that avoids the constitutional doubt if that is the right one' produces precisely the same result as 'adopt the right interpretation.' Rather, the doctrine of constitutional doubt comes into play when the statute is 'susceptible of' the problem-avoiding interpretation, *Delaware & Hudson Co., 213 U.S. at 408*—when that interpretation is reasonable, though not necessarily the best." Almendarez–Torres v. United States, 523 U.S. __, __ (SCALIA, J., dissenting).

As the majority's discussion amply demonstrates, there would be considerable doubt about the constitutionality of § 504(c) if it did not permit jury determination of the amount of statutory damages. Because an interpretation of § 540(c) that avoids the Seventh Amendment question is at least "fairly possible," I would adopt that interpretation, prevent the invalidation of this statute, and reserve the constitutional issue for another day.

MARKMAN v. WESTVIEW INSTRUMENTS, INC.

Supreme Court of the United States, 1996.
517 U.S. 1384, 116 S.Ct. 1384, 134 L.Ed.2d, 577.

Justice SOUTER delivered the opinion of the Court.

The question here is whether the interpretation of a so-called patent claim, the portion of the patent document that defines the scope of the patentee's rights, is a matter of law reserved entirely for the court, or subject to a Seventh Amendment guarantee that a jury will determine the meaning of any disputed term of art about which expert testimony is offered. We hold that the construction of a patent, including terms of art within its claim, is exclusively within the province of the court.

I

* * * It has long been understood that a patent must describe the exact scope of an invention and its manufacture to "secure to [the patentee] all to which he is entitled, [and] to apprise the public of what is still open to them." *McClain v. Ortmayer*, 141 U.S. 419, 424, 12 S.Ct. 76, 77, 35 L.Ed. 800 (1891). Under the modern American system, these objectives are served by two distinct elements of a patent document. First, it contains a specification describing the invention "in such full, clear, concise, and exact terms as to enable any person skilled in the art ... to make and use the same." 35 U.S.C. § 112 * * *. Second, a patent includes one or more "claims," which "particularly poin[t] out and distinctly clai[m] the subject matter which the applicant regards as his invention." 35 U.S.C. § 112.

* * * Victory in an infringement suit requires a finding that the patent claim "covers the alleged infringer's product or process," which in turn necessitates a determination of "what the words in the claim mean." [H. Schwartz, Patent Law and Practice 80 (2d Ed. 1995)] * * *.

[Petitioner Markman's] patent describes a system that can monitor and report the status, location, and movement of clothing in a dry-cleaning establishment. The Markman system consists of a keyboard and data processor to generate written records for each transaction, including a bar code readable by optical detectors operated by employees, who log the progress of clothing through the dry-cleaning process. Respondent Westview's product also includes a keyboard and processor, and it lists charges for the dry-cleaning services on bar-coded tickets that can be read by portable optical detectors.

Markman brought an infringement suit against Westview and Althon Enterprises, an operator of dry-cleaning establishments using Westview's products (collectively, Westview). Westview responded that Markman's patent is not infringed by its system because the latter functions merely to record an inventory of receivables by tracking invoices and transaction totals, rather than to record and track an inventory of articles of clothing. Part of the dispute hinged upon the meaning of the word "inventory," a term found in Markman's independent claim 1, which states that Markman's product can "maintain an inventory total" and "detect and localize spurious additions to inventory." The case was tried before a jury, which heard, among others, a witness produced by Markman who testified about the meaning of the claim language.

After the jury compared the patent to Westview's device, it found an infringement of Markman's [claim 1] * * *. The District Court nevertheless granted Westview's deferred motion for judgment as a matter of law, one of its reasons being that the term "inventory" in Markman's patent encompasses "both cash inventory and the actual physical inventory of articles of clothing." 772 F.Supp. 1535, 1537–1538 (E.D.Pa.1991). Under the trial court's construction of the patent, the production, sale, or use of a tracking system for dry cleaners would not infringe Markman's patent unless the product was capable of tracking articles of clothing throughout the cleaning process and generating reports about their status and location. Since Westview's system cannot do these things, the District Court directed a verdict on the ground that Westview's device does not have the "means to maintain an inventory total" and thus cannot "detect and localize spurious additions to inventory as well as spurious deletions therefrom," as required by claim 1. *Id.*, at 1537.

Markman appealed, arguing it was error for the District Court to substitute its construction of the disputed claim term "inventory" for the construction the jury had presumably given it. The United States Court of Appeals for the Federal Circuit affirmed, holding the interpretation of claim terms to be the exclusive province of the court and the Seventh Amendment to be consistent with that conclusion. 52 F.3d 967 (1995). Markman sought our review on each point, and we granted certiorari. 515 U.S. 1192, 116 S.Ct. 40, 132 L.Ed.2d 921 (1995). We now affirm.

II

* * *

A

* * * As to * * * the character of the cause of action, "[t]he form of our analysis is familiar. 'First we compare the statutory action to 18th-century actions brought in the courts of England prior to the merger of the courts of law and equity.'" *Granfinanciera, S.A. v. Nordberg*, 492 U.S. 33, 42, 109 S.Ct. 2782, 2790, 106 L.Ed.2d 26 (1989) (citation omitted). Equally familiar is the descent of today's patent infringement action from the infringement actions tried at law in the 18th century, and there is no dispute that infringement cases today must be tried to a jury, as their predecessors were more than two centuries ago. See, *e.g.*, *Bramah v. Hardcastle*, 1 Carp. P.C. 168 (K.B.1789).

B

This conclusion raises the second question, whether a particular issue occurring within a jury trial (here the construction of a patent claim) is itself necessarily a jury issue, the guarantee being essential to preserve the right to a jury's resolution of the ultimate dispute. In some instances the answer to this second question may be easy because of clear historical evidence that the very subsidiary question was so regarded under the English practice of leaving the issue for a jury. But when, as here, the old practice provides no clear answer * * * we are forced to make a judgment about the scope of the Seventh Amendment guarantee without the benefit of any foolproof test.

The Court has repeatedly said that the answer to the second question "must depend on whether the jury must shoulder this responsibility *as necessary to preserve the 'substance of the common-law right of trial by jury.' " Tull v. United States, supra,* at 426, 107 S.Ct., at 1840 (emphasis added) (quoting Colgrove v. Battin, 413 U.S. 149, 156, 93 S.Ct. 2448, 2452, 37 L.Ed.2d 522 (1973)); * * *.

[We should] classify a mongrel practice (like construing a term of art following receipt of evidence) by using the historical method, much as we do in characterizing the suits and actions within which they arise. Where there is no exact antecedent, the best hope lies in comparing the modern practice to earlier ones whose allocation to court or jury we do know, * * * seeking the best analogy we can draw between an old and the new, * * *.

C

* * *

At the time relevant for Seventh Amendment analogies, * * * it was the specification, [i.e., the description and drawings and not the inventor's claim] that represented the key to the patent. Thus, patent litigation in that early period was typified by so-called novelty actions, testing whether "any essential part of [the patent had been] disclosed to the public before," *Huddart v. Grimshaw,* Dav. Pat. Cas. 265, 298 (K.B. 1803), and "enablement" cases, in which juries were asked to determine whether the specification described the invention well enough to allow members of the appropriate trade to reproduce it, see, *e.g., Arkwright v. Nightingale,* Dav. Pat. Cas. 37, 60 (C.P. 1785).

The closest 18th-century analogue of modern claim construction seems, then, to have been the construction of specifications, and as to that function the mere smattering of patent cases that we have from this period shows no established jury practice sufficient to support an argument by analogy that today's construction of a claim should be a guaranteed jury issue. Few of the case reports even touch upon the proper interpretation of disputed terms in the specifications at issue, * * * and none demonstrates that the definition of such a term was determined by the jury. This absence of an established practice should not surprise us, given the primitive state of jury patent practice at the end of the 18th century, when juries were still new to the field. * * *

Markman seeks to supply what the early case reports lack in so many words by relying on decisions like *Turner v. Winter,* 1 T.R. 602, 99 Eng. Rep. 1274 (K.B.1787), and *Arkwright v. Nightingale,* Dav. Pat. Cas. 37 (C.P. 1785), to argue that the 18th-century juries must have acted as definers of patent terms just to reach the verdicts we know they rendered in patent cases turning on enablement or novelty. But the conclusion simply does not follow. There is no more reason to infer that juries supplied plenary interpretation of written instruments in patent litigation than in other cases implicating the meaning of documentary terms, and we do know that in other kinds of cases during this period judges, not juries, ordinarily construed written documents. The probability that the judges were doing the same thing in the patent litigation of the time is confirmed by the fact that as soon as the English reports did begin to describe the construction of patent documents, they show the judges construing the terms of the specifications. See *Bovill v. Moore*, Dav. Pat. Cas. 361, 399, 404 (C.P. 1816) (judge submits question of novelty to the jury only after explaining some of the language and "stat[ing] in what terms the specification runs"); cf. *Russell v. Cowley & Dixon*, Webs. Pat. Cas. 457, 467–470 (Exch.1834) (construing the terms of the specification in reviewing a verdict); *Haworth v. Hardcastle*, Webs. Pat. Cas. 480, 484–485 (1834) (same). This evidence is in fact buttressed by cases from this Court; when they first reveal actual practice, the practice revealed is of the judge construing the patent. See, *e.g. Winans v. New York & Erie R. Co.*, 21 How. 88, 100, 16 L.Ed. 68 (1859); *Winans v. Denmead*, 15 How. 330, 338, 14 L.Ed. 717 (1854); *Hogg v. Emerson*, 6 How. 437, 484, 12 L.Ed. 505 (1848); cf. *Parker v. Hulme*, 18 F. Cas. 1138 (No. 10,740) (CC ED Pa. 1849). These indications of our patent practice are the more impressive for being all of a piece with what we know about the analogous contemporary practice of interpreting terms within a land patent, where it fell to the judge, not the jury, to construe the words.

D

Losing, then, on the contention that juries generally had interpretive responsibilities during the 18th century, Markman seeks a different anchor for analogy in the more modest contention that even if judges were charged with construing most terms in the patent, the art of defining terms of art employed in a specification fell within the province of the jury. Again, however, Markman has no authority from the period in question, but relies instead on the later case of *Neilson v. Harford*, Webs. Pat. Cas. 328 (Exch.1841). There, an exchange between the judge and the lawyers indicated that although the construction of a patent was ordinarily for the court, *id.*, at 349 (Alderson, B.), judges should "leav[e] the question of words of art to the jury," *id.*, at 350 (Alderson, B.); see also *id.*, at 370 (judgment of the court); *Hill v. Evans*, 4 De. G.F. & J. 288, 293–294, 45 Eng. Rep. 1195, 1197 (Ch. 1862). Without, however, in any way disparaging the weight to which Baron Alderson's view is entitled, the most we can say is that an English report more than 70 years after the time that concerns us indicates an exception to what probably had been occurring earlier. In place of Markman's inference that this exceptional practice existed in 1791 there is at best only a possibility that it did, and for anything more than a possibility we have found no scholarly authority.

III

Since evidence of common law practice at the time of the Framing does not entail application of the Seventh Amendment's jury guarantee to the construction of the claim document, we must look elsewhere to characterize this determination of meaning in order to allocate it as between court or jury. We accordingly consult existing precedent and consider both the relative interpretive skills of judges and juries and the statutory policies that ought to be furthered by the allocation.

A

* * * [There are] two elements of a simple patent case, construing the patent and determining whether infringement occurred * * *. "The first is a question of law, to be determined by the court, construing the letters-patent, and the description of the invention and specification of claim annexed to them. The second is a question of fact, to be submitted to a jury." *Winans v. Denmead*, 15 How., at 338 * * *.

In arguing for a different allocation of responsibility for the first question, Markman relies primarily on two cases, *Bischoff v. Wethered*, 9 Wall. 812, 19 L.Ed. 829 (1870), and *Tucker v. Spalding*, 13 Wall. 453, 20 L.Ed. 515 (1872). These are said to show that evidence of the meaning of patent terms was offered to 19th-century juries, and thus to imply that the meaning of a documentary term was a jury issue whenever it was subject to evidentiary proof. That is not what Markman's cases show, however.

In order to resolve the *Bischoff* suit implicating the construction of rival patents, we considered "whether the court below was bound to compare the two specifications, and to instruct the jury, as a matter of law, whether the inventions therein described were, or were not, identical." 9 Wall., at 813 (statement of the case). We said it was not bound to do that, on the ground that investing the court with so dispositive a role would improperly eliminate the jury's function in answering the ultimate question of infringement. On that ultimate issue, expert testimony had been admitted on "the nature of the various mechanisms or manufactures described in the different patents produced, and as to the identity or diversity between them." *Id.*, at 814. Although the jury's consideration of that expert testimony in resolving the question of infringement was said to impinge upon the well-established principle "that it is the province of the court, and not the jury, to construe the meaning of documentary evidence," *id.*, at 815, we decided that it was not so. We said that

> "the specifications ... profess to describe mechanisms and complicated machinery, chemical compositions and other manufactured products, which have their existence in pais, outside of the documents themselves; and which are commonly described by terms of the art or mystery to which they respectively belong; and these

descriptions and terms of art often require peculiar knowledge and education to understand them aright.... Indeed, the whole subject-matter of a patent is an embodied conception outside of the patent itself.... This outward embodiment of the terms contained in the patent is the thing invented, and is to be properly sought, like the explanation of all latent ambiguities arising from the description of external things, by evidence in pais." *Ibid.*

Bischoff does not then, as Markman contends, hold that the use of expert testimony about the meaning of terms of art requires the judge to submit the question of their construction to the jury. It is instead a case in which the Court drew a line between issues of document interpretation and product identification, and held that expert testimony was properly presented to the jury on the latter, ultimate issue, whether the physical objects produced by the patent were identical. The Court did not see the decision as bearing upon the appropriate treatment of disputed terms. As the opinion emphasized, the Court's "view of the case is not intended to, and does not, trench upon the doctrine that the construction of written instruments is the province of the court alone. *It is not the construction of the instrument, but the character of the thing invented, which is sought in questions of identity and diversity of inventions." Id.,* at 816 (emphasis added). *Tucker*, the second case proffered by Markman, is to the same effect. Its reasoning rested expressly on *Bischoff*, and it just as clearly noted that in addressing the ultimate issue of mixed fact and law, it was for the court to "lay down to the jury the law which should govern them." *Tucker, supra,* at 455. * * *

If the line drawn in these two opinions is a fine one, it is one that the Court has drawn repeatedly in explaining the respective roles of the jury and judge in patent cases, * * *.

In sum, neither *Bischoff* nor *Tucker* indicates that juries resolved the meaning of terms of art in construing a patent * * *.

B

Where history and precedent provide no clear answers, functional considerations also play their part in the choice between judge and jury to define terms of art. We said in *Miller v. Fenton*, 474 U.S. 104, 114, 106 S.Ct. 445, 451, 88 L.Ed.2d 405 (1985), that when an issue "falls somewhere between a pristine legal standard and a simple historical fact, the fact/law distinction at times has turned on a determination that, as a matter of the sound administration of justice, one judicial actor is better positioned than another to decide the issue in question." So it turns out here, for judges, not juries, are the better suited to find the acquired meaning of patent terms.

The construction of written instruments is one of those things that judges often do and are likely to do better than jurors unburdened by training in exegesis. Patent construction in particular "is a special occupation, requiring, like all others, special training and practice. The judge, from his training and discipline, is more likely to give a proper interpretation to such instruments than a jury; and he is, therefore, more likely to be right, in performing such a duty, than a jury can be expected to be." *Parker v. Hulme*, 18 F. Cas., at 1140. Such was the understanding nearly a century and a half ago, and there is no reason to weigh the respective strengths of judge and jury differently in relation to the modern claim; quite the contrary, for "the claims of patents have become highly technical in many respects as the result of special doctrines relating to the proper form and scope of claims that have been developed by the courts and the Patent Office." Woodward, Definiteness and Particularity in Patent Claims, 46 Mich. L.Rev. 755, 765 (1948).

Markman would trump these considerations with his argument that a jury should decide a question of meaning peculiar to a trade or profession simply because the question is a subject of testimony requiring credibility determinations, which are the jury's forte. It is, of course, true that credibility judgments have to be made about the experts who testify in patent cases, and in theory there could be a case in which a simple credibility judgment would suffice to choose between experts whose testimony was equally consistent with a patent's internal logic. But our own experience with document construction leaves us doubtful that trial courts will run into many cases like that. In the main, we expect, any credibility determinations will be subsumed within the necessarily sophisticated analysis of the whole document, required by the standard construction rule that a term can be defined only in a way that comports with the instrument as a whole. * * * Thus, in these cases a jury's capabilities to evaluate demeanor, cf. *Miller, supra*, at 114, 117, 106 S.Ct., at 451, 453, to sense the "mainsprings of human conduct," *Commissioner v. Duberstein*, 363 U.S. 278, 289, 80 S.Ct. 1190, 1198, 4 L.Ed.2d 1218 (1960), or to reflect community standards, *United States v. McConney*, 728 F.2d 1195, 1204 (C.A.9 1984) (en banc), are much less significant than a trained ability to evaluate the testimony in relation to the overall structure of the patent. The decisionmaker vested with the task of construing the patent is in the better position to ascertain whether an expert's proposed definition fully comports with the specification and claims and so will preserve the patent's internal coherence. We accordingly think there is sufficient reason to treat construction of terms of art like many other responsibilities that we cede to a judge in the normal course of trial, notwithstanding its evidentiary underpinnings.

C

Finally, we see the importance of uniformity in the treatment of a given patent as an independent reason to allocate all issues of construction to the court. As we noted in *General Elec. Co. v. Wabash Appliance Corp.*, 304 U.S. 364, 369, 58 S.Ct. 899, 902, 82 L.Ed. 1402 (1938), "[t]he limits of a patent must be known for the protection of the patentee, the encouragement of the inventive genius of others and the assurance that the subject of the patent will be dedicated ultimately to the public." Otherwise, a "zone of uncertainty which enterprise and experimentation may enter only at the risk of infringement claims would discourage invention only a little less than unequivocal foreclosure of the field," *United Carbon Co. v. Binney & Smith Co.*, 317 U.S. 228, 236, 63 S.Ct. 165, 170, 87 L.Ed. 232 (1942), and "[t]he public [would] be deprived of rights supposed to belong to it, without being clearly told what it is that limits these rights." *Merrill v. Yeomans*, 94 U.S. 568, 573, 24 L.Ed. 235 (1877). * * *

Uniformity would, however, be ill served by submitting issues of document construction to juries. Making them jury issues would not, to be sure, necessarily leave evidentiary questions of meaning wide open in every new court in which a patent might be litigated, for principles of issue preclusion would ordinarily foster uniformity. Cf. *Blonder–Tongue Laboratories, Inc. v. University of Ill. Foundation*, 402 U.S. 313, 91 S.Ct. 1434, 28 L.Ed.2d 788 (1971). But whereas issue preclusion could not be asserted against new and independent infringement defendants even within a given jurisdiction, treating interpretive issues as purely legal will promote (though it will not guarantee) intrajurisdictional certainty through the application of stare decisis on those questions not yet subject to interjurisdictional uniformity under the authority of the single appeals court.

* * *

Accordingly, we hold that the interpretation of the word "inventory" in this case is an issue for the judge, not the jury, and affirm the decision of the Court of Appeals for the Federal Circuit.

It is so ordered.

ORTIZ v. FIBREBOARD CORP.

Supreme Court of the United States, 1999.
527 U.S. 815, 119 S.Ct. 2295, 144 L.Ed.2d 715.

[Fibreboard was and is the subject of many personal injury lawsuits arising from exposure to its asbestos products. It had already settled some 45,000 claims when, along with its insurers, it decided, along with a group of plaintiffs' lawyers, on a plan to effect a "Global Settlement" of the majority of its remaining liability. Basically, Fibreboard and its insurers would put up $1,535 billion for claimants who would file a Federal Rule 23(b)(1)(B) class action, based on the notion that there existed a "limited fund" to pay members of the class. A major feature of such a class is that its members do not have the ability to opt out of the class in order to bring their separate suits.

At the time of the settlement agreement a lawsuit was before a California court of appeal to determine to what extent, if any, the insurers were liable for a majority of the plaintiffs' damages. Thus the agreement, if approved, would include a settlement of that dispute. A separate agreement, the "Trilateral Settlement Agreement," was reached by which the issuers would put up $2 billion to cover the situation that would exist if the class action was not approved by the federal courts. Suit was then brought in the federal court in the Eastern District of Texas. The plan called upon Fibreboard and its insurers to place the agreed upon amount in a trust. Individual claimants were provided with a process for settling their claims with the trust. If no settlement could be reached, claimants would be required to engage in mediation, arbitration, and a mandatory settlement conference. After exhausting that process a claimant could bring a court proceeding against the trust, but there would be a $500,000 limit on recovery and punitive damages and prejudgment interest would be barred.

It should be noted that the class did not cover all claimants. Some 45,000 individuals who had already settled their claims were excluded along with some 53,000 who had suits pending.

The trial court, after extensive hearings, found that the class action met the requirements of Rule 23(a), and fell within the "limited fund" provision of Rule 23(b)(1)(B). It determined that the plan provided a "fair, adequate, and reasonable" settlement under Rule 23(e). On appeal the Fifth Circuit affirmed both the certification of the class and the adequacy of the settlement. The Supreme Court granted certiorari.]

Justice Souter delivered the opinion of the Court.

I

Like *Amchem Products, Inc. v. Windsor*, 521 U.S. 591, 117 S.Ct. 2231, 138 L.Ed.2d 689 (1997), this case is a class action prompted by the elephantine mass of asbestos cases, and our discussion in Amchem will suffice to show how this litigation defies customary judicial administration and calls for national legislation. * * *

III

A

* * *

Rule 23(b)(1)(B) speaks from "a vantage point within the class, [from which the Advisory Committee] spied out situations where lawsuits conducted with individual members of the class would have the practical if not technical effect of concluding the interests of the other members as well, or of impairing the ability of the others to protect their own interests." Kaplan, Continuing Work of the Civil Committee: 1966 Amendments of the Federal Rules of Civil Procedure (I), 81 Harv. L.Rev. 356, 388 (1967) (hereinafter Kaplan, Continuing Work). Thus, the subdivision (read with subdivision (c)(2)) provides for certification of a class whose members have no right to withdraw, when "the prosecution of separate actions ... would create a risk" of "adjudications with respect to individual members of the class which would as a practical matter be dispositive of the interests of the other members not parties to the adjudications or substantially impair or impede their ability to protect their interests." Fed. Rule Civ. Proc. 23(b)(1)(B). Classic examples of such a risk of impairment may, for example, be found in suits brought to reorganize fraternal-benefit societies, see, e.g., *Supreme Tribe of Ben-Hur v. Cauble*, 255 U.S. 356, 41 S.Ct. 338, 65 L.Ed. 673 (1921); actions by shareholders to declare a dividend or otherwise to "fix [their] rights," Kaplan, Continuing Work 388; and actions charging "a breach of trust by an indenture trustee or other fiduciary similarly affecting the members of a large class" of beneficiaries, requiring an accounting or similar procedure "to restore the subject of the trust," Advisory Committee's Notes on Fed. Rule Civ. Proc. 23, 28 U.S.C.App., p. 696 (hereinafter Adv. Comm. Notes). In each of these categories, the shared character of rights claimed or relief awarded entails that any individual adjudication by a class member disposes of, or substantially affects, the interests of absent class members.

* * * One recurring type of such suits was the limited fund class action, aggregating "claims ... made by numerous persons against a fund insufficient to satisfy all claims." Adv. Comm. Notes 697; cf. Newberg § 4.09, at 4–33 ("Classic" limited fund class actions "include claimants to trust assets,a bank account, insurance proceeds, company assets in a liquidation sale, proceeds of a ship sale in a maritime accident suit, and others"). * * * As the Advisory Committee recognized * * *, equity required absent parties to be represented, joinder being impractical, where individual claims to be satisfied from the one asset would, as a practical matter, prejudice the rights of absent claimants against a fund inadequate to pay them all.

Equity, of course, recognized the same necessity to bind absent claimants to a limited fund when no formal imposition of a constructive trust was entailed. In *Guffanti v. National Surety Co.*, 196 N.Y. 452, 458, 90 N.E. 174, 176 (1909), for example, the defendant received money to supply steamship tickets and had posted a $15,000 bond as required by state law. He converted to personal use funds collected from more than 150 ticket purchasers, was then adjudged bankrupt, and absconded. One of the defrauded ticket purchasers sued the surety in equity on behalf of himself and all others like him. Over the defendant's objection, the New York Court of Appeals sustained the equitable class suit, citing among other considerations the fact that all recovery had to come from a "limited fund out of which the aggregate recoveries must be sought" that was inadequate to pay all claims, and subject to pro rata distribution. Id., at 458, 90 N.E. 174, 90 N.E., at 176. * * * ("[Guffanti] explained that when a debtor's assets were less than the total of the creditors' claims, a binding class action was not only permitted but was required; otherwise some creditors (the parties) would be paid and others (the absentees) would not"). See also *Morrison v. Warren 174 Misc. 233*, 234, 20 N.Y.S.2d 26, 27 (1940) (suit on behalf of more than 400 beneficiaries of an insurance policy following a fire appropriate where "the amount of the claims ... greatly exceeds the amount of the insurance"); *National Surety Co. v. Graves*, 211 Ala. 533, 534, 101 So. 190 (1924) (suit against a surety company by stockholders "for the benefit of themselves and all others similarly situate who will join the suit" where it was alleged that individual suits were being filed on surety bonds that "would result in the exhaustion of the penalties of the bonds, leaving many stockholders without remedy"). * * *

B

The cases forming this pedigree of the limited fund class action as understood by the drafters of Rule 23 have a number of common characteristics, despite the variety of circumstances from which they arose. The points of resemblance are not necessarily the points of contention resolved in the particular cases, but they show what the Advisory Committee must have assumed would be at least a sufficient set of conditions to justify binding absent members of a class under Rule 23(b)(1)(B), from which no one has the right to secede.

The first and most distinctive characteristic is that the totals of the aggregated liquidated claims and the fund available for satisfying them, set definitely at their maximums, demonstrate the inadequacy of the fund to pay all the claims. The concept driving this type of suit was insufficiency, which alone justified the limit on an early feast to avoid a later famine. See, e.g., *Guffanti*, supra, at 457, 90 N.E., at 176 ("The total amount of the claims exceeds the penalty of the bond.... A just and equitable payment from the bond would be a distribution pro rata upon the amount of the several embezzlements. Unless in a case like this the amount of the bond is so distributed among the persons having claims which are secured thereby, it must necessarily result in a scramble for precedence in payment, and the amount of the bond may be paid to the favored, or to those first obtaining knowledge of the embezzlements"); *Graves*, supra, at 534, 101 So., at 190 ("The primary equity of the bill is the adjustment of claims and the equitable apportionment of a fund provided by law, which is insufficient to pay claimants in full"). The equity of the limitation is its necessity.

Second, the whole of the inadequate fund was to be devoted to the overwhelming claims. * * * It went without saying that the defendant or estate or constructive trustee with the inadequate assets had no opportunity to benefit himself or claimants of lower priority by holding back on the amount distributed to the class. The limited fund cases thus ensured that the class as a whole was given the best deal; they did not give a defendant a better deal than seriatim litigation would have produced.

Third, the claimants identified by a common theory of recovery were treated equitably among themselves. The cases assume that the class will comprise everyone who might state a claim on a single or repeated set of facts, invoking a common theory of recovery, to be satisfied from the limited fund as the source of payment. * * *

In sum, mandatory class treatment through representative actions on a limited fund theory was justified with reference to a "fund" with a definitely ascertained limit, all of which would be distributed to satisfy all those with liquidated claims based on a common theory of liability, by an equitable, pro rata distribution.

C

The Advisory Committee, and presumably the Congress in approving subdivision (b)(1)(B), must have assumed that an action with these characteristics would satisfy the limited fund rationale cognizable under that subdivision. The question remains how far the same characteristics are necessary for limited fund treatment. While we cannot settle all the details of a subdivision (b)(1)(B) limited fund here (and so cannot decide the ultimate question whether settlements of multitudes of related tort actions are amenable to mandatory class treatment), there are good reasons to treat these characteristics as presumptively necessary, and not merely sufficient, to satisfy the limited fund rationale for a mandatory action. At the least, the burden of justification rests on the proponent of any departure from the traditional norm.

It is true, of course, that the text of Rule 23(b)(1)(B) is on its face open to a more lenient limited fund concept, just as it covers more historical antecedents than the limited fund. But the greater the leniency in departing from the historical limited fund model, the greater the likelihood of abuse in ways that will be apparent when we apply the limited fund criteria to the case before us. The prudent course, therefore, is to presume that when subdivision (b)(1)(B) was devised to cover limited fund actions, the object was to stay close to the historical model. As will be seen, this limiting construction finds support in the Advisory Committee's expressions of understanding, minimizes potential conflict with the Rules Enabling Act, and avoids serious constitutional concerns raised by the mandatory class resolution of individual legal claims, especially where a case seeks to resolve future liability in a settlement-only action.

* * * [I]t is clear that the Advisory Committee did not contemplate that the mandatory class action codified in subdivision (b)(1)(B) would be used to aggregate unliquidated tort claims on a limited fund rationale. See Monaghan, Antisuit Injunctions and Preclusion Against Absent Nonresident Class Members, 98 Colum. L.Rev. 1148, 1164 (1998) ("The 'framers' of Rule 23 did not envision the expansive interpretations of the rule that have emerged.... No draftsmen contemplated that, in mass torts, (b)(1)(B) 'limited fund' classes would emerge as the functional equivalent to bankruptcy by embracing 'funds' created by the litigation itself"); see also Schwarzer, Settlement of Mass Tort Class Actions:

Order Out of Chaos, 80 Cornell L.Rev. 837, 840 (1995) ("The original concept of the limited fund class does not readily fit the situation where a large volume of claims might eventually result in judgments that in the aggregate could exceed the assets available to satisfy them"); Marcus, They Can't Do That, Can They? Tort Reform Via Rule 23, 80 Cornell L.Rev. 858, 877 (1995). None of the examples cited in the Advisory Committee Notes or by Professor Kaplan in explaining Rule 23(b)(1)(B) remotely approach what was then described as a "mass accident" case. While the Advisory Committee focused much attention on the amenability of Rule 23(b)(3) to such cases, the Committee's debates are silent about resolving tort claims under a mandatory limited fund rationale under Rule 23(b)(1)(B). It is simply implausible that the Advisory Committee, so concerned about the potential difficulties posed by dealing with mass tort cases under Rule 23(b)(3), with its provisions for notice and the right to opt out, see Rule 23(c)(2), would have uncritically assumed that mandatory versions of such class actions, lacking such protections, could be certified under Rule 23(b)(1)(B). We do not, it is true, decide the ultimate question whether Rule 23(b)(1)(B) may ever be used to aggregate individual tort claims, cf. Ticor Title Ins. Co. v. Brown, 511 U.S. 117, 121, 114 S.Ct. 1359, 128 L.Ed.2d 33 (1994) (per curiam). But we do recognize that the Committee would have thought such an application of the Rule surprising, and take this as a good reason to limit any surprise by presuming that the Rule's historical antecedents identify requirements.

The Rules Enabling Act underscores the need for caution. * * * Petitioners argue that the Act has been violated here, asserting that the Global Settlement Agreement's priorities of claims and compromise of full recovery abrogated the state law that must govern this diversity action under 28 U.S.C. § 1652. See Brief for Petitioners 31–36. Although we need not grapple with the difficult choice-of-law and substantive state-law questions raised by petitioners' assertion, we do need to recognize the tension between the limited fund class action's pro rata distribution in equity and the rights of individual tort victims at law. Even if we assume that some such tension is acceptable under the Rules Enabling Act, it is best kept within tolerable limits by keeping limited fund practice under Rule 23(b)(1)(B) close to the practice preceding its adoption.

Finally, if we needed further counsel against adventurous application of Rule 23(b)(1)(B), the Rules Enabling Act and the general doctrine of constitutional avoidance would jointly sound a warning of the serious constitutional concerns that come with any attempt to aggregate individual tort claims on a limited fund rationale. First, the certification of a mandatory class followed by settlement of its action for money damages obviously implicates the Seventh Amendment jury trial rights of absent class members. We noted in *Ross v. Bernhard*, 396 U.S. 531, 90 S.Ct. 733, 24 L.Ed.2d 729 (1970), that since the merger of law and equity in

1938, it has become settled among the lower courts that "class action plaintiffs may obtain a jury trial on any legal issues they present." Id., at 541, 90 S.Ct. 733. By its nature, however, a mandatory settlement-only class action with legal issues and future claimants compromises their Seventh Amendment rights without their consent.

Second, and no less important, mandatory class actions aggregating damage claims implicate the due process "principle of general application in Anglo–American jurisprudence that one is not bound by a judgment in personam in a litigation in which he is not designated as a party or to which he has not been made a party by service of process," *Hansberry v. Lee*, 311 U.S. 32, 40, 61 S.Ct. 115, 85 L.Ed. 22 (1940) * * *.

The inherent tension between representative suits and the day-in-court ideal is only magnified if applied to damage claims gathered in a mandatory class. Unlike Rule 23(b)(3) class members, objectors to the collectivism of a mandatory subdivision (b)(1)(B) action have no inherent right to abstain. The legal rights of absent class members (which in a class like this one would include claimants who by definition may be unidentifiable when the class is certified) are resolved regardless either of their consent, or, in a class with objectors, their express wish to the contrary. And in settlement-only class actions the procedural protections built into the Rule to protect the rights of absent class members during litigation are never invoked in an adversarial setting * * *.

IV

The record on which the District Court rested its certification of the class for the purpose of the global settlement did not support the essential premises of mandatory limited fund actions. It failed to demonstrate that the fund was limited except by the agreement of the parties, and it showed exclusions from the class and allocations of assets at odds with the concept of limited fund treatment and the structural protections of Rule 23(a) explained in Amchem.

A

The defect of certification going to the most characteristic feature of a limited fund action was the uncritical adoption by both the District Court and the Court of Appeals of figures agreed upon by the parties in defining the limits of the fund and demonstrating its inadequacy. When a district court, as here, certifies for class action settlement only, the moment of certification requires "heightene[d] attention," *Amchem*, 521 U.S., at 620, 117 S.Ct. 2231, to the justifications for binding the class members. * * * Thus, in an action such as this the settling parties must present not only their agreement, but evidence on which the district court may ascertain the limit and the insufficiency of the fund, with support in findings of fact following a proceeding in which the evidence is subject to challenge, see *In re Bendectin Products Liability Litigation*, 749 F.2d 300, 306 (C.A.6 1984) ("'[T]he district court, as a matter of law, must have a fact-finding inquiry on this question and allow the opponents of class certification to present evidence that a limited fund does not exist"); see also *In re Temple*, 851 F.2d 1269, 1272 (C.A.11 1988) ("Without a finding as to the net worth of the defendant, it is difficult to see how the fact of a limited fund could have been established given that all of [the defendant's] assets are potentially available to suitors"); *In re Dennis Greenman Securities Litigation*, 829 F.2d 1539, 1546 (C.A.11 1987) (discussing factual findings necessary for certification of a limited fund class action).

We have already alluded to the difficulties facing limited fund treatment of huge numbers of actions for unliquidated damages arising from mass torts, the first such hurdle being a computation of the total claims. It is simply not a matter of adding up the liquidated amounts, as in the models of limited fund actions. Although we might assume arguendo that prior judicial experience with asbestos claims would allow a court to make a sufficiently reliable determination of the probable total, the District Court here apparently thought otherwise, concluding that "there is no way to predict Fibreboard's future asbestos liability with any certainty." 162 F.R.D., at 528. Nothing turns on this conclusion, however, since there was no adequate demonstration of the second element required for limited fund treatment, the upper limit of the fund itself, without which no showing of insufficiency is possible.

The "fund" in this case comprised both the general assets of Fibreboard and the insurance assets provided by the two policies, see 90 F.3d, at 982 (describing fund as Fibreboard's entire equity and $2 billion in insurance assets under the Trilateral Settlement Agreement). As to Fibreboard's assets exclusive of the contested insurance, the District Court and the Fifth Circuit concluded that Fibreboard had a then-current sale value of $235 million that could be devoted to the limited fund. While that estimate may have been conservative, at least the District Court heard evidence and made an independent finding at some point in the proceedings. The same, however, cannot be said for the value of the disputed insurance. * * *

We do not, of course, know exactly what an independent valuation of the limit of the insurance assets would have shown. It might have revealed that even on the assumption that Fibreboard's coverage claim was sound, there would be insufficient assets to pay claims, considered with reference to their probable timing; if Fibreboard's own assets would not have been enough to pay the insurance shortfall plus any claims in excess of policy limits, the projected insolvency of the insurers and Fibreboard would have indicated a truly limited fund. (Nothing in the record, however, suggests that this would have been a supportable finding.) Or an independent valuation might have revealed assets of insufficient value to pay all projected claims if the assets were discounted by the prospects that the insurers would win the coverage cases. Or the Court's independent valuation might have shown, discount or no dis-

479

count, the probability of enough assets to pay all projected claims, precluding certification of any mandatory class on a limited fund rationale. Throughout this litigation the courts have accepted the assumption that the third possibility was out of the question, and they may have been right. But objecting and unidentified class members alike are entitled to have the issue settled by specific evidentiary findings independent of the agreement of defendants and conflicted class counsel.

B

The explanation of need for independent determination of the fund has necessarily anticipated our application of the requirement of equity among members of the class. There are two issues, the inclusiveness of the class and the fairness of distributions to those within it. On each, this certification for settlement fell short.

The definition of the class excludes myriad claimants with causes of action, or foreseeable causes of action, arising from exposure to Fibreboard asbestos. While the class includes those with present claims never filed, present claims withdrawn without prejudice, and future claimants, it fails to include those who had previously settled with Fibreboard while retaining the right to sue again "upon development of an asbestos related malignancy," plaintiffs with claims pending against Fibreboard at the time of the initial announcement of the Global Settlement Agreement, and the plaintiffs in the "inventory" claims settled as a supposedly necessary step in reaching the global settlement, see 90 F.3d, at 971. The number of those outside the class who settled with a reservation of rights may be uncertain, but there is no such uncertainty about the significance of the settlement's exclusion of the 45,000 inventory plaintiffs and the plaintiffs in the unsettled present cases, estimated by the Guardian Ad Litem at more than 53,000 as of August 27, 1993, see App. in No. 95–40635(CA5), 6 Record, Tab 55, p. 72 (Report of the Guardian Ad Litem). It is a fair question how far a natural class may be depleted by prior dispositions of claims and still qualify as a mandatory limited fund class, but there can be no question that such a mandatory settlement class will not qualify when in the very negotiations aimed at a class settlement, class counsel agree to exclude what could turn out to be as much as a third of the claimants that negotiators thought might eventually be involved, a substantial number of whom class counsel represent, see App. to Pet. for Cert. 321a (noting that the parties negotiating the global settlement agreed to use a negotiating benchmark of 186,000 future claims against Fibreboard).

Might such class exclusions be forgiven if it were shown that the class members with present claims and the outsiders ended up with comparable benefits? * * * As for the settled inventory claims, their plaintiffs appeared to have obtained better terms than the class members. They received an immediate payment of 50 percent of a settlement higher than the historical average, and would get the remainder if the global settlement were sustained (or the coverage litigation resolved, as it turned out to be by the Trilateral Settlement Agreement); the class members, by contrast, would be assured of a 3–year payout for claims settled, whereas the unsettled faced a prospect of mediation followed by arbitration as prior conditions of instituting suit, which would even then be subject to a recovery limit, a slower payout and the limitations of the trust's spendthrift protection. * * * Finally, as discussed below, even ostensible parity between settling nonclass plaintiffs and class members would be insufficient to overcome the failure to provide the structural protection of independent representation as for subclasses with conflicting interests.

On the second element of equity within the class, the fairness of the distribution of the fund among class members, the settlement certification is likewise deficient. Fair treatment in the older cases was characteristically assured by straightforward pro rata distribution of the limited fund. * * * While equity in such a simple sense is unattainable in a settlement covering present claims not specifically proven and claims not even due to arise, if at all, until some future time, at the least such a settlement must seek equity by providing for procedures to resolve the difficult issues of treating such differently situated claimants with fairness as among themselves.

First, it is obvious after Amchem that a class divided between holders of present and future claims (some of the latter involving no physical injury and to claimants not yet born) requires division into homogeneous subclasses under Rule 23(c)(4)(B), with separate representation to eliminate conflicting interests of counsel. See *Amchem*, 521 U.S., at 627, 117 S.Ct. 2231 (class settlements must provide "structural assurance of fair and adequate representation for the diverse groups and individuals affected"); * * * No such procedure was employed here, and the conflict was as contrary to the equitable obligation entailed by the limited fund rationale as it was to the requirements of structural protection applicable to all class actions under Rule 23(a)(4).

Second, the class included those exposed to Fibreboard's asbestos products both before and after 1959. The date is significant, for that year saw the expiration of Fibreboard's insurance policy with Continental, the one which provided the bulk of the insurance funds for the settlement. Pre–1959 claimants accordingly had more valuable claims than post–1959 claimants, see 90 F.3d, at 1012–1013 (SMITH, J., dissenting), the consequence being a second instance of disparate interests within the certified class. While at some point there must be an end to reclassification with separate counsel, these two instances of conflict are well within the requirement of structural protection recognized in Amchem.

* * * Here, just as in the earlier case, the proponents of the settlement are trying to rewrite Rule 23; each ignores the fact that Rule 23 requires protections under subdivisions (a) and (b) against inequity

and potential inequity at the pre-certification stage, quite independently of the required determination at postcertification fairness review under subdivision (e) that any settlement is fair in an overriding sense. A fairness hearing under subdivision (e) can no more swallow the preceding protective requirements of Rule 23 in a subdivision (b)(1)(B) action than in one under subdivision (b)(3).

C

A third contested feature of this settlement certification that departs markedly from the limited fund antecedents is the ultimate provision for a fund smaller than the assets understood by the Court of Appeals to be available for payment of the mandatory class members' claims; most notably, Fibreboard was allowed to retain virtually its entire net worth. Given our treatment of the two preceding deficiencies of the certification, there is of course no need to decide whether this feature of the agreement would alone be fatal to the Global Settlement Agreement. To ignore it entirely, however, would be so misleading that we have decided simply to identify the issue it raises, without purporting to resolve it at this time.

Fibreboard listed its supposed entire net worth as a component of the total (and allegedly inadequate) assets available for claimants, but subsequently retained all but $500,000 of that equity for itself. On the face of it, the arrangement seems irreconcilable with the justification of necessity in denying any opportunity for withdrawal of class members whose jury trial rights will be compromised, whose damages will be capped, and whose payments will be delayed. With Fibreboard retaining nearly all its net worth, it hardly appears that such a regime is the best that can be provided for class members. Given the nature of a limited fund and the need to apply its criteria at the certification stage, it is not enough for a District Court to say that it "need not ensure that a defendant designate a particular source of its assets to satisfy the class' claims; [but only that] the amount recovered by the class [be] fair." 162 F.R.D., at 527.

The District Court in this case seems to have had a further point in mind, however. One great advantage of class action treatment of mass tort cases is the opportunity to save the enormous transaction costs of piecemeal litigation, an advantage to which the settlement's proponents have referred in this case. Although the District Court made no specific finding about the transaction cost saving likely from this class settlement, estimating the amount in the "hundreds of millions," * * * it did conclude that the amount would exceed Fibreboard's net worth as the Court valued it, * * *. (Fibreboard's net worth of $235 million "is considerably less than the likely savings in defense costs under the Global Settlement"). If a settlement thus saves transaction costs that would never have gone into a class member's pocket in the absence of settlement, may a credit for some of the savings be recognized in a mandatory class action as an incentive to settlement? It is at least a legitimate question, which we leave for another day. * * *

VI

In sum, the applicability of Rule 23(b)(1)(B) to a fund and plan purporting to liquidate actual and potential tort claims is subject to question, and its purported application in this case was in any event improper. The Advisory Committee did not envision mandatory class actions in cases like this one, and both the Rules Enabling Act and the policy of avoiding serious constitutional issues counsel against leniency in recognizing mandatory limited fund actions in circumstances markedly different from the traditional paradigm. Assuming arguendo that a mandatory, limited fund rationale could under some circumstances be applied to a settlement class of tort claimants, it would be essential that the fund be shown to be limited independently of the agreement of the parties to the action, and equally essential under Rule 23(a) and (b)(1)(B) that the class include all those with claims unsatisfied at the time of the settlement negotiations, with intraclass conflicts addressed by recognizing independently represented subclasses. In this case, the limit of the fund was determined by treating the settlement agreement as dispositive, an error magnified by the representation of class members by counsel also representing excluded plaintiffs, whose settlements would be funded fully upon settlement of the class action on any terms that could survive final fairness review. Those separate settlements, together with other exclusions from the claimant class, precluded adequate structural protection by subclass treatment, which was not even afforded to the conflicting elements within the class as certified.

The judgment of the Court of Appeals, accordingly, is reversed, and the case is remanded for further proceedings consistent with this opinion.

It is so ordered.

Chief Justice REHNQUIST, with whom Justice SCALIA and Justice KENNEDY join, concurring.

Justice BREYER'S dissenting opinion highlights in graphic detail the massive impact of asbestos-related claims on the federal courts. * * * Were I devising a system for handling these claims on a clean slate, I would agree entirely with that dissent, which in turn approves the near-heroic efforts of the District Court in this case to make the best of a bad situation. Under the present regime, transactional costs will surely consume more and more of a relatively static amount of money to pay these claims.

But we are not free to devise an ideal system for adjudicating these claims. Unless and until the Federal Rules of Civil Procedure are revised, the Court's opinion correctly states the existing law, and I join it. But the "elephantine mass of asbestos cases" * * * cries out for a legislative solution.

Justice BREYER, with whom Justice STEVENS joins, dissenting.

This case involves a settlement of an estimated 186,000 potential future asbestos claims against a single company, Fibreboard, for approximately $1.535 billion. The District Court, in approving the settlement, made 446 factual findings, on the basis of which it concluded that the settlement was equitable, that the potential claimants had been well represented, and that the distinctions drawn among different categories of claimants were reasonable. 162 F.R.D. 505 (1995); App. to Pet. for Cert. 248a–468a. The Court of Appeals, dividing 2 to 1, held that the settlement was lawful. 134 F.3d 668 (C.A.5 1998). I would not set aside the Court of Appeals' judgment as the majority does. Accordingly, I dissent.

I

A

Four special background circumstances underlie this settlement and help to explain the reasonableness and consequent lawfulness of the relevant District Court determinations. First, as the majority points out, the settlement comprises part of an "elephantine mass of asbestos cases," which "defies customary judicial administration." * * * In the Eastern District of Texas, for example, one out of every three civil cases filed in 1990 was an asbestos case. * * * In the past decade nearly 80,000 new federal asbestos cases have been filed; more than 10,000 new federal asbestos cases were filed last year. See U.S. District Courts Civil Cases Commenced by Nature of Suit, Administrative Office of the Courts Statistics (Table C2–A) (Dec. 31, 1994–1998) (hereinafter AO Statistics).

The Judicial Conference found that asbestos cases on average take almost twice as long as other lawsuits to resolve. * * * Judge Parker, the experienced trial judge who approved this settlement, noted in one 3,000–member asbestos class action over which he presided that 448 of the original class members had died while the litigation was pending. *Cimino v. Raymark Industries, Inc.*, 751 F.Supp. 649, 651 (E.D.Tex. 1990). And yet, Judge Parker went on to state, if the district court could close "thirty cases a month, it would [still] take six and one-half years to try these cases and [due to new filings] there would be pending over 5,000 untouched cases" at the end of that time. Id., at 652. * * *

Second, an individual asbestos case is a tort case, of a kind that courts, not legislatures, ordinarily will resolve. It is the number of these cases, not their nature, that creates the special judicial problem. The judiciary cannot treat the problem as entirely one of legislative failure, as if it were caused, say, by a poorly drafted statute. Thus, when "calls for national legislation" go unanswered, * * * judges can and should search aggressively for ways, within the framework of existing law, to avoid delay and expense so great as to bring about a massive denial of justice.

Third, in that search the district courts may take advantage of experience that appellate courts do not have. Judge Parker, for example, has written of "a disparity of appreciation for the magnitude of the problem," growing out of the difference between the trial courts' "daily involvement with asbestos litigation" and the appellate courts' "limited" exposure to such litigation in infrequent appeals. Cimino, 751 F.Supp., at 651.

Fourth, the alternative to class-action settlement is not a fair opportunity for each potential plaintiff to have his or her own day in court. Unusually high litigation costs, unusually long delays, and limitations upon the total amount of resources available for payment, together mean that most potential plaintiffs may not have a realistic alternative. And Federal Rule of Civil Procedure 23 was designed to address situations in which the historical model of individual actions would not, for practical reasons, work. See generally Advisory Committee's Notes on Fed. Rule Civ. Proc. 23, 28 U.S.C.App., p. 696 (discussing, in relation to Rule 23(b)(1)(B), instances in which individual judgments, "while not technically concluding the other members, might do so as a practical matter").

For these reasons, I cannot easily find a legal answer to the problems this case raises by referring, as does the majority, to "our 'deep-rooted historic tradition that everyone should have his own day in court.'" * * * (citation omitted). Instead, in these circumstances, I believe our Court should allow a district court full authority to exercise every bit of discretionary power that the law provides. See generally *Califano v. Yamasaki*, 442 U.S. 682, 703, 99 S.Ct. 2545, 61 L.Ed.2d 176 (1979) ("[M]ost issues arising under Rule 23 ... [are] committed in the first instance to the discretion of the district court"); *Reiter v. Sonotone Corp.*, 442 U.S. 330, 345, 99 S.Ct. 2326, 60 L.Ed.2d 931 (1979) (district courts have "broad power and discretion ... with respect to matters involving the certification" of class actions). And, in doing so, the Court should prove extremely reluctant to overturn a fact-specific or circumstance-specific exercise of that discretion, where a court of appeals has found it lawful. * * *

B

The case before us involves a class of individuals (and their families) exposed to asbestos manufactured by Fibreboard who, for the most part, had not yet sued or settled with Fibreboard as of August 1993. * * * [T]here is no doubt that a realistic assessment of the value of these claims far exceeds Fibreboard's total net worth.

But, as of 1993, one potentially short-lived additional asset promised potential claimants a greater recovery. That asset consisted of two insurance policies, one issued by Continental Casualty, the other by Pacific Indemnity. If the policies were valid (i.e., if they covered most of the relevant claims), they were worth several billion dollars; but if they were invalid, this asset was worth nothing. At that time, a separate case brought by Fibreboard against the insurance companies in California state court seemed likely to resolve the value of the policies in the near future. That separate litigation had a settlement value for the insurance companies. At the time the parties were negotiating, prior to the California court's decision, the insurance policies were worth, as the majority puts it, the value of "unlimited policy coverage" (i.e., perhaps the insurance companies' entire net worth) "discounted by the risk that Fibreboard would ultimately lose the coverage dispute litigation." * * *

The insurance companies offered to settle with both Fibreboard and those persons with claims against Fibreboard (who might have tried to sue the insurance companies directly). The settlement negotiations came to a head in August 1993, just as a California state appeals court was poised to decide the validity of the insurance policies. This fact meant speed was important, for the California court could well decide that the policies were worth nothing. It also meant that it was important to certify a non opt-out class of Fibreboard plaintiffs. If the class that entered into the settlement were an opt-out class, then members of that class could wait to see what the California court did. If the California court found the policies valid (hence worth many billions of dollars), they would opt out of the class and sue for everything they could get; if the California court found the policies invalid (and worth nothing), they would stick with the settlement. The insurance companies would gain little from that kind of settlement, and they would not agree to it. See *In re Asbestos Litigation*, 90 F.3d 963, 970 (C.A.5 1996).

After eight days of hearings, the District Court found that the insurance policies plus Fibreboard's net worth amounted to a "limited fund," valued at $1.77 billion (the amount the insurance companies were willing to contribute to the settlement plus Fibreboard's value). See App. to Pet. for Cert. 492a. The court entered detailed factual findings. See generally 162 F.R.D., at 518–519. It certified a "non opt-out" class. And the court approved the parties' Global Settlement Agreement. The Global Settlement Agreement allows those exposed to asbestos (and their families) to assert their Fibreboard claims against a fund that it creates. It does not limit recoveries for particular types of claims, but allows for individual determinations of damages based on all historically relevant individual factors and circumstances. See 90 F.3d, at 976. It contains spendthrift provisions designed to limit the total payouts for any particular year, and a requirement that the claimants with the most serious injuries be paid first in any year in which there is a shortfall. It also permits an individual who wishes to retain his right to bring an ordinary action in court to opt out of the arrangement (albeit after mediation and nonbinding arbitration), but sets a ceiling of $500,000 upon the recovery obtained by any person who does so. See generally 162 F.R.D., at 518–519.

The question here is whether the court's certification of the class under Rule 23(b)(1)(B) violates the law. The majority seems to limit its holding (though not its discussion) to that question, and so I limit the focus of my dissent to the Rule 23(b)(1)(B) issues as well.

II

* * *

The majority thinks this class could not be certified under Rule 23(b)(1)(B). I, on the contrary, think it could.

The case falls within the Rule's language as long as there was a significant "risk" that the total assets available to satisfy the claims of the class members would fall well below the likely total value of those claims, for in such circumstances the money would go to those claimants who brought their actions first, thereby "substantially impair[ing]" the "ability" of later claimants "to protect their interests." And the District Court found there was indeed such a "risk." 162 F.R.D., at 526. * * *

I need not pursue the conceptual matter further, however, for the majority apparently concedes the conceptual point that a fund's limit may equal its "value discounted by risk." * * * But the majority sets forth three additional conditions, which it says are "sufficient ... to justify binding absent members of a class under Rule 23(b)(1)(B), from which no one has the right to secede." * * * Those three conditions are:

Condition One: That "the totals of the aggregated liquidated claims and the fund available for satisfying them, set definitely at their maximum, demonstrate the inadequacy of the fund to pay all the claims." * * *

Condition Two: That "the claimants identified by a common theory of recovery were treated equitably among themselves." * * *

Condition Three: That "the whole of the inadequate fund was to be devoted to the overwhelming claims." * * *

I shall discuss each condition in turn.

A

In my view, the first condition is substantially satisfied. No one doubts that the "totals of the aggregated" claims well exceed the value of the assets in the "fund available for satisfying them," at least if the fund totaled about what the District Court said it did, namely, $1.77 billion at most. The District Court said that the limited fund equaled in value "the sum of the value of Fibreboard plus the value of its insurance coverage," or $235 million plus $1.535 billion. App. to Pet. for Cert. 492a. The Court of Appeals upheld the finding. 90 F.3d, at 982. And the finding is adequately supported.

The District Court found that the insurance policies were not worth substantially more than $1.535 billion in part because there was a "significant risk" that the insurance policies would soon turn out to be worth nothing at all. 162 F.R.D., at 526. The court wrote that "Fibreboard might lose" its coverage, i.e., that it might lose "on one or more issues in the [California] Coverage Case, or that Fibreboard might lose its insurance coverage as a result of its assignment settlement program." Ibid.

Two California insurance law experts, a Yale professor and a former state court of appeals judge, testified that there was a good chance that Fibreboard would lose all or a significant part of its insurance coverage once the California appellate courts decided the matter. 90 F.3d, at 974. And that conclusion is not surprising [in light of the limited time the policies were in effect and the scope of the language as to coverage]. * * *

The District Court arrived at the present value of the policies ($1.535 billion) by looking to a different settlement, the settlement arrived at in the insurance coverage case itself as a result of bargaining between Fibreboard and the insurance companies. * * * That settlement, embodied in the Trilateral Agreement, created a backup fund by taking from the insurance companies $1.535 billion (plus other money used to satisfy claims not here at issue) and simply setting it aside to use for the payment of claims brought against Fibreboard in the ordinary course by members of this class (in the event that the federal courts ultimately failed to approve the Global Settlement Agreement).

The Fifth Circuit approved this method of determining the value of the insurance policies. See 90 F.3d, at 982 (discussing value of Trilateral Agreement plus value of Fibreboard). And the majority itself sees nothing wrong with that method in principle. * * *

The majority rejects the District Court's valuation for a different reason. It says that the settlement negotiation that led to the valuation was not necessarily a fair one. The majority says it cannot make the necessary "arms-length bargaining" assumption because "[c]lass counsel" had a "great incentive to reach any agreement" in light of the fact that "some of the same lawyers ... had also negotiated the separate settlement of 45,000" pending cases, which was partially contingent upon a global settlement or other favorable resolution of the insurance dispute. * * *

The District Court and Court of Appeals, however, did accept the relevant "arms-length" assumption, with good reason. The relevant bargaining (i.e., the bargaining that led to the Trilateral Agreement that set the policies' value) was not between the plaintiffs' class counsel and the insurance companies; it was between Fibreboard and the insurance companies. And there is no reason to believe that that bargaining, engaged in to settle the California coverage dispute, was not "arms-length." That bargaining did not lead to a settlement that would release Fibreboard from potential tort liability. Rather, it led to a potential backup settlement that did not release Fibreboard from anything. It created a fund of insurance money, which, once exhausted, would have left Fibreboard totally exposed to tort claims. Consequently, Fibreboard had every incentive to squeeze as much money as possible out of the insurance companies, thereby creating as large a fund as possible in order to diminish the likelihood that it would eventually have to rely upon its own net worth to satisfy future asbestos plaintiffs.

* * *A perfect valuation, requiring lengthy study by independent experts, is not feasible in the context of such an unusual limited fund, one that comes accompanied with its own witching hour. Within weeks after the parties' settlement agreement, the insurance policies might well have disappeared, leaving most potential plaintiffs with little more than empty claims. The ship was about to sink, the trust fund to evaporate; time was important. Under these circumstances, I would accept the valuation findings made by the District Court and affirmed by the Court of Appeals as legally sufficient. * * *

B

I similarly believe that the second condition is satisfied. * * * The District Court found equitable treatment, and the Court of Appeals affirmed. But a majority of this Court now finds significant inequities arising out of class counsel's "egregious" conflict of interest, the settlement's substantive terms, and the District Court's failure to create subclasses. * * * But nothing I can find in the Court's opinion, nor in the objectors' briefs, convinces me that the District Court's findings on these matters were clearly erroneous, or that the Court of Appeals went seriously astray in affirming them.

The District Court made 76 separate findings of fact, for example, in respect to potential conflicts of interest. * * * Of course, class counsel consisted of individual attorneys who represented other asbestos claimants, including many other Fibreboard claimants outside the certified class. Since Fibreboard had been settling cases contingent upon resolution of the insurance dispute for several years, any attorney who had been involved in previous litigation against Fibreboard was likely to suffer from a similar "conflict." So whom should the District Court have appointed to negotiate a settlement that had to be reached soon, if ever? Should it have appointed attorneys unfamiliar with Fibreboard and the history of its asbestos litigation? Where was the District Court to find those competent, knowledgeable, conflict-free attorneys? The District Court said they did not exist. Finding of Fact ¶ ;372 says there is "no credible evidence of the existence of other 'conflict-free' counsel who were qualified to negotiate" a settlement within the necessary time. * * * Finding of Fact ¶ 317 adds that the District Court viewed it as "crucial ... to appoint asbestos attorneys who were experienced, knowledgeable, skilled and credible in view of the extremely short window of opportunity to negotiate a global settlement, and the very high risk to future claimants presented by the Coverage Case appeal." * * * Where is the clear error?

In addition, more than 150 findings of fact, made after an 8-day hearing, support the District Court's finding that overall the settlement is "fair, adequate, and reasonable." * * *

The Fifth Circuit found that "[t]he record amply supports" these District Court findings. 90 F.3d, at 978. Does the majority mean to set them aside? If not, does it mean to set forth a rigid principle of law, such as the principle that asbestos lawyers with clients outside a class, who will potentially benefit from a class settlement, can never represent a class in settlement negotiations? And does that principle apply no matter how unusual the circumstances, or no matter how necessary that representation might be? Why should there be such a rule of law? If there is not an absolute rule, however, I do not see how this Court can hold that the case before us is not that unusual situation.

Consider next the claim that "equity" required more subclasses. * * * To determine the "right" number of subclasses, a district court must weigh the advantages and disadvantages of bringing more lawyers into the case. The majority concedes as much when it says "at some point there must be an end to reclassification with separate counsel." * * * The District Court said that if there had "been as many separate attorneys" as the objectors wanted, "there is a significant possibility that a global settlement would not have been reached before the Coverage Case was resolved by the California Court of Appeal." * * * Finding of Fact & ¶ 346 lists the shared common interests among subclasses that argue for single representation, including "avoiding the potentially disastrous results of a loss ... in the Coverage Case," "maximizing the total settlement contribution," "reducing transactions costs and delays," "minimizing ... attorney's fees," and "adopting" equitable claims payment "procedures." * * * Surely the District Court was within its discretion to conclude that "the point" to which the majority alludes was reached in this case.

* * * The Fifth Circuit found that the District Court "did not abuse its discretion in finding that the class was adequately represented and that subclasses were not required." 90 F.3d, at 982. This Court should not overturn these highly circumstance-specific judgments.

C

The majority's third condition raises a more difficult question. It says that the "whole of the inadequate fund" must be "devoted to the overwhelming claims." * * * Fibreboard's own assets, in theory, were available to pay tort claims, yet they were not included in the global settlement fund. Is that fact fatal?

I find the answer to this question in the majority's own explanation. It says that the third condition helps to guarantee that those who held the

> "inadequate assets had no opportunity to benefit [themselves] or claimants of lower priority by holding back on the amount distributed to the class. The limited fund cases thus ensured that the class as a whole was given the best deal; they did not give a defendant a better deal than seriatim litigation would have produced." * * *

That explanation suggests to me that Rule 23(b)(1)(B) permits a slight relaxation of this absolute requirement, where its basic purpose is met, i.e., where there is no doubt that "the class as a whole was given the best deal," and where there is good reason for allowing the third condition's substantial, rather than its literal, satisfaction.

Rule 23 itself does not require modern courts to trace every contour of ancient case law with literal exactness. Benjamin Kaplan, reporter to the Advisory Committee on Civil Rules that drafted the 1966 revisions, upon whom the majority properly relies for explanation, see, e.g., ante, at ___, ___, ___, wrote of Rule 23:

> "The reform of Rule 23 was intended to shake the law of class actions free of abstract categories ... and to rebuild the law on functional lines responsive to those recurrent life patterns which call for mass litigation through representative parties. ...And whereas the old Rule had paid virtually no attention to the practical administration of class actions, the revised Rule dwelt long on this matter—not, to be sure, by prescribing detailed procedures, but by confirming the courts' broad powers and inviting judicial initiative." A Prefatory Note, 10 B.C. Ind. & Com. L.Rev. 497 (1969).

The majority itself recognizes the possibility of providing incentives to enter into settlements that reduce costs by granting a "credit" for cost savings by relaxing the whole-of-the-assets requirement, at least where most of the savings would go to the claimants. * * *

There is no doubt in this case that the settlement made far more money available to satisfy asbestos claims than was likely to occur in its absence. And the District Court found that administering the fund would involve transaction costs of only 15%. * * * A comparison of that 15% figure with the 61% transaction costs figure applicable to asbestos cases in general suggests hundreds of millions of dollars in savings—an amount greater than Fibreboard's net worth. And, of course, not only is it better for the injured plaintiffs, it is far better for Fibreboard, its employees, its creditors, and the communities where it is located for Fibreboard to remain a working enterprise, rather than slowly forcing it into bankruptcy while most of its money is spent on asbestos lawyers and expert witnesses. I would consequently find substantial compliance with the majority's third condition.

Because I believe that all three of the majority's conditions are satisfied, and because I see no fatal conceptual difficulty, I would uphold the determination, made by the District Court and affirmed by the Court of Appeals, that the insurance policies (along with Fibreboard's net value) amount to a classic limited fund, within the scope of Rule 23(b)(1)(B). * * *

RUHRGAS AG v. MARATHON OIL CO.

Supreme Court of the United States.
526 U.S. 574, 119 S. Ct. 1563, 143 L.Ed.2d 760.

Justice Ginsburg delivered the opinion of the Court.

[Defendant removed the case from a state court to a federal district court. Plaintiff moved to remand the case for lack of federal subject-matter jurisdiction. Defendant moved to dismiss the case for lack of personal jurisdiction. The federal trial judge dismissed the case for lack of personal jurisdiction without deciding the question of subject-matter jurisdiction. A panel of the 5th Circuit Court of Appeals reversed the decision, holding that subject-matter jurisdiction must be determined first. The 5th Circuit Court of Appeals, sitting en banc, by a 9 to 7 vote, agreed with the panel. Judge Higgenbotham wrote the dissenting opinion. The Supreme court granted certiorari. After discussing the different policies behind the two types of jurisdiction, the Court continued as follows:]

A

* * *

These distinctions do not mean that subject-matter jurisdiction is ever and always the more "fundamental." Personal jurisdiction, too, is "an essential element of the jurisdiction of a district ... court," without which the court is "powerless to proceed to an adjudication." *Employers Reinsurance Corp. v. Bryant*, 299 U.S. 374, 382, 57 S.Ct. 273, 81 L.Ed. 289 (1937). In this case, indeed, the impediment to subject-matter jurisdiction on which Marathon relies—lack of complete diversity—rests on statutory interpretation, not constitutional command. Marathon joined an alien plaintiff (Norge) as well as an alien defendant (Ruhrgas). If the joinder of Norge is legitimate, the complete diversity required by 28 U.S.C. § 1332 (1994 ed. and Supp. III), but not by Article III, see *State Farm Fire & Casualty Co. v. Tashire*, 386 U.S. 523, 530–531, 87 S.Ct. 1199, 18 L.Ed.2d 270 (1967), is absent. In contrast, Ruhrgas relies on the constitutional safeguard of due process to stop the court from proceeding to the merits of the case. See *Insurance Corp. of Ireland*, 456 U.S., at 702, 102 S.Ct. 2099 ("The requirement that a court have personal jurisdiction flows ... from the Due Process Clause.").

While *Steel Co. [v. Citizens for Better Environment, 523 U.S. 83, 118 S.Ct. 1003, 140 L.Ed.2d 210 (1998)]* reasoned that subject-matter jurisdiction necessarily precedes a ruling on the merits, the same principle does not dictate a sequencing of jurisdictional issues. "[A] court that dismisses on . . . non-merits grounds such as . . . personal jurisdiction, before finding subject-matter jurisdiction, makes no assumption of law-declaring power that violates the separation of powers principles underlying * * * Steel Company." *In re Papandreou*, 139 F.3d 247, 255 (C.A.D.C.1998). It is hardly novel for a federal court to choose among threshold grounds for denying audience to a case on the merits. Thus, as the Court observed in *Steel Co.*, district courts do not overstep Article III limits when they decline jurisdiction of state-law claims on discretionary grounds without determining whether those claims fall within their pendent jurisdiction, see *Moor v. County of Alameda*, 411 U.S. 693, 715–716, 93 S.Ct. 1785, 36 L.Ed.2d 596 (1973), or abstain under *Younger v. Harris*, 401 U.S. 37, 91 S.Ct. 746, 27 L.Ed.2d 669 (1971), without deciding whether the parties present a case or controversy, see *Ellis v. Dyson*, 421 U.S. 426, 433–434, 95 S.Ct. 1691, 44 L.Ed.2d 274 (1975). * * *

B

Maintaining that subject-matter jurisdiction must be decided first even when the litigation originates in federal court, see Tr. of Oral Arg. 21; Brief for Respondents 13, Marathon sees removal as the more offensive case, on the ground that the dignity of state courts is immediately at stake. If a federal court dismisses a removed case for want of personal jurisdiction, that determination may preclude the parties from relitigating the very same personal jurisdiction issue in state court. See *Baldwin v. Iowa State Traveling Men's Assn.*, 283 U.S. 522, 524–527, 51 S.Ct. 517, 75 L.Ed. 1244 (1931) (personal jurisdiction ruling has issue-preclusive effect).

* * *

Most essentially, federal and state courts are complementary systems for administering justice in our Nation. Cooperation and comity, not competition and conflict, are essential to the federal design. A State's dignitary interest bears consideration when a district court exercises discretion in a case of this order. If personal jurisdiction raises "difficult questions of [state] law," and subject-matter jurisdiction is resolved "as eas[ily]" as personal jurisdiction, a district court will ordinarily conclude that "federalism concerns tip the scales in favor of initially ruling on the motion to remand." *Allen v. Ferguson*, 791 F.2d 611, 616 (C.A.7 1986). In other cases, however, the district court may find that concerns of judicial economy and restraint are overriding. See, *e.g., Asociacion Nacional de Pescadores v. Dow Quimica*, 988 F.2d 559, 566–567 (C.A.5 1993) (if removal is nonfrivolous and personal jurisdiction turns on federal constitutional issues, "federal intrusion into state courts' authority . . . is minimized"). The federal design allows leeway for sensitive judgments of this sort. * * *

The Fifth Circuit and Marathon posit that state-court defendants will abuse the federal system with opportunistic removals. A discretionary rule, they suggest, will encourage manufactured, convoluted federal subject-matter theories designed to wrench cases from state court. See 145 F.3d, at 219; Brief for Respondents 28–29. This specter of unwarranted removal, we have recently observed, "rests on an assumption we do not indulge—that district courts generally will not comprehend, or will balk at applying, the rules on removal Congress has prescribed. . . . The well-advised defendant . . . will foresee the likely outcome of an unwarranted removal—a swift and nonreviewable remand order, see 28 U.S.C. §§ 1447(c), (d), attended by the displeasure of a district court whose authority has been improperly invoked." *Caterpillar Inc. v. Lewis*, 519 U.S. 61, 77–78, 117 S.Ct. 467, 136 L.Ed.2d 437 (1996).

C

In accord with Judge Higginbotham, we recognize that in most instances subject-matter jurisdiction will involve no arduous inquiry. See 145 F.3d, at 229 ("engag[ing]" subject-matter jurisdiction "at the outset of a case . . . [is] often . . . the most efficient way of going"). In such cases, both expedition and sensitivity to state courts' coequal stature should impel the federal court to dispose of that issue first. See *Cantor Fitzgerald, L.P. v. Peaslee*, 88 F.3d 152, 155 (C.A.2 1996) (a court disposing of a case on personal jurisdiction grounds "should be convinced that the challenge to the court's subject-matter jurisdiction is not easily resolved"). Where, as here, however, a district court has before it a straightforward personal jurisdiction issue presenting no complex question of state law, and the alleged defect in subject-matter jurisdiction raises a difficult and novel question, the court does not abuse its discretion by turning directly to personal jurisdiction.

* * *

For the reasons stated, the judgment of the Court of Appeals is reversed, and the case is remanded for proceedings consistent with this opinion.

It is so ordered.

Part IX

Proposed Federal Statutes and Rules Regulating Civil Procedure

TABLE OF CONTENTS

**Proposed Amendments to the Federal Rules of Civil Procedure
As Approved by the Supreme Court of the United States, April 2000,
and Referred to Congress
(Unless Congress intervenes these rules will take effect on
December 1, 2000.)**

Rule	Page
4(i)(2), (3)	496
5(d)	496
12(a)(3)	496
14(a), (c)	496
26(a), (b), (d), (f)	497
30(d), (f)(1)	500
37(c)(1)	501
Supplemental Rule B(1), (2)	501
Supplemental Rule C(2), (3), (4), (6)	502
Supplemental Rule E(3), (7), (8), (9)(b), (10)	505

**Proposed Amendments to the Federal Rules of Civil Procedure
As Circulated for Comment by the Committee on Rules of
Practice and Procedure**

Rule	Page
5(b)	506
6(e)	507
65(f)	507
77(d)	507
81(a)	508

Proposed Legislative Alteration of a Federal Rule of Procedure

11(c)	508

**Proposed Changes and Additions to the United States
Code Provisions Regulating Procedure**

Proposed Statutes   Page

28 U.S.C. §§ 1369, 1407 (to modify 28 U.S.C. §§ 1332, 1391, 1407, and 1441, and to add § 1660 regarding choice of law, in certain multiparty, multiforum suits) 508

28 U.S.C. §§ 1332, 1453 (to modify provisions regarding jurisdiction over plaintiff class actions) 513
28 U.S.C. § 1453 (to modify 28 U.S.C. § 1441 with regard to plaintiff class actions)... 514
28 U.S.C. §§ 1712, 1713 (to add sections requiring notification of proposed class-action settlements to federal and state attorneys general and to regulate notices provided to class members) 515
28 U.S.C. § 1714 (to add a section limiting attorney fees in class actions).... 518

PROPOSED AMENDMENTS TO THE FEDERAL RULES OF CIVIL PROCEDURE
As Approved by the Supreme Court of the United States, April, 2000
(Unless Congress intervenes these rules will take effect on December 1, 2000.)

Rule 4(i)(2), (3)

The proposal would provide that whenever an officer or employee (or former officer or employee) of the United States is sued in an individual capacity for acts or omissions in connection with official duties for the United States, the United States, as well as the officer or employee, shall be served with a copy of the complaint.

Rule 5(d)

The proposal would amend Rule 5(d) to read as follows:

All papers after the complaint required to be served on a party, together with a certificate of service, must be filed with the court within a reasonable time after service, but disclosures under Rule 26(a)(1) or (2) and the following discovery requests and responses must not be filed until they are used in the proceeding or the court orders filing: (i) depositions, (ii) interrogatories, (iii) requests for documents or to permit entry upon land, and (iv) requests for admissions.

Rule 12(a)(3)

The proposal would provide that the United States and its officers and employees have 60 days in which to respond to a claim, cross-claim, or counterclaim against an officer or employee alleged to have acted improperly in connection with duties on behalf of the United States. See Proposed Rule 4(i)(2), (3) above.

Rule 14(a), (c)

The proposal would amend the current provision to permit a third-party admiralty or maritime claim by or against a person who asserts a right under proposed Supplemental Rule C(6)(b)(i). The latter proposed rule is set out below.

Rule 26(a), (b), (d), (f)

The proposal would make major changes in the current provision by altering them to read as follows:

(a) Required Disclosures; Methods to Discover Additional Matter.

    (1) Initial Disclosures. Except in categories of proceedings specified in Rule 26(a)(1)(E), or to the extent otherwise stipulated or directed by order, a party must, without awaiting a discovery request, provide to other parties:

        (A) the name and, if known, the address and telephone number of each individual likely to have discoverable information that the disclosing party may use to support its claims or defenses, unless solely for impeachment, identifying the subjects of the information;

        (B) a copy of, or a description by category and location of, all documents, data compilations, and tangible things that are in the possession, custody, or control of the party and that the disclosing party may use to support its claims or defenses, unless solely for impeachment;

        (C) a computation of any category of damages claimed by the disclosing party, making available for inspection and copying as under Rule 34 the documents or other evidentiary material, not privileged or protected from disclosure, on which such computation is based, including materials bearing on the nature and extent of injuries suffered; and

        (D) for inspection and copying as under Rule 34 any insurance agreement under which any person carrying on an insurance business may be liable to satisfy part or all of a judgment which may be entered in the action or to indemnify or reimburse for payments made to satisfy the judgment.

        (E) The following categories of proceedings are exempt from initial disclosure under Rule 26(a)(1): (i) an action for review on an administrative record; (ii) a petition for habeas corpus or other proceeding to challenge a criminal conviction or sentence; (iii) an action brought without counsel by a person in custody of the United States, a state, or a state subdivision; (iv) an action to enforce or quash an administrative summons or subpoena; (v) an action by the United States to recover benefit payments; (vi) an action by the United States to collect on a student load guaranteed by the United States; (vii) a proceeding ancillary to proceedings in other courts; and (viii) an action to enforce an arbitration award.

These disclosures must be made at or within 14 days after the Rule 26(f) conference unless a different time is set by stipulation or court order, or unless a party objects during the conference that initial disclosures are not appropriate in the circumstances of the action and states the objection in the Rule 26(f) discovery plan. In ruling on the objection, the court must determine what disclosures—if any—are to be made, and set the time for disclosure. Any party first served or otherwise joined after the Rule 26(f) conference must make these disclosures within 30 days after being served or joined unless a different time is set by stipulation or court order. A party must make its initial disclosures based on the information then reasonably available to it and is not excused from making its disclosures because it has not fully completed its investigation of the case or because it challenges the sufficiency of another party's disclosures or because another party has not made its disclosures.

(3) Pretrial Disclosures. In addition to the disclosures required by Rule 26(a)(1) and (2), a party must provide to other parties and promptly file with the court the following information regarding the evidence that it may present at trial other than solely for impeachment:

    (A) the name and, if not previously provided, the address and telephone number of each witness, separately identifying those whom the party expects to present and those whom the party may call if the need arises;

    (B) the designation of those witnesses whose testimony is expected to be presented by means of a deposition and, if not taken stenographically, a transcript of the pertinent portions of the deposition testimony; and

    (C) an appropriate identification of each document or other exhibit, including summaries of other evidence, separately identifying those which the party expects to offer and those which the party may offer if the need arises.

Unless otherwise directed by the court, these disclosures shall be made at least 30 days before trial. Within 14 days thereafter, unless a different time is specified by the court, a party may serve and promptly file a list disclosing (i) any objections to the use under Rule 32(a) of a deposition designation by another party under Rule 26(a)(3)(B), and (ii) any objection, together with the grounds therefor, that may be made to the admissibility of materials identified under Rule 26(a)(3)(C). Objections not so disclosed, other than objections under Rules 402 and 403 of the Federal Rules of Evidence, shall be deemed waived unless excused by the court for good cause.

(4) Form of Disclosures. Unless the court orders otherwise, all disclosures under Rules 26(a)(1) through (3) must be made in writing, signed, and served.

(b) Discovery Scope and Limits. Unless otherwise limited by order of the court in accordance with these rules, the scope of discovery is as follows:

(1) In General. Parties may obtain discovery regarding any matter, not privileged, that is relevant to the claim or defense of any party, including the existence, description, nature, custody, condition, and location of any books, documents, or other tangible things and the identity and location of persons having knowledge of any discoverable matter. For good cause shown, the court may order discovery of any information relevant to the subject matter involved in the action. Relevant information need not be admissible at the trial if the discovery appears reasonably calculated to lead to the discovery of admissible evidence. All discovery is subject to the limitations imposed by Rule 26(b)(2)(i), (ii), and (iii).

(2) Limitations. By order, the court may alter the limits in these rules on the number of depositions and interrogatories, or the length of depositions under Rule 30. By order or local rule, the court may also limit the number of requests under Rule 36. The frequency or extent of use of the discovery methods otherwise permitted under these rules and by any local rule shall be limited by the court if it determines that: (i) the discovery sought is unreasonably cumulative or duplicative, or is obtainable from some other source that is more convenient, less burdensome, or less expensive; (ii) the party seeking discovery has had ample opportunity by discovery in the action to obtain the information sought; (iii) the burden or expense of the proposed discovery outweighs its likely benefit, taking into account the needs of the case, the amount in controversy, the parties' resources, the importance of the issues at stake in the litigation, and the importance of the proposed discovery in resolving the issues. The court may act upon its own initiative after reasonable notice or pursuant to a motion under Rule 26(c).

(d) Timing and Sequence of Discovery. Except in categories of proceedings exempted from initial disclosure under Rule 26(a)(1)(E), or when authorized under these rules or by order or agreement of the parties, a party may not seek discovery from any source before the parties have conferred as required by Rule 26(f). Unless the court upon motion, for the convenience of parties and witnesses and in the interests of justice, orders otherwise, methods of discovery may be used in any sequence, and the fact that a party is conducting discovery, whether by deposition or otherwise, shall not operate to delay any other party's discovery.

(f) Conference of Parties; Planning for Discovery. Except in categories of proceedings exempted from initial disclosure under Rule 26(a)(1)(E) or when otherwise ordered, the parties must, as soon as practicable and in any event at least 21 days before a scheduling order is due under Rule 16(b), confer to consider the nature and basis of their claims and defenses and the possibilities for a prompt settlement or resolution of the case, to make or arrange for the disclosures required by Rule 26(a)(1), and to develop a proposed discovery plan that indicates the parties' views and proposals concerning:

(1) what changes should be made in the timing, form, or requirement for disclosures under Rule 26(a), including a statement as to when disclosures under Rule 26(a)(1) were made or will be made;

(2) the subjects on which discovery may be needed, when discovery should be completed, and whether discovery should be conducted in phases or be limited to or focused upon particular issues;

(3) what changes should be made in the limitations on discovery imposed under these rules or by local rule, and what other limitations should be imposed; and

(4) any other orders that should be entered by the court under Rule 26(c) or under Rule 16(b) and (c).

The attorneys of record and all unrepresented parties that have appeared in the case are jointly responsible for arranging the conference, for attempting in good faith to agree on the proposed discovery plan, and for submitting to the court within 14 days after the conference a written report outlining the plan. A court may order that the parties or attorneys attend the conference in person. If necessary to comply with its expedited schedule for Rule 16(b) conferences, a court may by local rule (i) require that the conference between the parties occur fewer than 21 days before the scheduling conference is held or a scheduling order is due under Rule 16(b), and (ii) require that the written report outlining the discovery plan be filed fewer than 14 days after the conference between the parties, or excuse the parties from submitting a written report and permit them to report orally on their discovery plan at the Rule 16(b) conference.

Rule 30(d), (f)(1)

(d) The proposal, in (d)(1), would eliminate the words "to evidence" and would exchange the word "person" for the word "party" with respect to who can instruct a deponent not to answer and when such an instruction is proper. The reference to "paragraph 3" at the end of (d)(1) would be changed to "Rule 30(d)(4)."

The proposal would revise (d)(2), splitting it into a new (d)(2) and (d)(3). Current (d)(3) would be renumbered (d)(4). The revised (d)(2) and (3) would read as follows:

(2) Unless otherwise authorized by the court or stipulated by the parties and the deponent, a deposition is limited to one day of seven hours. The court shall allow additional time consistent with Rule 26(b)(2) if needed for a fair examination of the deponent or if the deponent or another person, or other circumstance, impedes or delays the examination.

(3) If the court finds that any impediment, delay, or other conduct has frustrated the fair examination of the deponent, it may impose upon the persons responsible an appropriate sanction, including the reasonable costs and attorney's fees incurred by the parties as a result thereof.

(f)(1) The proposal would merely change the word "shall" whenever it appears in (f)(1) to the word "must."

Rule 37(c)(1)

The proposal would alter the first sentence of the current rule by adding the words "or to amend a prior response to discovery as required by Rule 26(e)(2)" after the words "26(e)(1)."

Supplemental Rule B(1), (2)

The proposal would retitle Rule B to read "In Personam Actions: Attachment and Garnishment" and would require Rule B(1) and (2) to read as follows:

(1) When Available; Complaint, Affidavit, Judicial Authorization, and Process. In an in personam action:

(a) If a defendant is not found within the district, a verified complaint may contain a prayer for process to attach the defendant's tangible or intangible personal property—up to the amount sued for—in the hands of garnishees named in the process.

(b) The plaintiff or the plaintiff's attorneys must sign and file with the complaint an affidavit stating that, to the affiant's knowledge, or on information and belief, the defendant cannot be found within the district. The court must review the complaint and affidavit and, if the conditions of this Rule B appear to exist, enter an order so stating and authorizing process of attachment and garnishment. The clerk may issue supplemental process enforcing the court's order upon application without further court order.

(c) If the plaintiff or the plaintiff's attorney certifies that exigent circumstances make court review impracticable, the clerk must issue the summons and process of attachment and garnishment. The plaintiff has the burden in any post-attachment hearing under Rule E(4)(f) to show that exigent circumstances existed.

(d)(i) If the property is a vessel or tangible property on board a vessel, the summons, process, and any supplemental process must be delivered to the marshal for service.

(ii) If the property is other tangible or intangible property, the summons, process, and any supplemental process must be delivered to a person or organization authorized to serve it, who may be (A) a marshal; (B) someone under contract with the United States; (C) someone specially appointed by the court for that purpose; or (D) in an action brought by the United States, any officer or employee of the United States.

(e) The plaintiff may invoke state-law remedies under Rule 64 for seizure of person or property for the purpose of securing satisfaction of the judgment.

(2) Notice to Defendant. No default judgment may be entered except upon proof—which may be by affidavit—that:

(a) the complaint, summons, and process of attachment or garnishment have been served on the defendant in a manner authorized by Rule 4;

(b) the plaintiff or the garnishee has mailed to the defendant the complaint, summons, and process of attachment or garnishment, using any form of mail requiring a return receipt; or

(c) the plaintiff or the garnishee has tried diligently to give notice to the action to the defendant but could not do so.

Supplemental Rule C(2), (3), (4), (6).

The proposed would retitle Rule C to read "In Rem Actions: Special Provisions" and would rewrite sections (2), (3), (4), and (6) to read as follows:

(2) Complaint. In an action in rem the complaint must:

(a) be verified;

(b) describe with reasonable particularity the property that is the subject of the action;

(c) in an admiralty and maritime proceeding, state that the property is within the district or will be within the district while the action is pending;

(d) in a forfeiture proceeding for violation of a federal statute, state:

(i) the place of seizure and whether it was on land or on navigable waters;

(ii) whether the property is within the district, and if the property is not within the district the statutory basis for the court's exercise of jurisdiction over the property; and

(iii) all allegations required by the statute under which the action is brought.

(3) Judicial Authorization and Process.

(a) Arrest Warrant.

(i) When the United States files a complaint demanding a forfeiture for violation of a federal statute, the clerk must promptly issue a summons and a warrant for the arrest of the vessel or other property without requiring a certification of exigent circumstances.

(ii)(A) In other actions, the court must review the complaint and any supporting papers. If the conditions for an in rem action appear to exist, the court must issue an order directing the clerk to issue a warrant for the arrest of the vessel or other property that is the subject of the action.

(B) If the plaintiff or the plaintiff's attorney certifies that exigent circumstances make court review impracticable, the clerk must promptly issue a summons and a warrant for the arrest of the vessel or other property that is the subject of the action. The plaintiff has the burden in any post-arrest hearing under Rule E(4)(f) to show that exigent circumstances existed.

(b) Service.

(i) If the property that is the subject of the action is a vessel or tangible property on board a vessel, the warrant and any supplemental process must be delivered to the marshal for service.

(ii) If the property that is the subject of the action is other property, tangible or intangible, the warrant and any supplemental process must be delivered to a person or organization authorized to enforce it, who may be: (A) a marshal; (B) someone under contract with the United States; (C) someone specially appointed by the court for that purpose; or (D) in an action brought by the United States, any officer or employee of the United States.

(c) Deposit in court. If the property that is the subject of the action consists in whole or in part of freight, the proceeds of property sold, or other intangible property, the clerk must issue—in addition to the warrant—a summons directing any person controlling the property to show cause why it should not be deposited in court to abide the judgment.

(d) Supplemental process. The clerk may upon application issue supplemental process to enforce the court's order without further court order.

(4) Notice. No notice other than execution of process is required when the property that is the subject of the action has been released under Rule E(5). If the property is not released within 10 days after execution, the plaintiff must promptly—or within the time that the court allows—give public notice of the action and arrest in a newspaper designated by court order and having general circulation in the district, but publication may be terminated if the property is released before publication is completed. The notice must specify the time under Rule C(6) to file a statement of interest in or right against the seized property and to answer. This rule does not affect the notice requirements in an action to foreclose a preferred ship mortgage under 46 U.S.C. § 31301 et seq., as amended.

(6) Responsive pleading; Interrogatories.

(a) Civil Forfeiture. In an in rem forfeiture action for violation of a federal statute:

(i) a person who asserts an interest in or right against the property that is the subject of the action must file a verified statement identifying the interest or right:

(A) within 20 days after the earlier of (1) receiving actual notice of execution of process, or (2) completed publication of notice under Rule C(4), or

(B) within the time that the court allows;

(ii) an agent, bailee, or attorney must state the authority to file a statement of interest in or right against the property on behalf of another; and

(iii) a person who files a statement of interest in or right against the property must serve an answer within 20 days after filing the statement.

(b) Maritime Arrests and Other Proceedings. In an in rem action not governed by Rule C(6)(a):

(i) A person who asserts a right of possession or any ownership interest in the property that is the subject of the action must file a verified statement of right of interest:

(A) within 10 days after the earlier of (1) the execution of process, or (2) completed publication of notice under Rule C(4), or

(B) within the time that the court allows;

(ii) the statement of right or interest must describe the interest in the property that supports the person's demand for its restitution or right to defend the action;

(iii) an agent, bailee, or attorney must state the authority to file a statement of right or interest on behalf of another; and

(iv) a person who asserts a right of possession or any ownership interest must file an answer within 20 days after filing the statement of interest or right.

(c) Interrogatories. Interrogatories may be served with the complaint in an in rem action without leave of court. Answers to the interrogatories must be served with the answer to the complaint.

Supplemental Rule E(3), (7), (8), (9)(b), (10)

The proposal would rewrite sections (3), (7), (8), and (9), and would add a new section (10) as follows:

(3) Process.

(a) In admiralty and maritime proceedings process in rem or of maritime attachment and garnishment may be served only within the district.

(b) In forfeiture cases process in rem may be served within the district or outside the district when authorized by statute.

(c) Issuance and Delivery. Issuance and delivery of process in rem, or of maritime attachment and garnishment, shall be held in abeyance if the plaintiff so requests.

(7) Security on Counterclaim.

(a) When a person who has given security for damages in the original action asserts a counterclaim that arises from the transaction or occurrence that is the subject of the original action, a plaintiff for whose benefit the security has been given must give security for damages demanded in the counterclaim unless the court, for cause shown, directs otherwise. Proceedings on the original claim must be stayed until this security is given, unless the court directs otherwise.

(b) The plaintiff is required to give security under Rule E(7)(a) when the United States or its corporate instrumentality counterclaims and would have been required to give security to respond in damages if a private party but is relieved by law from giving security.

(8) Restricted Appearance.
An appearance to defend against an admiralty and maritime claim with respect to which there has issued process in rem, or process of attachment and garnishment, may be expressly restricted to the defense of such claim, and in that event is not

505

an appearance for the purposes of any other claim with respect to which such process is not available or has not been served.

(9) Disposition of Property; Sales.

(b) Interlocutory Sales; Delivery.

(i) On application of a party, the marshal, or other person having custody of the property, the court may order all or part of the property sold—with the sales proceeds, or as much of them as will satisfy the judgment, paid into court to await further orders of the court—if:

(A) the attached or arrested property is perishable, or liable to deterioration, decay, or injury by being detained in custody pending the action.

(B) the expense of keeping the property is excessive or disproportionate; or

(C) there is an unreasonable delay in securing release of the property.

(ii) in the circumstances described in Rule (E)(9)(b)(1), the court, on motion by a defendant or a person filing a statement of interest or right under Rule C(6), may order that the property, rather than being sold, be delivered to the movant upon giving security under these rules.

(10) Preservation of Property. When the owner or another person remains in possession of property attached or arrested under the provisions of Rule E(4)(b) that permit execution of process without taking actual possession, the court, on a party's motion or on its own, may enter any order necessary to preserve the property and to prevent its removal.

PROPOSED AMENDMENTS TO THE
FEDERAL RULES OF CIVIL PROCEDURE
(As Circulated for Comment by the Committee on Rules of Practice and Procedure)

Rule 5(b)

Rule 5(b) is revised as follows:

(b) Making Service.

(1) Service under Rules 5(a) and 77(d) on a party represented by an attorney is made on the attorney unless the court orders service on the party.

(2) Service under Rule 5(a) is made by:

(A) Delivering a copy to the person served by:

(i) handing it to the person:

(ii) leaving it at the person's office with a clerk or other person in charge, or if no one is in charge leaving it in a conspicuous place in the office; or

(iii) if the person has no office or the office is closed, leaving it at the person's dwelling house or usual place of abode with someone of suitable age and discretion residing there.

(B) Mailing a copy to the last known address of the person served. Service by mail is complete on mailing.

(C) If the person served has no known address, leaving a copy with the clerk of the court.

(D) Delivering a copy by any other means, including electronic means, consented to by the person served. Service by electronic means is complete on transmission; service by other consented means is complete when the person making service delivers the copy to the agency designated to make delivery. If authorized by local rule, a party may make service under this subparagraph (D) through the court's transmission facilities.

Rule 6(e)

The proposal would conform Rule 6(e) to the proposed changes in Rule 5(b) as follows:

(e) Additional Time After Service under Rule 5(b)(2)(B), (C), or (D). Whenever a party has the right or is required to do some act or take some proceedings within a prescribed period after the service of a notice or other paper upon the party and the notice or paper is served upon the party under Rule 5(b)(2)(B), (C), or (D), 3 days shall be added to the prescribed period.

Rule 65(f)

The proposal would eliminate an inconsistency between Rule 65 and a special copyright Rule of Practice.

(f) Copyright Impoundment. This rule applies to copyright impoundment proceedings.

Rule 77(d)

The proposal reflects proposed changes in Rule 5(b).

(d) Notice of Orders or Judgments. Immediately upon the entry of an order or judgment the clerk shall serve a notice of the entry in the manner provided for in Rule 5(b) upon each party who is not in default for failure to appear, and shall make a note in the docket of the mailing. Any party may in addition serve a notice of such entry in the manner provided in Rule 5(b) for the service of papers. Lack of notice of the entry by the clerk does not affect the time to appeal or relieve or authorize the court to relieve a party for failure to appeal within the time allowed, except as permitted in Rule 4(a) of the Federal Rules of Appellate Procedure.

Rule 81(a)

(a) Proceedings to Which the Rules Apply

(1) These rules do not apply to prize proceedings in admiralty governed by Title 10, U.S.C., §§ 7651–7681. They do apply to proceedings in bankruptcy as provided by the Federal Rules of Bankruptcy Procedure.

PROPOSED LEGISLATIVE CHANGES TO THE FEDERAL RULES OF CIVIL PROCEDURE

Rule 11(c)

Senate Bill 353, 106th Cong., 1st Sess., proposed amendments to Rule 11(c):

(1) in the first sentence by striking "may, subject to the conditions stated below," and inserting "shall";

(2) in paragraph (2) by striking the first and second sentences and inserting "A sanction imposed for violation of this rule may consist of reasonable attorneys' fees and other expenses incurred as a result of the violation, directives of a nonmonetary nature, or an order to pay penalty into court or to a party."; and

(3) in paragraph (2)(A) by inserting before the period ", although such sanctions may be awarded against a party's attorneys".

PROPOSED CHANGES AND ADDITIONS TO PROVISIONS OF THE UNITED STATES CODE REGULATING PROCEDURE

28 U.S.C. § 1369   (modifying §§ 1332, 1391, 1407, 1441 and adding § 1660 regarding choice of law)

House Bill 2112, 106th Cong., 1st Sess. would govern multiparty, multiforum cases by amending § 1407 and adding a new § 1369 that specifically modifies §§ 1391, 1407, and 1441 and would have the effect of altering current practice under § 1332. The bill was passed by the House of Representatives on September 13, 1999. On October 29, 1999, the Senate passed the bill with one amendment, to proposed § 1407(i)(1). On November 17, 1999, the House requested a conference to resolve the difference.

(a) Subject–Matter Jurisdiction.

(a) IN GENERAL—The district courts shall have original jurisdiction of any civil action involving minimal diversity between adverse parties that arises from a single accident, where at least 25 natural persons have either died or incurred injury in the accident at a discrete location and, in the case of injury, the injury has resulted in damages which exceed $75,000 per person, exclusive of interest and costs, if—

(1) a defendant resides in a State and a substantial part of the accident took place in another State or other location, regardless of whether that defendant is also a resident of the State where a substantial part of the accident took place;

(2) any two defendants reside in different States, regardless of whether such defendants are also residents of the same State or States; or

(3) substantial parts of the accident took place in different States.

(b) SPECIAL RULES AND DEFINITIONS—For purposes of this section—

(1) minimal diversity exists between adverse parties if any party is a citizen of a State and any adverse party is a citizen of another State, a citizen or subject of a foreign state, or a foreign state as defined in section 1603(a) of this title;

(2) a corporation is deemed to be a citizen of any State, and a citizen or subject of any foreign state, in which it is incorporated or has its principal place of business, and is deemed to be a resident of any State in which it is incorporated or licensed to do business or is doing business;

(3) the term "injury" means—

(A) physical harm to a natural person; and

(B) physical damage to or destruction of tangible property, but only if physical harm described in subparagraph (A) exists;

(4) the term "accident" means a sudden accident, or a natural event culminating in an accident, that results in death or injury incurred at a discrete location by at least 25 natural persons; and

(5) the term "State" includes the District of Columbia, the Commonwealth of Puerto Rico, and any territory or possession of the United States.

(c) INTERVENING PARTIES—In any action in a district court which is or could have been brought, in whole or in part, under this section, any person with a claim arising from the accident described in subsection (a) shall be permitted to intervene as a party plaintiff in the action, even if that person could not have brought an action in a district court as an original matter.

(d) NOTIFICATION OF JUDICIAL PANEL ON MULTIDISTRICT LITIGATION—A district court in which an action under this section is pending shall promptly notify the judicial panel on multidistrict litigation of the pendency of the action.

(b) Venue.

Section 1391 of title 28, United States Code, is amended by adding at the end the following:

(g) A civil action in which jurisdiction of the district court is based upon section 1369 may be brought in any district in which any defendant resides or in which a substantial part of the accident giving rise to the action took place.

(c) Multidistrict Litigation.

Section 1407 of title 28, United States Code, is amended ... [first, by inserting in the third sentence of subsection (a), after the word "terminated" the following phrase "or ordered transferred to the transferee or other district under subsection (i)," and second, by adding the following new subsections (i) and (j) at the end:]

(i)(1) Subject to paragraph (2) and except as provided in subsection (j), any action transferred under this section by the panel may be transferred for trial purposes, by the judge or judges of the transferee district to whom the action was assigned, to the transferee or other district in the interest of justice and for the convenience of the parties and witnesses.

(2) Any action transferred for trial purposes under paragraph (1) shall be remanded by the panel for the determination of compensatory damages to the district court from which it was transferred, unless the court to which the action has been transferred for trial purposes also finds, for the convenience of the parties and witnesses and in the interests of justice, that the action should be retained for the determination of compensatory damages.

Note: The Senate Amendment to House Bill 2112 eliminated the words "and except as provided in subsection (j)" in subsection (i)(l). That is the only difference between the versions of the bill passed by the House and Senate.

(j)(1) In actions transferred under this section when jurisdiction is or could have been based, in whole or in part, on section 1369, the transferee district court may retain actions so transferred for the determination of liability and punitive damages notwithstanding any other provision of this section. An action retained for the determination of liability shall be remanded to the district court from which the action was transferred, or to the State court from which the action was removed, for the determination of damages, other than punitive damages, unless the court finds, for the convenience of parties and witnesses and in the interest of justice, that the action should be retained for the determination of damages.

(2) Any remand under paragraph (1) shall not be effective until 60 days after the transferee court has issued an order determining liability and has certified its intention to remand some or all of the transferred actions for the determination of damages. An appeal with respect to the liability determination and the choice of law determination of the transferee court may be taken during that 60–day period to the court of appeals with appellate jurisdiction over the transferee court. * * *

(d) Removal of Actions.

Section 1441 of title 28, United States Code, is amended—

* * *

(2) by inserting after subsection (d) the following:

(e)(1) Notwithstanding the provisions of subsection (b) of this section, a defendant in a civil action in a State court may remove the action to the district court of the United States for the district and division embracing the place where the action is pending if—

(A) the action could have been brought in a United States district court under section 1369 of this title; or

(B) the defendant is a party to an action which is or could have been brought, in whole or in part, under section 1369 in a United States district court and arises from the same accident as the action in State court, even if the action to be removed could not have been brought in a district court as an original matter.

The removal of an action under this subsection shall be made in accordance with section 1446 of this title, except that a notice of removal may also be filed before trial of the action in State court within 30 days after the date on which the defendant first becomes a party to an action under section 1369 in a United States district court that arises from the same accident as the action in State court, or at a later time with leave of the district court.

(2) Whenever an action is removed under this subsection and the district court to which it is removed or transferred under section 1407(j) has made a liability determination requiring further proceedings as to damages, the district court shall remand the action to the State court from which it had been removed for the determination of damages, unless the court

finds that, for the convenience of parties and witnesses and in the interest of justice, the action should be retained for the determination of damages.

(3) Any remand under paragraph (2) shall not be effective until 60 days after the district court has issued an order determining liability and has certified its intention to remand the removed action for the determination of damages. An appeal with respect to the liability determination and the choice of law determination of the district court may be taken during that 60–day period to the court of appeals with appellate jurisdiction over the district court. In the event a party files such an appeal, the remand shall not be effective until the appeal has been finally disposed of. Once the remand has become effective, the liability determination and the choice of law determination shall not be subject to further review by appeal or otherwise.

(4) Any decision under this subsection concerning remand for the determination of damages shall not be reviewable by appeal or otherwise.

(5) An action removed under this subsection shall be deemed to be an action under section 1369 and an action in which jurisdiction is based on section 1368 of this title for purposes of this section and sections 1407, 1660, 1697, and 1785 of this title.

(6) Nothing in this subsection shall restrict the authority of the district court to transfer or dismiss an action on the ground of inconvenient forum.

(e) Choice of Law * * *

(a) FACTORS—In an action which is or could have been brought, in whole or in part, under section 1369 of this title, the district court in which the action is brought or to which it is removed shall determine the source of the applicable substantive law, except that if an action is transferred to another district court, the transferee court shall determine the source of the applicable substantive law. In making this determination, a district court shall not be bound by the choice of law rules of any State, and the factors that the court may consider in choosing the applicable law include—

(1) the place of the injury;

(2) the place of the conduct causing the injury;

(3) the principal places of business or domiciles of the parties;

(4) the danger of creating unnecessary incentives for forum shopping; and

(5) whether the choice of law would be reasonably foreseeable to the parties.

The factors set forth in paragraphs (1) through (5) shall be evaluated according to their relative importance with respect to the particular action. If good cause is shown in exceptional cases, including constitutional reasons, the court may allow the law of more than one State to be applied with respect to a party, claim, or other element of an action.

(b) ORDER DESIGNATING CHOICE OF LAW—The district court making the determination under subsection (a) shall enter an order designating the single jurisdiction whose substantive law is to be applied in all other actions under section 1369 arising from the same accident as that giving rise to the action in which the determination is made. The substantive law of the designated jurisdiction shall be applied to the parties and claims in all such actions before the court, and to all other elements of each action, except where Federal law applies or the order specifically provides for the application of the law of another jurisdiction with respect to a party, claim, or other element of an action.

(c) CONTINUATION OF CHOICE OF LAW AFTER REMAND—In an action remanded to another district court or a State court under section 1407(j)(1) or 1441(e)(2) of this title, the district court's choice of law under subsection (b) shall continue to apply.

28 U.S.C. §§ 1332, 1453 (modifying § 1441)

House Bill 1875, 106 Cong., 1st Sess., passed by the House of Representatives on September 23, 1999, and currently before the Senate Committee on the Judiciary, would expand diversity-of-citizenship jurisdiction over class actions, initially and upon removal, as follows:

Section 1332   * * *

[S]ubsections (b), (c), and (d) . . . are redesignated (c), (d), and (e) and the following new (b) is substituted and (f) is added.

(b)(1) The district courts shall have original jurisdiction of any civil action which is brought as a class action and in which—

(A) any member of a proposed plaintiff class is a citizen of a State different from any defendant;

(B) any member of a proposed plaintiff class is a foreign state and any defendant is a citizen of a State; or

(C) any member of a proposed plaintiff class is a citizen of a State and any defendant is a citizen or subject of a foreign state.

As used in this paragraph, the term 'foreign state' has the meaning given that term in section 1603(a).

(2)(A) The district courts shall not exercise jurisdiction over a civil action described in paragraph (1) if the action is—

(i) an intrastate case;

(ii) a limited scope case; or

513

(iii) a State action case.

(B) For purposes of subparagraph (A)—

(i) the term 'intrastate case' means a class action in which the record indicates that—

(I) the claims asserted therein will be governed primarily by the laws of the State in which the action was originally filed; and

(II) the substantial majority of the members of all proposed plaintiff defendants, are citizens of the State in which the action was originally filed;

(ii) the term 'limited scope case' means a class action in which the record indicates that all matters in controversy asserted by all members of all proposed plaintiff classes do not in the aggregate exceed the sum or value of $1,000,000, exclusive of interest and costs, or a class action in which the number of members of all proposed plaintiff classes in the aggregate is less than 100; and

(iii) the term 'State action case' means a class action in which the primary defendants are States, State officials, or other governmental entities against whom the district court may be foreclosed from ordering relief.

(3) Paragraph (1) shall not apply to any claim concerning a covered security as that term is defined in section 16(f)(3) of the Securities Act of 1933 and section 28(f)(5)(E) of the Securities Exchange Act of 1934.

(4) Paragraph (1) shall not apply to any class action solely involving a claim that relates to—

(A) the internal affairs or governance of a corporation or other form of business enterprise and that arises under or by virtue of the laws of the State in which such corporation or business enterprise is incorporated or organized; or

(B) the rights, duties (including fiduciary duties), and obligations relating to or created by or pursuant to any security (as defined under section 2(a)(1) of the Securities Act of 1933 and the regulations issued thereunder).

(f) For purposes of subsection (b), a member of a proposed class shall be deemed to be a citizen of a State different from a defendant corporation only if that member is a citizen of a State different from all States of which the defendant corporation is deemed a citizen.

Section 1453   * * *

(a) IN GENERAL.—A class action may be removed to a district court of the United States in accordance with this chapter, but without regard to whether any defendant is a citizen of the State in which the action is brought, except that such action may be removed—

(1) by any defendant without the consent of all defendants; or

(2) by any plaintiff class member who is not a named or representative class member of the action for which removal is sought, without the consent of all members of such class.

(b) WHEN REMOVABLE.—This section shall apply to any class action before or after the entry of any order certifying a class, except that a plaintiff class member who is not a named or representative class member of the action may not seek removal of the action before an order certifying a class of which the plaintiff is a class member has been entered.

(c) PROCEDURE FOR REMOVAL.—The provisions of section 1446(a) relating to a defendant removing a case shall apply to a plaintiff removing a case under this section. With respect to the application of subsection (b) of such section, the requirement relating to the 30-day filing period shall be met if a plaintiff class member who is not a named or representative class member of the action for which removal is sought files notice of removal no later than 30 days after receipt by such class member, through service or otherwise, of the initial written notice of the class action provided at the court's direction.

(d) EXCEPTIONS.—

(1) COVERED SECURITIES.—This section shall not apply to any claim concerning a covered security as that term is defined in section 16(f)(3) of the Securities Act of 1933 and section 28(f)(5)(E) of the Securities Exchange Act of 1934.

(2) INTERNAL GOVERNANCE OF BUSINESS ENTITIES.—This section shall not apply to any class action solely involving a claim that relates to—

(A) the internal affairs or governance of a corporation or other form of business enterprise and that arises under or by virtue of the laws of the State in which such corporation or business enterprise is incorporated or organized; or

(B) the rights, duties (including fiduciary duties), and obligations relating to or created by or pursuant to any security (as defined under section 2(a)(1) of the Securities Act of 1933 and the regulations issued thereunder).

* * *

28 U.S.C. §§ 1712, 1713 (governing notice of class action certification and of settlements)

Senate Bill 353, 106th Cong., 1st Sess. would require notice in federal and certain state class action suits as follows:

Section 1712

This chapter shall apply to—

(1) all plaintiff class actions filed in Federal court; and

(2) all plaintiff class actions filed in State court in which—

(A) any class member resides outside the State in which the action is filed; and

(B) the transaction or occurrence that gave rise to the class action occurred in more than 1 State.

Section 1713

(a) Not later than 10 days after a proposed settlement in a class action is filed in court, class counsel shall serve the State attorney general of each State in which a class member resides and the Attorney General of the United States as if such attorneys general and the Department of Justice were parties in the class action with—

(1) a copy of the complaint and any materials filed with the complaint and any amended complaints (except such materials shall not be required to be served if such materials are made electronically available through the Internet and such service includes notice of how to electronically access such material);

(2) notice of any scheduled judicial hearing in the class action;

(3) any proposed or final notification to class member of—

(A)(i) the members' rights to request exclusion from the class action; or

(ii) if no right to request exclusion exists, a statement that no such right exists; and

(B) a proposed settlement of a class action;

(4) any proposed or final class action settlement;

(5) any settlement or other agreement contemporaneously made between class counsel and counsel for the defendants;

(6) any final judgment or notice of dismissal;

(7)(A) if feasible the names of class members who reside in each State attorney general's respective State and the estimated proportionate claim of such members to the entire settlement; or

(B) if the provision of information under subparagraph (A) is not feasible, a reasonable estimate of the number of class members residing in each attorney general's State and the estimated proportionate claim of such members to the entire settlement; and

(8) any written judicial opinion relating to the materials described under paragraphs (3) through (6).

(b) A hearing to consider final approval of a proposed settlement may not be held earlier than 120 days after the date on which the State attorneys general and the Attorney General of the United States are served notice under subsection (a).

(c) Any court with jurisdiction over a plaintiff class action shall require that—

(1) any written notice provided to the class through the mail or publication in printed media contain a short summary written in plain, easily understood language, describing—

(A) the subject matter of the class action;

(B) the legal consequences of being a member of the class action;

(C) the ability of a class member to seek removal of the class action to Federal court if—

(i) the action is filed in a State court; and

(ii) Federal jurisdiction would apply to such action under section 1332(d);

(D) if the notice is informing class members of a proposed settlement agreement—

(i) the benefits that will accrue to the class due to the settlement;

(ii) the rights that class members will lose or waive through the settlement;

(iii) obligations that will be imposed on the defendants by the settlement;

(iv) the dollar amount of any attorney's fee class counsel will be seeking, or if not possible, a good faith estimate of the dollar amount of any attorney's fee class counsel will be seeking; and

(v) an explanation of how any attorney's fee will be calculated and funded; and

(E) any other material matter; and

(2) any notice provided through television or radio to inform the class members of the right of each member to be excluded from a class action or a proposed settlement, if such right exists, shall, in plain, easily understood language—

(A) describe the persons who may potentially become class members in the class action; and

(B) explain that the failure of a person falling within the definition of the class to exercise such person's right to be excluded from a class action will result in the person's inclusion in the class action.

(d) Compliance with this section shall not provide immunity to any party from any legal action under Federal or State law, including actions for malpractice or fraud.

(e)(1) A class member may refuse to comply with and may choose not to be bound by a settlement agreement or consent decree in a class action if the class member resides in a State where the State attorney general has not been provided notice and materials under subsection (a).

(2) The rights created by this subsection shall apply only to class members or any person acting on a class member's behalf, and shall not be construed to limit any other rights affecting a class member's participation in the settlement.

(f) Nothing in this section shall be construed to impose any obligations, duties, or responsibilities upon State attorneys general or the Attorney General of the United States.

28 U.S.C. § 1714   (limiting attorney's fees in class actions)

Senate Bill 353, 106th Cong., 1st Sess., would limit attorney fees in both federal and state class actions as follows:

(a) In any class action, the total attorney's fees and expenses awarded by the court to counsel for the plaintiff class may not exceed a reasonable percentage of the amount of—

(1) any damages and prejudgment interest actually paid to the class;

(2) any future financial benefits to the class based on the cessation of alleged improper conduct by the defendants; and

(3) costs actually incurred by all defendants in complying with the terms of an injunctive order or settlement agreement.

(b) Notwithstanding subsection (a), to the extent that the law permits, the court may award attorney's fees and expenses to counsel for the plaintiff class based on a reasonable lodestar calculation. * * *

Part X

Index to Comparative Provisions

Federal Provisions

	Page
United States Constitution 7th Amendment	122
United States Code	
Tit. 15, § 15(a)	249
United States Code	
Tit. 42, § 1981a (jury trial in Title VII cases)	122
United States Supreme Court Rule 10	240
United States District Court, District of Columbia, Rule 7.1(m)	120
United States District Court, District of Connecticut, Local Rule of Civil Procedure 16(a)	125
United States District Court, Southern District New York, Civil Rule 33.4(a)	109
Proposed Consumer Class Action Act	249

State Provisions

Alabama Code	
§ 12–2–13	290
Arizona Rules of Civil Procedure 26.1(a)	90
California Constitution	
Art. 6, § 11	238
Art. 6, § 12	238
California Civil Procedure Code	
§ 382	73
§ 386	66
§ 396	43
§ 415.30	21
§ 425.10(b)	28
§ 430.10	45
§ 431.30(d)	30
§ 436	154
§ 437c	151
§ 446(a)	30
§ 469	52
§ 470	52
§ 471	52
§ 583.210	125
§ 583.310	125
§ 583.320	126
§ 583.330	126
§ 583.360	126
§ 583.410(a)	126
§ 583.420	126
§ 597	44
§ 597.5	45
§ 909	290
§ 2023	120
§ 2030(f)(2)	109

Page

California Rules of Court
28 -- 238
29 -- 240
228 --- 134

Colorado Rules of Civil Procedure
8(e)(1) --- 31

Connecticut Superior Court Rules of Civil Procedure
§ 17–55 --- 280

Florida Rules of Civil Procedure
1.500 --- 149

Georgia Constitution
Art. VI, § 1, ¶ 8 --- 241
Art. VI, § 5, ¶ 5 --- 241
Art. VI, § 6, ¶ 2 --- 241
Art. VI, § 6, ¶ 3 --- 241
Art. VI, § 6, ¶ 5 --- 241

Georgia Code Annotated
§ 5–5–24 -- 140
§ 9–10–111 -- 38
§ 9–11–8(a)(2) -- 28
§ 9–11–8(e)(2) -- 31
§ 9–11–11(b) -- 38
§ 9–11–54(c)(1) --- 148
§ 9–11–60 --- 159
§ 19–5–5(a) --- 38

Illinois Compiled Statutes ch. 735, 5/2
104(a) -- 257
104(b) -- 43, 257
201(a) -- 17
202 --- 18
203(a) -- 18
204 --- 18
205 --- 18
205.1 --- 19
206(a) -- 20
207 --- 20
208 --- 19
211 --- 19
212 --- 19
301 --- 44
603(b) -- 35
604 --- 28
610 --- 30
613(a) -- 35
616(d) -- 53
1009(a), (c) -- 124

Illinois Compiled Statutes ch. 735, 5/4
101 --- 20
126 --- 21

Illinois Supreme Court Rules
Rule 20 --- 263
Rule 239 -- 141

Page

Indiana Rules of Trial Procedure
    Trial Rule 8(E)(3) 42
    Trial Rule 41(E) 127
    Trial Rule 50 138
Kansas Statutes Annotated
    § 60–203(a) 11
Maryland Rules
    2–321 41
Massachusetts General Laws Annotated
    c. 233, § 45 266
Michigan Court Rules
    2.113(F) 35
    2.113(G) 36
    2.203 60
    2.203(B) 48
    2.206(A) 64
    2.302(B)(4)(d) 106
    2.308(A) 106
Minnesota Constitution
    Art. 1, § 4 135
Minnesota Rules of Civil Appellate Procedure
    103.03 244
Minnesota Rules of Civil Procedure
    4.04(a)(2)(B) 44
    26.02(c) 91
    33.01(a) 109
    35.01 113
    51 140
    59.01 157
    59.03 158
Mississippi Code Annotated
    § 11–7–155 140
Missouri Statutes Annotated
    § 510.330 158
Missouri Rules of Civil Procedure
    55.25(a) 42
    78.01 159
Nebraska Revised Statutes
    § 25–803 26
    § 25–804 29
    § 25–806 42
    § 25–807 42
    § 25–808 42
    § 25–810 42
    § 25–811 49
    § 25–820 26
    § 25–833 46
    § 25–842 31
    § 25–1223 133
    § 25–1224 134
    § 25–1227(1) 134
    § 25–1228(1) 134

Page

New Jersey Civil Practice Rules
　4:5–8(b) _____ 33
　4:9–3 _____ 52
　4:17–7 _____ 93
　4:25–1 _____ 57
　4:41–5(b) & (c) _____ 145

New York Civil Practice Law and Rules
　216 _____ 66
　302(a) _____ 284
　320(c) _____ 44
　602 _____ 127
　1002(a) & (b) _____ 65
　1002(c) _____ 128
　3013 _____ 29
　3015 _____ 32
　3016 _____ 33
　3017(c) _____ 29
　3018(a) _____ 31
　3018(b) _____ 31
　3019(b) _____ 49
　3024(b) _____ 46
　3025(a) & (b) _____ 51
　3041 _____ 29
　3043 _____ 29
　3101 _____ 91
　3102(c) _____ 95
　3106 _____ 93
　3120 _____ 111
　3121(b) _____ 113
　3130 _____ 109
　3211 _____ 46
　3219 _____ 167
　3220 _____ 167
　3221 _____ 168
　4103 _____ 123
　4317 _____ 145
　4404(a) _____ 138
　5205 _____ 168
　5206 _____ 170
　5601 _____ 241
　5602 _____ 239
　5701 _____ 245
　6201 _____ 162
　6301 _____ 165
　6401 _____ 166

North Carolina General Statutes
　§ 1–75.2 _____ 285
　§ 1–75.4 _____ 285
　§ 1–75.7 _____ 288
　§ 1–75.8 _____ 288

North Carolina Rules of Civil Procedure
Form (3) Complaint for Negligence _____ 191

Page

Ohio Revised Code Annotated
§ 2307.27 77

Oklahoma Statutes Annotated
Tit. 12, § 611 142

Pennsylvania Constitution
Art. 1, § 6 122

Pennsylvania Rules of Civil Procedure
1024 38

Rhode Island General Laws Annotated
§ 9–5–33(a) 288

South Carolina Code
§ 14–7–1020 135

Texas Rules of Civil Procedure
301 148

Virginia Code
§ 8.01–359 135

Virginia Constitution
Art. 1, § 11 122

Wisconsin Statutes Annotated
§ 801.63 256
§ 805.12(1) 136
§ 805.12(2) 137

Uniform Acts

Uniform Declaratory Judgments Act
§ 6 281

Uniform Enforcement of Foreign Judgments Act (1964 Revision)
§ 2 279
§ 6 279

Uniform Interstate and International Procedure Act
§ 1.02 289
§ 1.03 289
§ 1.05 289

Uniform Parentage Act
§ 8(b) 289

†